le to

grity

LAN Times Guide to Security and Data Integrity

Marc Farley,
Tom Stearns, and
Jeffrey Hsu

Osborne **McGraw-Hill**

Berkeley   New York   St. Louis   San Francisco
Auckland   Bogotá   Hamburg   London   Madrid
Mexico City   Milan   Montreal   New Delhi   Panama City
Paris   São Paulo   Singapore   Sydney
Tokyo   Toronto

Osborne **McGraw-Hill**
2600 Tenth Street
Berkeley, California 94710
U.S.A.

For information on translations or book distributors outside the U.S.A., or to arrange bulk purchase discounts for sales promotions, premiums, or fundraisers, please contact Osborne **McGraw-Hill** at the above address.

LAN Times Guide to Security and Data Integrity

1234567890 DOC 99876

ISBN 0-07-882166-5

Acquisitions Editor	**Computer Designer**
Cindy Brown	Peter Hancik
Project Editor	**Illustrators**
Janet Walden	Loretta Lian Au
	Richard Whitaker
Copy Editor	**Cover Design**
Gary Morris	Emdesign
Proofreader	**Quality Control Specialist**
Linda Medoff	Joe Scuderi
Indexer	
David Heiret	

About the Authors...

Marc Farley lives in San Jose, California and works as a product manager for Hitachi Data Systems. He has a wealth of experience helping end users select and implement backup and recovery systems for their LANs. He has also worked with storage experts throughout the computer industry, assisting them in the development and delivery of LAN backup and recovery solutions to their customers.

Tom Stearns is a computer consultant in Salt Lake City, Utah, specializing in Xbase work. He has lead training in FoxPro, and is a freelance product reviewer for *LAN Times* magazine. He is also the coauthor of *Visual FoxPro Programming Basics*.

Jeffrey Hsu is an experienced author, consultant, and journalist specializing in the area of computers and scientific technologies. He is completing a Ph.D. in information systems, holds a master's degree in computer science and an M.B.A. in management, and also several computer certifications, including a Novell Master CNE. He has over a decade of teaching and training experience and is currently a Professor of Information Systems at Montclair State University.

Contents at a Glance

Contents

Acknowledgments

A special word of thanks goes to Brad Shimmin, who had the original idea to create a cross-disciplinary book on this topic and got the ball rolling. A big thanks also to Cindy Brown and Janet Walden at Osborne/McGraw-Hill for keeping this project alive while authors and editors were changing and moving around the country. And thanks to Ian Vogelesang for providing the lion's share of the material used in Chapter 10.

Finally, thanks to my family for putting up with their distracted daddy over the last few months. This book never would have been finished without their generosity and understanding.

— Marc Farley

Introduction

The old Chinese proverb, "May you live in interesting times," applies as much today as it ever has, especially in the world of computer networking. The rapid growth of the Internet in the last 18 months has left many networking professionals wondering what will come next.

Foremost among their concerns are questions about data protection. While many people view the Internet enthusiastically as the next great computing renaissance, many of the people who responsibly manage networks that attach to the Internet fear the unknown risks to their data that it may introduce.

But the Internet is not the only cause for alarm. Indeed, most of the changes on networks today are internally generated. Companies are increasingly dependent on their LANs to support important business functions, resulting in an increase in LAN-resident data and a healthy concern over its safety. As the amount of data grows on LANs, the difficulty of managing this data also increases and forces LAN administrators to look for new technologies and techniques that provide the protection they need.

This book was written to help LAN administrators understand the issues and technology of data protection in this changing world. The concept was to use a multidisciplinary approach to give the reader a broad perspective. Therefore, a wide range of topics are presented, including backup and recovery, archiving, hierarchical storage management (HSM), redundant systems, system security, user security management and policies, authentication, encryption, viruses, and disaster recovery planning.

The first two chapters are intended to familiarize readers with the status of network data protection today, including an examination of the threats that could cause data to be lost or stolen. Chapter 3 is an in-depth analysis of LAN backup, the foundation of any data protection scheme. It includes a discussion of the problems that cause backup systems to fail and the various technologies that can be employed to solve the problems. Chapter 4 looks at ways to manage data growth more effectively through archiving and HSM techniques. In Chapter 5, we examine several ways to implement redundancy to protect your LAN systems and data.

Chapter 6 switches the focus to database systems, particularly the problems of backing up database systems on LANs. The issues of database protection are continued in Chapter 7, which discusses the issues of security problems associated with database systems.

The topic of security on LANs is continued in Chapters 8 through 11. Chapter 8 looks at general system security and is expanded upon in Chapter 9 where the issues of network security are discussed. Chapter 10 introduces the advanced technologies that provide authentication and encryption on networks. Considering the amount of concern over Internet security, this chapter should be of interest to many readers. Viruses and virus protection are the subject of Chapter 11.

The last two chapters of the book deal with future considerations. Chapter 12 looks at disaster recovery planning, and how the reader might best prepare to avoid the business-ruining calamity that could happen someday. Finally, Chapter 13 examines developing trends in computing technology today and attempts to predict where some potentially dangerous exposures lie for data in the future.

CHAPTER ONE

Networks and Data

It's human nature to preserve one's well-being by anticipating future problems. Readers of this book are probably wondering what they can do to protect their data now, and in the future. Unfortunately, there are no good templates to simply plug into or recipes to follow that create a secure and safe environment for your data.

The beginning of this work is to get a good handle on the current environment. These are certainly interesting times in the computer industry. Every day, the amount of data stored on computers increases, along with the number of people who want to access it. Along with these increases, the potential for data integrity and security "surprises" also increases.

This chapter is intended to help the reader understand the LAN environment better by analyzing the capabilities of both customers and producers of technology to provide reliable, secure systems.

Data Integrity and Security

Data on networked systems is subject to a wide variety of hazards that can make life miserable for systems administrators. The old saying "Garbage in, garbage out" is as true today as it was when it was first spoken—nobody wants to get bad or worthless information from their systems. *Data integrity* is a broad term used to describe the state of the data relative to corruption or loss; it generally means that the data can be counted on to be secure and accurate. Compromised, or poor, data integrity implies that the data may be invalid or incomplete.

The term *data security* describes the state of data relative to its intentional theft or destruction. Just as businesses employ security guards to protect their capital assets from theft or willful destruction, computer professionals use security products to guard their data assets from these threats.

As systems administrators, it makes sense for us to take the steps to ensure we can provide the best data integrity and security possible to others in our organizations. This book explores the most common causes of lost, corrupted, destroyed, or stolen data on LAN systems and discusses technologies and techniques to prevent them.

The following analogy, illustrated in Figure 1-1, may help clarify data integrity and security terms and set the stage for subsequent discussions. Getting accurate information from a computer is like baking a cake. The eggs, flour, baking powder, milk, and the other ingredients are equivalent to the raw data. The oven that bakes the cake is similar to the computer and software that transform the data into information. And the finished cake is akin to the information that is gained from this process. So, what happens if you mistakenly use baking soda instead of flour in the cake recipe? It will taste awful and you will probably have a lot of leftovers on your hands. In a similar vein, what happens if you try to bake bread, but discover that you are missing ingredients, or that the oven is not working? You will not bake bread. Perhaps you developed a new recipe for German chocolate cake and spent months perfecting it for a national contest. Then, a neighbor copies your recipe, changes it slightly, enters the contest, and wins. Would you be upset? Probably, especially if there was a cash prize

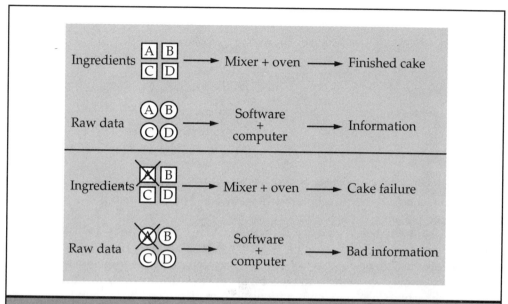

Figure 1-1. *The spoiling or loss of ingredient A results in a cake that doesn't turn out right. Similarly, the corruption or loss of raw data A results in bad information*

to go along with the award. Similarly, where data integrity is concerned, if your data becomes altered, lost, or stolen, the information may be invalid, inaccessible, or used by others to their advantage.

This analogy illustrates the key issues in data integrity: the data in storage should be exactly the same as it was when it was entered or last updated; the computers, peripherals, and components needed to create information should be working correctly; and the data should be safe from others who would use it at your expense.

The Role of Data

The twentieth century has produced profound changes in technology, economics, and culture. One hundred years ago there were no telephones. Most of the tasks performed in business, including correspondence, were done manually. In this century the earth has evolved from an enormous, mysterious place to a relatively small world that can be traversed in hours by air and where people can have telephone conversations between almost any city anywhere. Our cultural framework has changed from a collection of local cultures supporting time-honored local traditions to a globally aware web of ideas where the images of any and all cultures are mixed together. To a large extent, this fundamental change in our lives has occurred because of the accessibility of information. The following table lists some of the changes that have occurred in the second half of this century that facilitate global communications.

1950	**1996**
Telephone/Telegraph system	Satellites
Postal service	Computer networks
Rotary phones	Touch-tone phones
Electro-mechanical switches	Computerized switches
Copper cabling	Fiber-optic cabling

As this century draws to a close, we continue to see rapid advancements in information technology. Many scholars believe we have passed out of the industrialized age of mass-market production and into the information age of highly customized, individualized products and services. Many people today are truly part of a global electronic village, thanks to the recent growth of online services and the Internet. People use these services to exchange personal as well as professional mail, order groceries, schedule travel, and meet others with similar interests and points of view. Asynchronous electronic conversations via e-mail, bulletin boards, and electronic conferences allow people to make informed decisions and receive assistance at their own convenience. Many of us have become "information workers" whose job it is to provide the information infrastructure to our organizations. Information becomes more important to us every day.

To gain a perspective on data, it is interesting to consider the question: "Which is more valuable, the manufacturing or the marketing of goods?" When the leverage from marketing and value-added services becomes more important than the leverage from manufacturing, it can be argued that industrialization has been replaced by information as the force that drives the economic machinery of the world. Whether we are in the information age or not, information is an extremely important part of our lives. We pursue and value education, particularly technical education, because we believe it will improve our position and income. Part of the excitement of the Internet is the potential to acquire knowledge that will help us somehow. Figure 1-2 shows the relative contribution of manufacturing and information processing to profitability.

Information is valuable, not only for how it is shared, but for how it is protected from others. A great deal of information is treated confidentially by the organization that owns it because it gives them competitive advantages. Such information is closely guarded by legal agreements, patents, and other security measures. If a company invests years of market, technology, and product research in a new product, they want to make sure a competitor won't be able to duplicate it and sell it for less simply by reading the documents and diagrams that describe it. Although patent law is designed to protect companies from such activities, they should still make the effort to ensure that competitors cannot easily obtain proprietary information. Industrial espionage is an unfortunate reality in our world, even involving governments, as evidenced by the

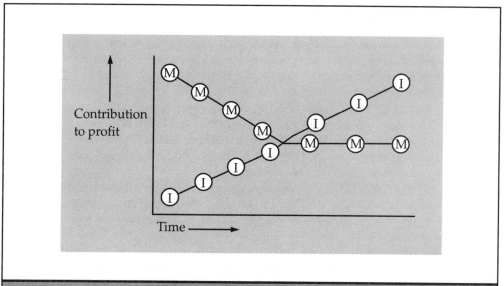

Figure 1-2. *Over time, the ability to control information is becoming more valuable to a company than the ability to manufacture goods*

feud between the United States and France over accusations of spying on each other's aerospace industries.

Our Increasing Dependence on Data

In a network environment, what do we use data for? Office automation, personal productivity, accounting, manufacturing, software development—you name it. It is becoming difficult to perform our jobs without the assistance of data that exists in a network. For many of us, the amount of data we need to perform our jobs vastly exceeds our human ability to remember or reconstruct it all. Therefore, we depend heavily on the data in networked systems for almost every aspect of our businesses, including the process of making strategic decisions on directions and policy.

Our dependence on computers has steadily increased over the past 30 years. In the 1960s, mainframe systems became standard equipment in many companies. The 1970s saw the advent of smaller minicomputers, which allowed smaller businesses and departments to automate their processes. The 1980s ushered in the personal computer, which gave individuals the chance to take advantage of automation. In each case, a greater number of people were introduced to computers and became dependent on them to support their work.

If organizations need more leverage from their information resources, employees need to be able to access information. While the individual PC gives workers the most flexibility and control, it doesn't provide the best scenario for businesses that need to regulate the cost of computing and the use of information. One of the reasons why LANs have flourished is that, compared to mainframe systems, they allow end users and departments greater freedom in how they choose to work, while simultaneously providing control of information and employees. Figure 1-3 shows a comparison of LAN-based computing to other possibilities.

It's too early to say what the 1990s will be known for—it could be introduction of the PDA (personal digital assistant). Some companies are already developing LAN connectivity solutions for workers with PDAs so they can connect their field workers with their office workers in one logical network system. PDAs represent the ultimate in flexible computing but are also the most difficult environment for protecting data integrity. Because they are small and designed to go anywhere the worker goes, they can easily be lost or stolen. In addition, they are subject to the same sorts of interference and broadcasting problems as cellular phones, which makes them susceptible to unauthorized frequency monitoring and transmission inaccuracy.

With or without PDAs, it is likely that our dependence on LAN automated systems will increase. But this will depend on the value of the information they provide, which in turn will depend on accurate and available data. Data is the cornerstone of all data processing, and as our dependence on data processing grows, the integrity, control, and availability of data becomes increasingly important.

An Equation for Trouble: Competition + Cost = Compromise

There are many ways to think about LAN systems. If you are interested in maintaining data integrity, you will use a conservative approach to implement your LANs that results in a more stable environment. Increasing the stability of your network through the implementation of mature products will increase your availability to data by minimizing downtime. However, if you need to maximize the performance or

	Equipment cost	System operators	Management control	Personal productivity
Mainframe	$$$$	Few	Strict	Minimal
Minicomputer	$$$	Few	Good	Minimal
PC	$	Everybody	Minimal	Excellent
LAN	$$	Few	Good	Excellent

Figure 1-3.   *Why LANs are used: Relatively low cost and better business control while promoting productivity*

capacity, you may need to implement newer, leading-edge, products that are not as well known or tested.

It is difficult to separate technology from marketing in the networking industry. The rapid expansion of this industry could not have happened without substantial marketing efforts by the entire industry. As the industry continues to grow, the sheer number of products competing for your attention also grows, making it very difficult for companies to become noticed above the din and convey their messages to the market.

This situation creates an environment where market hype almost becomes necessary for survival. This is certainly no surprise to most readers. In fact, it is well recognized that promoting vaporware and exaggerating features and capabilities is "good" marketing—the better the spin doctors are at concocting product stories, the faster their careers advance. Many of the most successful companies have established themselves through aggressive marketing campaigns doing such things as hyping products not due to ship for another six months or more. These practices, for better or worse, have set the trend in marketing in the LAN industry.

Criticizing marketing practices is easy, but it is important to realize that the market seems to respond enthusiastically to these practices. Sometimes the response approaches hysteria. Anyone who has been to the Comdex trade show in Las Vegas knows what this is all about—it is a virtual feeding frenzy for technology. The quest to establish a technology or knowledge advantage drives both manufacturers and customers. Indeed, there is an element of personal expression in the selection of technology. Just as fortunes have been built within the companies creating technology, personal careers have been built inside businesses and corporations based on successes in implementing LAN technology. The higher the expectation and hype for new technology, the greater the chance to be disappointed, as illustrated here:

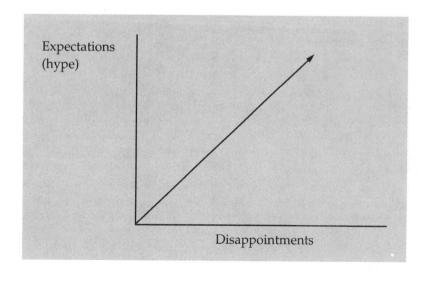

This is especially true for software products, where bugs are unavoidable and can be difficult to troubleshoot and fix. In more colorful terms, the road of technology littered with the wrecks of better ideas. If such disappointments are related to compromises in data integrity or security, the results can be devastating.

Sometimes the selection of technology is aggressive, to say the least, in terms of the integration effort involved. Consider an OLTP application running on an Oracle database on a 75GB NetWare 4.1 server that services 1,500 users in all 50 states and Canada. On paper, this really doesn't sound so terrible, but consider what it would be like to have your job on the line ensuring that this system was available 24 hours a day, every day for the next two years. Whom do you trust to help you implement this monster and ensure its stability, your local Oracle or Novell sales offices? And therein lies both the strength and weakness in LAN systems: they can be highly customized to fit each customer's needs. They are formed by the combination of variable machines running variable operating systems with variable application systems, connected by variable wiring and protocols. The number of degrees of freedom becomes staggering. Although there are standards supporting this scenario, you should respect the complexity involved and not take it for granted.

Open systems products are appealing for their use of industry standards, the competitive environment they create, and the corresponding downward pressure on prices, which make it possible to pay very little for a system with enormous capabilities. But lower prices and lower margins create problems for supporting and testing products because manufacturers cannot afford to test their products the way customers expect. This is one reason why new products tend to have a lot of bugs.

System incompatibilities or bugs affect data integrity in just about any way imaginable. There have been cases where products that were sold to protect data actually deleted it due to a bug. Incompatible products may not always destroy your data, but they could result in systems that are unreliable. For instance, if the backup systems fail once a week, does that create an exposure to the business in terms of loss of assets? If data is lost due to a failed backup on a network you support, does that affect your employment outlook?

Open systems-based standards can go a long way toward making products operate together correctly. Either de facto standards developed by industry leaders or industry standards developed by standards organizations like the IEEE (Institute of Electrical and Electronics Engineers) and ISO (International Organization for Standardization) can significantly reduce the amount of testing and frustration. The purpose of standards is to provide well-defined general interfaces that manufacturers can implement to allow their products to work with any other product that also implements that interface.

However, just because there are standards to follow does not mean that all the off-the-shelf components you buy will work. Sometimes standards are so broad that it becomes difficult for the industry to ascertain what a minimal set of functions should be, and without agreement on this, there is no guarantee that two standards-compliant products will work together. It is also common for a standards definition to be in a state of flux as new capabilities are added to future revisions.

Often companies will differentiate their products by using extensions or options to the standard that make their products more competitive—but this could also make their products incompatible with others. So, even though there are standards in the market, products still need to be tested; but the sheer number of product combinations is far too large for any company to handle. Figure 1-4 shows two processes, using the same standard, which yield incompatible results.

Consider another scenario. You recently purchased a new IBM PC Server 300 to run Microsoft Corporation's Windows NT for a new customer service application that you developed to run on your network. All other servers are running Novell NetWare. You back up your network to an HP Surestore 4mm tape library system, which works fine with the Cheyenne backup software you own. You now need to start backing up the new Windows NT application. You have two choices: back it up with the existing system or put an additional tape device (HP DAT drive, in accordance with purchasing directives in your company) on the new server and back it up separately.

You purchased these products because they come from some of the largest names in the business, all claiming support for industry standards. Therefore, they should all work together fairly well. Unfortunately, they might not. Shocking as it may seem, it is likely that nobody has tested this exact configuration before and it is unknown if any engineering difficulties exist. The following table, which uses tape backup as an

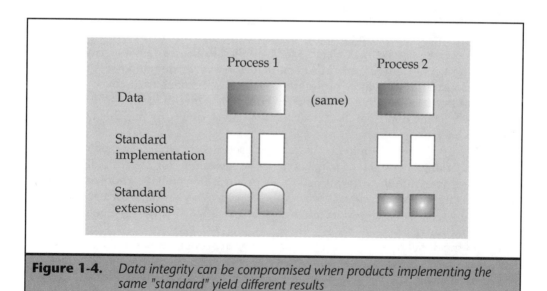

Figure 1-4. *Data integrity can be compromised when products implementing the same "standard" yield different results*

example, shows the difficulty in testing all the various combinations—7,500,000 possible—of components.

Component	Number of models/vendors
Server systems	30
SCSI adapters	10
Tape drives	100
Backup software	25
Tape brands	10

From a perspective of ensuring data integrity, you could realistically describe LANs as a collection of loosely coupled, untested, randomly distributed machines that provide computing functionality within organizations. This is not particularly flattering. Of course, many LAN professionals have years of experience and have learned a great deal about the technology and environment. This does not make it easy, however. That is why it is common for seasoned veterans who have been burned in the past to test most new products in an isolated test environment for several weeks before they roll them into their production environments.

Data in Networks, Risky Business

If data is becoming increasingly important to us, and if LANs are best suited to conform to the structure within a company, and if LANs are complex integration efforts combining many unlike components, what does this say for managing data security and data integrity on LANs?

It means a conscious effort will have to be applied to ensure data integrity problems are kept to a minimum. Most companies, however, do not possess the skills or resources to adequately protect their data. It is shocking to discover the amount of finger crossing that is going on in corporate America today as MIS employees can only hope that their systems don't break down, forcing them to restore them from backup media.

Most companies are ill-prepared to deal with serious data integrity problems. Ask yourself how long it would take to generate a purchase order for replacement equipment if your building was burned to the ground. Do you have a way to monitor, detect, and support security breaches in your company? If your database becomes corrupt, how long will it take to restore it and when did you get the last good, complete backup of it?

Part of the difficulty in preparing for data integrity problems lies in the current trend to downsize business organizations. LAN professionals understand only too well what it is like to be asked to do more things than one can do well. Many companies assume that their LAN staff can be smaller than it ought to be. Data processing is a cost that adversely affects the bottom line of the business; therefore LAN staffs often do not increase commensurate with the growth and complexity of the systems they manage. It is typical for a few people to perform a wider variety of job functions than they can realistically do.

Another reason for the lack of preparation is assumptions made by higher-level IS managers with backgrounds in mainframe systems. On mainframe systems, data integrity issues have been studied and developed over many years, and it is sometimes assumed that similar systems exist for LANs. Those who make this assumption are often unpleasantly surprised to find out that mainframe-like systems do not exist on LANs because, as discussed earlier, LAN products do not receive the same amount of rigorous systems testing as mainframe systems do. On top of that, LAN systems are a newer technology than mainframes and do not have the same kinds of systems data integrity tools that mainframes do.

As an example, consider a high-speed tape backup device. A mainframe high-speed half-inch tape drive may be priced in the neighborhood of $30,000. This drive will move data much faster than most PCs can transfer data to it and could conceivably provide mainframe-like capabilities. But who would want to spend $30,000 for a tape drive to run on an $8,000 server? Actually, there are probably a few systems professionals managing client/server database systems who would do this if it meant their data, which could be worth millions, could be protected adequately.

Not all technology scales in the same way, nor does the cost of manufacturing change at the same rate. The cost of PC hardware has decreased rapidly due to the enormous market and the ability of chip manufacturers to provide technological advances inexpensively in silicon. The dynamics of this market do not exist, however, in all parts of the industry. Customers should seriously evaluate the value of their data and select products to protect it based on the capability of the product as opposed to its price tag. While it may not make sense on the surface to purchase a $4,000 tape

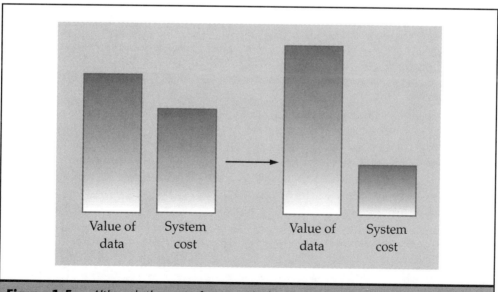

Figure 1-5. *Although the cost of systems is decreasing, the value of the data on them is increasing*

device or software option for a $3,000 server, it may be quite sensible if you consider the data to be worth much more than that. Figure 1-5 illustrates the concept that, while the cost of systems is decreasing, the value of data is actually increasing. Given the dynamics shown in Figure 1-5, one would be well advised to watch out for low-price purchasing policies regarding data integrity and security-oriented products.

The good news is that the technology of network backup, database, and security products continues to get better all the time. The bad news is that the means to control the network and ensure data integrity is always trying to catch up with the swarm of new technologies introduced into the market. Ensuring data integrity on heterogeneous distributed systems is an overwhelming problem: the differences in file systems, operating systems, security systems, communication facilities, protocols, administrative tools, language, peripherals, and so on create an enormous challenge to any vendor bold enough to attempt it. Economics also plays a role in the future development of network data integrity products; whether or not companies will take the risk and pay for increased development of such products remains to be seen.

This book takes a look at some of the technologies available and the environments that influence their operations and effectiveness. You will gain a firm understanding of the issues and technologies surrounding data integrity and security, including some of the more common problems and the solutions to these problems.

CHAPTER TWO

An Overview of Data Integrity and Security

As we have learned through centuries, human beings have a tendency to make mistakes. One of the other constants is that if you tempt fate, it will take advantage of you. Efforts to maintain data integrity and security must be made to negate these constants in networked computer systems.

In this chapter we will discuss data integrity and security and give you a brief overview of the tools used to help LAN administrators protect their data from human nature as well as equipment failures.

Data integrity and security are closely related through their common purpose of protecting data from some potential danger. In the case of data integrity, the danger is often some simple miscalculation, confusion, or mistake in judgment by a human being, or an equipment failure that results in data becoming lost, corrupted, or improperly changed. As for security, people intentionally try to infiltrate another company's systems in order to steal or damage information for their own advantage.

Not all security breaches are malevolent, however; sometimes a hacker will attempt to access data just because it's a challenge. This results from another common human trait—we do things just because they seem interesting and we are curious. This natural curiosity of ours is a real Pandora's box when it comes to how we use computers in the workplace. A user's workstation can be a trigger for incredible creativity or incredible boredom, depending on what the user is working on. Unfortunately, what the user *should* be doing may be dull enough to inspire mischief and entertainment that is more interesting. Sometimes this involves mangling a document by trying to give it more sizzle, like importing a graphics files into it; and sometimes it involves snooping around the network trying to find interesting information such as the CEO's private e-mail.

Data Integrity

The dictionary defines *integrity* as "an unimpaired condition" and "the quality or state of being complete or undivided." This book will use this definition to distinguish data integrity from security, which is used primarily to ensure that outside entities do not have access to data.

Using this definition, the goal of data integrity is to keep the data and information in computer systems in a whole and unimpaired condition. This means that data will not be altered or lost due to any accidental or intentional event. A loss of data integrity means that something happened that resulted in lost or altered data. In the following section we will examine some of the most common causes for losses of data integrity.

Types of Data Integrity Problems

Maintaining the integrity of data in a distributed environment of PCs, workstations, servers, midrange machines, and mainframes is becoming more difficult every day. Many organizations use various combinations of platforms in order to provide the best possible services to their users. This means that an organization is likely to have machines with dissimilar file systems and system services as well as different hardware platforms. E-mail interchange systems are rapidly becoming a requirement for corporate networks, and along with them comes the need for document interchange and conversion. Protocols may be different, requiring gateway or protocol conversion, and the system development languages and compilers are different also, making communications between systems suspect. Add to this list the problem of manufacturers' inability to provide the kind of testing that a distributed system needs and you have a potentially volatile and unpredictable situation.

The five most common sources of threats to data integrity are shown in Figure 2-1. In the following sections, we will explore hypothetical situations that illustrate how these threats could impact your network.

Humans: The Protein Robot Strikes Again!

Despite these challenges, the weakest links in the chain of distributed systems are the people who use them. The fallibility of the human race is a well-documented wellspring of inexplicable errors that never seems to dry up. You have probably been involved in competitive conversations with LAN administrators boasting over the "stupid" antics of end users. In a large percentage of such stories, the end user tells the administrator that "Nothing has changed, it was the same as I left it yesterday." Of

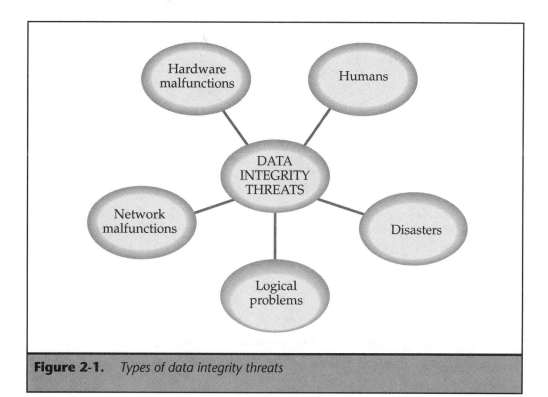

Figure 2-1.   *Types of data integrity threats*

course, in reality, the LAN administrator uncovers through trickery or genius that the end user was doing something like looking through his or her system configuration files and got confused, flipped a bunch of bits just for the heck of it, crashed the machine, and went home for the day.

But it is not only end users who make mistakes. Unfortunately, stories also abound of LAN administrators who stayed up all night recovering data after they blew away a "bunch of data" while performing a simple operation like a server volume reorganization to redistribute data among their servers to balance the load. This type of mistake is not fun to deal with, but it is easy to understand how it happens when you consider the environment that many network administrators work in, managing extremely complex systems with relatively few resources.

Figure 2-2 summarizes the most common threats that humans present to data integrity. Each of these threats will be discussed in the following sections.

Figure 2-2. *Threats that humans pose to data integrity*

ACCIDENTS   Accidents happen. Somebody says red and you hear blue. You transpose the last two digits of a phone number. You press the OK button when you mean to press the Cancel button. You log into the wrong server and start pruning the file system before you realize there's something wrong and you get that sinking feeling in your stomach. The only real explanation for this sort of thing is that you may have been thinking about one thing while working on something else.

INEXPERIENCE   Let's say your e-mail coordinator is on vacation in Alaska for two weeks, during which time the corporate e-mail system runs amok and brings your e-mail server to its knees. Your boss assigns you to solve this problem immediately because it is costing your company $1,000 per hour. You know everything there is to know about directory services, protocols, remote dial-in, and so on, but strangely enough, you have never worked on the e-mail system. Do you think there is a possibility that wrong decisions might be made as you try to resolve the problem and get the business profitable for the day?

STRESS/PANIC   Lets face it, sometimes the stress of being a LAN administrator can be intense. It's the Friday before the 4th of July weekend at 8:45 A.M. The phone is ringing off the hook. End users are complaining about response time because one of the servers is still running last night's backups, accounting is all over you because their month-end reports didn't print the night before, and the VP of sales is demanding to know when the voice-mail system will be fixed because he is missing sales opportunities. While all this is going on, HR calls to tell you that John Doe has been fired and requests you to remove his user accounts from any systems he might have access to.

This is a morning where caffeine consumption only makes things more interesting than they already are. You have a little shortness of breath, your heart is pounding, but gradually you work through the issues one by one and become the hero of the day. E-mail doesn't really get much attention from you today, even the helpful reminder from HR about John Doe's accounts. You go home exhausted, hoping to have a great holiday weekend so you can forget it all and come back for more next week.

Unfortunately, over the weekend, the most recent disgruntled ex-employee dials in from a remote machine and starts deleting all the files he can reach.

MISSED COMMUNICATIONS   This is touched upon in the example above but deserves further analysis. A coworker of yours is reorganizing servers for an upcoming server consolidation project. Part of this involves moving information from one server to another as a temporary storage container. You have the responsibility for backups on all servers on a daily basis. It just so happens that one of the backup systems isn't working due to a tape drive problem and that server hasn't been backed up for a week. You send your coworker an e-mail message detailing the situation and noting that this should be taken into account during work.

Well, it's been a busy week, and your coworker just hasn't had the time to dig through all his or her e-mail. While copying files from the temporary server, the system falls off a table and breaks into pieces on the floor. Data is lost as a result. Where is the problem? There are many places to point to, but one of the main problems was your expectation that the message you sent was received, understood, and acted upon by your coworker. Just because communication systems exist doesn't mean that they can be trusted to deliver a message for you, or that the message will be read.

REVENGE   As in the scenario above where John Doe is fired and wipes out files from a remote machine, employees will sometimes seek to damage the company they work for or other individuals in the company. This sort of behavior is most threatening to data when the employee actually hasn't left the company and does damage while on the job.

AVARICE   Financial gain influences some people more than others. There will probably never be an end to the scams that help creative people make something for nothing. One way to do it is to adjust the data records that determine a person's earnings. A tweak here, a tweak there, and voila!—there's a new BMW in the parking lot.

Hardware Malfunctions

People aren't the only things that fail in this world. High-performance machinery of any kind can only run for so long; this includes computer components. Figure 2-3

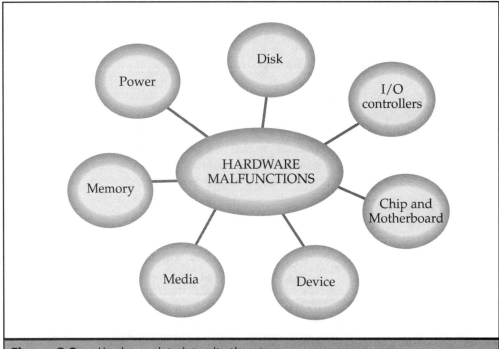

Figure 2-3.   *Hardware data integrity threats*

summarizes some of the more common electrical and mechanical failures that happen with computing equipment. Each of these types of failures are discussed in the following sections.

DISK FAILURES   One of the most common problems in computing is disk failure. A hard disk is a fairly remarkable piece of equipment that users expect to run like clockwork. However, don't blindly trust the mean time between failure (MTBF) numbers, as manufacturers are prone to exaggeration due to marketing pressures. Instead, you are better off planning to replace your drives before they become too risky. For instance, it may make sense to replace your drives before the bearings wear out. Since a disk is relatively inexpensive, it doesn't make sense to risk expensive data on stretching your disk life. There is nothing quite like the realization that a disk has crashed to make you feel vulnerable. That is why RAID (redundant array of inexpensive disks) subsystems that have built-in redundancy to cover disk failures are gaining in popularity.

I/O CONTROLLER FAILURES   There are few things as potentially damaging to the integrity of data as a disk controller that makes sporadic write errors. At least with a disk crash you can send the disk to a company like Ontrack Data Recovery that specializes in recovering data from damaged disks. With a controller failure, the data written to disk is already corrupted and there is no known process that can recover your data for you. Controller failures don't happen that often, but they do happen. If it ever happens to you, you will appreciate the value of disk duplexing, which is discussed in more detail in Chapter 5.

POWER FAILURES   Power failures come in two varieties: either the source of power coming into the machine from the outside is lost or the power supply inside the machine fails. In either case, the potential to lose or corrupt data is significant due to the unpredictable behavior of the system as power is lost. Data in volatile memory will be lost when the power is suddenly removed from the system.

It is a very good idea to install power conditioning equipment and battery backup systems with servers to help ensure a smooth shutdown prior to power loss. The power grid outside your building is way out of your control, and there is no predicting what sort of calamity is waiting to bring it down. There are virtually no locations in the world immune from power problems. Chapter 5 discusses power issues further.

MEMORY FAILURES   Occasionally RAM chips fail. Blame it on wayward gamma rays or sloppy etching in the wafer or even strong electromagnetic fields, but whatever the cause, memory chips can have their data altered by things that are impossible to see and determine. If a memory error occurs in an area where data is being stored, you will end up with corrupted data and you probably won't be aware of the problem until sometime later when somebody discovers the data is wrong. If the memory error occurs where executable code is stored, sooner or later your system will try to run the faulty code segment and the process that was running will stop.

When this happens you will probably learn of your memory problem from your machine diagnostics, but you will not likely know which data files may have become trashed. Server systems that incorporate memory parity checking can help combat this type of problem by identifying corrupt code segments and preventing them from running.

MEDIA, DEVICE, AND OTHER BACKUP FAILURES   Data stored on removable media for backup and recovery purposes contains copies of the data. Anything wrong with your storage device or the media that it uses could result in lost data if your server is also lost or damaged. Problems with tape backup systems are extremely common. Strategic Research, a Santa Barbara-based consulting company dedicated to the study of distributed storage concerns, indicates from their research that, on the average, LAN-based backups fail in completing their job almost three times per week. This is an astounding figure but not entirely due to hardware failures or media problems; the software part of backup can certainly cause difficulties, too. LAN administrators tell horror stories about how one of their servers lost all its data as the result of a disk crash or disaster, but when they went to restore their files from a backup tape, none of their tapes had data on them. Chapter 3 goes into detail on backup and restore issues.

CHIP AND MOTHERBOARD MALFUNCTIONS   No book on data integrity should miss the opportunity to comment on the Pentium chip division error scandal of 1994. This event highlighted the fundamental weakness within the PC industry in relation to data integrity—the notion that such an error is inconsequential because it only affects a small minority of Intel's customers. When one of the giants in the PC and networking industry takes such an attitude, it is hard to imagine trusting any PC system completely ever again. Most of the news concerning this discussed the arguments between Intel and others about the order of magnitude of the error (number of decimal places where it would occur) and how the company handled it publicly (PR policy lesson). The exposure of the flaw became more important than the flaw itself. It is perhaps unfortunate that the industry and market were not able to learn more about the concept of trusted systems, as opposed to public relations strategies. So, as we have learned from this, CPUs can inject errors, motherboards can fail, you name it—if people make something, it can fail, especially if it is complex in nature.

Network Malfunctions

In a LAN, data is transferred from one machine to another at very high speeds. Electrical signals are generated in a computer and broadcast onto a network of some sort. The wiring that is used to connect the machines is exposed to a variety of hazards including interference and physical damage. Anything that makes it difficult or impossible for two computers to communicate could result in corrupted or lost data. In the following sections we examine some of the common ways network equipment can malfunction, causing data loss. These are also summarized in Figure 2-4.

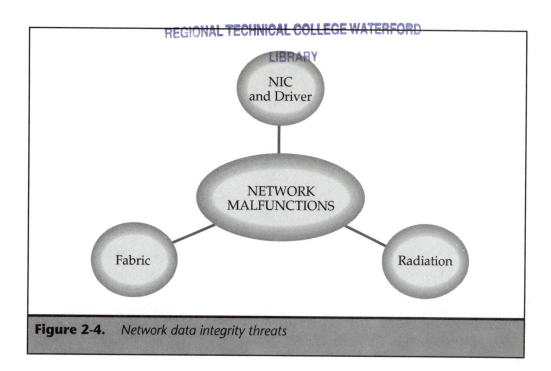

Figure 2-4.   *Network data integrity threats*

NIC AND DRIVER PROBLEMS   The network interface card and the driver that controls it are virtually inseparable. While these components combined could be considered part of the machine's hardware, it also makes sense to include them as networking components. NICs do fail and drivers can be even worse. Any experienced LAN administrator who has run a token ring network over the last several years has probably dealt with driver upgrades for their network. Most of the time, NIC/driver problems do not harm data; they simply prevent users from accessing data. But when a NIC card fails on a server, the server is likely to stop in its tracks, and at that point it is very difficult to know what open files may be corrupted.

FABRIC PROBLEMS   LAN administrators often take pride in their network wiring schemes. The selection of which routers to buy and which WAN services to use becomes a personal expression for many LAN administrators. Unfortunately, when network fabric products are being evaluated, it is rare for them to be tested for reliability and accuracy under the workloads imposed by backup and recovery systems. In case you haven't thought of it before, nothing stresses a network like moving all your data through it. Any weaknesses in your fabric will likely affect your backup system. For example, buffers in routers and bridges that are not large enough can become overstuffed by backup operations, resulting in dropped packets. Conversely, the router or bridge may have plenty of buffer capacity, but the latency incurred from handling so much traffic could ultimately cause session time-outs.

RADIATION PROBLEMS   As much as we would like to think we got rid of radiation threats when the Soviet Union dissolved, it is all around us as electromagnetic waves and other wave/particle phenomena. And just as portable computers can emit radiation that could foul up an aircraft's navigation system, other things emit radiation that can foul up your computers. Since just about everything in a computer comes down to the movment of electrons, and radiation has the capability of moving electrons, it follows that radiation and computers can combine to form some pretty weird science, if not bad data. The difficult thing about radiation is that you have very little control over it, so the best policy is to try and avoid it altogether.

Logical Problems

After users, hardware, and networks, what else could go wrong and threaten your data? Software, of course! The following section looks at some of the ways software can contribute to loss of data integrity (see also Figure 2-5).

BUGS   When was the last time that you bought a software product that didn't have some bug in it? Do you ever wait to buy a new product to let the developer get it right so you don't have to debug it for them? Bugs cover a wide range of flaws, usually related to applications logic. As a consumer there is very little you can do to protect yourself from bugs because no development organization can test every possibility of use.

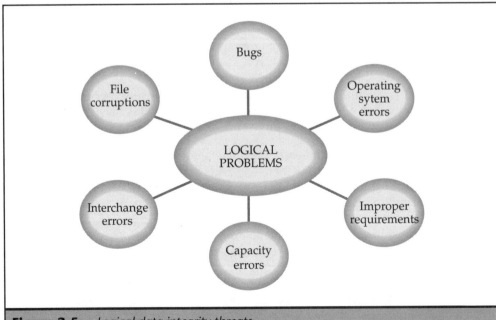

Figure 2-5.   *Logical data integrity threats*

FILE CORRUPTIONS Files can become corrupted as the result of some physical or network problem. They can also become corrupted by some flaw in system control or application logic. If the corrupt file is itself used by other processes to create data, the resulting data can be erroneous. This is a very nasty type of problem to solve, incidentally, because it is usually not obvious to the end user what files contribute to the overall process.

INTERCHANGE ERRORS Interchanging data files between applications is a common occurrence. So is cursing and foaming at the mouth when the conversion process turns out a mangled document that won't format correctly. Any time data must be run through a conversion process, such as between two different word processors, data integrity is at risk.

CAPACITY ERRORS By now, users should always be on the lookout for capacity-related causes of crashing or flaky behavior—like memory. When was the last time you completely filled up a Novell NetWare volume? Stressing a system to its limits conserves money, but it is dangerous. Any time a system gets bloated, all kinds of extra work needs to be done by the system to accommodate it. Eventually the machine will run out of room and leave you at the mercy of whatever contingencies exist in the operating system for this condition. Even if the machine gracefully shuts itself down, there are likely to be open files that do not get updated correctly.

OPERATING SYSTEM ERRORS Remember Windows 3.0 and the ever-threatening "Unrecoverable Application Error" dialog box? All operating systems have their own set of bugs. Convincing the developer of the operating system that you think there may be a bug in their system can be a stout challenge of willpower. Considering the complexity of operating systems, it really shouldn't come as a surprise when they are found. One of the more frustrating places for bugs is in one of the system's application programming interface, or API, codes. An API is used by third-party software and hardware developers to request or provide services to end users. These third-party companies write their products trusting that the APIs will work as advertised. What happens if they don't? In some cases data can be corrupted.

Because network operating systems are fairly complicated, you can always count on something not working correctly—often it is backup. Chapter 3 has more detail on backing up various network operating systems.

IMPROPER REQUIREMENTS Software developers have a habit of sequestering themselves in sanctuaries and developing better mousetraps. The problem with this approach, however, is that you've got rats, not mice. How often have you heard or uttered the plea: "Why on earth doesn't somebody finally build me something I can use?" If the software's requirements do not correctly describe the work that the user needs to do, the system could end up creating bad data. This typically happens where some numerical field is constrained and an entry is made that exceeds the boundaries. If error-checking code doesn't catch it, bad data will be created. For example, a tax product could allow you to enter a number of dependents, but it is a single digit field.

As it turns out, you have 12 dependents, but the software enters the last digit you entered, which is 2.

Disasters

There is nothing like a complete wipeout of your building or site to challenge the data integrity of your systems. Disaster recovery planning has been a staple of mainframe installations for the past 15 years; however, the distributed nature of the LAN environment has made it very difficult to implement there. Chapter 12 looks at disaster recovery planning and procedures. Figure 2-6 shows the most common types of disasters. The following sections examine each one briefly.

FIRES   Few things are as devastating as a fire. The destruction of resources from heat is only the beginning. Smoke damage, water damage, and the other resulting residue, especially PCBs, can make it impossible to ever restore anything following a fire. Software license agreements that show proof of purchase are not usable after they have turned to ashes; neither are purchase order forms.

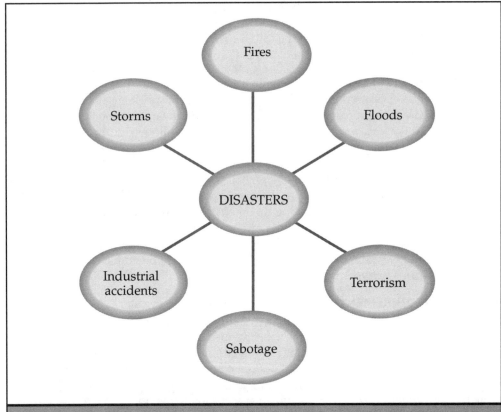

Figure 2-6.   *Disaster threats to data integrity*

FLOODS   Flooding is the most common disaster. Indeed, one cannot read the news on a regular basis without being aware of flooding occurring somewhere that week. The causes of floods are many and can be somewhat bizarre. The underground tunnel system flood in downtown Chicago in 1993 is an example of a completely unexpected flood. Internal water pipes breaking are another cause of unusual and unexpected floods.

STORMS   Tornadoes, hurricanes, ice storms, high winds, and even tidal waves are examples of storms that can either demolish a building, or at least completely wipe out power and water services.

INDUSTRIAL ACCIDENTS   Cables get cut by uninformed backhoe operators. Dangerous gases escape as the result of some accident at the plant or in transit. Nuclear power plants can malfunction. Industrial accidents may wipe out your building, in which case you've probably got more urgent problems on your hands than just data integrity. More likely, however, an industrial accident will make it impossible for you to access your equipment. The EPA or some other agency will quarantine an area until the threat of harm passes. This can take a lot more time than you would realize and also applies to fires, by the way.

SABOTAGE/TERRORISM   Unfortunately, there are people who believe it is their right to hurt or destroy equipment, buildings, and other people. The bombing of the federal building in Oklahoma City and the World Trade Center bombing are examples that made front page news. It would be wonderful if all terrorist activities would suddenly stop, but that's not likely to happen.

There are many instances of similar events that occur on a smaller scale that don't get publicized nearly as much. Disgruntled employees have been known to discharge firearms into data processing equipment. You may feel lucky if an angry employee limits his or her destructive activities to computers, but it does mean that you have a data integrity problem on your hands.

Security

The dictionary defines *security* as "the quality or state of being free from danger" and "measures taken to guard against espionage or sabotage, crime, attack, or escape." This section explores some of the ways data is put at risk. The term "security threat" is used in this book to identify a state or activity that could be exploited or used to gain unauthorized access to data.

Types of Security Threats

Security threats on distributed systems are challenging, to say the least. The different types of systems in use make it virtually impossible to implement consistent security measures across all systems in the organization, and centralized security on a network is intrinsically compromised. For example, if you or any process need to send information across the wire to execute security measures, the wire transfer alone makes the whole system suspect. Figure 2-7 shows the basic types of security threats. Each one will be examined briefly in the sections that follow.

Physical

Physical security is a fairly simple concept: don't let anybody get what you have, and don't let them spy on you either. The most common physical security threats are discussed in the following sections (see also Figure 2-8).

THEFT   There is a school of thought in law enforcement that says if you want to catch a criminal, you should think like one. Don't underestimate the bold bravado of thieves who use simple brute force methods to get what they want. If they want something they can't afford, they steal it. If they need money, they steal something and sell it. If the thing they want is in a safe, they steal the safe. If the thing they want is in a computer, they'll steal the entire computer.

Of course, another way to get information from a computer is to read it on a monitor. So how does one get access to a monitor? The brute force approach says you

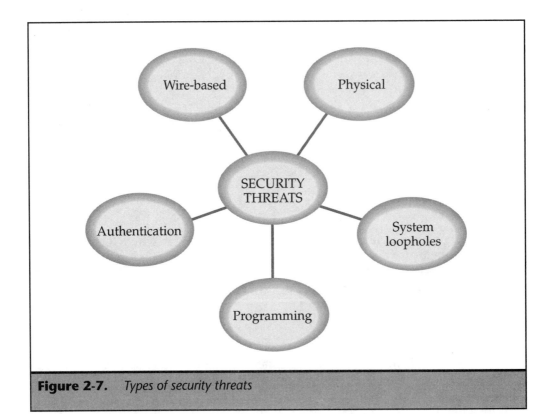

Figure 2-7.   *Types of security threats*

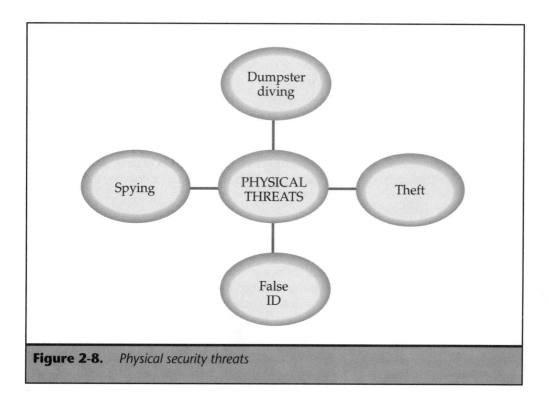

Figure 2-8. *Physical security threats*

pick the lock or steal the key, open the door, and walk right up to it; not very creative but it works.

DUMPSTER DIVING   Scavenging through trash looking for some printed materials or diskettes is a great way to spend an evening or weekend, especially if you can do it with someone you love. Some might call it clever, others call it dumpster diving, still others call it the perfect union of environment and personality. Enough said, but it happens.

SPYING   Face it, you have probably done it yourself sometime or another, even if by accident. You watch somebody enter his or her password on the keyboard and you learn it. Quite often this happens when you are helping somebody troubleshoot a problem and you end up logging in and out a hundred times. Maybe this isn't really spying, but there are people who *do* watch for these things and use them at your expense.

What you probably haven't done is walk around a competitor's building at night looking in windows and reading the information glowing in the dark on some stranger's monitor. Industrial espionage is very real. Governments even get into the act once in a while. This is certainly disquieting, but common enough; organizations will do all kinds of unethical things to save money and learn competitive secrets.

FALSE ID   Need a passport, a drivers license, a birth certificate, or an encoded security card? Somebody out there can make you one. Anybody who actually does something like this at least has a little bit of courage, technical aptitude, and cunning. This is where the brute force method meets some sophistication and skill. The people perpetrating such activities are also probably fairly serious about their plan and know what they are looking for; therefore they pose a significant threat to your data.

Wire-Based

The use of computer networks creates additional security threats to data. Several of the more common problems are discussed in the following sections (see also Figure 2-9).

EAVESDROPPING   The nature of distributed computing is that various discrete computers communicate over some type of media. It follows that you could "listen in" on the session traffic and gather information. This type of electronic eavesdropping does not even require that the listening device be physically attached to the wire; sometimes it is possible to pick up the signals from the radiation emitted across the wire. Given the confidential nature of internal communications in an organization, they may want to use encryption to prevent their messages from being easily decoded.

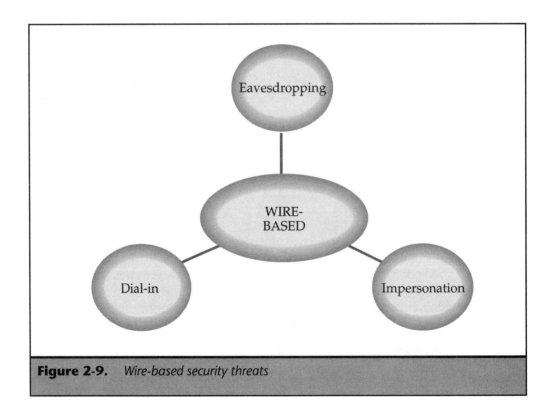

Figure 2-9.   *Wire-based security threats*

DIAL-IN   Anybody with a modem and a phone number to call can try to access your network through your remote dial-in facility, especially if they have a stolen laptop from somebody within your organization.

IMPERSONATION   The term *impersonation* refers to the ability of a machine on the network to appear as if it is another machine—the "evil twin" concept put to work. This is not easy to accomplish and means that somebody within your organization is probably involved who knows your network and operating procedures.

Authentication

Authentication refers to the process whereby a computer determines that you are authorized to request and provide certain services on the server. Without authentication there would be no useful security on LAN systems today. Common authentication security threats are summarized in Figure 2-10 and in the following sections. (Chapters 8 and 9 look at authentication in more detail.)

PASSWORD TRAPS   *Password traps* are one of the truly clever scams in computing and are related to the idea of impersonation discussed above. Somebody writes and compiles a code module that looks exactly like your logon screen. This is inserted in the logon sequence before the system asks for a logon. All the end user sees are two logon screens, one after the other; the first logon apparently fails, so the end user is asked to enter his or her ID again. In reality, however, the first logon attempt did not fail; it wrote the logon data such as Userid and password into a data file where it can be retrieved later.

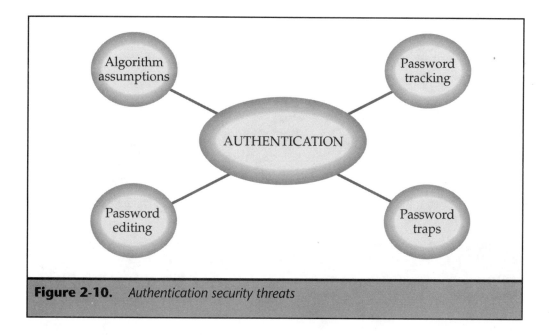

Figure 2-10.   *Authentication security threats*

PASSWORD CRACKING   Trying to crack a password on a computer is like trying to figure out the combination to a bicycle lock. And just as in any field, the professionals have a much higher skill and success rate than the amateurs.

ALGORITHM ASSUMPTIONS   Password screening works on a set of requirements that somebody somewhere coded and is based on some sort of algorithm. It is possible that these algorithms might not work for a given set of input. There are known cases of password algorithms that have been broken by clever intruders who intelligently used passwords of extended length to break into systems.

PASSWORD EDITING   Like many security compromises, *password editing* requires an inside breach. Quite simply, somebody inside a company sets up a bogus account or changes the password of an existing dormant account. Then the machine can be accessed by anybody who knows that user ID and password.

Programming

The truly interesting and diabolical security breaches originate in code (see Figure 2-11). Sometimes these attacks are benign in nature, as a test to see if they can be done. Most of the time, however, they are consciously destructive and will destroy data. Therefore viruses threaten both security and data integrity.

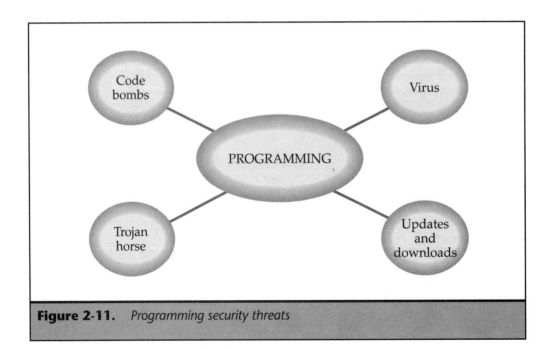

Figure 2-11.   *Programming security threats*

VIRUS   A *virus* is a piece of code that replicates itself by attaching to another program in the machine and moving into other machines when that program is transferred to it. This transfer could be via BBS downloads, diskettes that are traded, or any other way you get new stuff in your machine. Some of the most disturbing virus problems have occurred when shrink-wrapped commercial products had viruses embedded in the distribution diskettes that infiltrated machines when the software was installed. Chapter 11 explores viruses in more detail.

There have been many well-publicized viruses over the past several years. One of the most important ones, the Internet Worm, was not really a virus. The Internet Worm began as a person's quest to see if he could write something that would infiltrate the Internet and spread itself throughout the network. Using known UNIX security loopholes, it succeeded brilliantly in spreading itself all over the network and causing severe performance degradation problems for many systems on the Internet. It was not intended to be damaging, but unfortunately, it did have some damaging side effects by replicating itself within the systems that it infiltrated and eating up storage space. Overall, however, the Internet Worm probably did more good than harm by exposing serious security problems within the Internet and distributed computing in general.

CODE BOMBS   Most destructive viruses also function as *code bombs*. The idea of a code bomb is that on a given date and time, or based on some sequence of operations in the machine, the code bomb will be triggered and do its dirty work.

Code bombs do not have to spread like viruses, however; there have been plenty of cases where code bombs were written into a machine by the systems programmers working on them. The greedy programmer in the book and movie *Jurassic Park*, by Michael Crichton, uses a code bomb to turn off the electronic security system so he can steal the dinosaur DNA and smuggle it to a competitor. Schemes similar to this have been played out several times by people in real life. The idea is to write a code bomb that creates a bug in the system that nobody can figure out, at which point the devious programmer is invited back in to fix the problem he or she created, becoming an instant hero and making a fair amount of money in the process. It is high-tech blackmail where the victims don't even know they are being blackmailed, or if they suspect it, cannot prove it.

TROJAN HORSE   The moniker *Trojan horse* is a general term for the range of malevolent code threats that include viruses, bombs, worms, and the like. Like the name implies, a Trojan horse gets itself installed in a foreign machine and does the work of the unknown coder. Quite often the Trojan horse destroys data; sometimes it masquerades as another program that exists on your system, sometimes it creates user IDs and passwords.

UPDATES AND DOWNLOADS   Not to be confused with the ways Trojan horses wind up in your PC, some computer systems allow firmware and operating system updates via modem. There have been cases where intruders were able to break the access code for such processes and provide their own unauthorized updates.

System Loopholes

System loopholes are also known as *trapdoors*. Trapdoors are usually put into an operating system by developers to allow them to gain access to systems in the event a customer loses all knowledge of his or her authorized access. For example, VMS includes a standard maintenance ID and password that allow digital engineers to access their systems in case their customers forgot theirs. But sometimes these trapdoors result from system bugs, which means that nobody understands how they work except the people that discover them, and even they might not understand the process, just the result. Figure 2-12 summarizes the various security threats posed by system loopholes.

PIGGYBACKING   *Piggybacking* refers to a situation where one user stops communicating with another system, but for some reason the port stays active on the other system. Then another user can start communicating with the other system through the same port without passing any security checks.

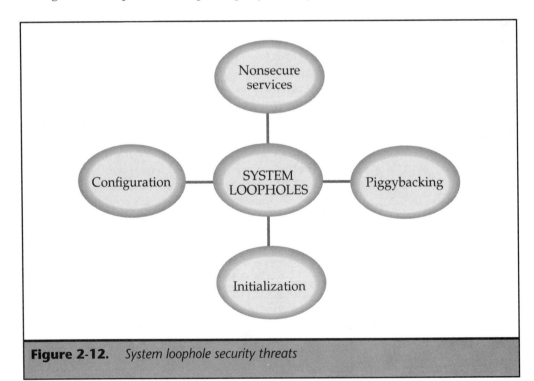

Figure 2-12.   *System loophole security threats*

NONSECURE SERVICES   Sometimes services of an operating system may bypass the machine's security system. The Internet Worm discussed previously in the section on viruses was able to exploit three such bypass mechanisms in the Berkeley UNIX system.

CONFIGURATION AND INITIALIZATION   Imagine having to down one of your servers for maintenance on one of its subsystems. A few days after you bring it back up, you are faced with a slew of end users complaining of missing or garbled files. What happened? It is possible that in reinitializing the system, the security system did not initialize correctly, leaving security holes for others to exploit, which they did. A related problem can occur when a Trojan horse program makes updates to system security configuration files.

General Solutions to Data Integrity and Security Threats

In the following sections we will briefly explore some of the broad techniques that can be used to maintain data integrity and system security. The remaining chapters in this book go into these topics in greater detail.

Tools for Improving Data Integrity

The following table lists some of the techniques for restoring data integrity or preventing a loss of data integrity. The column on the left lists the technique; the column on the right indicates if it is preventive or corrective. Preventive techniques are designed to keep data integrity from occurring, while corrective measures are used to restore data integrity following a loss.

Backup	Corrective
Mirroring	Preventive
Archiving	Preventive
Vaulting	Corrective
HSM	Preventive
Parity checking	Preventive
Disaster recovery planning	Corrective
Predictive failure analysis	Preventive
Power conditioning	Preventive
System security implementation	Preventive

Backup

The *backup system* is the most common method used to restore a compromised system. If you lose the data integrity of your system, restore an older snapshot of your system from your backup system. There is no excuse not to perform backups. The problem is that in LAN environments the backup operation is prone to failure. We will discuss backups in detail in Chapter 3.

Mirroring

Mirroring refers to copying data as it is written from one device or machine to another. Mirroring can be performed logically to replicate segments of a machine's file system somewhere else on the network. It can also be performed strictly on a physical level by mirroring disk drives, I/O drive subsystems, and entire machines. This topic is explored in Chapter 5.

Archiving

Archiving is a term that means many different things, depending on whom you are talking to. In this book, archiving refers to the process of removing files from network online storage and copying them to long-term shelf storage on tape or optical media. Although the primary purpose of archiving may be to create space on storage volumes by removing old files, it can also be done to enhance the protection of the file system by removing data from online storage and putting it in shelf storage, thereby protecting it from the funny things that can happen to files online. Archiving is examined in greater detail in Chapter 4.

Vaulting

Vaulting is a very simple concept: if your building gets wiped out, you need to recover data using a backup system and tapes stored at an off-site facility. Vaulting is how those tapes get somewhere else. Although data vaulting services are common, many LAN administrators do their own vaulting by using their briefcase or some other means of shuttling tapes. This last scenario is better than nothing, but a long way from providing the protection you really need. Chapter 3 discusses vaulting and vault rotation systems.

HSM

HSM, or *hierarchical storage management*, is an automated system for the archiving and recall of files from online storage to near-line storage and back again. It is quite closely related to archiving but presents additional benefits and risks to data integrity. Chapter 4 discusses these issues at some length.

Parity Checking

Parity checking is a feature of high-end server machines. It provides a watchdog mechanism for ensuring that unexpected memory failures do not result in server failures and loss of data integrity. Parity checking is discussed in greater detail in Chapter 5.

Disaster Recovery Planning

If you are left with virtually nothing after some disaster, where do you start, who do you call, and what if they can't make it? A *disaster recovery plan* is a road map to rebuilding your systems from scratch. Writing a disaster recovery plan could be the most valuable thing you will do this year. Distributed systems pose some difficult challenges, mostly because they change so frequently that a plan older than one year is likely to be obsolete. This topic is covered in Chapter 12.

Predictive Failure Analysis

It is rare for a component to fail all at once. If you could watch a device fail, you might notice that it started acting strangely for some time with an increasing number of errors. Components like disk drives are being developed that will tell you if they are starting to fail. Could this be a scam to get everyone to purchase more disk drives? Perhaps, but at prices less than 30 cents per megabyte for disk storage, it might not matter.

Power Conditioning

Like the backup system, an uninterruptible power supply is an essential element of a complete server system that supplies battery backup in case you lose power. These devices do more than provide battery backup, however; they also provide a consistent, smooth voltage to the machine. This is valuable because the power grid that supplies power fluctuates with load changes that can affect the operation of the system. Chapter 5 has more on this topic.

System Security Implementation

A major part of this book is about security. Keeping disgruntled employees, con artists, and competitors away from your systems will help maintain your data integrity. Chapter 8 discusses this topic in more detail.

Tools for Reducing Security Threats

The following is a short list of recommendations to provide adequate security to your systems. The column on the left lists the recommendation, while the column on the right indicates whether it can be implemented on your systems or if it is a personnel policy that must be communicated to your organization's employees.

Eliminating system loopholes	System
Virus scanning	System
Physical security	Policy
Unattended machine policy	Policy

Disposal policy	Policy
Password policy	Policy
Encryption	System
Authentication enforcement	System
Internet firewalls	System
Intruder entrapment	System

Eliminating System Loopholes

If you discover a loophole in your system, you may want to have it closed. Obviously, this could be a problem for you in the future if you end up with a system problem that requires the loophole to access the system. But how often have you had to bring in somebody from the manufacturer to do something like this? This is probably less risky than having somebody find out about it, access your system, and steal or destroy data.

Virus Scanning

Virus scanning is another item similar to backup and uninterruptible power supplies that is of critical importance to you. There are many virus scanning products on the market to help prevent virus intrusion. Virus scanners can run on LAN clients as well as on servers. You may find yourself implementing a strategy incorporating multiple virus systems if you feel you are prone to virus attacks. Viruses are discussed in Chapter 11.

Physical Security

Equipment that is locked up in rooms where most people can't see it is safer from security threats than equipment that is out in the open where anybody can walk up to it and study it and contemplate how neat it would look in their basement office. Although the equipment room may be fun to show off, it's probably only *really* interesting to you and your coworkers and anybody who wants to access it when nobody else is around.

Unattended Machine Policy

This is a clunky way of saying you might want to consider a corporate policy to make sure that screen savers and keyboard passwords are implemented. While almost everybody likes looking at new screen savers, most people dislike keyboard locks. At least there should be a policy that says machines should be powered off at night and over the weekends.

Disposal Policy

How do you throw away your old garbage? Shredded? Degaussed? Perhaps confidential documents on paper and in electronic format should be treated that way to foil the dumpster divers in your neighborhood.

Password Policy

How often do you force password changes? This should be done on a periodic basis. (Passwords shold not be reusable and should not be based on such things as family names or phone numbers.) This topic is discussed in depth in Chapter 8.

Encryption

Encryption scrambles data so it cannot be used unless it is first unencrypted. This keeps electronic peeping toms from getting too much of a thrill when they listen in on your network. If it is used on disk files, it keeps others from making copies of files and reading them on another machine somewhere else. Encryption of credit card information on the Internet is considered one of the primary functions necessary to reduce credit card fraud and promote electronic commerce.

The weakness in all encryption schemes is the use of an algorithm that can be decoded eventually by somebody else. This is especially true since the dissolution of the Soviet Union; there is an abundance of highly skilled cold-war mathematicians from both sides who have expertise and experience in this area. Chapter 10 has an analysis of encryption technology and techniques.

Authentication Enforcement

How do you tell who is doing what on your network anymore? You may not be accessing another machine directly, but some program you are running might be doing it without your knowledge. It is possible that somebody else who is trying to access your systems knows what is going on and how to take advantage of it. Authentication ensuring the validity of the person or program on the other end of the session is extremely important to many organizations. Kerberos, in the UNIX environment, is a product that does this. Chapter 10 discusses authentication.

Internet Firewalls

If you are going to be on the Internet, get a firewall installed. There are far too many hackers who know more about the intricacies of your systems than you do.

Intruder Entrapment

Turn the tables on people trying to hack their way into your system by using a product that tries to identify who they are and where they are working. The idea is to make intruders believe they are actually getting into your system while you simultaneously try to trace their source node.

CHAPTER THREE

Network Backup
Systems

As discussed in the previous chapter, computer systems fail for many reasons. What does this mean for organizations that depend on them? It means there must be some way to rebuild the computer system should it become necessary. While new equipment can be assembled to replace damaged parts, there is no way to buy new data from a vendor. The only way to put your data back into a machine is to restore it from some storage device or media that you put it on, typically as the result of running backup operations. There are other sorts of dangers to your network data as well, such as those caused by viruses or disgruntled employees. Of course, human fallibility also makes backups a necessity. As people make the minor and major errors they occasionally do when working with their files, it may become necessary to restore previous versions of those files.

For whatever reason you need to restore from backups, this chapter should help you understand the technology involved and give you a perspective to help you improve your backup operations.

Requirements of a Backup System

Backup systems exist for one purpose: to completely restore the data and systems information needed to run a computer system as quickly as possible. This is not conceptually difficult; most of us have been dumping and filling containers since we were children.

However, as LAN systems grow in complexity with an increasing variety of operating systems and network applications, it becomes much more difficult to achieve the thoroughness that is required. This means that adjustments are often made that compromise the goals of the simple requirements stated above. It is not uncommon for LAN professionals to adopt a compromised strategy where complete backup coverage is attempted, but rarely attained, to ensure that backups don't run into the regular workday and adversely affect network performance. This, of course, is a risky approach because data that does not get backed up cannot be restored.

The most dangerous response to backup problems is to give up on backups entirely. Surprisingly enough, this happens, and the results can be disastrous. This chapter presents a broad range of technologies and techniques that should help you analyze your own backup requirements so you can implement solutions that will work for you.

Operating System Backup Utilities

If many of the available operating systems today, such as Novell, Inc.'s NetWare, Microsoft Corporation's Windows NT, and many varieties of Unix, all come with their own backup products built in, the question is "Why would you ever want to spend money on something you can get for free?" The answer is simple. The operating system backup utilities are rudimentary and do not provide much in the way of automation and file management.

Although backup appears simple enough on the surface, there is a great deal of complexity involved in providing full-featured backup and recovery services. Incorporating more complicated backup capabilities into the operating system would add considerable overhead to any operating system development effort and could have a negative impact on product schedules. However, in today's world of mergers and acquisitions, this scenario could change at any time; an operating system company could control a backup software company and decide to more tightly integrate the backup technology with the operating system.

Network Backup Building Blocks

Before analyzing LAN backup systems, there are four basic network components to identify and become familiar with.

- **Target** A *target* is any system that is being backed up or restored.
- **Engine** The *engine* is the system that performs backup tasks, such as copying data from a target to tape.
- **Device** For the purposes of this chapter, *device* means a *storage* device that writes data on removable media, usually tape.
- **SCSI bus** The *SCSI bus* is the physical and electrical cables and connectors that link devices to networked computers. For LAN backup, the SCSI bus usually connects devices to the backup engine system.

Two Basic Backup Systems

The simplest backup system is one that combines the four components discussed in the previous section in one machine. Figure 3-1 shows a stand-alone server backup system that consists of a single server that backs itself up to a SCSI attached tape drive.

A variation of this approach takes the engine, SCSI bus, and device and moves them to a dedicated workstation on the network. Figure 3-2 shows this type of system.

Server to Server Backup

Figure 3-3 shows a server to server backup system. It is similar to both stand-alone server backup and workstation-based backup. Server B backs itself up to an attached device—and also backs up servers A, B, and C. This is the most common implementation of LAN backup in use today.

Dedicated Network Backup Server

Because of problems that can occur with backups running on production servers (to be discussed later in this chapter), some organizations place the engine, SCSI bus, and device components on dedicated server systems. This concept is very close to the

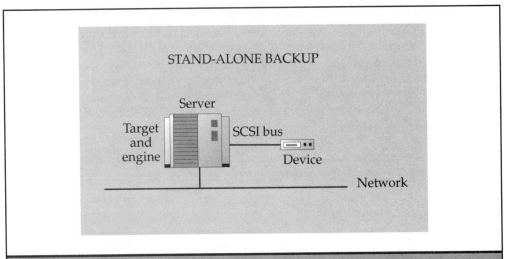

Figure 3-1.   *In stand-alone backup, the server backs itself up to the attached device*

workstation backup method shown in Figure 3-2, except the workstation is replaced with a server for performance and compatibility purposes. Figure 3-4 is a diagram of a dedicated network backup server system.

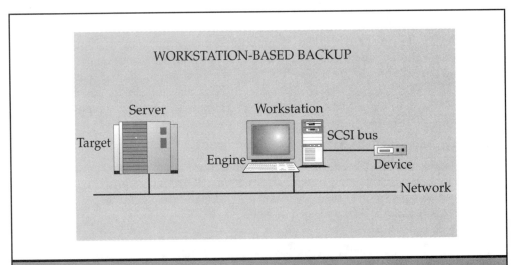

Figure 3-2.   *In workstation-based backup, the server data is transferred to the workstation and written to the device*

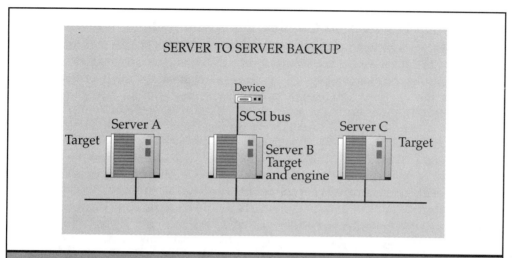

Figure 3-3.   *In server to server backup, server B backs itself up, as well as backing up servers A and C*

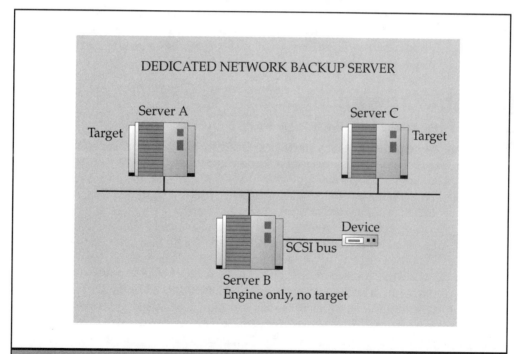

Figure 3-4.   *Server B is dedicated to backup processing and backs up servers A and C to its attached device*

A Systems Approach to Backup

Now imagine your own network. Think of all the servers and PCs on it, including machines with databases and application systems such as electronic mail; don't forget to consider the operating systems on these machines and the file systems within them. Next, think of your network fabric: cabling routers, bridges, NICs, even device drivers. Now add to this mental picture all of the storage equipment, including disk drives, tape drives, and the like; don't forget to consider SCSI controllers or other peripheral controllers.

While you are visualizing your entire network, try to convince yourself that the sole purpose of this network is to run backup operations. Imagine that database machines and high-capacity servers exist only to provide data for being backed up. Think about the amount of data on each machine, and try to imagine it is there for the express purpose of being backed up. Think about the flow of traffic on the network during backup operations and how the data is transferred from a disk drive, over the system bus, onto the network, through the backup system, and finally onto the tape drives or other equipment where it is stored.

Referring to Figures 3-1 and 3-2, you may be able to see where bottlenecks can occur in your network backup system. If servers A, B, or C are performance-constrained, data transfers could be slow. This could be caused by such things as protocol and communication inefficiencies, operating system overhead, target software performance, disk fragmentation, slow I/O or SCSI controllers, lack of caching, and processor overload.

A Thought Experiment: Putting Network Backup First

To continue the systems approach started earlier, we'll now examine several other ways to improve the performance of a backup-only network.

If you wanted to optimize backup performance, you would make sure servers A, B, and C ran on the same hardware platforms and operating systems. This would make it easy to balance the work and provide some degree of predictability. You could also tune your protocol and driver configurations for backup operations and use a prioritization scheme for disk I/O that gives backups the highest priority. Special adapter cards could be used to speed the transfers of data from the disk to the LAN.

As for the network, you would use a dedicated network that wasn't available to any other applications. The higher performance the network, the better. You might even want to use multiple network cards in the backup system and give servers A, B, and C their own dedicated backup segments through a network switch.

Your backup systems would have fast CPUs, possibly even multiprocessor systems with very fast I/O characteristics. The system would be capable of streaming data to multiple devices at the same time, and it would have the intelligence to do the most efficient selection of files. Every time you placed a new system on the network, you would make sure it integrated with your existing backup system first, to minimize the impact it had on your backup system.

Back to Reality

However, the scenario outlined above is only a conceptual experiment. Backup is probably not in the forefront of your thoughts every day. Unfortunately, it is normally one of the last budget items considered when new LAN systems are installed. The technology of building a network is fascinating, and we tend to get caught up in the thrills and challenges of installing and optimizing our network applications. Most of the time, backup doesn't make the radar screen until the last minute.

This exercise might point out weaknesses in your network that you were not aware of. Perhaps you shouldn't expect your backup system to be adequate for the systems that are running on it. Your bridges, routers, hubs, and switches may not be able to gracefully handle all your data moving across them during backups. If you planned your network to handle peak traffic loads that occur during normal working hours only, you may find yourself running out of bandwidth for backups before you realize it. When you install new systems in your environment, do you consider whether or not your current backup system will work?

Unfortunately, identifying such problems doesn't necessarily solve your problem. You may find yourself in a quandary because the backup technology you need isn't available. Perhaps the database vendor doesn't provide adequate tools for facilitating backup, making it a manual process. Perhaps your network didn't have the bandwidth to move all the data you were planning to create. Maybe the new operating system had relatively weak support from the backup companies, or the system bus of your backup system is not fast enough to keep pace with the new high-speed tape devices you bought, throwing off all your careful calculations for backup performance.

The point here is simple: backup must be thought of as a systems process if it is going to work for you. Don't just blame the tape drive or the software for difficulties; you need to think broadly to understand how to back up your network.

Historical Development of LAN Backup

LAN backup products have a relatively short history. In the mid to late '80s, network backup started to receive the attention of LAN administrators. The first LAN backup products were designed primarily to back up Novell NetWare servers. The first backup products for PC LANs were DOS based, meaning that server data was copied over the network to a PC running a backup application and written to a tape drive connected to the PC.

With the introduction of NetWare's NLM architecture with NetWare 3.x, backup companies started designing their applications to reside on the server and execute as server processes, resulting in less network traffic and higher performance.

Today, most LANs have many different types of operating systems and network applications within them. As a result, we are starting to see the backup companies respond with products that are evolving toward a distributed multiplatform model, but there is still a great deal of progress to be made in this area.

Backup System Components

If you consider backup to be a system, what is the system composed of? Table 3-1 shows the various parts of a generic backup system along with a brief explanation of their roles.

As you can see there are many pieces to the puzzle, all having to work together to form a well-oiled, reliable system. When making changes to your backup system, you may want to keep these components in mind to make sure that the solution you implement is balanced. If it is not, you may find yourself wasting money on products that you thought would provide the performance you need but cannot due to other system constraints.

We will now look at these components in more detail in the following sections.

Component	Description
Physical host system	Machine where primary backup logic executes
Logical host system	Operating system for above
I/O bus	Machine's internal bus, also external buses like SCSI
Peripheral devices	Tape drives, disk drives, optical drives
Device driver software	The low-level code that interfaces with devices
Backup storage media	Magnetic tape, optical platters, etc.
Operations scheduler	Determines what to do each day backups run
Operations executor	The code that performs the backup operation
Physical target system	The machine data is being copied from
Logical target system	The operating system and environment for it
Network fabric	Routers, bridges, switches, cabling
Network protocol(s)	Transport protocols: IPX/SPX, TCP/IP, etc
System metadata	Knowledge base of backup file information
System console	Administrator's interface
Systems management	SNMP or other ways to manage the system

Table 3-1.   *Backup System Components*

Physical Host System

This is the system where the "brains" of the backup application reside. This could be a 100Mhz Dual Pentium PCI bus PC, a 16Mhz 386-based PC, a Unix workstation, a Power PC, an Apple Macintosh, a Digital Alpha-based machine, or any other piece of hardware from which backups are run. These machines all have different CPUs with different performance characteristics as well as different system I/O buses (discussed in the following sections). Hence the performance of backup may be limited by some bottleneck inherent in the machine.

Logical System Host

This is the operating system (OS), where the main body of the backup system resides. The OS provides I/O functionality according to its internal architecture. For that reason, the operating system can become a limiting factor in backup performance.

I/O Bus

There are two parts to the I/O bus: the first is the internal system bus that the machine uses to transfer data, and the second is the external storage bus that is often used to connect storage devices.

There are several system buses in use on LAN-connected computers today that the various manufacturers tout as being fastest. Often these claims don't mean much to the customer because the systems never come close to exercising the full bandwidth of the bus. This is not necessarily true for backups, however; once you have a fast enough processor in your host system, this is the next most likely place to find a bottleneck. Moving the entire contents of the file system through the system bus will probably test the performance of the system bus. Any bottlenecks here will show up if your storage bus and devices are fast enough. Most PC systems, including systems utilizing high-speed bus architectures such as EISA and PCI, cannot move data faster than 5MB per second (MBps)—most of them are much slower, in fact. If you hit this limitation, you are in the land of the "I/O bound," and you also have some relatively fast storage hardware. Some Unix systems, on the other hand, have bus architectures that are much faster, in the range of 10 to 15MB per second.

The most common bus for storage device connection today is SCSI (Small Computer Systems Interface). There are several SCSI implementations that are worth knowing about, and you may find it helpful to have a clear understanding of what they are and how you might use them. Table 3-2 indicates the various SCSI bus specifications, including the number of devices that can be attached to each SCSI controller. Single-ended SCSI is the most common connector implemented, which means that SCSI bus lengths should not exceed three meters: this does not mean that individual cables cannot exceed three meters, but that all cables combined on the bus, including internal cables inside machines, cannot exceed three meters. Differential SCSI connectors circumvent this problem by allowing the SCSI bus to be up to 15 meters in length; the problem, however, is that relatively few products use differential SCSI connectors.

SCSI Bus	Speed (MBps)	Number of Devices That Can Be Attached
Regular SCSI, 8-bit transfers	5	7
Fast SCSI (Fast uses an enhanced protocol)	10	7
Wide SCSI, 16-bit transfers	10	15
Fast-wide SCSI	20	15
Ultra SCSI, 8-bit	20	15
Ultra SCSI, 16-bit	40	15

Table 3-2.   *SCSI Technology Comparison*

What is interesting to note about the SCSI speeds is that most of them exceed the speed of the system bus. So even if SCSI will support 10MBps transfers, your system will never see anything close to that today. Therefore, if you think you will need very fast storage subsystems, it is a good idea for you to start paying attention to developments in technology that can move data using PCI (peripheral component interconnect) bus mastering technology. PCI is a scaleable architecture that will be able to accommodate high-speed data transfers.

Although bus mastering adapters have been on the market for some time—ever since the PC bus wars between EISA and Microchannel (MCA)—they have been built for general-purpose activities such as network connections and disk controllers with the intention of off-loading the CPU and enabling better overall system performance. Truly high-speed, high-throughput, peer-to-peer bus mastering adapters capable of handling massive data transfers between storage devices have not existed, partly because of limitations in available system buses, but also because that level of performance has not been required.

Over the last several years a great deal has been written about how PC-based systems will eventually replace mainframe systems for much of data processing due to the cost advantages and rapid improvement in technology in PC processing power. People planning on shifting operations from mainframes to PC platforms are advised to be aware of the data transfer limitations of PC systems and what that means for data protection.

Multiple SCSI devices are connected to a single SCSI PC adapter using a technique called "daisy-chaining." Figure 3-5 shows a string of daisy-chained devices connected to a single SCSI adapter in a server system, and Figure 3-6 shows a detail of SCSI device connectors.

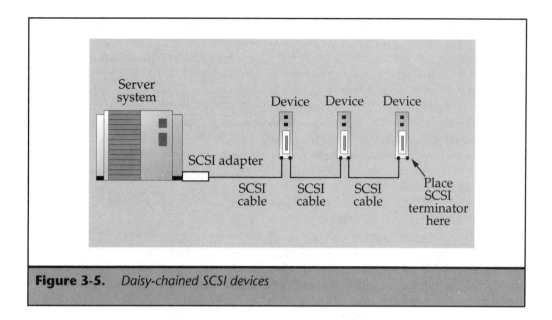

Figure 3-5.   *Daisy-chained SCSI devices*

Peripheral Devices

The peripheral devices are the disk drives, tape drives, optical drives, RAID systems—whatever you read and write data to. Most of these devices are slower than the system bus and none can fully utilize the SCSI bus.

The performance limitations for storage devices are usually physical. The faster the data can be moved past a recording head, the better the performance will be. For

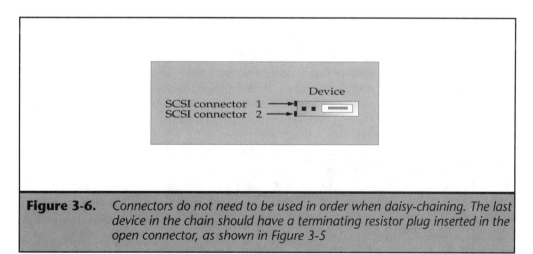

Figure 3-6.   *Connectors do not need to be used in order when daisy-chaining. The last device in the chain should have a terminating resistor plug inserted in the open connector, as shown in Figure 3-5*

disks, performance is limited by the rotation speed of the disk; that's why high-RPM (revolutions per minute) drives are faster than lower-RPM drives: the faster the drive spins, the faster data can be read from it. For tape drives, the limitation is how fast the tape transfer can keep tape moving past the heads at a high rate of speed while depositing data on it. This is known as tape streaming.

RAID (Redundant Array of Inexpensive Disks) technology allows faster performance by writing data to multiple devices in sequence. The devices have coordinated movement mechanisms that allow a single data stream to be written to each device in turn, without having to wait for them to catch up. Because there are other devices sharing the load, no single device will limit the performance. RAID is discussed in more detail in Chapter 5.

Device Driver Software

The SCSI chip set manufacturers all use programmable device drivers that control the operations of their hardware via some application programming interface. Adaptec's ASPI (Advanced SCSI Programming Interface) has become a pseudo-standard in the PC network marketplace, and, as a result, most of the backup software supports ASPI.

Figure 3-7 shows the relationship between the backup software, device drivers, SCSI connector, and recording media.

Differences in device drivers can have a significant impact on both the performance and reliability of the SCSI subsystem. Sometimes you might be tempted to try out a new upgrade of a driver, but in general, it is not a good idea to change your SCSI drivers unless you have a good reason for it. As a rule of thumb, if it's not broken, you're better off not fixing it.

Backup Storage Media

Media and the devices that write to them are virtually inseparable. The devices, of course, have a lot more features than media and cost a lot more money. For that reason, people implementing backup products often focus their attention on the devices and don't give much thought to the media. This is understandable but a bit shortsighted, because the data actually resides on the media, not on the drive; and if you ever need to restore from your backup system, you can always replace the drive but not the particular tape that has the file versions you're looking for. In general, the wider the tape, the better the reliability and capacity. Media is discussed in greater detail later in this chapter.

Operations Scheduler

This is the part of the backup system that determines what data to copy to backup media for a given set of circumstances. These usually include day of the week, business cycles like monthly accounting closing, and other cyclical or calendar-based data. Some backup systems allow a great deal of flexibility in scheduling and automating your backup operations. This topic is sometimes referred to mistakenly as tape rotation, which is covered later in the chapter.

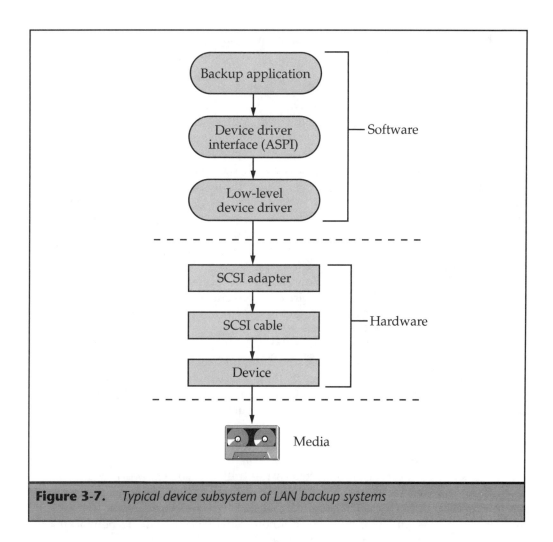

Figure 3-7.   *Typical device subsystem of LAN backup systems*

Operations Executor, or Backup Engine

This is the software that most people associate with a backup and recovery engine. Think of it as the program responsible for the bulk of the work during backup operations. It is also the lifeblood of most software companies writing backup software. Mistakes in this part of the software can make for inefficient operations or serious nightmares during futile restore operations.

Physical Target System

The target system is the machine that has data on it that you want to back up. The word "physical" refers to the actual hardware platform. Just as the hardware platform of the backup host system can make a significant impact, the hardware platform of the target can have significant impact on overall backup performance.

Logical Target System, or Agent

The target, of course, has an operating system and applications running on it. It also has an end user who occasionally uses it. For the purposes of backup, however, the primary logical component of the target is an agent that responds to requests from the operations executor (or backup engine) described previously. This agent is responsible for handing off files and other system data through some pipeline to be read by the backup engine. It must be able to handle the target's file system details and other system data that does not reside within the target's file system. Targets are sometimes referred to as clients, which can be confusing, due to the way the term "client" is used to describe client/server computing. The primary difference between "target" and "client" is that targets refer to any system that is being backed up, including servers, whereas clients usually refer to end user workstations or PCs.

Target software that is buggy or slow can have a severe impact on overall backup operations. Problems with target software can even crash the backup engine. Also, if the backup operation processes each target in sequence, a particularly slow target could prevent the entire backup from finishing on time.

Due to the high availability requirements of database and other application systems, it may not be possible to close those files for backup. This introduces the requirements to have special target agents that can adequately address the intricacies of such systems. You can expect to see increasingly more of these specialized application target agents from companies in the backup industry. Chapter 6 discusses this in more detail.

Network Fabric

Network fabric is a term for the stuff that carries traffic on your network: routers, bridges, hubs, concentrators, switches, cabling, and anything else that sits between computers on your network. It's common to discover your network fabric's weaknesses when running backups. A common scenario occurs when a networking device is overrun with files and drops packets. When packets are dropped, many problems can occur, including file corruption, missed targets, and even backup system failure. For this reason, it's a good idea to have some realistic understanding of the backup system's load on the network before making a large investment in network fabric. Figure 3-8 shows network fabric in an interconnected LAN.

Network Protocols

This is one of the major pains in LAN backup—what types of services are available through what protocols, and how reliable are they? Just as backup will test network fabric, it will also test your protocol stacks because the volume of traffic is so great. Inefficiencies in the protocol stack may not be noticeable in daily traffic; but during

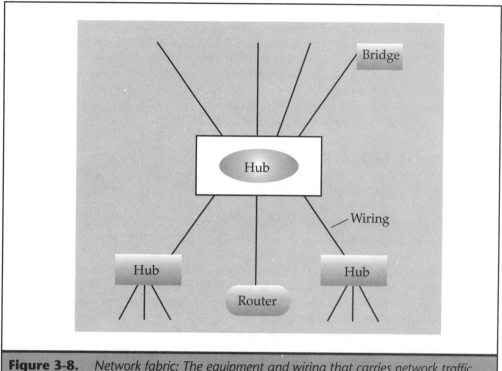

Figure 3-8.   *Network fabric: The equipment and wiring that carries network traffic*

backups it will result in poor performance and even cause the communication session to disconnect and fail, which triggers unpredictable behavior in the backup system.

System Metadata

Think of the system metadata as the database that holds all the detailed records about which files were backed up to which device, when they were backed up, what the file system attributes were, and anything else the backup engine developer thought was important. While a database system is not essential, that is how most metadata systems are implemented.

Considering the huge number of transactions occurring in backups, it is important that the metadata system be set up in a way that allows rapid updating and that there is a way to control the size of the metadata files. A backup application design that overlooks this part of the application can result in serious problems, as this subsystem is core to the operation of the entire backup system.

System Console

The backup system has a console someplace where you observe and operate the backup system. Usually this is implemented on a platform with a GUI interface as a client machine, as in client/server computing, while the system with devices attached is the server. Performance of the backup system can be degraded while observing backups at the console due to the additional load of sending this information over the network. For that reason, you are probably better off not leaving the system console interface running when you are not actually there to view it.

Figure 3-9 shows a backup console running on a PC controlling and monitoring the engine running on server B. Backup consoles are developed specifically for each engine and vary considerably in look and feel.

Systems Management

As network systems continue to grow in number of machines and storage capacity, it is becoming increasingly important to be able to quickly view the status of many backup systems on the network. Some sort of network management capability to do this is quickly becoming a requirement. This can be a proprietary method for viewing backup installations, which could provide you with detailed information, or it could be done within your network management console, most likely via SNMP (Simple Network Management Protocol), to indicate any alerts or other troubles. While SNMP seems like the logical choice, there are no standard MIBs (Management Information Bases) for backup systems. Without a standard MIB, the messages and warnings from different backup systems will be inconsistent.

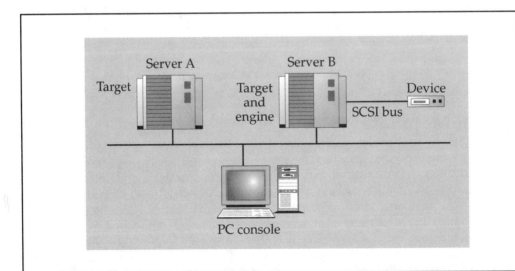

Figure 3-9.   *The backup system console gives the administrator control of the backup engine on server B. Notice the console does not need to be a target for backup*

Devices and Media

There is a certain mystique surrounding the devices and media used for backup and recovery, probably due to the wishful thinking that accompanies their use. To many, tapes and tape drives are a black art—you may not know how something works or how it fails, but you know that if you spin around on one foot three times humming your favorite golden oldies everything seems to go better. Trying to work, or even troubleshoot a problem, in this manner can take a great deal of time and is not recommended. The following section gives some background in this area so you can appreciate the technology and also save yourself some headaches in the future.

Tape Media

Data-grade tape media is much more difficult to design and manufacture than most people realize. It is made up of several layers of materials with different characteristics. Among these are tensile strength, so it won't break; flexibility, so it can be wound tightly and then change shape rapidly as it moves through the tape drive; and magnetic properties, so the tape can be erased and overwritten with new data without being affected by the constant presence of low-level magnetic images on other parts of the media. On top of all that, it needs to stay together without having its layers separate or fall apart.

For these reasons, and others discussed here, you are advised to use tapes designated specifically for data recording. Other tapes, such as audio or videotape, may not be good enough for your data. Audio and videotapes are made with the philosophy that a few bits lost here and there do not make a substantial difference in the results. A few bits of data dropped, however, can ruin everything you're working on.

Error Correction on Tape

It probably comes as no surprise, then, that tape recording methods for data implement sophisticated error-correction techniques to ensure that data is written and read correctly. As a rule of thumb, 30 percent of the tape's surface is used for error-correction information. As data is successfully written to tape, the error-correction data is written along with it in case the tape degrades in storage before it is needed for restoring data. If the raw data on the tape cannot be read, the error-correction information is used to try to calculate the values of the missing bits. If the data cannot be reconstructed by the drive, the drive will issue a media failure message to the SCSI host, alerting the system to the media failure.

During the write phase, there is a read-after-write test that is done with a secondary head to determine that the data just written can be read again. If this test fails, the tape is forwarded to a new position and the write attempt is tried again. After so many retries, the drive will give up and issue a fatal media error to the SCSI host. At that point your backup operation fails until new media is loaded.

Tape Drive Cleaning

Clean your tape drives regularly! This should not be trivialized or ignored. Think about all the weird stuff that tape has to be able to do and the performance you expect from it. This all happens on a microscopic level between the tape drive heads and the tape media. Smoke and most other airborne particles have magnetic charges that are attracted to magnetic fields created by tape drives. This means your tape drive acts like a miniature vacuum cleaner to help clean the air of floating dirt—depositing it right on your tape drive's heads. You can guess what that means to the head/tape interaction—that there can be a lot of extra garbage in there wrecking the efficiency of the system.

The other thing that causes tape to get dirty is that the tapes themselves flake off particles onto the heads. It is impossible to prevent this, even though the tape manufacturers may have bright and talented people working full time to improve the situation. Simply reading and writing tapes makes tape heads get dirty. It's one of the byproducts of the technology—like automobile engines getting dirty because they are constantly creating explosions, which in turn creates carbon that results from the combustion.

Clean your tape drive heads and try to follow the manufacturer's suggested schedule. As a rule of thumb, do this every thirty hours of operation. If this is difficult, do it at least once a week, and be sure to use a nonabrasive cleaning cartridge for the task; otherwise you could destroy the heads on your drive. It is unfortunate but true that many times data is lost because tape drives are too dirty to function properly and the media becomes damaged in the process.

Tape Head Failures

You may start receiving an increase in tape errors from your backup system, even using new tapes. When this happens you should be suspicious of the condition of your tape heads. Clean and reclean your heads, and then test the drive with brand new data-grade tapes. If you receive a high level of errors, the heads are suspect and may need replacing. Keep in mind that you will receive a much faster response from the drive manufacturer if you have already done these things in advance—they almost certainly will ask you to do them first, so you might as well save yourself the time.

Also, do not think that you can fool the manufacturers and get a free replacement by telling them you clean the drive every week when in fact you don't. Some drives sold today have internal circuitry and data blocks that track cleanings, so if you end up sending in your drive for inspection or replacement, they may know if you are stretching the truth about your cleaning history.

Shelf Maintenance

Tape that sits on a shelf for a long period of time should be "exercised" once a year. This helps keep the tape flexible and improves its reliability. Exercising the tape is easily accomplished by reading to the end of the tape and rewinding.

QIC Technology

QIC stands for quarter-inch cartridge. This is the same width tape that has been used for years in audio recording. The technology is well understood and very stable. This media has been viewed as a low-end solution for stand-alone backup systems and therefore is not applicable to LAN systems because capacities and speeds are too low.

QIC has an active industry standards group that meets regularly to discuss pertinent issues. Recently, QIC has added 5GB-capacity drives and will have a 13GB drive with MR (magneto-resistive) heads, which allow much greater density of tracks on the tape. These new drives should help move QIC from the ranks of the low end into mainstream LAN backup.

4mm Technology

Another technology whose roots are in audio recording is 4mm tape. First introduced as digital audio tape, or DAT, Hewlett-Packard and Sony led the development of a DAT tape standard for use in data storage. Several other companies also joined the DAT standards effort and manufacture DAT tape equipment. Such tapes are signified by the acronym DDS, for digital data storage.

The original DDS tape was 60 meters in length and held 1.3GB of uncompressed data. After 90-meter tapes were introduced, DAT tapes boosted their capacity to 2GB. With the addition of compression, these tapes grew to a capacity (calculated for average file compressibility) of 4GB. DDS II tapes have a native capacity of 4GB with a compressed capacity in the ballpark of 8GB. DDS III technology is under development with availability set for the summer of 1996 that is expected to significantly increase DAT's capacities again to 8GB, without compression.

To accommodate different capacity media easily, the DAT tape industry has adopted a technology called the *media recognition system*, or MRS.

MRS media can be positively identified by newer DAT tape drives that have the ability to sense information encoded on the exterior of the tape cartridge. Such information can greatly help reduce confusion and help administrators manage backups more effectively.

8mm Technology

The technology of 8mm tapes was derived from videotape recorders. Exabyte Corporation seized the opportunity and developed 8 mm tape and drives for data recording. It's possible that other manufacturers of videotape recorders may enter this market.

Capacities of 8mm tapes started at 2.2GB and now are 7GB native and 14GB using extended length tapes (160 meters) and compression. The next generation drive from Exabyte, which has been in development for some time, is referred to as "Mammoth." It is touted as having capacities in the 20GB range and transfer rates of 3GB per second (GBps).

One of the advantages of 8mm tapes is the fact that they are readily available and exist on many systems. This means that data interchangability between systems is somewhat easier than with 4mm tape. Please note, however, that tape format differences in the various manufacturer's software packages could likely result in interchange incompatibilities.

Digital Linear Tape

Digital linear tape, or DLT, was developed by Digital Equipment Corporation for use on VAX midrange systems. The tape is a half-inch wide in a sturdy cartridge that can withstand a great deal of stress and vibration. DLT has excellent characteristics for reliability and shelf life, and it also costs more.

DLT tape cartridges have one internal reel, the other reel is situated inside the tape drive mechanism. This provides an extra level of protection for the tape because no part of the tape is exposed when it is out of the drive. The disadvantage of this design is that DLT tapes usually take slightly longer to load than other technologies.

Quantum Corporation acquired the technology for DLT from Digital in 1994, along with Digital's disk drive technology. As with Exabyte and 8mm drives, Quantum is currently the sole manufacturer of DLT hardware, although other companies are selling it under their brand names. One of the biggest questions surrounding DLT is whether the equipment can be manufactured in quantity. Supply has been an issue with these drives.

Performance and capacities of DLT tapes are also excellent. The DLT 2000 drive writes 10GB native and 20GB compressed to a single cartridge. The DLT 4000 has a native capacity of 20GB and 40GB with compression.

3480/3490

The 3480/3490 tapes are a media used in the mainframe world for high-speed devices. These tapes have historically had extremely high transfer rates and relatively small capacities in the 250 to 500MB range. They are not widely supported in the LAN marketplace because of the cost of the devices. However, this situation could change as LAN systems increase in storage capacity and online database systems requiring short backup interruptions evolve. Still the newest tape cartridge in this family, the 3490-E has been slow to gain acceptance and has a comparatively small native capacity of 1GB.

Optical Media

Optical media is based on interpreting the reflections of laser light off the surface of the media. The zero and one bits on optical media reflect light differently, allowing the optical drive to shine a laser light on the tracks and determine the differences in the reflection. In general, it is much more robust than tape because the media is static, which means it doesn't move through tape transports and get wrapped around spools at high speed. Also, the media doesn't generate its own dirt. On the down side, the challenges of writing to optical media are much greater than those involved with tape and will be discussed later in this chapter.

Magneto-Optical

Magneto-optical technology is based on the interaction of magnetic and laser technologies. The term "magnetic susceptibility" refers to the relative ease with which the magnetic alignment of molecules within some material can be changed. As it turns out, magnetic susceptibility is related to the temperature of the material; typically, the hotter the material, the higher its susceptibility. In other words if you raise the temperature of the material, you make it easier to write magnetic information on it.

On a miniature level, magneto-optical technology works by raising the temperature of the material on the platter and then quickly altering its magnetic alignment. The media cannot have its magnetic properties altered at normal operating temperatures, which is one of the reasons for the long life span of data on magneto-optical data cartridges. Writing data to magneto-optical platters requires two passes, one to first erase the old data and the other to write the new data.

Magneto-optical cartridges, or MO for short, have the best longevity and resistance to wear and tear of all available media. Unlike tape, there is no particulate matter that flakes off the surface. As a platter, it is a random-access media that allows extremely fast recall of data, making it excellent for hierarchical storage management applications or any other system where transparent recall of near-line data is important. In addition, there are several companies manufacturing MO equipment and a few standards bodies attempting to ensure interchangeability of the technology between manufacturers.

However, the capacity of MO does not match the capacity of tape, and for that reason it is not widely used as a backup media. MO media began as a 650MB platter on 5.25" media. These platters held 325MB per side. The original 3.5" MO cartridges held 128MB of data, not even close to being useful for LAN applications. There are also 12" MO drives that have platters with capacities of 4GB, 2GB per side, but the cost of this equipment has kept it from being supported in the LAN world.

Today, there are a few manufacturers with 5.25" MO drives having a combined capacity of 2GB; 1GB per side. The 3.5" media can now hold up to 256MB of data, still too small for network applications. (But, keep in mind, those capacities continue to increase.) In general, the threat from large magnetic disks; high-speed, high-reliability tapes like DLT; and CD-R technology may put the entire magneto-optical industry out of business. This would be unfortunate, as MO is an excellent media for backup and archiving purposes, having the best characteristics for long-term data storage of all media.

CD-Recordable

In all likelihood, CD-recordable (CD-R) media will become the most widely used optical media in the near future due to its cost and familiarity. CD-R is based on a smooth, clear surface platter with a dyed background that can be changed to signify the difference between bits. The writing laser is capable of changing the dye, thus writing data to the CD. At the present time, this is a one-shot deal, and CDs should be thought of as a WORM (write once, read many) device. This limits its use as a media for backup operations.

CD-ROM–recordable devices are making their way into the market. At the current time they are not adequate for network backup operations due to their slow performance and technical difficulties with multisession media writing. To comply with the ISO 9660 standard for CD-ROM media, the data must be written in one uninterrupted operation. The unpredictable nature of traffic makes it virtually impossible to ensure this could happen; in network backup, it can be impossible to keep that type of data stream flowing to the device.

Performance Comparisons

Table 3-3 shows the optimum uncompressed write performance characteristics of the various media previously discussed.

Achieving Maximum Performance from Your Devices

When you have a lot of data to back up, performance is important. This section looks at some of the technology that can be applied to improve backup performance.

RAID

The time it takes tape to move over recording heads is a bottleneck where performance is an issue. Data General, Ultera Systems, and HI-PAR Systems have developed tape RAID systems to address the performance issues of tape backup in the LAN market. The concept of tape RAID is similar to disk RAID in that data is "striped" across multiple tape devices, thereby achieving extremely fast transfer rates. Pinnacle Micro has built an MO RAID called "Orray" that uses color-coded 5.25" MO platters.

Media	Write Performance (MBps)
QIC	1.0
4mm, DDS IIDAT	0.6
8mm	0.5
DLT	2.0
3480/3490	3.0
Magneto-optical	1.0

Table 3-3. *Write Performance for Backup Media*

This device is not being marketed as a backup device, but could probably be used effectively for it in some situations.

The RAID controller sends a data block to the tape drive, which immediately places the data in buffer memory; this is a very fast operation for most devices. The tape RAID controller moves from device to device, filling the buffers of each one in sequential order. The drives all empty their buffers onto media after receiving a transfer, and then wait for the next transfer into their buffers. Figure 3-10 shows data being striped across four devices onto four tapes.

One of the potential problems with this scheme could occur if the drive empties its buffers and then has to stop to wait for another buffer refill. This would cause the drive to stop moving tape, which results in much slower performance as the tape drive continually stops and restarts. Also, there are questions about the reliability of recovery operations due to the need to precisely position and time multiple tape devices in order to recover the data correctly. Given the amount of variables involved with tape recording, this could prove to be a difficult task.

That said, this is promising technology for situations where the highest speed and capacity are required.

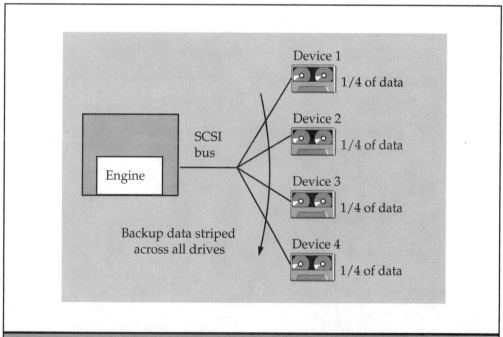

Figure 3-10. *To increase performance on large servers where tape speed is the limiting factor, the backup data is striped across all four devices sequentially, resulting in four times the performance of a single device*

Device Streaming

Device streaming is the state a tape drive is in when the tape is moving at an optimal rate while writing or reading data. It follows, then, that your tape drives need to be streaming in order for you to achieve maximum performance. For the best performance on a tape RAID system, it follows that you want to see all the drives in the RAID subsystem streaming.

In order to keep the device streaming, the SCSI host adapter must continuously be filling the device's buffer with data. For the SCSI host adapter to do this, it must have enough data being given to it from the backup application as shown previously in Figure 3-8. Unfortunately, the transfer capabilities of most LANs are unable to provide the data to the backup application fast enough to keep the device's buffers filled, which means that it is very difficult to keep devices streaming when the backup system is backing up other systems on the LAN.

Tape Interleaving

Some backup software companies have solved the problem described above by using a technique called *tape interleaving*. Tape interleaving combines data from several targets being backed up simultaneously onto a single device and single tape.

In essence, interleaving braids data together on tape. Figure 3-11 shows data from three targets being interleaved together on one tape. Individually, the transfer of data from any of the targets would not be able to allow the tape drive to stream, but the combined transfers from all three targets allows the device to stream.

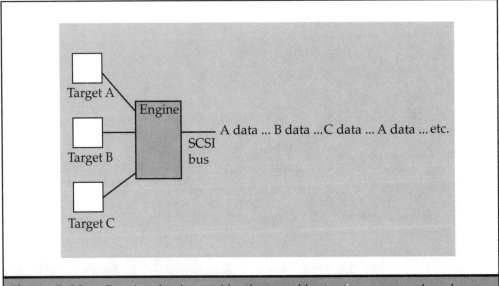

Figure 3-11.   *Tape interleaving enables the tape drive to stream, even when slower targets are being backed up across the network*

Parallel SCSI Controllers

If you really want to make your SCSI devices haul, try limiting the number of backup devices to no more than three devices per SCSI host adapter. In large backup systems it can make a significant impact.

Network Performance

LANs that offer high-bandwidth transmissions can be built to allow devices to stream data from cross-network systems. Some companies even install special high-speed backup backbones that they use only for backup purposes. By dedicating the backbone, they never run into surprising degradation problems from other systems or applications.

There are many approaches one could take along this path: Any of the 100MB+ networks, such as FDDI, 100baseT, ATM, or 100VG AnyLAN, seem to work pretty well; but even they can become saturated when there is enough traffic, particularly backup traffic. You might also find that implementing duplexed switched network connections, such as ethernet switching hubs, for high-traffic backup links can do wonders for your backup performance. Dedicated, switched network technology, such as ATM, also holds a great deal of promise for backup performance problems.

Compression

Devices that have internal compression chips that compress data as it is written to media can provide substantial performance advantages, usually slightly less than or equal to the compression ratio in effect. For example, a compression ratio of 2:1 can be expected for most PC LAN data, although some data, such as graphics files, are usually not compressible. This means that the streaming speed of the device when it is compressing data is twice as fast as when it is not compressing data. If the tape drive you have has an uncompressed sustained streaming speed of 30MB per minute (MBpm), using compression it will stream data at 60MBpm. The challenge for network backup, as discussed earlier, is supplying the drive with data fast enough to keep it streaming.

Automated Devices

Because backup usually runs in the middle of the night, you may wish to use automated robotics tape-changing equipment to help ensure backup operations complete successfully without human oversight and intervention. You may know such devices as stackers, jukeboxes, libraries, changers, and autoloaders. Figure 3-12 shows the differences between stackers, autoloaders, libraries, and jukeboxes. The following discussion will clarify the differences between them.

Typically, these devices are connected to the host system via a single SCSI cable. Circuitry inside the autoloader system allows different SCSI addresses to be set up for the drives as well as the robotics mechanism. Sometimes the robotics are controlled via a serial connection instead of SCSI. The capacity and physical size of these devices

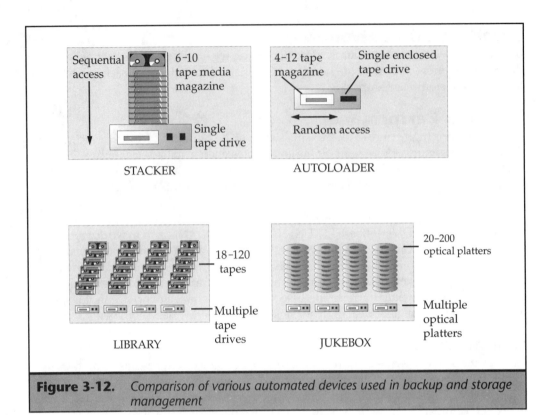

Figure 3-12. *Comparison of various automated devices used in backup and storage management*

varies enormously. The smallest changers hold four DAT tapes and fit in a full-height bay in a PC. The largest of these machines, called *silos*, can fill an entire room and holds hundreds of tapes.

Tape Stackers

A *stacker*, or *changer*, is a sequential access device that uses tapes in the order they are loaded in the changer. The primary advantage of this system is that operations that exceed the capacity of a single piece of media can continue with the next one. This obviously assumes that the tapes in the changer can all be overwritten by the next backup operation. Stackers are not very forgiving if the wrong tapes are inserted or if they are in the wrong order; therefore, they work best when applied to single-system backup where there is little confusion over tapes. Although they offer some benefits during restore operations, they are less suitable for selective restore operations where files and tapes are selected at random.

Stackers are also usually single-drive systems. This means that the performance advantages of parallelism, discussed in "Software Performance Techniques" later in this chapter, may not be possible when using them.

Libraries and Autoloaders

Libraries and autoloaders generally refer to a more sophisticated device than stackers. A library system is a random-access device that allows any piece of media to be selected and loaded into an available drive. It is common for this class of machine to have multiple drives to achieve parallel or concurrent operations. The advantage to this is that one device could be writing data to one piece of media while another device is writing or possibly reading data from another.

The biggest advantage of these machines, however, is their random-access capabilities. This allows the tapes to be loaded in the system in any way possible and the system will adjust and use the media appropriately. This in itself reduces the amount of human errors related to media selection. For organizations with remote sites without LAN administration skills, this can significantly improve data protection.

In addition, the time it takes to restore data can be reduced by using library systems. Any piece of media can be accessed quickly, inserted in a drive, and positioned at any specific file that is requested. Some software systems even allow end users to make such requests, freeing the LAN administrator from having to run the restore operation. Furthermore, using bar code technology, media can be identified even faster. Bar coding is important for larger libraries; without it, the library would have to insert every tape in a drive to learn the electronic label from the tape. Bar coding also comes in handy for systems management tasks, including off-site media transfers.

One of the other important advantages of autoloaders is the ability to set up automated head cleaning for tape drives. A tape-cleaning cartridge can be inserted into an autoloader and either through software control or firmware logic in some of the autoloaders, cleaning will be triggered automatically and you will not have to worry about doing it yourself. Keep in mind that cleaning cartridges don't last forever and are only good for a limited number of uses.

Jukeboxes

A jukebox for data storage normally refers to an optical autoloader system. Jukeboxes are very similar to libraries in their random-access capabilities. The primary advantage of jukeboxes for data integrity is the time it takes to restore data: not only can the media be located and loaded very quickly, but once it's in the drive it can be read far faster than comparable tape equipment. This makes jukeboxes the leading near-line storage component in HSM (hierarchical storage management) systems discussed in Chapter 4.

Software and Logic of LAN Backup

The basic requirements for a backup system were stated at the beginning of the chapter: "to completely restore the data and systems information needed to run a computer system as quickly as possible." We've just looked at a variety of media and devices, so now we'll do the same thing for software. Software's job is to control the transfer of data from systems onto media. It sounds easy on the surface, but there are many difficult problems to be solved beyond the basic dumping and filling data from a single machine. LAN backup systems deal with an astounding number of unpredictable variables, which makes it difficult to assure the success of the backup on a daily basis.

You may have many different machines on your LAN, but the systems you are most concerned about are your network and application servers, which usually contain the data that your end users need to perform their jobs. For this reason, the typical goal of many organizations' LAN backup strategy is to be able to restore their server machines quickly and then worry about the rest of the systems when the time arises. Another common requirement for LAN backup is that it not interfere with normal business operations. This means that there are only certain hours of the day, known as the *backup window* when backups can be run.

In the following sections we will examine some of the common implementations used in LAN backup software and try to help you understand why they exist and how they could be useful to you.

What Is Your Backup Strategy?

Probably the most important thing about using a backup system is knowing what to expect from it. Because backup is one of those things that people don't really like to think about—after all, its not as exciting as other technology—many LAN administrators don't really work with their backup system enough to know it well, and hence have unrealistic expectations about what it will do for them. In addition, many of these same people have some expectations that their backup system will bail them out when their job is on the line. You could say that this attitude verges on the insane.

You will be able to avoid such an approach to backup and recovery by knowing what you are doing before a crisis hits you. Chapter 12 on disaster recovery planning covers this in more detail. At the very least you should have a very good idea about what data should be backed up, what the frequency of those backups should be, how long you need to keep those backups, and where you should keep them. This sounds fairly simple in principle, but it can be difficult to gain agreement on it because the desired approach may not be possible without making major changes to your backup operations.

Somebody, somewhere in your organization probably has some idea of what data needs to be backed up and how long to keep it safe from a disaster. If you want to be a hero following some disaster, get this information and adhere to it with daily backup operations. Many backup strategies are not described in documents, rather they are merely some individual's understanding of what needs to be done. This approach works but is subject to all kinds of personnel-related problems and is not as useful as written guidelines if you ever attempt to analyze your situation.

Managed Redundancy

Another way to view backup software is as a mechanism for managing redundant copies of data. Managing redundant data is a slightly different approach than trying to merely attain backup perfection. Managed redundancy implies that some thought has been applied to the problems of maintaining access to LAN data as well as swift recovery of that data, even if your building is destroyed. This approach may help you put together a strategy based on ensuring enough copies of your data exist in places where they can be accessed in a relatively short period of time. Note that managed redundancy may not even include backup, but instead may rely on mirroring techniques.

Types of Backup Operations

The fundamental question of backup is "How much do I need to back up and when do I need to do it in order to enable me to restore all my systems?" There are several approaches that can be taken, described in the following sections.

FULL BACKUPS   *Full backups,* where all files are written to backup media, are popular because brute force methods appeal to our insecurities. This way we know we can recover everything about a system from whatever day we ran the backup. However, there is often too much data to back up completely every day, so we can only run full backups on the weekends. Also, few of us like to practice overkill on a daily basis for a number of reasons, including the fact that it's harder on the equipment. So we try to find more efficient methods.

INCREMENTAL BACKUPS   The next most obvious solution is to back up only those files that have changed since the last backup, also known as *incremental backup.* Incremental backup is the most efficient way to run backups. If all we did every day was an incremental backup, performance and capacity problems would be greatly diminished.

However, the time it would take to restore data from all your tapes would send you into lunar orbit after a while. One of the other problems with incremental backup is that it usually depends on the file system change attribute to identify changed files, which is not always a dependable method. It is possible to implement a file system database or record of some sort to identify newly changed files. Such an approach may be more accurate, but also more prone to other system problems.

Incremental backups are commonly used with full backups to provide fast backups, as well as reduce the number of tapes required for a restore. As an example, many companies run full backups over the weekend starting on Friday night and then run incremental backups on Monday through Thursday.

DIFFERENTIAL BACKUPS   *Differential backups* are a way to back up all the files that have changed since the last full backup. They are similar to incremental backups, except that for each subsequent day since the last full backup, the aggregate group of files that have changed since the last full backup is written; therefore, daily backups gradually take longer to run until the next full backup operation. This can be done either by using file system change attributes or by tracking changed files.

The primary advantage of differential backups is that the entire system should be able to be restored from just two tapes: the last full backup and the last differential backup.

Figures 3-13, 3-14, and 3-15 show the differences between full, incremental, and differential backups.

ON-DEMAND BACKUPS   *On-demand backups* refers to the operations that are done outside of the regular backup schedule. There are many reasons you might want to run nonscheduled backups: for example, maybe you just want to back up a few files or directories, or maybe you want to take a full snapshot of a server prior to upgrading it. On-demand backups can also be used to augment your normal scheduled backups for the purposes of redundancy or long-term vaulting.

EXCLUSIONS   These aren't really an operation, per se, they are just files that you don't want backed up. There are ways to make sure these files are not copied to media. Perhaps the file is huge but not important, or maybe the file always causes problems with backup operations and you haven't been able to troubleshoot the problem yet.

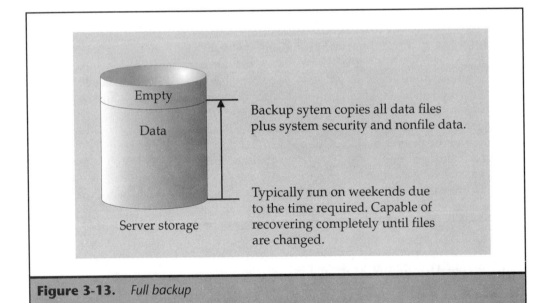

Figure 3-13.   *Full backup*

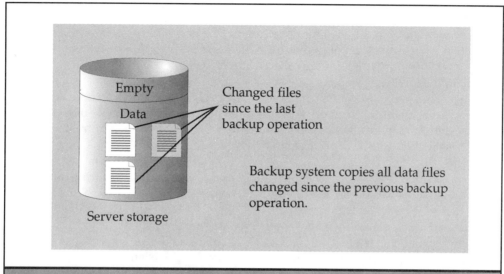

Figure 3-14.   *Incremental backup*

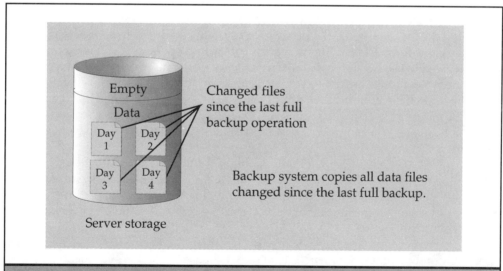

Figure 3-15.   *Differential backup*

Types of Restore Operations

Restore operations typically fall into two camps. The first is full system restores, and the second is the restoration of individual files. There is an additional type of restore operation that is worth mentioning called *redirected restores*. We'll talk about each one of them in the following sections.

In general, restore operations are much more problematic than backups. While backups just copy information off a disk, restores actually have to create files on the target system, and there are many extra things that can go wrong when creating files. These include hitting capacity limitations, authorization restrictions, and file overwrite errors.

Backups don't need to "know" much about the system prior to restoring data, they just copy what they are supposed to. Restores, on the other hand, need to understand which files to restore and which ones not to. Consider a large old application that has been deleted and replaced by a new application that takes up all the space the old one did. Now assume that later in the week the system fails and needs to be restored from tape. It is very important that the backup system detect the deletion of the old application so it doesn't try to restore both the old application and the new one, overfilling the server during the restore and crashing the system again. Don't assume that your current backup system developer or the one you may be considering deals with this problem adequately; check with somebody in their support organization who can describe how this situation is handled.

FULL RESTORES   Full restores are used to recover from catastrophic events or when performing system upgrades and system reorganizations and consolidations. The idea is simple: take the data on media for the given system and dump it all back where it originally came from. Depending on the type of backup operations you were using you may need to use several tapes. For instance, let's assume you work at a company where the system is used seven days a week and you are using a monthly rotation, changing tapes daily and running incremental operations. If you experienced a failure on the morning of the 21st, you would need to use all previous 20 tapes for each day of the month so far, to restore the complete system. Ugly—unless you have an autoloader.

This raises an interesting point that you might want to be aware of when considering backup software. If the same database file existed on each one of these 20 tapes, how many times would you actually restore this file, only to have it overwritten by a newer version on the next tape? As you might guess, this could add considerable time to your restore scenario.

Say you are using a GFS rotation, discussed later in this chapter, with incremental operations on weekdays, and there is a 900MB database file on the system. Some products will restore the last full backup first, including the database file, and then restore it again and again for each subsequent incremental tape. If you had a failure on a Thursday, this would result in restoring the file unnecessarily four times; in other words, restoring 3.6GB of data that you didn't need to.

As a rule of thumb, if possible you should use the last tape you used for backup as the first tape to restore from because it will have the files that are currently being worked on, and your end users will need them as soon as the system is ready. Then use the last full backup tape or any other tape with a majority of files on it. After that, the order doesn't matter much as long as all relevant tapes get used.

One other thing to watch out for is the assumption that all your files exist, say, on the last full and last differential backup tapes. There are usually a few files that don't get backed up during backup operations because they were left open by an end user who didn't log out at night or for some other reason. So, after restoring, you may want to review your recent error logs to look for any files that may have slipped through the cracks.

INDIVIDUAL FILE RESTORES   It is probably far more common for you to be asked to restore individual files than to run full restore operations. Why is this? Defective end users, that's why.

Usually they need the last version of the file that was written to media because they just finished ruining or deleting the online version. For most backup products this is a relatively simple operation—look through the backup database or catalog, select the file, and submit a restore job. Most products also allow you to select the file from a listing of the media journal.

Sometimes you want to go a little further back in time to restore an older version; again, most of the products today provide methods for doing this, some better than others. Products that use a file system orientation to select historical versions of files are usually faster to work with than products that use a session-based interface to look for older file versions. This is because the file system view requires a single search, whereas the session-based method makes you look through each session log until you find the right version. Indexing over session log boundaries alleviates that problem.

REDIRECTED RESTORES   A *redirected restore* is one where the file(s) you are restoring are returned to a different location or system than the one they were copied from during the backup operation. They can be either full restores or restores of individual files.

Redirected restores can be unusually problematic if you do not pay close attention to detail. Remember that if you rename your servers or completely reorganize your server's storage and volume names, any time you restore files from tapes that were made prior to the reorganization you will need to use a redirected restore. Try not to forget the name and path information of the original server; you should always be able to get it from the media journal, but that adds time and suspense to the process.

Also remember that the new system probably uses different security information than the old one and that this may cause file ownership to not translate correctly upon restore.

Tape Rotation

One of the first things you will run into when establishing a backup policy is tape rotation. Tape rotation is a scheme that determines what pieces of media should be used according to some predetermined schedule. You want to do this because your data is actually on tape cartridges and if you ever want to retrieve your data, you may find a system of organization helps you immensely. Tape is relatively cheap, but that doesn't mean that it makes sense to use a brand new tape every day. Not only is there a cost involved, but managing an ever-increasing pool of tapes makes it extremely difficult to get organized for a restore operation.

The primary function of tape rotation is to determine when the data on tape can be overwritten with new data, or conversely, over which time period data on tape should *not* be overwritten. For example, if your policy determines that your backups on the last day of every month need to be kept for six months, your tape rotation scheme should help ensure that the data written by those operations are not overwritten before those six months have transpired.

This idea of protecting data on tape really strikes at the heart of why tape rotation methods are important: they help reduce the likelihood of human errors in the backup process. Inserting the wrong tape at the wrong time may result in loss of data that you may never be able to capture again. A closely followed tape schedule can help prevent this from happening.

One of the other advantages of tape rotation is that it enables you to implement autoloader systems. Combining an autoloader with a tape rotation schedule gives you a predictable set of operations that you can have some level of confidence in. That does not mean that such a system does not need to be verified for correct operations, but it does mean that you don't have to wonder if the right tapes are being put in the drives on a daily basis.

A/B ROTATION   A simple rotation model is an A/B model where you have a tape called "A" and one called "B" and you use these tapes every other day. This means that "A" is used on even-number days and "B" is used on odd-number days. This model does not allow you to retain data very long, but at least you know which tapes you would use for a restore. The A/B model lends itself primarily to brute force scenarios where full backups are taken daily.

WEEKLY ROTATION   Another approach is to change tapes once a week, leaving the same tape in the drive for the entire week. This works well if the amount of data is small enough or if you are using an autoloader that can change media if the previous tape fills. This technique actually allows you to use a single tape all week, which means that a restore operation would only need to use one tape. The idea is to run a full backup first and then append incremental backups to the end of the tape.

Figure 3-16 shows how data is typically written to tape using weekly rotation. The first backup is the weekend full backup. On each day following, incremental backup jobs are run.

DAILY ROTATION   A slightly more interesting rotation model is to change tapes every day of the week. This means you could have seven tapes labeled the days of the week, five tapes for Monday through Friday, or any other combination of days of the

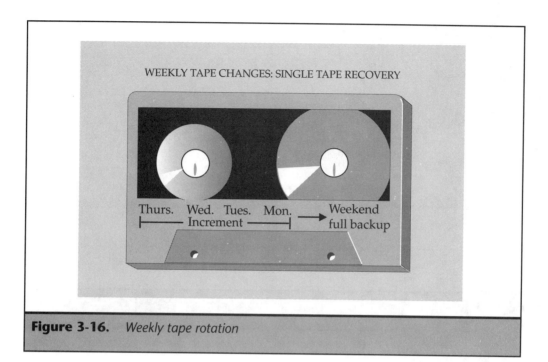

Figure 3-16. *Weekly tape rotation*

week. This scenario works well with the combination of full backups and either differential or incremental backups. Figures 3-17 and 3-18 show daily rotation schemes.

MONTHLY ROTATION An extension to the previous method is to use a monthly rotation. While this is not particularly common, it is sometimes employed as a means to reduce the number of full backup operations. It is usually implemented as a full backup at the beginning of the month and then incremental operations on other tapes the remainder of the month, with tapes being changed either daily or weekly. It can also be done using a differential backup every day, although these can get pretty large by the end of the month.

GRANDFATHER, FATHER, SON (GFS) The most common rotation model in use today is the Grandfather, father, son model. It is a combination of the daily, weekly, monthly models discussed above and the idea is fairly simple: there are four tapes designated for daily use on Monday through Thursday, four tapes designated for use on each weekend of the month (first weekend, second weekend, and so on), and one tape designated for the end of the month. Slight adjustments are made to accommodate the few extra days each month, but the pattern stays the same.

The main advantage of GFS is that it matches up nicely with the calendar and business cycles. It provides a balance of brute force protection with full backups on

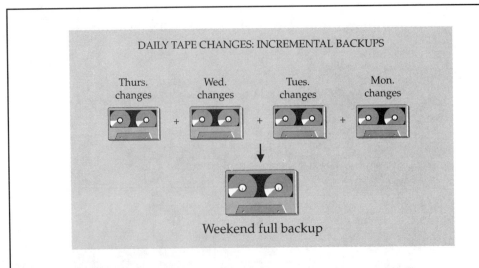

Figure 3-17. *Daily rotation with incremental backups*

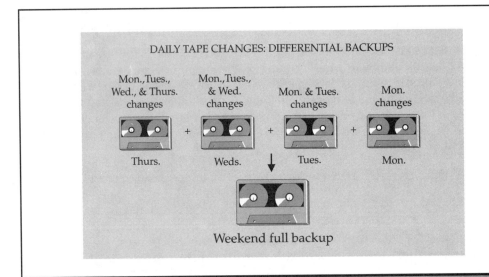

Figure 3-18. *Daily rotation with differential backups*

weekends combined with more efficient differential or incremental backups on weekdays. In addition, it is easy to explain how to work with it to your operations staff, and it works relatively well with autoloader systems.

TOWER OF HANOI   The Tower of Hanoi rotation model is based upon the ancient oriental puzzle of the same name. The game is set up with three poles. On one of the poles is a stack of disks in increasing sizes where the largest disk is on the bottom, the next largest disk is immediately above it, and so on until the smallest disk is at the top of the stack. The object of the game is simple: transfer the stack of disks to another pole. There are only two rules: you can only move one disk at a time, and you cannot put a larger disk on top of a smaller one.

While the game is somewhat interesting, it doesn't really help explain the algorithm very well. The best way to think of this rotation model is to consider the bits in a binary register. Each bit corresponds to a tape in the rotation. Starting from a zero value (all zero bits), begin incrementing the register by one. After each increment, read from the least-significant bit to the most-significant bit looking for the first occurrence of a one bit. The column this bit is in corresponds to the tape you would use in the Tower algorithm. Table 3-4 shows the progression of bits as this register is incremented and the corresponding tape the Tower algorithm would call for.

The Tower algorithm can be fascinating to play around with as an intellectual exercise, but for operators it is best left alone. The primary advantage of the Tower of Hanoi is that it is more efficient in its use of tapes and provides an extended length for data retention, depending on the number of tapes you employ.

For example, the GFS rotation scheme above uses nine tapes and allows the weekend tapes to be kept for a period of one month. Using the same number of tapes, the Tower of Hanoi algorithm would allow you to keep data on the least-frequently used tape for 256 days, or well over eight months. If weekly rotation was used, this would mean you could keep data for up to 256 weeks; however, you should keep in mind that this represents a single operation and that the next closest copy of data would be from 128 weeks, or over two years, earlier. So while the retention in the Tower may be good for extending the time you keep data, the number of samples of that data may not be sufficient.

The Tower of Hanoi is a good rotation model for automated environments implementing autoloaders. However, it is generally too demanding to understand for manual operations. You probably have better things to do than spend your time trying to figure out where in the cycle you are at any given time, trying to predict what to expect next.

CALENDAR-BASED ROTATION SCHEDULING   Probably the best way to schedule media rotation is by using a calendar to plan your operations. This way you can take into account holidays and significant business events that may force you to change your schedule. Using calendar-based rotation you can set the data retention period for each operation, as opposed to setting it for a certain class of periodic tapes. It also

Bit 0 = A	Bit 1 = B	Bit 2 = C	Bit 3 = D	Bit 4 = E	Selection
0	0	0	0	0	0
①	0	0	0	0	A
0	①	0	0	0	B
①	1	0	0	0	A
0	0	①	0	0	C
①	0	1	0	0	A
0	①	1	0	0	B
①	1	1	0	0	A
0	0	0	①	1	D
①	0	0	1	0	A
0	①	0	1	0	B
①	1	0	1	0	A
0	0	①	1	0	C
①	0	1	1	0	A
0	①	1	1	0	B
①	1	1	1	0	A
0	0	0	0	①	E

Table 3-4. *Tower of Hanoi Rotation Model Sequence*

allows you to communicate the schedule in a very clear fashion to operations staff, who can simply look at the calendar/scheduler to understand what they should do.

The problem with calendar-based scheduling is that there is no inherent mechanism for reusing tapes periodically. While you could set up the system this way, the system itself will not try to enforce a periodic scheme but will require management to make sure it's all working as you had anticipated. The other caveat is that you or your coworkers may set up a deficient rotation schedule that does not provide the coverage you really want.

HYBRID ROTATION If you are like most LAN administrators, you will probably need to create some variation from whatever rotation model ships with the software you purchased. This may mean performing some manual, on-demand backups to augment your normal schedule. A product that will allow you to automate or schedule your on-demand operations will help minimize problems that come from forgetfulness and other human weaknesses.

PERPETUAL INCREMENTAL   This is perhaps the most intriguing rotation method of all, but requires a level of sophistication not shown by today's leading LAN backup software products. The idea of this model is that you only take a full backup once, the first time you run the system. From that point forward you only run incremental backup operations. To facilitate restore operations, the system should be able to merge backup from multiple backups onto other larger contiguous blocks of media.

Accurate database operations are necessary for this sort of rotation to work since the backup merge operation would require a lot of detailed information about small backup sessions on a large number of media. Harbor, from New Era Systems, is a mainframe-based LAN backup product that implements such facilities for very efficient backup operations.

BASELINE DIFFERENCE OPERATIONS   The idea of a baseline is to build redundant protection for a group of files that are stable and don't change. Examples of this type of files are application executable files and system files that are used often but are never updated. Other files that fit this category are old data files that are in server storage but have outlived their purpose and will never be updated again.

If these files can be copied to multiple pieces of media for redundant protection and if this media can be kept for an extended period of time, it follows that you should be able to skip over these files during normal backup operations. If a full restore is ever needed, the system files and older data files can be recovered from these tapes. In an automated backup system where autoloaders are used, this can be done without difficulty.

This is a clever way to work that can save over 50 percent of the time it normally takes to perform full backups. Palindrome Corporation has used this technique for many years. Although many of their customers would say this is a benefit of the Tower of Hanoi rotation model, it isn't. A variation of this technique is to exclude system and application files from backup altogether. If a full restore is ever needed, these files can be restored from the floppy disks or CD-ROM platters that they originally came on. This process could be made safer by keeping on-demand backup tapes of only these files in case there are problems with the diskette or CD-ROM media.

OFF-SITE ROTATIONS   If your building gets smoked or otherwise ruined, you can bet that your tapes inside it will probably be unreadable. A fireproof safe might help you if you can even get in the building to retrieve it. Having data off-site in case of such a disaster is an excellent way of saving the company. There can be significant benefits to using a rotation scheme that fits your off-site rotation schedule; this is most likely going to be a GFS or a calendar-based rotation. There is a lot more to this than just shuttling tapes off-site, and we will explore this topic in Chapter 12.

One of the most difficult problems can be figuring out what data you want to have on-site and what data you need on-site on a daily basis. For instance, it makes sense to have the previous night's backup on site the next day because this is when you are most likely to use it—to restore files for end users who are behaving normally.

However, you might also want this tape off-site right away to ensure that you can perform a full recovery, as would be a common requirement for full backup operations.

A simple technique that you might find useful is making copies of the previous night's tapes and sending the copies off-site while keeping the originals on-site. This can be confusing as you start rotating off-site media back in for reuse, but it shouldn't be too difficult if you clearly identify media that is used for copies and only take those off-site. Some of the software packages will do this for you, but this can also be implemented in hardware, either through tape mirroring or through after-operations automated copying.

The Backup Knowledge Base

The more sophisticated backup products today allow you to restore data and system objects with relative ease through the integration of relational database technology. If you can identify a file by name, location, or, in the future, by keywords, the backup system will identify the tapes you can use. Once the file and the tape have been identified, restoring the data is relatively simple; you put the tape in the drive and run the restore operation. If you have an autoloader, the process is even simpler.

This is not done without some pain, however, because implementing a database that tracks files as they are backed up is technically challenging. You may find it difficult to believe that with today's database systems, this would be difficult. But backup is one application that can easily exceed the capabilities of your database's performance and capacity. This might seem surprising, but when you stop to consider the number of transactions required to track every file, you see it can be a large number. A large server can easily have a file system with a few hundred thousand files. This is a lot of transactions to write during a full backup. Not only that, but if your backup system keeps file history records of older backup sessions like most do, you can wind up having a fairly large database, which slows down performance and eats disk space.

For that reason LAN backup packages usually employ proprietary database structures in order to keep the size of them manageable and the transaction speed running fast. There are some who believe this is the only way to solve the problems of performance and size; but considering the performance-intensive competition among database companies today, it would not be surprising to see backup developers include the capability of using the leading database engines as the file management tool inside their backup software.

So why do these databases get so big anyway? Well, what do you want to know about the files that you store on tape? You want to know the filename, its path, the machine and volume it came from, its access date, its create/modify date, its owner, its security restrictions and access information, its size, the media it was written to, where on the media you can find it, the date and time it was written to media, the session identifier, and any other relevant data that would help you locate this file and restore it. Then you may want to link all records for this file to enable easier file restores. As it turns out, there are a large number of variables that make perfect sense to store in a database to help restore your data. Then there are all the possible indexes that you might find useful.

During the backup operation, there is a lot of stuff to write and analyze and it takes its toll on the backup system one way or another. There are two common ways to deal with this issue: real-time database updates or batch updates. In the real-time update, each file has its record created as it is being written to tape. This obviously requires some sophisticated multithreaded code, but it may still be too slow due to the database work causing shortfalls in the data transfer and the drive failing to stream. With batch updates, all the data is transferred to media and then a list of files is updated against the database. The problem with this approach is that something could occur to stop backup operations and the database would know nothing about any of the files that were on the tape.

Some backup products do not use relational database technology as their operations infobase. Instead they keep journals, or lists of what files were backed up in any given operation. This approach works well for situations where there is not a requirement to restore individual files and the goal of the backup system is simply to provide bulk dump and restore functionality.

So how does one control the size of their databases? Through automated database pruning or through manual methods. Most LAN backup products today provide automated tools to delete records for files from the database that are no longer on tape. The reason they are no longer on tape is because the tape has been rotated in again and old data overwritten on it, or the dog ate it, or some event zapped it. In any case, the database should be updated to reflect the fact that data cannot be restored from those tapes any longer. Most LAN backup systems allow manual tools for deleting database records.

But the backup system should also be smart enough to know if it zapped a tape and to perform the maintenance itself. An example of this occurs when an operator loads the wrong tape in the drive and the system is scheduled for a full backup tonight. Now the logic in the system can do one of two things—it can keep all the old data that hasn't expired yet and try to append to the end of the tape, or it can delete all the old information and overwrite it with new. The problem with the first approach is that tonight's full backup probably won't finish, leaving some of your most recent data unprotected. The problem with the second approach is that your system just deleted data that you didn't expect to delete yet.

This illustrates one of the additional benefits of using autoloader systems; you have a much better chance of avoiding this scenario if an autoloader can present a choice of tapes to use, instead of one take-it-or-leave-it ultimatum that you have with an unattended tape drive.

Software Performance Techniques

The answer to performance in backup is parallelism. If you need to move a lot of data, the best way to do it is to give the backup system as many paths to use as possible. For example, it would take much longer to back up ten servers with one backup system than if you used ten backup systems, one per server. However, parallelism is not the only way to speed things up; brute force and cunning can be applied to great advantage also.

Eliminate the Network: Remote Control of Devices

Performance of LAN backup is primarily constrained by the network. If you are really going to make network backup perform the fastest, you need to get the network out of the equation by using devices directly connected to your systems. One way to do this is for the backup system to put the SCSI bus and device components on the target and control them remotely from the engine on another machine. Figure 3-19 shows this type of arrangement.

Parallel SCSI Devices

Another effective brute force technique to speed up backup is to use multiple devices simultaneously. This can be done because the SCSI bus has much more bandwidth than the devices and is sitting idle much of the time anyway. Do not expect the performance on a single SCSI bus to be linear, however. Just because you get transfer rates of 30MBpm with one device, don't expect four devices to yield 120MBpm. You will start to see bus degradation after three devices, if your devices are big and fast.

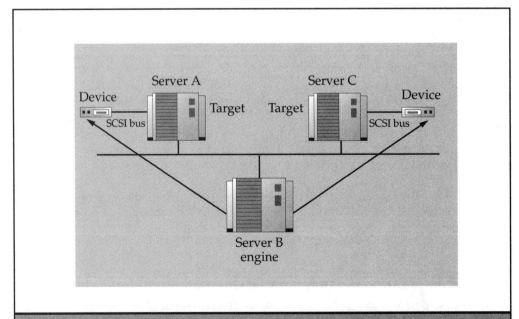

Figure 3-19. *The engine on server B controls remote devices on servers A and C*

This technique also works fairly well for backing up targets over the network. Similar to tape interleaving discussed earlier in this chapter, using parallel devices allows the data from multiple devices to be transferred from targets to the engine simultaneously. Although not as efficient as tape interleaving, because it uses several devices whereas tape interleaving uses one, parallel devices also provide a level of device redundancy that could be desirable. Figure 3-20 shows a LAN backup system using parallel device operations to back up several targets simultaneously.

Prereading and Caching Files

If you are logically working with only one file at a time within a target system, you are not really getting the best performance out of the target system. A smarter system uses techniques that preread files and place them in fast cache, enabling most of the backup transfers to originate from fast memory as opposed to waiting for the target machine to perform disk I/O. This is a technology that could easily be implemented in target software.

Push Versus Pull

Most LAN software packages use a *pull architecture*. This means the host backup system initiates all data transfers and requests each file. Meanwhile, the target system may be idly waiting for something to do.

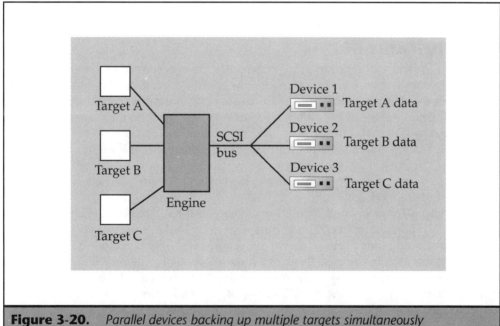

Figure 3-20.   *Parallel devices backing up multiple targets simultaneously*

Some LAN backup systems, such as Tecmar's Proserve and Arcada's Backup Exec, have developed target software that prereads and caches files before pushing them across the network to the engine. This cuts down on the processing cycles at the engine and eliminates some protocol overhead, plus taking advantage of the target system's CPU cycles so the engine doesn't have to do all the processing work. This approach is called a *push architecture*. While it appears to have several merits, the one flaw to keep in mind is the potential for pushing targets to saturate the LAN and degrade performance considerably. For a push architecture to work well, there needs to be some control, called *pacing*, that determines when each target can send its data over the network.

Overall, it is not clear if using a push architecture is actually faster than using effective prereading and caching in a pull architecture.

Disk Buffering

Similar to multiplexed sessions as discussed above, backup traffic from multiple targets can be buffered onto a large hard disk at the host backup system before writing to tape. While this adds an extra device to the process, disk drives tend to be much faster than tape drives and certainly outperform network transfer speeds. The main benefit of this approach is that the data from each target is written in larger contiguous blocks on backup media, which you might appreciate during restores. Also, in large backup systems where tape management is an issue, the less your data is spread across multiple tapes the better off you are.

Balancing Backup and Restore Time Requirements

One of the keys to a successful backup strategy is to always consider what the effect will be on restore operations if you change your backup operations. Any operation that reduces the amount of data written during backup operations probably increases the time it takes to restore, in addition to requiring more tapes. To make matters worse, you may find that some of your tapes are at another location and need to be retrieved. Although you live with backup operations every day, it is important to keep things in perspective and to remember that any shortcuts you take during backups will show their restore weaknesses after it is too late and you are working through the problems of restoring data.

For example, consider an A/B rotation where you run full backups every day onto two different tapes, or tape sets. This means your daily backups are not very efficient and may take a long time to run, but any full restores will only need to use the tapes from the last backup. In contrast, think of a monthly rotation scheme where the full backup is done on the first day of the month followed by incremental backups to different tapes every day thereafter. While backups would be very fast, full restores could require many tapes, depending on the day of the month.

You might also consider implementing autoloader systems to reduce the potential errors of changing tapes during restores, even if you don't have the need for them during backup operations. Using the monthly rotation example again, with a full backup on the first of the month and incremental backups every other day to new tapes, you really wouldn't need an autoloader for backups (except possibly on the first of the month). But you would definitely benefit from having one during a restore.

Backup Standards

In networking, we tend to look for standards that help us integrate products from different manufacturers to meet our requirements. Unfortunately, there are no universal standards in the backup world. That is not to say that standards have not been proposed, or even implemented, but the fact is that interoperability among backup products is minimal.

Novell's Storage Management Services

Novell file system APIs tend to change with each new major release, and sometimes with point releases, too. This created a problem for LAN administrators who found that their API-dependent backup products would not work with the new release. Not only that, but because of the time it took for the backup developers to adjust to the new APIs, including testing, the customers could be without backups for months.

To fix this problem, Novell designed and implemented an API set that backup developers are advised to use when working with NetWare systems. This API set is part of an overall approach for server backup called SMS, or Storage Management Services. The SMS API is intended to stay consistent for all future releases of NetWare, so that if a backup product works on your system today, it will also work for new upgrades when they are released. There is no other way to completely back up a NetWare 4.x server, including the NetWare Directory Services and name spaces, so backup software developers are left with no choice but to use SMS for backing up NetWare 4.x networks.

The other major component of SMS is a tape format called SIDF (systems independent data format). SIDF originated inside Novell as part of SMS and was subsequently taken over by a consortium of backup developers who continued the specification and interoperability work.

Novell's goal was to create an architecture that would be adopted by the backup developers, making it possible to implement plug-and-play backup components from various manufacturers. However, to date, this dream has not really materialized. Changes between the SMS implementation in NetWare 3.x and 4.x hurt the integrity of the concept. In addition, as is common in networking, the standards-based products suffered from compromised performance while the proprietary, higher performance solutions have naturally won the majority of the market so far.

One of the components of SMS is something called the TSA, or target service agent, which is, appropriately, target software. Novell originally had big plans to put

TSAs on all client systems that you would find on NetWare networks. These TSAs would use the same APIs as those used on NetWare servers, making it easier for backup software developers to build consistent mechanisms for all systems on the network. The TSA handles all the intricate file system and operating system details, so the backup system only has to worry about the proper and safe storage of the data. While the promise of this was nice, the delivery has been disappointing to date. Limited client platform support, quality issues, poor performance, schedule delays in shipping certain clients, and functional limitations in the client TSAs from Novell have kept the dream of SMS from becoming a reality.

This said, some of the backup software developers are starting to release their own TSAs for various platforms or applications, including databases. However SMS products become more widely available, that does not mean that they will be adopted. It remains to be seen whether or not SMS will ever move beyond a system for backing up NetWare servers.

IEEE 1244 Reference Model for OSSI

The IEEE (Institute of Electrical and Electronics Engineers) Storage Systems Standards Working Group has a project underway to identify areas where standardization would be useful to strengthen the capabilities of distributed storage systems. This project, #1244, is known as the Reference Model for Open Storage Systems Interconnection (OSSI).

There are three important things to note in relation to this effort: (1) from its conception it was intended to be an open standard, not pushed from the development labs of any one organization, as is the case with Novell's SMS; (2) the organizations participating in this effort have vast expertise in the areas of storage management, mostly on large Unix systems; and (3) implementations of parts of the reference model are now commercially available.

The 1244 Reference Model is a generalized approach for handling all applications that utilize removable media, not just backup. Its facilities could be used by document management, imaging, workflow automation, HSM, and archiving systems. It is still very young in its development, and it is not clear if any of its components will be utilized by the broad storage market.

The most interesting and tangible parts of Project 1244 are described in the following sections.

OBJECT IDENTIFIER (SOID 1244.1)   Think of a big network and the chance that many of the files in this network have the same name and are in the same path but on different servers. The object identifier is intended to uniquely identify all system objects, as well as the algorithms used for such labels.

PHYSICAL VOLUME LIBRARY (PVL 1244.2)   If you have drives and autoloaders scattered all over your network, wouldn't it be nice if there was a way to manage all the media in those devices and optimize the use of devices within autoloaders? That's what the PVL is for: it manages the overall media library. The use of the word *library* here refers to the collection of tapes, not to a specific automated hardware device.

PHYSICAL VOLUME REPOSITORY (PVR 1244.3)   The PVR defines services and processes for the storage of removable media in automated devices.

DATA MOVER (MVR 1244.4)   The Data Mover is the storage system's interface to services that provide data transfers. Note that this does not introduce any new transfer protocols, but it does provide an interface to execute transfers that utilize them.

STORAGE SYSTEM MANAGEMENT (MGT 1244.5)   Just as there is network management in the form of SNMP and CMIP, this specification defines how you would manage distributed storage. It is not clear yet if SNMP or CMIP can be effective protocols for managing large amounts of data. Rather than waiting and seeing, a new management scheme intended for storage-specific problems is being developed by the committee.

VIRTUAL STORAGE SERVICE (VSS 1244.6)   With data and media and machines scattered all over the place, how do you present this as a single entity to facilitate management? VSS.

Of the above components, the PVL and PVR are finding their way into fledgling products in the market, probably because they can be sold as device-driver and media management mechanisms for other storage applications.

Limitations to Watch Out for When You Select a Backup System

Scalability is probably the single biggest issue facing networking professionals. Sooner or later, the network bursts at the seams, and new technology has to be found to replace a constrained technology that's causing a system bottleneck. The following list identifies three areas to look out for in backup products.

- **Spanning media** Does the backup system allow you to span media, that is, continue with another piece of media when the first one fills? Probably. How about files? Can you copy a file that is larger than the media you are using? Maybe not.

- **Operation limitation** Some backup products do not allow you to have a single session exceed a given size, say 4GB. If you have to manually balance the work to fit underneath such a restriction, can you still find your files easily? Behind the scenes here is a question about the backup system's database.

- **File size limitation** Some backup systems have limitations on the size of individual files. This is similar to the first item in this list, but it does not have to be a function of media size.

Workstation Backup

Most backup systems have some facility for backing up end user workstations (not only PCs but also Unix desktop machines). But because they are optimized for server backup operations, they do not always perform well for workstation backup. The main problem with workstation backup is that it is slow. Using a product that interleaves data from several targets simultaneously onto tape can garner big efficiency savings. A perpetual incremental rotation system would also be used to excellent advantage to enable the backup of many workstations.

Although logically you should be able to back up workstations with the same product you use to back up servers, that may not be a valid assumption. For starters, workstations and workstation communications features are not typically as robust as servers. If you think about this, you'll agree—when you're backing up a workstation, you're really asking the workstation to act like a file server and give you a whole bunch of files as fast as it can. That's why network operating systems exist. If flaky behavior from workstations puts your server backup in jeopardy, you may want to try a solution that is dedicated to workstations.

Most companies don't back up end user machines. Policies exist that state that if the user needs a system backup, he or she should copy the files to the server. This approach solves the problem, but also adds complexity to the restore side of the equation because the user then needs to remember which server directory the file was temporarily placed in. Not impossible, just extra confusion and room for errors.

The other problem with this approach is that the data on workstations is often very valuable to the organization, and if for any reason it was lost, it would cost a great deal of money to replace it. Does the organization really want to place the responsibility for intellectual and corporate property in the hands of its end users? Logically no, but that's the norm today.

For LAN administrators this causes a few problems. The job should be done, but the tools for doing it are not very good; and if you do it with your server backup, it might make the whole system fail. A server-based system that you dedicate to workstation backup that multiplexes data from multiple clients onto tape is probably your best choice until products dedicated to workstation backup are introduced to the market.

Management of Backup Systems

The tools to manage distributed backup systems are not very well developed currently. About the best you should hope for is a blinking light showing up on your network management console. Some of the backup software development companies have announced consoles for their products, but there is not an industry standard yet to deal with this issue. In the future you may see storage management and backup as a subset of network management, or you may see a whole new class of products developed specifically for network storage management. The IEEE 1244 Reference

Model's Storage System Management component (MGT) may very well be the best approach available today.

Summary

We introduced the idea of the backup system as a complete network application system. By viewing your backup system in its entirety, you may be able to clearly see any problems or bottlenecks that come your way.

CHAPTER FOUR

Archiving and Hierarchical Storage Management (HSM)

In this chapter we'll examine two different ways to remove data from online systems: archiving and hierarchical storage management (HSM). As the data on your network continues to increase, you need to be aware of and understand this technology in order to make informed decisions about how your organization can most effectively manage your network data.

Archiving

Backup is an effective brute force solution to recovery from disasters and system failures. However, backup by itself may not provide all the functionality that an organization needs to protect and manage its data. For example, backup systems are designed to recover data within a few days or weeks of when it was backed up, but they are typically not designed to archive data for more than two or three years. So what do you do with data that you want to save for many years but you only have one chance to record it—for example, exit poll data from the last presidential election? (See Figure 4-1.)

As discussed in Chapter 2, data integrity can be compromised by problems with online systems, possibly from system failures or bugs, but also from human mistakes or willful damage. One of the ways to decrease this sort of problem is to remove data from online systems onto offline storage. Removable media is certainly one of the best ways to take data away from your site to protect it from any threats that exist there. If the data is not available online, it follows that it is not exposed to the things that threaten online data.

Archiving Defined

The term *archive* has been used by some LAN backup companies interchangeably with *backup*. For others, however, there are significant differences in the two words that

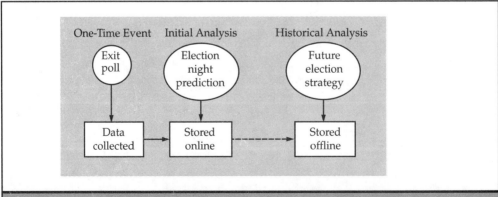

Figure 4-1. *Data online can be protected by backup copies, but data stored offline has no regular mechanism to ensure its integrity*

clearly distinguish their functions. For our purposes, we will define the word *archive* to mean to copy or package data for the purpose of historical preservation over an extended period of time. And we will define *backup* to mean to copy data for the purposes of disaster protection and incidental file restorations within a moderate period of time.

One of the uses for archiving is intuitively obvious: you have data that you know is valuable and you want to keep it safely for a long time. Another use of archiving is to help the LAN administrator delete files from server disks, preferably while maintaining a way to access them from offline storage. With so much data on the network, you might not know if the files you are removing are important, so you need to make sure you can recover them.

Difference Between Backup and Archiving

Backup data is only intended to be kept for a relatively short period of time; a day, a week, a month, or even a few years, but usually not for more than a couple of months. The main purpose of backup is to recover data that somehow becomes corrupt or lost; backup operations are scheduled to provide this type of functionality.

Archived data, on the other hand, could be kept indefinitely. This has serious implications for the type of media you use and the operations needed to maintain it. See the section "Media, Redundancy, and Archiving" later in this chapter. While backups are generally performed daily, archiving is usually done less frequently. We now look at the two main types of archiving operations: historical archiving and capacity management.

Historical Archiving

As mentioned previously, one reason for archiving is to preserve data for a long time. What files within your organization might you want to archive? Corporate human resources information, engineering drawings, detailed financial analysis, medical research data, digital photographs, maybe even old versions of software are all types of data that you or your company might want to keep for an extended period of time. Try to think of instances where you needed to recover files that had been deleted. Perhaps you know what it feels like to restore them from diskettes or tape. Perhaps you know what it feels like to *not* be able to restore them. LAN administrators can be heroes in the eyes of their end users if they can help them restore the data they need.

Capacity Management

One of the other reasons to archive data is because your online systems become bloated with data and you need to find some other place to store some of it. One of the great thrills of LAN administration occurs when your server's disk space becomes so full that it threatens the operation of the server. What happens when disk space overfills? Consider what the operating system is trying to accomplish if it tries to put more onto a disk than the disk can hold, there is a good chance that data integrity is compromised. In a LAN environment this could affect the data of many users simultaneously.

Consider a scenario where users have loaded files from their network server drives onto their PCs for processing. While most users are busy performing their normal everyday work, one of the users is reorganizing his PC and, in the process, unknowingly copies a large number of files onto the server, which fills the server disk to its capacity, making it impossible for anybody else to store their data on the server. At this point, all the other users have a problem finding a place to save the files they've been working on all afternoon. If these files can't be saved on their PCs or if the power is temporarily cut to their PCs, their data files may be lost and have to be re-created (see Figure 4-2).

One of the most common approaches to solving disk capacity problems is for the LAN administrator to panic and begin deleting files and directories that they believe are not important. Hopefully, their backup system can bail them out if they make a mistake. It is hardly optimal to have somebody working under pressure making fast decisions about which files to delete. Clearly, this is a threat to data integrity. Perhaps you have already experienced that sinking feeling of explaining to an end user that the file he or she is looking for is gone, and this, of course, after looking through backup logs and tapes for hours trying to find it.

Can't I Just Keep Buying More Disks?

Magnetic disks are becoming incredibly cheap. The cost per megabyte is now well below 25 cents, while capacity continues to rise. For example, the 9GB disk models

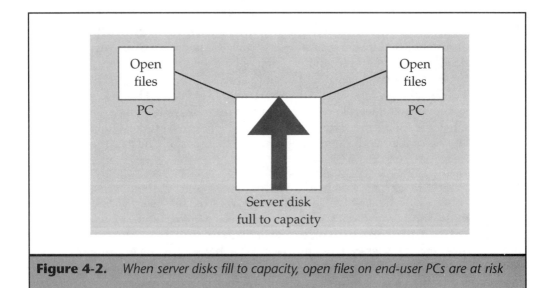

Figure 4-2.   *When server disks fill to capacity, open files on end-user PCs are at risk*

available today will soon be available as 18GB disks for roughly the same cost per megabyte.

So it appears that one possible solution to those bloated file servers is to simply buy more disk space. On the surface this is a reasonable approach—you are probably already doing it with some regularity. In fact, disk installation may be gradually taking up more and more of the time spent managing the network.

However, if you take a slightly longer range view of this practice, you might discover a few things about it that bother you. As you add more disks, you probably find that they get filled up with data as fast as they ever did. Therefore, you know you will need to add disks again. But the next time, you may have difficulty adding the same percentage of extra disk space. For example, if you add 4GB to your existing 4GB server, you have doubled your disk capacity. However, the next time you add a 4GB disk, you have only increased your disk capacity by 50 percent. Does this mean that the advantages of adding disk over time may be diminishing? Perhaps.

Let's assume that is not the case, however, and adding extra disks is something you can plan for and that you have no problem implementing this strategy. The next problem you may encounter is not being able to back up everything during the hours available to do it (see Figure 4-3). Not only that, but restores will also take longer (see Figure 4-4). Even individual file restores will suffer as the backup system now has to wade through much more data than it used to in order to find the files you need. In addition, the database of the backup system will also grow much larger, affecting performance negatively. So, you might anticipate having more problems with backup than you have today and your data will be at greater risk for loss.

But perhaps you already have a backup strategy that will scale with your network storage capacity and backup is not a problem for you. There are other problems not related to backup that you may already be seeing in your organization. As the

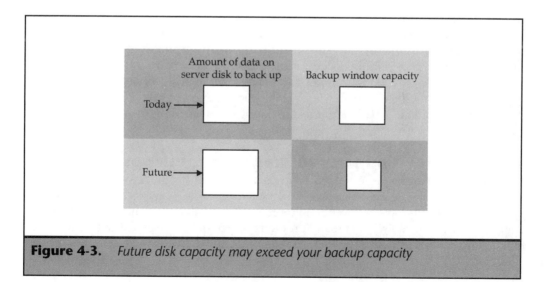

Figure 4-3.   *Future disk capacity may exceed your backup capacity*

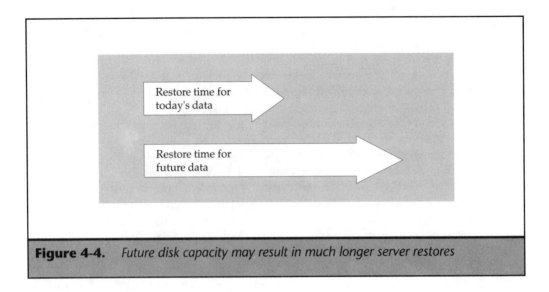

Figure 4-4. *Future disk capacity may result in much longer server restores*

network file system grows, users may find themselves having a harder time finding files because they now have many more to search through. Maybe you've noticed some drop in overall network productivity as users search through larger and larger directories of information in their Windows pick lists. Bigger disks also allow you to increase the size of your electronic mail database files. This lets you ignore them a little bit longer, but performing maintenance on them is now a much bigger job. There are probably other application systems that use database technology that now becomes more difficult to maintain. Finally, as available disk space expands and fills, it becomes increasingly difficult to know which files are useful and which are just taking up space and getting in the way—and the cycle repeats itself all over again.

So we see that increasing the size of your network file system poses some potentially serious problems that may be difficult to manage effectively. Another subtle problem with increasing disk capacity is that it is very painful to backtrack and return to your previous configuration with less disk space in case you experience problems managing the new disk space. Think about removing 50 percent of your disk space—could you do it? That's why most disk upgrades are permanent changes to your network.

Archiving for Capacity Management Purposes

The idea of archiving to preserve disk space is hardly new. People have been doing it for a long time using whatever methods they have available. The good news is that file system management tools are becoming more readily available and have more power. Unfortunately, there are still not many products that perform the entire archiving function from file selection to media management. They are either adapted from backup products and do not have sophisticated file selection capabilities, or they are good at selecting files but do not provide the device and media support that's needed.

Selecting Files to Archive (Size, Age, Project, Others)

If you decide to start archiving data, one of the first things you'll want to think about is what files you want to archive. There are four file system variables that are commonly used to make those selections. You may find that combining these variables works best for you, but you may also find that having a simple strategy is easier to manage. Table 4-1 lists them and indicates if they would be used primarily for historical archiving or capacity management.

Methods and Tools for Archiving

There are a number of products available today to help you archive your files. Some of them are application oriented, while others are system software. The following section reviews some of the methods available.

Document Management

Almost all document management software includes a scheme to archive files, both for capacity management and historical archiving. At this time, none of the products have imbedded device support for tape or optical drives, so the archiving function is rather limited in its archiving capability and only provides a mechanism for depositing files selected for archiving in a special directory.

Variable	Use	Example
File size	Capacity management	Archive all files larger than 100MB.
File age (time since last update)	Capacity management Historical archiving	Archive all files that haven't been updated in over a year.
Directory	Historical archiving Capacity management	A directory is used as an archival repository; everything placed in it is archived.
Ownership	Historical archiving	Files created by an individual, group member, or project member are archived.

Table 4-1. *File System Variables Used in Archiving*

The document management system typically manages some defined group of documents on the network. It enables fast retrieval of documents via a variety of search criteria including keywords, text strings, titles, ownership, and in some cases, even fuzzy language-matching algorithms. The idea is to help organizations with heavy document processing requirements retrieve documents in a timely fashion.

These systems will clean up their directory structures by selecting document files that meet some archiving criteria, usually age (time since last update). The document management system then moves these files to a designated directory that serves as a holding tank until they are written to removable media or deleted (see Figure 4-5).

Periodically, the document management system administrator is expected to check on the status of this directory and write these files to removable media, usually tape. This process is mostly manual, with the administrator performing the actual media writing operation with another product. This includes verification that the files were actually written to tape and giving the tape a name that can be identified from within the document management system. After the files have been transferred to tape, the administrator runs an operation in the document management system that deletes those files from the archive directory and resets the location of those files to the tape they were written to.

Although it works, there are significant weaknesses to this approach, primarily the fact that there is no redundancy built into the tape management and if the tape becomes unreadable for whatever reason, the data is lost. The other major weakness is that the process is a mix of manual and automatic operations that have no integrated checking—there is no way for the document management system to verify that all the files were actually written to tape before deleting them.

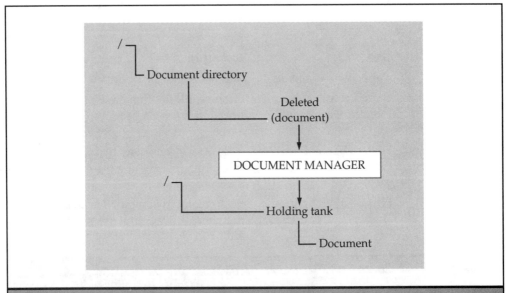

Figure 4-5.   *The document management system removes a document from its original directory and places it in a "holding tank" directory*

Compression Archiving

This is overwhelmingly the most popular method of archiving data on PC networks, although it is highly susceptible to major failures. The basic concept is to compress the data with a data compression utility so it takes less room on the disk, and then periodically copy it off somewhere else or delete it. It's a similar approach to the one described earlier for document management except there is no automated, system-configured selection of files, nor is there a defined holding tank directory where files for archival are stored.

Administrators using compression archiving typically use file system utilities to identify and select files based on size, age, or owner. After reviewing this selection list, the administrator uses a compression utility to compress the files and deletes the originals, and by doing so, can often save up to 70 percent of disk space. Often the files are not compressed on a one-to-one basis, where one compressed file corresponds to one unique original file, but instead files are grouped together by the compression utility in one larger compressed file. Figure 4-6 shows compression software "zipping" three files into one.

While it is possible to search these compressed files for their contents, such a process leaves a lot to be desired as a method for responsible data management. It is truly a brute force scenario where the LAN administrator must keep close track of all the variables including the directories, tapes, and compressed files where the data has been moved. On top of that, there is no simple tool for your end users to help you find the files the are looking for, unlike with a document management system. Like the document management system, there is no enforced redundancy policy to ensure that you have adequate protection should your media fail.

Perhaps the biggest problem with this approach, however, is that it does not lend itself to documentation or cross-training; instead, it tends to be a highly personalized

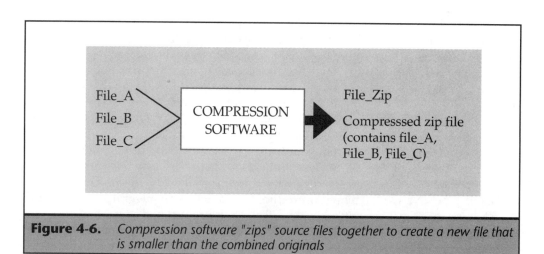

Figure 4-6.   *Compression software "zips" source files together to create a new file that is smaller than the combined originals*

way of working. This makes it very difficult for somebody else to find anything and restore it should the person who implemented it become unavailable for any reason.

Archiving with Your Backup System

Another common way to archive data is with your backup system. First you need to identify what files to archive, then you run a backup operation to store them on removable media, and then you delete the files. This provides the functionality that both compression archiving and document management systems lack, that is, the device and media writing operations.

The leading LAN backup products all provide some capability for archiving files. These functions are called *disk grooming* or *file migration*. Unfortunately, like the compression archiving schemes discussed above, most of the backup systems' archiving features do not provide a sure-fire plan to locate files on media after they have been removed. Your backup system probably has some session log or database to track files, but this is not always available for your end users to access.

You should be aware that your backup system's logging facility or database may not stand the test of time. In fact, there is an excellent chance that your session logs or databases will be long gone years from today when you want to retrieve your archived data. Just ask the technical support people of your backup software company.

This topic is discussed more completely in Chapter 3, but as it turns out, tracking all the files of a backup job is a huge amount of work, and this tracking mechanism is one of the primary problem areas for technical support in backup companies. If backups fail because your database is fouled up, you will probably be told to wipe out your database and re-create a new one—not very good for using the database for recovering data later. For that reason it is a good idea to back up your logs or database files onto the same tape as your archived files. You may even want to employ a separate system to help you track archived data. This will require extra work on your part but could be well worth the effort later.

Even though archiving with your backup system provides the device operations for you, there is no media redundancy built into this scheme unless you provide it yourself. This could be done by writing the same data multiple times to different tapes; for instance, three different backup operations to three different tapes. It could also be covered by performing a media-to-media copy operation, provided you have an extra tape device that's clean and in good operating condition. Don't assume that your backup software will support copying between two unlike devices; you may want to check for this capability before you adopt it as a strategy. Figure 4-7 shows two ways to create redundant tape copies using your backup system.

Also, be advised that tapes from your backup system that you use for archiving could be overwritten if they are inadvertently placed in the drive by mistake for a backup operation. This is an example of why redundancy is highly desirable.

Palindrome's Network Archivist introduced archiving as an integrated component of LAN backup when it was introduced in 1990. Their product had several distinct advantages in that it electronically labeled archive data sets on media so that an operator error would not result in overwritten data. By default, it enforced media

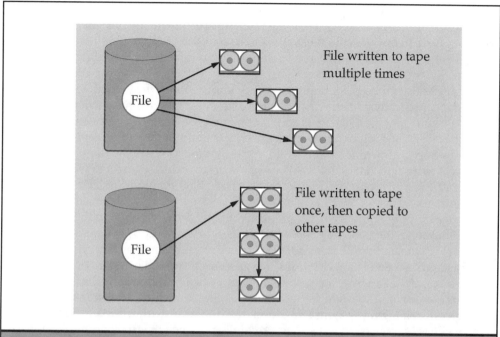

Figure 4-7. *Creating redundant archive copies with your backup system*

redundancy by ensuring that any file selected by the system for archival would have at least three copies on different pieces of media. In addition, it implemented automated file migration, which included both archiving and file deletion as part of backup operations. It even allowed end users to submit restore requests to the LAN administrator or to an autoloader system. Finally, its databases were written to each tape to ensure they could be recovered later should online database problems become an issue.

It sounds wonderful, but it suffered from some serious ease-of-use problems. The fact that this was done automatically left many users feeling out of control. The media rotation and naming scheme were confusing and customers were not comfortable about where their data was on tape. As a result, trusting it to migrate files was not something they were eager to do. Also, the integration of archiving with backup made it difficult to perform archiving operations on demand. In short, the archiving capabilities were very good, but the implementation of archiving as part of backup was too confusing to be generally useful.

Imaging Systems

Although they do not work on the broad file system, imaging systems provide archiving functionality for certain high-volume applications. An imaging system is similar to a document management system in the way it helps users locate files easily. The major difference, however, is that the imaging system usually has integrated device support. In fact, most of them are sold as part of a package that includes an optical jukebox. Jukebox storage allows the system to run efficiently without filling the magnetic disk storage on the server.

Imaging is used mostly for paperless-office applications where documents are captured electronically and stored as records. Organizations that need extensive audit trails of account activities, like insurance companies, use imaging solutions to quickly and efficiently store documents they may need to call up in the future, replacing older technology such as microfiche. You could argue that this is not really file system archiving, because the data never really is intended to reside on a server for any length of time, but it is a way of providing access to a large amount of historical information on the network.

Because they are online systems, requested files are read directly off the optical media without having to be first copied back onto server disks. This would be a wonderful way to archive all your data but, unfortunately, imaging is a specialized type of application that is not applicable for general-purpose file system operations. In order to store files in an imaging system, they must be input through whatever input technology the imaging system uses, whether paper scanner, medical scanner, or printing image. Imaging systems are not intended to work with raw data; instead, as the name implies, they store *image* data. Archiving, on the other hand, must be able to cover all types of data to be useful.

Jukebox as Mounted Disk

There are software products available that turn optical jukeboxes into mountable file systems. In general, these solutions work well for archiving or any other scenario where the amount of input/output processing is relatively light. The challenge in implementing such a system for archiving is figuring out what to do when you run out of capacity in the jukebox. Specifically, one needs to know how the jukebox's file system is implemented and whether or not it continues to reference media that has been removed for restoring data. If the system doesn't allow you to remove platters and easily find data on them, does it make sense to use it for archiving? If not, perhaps a high-capacity magnetic disk dedicated for archiving would be better. Figure 4-8 shows three ways to implement a file system on an optical jukebox.

As with any technology, you should try to understand what the jukebox system can do for you before you implement it. Make sure you understand such issues as how the jukebox accesses files, including where the file system lookup information is kept. Is there a disk cache that contains the file system lookup information, or is this kept on the platters themselves? You may find that a dual drive or larger jukebox will significantly increase performance.

How long will it take to back up—hours or days? If the file system lookup information is distributed on each platter, the jukebox could spend all its time thrashing, moving platters in and out of drives. Keep in mind that typical network

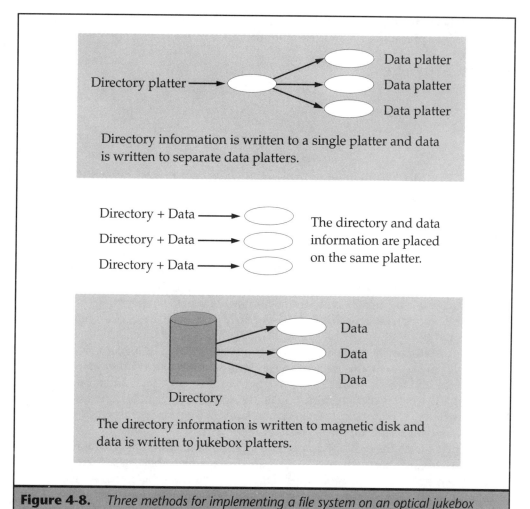

Figure 4-8.   *Three methods for implementing a file system on an optical jukebox*

traffic is random file reading and writing, and that these operations will normally be much slower than reading directly from magnetic hard disks.

Media, Redundancy, and Archiving

Backup tapes are usually kept for a short period of time depending on your off-site rotation policy: days, weeks, months, or at the most, a few years. Most organizations do not need to keep backup data for more than a couple years. In that case, there is less need to take special precautions to maintain your media (this doesn't give you a license for being negligent). However, if you plan to implement archiving, you are advised to take precautions and implement processes to maintain your media.

Media Storage

The following is a list of the environmental variables that can shorten the life of data stored on tape:

- Warm/Hot temperatures
- Humidity
- Electromagnetic radiation
- Pollutants, Smoke

So, how are you supposed to keep this data available for years and years? For starters, you need to understand that both heat and humidity are your worst enemies. You want to keep your media in the best environment possible. A temperature of 40 degrees Fahrenheit and less than 30 percent relative humidity are optimal but difficult to achieve and can be expensive to implement. Since you probably can't do this, try your best to obtain a climate-controlled environment for both temperature and humidity. If you cannot control either of these variables, do not expect your media to last as long as you would like.

Of course, storing media near large electromagnetic fields is not a good idea either. In an office environment, this includes near elevator shafts or any other place electrical cabling exists and moves a large amount of current. Radar systems and arc-welders are among the worst sources of high-powered electromagnetic noise, and both have been known to render media useless. Storing tapes in a sturdy metal box or safe can help prevent data destruction in such an environment.

Tape that sits on the shelf for an extended period of time becomes brittle and assumes its wound shape. This causes it to shed its magnetic particles when it is used again, which can result in dropouts and data loss. To prevent this from happening, exercise your tapes by running them from end to end through a clean tape drive a couple of times a year. This winding/unwinding helps preserve the flexibility of the tape.

Redundancy

Media becomes trashed; this is a fact of computer life. It gets stepped on, thrown away, baked, soaked, exposed to high humidity, eaten by animals, overwritten by mistake, and subjected to many other calamities; there are countless ways that media becomes useless. So, if you are going to archive data that you expect to use in the future, make sure that you have sufficient copies of your media in case some are destroyed.

There are two basic methods for building redundancy: run multiple operations or make media copies. In the first case, perform your archiving operations two or three times on different media. In the second case, perform the archiving operation once and copy the media onto other pieces of media.

If you are going to keep data for a long period of time, say ten years or more, make sure you are following sound media maintenance practices. In addition, you might need to implement a policy to make fresh copies of aging media. Every five years or so, you might want to make copies of these tapes to new tapes to ensure longer life of the data. Think about what NASA has to go through to ensure its data is retained; they can't just build a new satellite every time they lose data and need to recapture it. You may have a similar scenario where data was captured once and can never be captured again.

Tape Versus Optical

The best media for archiving is optical, but be warned that CD-recordable may not stand up well over time. Magneto-optical is probably your best bet, but be aware that optical media uses metal particles that are susceptible to oxidation and corrosion and therefore should be treated with care and stored under reasonable conditions. Kept under good conditions, the life expectancy of magneto-optical media is over 30 years. Keep in mind that extremes in temperature and humidity will shorten its longevity.

Tape will work for archiving but requires more deliberate care than optical. Also, not all tape is equal; in general, linear serpentine format tapes experience less physical distortion problems than helical scan tapes due to the additional variable of track angle and how it changes in relation to tape stretching. One more word about tape: longer tape is thinner tape, which is more susceptible to environmental damage. For that reason, you may choose to use shorter tape for archiving purposes. The life expectancy of tape ranges from 5 to 30 years. Keep in mind that manufacturer's claims regarding tape life may not be realizable due to the environment assumptions that were made.

Hierarchical Storage Management (HSM)

Hierarchical storage management, or HSM, is an automated system that provides archiving functionality transparently to users and administrators alike. The one key component that differentiates HSM from archiving is that the HSM system does not delete files per se, but instead leaves a small placeholder (stub) file in place of the original. This stub file is used to trigger automated recalls of the original when an end user attempts to access the file. Another difference is that HSM systems use the term *migrate* in place of the term *archive*.

Briefly, HSM works like this: Files are selected for migration by the HSM system and then copied to the HSM's media. After the file is copied correctly, a stub file is created with the same name as the original file, but it takes up much less space on the disk. Later, when a user tries to access the stub file, the HSM system intervenes and restores the original file from the appropriate HSM media.

The hierarchical part of HSM comes from the fact that data is moved from one type of repository to another as the data ages. HSM implies a structure that makes efficient use of media and storage subsystems to optimize performance and save money.

Studies show that the more recently a file has been updated, the more likely it will be recalled; so the most recently used data that is migrated is placed on the most expensive media on the fastest performing systems, and as the data ages and becomes less likely to need recalling, it is moved to less expensive media and slower, more cost-effective devices. Figure 4-9 shows the relationship between the three most common hierarchies in an HSM system: online, near-line, and offline. Online data is on the system's disk. Near-line data has been moved to a storage repository that is typically less costly than disk and from which it can be recalled quickly. And offline data has been moved again to less expensive media and may not be retrievable via automation if it is in shelf storage.

Functional Components of HSM

Figure 4-9 shows the relationship between devices and media in an HSM system. This is only part of the story, however. There needs to be corresponding software, or functional components that make it all work together. HSM is built on three simple functional ideas: automatic migration; automatic recall; and the stub file, or placeholder. Although these ideas are fairly easy to understand, as usual, the implementation of them can get a bit tricky. We'll now look at each of these functional components individually.

Automatic Migration

Migration is the operation that performs the archiving function. In other words, migration copies files to removable media and then deletes those files from the server.

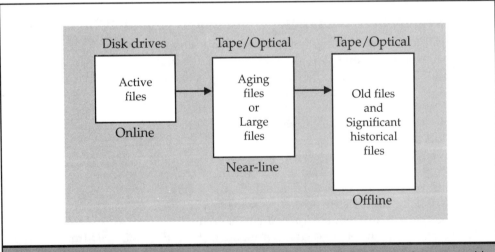

Figure 4-9. *HSM systems move files from online storage to less expensive, removable near-line and offline storage*

In HSM, the migration component is also responsible for the creation of the stub file. The idea is that some set of parameters can be established that determine when files are to be archived and which files to archive. Figure 4-10 shows this process.

Auto migration is usually triggered by a system storage capacity threshold being passed or according to a configured schedule. For instance, the system might be set up with a watchdog process that monitors if system disk capacity exceeds 95 percent. If that happens, the HSM system will kick in and begin copying and deleting files. The capacity level is referred to as a high-water mark. Typical high-water marks are between 85 and 95 percent of disk capacity.

Once the disk capacity has settled past a certain point, it can become a problem if the migration continues and starts removing files you need online. So there is a corresponding threshold that indicates when the migration operation is to stop. This threshold is called the low-water mark. Typical threshold levels for low-water marks are in the range of 60 to 70 percent disk full.

Automatic Recall

Automatic recall is the function that restores a file from the HSM system when a user tries to access a stub file. The more transparent this is to users and the faster it is done, the better.

Here's how it works. There is a mechanism installed in the system that identifies the file as a stub file. This can be implemented either as a watchdog process that traps every file open request, or it can be done as a file system modification, so the file system itself recognizes the stub file as such. Once the stub file is recognized, a small amount of information is derived from it and passed to the HSM system. Then the HSM system takes this information and determines the media to use for the restore operation. The correct media is loaded and the file is retrieved to disk, overwriting the stub file with the original (see Figure 4-11).

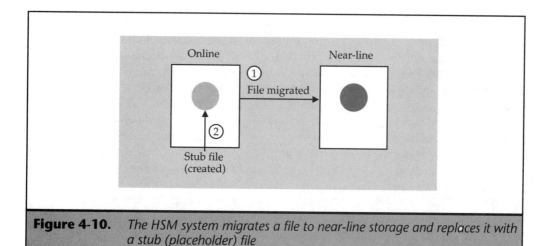

Figure 4-10.   *The HSM system migrates a file to near-line storage and replaces it with a stub (placeholder) file*

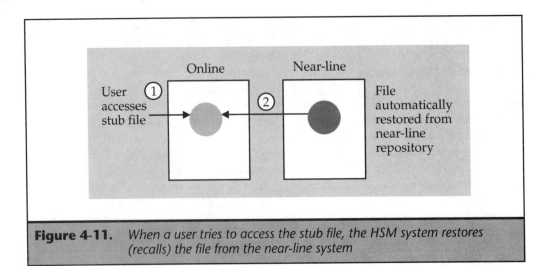

Figure 4-11. *When a user tries to access the stub file, the HSM system restores (recalls) the file from the near-line system*

One of the key problems with automatic recall is the time it takes to restore the file from the HSM system's media and the expectations of end users who might become impatient or suspect their system has hung and reboot. An HSM system that uses tape is likely to be much slower than one that uses optical media. An HSM system that keeps its restore programs loaded, but sleeping, is faster than a system where the restore program must be loaded before it can service a recall request.

The Stub File, or Placeholder

As mentioned above, the unique component of HSM is the stub file that is created to replace the original file. The stub file has the same name as the original file, but is much smaller and contains a small amount of information related to the location of the original file on removable media.

Although it is a simple idea, you should be careful to understand how this works in any HSM system you implement. Portability of the stub file could be very important to you. For the stub to be portable, it should be self-describing and contain information about its location at the time it was created. For instance, say you have a directory named JOES_DIR that you migrate files from with your HSM system and create stub files. Later you rename JOES_DIR to JANS_DIR and nothing else changes in your system. When users try to access their migrated files, they open the stub file and the recall operation begins. The restore operation begins, but the system notices that the directory is not the same; what should the system do? The simple answer is that it should recall the file, but the restore operation might only be set up for restoring files to their original location.

So now you have a scenario where the system transparently removed a file but won't transparently restore it for an end user who changed his directory name from

Joe to Jan. This is a simple scenario, but it points out some of the profound challenges of HSM.

You may find yourself wanting to manage stub files like your other files. This makes a great deal of sense because the idea of the stub file is to blend in with the file system as transparently as possible. Now consider a situation where you decide to create, or re-create, a file with the same name as one that has been migrated. There are several reasons why you might want to do this; for instance, the file is made by a process you run twice a year or it periodically gets big and needs to be removed and started from scratch again. You may be familiar with this sort of phenomenon in your network.

The problem is that a new file with the same name as the stub file will overwrite the stub file, making it impossible to restore the previous version that the stub was created for. So, the question is, can the HSM system watch for this situation and provide a way to rename the stub file so it can still be used if an older version must be restored? Unfortunately, existing LAN-based HSM systems do not provide this functionality and probably won't for several years.

Another potential stub file problem occurs when you reorganize, split, or consolidate your servers. If you have an HSM system can you move stub files from one server to another? And once they get there, will they work properly? Consider the following scenario: Even though you have an HSM system, you've outgrown your primary server because you have too many new users. So you decide to install a new server, B, to help balance the load. Your calculations of disk capacity are all made using the size of the stub files that are on the system, not the original file sizes.

You get B up and running on the network, and then you decide to copy a chunk off the file system tree from A to B. Does the copy command access all the files and recall them to A prior to copying them to B? If this is the case, not only will you likely overfill A's disks, and then possibly B's, but it will take an incredible amount of time to recall all of those files. It's the sort of thing that you would probably notice and stop the job before finding yourself with a real mess, but you are also suddenly left with an extremely difficult problem to solve. Fortunately, utilities to manage the movement of stub files have been provided by some of the HSM software companies as of the end of 1995.

The Hierarchical Structure

HSM commonly is described as a multi-tiered media system, as shown in Figure 4-9. In this approach, data is moved between different media layers. Although it makes pretty pictures, this technology is, in the final analysis, less important than the implementation of the stub file. Still, no chapter on HSM would be complete without a discussion of the possible media strategies outlined in the sections that follow.

One of the concepts used in HSM discussions is near-line storage. Near-line storage refers to the subsystem that is used for rapid recovery of migrated files. In general, near-line storage is typically comprised of an autoloader or jukebox with media containing migrated files in them. Studies show that the most common recall operations are done on files that are most recently updated, meaning the newest HSM media is more likely to have the files users want to work with.

This near-line media is normally not directly mounted as usable storage space, but there are people who attempt to do this with optical jukebox equipment. Before you try to use a jukebox for both HSM and for mountable volumes, check to see if anybody has written the software yet to allow different applications and device driver software to share the same device and media safely. Today, you would find that you could run either the mounted volume software or the HSM software, but not both at the same time, defeating the purpose of simple transparent storage services.

Two-Tiered

A two-tiered HSM system is built around the idea that you only need one repository for migrated data—the near-line store. When the capacity of the device is exceeded, just remove the oldest media from it and store it in a cool, dry place. This is consistent with the HSM model depicted in Figure 4-9, although there is no automatic migration of data from near-line to offline. Another way to think of a two-tiered system is as a file system extension for the online system. Such a system should be adequate for many LANs.

Three-Tiered

The three-tiered HSM system is the most common. As described previously, migrated files are first placed in a near-line device for rapid retrieval; then, in time, they are further moved onto offline storage. There is nothing that says that offline storage could not be another type of automated system, like a large tape library. Along with an optical jukebox for the near-line store, such a tape library would provide slow but automatic recall of files from the offline storage subsystem.

Near-Line Media and Devices

Near-line storage is optimized for performance by using magnetic disks. The problem with this approach for near-line storage is that the near-line store may not have the capacity you want because it cannot expand as easily as a removable media system. For instance, if your near-line device is a 9GB disk, you may run into problems when you fill this up. But this should only be a problem if you experience difficulties moving data from the near-line to the offline system or if you have a two-tiered system.

The next best device for a near-line device is an optical jukebox. Today these are magneto-optical devices, but in the future they are likely to be CD-recordable subsystems. Multidrive machines are far better than single-drive machines for the purpose of HSM because you can serve multiple requests much more efficiently.

Tape will also work for near-line storage, but it takes a lot longer to load and find the data once the tape is loaded. Depending on your tape device, this could take quite awhile. All tapes are sequential media, which means you have to fast forward to the place where the data is. The problem is that some older tape systems, like the 8mm

2.2GB drives, don't have a true fast-forwarding mechanism, also called QFA for quick file access. If you decide to use tape for your near-line store, a multidrive autoloader is recommended to facilitate multiuser file recalls.

The choice of which tape drive to use for a near-line store is interesting. DLT has the best characteristics for maintenance and capacity, but takes much longer to load than a near-line device should. The 4mm and 8mm devices load tapes much faster. If you use a DLT system, you would want to ensure that you have a tape always loaded with the most recent data on it. As mentioned previously in the section on automatic recall, you also want a software system where the recall system is loaded but asleep, rather than a system that must first load itself before it can respond to a recall request.

If you use tape for near-line storage, take the precaution of cleaning your tape drives daily. The use they will receive loading tapes with lots of fast forwarding and rewinding will make the heads become dirtier faster than normal streaming backup and restore operations.

Offline Media and Devices

Offline media is usually tape because it is least expensive. There is no reason it couldn't be another media. In the future, CD-recordable may become the best media for offline storage as well. Be aware, however, the CD-recordable may not have the expected life of other media, including tape stored in a good environment. The dyes used for CD-recordable may end up deteriorating faster than the magnetic particles on tape.

If you want to provide automated restores of data from the offline system (admittedly a bit of an oxymoron), you can do this with a jukebox or library system. You should expect at some point, however, that you could overfill the capacity of such a device and need to use shelf storage, too.

Network Structure and Impact of HSM

Your HSM system can be set up on a one-to-one basis with the server that it is attached to, or it can be set up to migrate data from multiple servers. If it is set up on a one-to-one basis, it may not have any impact on the network, and all data transfers may be accomplished across the system's SCSI bus. However, a one-to-one ratio does not guarantee that you will not have network traffic to consider; the HSM system may perform all its work over the network anyway.

The reason this should be a consideration is as follows: Suppose you have a superserver on your network with over 20GB of capacity on it. Your HSM system is configured with a high-water mark of 95 percent and a low-water mark of 70 percent. In the middle of some busy day, your server's capacity goes over the high-water mark and you begin migrating files. Does your network have the bandwidth to accommodate the rapid movement of 5GB of data across the wire in the middle of the workday? If not, you will want to implement other procedures to assure this doesn't bring your network to its knees in the middle of the day. For this reason you may want to plan your HSM implementation so it doesn't move data across bridges or routers and saturate them.

One way some HSM systems deflect this issue is by prestaging migrated data. This is a technique where the HSM system tries to predict which files would be migrated next and copies them to its near-line store in nonbusy off-hours. This way a large percentage of the actual data needing to be moved during migration operations is minimal, and the majority of the work is to delete files and replace them with their stubs.

HSM Redundancy Issues and Integration of HSM and Backup

Sooner or later you will come around to wondering what needs to be done in order to protect your near-line and offline media from a catastrophe. Sure, if your primary system is lost, you will use backup to restore it, but what about your near-line store or even your offline store?

One of the solutions to this problem is to back them up as discrete systems and restore them following a disaster. This is not a bad solution, but it adds some complexity to the restore scenario—complexity that you will not enjoy. In the best case, these backups would be media copy operations, where you copy from your near-line media to exactly the same type of media and then move the copies to a storage vault. In this way, all you need to do is load your media copies into a similar device and you are on your way.

Another solution integrates the backup system with the HSM system so that the HSM system's data can be restored from media that is used for backup. Notice that this doesn't necessarily mean that you can easily restore your HSM system, but at least the data can be retrieved. This approach is much easier for sustaining smooth daily operations than the approach where the HSM system needs to be backed up separately. Unfortunately, following a disaster, your HSM recall may not work at all, forcing you to perform recall operations manually.

But this leads to another interesting question: how does backup and recovery integrate with your HSM system during backups? Obviously, the backup system cannot demigrate every file that it tries to back up. You only want the backup system to copy the stub files onto tape.

One way to prevent a massive demigration is to employ a user registration scheme whereby the backup ID registers with the HSM system so the HSM system will not demigrate any files the backup system requests. This works until somebody changes the backup system ID some day while you are on vacation. A better method uses an API call to inform the HSM system that a backup system is accessing the file and that it should not be migrated.

This type of mechanism is not foolproof either, but is less likely to fail through human fallibility. Expect to see this type of capability built into future operating systems. For instance, Microsoft is working with Avail Systems, one of the leading

HSM companies in the LAN market, to provide HSM capability in future versions of their operating systems.

3M's National Media Lab

A great source of information on media issues and characteristics, including life expectancy, can be found on 3M Corporation's National Media Lab web site on the Internet. Their URL is http://www.nml.org. Most of what they do is geared toward understanding the requirements of government and research data storage, so their materials tend to have a research and academic orientation. However, a great deal of this information is relevant to LAN systems and they study all types of media and recording devices, including those used on LANs. It is also one of the only places where you can go to get a relatively unbiased perspective on recording technology coupled with an incredible in-depth knowledge of the subject.

CHAPTER FIVE

High-Availability Systems for Reducing Downtime

Backup is something you want to ensure is done correctly every day, like clockwork. Restores, on the other hand, are something you want to avoid doing because it means that files have been lost. This is especially true of complete system restores of your network servers, because so many people depend on them.

The fact that people depend on the availability of their servers makes your goal slightly different than just being able to recover lost data. The real goal of the LAN administrator should be system availability. To increase your servers' availability, you decrease the time they are unavailable by implementing redundant or fault-tolerance components that can step in and take over the responsibilities of the failed components. This chapter looks at several ways of implementing redundancy and fault-tolerant technologies that can help you reduce the amount of time your network data is unavailable to users following a server failure.

Fault Tolerance

If you're like most people, you like some amount of predictability and stability in your life and do not want to feel threatened. As a LAN professional, you also like some stability and predictability on the job. In addition, you do not like to be surprised by your network very often because surprises on a LAN usually mean that whatever you planned for the day will now have to wait while you attend to fixing the surprise.

Today, the financial services industry is very large thanks to the concern investors have about their financial well-being and stability. Investors of all types want to have timely access to information about their accounts and transactions in order to determine their current financial status. The faster information about transactions can be known to investors, the more secure they can feel. Therefore, financial institutions compete in the market by providing information services that offer data on demand, either over the telephone or more recently through online services and ATMs (automated teller machines). These services help their customers feel good about their finances and give them a sense of control.

So, given the fact that financial services compete with each other by offering their customers fast access to their financial information, it follows that the financial services industry would, as a group, be concerned about maintaining the availability of their systems. After all, if customers can't find out about their account due to a system failure, they may decide to take their business someplace else where they feel more confidence.

It is not terribly surprising, then, that the financial services industry helped lead the way in establishing system requirements that include the elimination of all downtime. While the requirement for zero downtime may be impossible to meet, the goal of minimizing downtime has led to development of what are called *fault-tolerant systems*, where the responsibility of finishing a task is shared among two or more components.

There are several generic ways to achieve fault tolerance depending on the task being performed and the cost people are willing to pay for it. We will examine some of these in the following sections.

Idle Spares

One way to provide fault tolerance is to have a spare component in an idle state, ready to replace the functions of the primary component if it should fail. A simple example of this type of fault tolerance would be the use of an older, slow printer that you keep online for network printing but only use as a backup in case you have a problem with your current system.

Hot-"Swappable" Modules

It is possible to have memory and processor chips on modular "hot-pluggable" circuit boards that can be used to replace malfunctioning primary components. This type of capability can be employed on a system where a memory or processor failure only affects part of the system and does not cause a complete system failure. For example, routers that use modular circuit boards for routing particular network segments can afford to lose some routing capability and still function to route other traffic. As soon as the failed board is replaced, the router is back to normal.

By contrast, if memory or the processor in an average PC or workstation fails, it will result in a complete system failure, which requires the replacement of parts while the system is powered off (not fault tolerant).

Load Balancing

Another way to provide fault tolerance is to have two components sharing a task and, if one fails, the other component takes on the complete workload of both. This is commonly done with dual power supplies in server systems. If one power supply fails, the other takes on a double load. By the way, just because a system has dual power supplies does not mean they are load balancing. For instance, it would be possible to use one power supply for the system board and cooling fans and the other for storage devices. If you want load balancing and fault-tolerant power, make sure you clarify with the vendor that they indeed work this way.

Symmetric Multiprocessing

Multiprocessing systems are becoming more common on network servers. There are two fundamental types of multiprocessing for network systems: symmetric and asymmetric, as shown in Figure 5-1. In symmetric multiprocessing, each processor in the system is capable of performing any of the work in the system; in other words, it works by balancing the tasks among the various processors. For this reason, symmetric multiprocessing has the capability to provide fault tolerance at the CPU level.

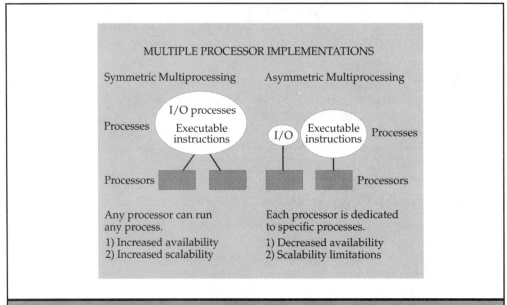

Figure 5-1. *Symmetric multiprocessing shares the work among all processors, while asymmetric multiprocessing dedicates processes to certain tasks*

This does not mean that the process running on a particular CPU can be finished completely by another processor. The challenges of managing the system memory, caches, and virtual memory make this extremely difficult. However, it does mean that the system may be able to continue to successfully run the other processes without stopping.

Asymmetric processing, on the other hand, is like using separate power supplies for different parts of the system. A typical asymmetric processing model uses one processor for executing code and the other for managing system I/O. In this case, if either CPU fails, the entire system fails. In fact, now that there are two components, each of which is capable of causing a system failure, the likelihood of a complete system failure just doubled. For that reason, asymmetric multiprocessing is not recommended for situations where high availability is desired.

Mirroring

In *mirroring*, two components perform exactly the same work in lockstep, and if one of them fails, the other system continues working. This is most commonly implemented in disk subsystems where two disks and two controllers write identical data to the same sectors on identical disk drives.

In mirroring, the two systems are peers and do not complete a task until both systems complete it. When a failure occurs, the system identifies it and switches over to single subsystem operations. Mirroring works well for disks, but has proven to be quite challenging for complete systems due to the difficulty in mirroring events that occur as rapidly as internal bus transfers and problems with software-generated system failures that are mirrored on both machines.

Replication

A variation of mirroring in networks is *delayed mirroring*, or *replication*, where a secondary system receives data from the primary system, but after some delay. If the primary fails, the secondary comes online, substituting for the primary system, and allows workers to pick up working close to where they left off. Because these systems have some lag time between when the data was created on the primary and copied to the secondary, they are not precise mirrors, so the work interruption is not seamless. However, these systems can be designed and implemented so that the replication happens very quickly after the primary writes the data to disk, minimizing the loss of data on the network.

One of the key challenges to this type of product is bringing the replication system up on the network, posing as the primary. For the replication system to function as a replacement, it must also replicate the primary system's security information and mechanisms, such as user IDs, group memberships, login initialization, and any other authorization processes. This is not necessarily automatic with some of the replication products in the market, which means that the LAN administrator must manually set up system security to ensure that users can log in with full security. This obviously can slow down the effectiveness of replication products.

The Impossibility of Fault Tolerance

A common misconception about fault tolerance is that nothing will go wrong with a fault-tolerant system. The key word is "tolerance," which is sometimes interpreted to mean "bullet-proof." The words "fault tolerance" really mean that the system can continue operating after recovering from certain types of failures. In other words, the system is tolerant of some kinds of faults. It does not mean that the system will recover from every possible failure, because there is no way to predict all the ways a system could fail.

Continuous Uptime

If you can't buy perfect fault tolerance for your network, you may try for the next best thing. A more realistic goal is to provide continuous uptime, or in other words, as little downtime as possible. The idea here is to keep users working without noticeable periods of time when productivity is lost due to network failures.

What you accept as a reasonable amount of downtime is key to what you can implement. Recovery capability that is totally seamless to end users and customers will cost you significant resources to implement and maintain. On the other hand, if your goal is to provide reasonable uptime with outages less than five minutes while you switch over to alternate systems, you can probably save yourself a lot of time and money.

To provide adequate alternative systems, you need to cover the following items:

- **Network access**   If your primary network fails, is there alternative access to your systems?

- **Data access**   Are there alternative storage subsystems that you can access to get at your data?

- **Power access**   Do you have alternative power sources if the line fails?

- **System access**   If your system fails, is there an alternative system available and ready?

Redundant System Components

Within any given system, several components can be duplicated to increase the tolerance to failures. Some of these must be designed into the system, but others can be added after the product is installed. Following is a brief examination of some of the ways this is done.

Main Processor

Once it is up and running, the main processor in a system will not often fail. Still, the engineering know-how exists to mount redundant CPUs in a system. For the most part, when the use of multiple CPUs is discussed, it is usually in the context of improving performance rather than system reliability.

The challenge of implementing redundant CPUs for fault tolerance is in the memory, cache, and task management. The secondary CPU must be able to accurately track the operations of the primary, but without getting in the way of the primary's operations. One way to do this is to mirror the state of the primary processor in the secondary processor. Then, if the primary fails, the secondary already has the information loaded into its internal memory and can take over control of the system. Of course, any bad information resulting from the failing primary could also be replicated in the secondary, causing errors when the secondary begins processing.

NetFrame Systems has developed fail-safe technology for their CPUs that it calls "Gemini" mode. The concept of Gemini is to use an alternate CPU that replicates the primary CPU a few cycles after the primary executes its instructions. This way, if the primary fails, the secondary is less likely to replicate bad data resulting from the failed CPU and continues processing from a time prior to the actual failure.

There has been a great deal written over the last several years about symmetric multiprocessing on server systems. Symmetric multiprocessing machines are constructed to allow multiple CPUs to split the work and provide some degree of fault tolerance. For instance, in a dual-CPU machine, if one CPU fails, the system can still be run on the other. However, the process running on the failed CPU will probably fail.

Multiprocessing depends heavily on the capabilities of the operating system to handle memory management between tasks running on different processors, including operating systems processors. It would not be surprising, therefore, if a failed processor in a multiprocessor system caused the machine to crash. If the system would run with a disabled CPU, that is fault tolerance at work.

In asymmetric multiprocessing systems, the CPUs are given specific tasks to manage. For instance, one CPU would perform I/O tasks and the other would execute the programs. In this case, a failed CPU would completely disable the machine and would not be recoverable running on a single processor.

Power Supplies

It's common for manufacturers to use dual power supplies in their high-end products. The dual power supplies balance the load; that is, they both provide power when the system is working, as shown in Figure 5-2. When one power supply fails, the other one has to carry the load. Obviously, you want to make sure that either power supply has the power capacity to handle the load by itself. For instance, a system that uses 500 watts of power should not have dual 400-watt power supplies.

You should also try to make sure that the machine has been properly engineered to remove heat from the system successfully. If you have a system with dual power supplies, you probably have other redundant components too, such as network

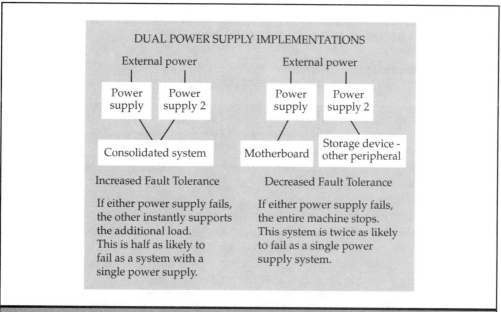

Figure 5-2. *Dual power supplies are used to improve availability, but can also reduce availability if they are dedicated to specific components*

interface cards, I/O cards, and disks. All of these devices take extra power and generate more heat. Power supplies also generate heat, and the bigger they are, the more heat they generate. All of this means that heat becomes a much more likely source of problems in redundant systems, and you want to make sure that the system has adequate ventilation to deal with all the extra heat.

I/O Devices and Channels

Transferring data from memory to magnetic storage is an everyday occurrence, but it is also quite complicated on a detailed level. As the requirements for storage capacity continue to increase, the components of disk and tape drives become smaller and smaller and engineering tolerances become much tighter. It is not surprising that storage devices occasionally fail.

To prevent losing data on account of a failed device, you may want to implement redundant devices and I/O controllers. Redundant disk pairs on a single controller is called *mirroring;* redundant disk pairs on redundant controllers is called *duplexing.* Duplexing is safer and faster than mirroring because the extra controller removes the system's disk controller as a single source of failure and the controllers can overlap disk reads for faster performance.

Storage Subsystem Redundancy

As mentioned above, one of the most likely sources of faults within a system is with the storage subsystems. So it's only natural that several approaches have been developed to provide fault tolerance in this area. The more popular ones are examined in the following sections.

Disk Mirroring

Disk mirroring sounds simple enough: just get two disks and then write all of what goes on one disk to the other. You run into problems, however, if the disks are formatted differently. The partition sizes of the primary and secondary should be the same. If the primary were larger than the secondary, it would be impossible to mirror all disk updates once the primary exceeded the secondary's capacity.

Disk mirroring carries some performance overhead on disk-write operations. The mirrored pair is not finished writing until both disks have written the same data. This takes a little longer than simply writing the data once to one disk. Disk reads, however, can be faster because the two disks can work independently and divide the work. Disk reads are constrained by the time it takes to position the disk arm correctly. Using disk mirroring, while one disk is reading data, the other one can be positioning to the next data block All in all, the data can be read faster than if you used a single drive because there is less latency waiting for heads to settle on the proper tracks.

Disk Duplexing

Disk duplexing is virtually the same as mirroring, except another I/O controller is added for the mirrored pair. Performance increases due to less contention on the I/O bus. It may not be obvious, but I/O buses are serial in nature, not parallel. This means that each device on an I/O bus shares the bus with other devices and that only one device at a time can be written to. Obviously, if you have a separate controller for each device in a mirrored disk pair, you will have slightly less bus congestion. Then again, if your system is not I/O bound in performance, you might never realize the difference.

As with mirrored disk pairs, it is highly recommended that you use the same manufacturer and model of controller for your duplexed drives. Mixing an older, slower controller with a new high-speed controller will effectively negate all the performance advantages of the new controller.

RAID

RAID stands for *redundant array of inexpensive disks*. The main idea of RAID is to be able to replace a failing, or failed disk drive, without experiencing any downtime. In other words, RAID was conceived as a way to ensure continuous uptime from disk subsystems.

The other advantage of RAID is its performance capabilities. One of the limiting factors in disk drive performance is the rotational speed. That's why disk drive manufacturers highlight the RPMs of their products. The higher the RPM rating of the drive, the faster data can be read from it, generally. But the rotation speed of the disk is still a limiting factor to I/O performance because the transfer speed of the bus far exceeds it. In other words, the bus has to wait for data to be read off the spinning disks. Therefore, striping data across multiple devices has emerged as a way to overcome rotational latency.

By transferring data to four different devices operating in sync with each other, the bus can continue to supply data much faster than it can to a single disk, where it must wait for the disk drive to complete a revolution. A simple RAID model uses four disks and has data transferring to each of these disks in sequence. Each disk is responsible for the transfer during a quarter revolution of its disk. Figure 5-3 shows a simple RAID 0 implementation and how the RAID controller writes to all the disks sequentially.

RAID LEVELS   RAID can be implemented several different ways, depending on the type of performance, cost, and uptime desired. The table that follows describes the various RAID levels in use today.

Level 0	Striping without parity
Level 1	Disk mirroring, not striping
Level 3	Striping, implemented with a dedicated parity disk
Level 5	Striping across five disks, where parity is also striped
Level 01 (or 10)	Striped data across two disks, each striped pair mirrored

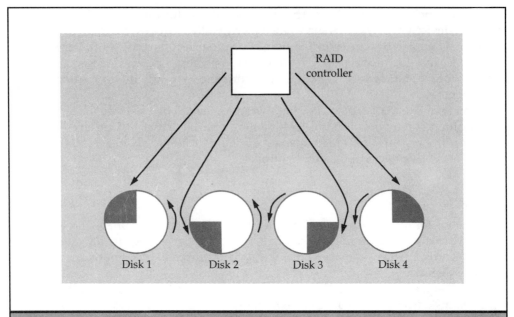

Figure 5-3. *RAID systems write consecutive data blocks to multiple synchronized disks*

RAID level 0 stripes data across four disks. There is no built-in redundancy in a RAID 0 system, which is intended for high-speed transfers where permanence of the data is not generally important. If any of the drives fails in a RAID 0 system, the data on all the drives will be lost. For this reason, some manufacturers now sell RAID systems where their RAID 0 implementation fills the disks sequentially rather than striping across them. The end result is slower performance, but the ability to retain three-quarters of the RAID system's data if one of the disks fail.

RAID level 1 is disk mirroring. In terms of RAID, it is the most expensive because there is one extra disk for redundancy for each disk of data. In other words, with disk mirroring you may purchase 4GB of storage on two 2GB disks, but you will only be able to use 2GB on your system. Because it doesn't stripe data across four synchronized disks, it is relatively slow for disk writes. On the other hand, it has generally good performance on read operations.

RAID level 3 stripes the data across four disks and then writes parity information on the fifth disk. This is a more economical way to buy disks because only 20 percent of your disks are being used for redundancy. For instance, if you buy five 1GB disks, 4GB would be used for data, while 1GB would be used for parity. If one of the disks fails in RAID 3, a new, empty disk is inserted in the RAID cabinet, and its data is then re-created by calculating its values from other disks and the parity disk. The following section on parity explains this in detail.

RAID level 5 is very similar to RAID 3, except that the parity information is spread among the five disks rather than being localized on one disk. As with RAID level 3, 20 percent of the disk capacity is used for redundancy and any disk can be replaced and rebuilt from the data on the other disks.

PARITY   RAID disks use an EXCLUSIVE OR algorithm to build the parity information that is written to disk. Obviously there must be some calculations made to create this parity information as data is being written to disk. This is a fairly fast calculation, especially when done on a hardware chip, as opposed to using processor memory. Although the calculation must be made and written with each outgoing data block, it is still faster than writing data to a single spinning disk and waiting for the rotations to complete.

It gets interesting, however, when a disk fails and must be replaced. The RAID system will continue to function without the missing disk by using a parity reconstruction algorithm that creates the missing data from the remaining disks. In a similar fashion, an empty replacement disk inserted in a RAID cabinet can be slowly repopulated by the RAID controller, which calculates the missing values from the same parity reconstruction algorithm. This is known as a *parity rebuild.*

Figure 5-4 shows the various stages of RAID activity. The first two parts of the figure show a RAID 3 array under normal operating conditions and when one of its disks fails. The third part of the figure shows how a new drive has replaced the failed one and has its data rebuilt using the inverse operation of the parity calculation.

Parity rebuilds are great in theory, but if the RAID cabinet is being heavily used when the parity rebuild starts, performance of the system will be significantly slowed. For all disk read requests in the system, the parity reconstruction must be made to regenerate the data. When the disk is idle, it will start working on the parity rebuild process. While this is going on, all other disk activities are suspended temporarily while the parity rebuild completes its block writes. It is highly likely that the parity rebuild will then be interrupted by some other disk request, so the parity rebuild has to be able to keep track of where it was working when it was interrupted. Keep in mind that the disks are synchronized and must write the data in concert with each other. The situation becomes even more involved as new updates are written to the disk.

The end result of all this is that parity rebuilds are best done when the system is idle and does not have to perform real-time work. Although this may seem to defeat the purpose of RAID, remember that data can still be retrieved from the system in the meantime. Delaying the parity rebuild until the system is quiet simply provides better system performance, although at some risk. The evolution of predictive failure analysis technology in disk drives (see the last section in this chapter) may provide you with the preventive means to schedule the replacement of RAID disks at your convenience, rather than on the demands of the smoking drive.

HOT SWAPPING   Hot swapping is the name used for the ability to pull out or insert devices into a RAID cabinet while the cabinet continues to operate and provide disk

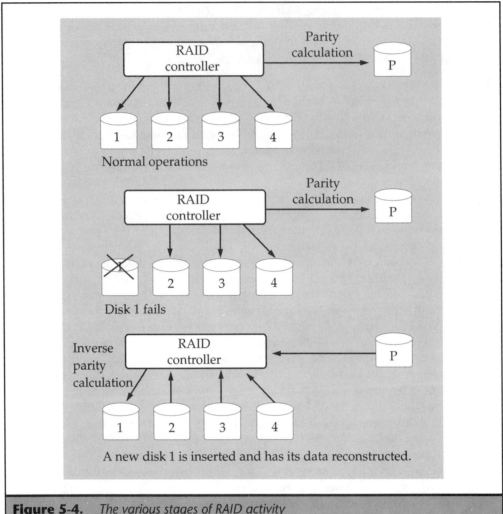

Figure 5-4. *The various stages of RAID activity*

I/O to the system it's attached to. This requires some interesting engineering that enables it to handle the power surges and the internal I/O bus interruptions that result from device insertions or removals. Although it is fun to try this out, it is not a good idea to tempt fate by experimenting with the hot-swapping capabilities of your RAID system. For starters, you may end up running parity rebuilds that you don't want to, but more importantly, you do not want to put undue stress on the connectors in the RAID systems backplane; although such connectors are built to last many insertions or removals, strange things can happen.

HOT SPARE   A hot spare is an extra drive in a RAID cabinet that can be used for automatic insertion into a RAID array should any of the disks fail. These are most commonly seen in RAID cabinets that hold multiple RAID arrays. Then, if any drive fails in any of the arrays inside the cabinet, the hot spare will automatically be used to fill in for the failed drive. Be aware that the use of such a hot spare will most likely begin an immediate parity rebuild, which you might prefer to avoid until later in the day. A large RAID cabinet with a hot spare drive is shown in Figure 5-5.

RAID CONTROLLERS   RAID systems are composed of several disks but look like one disk to the host system's I/O controller. There is another controller positioned inside the RAID system itself that actually performs all the disk I/O operations to the disks. This RAID controller is responsible for several operations, including parity creation during write operations and parity rebuild operations.

The structure of this controller determines many of the capabilities of the RAID system. For instance, the RAID 0 configuration where all drives are used in sequence,

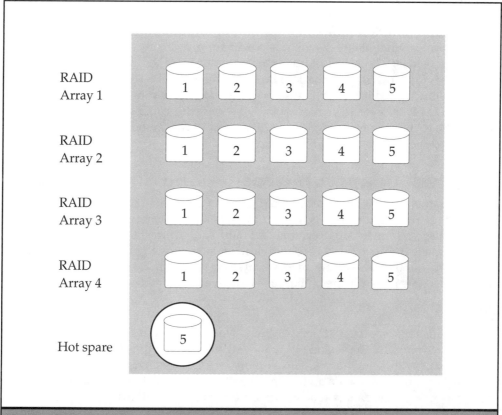

Figure 5-5.   *The hot spare drive can replace any other failed drive instantaneously*

as opposed to striping, is determined by firmware in the RAID system's controller. These RAID controllers vary in design and complexity, but almost all of them are expected to perform quickly and without errors. Another area to look at is what sort of redundancy is built into the controllers. Dual, redundant RAID controllers provide fault tolerance and build the fault tolerance of the RAID system. There are some RAID systems today that have dual controllers for redundancy but also work together for load balancing to improve performance when both are operational.

OTHER RAID FEATURES   There are several other approaches used in RAID systems to increase their fault tolerance and performance. One way storage systems differ is in the amount of cache they utilize and how the cache is designed to function. As far as RAID is concerned, a write-through cache is best for data integrity purposes because disk writes are immediately transferred to the disks, as opposed to caches where disk writes wait to be flushed. If data is held in the cache waiting to be flushed to disk, it is possible that a failure of some sort would result in lost data before it gets written to disk. This is especially true when working with database systems that have complicated data update mechanisms. The database assumes data is written to disk when it is sent to the device; if the device doesn't actually complete the writing immediately, you could end up with restore problems.

Of course, redundant, hot-swappable power supplies are recommended. You might also consider a battery backup for them if your line goes down. Some RAID systems have their own battery backup built into them. A UPS system on the server doesn't do much good if the RAID system doesn't also have some battery backup. Some RAID systems even have redundant hot-swappable cooling fans. Considering the way the RAID cabinet may be expected to support continuous uptime operations, having hot-swappable fans could be an advantage.

System Redundancy: Mirroring and Shadowing

Whole or partial systems can be replicated on another machine to provide redundancy. The advantage of this approach is that a component in a machine that isn't replicated will not cause a severe loss in downtime if it fails. For systems that require continuous uptime, it makes sense to build your individual machines with internal component redundancy, and then also create an identical spare of that machine to function as its mirror. We'll now review some of the ways to provide system mirroring.

SFT III

SFT III stands for system fault tolerant, three, to distinguish it from SFT II, which is a disk mirroring and duplexing utility in NetWare 2.*x*. SFT III is Novell's primary product for providing high-availability servers for PC LANs. The idea behind SFT III is to connect two machines via a fiber optic cable and then replicate the state of the primary within the secondary machine. Should the primary fail for any reason, the secondary will kick in and start up where the primary failed.

The concept of a state machine is important to understanding SFT III. At any given time, the two SFT III machines should be almost exactly alike. Every instruction and device operation that occurs on the primary is echoed in the secondary. This way, when the primary fails, the secondary can pick up the workload without missing an operation.

The most compelling feature of SFT III is its transparency; the cut-over to the secondary system is completely invisible to end users and administrators alike. There is no administration work required to keep it up and running. On the negative side, it is expensive to implement and poses some compatibility problems with other NLMs. Another problem with SFT III is that logical problems within the primary are echoed in the secondary. Therefore, a logical problem that causes the primary to fail will also cause the secondary to fail.

While it received a great deal of attention, SFT III was not widely implemented by the market. As Novell moves its company toward the production and marketing of NetWare 4.*x*, it is unknown if their SFT product will continue to be developed.

Vinca StandbyServer

Vinca Corporation of Orem, Utah, has developed a server disk replicating product called StandbyServer. StandbyServer differs from SFT III in that the secondary does not mirror the state of the entire primary system but uses NetWare's disk-mirroring capabilities to send disk writes to another machine over a high-speed serial link up to 50 feet away. In other words, StandbyServer replaces a disk in the primary system's disk-mirroring scheme with a communications link to a secondary machine. The secondary monitors the primary for failure, and if it determines that the primary has failed, the secondary puts itself online with the data it had mirrored to it.

This approach is significantly different than the state machine approach of SFT III. StandbyServer does not mirror the entire machine, it mirrors physical disks. This means that problems on the primary with such things as memory and task management will not be replicated on the secondary because the secondary only receives disk I/O.

One of the disadvantages of this approach is that you will not get the kind of performance you'd expect from mirrored disk pairs under NetWare. Normally, using mirroring, disk reads are staggered between the two drives, allowing the disk arms to position independently and thus faster. StandbyServer places all the responsibility for disk reads on the disk drive in the primary. In addition, it is likely that high-volume disk updates would suffer performance degradation using a StandbyServer mirrored disk.

Memory Technology's SOFT

Most server systems today in distributed environments use SCSI storage devices. One of the most restricting limitations of SCSI is the cable lengths allowed. Normal SCSI has a cable maximum of six meters, and differential SCSI, which is not widely implemented, has a maximum cable length of 25 meters. This makes it virtually impossible to mirror disks outside the boundaries of the room where the machine is.

An English company, Memory Technology, has designed, built, and begun marketing an optical transceiver for SCSI. Two such transceivers would allow you to mirror your SCSI devices up to 45 kilometers away over a dedicated fiber optic link. This transceiver system is called SOFT, for SCSI Over Fiber Transmission, and it has very little, if any, bandwidth degradation associated with it due to the extremely high bandwidth properties of fiber optic cable.

You may wonder why anybody would want to implement such a product, but the answer is simple: they want to have their data somewhere outside the proximity of the machine in case they have some site disaster. If they did have a site disaster, they could be up and running again without having to restore data from tape simply by having another machine available to plug into the remote storage device.

Although SOFT would not keep you from experiencing any downtime, it may very well limit the amount of downtime you experience following some disaster. Another big advantage of this kind of approach would be the ability to centralize the location of storage devices in an organization. If you could now run cables that connect your server systems on the department floors to SCSI devices located in a data center environment, would this be a benefit to you? It could very well reduce the amount of downtime you experience following a system failure on your network.

Shadowing

It may not be necessary to copy the complete system or disk to another machine to ensure the right amount of redundancy for your organization. There are other products available that enable the copying of certain files and/or directory structures to another system on the network. The idea is to have a file system watchdog that continuously scans for updates to certain configured files. If such an update occurs, the watchdog process calls another program that replicates the files or directories onto another machine on the network.

If the primary system fails, users and applications can access the replicated data on whatever server it was copied to. This would probably take some administrative work to make sure that drive mappings and rights were established correctly, or to rename the alternate server.

In fact, the terms *primary* and *alternate* do not apply very well to a shadowing product. One of the advantages of shadowing is that the redundancy is provided logically and that the alternate repository can be structured several ways. For instance, two servers could have their most important files and directories shadowed on the other one. Another way to implement shadowing would be to have one alternate server shadow all the other servers on the network; then if any of them failed, the alternate could substitute as the failed machine.

The primary problems with shadowing are that it uses network bandwidth to create redundant data and that the shadowing is not instantaneous—data could be lost between the last replication and the system failure. As mentioned, it also requires more administrative work than the solutions above. On the plus side, shadowing is relatively inexpensive to implement and is fairly easy to set up and maintain.

Figure 5-6 shows how shadowing is typically implemented on LANs. It is possible that a single server could act as a repository of "shadowed" files for many other servers on the network. Alternatively, two servers could be set up to shadow each other. Two products that provide shadowing are LAN Shadow by Horizons Technology and Double Take by NSI, Inc.

Storage Server

There is another class of device that has been discussed within the storage industry for some time now, referred to as a *network storage server*. The concept of the network storage server is to provide high availability for network servers with a single system that replicates data from those servers and can make it available should one of those servers fail.

The network storage server concept includes what are called "hot" backups of server machines. Hot backup is a continuous ongoing incremental backup (see Chapter 3 for a discussion of incremental backups), where files are replicated constantly as they are updated, or soon after. In its fastest implementation, a hot backup system would copy a file to a storage server at the same time the file is written to the server's own file system.

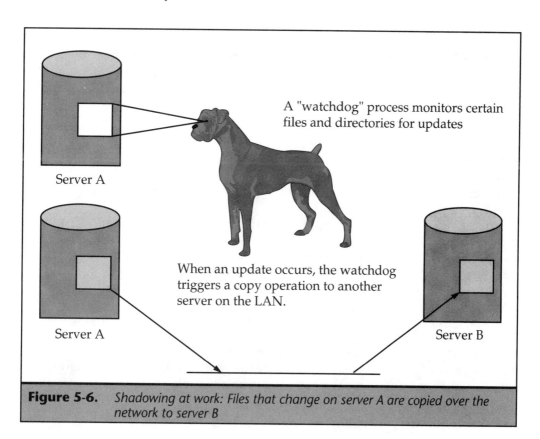

Figure 5-6. *Shadowing at work: Files that change on server A are copied over the network to server B*

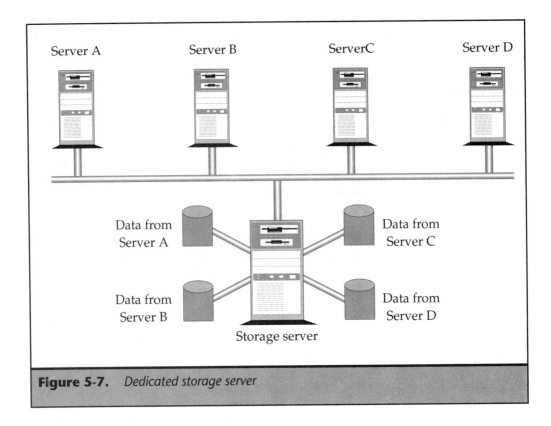

Figure 5-7.   *Dedicated storage server*

Let's assume that such a network storage server is installed and that it is backing up several primary file servers. If one of the primary servers fails, the storage server would create a mountable file system image of the failed primary and be made available on the network, masquerading as the failed primary server. The detailed technology of how the primary server's file system is made available is a design choice of the people who make the storage server.

For example, the storage server could use HSM technology to populate a disk with stub files from the primary server and then demigrate any files that users request. In other words, the storage server masquerades as the primary server with a virtual file system. As users and applications access the storage server, the files they call for would be restored to the disk in the storage server. While the performance of such a design would be slower than accessing files directly from a file system, it has the advantage of making the entire file system available very quickly, much faster than restoring all the data files first, before coming online.

Figure 5-7 shows one possibility for implementing a storage server. Dedicated disks on the storage server hold copies of data from network servers. Should any of servers A, B, C, or D fail, the storage server mounts the appropriate disk for network access and masquerades as the failed server.

Network Redundancy

If you have a wiring failure or some other problem with your network fabric, you have to have an alternative path to sustain uptime. Well-structured wiring that allows you to isolate segments on your network can greatly help you manage problems. Beyond having a well-designed wiring scheme, the next section discusses other ways to increase the reliability of your network.

Dual Backbones

Many networks use a backbone as part of their structured wiring approach. For those not familiar with the term, a *backbone* is the highest-level segment in a hierarchical network. As data passes between different network segments in a hierarchy, it travels to a higher level until it finds a direct route to the other network segment. Sometimes this is some level below the backbone, but sometimes it may have to travel over the backbone.

Backbones are also often used to connect servers and other service-providing machines on the network. Often these backbones are higher-speed networks to facilitate the best performance from the server machines. So, if the backbone is providing the network service to your servers, what happens if the backbone fails? The server machines are probably still functioning, but they are virtually unusable because access to them is cut off.

That's why some organizations implement dual-backbone networks. If the primary network goes down, the secondary network will carry the traffic. The concept is independent of topology, but it lends itself better to token ring, ethernet, and FDDI. Figure 5-8 shows two distinct backbone rings connecting a group of servers redundantly.

One of the things to watch out for in any high-traffic backbone is how to recover from something that destroys your cabling. For this reason, it is a good idea if the wiring for the secondary network follows a different path than the primary. There are many things that will destroy a network connection, but few do it so swiftly as construction work that snaps a cable in the midst of heavy machinery working. Unfortunately, when a backhoe rips your cabling out of the ground while it is digging a trench, the backhoe operator probably isn't even aware that the cable was destroyed. If your dual-backbone cabling is run next to each other, there is an excellent chance that both backbones were destroyed.

Intelligent Hubs, Concentrators, Switches

For switched 10BaseT and ATM networks, where each machine is connected to the network through some switching device, you can build redundancy into the network

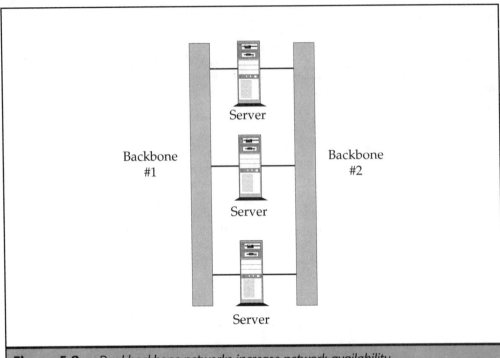

Figure 5-8. *Dual backbone networks increase network availability*

by providing alternative high-speed links between them. The ability of such network devices to precisely detect failed segments and channel traffic through alternate routes is a big advantage of this technology.

Another benefit of switching technology is that it can be managed with a network management console. Component failures can be viewed almost instantaneously on the console and responded to quickly. For example, configuration changes in the device can be made from the console to more effectively distribute the traffic. Another benefit is the advance warning of failing segments through notification of conditions that exceed normal traffic or error levels.

Finally, many switching devices are built modularly with hot-swappable circuit boards. If a chip fails on a board in the device, it can be replaced relatively quickly just by removing the failed card and sliding in a new one. In addition, dual power supplies and battery backups should be used on your switching devices whenever possible to increase the uptime of your network.

Routers

Routers usually have the most intelligence built into them and are therefore the most flexible network fabric devices. Routers do what their name implies—route traffic within the network. This makes them valuable for rerouting traffic in case some failure causes you to access servers at another location.

Suppose the room where your servers are running has had the electrical supply cut and you have run out of battery backup. So, you decide to start using an alternate room in your building for your servers. How do your users, who never had to move their equipment, access these alternate machines when there is no network connection established between them? By changing the router configurations, you may be able to use existing wiring to establish connections to the new server location.

In more extreme cases, where equipment must be moved to another site, you may need additional routers for the new site, as well as the assistance of the various telephone and network service providers to set up a temporary network to carry all the traffic between your users and your servers.

Communications Middleware

Although they are not widely implemented, there are communications middleware software products that allow you to bypass failed circuits on the network and route your traffic through other connections. An example of such a product is Pipes from Peerlogic in San Francisco. A Pipes network shares a directory service mechanism that identifies every possible routing alternative between machines running Pipes in the network. It also has intelligent error handling that gives Pipes the ability to dynamically and transparently reroute a network conversation to another path if the initial route fails, including paths using different communication protocols.

Figure 5-9 shows a conversation between two Pipes nodes on a network. The conversation started with a path through router A over TCP/IP. When a network segment fails between router A and node 2, Pipes automatically re-establishes the connection without application time-out errors by routing a completely different session through bridges B and C over the IPX protocol. Note that the new route was not created by an intelligent routing device, but by the Pipes software running in the two conversing nodes.

Middleware products such as Pipes are not intended to be deployed on every single machine on a network, but instead are typically used for developing robust distributed applications that need the redundancy and fault-tolerant services provided by the middleware development platform. Therefore, using middleware like Pipes requires some planning and development work, but the benefits of having transparent fault tolerance built into a distributed application are significant.

Predictive Failure Analysis

One of the more interesting recent developments in disk drive technology is predictive failure analysis. Introduced by IBM, it is now showing up in the products of other companies. The idea is simple: figure out what variables to measure that can indicate when a disk drive might be failing, monitor those variables, and report when they exceed some threshold that you set.

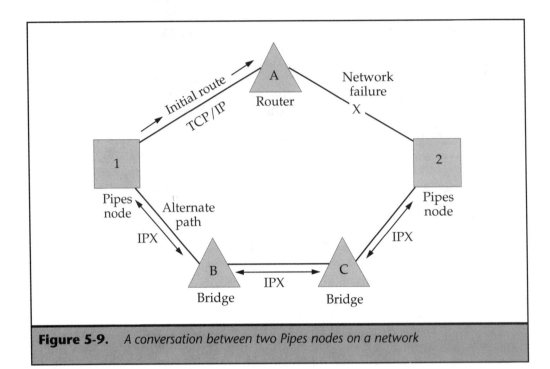

Figure 5-9. *A conversation between two Pipes nodes on a network*

It is a nice idea in theory, but is yet not understood in the market. The variables used to determine when a drive may be failing may not necessarily indicate with certainty when the drive is likely to fail. Receiving premature failure notices may become a real nuisance after a while. On the other hand, you could stop proactively replacing old drives and simply count on receiving notification when it is time to change a drive. In this case you may be unpleasantly surprised when you lose a disk that failed for some other reason than what is monitored by the predictive failure analysis.

One of the important benefits that should help build the reliability of distributed systems on LANs comes from using predictive failure analysis technology in a RAID cabinet. As discussed previously, the parity rebuild is something you would prefer to do when the RAID system is being exercised less. With notice of drives failing in advance, you could conceivably schedule your drive replacement and parity rebuild so you have less risk and experience less performance degradation during production hours. This, in turn, should provide a more predictable and stable environment for distributed computing.

CHAPTER SIX

Database Backup Considerations

A s discussed in Chapter 3, backup poses many challenges to LAN administrators. In this chapter we address the special circumstances of backing up databases. First, we'll cover the problems that make it a special backup topic. Then we'll examine some methods of dealing with them. Finally, we'll explore some of the issues involved in backing up client/server databases.

Characteristics of Databases

Databases are unlike most other applications found on networks. In the following sections we'll examine some characteristics of databases that make them challenging to back up.

Multiple Users

Although network servers are used for sharing resources, most of the files stored on them are intended for single-user access. Databases on LANs, however, are intended for multiuser access. This means that any database administration operations, including backups, that impact your users' productivity can affect many users.

High Availability

Compounding the problem of multiple users per database is the amount of time that database systems are required to be available for access and updates. Whereas office automation file servers can be relatively quiet during off-hours, database systems often need to be running much longer hours to accommodate batch job processing and access by users in other time zones.

The term "backup window" refers to the amount of time available to run backups between work shifts. It is commonly considered to be the amount of time that the LAN is "quiet," when no work is being done, and all the files are closed and thus can be backed up without interfering with users' work. Due to the high availability requirements databases have, however, their backup windows tend to be much shorter than for network file servers. Figure 6-1 graphically shows the backup window.

Frequent Updates

File servers typically do not have a high volume of disk writes during the day. After someone opens an office automation file, they may save their changes to it every 15 minutes or so. If there are 250 users working on that server, this means, on the average, a file is being saved every four seconds. Although this may seem like a lot, it is quite small compared to a database system that supports a workload of 50 transactions per second.

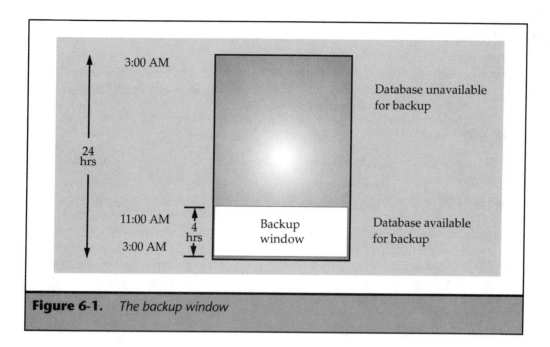

Figure 6-1. *The backup window*

Large File Sizes

Finally, database systems tend to have much larger files than standard office automation applications. The average size of files used for an office automation application such as word processing is in the range of 5 to 10Kb. Database files, on the other hand, are often several gigabytes in size.

To summarize, databases typically have more data to be backed up and less time available to get the job done. In addition, backups that extend beyond the backup window cause more problems with user access and performance due to the higher work levels that databases incur.

Risk Analysis

Before you can devise a plan to protect your databases, you must understand what you are protecting, its exposure to loss, the costs associated with losing it, and the costs associated with protecting it. It would not make sense to spend $50,000 a year protecting data that can be recovered for $10,000 and is likely to be lost only once every three years.

Cost Versus Risk

No endeavor can be said to be without cost.

Even though your databases may be used to run your company, you will still have to weigh the costs of various levels of backup protection. In examining these, you will have four critical questions to consider:

- **Can you afford it?**

Is the money in the budget? If you can't afford it, you'll have to scale back to something you can afford.

- **Will it make the situation better?**

There is no use in going from the frying pan to the fire. You may decide to equip your servers and tape drives with battery backups so that if the power fails at night, you will still be able to back up. But if your backup takes two hours and the battery is only good for 30 minutes, you have not really improved the situation. (There are other good reasons for using power conditioning; this is just an example.)

- **What other problems could it cause?**

If your approach excludes users during backups, what effect will that have on them? Will productivity decrease as a result?

- **Is it cost-effective?**

What is the cost of the worst case? If the system crashed as everyone was leaving to go home, losing a whole day's orders, what would it cost to re-create those orders? Careful analysis of the risks and costs will let you put your efforts where they will do the most good. Chapter 12 on disaster recovery planning examines this topic in more detail.

Pareto's Principle: The 80/20 Rule

Vilfredo Pareto was a late nineteenth-century economist and sociologist whose belief in an elite ruling class lead to the development of Italian fascism. He is also the person who discovered the so-called 80/20 rule, which claims that a majority of effects come from a small set of causes. Figure 6-2 illustrates this. When we prioritize our tasks, we consciously or unconsciously use the Pareto principle to help us make decisions about allocating our time and energies.

All or Nothing

When we think about database backup, however, we have to adjust our thinking from our accustomed 80/20 way of doing things. Database backup is usually an all or

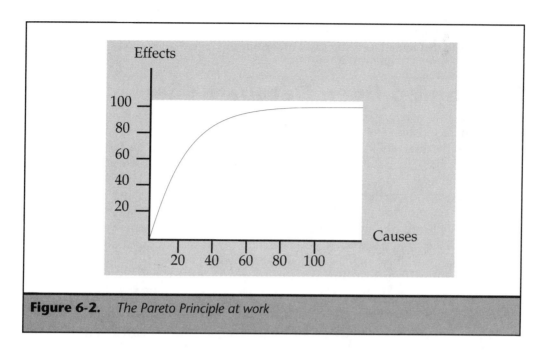

Figure 6-2. *The Pareto Principle at work*

nothing proposition—if you don't back up the entire database, you won't be able to use it after a recovery. For many database systems, any change to the database necessitates a complete backup of the entire database. Figure 6-3 illustrates this.

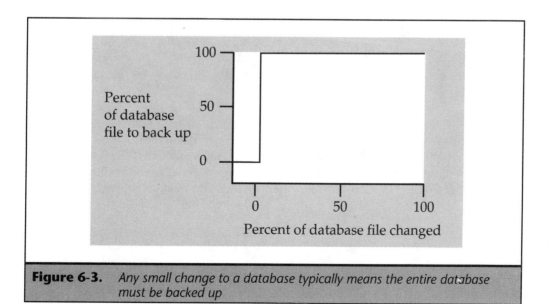

Figure 6-3. *Any small change to a database typically means the entire database must be backed up*

Next, we'll examine the reasons for this and see how backing up open database files can result in a loss of data integrity to the backup copy.

Backing Up Open Database Files

The fundamental problem of database backup is backing up open files. Among the primary characteristics of online databases, discussed earlier, are the frequency of updates and the accessibility for users to request them as they are needed. In order to provide this capability, database systems keep their database file(s) open while the database is running.

Keeping this view of databases in mind, we'll consider how backups are normally processed in order to find potential problems. Backup is a process that takes time, and the larger the file is the longer backup takes. For example, let's assume that at some time, say t=0, the backup starts. At a later time, say t=10, the backup should end. Halfway in between these points is a time, t=5, when the backup is halfway completed. This process is illustrated here:

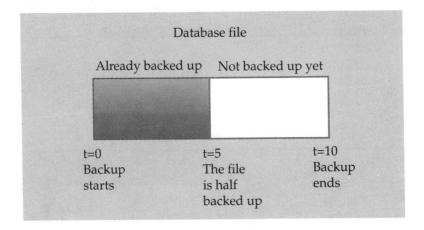

Now consider the situation where a database update occurs while the backup is processing. Let's say the database file is in the middle of backup at time t=5, roughly halfway through the file. At this time a database update is made that changes information that has already been backed up. The following illustration shows a database update being made to the file at point A, after the backup process has already copied this information.

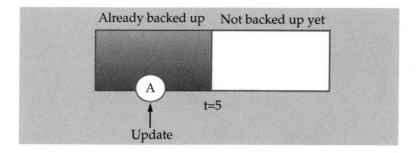

This is not necessarily a problem. The update occurred to an area of the file that was already copied, but had no effect on any other part of the file. To simplify things, we'll further assume that no other updates occurred during backup processing. The backed up file is still intact, the way it was before backup started. Assuming backup finished correctly, should the system need to be restored, the file could still be restored to its original state at time t=0. To bring the database up to its current state after it is restored requires reentering any updates that occurred after backup started.

Now we'll consider the opposite problem. Let's say the database file is in the middle of backup again at time t=5. This time, instead of the update occurring in an area of the file that has already been backed up, the update occurs to a part of the file that has not been backed up yet. The following illustration shows a database update being made to the file at point B, before the backup process has copied this information.

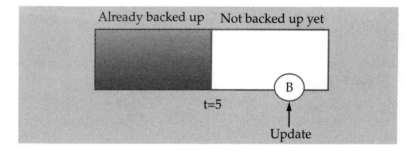

This is not necessarily a problem either. The update occurred to an area of the file that was not already copied and has no effect on any other part of the file. Again, we'll assume that no other updates occur and that the backup finished correctly. If the database system needed to be restored, the file could be restored to a complete state that includes the update to point B. To bring the file up to date now requires reentering all updates that occurred after backup finished.

Unfortunately, databases are complex systems that are made of many small interrelated parts. Database updates, or *transactions*, usually include updates to several parts of the database in rapid sequence. This is discussed later in this chapter in the section titled "Transaction Processing." Once again, assume that backup for the file is in progress at time t=5. We'll now consider the scenario shown here, where a single database transaction updates the file at both points A and B.

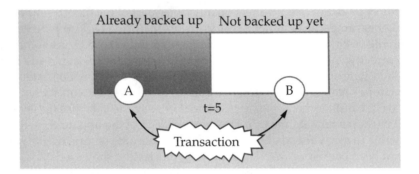

Now we are in real trouble because the backup copy of the file reflects an unchanged component from the update at point A and a changed component from the update at point B. The backup copy of the database file has now lost its integrity. When this happens, the data that results may be nonsensible and could even result in the database system crashing.

Cold Backups

Considering the challenges outlined in the preceding sections, it makes sense to try to back up your databases when there is no possibility of updates being written to them. The best way to prevent updates from occurring is to shut down the database prior to backing it up. This is called running a *cold backup* (also called an *offline backup*).

One of the best ways to automate cold backups for unattended operations in the middle of the night is to build a batch file that shuts down the database system at an appointed time, backs up the database, and then starts the database again. Avanti Technologies in Austin, Texas develops and sells an NLM batch file and scheduling system for Novell NetWare servers that many organizations use for this purpose. The algorithm for using this type of tool is fairly simple and is shown here. The step to clear workstation connections is included to ensure that no users are holding any files open in the database with records locked from the backup system.

```
At time = starttime, begin
clear workstation connections
shutdown database
begin backup operations
when backup ends, restart database
end
```

This backup of the database could be done by your normal backup system or by a dedicated backup system, depending on several variables—such as size, backup window, and importance of the database to your organization.

Common Applications of Databases on LANs

Before continuing with our discussion of database backup problems and solutions, it is appropriate to discuss some of the more common types of databases and database applications running on LANs today.

Database systems are currently implemented on the majority of LANs to support a wide variety of business applications. These database systems range in size from very small to over 100GB in size. For the purposes of this chapter, we'll focus our attention on large database systems, the unique problems they pose, and the difficulty in solving them.

Lotus Notes

One of the most popular and widespread database systems in use today is Lotus Notes. Notes database files contain many small documents that are linked together in a single large system. Notes users view and update these documents, which they share among groups of workers online. While the users see many documents, the file system only sees one large file to manage. This removes the burden on the file system of having to synchronize many small files. Conversely, a small change to just one of the documents in the Notes database will appear to have changed an entire large file in the file system.

This creates a challenging environment for backup. Because it's so easy for users to make minor changes to documents in the Notes database, the Notes files are almost always being updated everyday. To adequately protect this data with backup, the entire Notes file has to be backed up. When these files get to be over 1GB in size, this can take a great deal of time; and when they get quite large, such as 10GB, they may not be able to be backed up at all by many backup systems.

This is a real problem for many organizations because they use Lotus Notes as an important part of their corporate communications infrastructure. Notes provides a flexible development environment that many have used to develop LAN-based applications to run their businesses. If they lost their Lotus Notes data, they might not be able to perform many of their basic business functions.

Fortunately, Notes provides its own built-in facility for backup and recovery. Its ability to replicate Notes databases from server to server provides excellent protection from server failures and disasters. Figure 6-4 shows a Notes database on system A that has replicated a database to system B. Later, after system A fails, the database can be replicated back from B to A.

The problem with this approach is the amount of time that replication can take, especially if the databases are large and the bandwidth available is small. For this reason, complete local backup of the Notes database is prudent. Notes was initially introduced to run on OS/2, therefore the majority of Notes installations

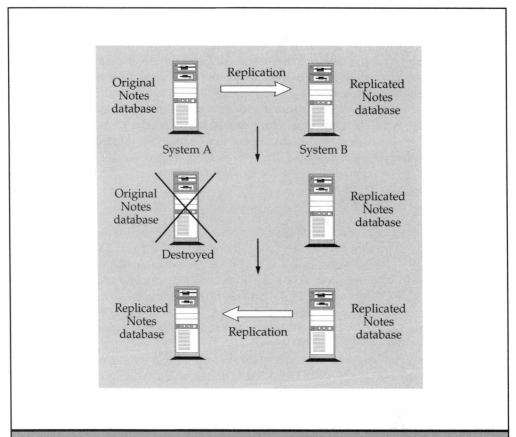

Figure 6-4. *Replication can be used as a means to back up and recover a Notes database*

run on OS/2. It follows that to correctly back up Notes locally, you need to have a backup product that correctly backs up OS/2. Considering the questionable future of OS/2 as an operating system, there are not many OS/2 native backup systems available on the market.

Electronic Mail

Electronic mail packages like cc:Mail, DaVinci eMail, and Microsoft Mail use database technology to store messages. It's easy to understand why databases are used when you consider that a single message sent to everybody in the company only has to be stored once. Recipients of the message do not receive separate copies; they are simply "joined" to the message with database pointers that direct their mailboxes to the message record in the database. This is much more efficient than actually making a copy for everybody in the company and storing the exact same message hundreds of times.

As you are probably aware, users tend to squirrel away e-mail messages in system folders, saving them for later if they need to explain a decision or remember a phone number. This results in electronic mail database files growing very large in size, sometimes several gigabytes. As is true with Lotus Notes, these databases are updated every day, which means they need to be backed up in their entirety to adequately protect the e-mail data in the organization.

While e-mail typically does not have the same capability for integration with business functions as Lotus Notes does, it is still a very important resource in many organizations. Losing the e-mail system can severely hinder productivity in an organization that depends on it.

Accounting Systems

Most LAN-based accounting packages, such as Great Plains Accounting or Platinum Software, have database technology incorporated in them. There are many database development tools in existence that are used as the basis for accounting systems. These systems usually don't have large files that need to be backed up; instead, they are typically made up of many small files that are all linked together in a large system, which together may be quite sizable.

The challenge in backing up such systems is ensuring that all the little files that belong together as a matched set are backed up together. The restore portion of the process is also complicated by the occurrence of so many small files. If one file out of 20 is not handled correctly, the database could be completely ruined.

Manufacturing Systems

Similar to accounting systems, there are many manufacturing systems on the market that implement database technology. One of the leading databases used for manufacturing systems on LANs is Advanced Revelation. These systems can be fairly sophisticated and provide extremely important support to manufacturing operations in such critical areas as cost accounting.

Manufacturing database systems are typically made up of many small files that are synchronized together as a single system. In some cases, however, not all the files that were updated by the system indicate to the file system that they have been updated. This has caused some fairly catastrophic problems for some organizations that were unable to restore their systems due to groups of files that were not correctly backed up together.

Customer Service, Marketing, and Sales Force Automation

Applications for finding, servicing, and keeping customers use database technology. These come in a wide variety of implementations, many of which are home-grown to fit the needs of a particular business application or industry. Examples are contact management systems for sales organizations, customer prospect databases for marketing organizations, and customer support systems for technical support departments.

There are many development toolkits available to help organizations build their own customer information systems. Among the more popular systems in use are Borland's Paradox and Microsoft's Access and FoxPro. Applications developed with these database development tools are generally not very large and can be shut down at night to allow them to be easily backed up.

These products are essentially PC databases that process data on workstations but store their files on the server. The server system is typically used for storage and multiuser file access. Occasionally, these systems will have a license file that counts the number of users and will not allow more than the licensed number of users to access its database files. It is somewhat common for these license files to be held open at all times, even if the database is not being used. It is also common for these files to not be accessible for backup in order to limit potential licensing workarounds.

If you find such a file in your database system, you should inquire with the developer's tech support department. The chances are good that if you ever suffered a system crash and needed to restore the database, this license file would be automatically re-created for you when the database is started again. There is no important data in such a license file, so it shouldn't bother you that it may become lost and need to be re-created. The files to worry about are those that have your data in them.

Client/Server Relational Databases

One of the major developments in LANs in the last five years has been the growth and acceptance of client/server computing. Although there are many reasons for this, the primary motivation has been cost: it's less expensive to acquire and operate client/server systems than mainframe database systems.

The leading companies in this area, Oracle, Sybase, and Informix, have all been quite successful selling their products as platform replacements for older mainframe applications. For the most part, these client/server databases have proven their capabilities and continue to improve themselves, especially in the area of performance.

Too Much Data, Too Little Time to Back Up

The primary problem with database backup is the amount of data that needs to be copied onto tape and the amount of time available to do the job. If all of the data can be transferred to tape within the backup window, there isn't a problem. If, however, all the data cannot be backed up within the backup window, then you have a potentially serious problem. In the next section we'll look at applying some of the techniques discussed in Chapter 3 to solving database backup problems.

Improving Database Backup Performance

There are a number of things you can do to increase the performance of your database backups. While most of them are related to buying faster hardware, there are a few software products that can help you as well.

Use Local Backup Devices

Backup performance is typically much faster when writing to devices that are locally attached than to devices that are attached to another system across the network. If you are going to take this approach, you should also make sure that the SCSI host adapter that connects is capable of high-speed extended data transfers. In addition to this, isolate your backup devices on their own SCSI hosts and do not exceed three devices per host if you use multiple devices.

If your network topology supports transfer rates in excess of 100 Mb per second, however, you may be running your backup devices at streaming speed already. In this case, moving the device to the database machine would not result in any backup performance improvements.

Use Faster Backup Devices

If your devices are locally attached to your database server, or if your network is fast enough to stream your devices but backups still take too long, the next performance bottleneck to deal with is the backup device itself. Chapter 3 discusses a variety of technologies that you could use to speed up your backups.

Back Up to Disk

Another common technique to accommodate high-speed backup of databases is to back up the database to disk, either on the same system or to another system on the LAN. After the database has been copied this way, tape backups can be made without encountering data integrity and access problems. Although it is expensive, this approach works the best if you can dedicate a complete volume or server as the backup disk. Although this approach can be somewhat labor intensive, it might be the only way to get the job done (see Figure 6-5).

Upgrade the Database System

In order to make backups work, you may need to upgrade the database system with more memory or more processing power.

Use Raw Disk Partition Backups

Reading data directly from the disk partition, as opposed to using file system API calls, can make backups run much faster. In the PC LAN environment, there are three products that allow you to do this: Columbia Data's Snapback, Stac's Replica, and Cheyenne's Jetstore. The weakness of such products for file system backup is their inability to perform anything but a full backup every operation. For large databases, however, this doesn't matter as much because large databases tend to take up a lot of the available space anyway.

St. Bernard Software's Open File Manager

An alternative approach to increasing performance is to instead provide systems software that removes the problems of open file backups discussed previously. This is precisely what St. Bernard Software has done with its Open File Manager product.

Open File Manager has the ability to recognize the backup process either by the NLM that is running or by specifying a unique user ID and password. The key to this

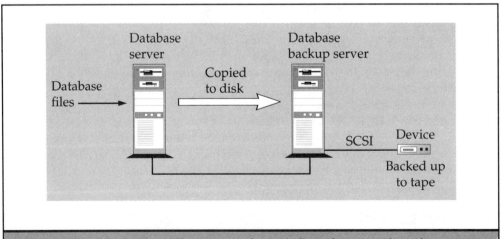

Figure 6-5. *The database files are copied to a dedicated system where they are subsequently backed up to tape*

product is its ability to capture disk block writes immediately before they occur, and to write the old data to a disk cache before allowing the update to overwrite the old data. Then, when the backup process reaches a disk block where this has occurred, the disk block information is read from the cache instead of the disk. This way, you can back up an open file with integrity to its state as of time t=0.

It also has the ability to link several small database files together and capture their updates to cache in a similar fashion, ensuring that all of them can be backed up as a single set of database files with complete integrity.

Appendix A contains edited excerpts from St. Bernard Software's white paper on Open File Manager. It is included to help provide deeper insight into the issues of open file backups.

System and Network Integrity

In addition to the performance techniques discussed in the preceding section, you will want to ensure that your systems and network are reliable enough to preserve the integrity of your databases.

The hardware and cabling that comprise your network are considered the "physical plant." The following sections will discuss some considerations for protecting that plant from failure. Figure 6-6 shows the different areas of concern.

Server Protection

Servers are the principal machines in most LANs. If you do nothing else, protect your servers.

Power Conditioning

Electricity is the heartbeat of your server. You should have quality power conditioning and battery backup capability. Buy enough battery capacity to keep your server running long enough to back up your databases.

Environmental Management

Heat is the major cause of failure in modern electronics. Consider an air-conditioned room for your servers to keep them cool, and keep the ventilation ports and ducts clean. Also, there is usually a mesh filter over the fan that will eventually get clogged enough to make the fan useless. Check and clean it regularly.

Security

As mentioned previously, you should consider getting a special room, with proper power and cooling, for your servers. You should also lock this room to prevent possible accidents—knocking over a server, accidentally resetting it, or turning it off. Chapters 8 and 9 cover this in more detail.

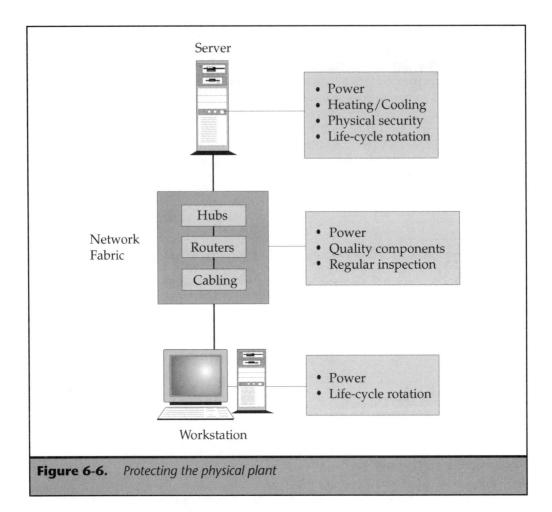

Figure 6-6. *Protecting the physical plant*

Hardware Expected Life/Rotation

All hardware will eventually fail. Therefore, you should consider a replacement scheme that keeps the reliable hardware in your servers. You should probably plan on one-and-a-half to two years as a respectable time for a database server.

Before you install that new server, you should do several days' worth of stress testing. Work the drives, memory, and CPU. The most common failures in computer equipment are not from old age but from youth. This tendency goes by the unattractive name of "infant mortality." What it boils down to is that if the equipment can survive its first few days (infancy), it will probably give a long life of service.

NetWare System Fault Tolerance

Introduced in Chapter 5, Novell's System Fault Tolerance III uses a complete secondary server for the purposes of providing real-time fail-over capabilities to protect against server failures. A high-speed line in the range of 100 Mb per second connects the primary server to the secondary. When the secondary server detects a failure in the primary server, it automatically begins operating on behalf of the primary.

Replication

Database replication through shadowing, or any of the other means described in Chapter 5, provides some level of fault tolerance. The system receiving replicated data has the ability to come online as the primary after the primary fails. This type of solution can be used to minimize loss on your network databases following a system failure but is incapable of preserving the integrity of a single transaction should the primary fail in the middle of a transaction.

Client Protection

Next are the clients or workstations. Clients are every bit as important to your databases as servers are; they are, after all, where the data comes from.

Power Conditioning

Power conditioning your workstations can help preserve data integrity. If a power failure occurs during a transaction between workstation and server, it will not help if the server is protected but the workstation is not.

You can purchase inexpensive power conditioning units for around $100. Battery support only needs to last long enough to save files and complete transactions. As a matter of policy, make sure your users know what to do when the power goes out.

Hardware Expected Life/Rotation

Previously, you saw the case made for regular replacement of server hardware. The same is true for workstations, although the failure of a particular workstation is unlikely to be catastrophic. The truth is that the workstation will probably be obsolete before it fails.

Network Fabric

Network fabric is the stuff between your workstations and servers: cabling, hubs, routers, punchdown blocks, and such. Make certain that the cabling is installed professionally using top-quality components. You probably want to monitor transmissions through your fabric with an SNMP network management tool.

Power Conditioning

Power conditioning that includes battery backup should be implemented in all fabric components. Without it, transactions between client and server will probably not be completed. Try to purchase UPS systems that will allow your fabric to run at least as long at your workstations following a power failure.

Redundant Paths

If possible, you should plan your networks to have secondary paths available for network connections. These could be dual backbones, as discussed in Chapter 5, or they could be implemented as switchable connections. The basic idea is to be able to respond to network fabric failures quickly and to re-establish connectivity for end users.

The problem with this, however, is the fact that transaction information would be lost when the initial failure occurs. This is why fault-tolerant middleware, also introduced in Chapter 5, that transparently keeps sessions alive while it reestablishes a new connection could be an excellent solution.

Relational Client/Server Backup Techniques

In addition to the techniques discussed previously for backing up databases on LANs, there are some additional techniques that are specific to the world of high-end relational client/server databases, such as Informix, Oracle, and Sybase. Before we proceed, there are some basic database concepts that are helpful to understand.

Transaction Processing

When discussing databases, the term *transaction* refers to a sequence of operations that results in a new interrelated set of data values. For instance, an airline reservation system completes a transaction when the passenger's name is entered along with the flight number and the fare information. If any of these items could not be updated completely for any reason, the transaction itself would not be complete and the database system would need to *roll back*, or undo, the updates that were made.

Continuing the discussion on transaction processing, let's look at a hypothetical scenario of a hardware distributor accounting system used by a chain of hardware stores and follow the steps of a transaction after an order for ten hammers is placed.

1. Verify customer number.
2. Verify sufficient inventory is on hand to fill the order.
3. Verify the customer is credit-worthy for the amount of the order.
4. Enter a purchase order record.
5. Subtract 10 units from the hammer inventory totals.
6. Add the order amount to the customer's invoice balance.
7. Generate a pick list for the warehouse.

All of these steps combined must be done in order for the transaction to be 100 percent complete. You can probably see the problems in trying to get a complete backup of this database when a single transaction has so many discrete steps to perform.

Transaction Logging

Because transactions can be so complex, requiring many machine instructions, system failures on database systems will almost certainly result in transactions that do not complete. If you are halfway through a transaction when the process is interrupted, how does the database know where you were in the process and what updates to remove to return the system to data integrity?

The answer is log files. As the database is working, it audits its internal processes and puts the contents of its instructions in the log file. Notice that the log does not have to store any real data—just the operation details. If the log ever has to be used to roll back a transaction, the data values stored in the database records are retrieved. Then the system determines the original data values and restores them to the appropriate record in the database.

Preserving Integrity of Relational Client/Server Databases

Restoring large client/server databases can be an extremely complex task composed of many steps to synchronize all components of the database. Usually, the DBA (database administrator) for the system will have the primary responsibility for reassembling the database components and making the system functional again. Because the DBA has this responsibility, he or she also has a vested interest in making sure backups are operating correctly and determining how they should be done. In some cases, the LAN administrator may be responsible for monitoring the completion of backups on these databases, but would not be responsible for restoring and re-creating the data.

Three Types of Database Backup: Cold, Hot, and Logical

There are basically three ways to back up databases; cold backup, hot backup, and logical backup. Each is explained briefly in the following sections.

Cold Backup

Cold backup was discussed previously in this chapter. The idea of cold backup is to shut down the database and back it up while no end users are working on it. This is the best approach where data integrity is concerned, but does not help much if the database is too big to fit in the backup window.

Hot Backup

Hot backups are done when the database is running and updates are being written to it. Hot backups depend heavily on the ability of log files to "stack up" transaction instructions without actually writing any data values into database records. While these transactions are stacking up, the database tables are not being updated, and therefore can be backed up with integrity.

There are some obvious shortcomings to this approach. Foremost, if the system crashes in the middle of backup, all the transactions stacking up in the log file would be lost. This would result in a loss of data. Second, it requires the DBA to carefully monitor system resources, so the log file does not run out of room and have to stop accepting transactions. Finally, the log file itself needs to be backed up at some point to be able to reconstruct data. Having additional files to worry about and synchronize together adds to the complexity.

But the alternative to this approach may be to not back up the database at all. Quite simply, there may be no other way to get the job done due to database size and system availability requirements. In some cases, incremental backups of databases may work, if the log files can determine which transactions updated which records since the beginning of the previous backup operation.

The client/server database companies have approached backup traditionally as a problem for the DBA, and not the LAN administrator. This is not such a bad idea considering the complexity of the problem. For instance, Rama Velpuri's book, *Oracle Backup and Recovery Handbook* (Osborne/McGraw-Hill, 1995), contains 384 pages of detailed analysis, tips, and techniques for performing backups and recoveries on Oracle databases. Obviously, some level of expertise is required to do the job.

Therefore, there were not many integration efforts designed to allow ordinary LAN backup systems to access these database systems during backup. However, this scenario has changed in the last few years. All the major database developers now have developer assistance programs and specialized APIs for backup vendors to integrate LAN backup with database backup. A great deal of this work has been to provide hot backup capability to LAN backup systems. It remains to be seen how well such efforts work.

Logical Backups

Logical backups use software techniques to extract data from the database and write the results in an export file. This export file is not a database table, but is an image of all the data that was in the table. You cannot actually run any database operations on this export file. For the major client/server databases, structured query language (SQL) is used to create the export file. This process is somewhat slow and not practical for performaing full backups of large databases. It is very good, however, for incremental backups where you only want to back up the records that have changed since the previous backup.

In order to restore data from an export file, the inverse SQL statements must be generated. This process is also fairly time-consuming, but it works reasonably well.

Rebuilding Database Servers

If you lose a database server and need to replace the system, there will be many options to think about. You will want to upgrade the capacity and performance of the system and perhaps consider some other features (reliability, perhaps?).

Certainly one of things to watch out for is not providing enough room for the database to run. The capacity shortfall could appear as system RAM, disk storage, or some other system resource. Remember, if you try to squeeze your database into a system that isn't big enough, you can expect a great deal of difficulty.

For that reason, you may want to keep records of your server configurations. While many LAN administrators know precisely how much RAM and disk storage is in each of their database servers, there are probably many more who think they have a pretty good idea, but do not know for certain. If you don't know, how do you know if you have enough?

Chapter 12 has more information about disaster recovery planning that you might find useful in helping you prepare for the unexpected.

A Final Word

It bears repeating that there is no one solution, no holy grail, for backups. Also remember that there are no perfect solutions, only trade-offs. In order to make a proper choice in backup options, you need to know your systems and know the costs involved with each proposed option.

Test and Practice

You do not want to be in the position of testing your parachute for the first time *after* you jump out of the plane. Test your plan fully and then practice it occasionally to see if it still works for you.

When the system is not in use, take the server offline and replace it with a backup server. Then do a complete restore and see if you can bring your backup server up properly. It is through these tests and practices that you will find the bugs and correct them.

A system crash is the wrong *time to find out if your procedures work.* There is supposed to be a saying among submarine commanders: "I know I'm paranoid, but am I paranoid enough?" Don't get lulled—test and practice regularly.

Chapter 12 on disastery recovery planning should help you understand how to prepare yourself for a disaster. Being familiar with your databases is the other part of a successful plan.

CHAPTER SEVEN

Database Security

This chapter addresses securing your live data. Data in databases poses a special trade-off of necessary availability and the threats of manipulation, corruption, and theft. Walking this tightrope is illustrated in Figure 7-1. The definition of "data" developed in Chapter 6 will be used here, too.

We begin with an examination of the threat you face. Next we cover some methods and tools for dealing with these threats. Finally, we discuss planning for security.

NOTE: Examining the threat and responses is the meat and potatoes of security. The security itself, however, comes from implementing measures on an ongoing basis. Too often security, even onerous security, fails because of minor slips. We will address this again later in this chapter. At the end of this chapter we offer an example of comprehensive security that failed dramatically because of a small enforcement failure. For now, remember that security only works if you use it.

The Threats

"There is no little enemy."—Benjamin Franklin, *Poor Richard's Almanac*, 1733

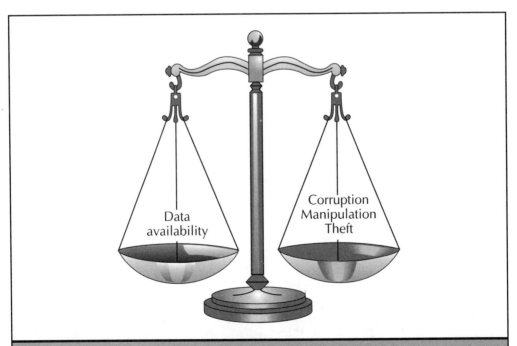

Figure 7-1.   *Effective data protection requires a balance between data availability and the potential manipulation, corruption, and theft that could occur*

As previously discussed, data is central to business today. Ignoring the threats to it, or judging them trivial, is like playing Russian roulette: for a while you may be lucky, but sooner or later your luck will run out.

The first thing to recognize is that there are threats. Unfortunately, most of the threats are invisible until it is too late. It is akin to wearing seat-belts: you perform the same, tedious, tasks—buckling and unbuckling your belts as you get in and out of your car—over and over again, rarely glimpsing the danger. Then, suddenly, when it is too late to do anything and there is no time to react, the crunch will come and those habits, that tedium, will pay off.

So, you need to recognize that you are in danger, even if it is not obvious. In the case of seat belts, you can come to that realization through other people's tragedies, the sight of a crumpled car or an ambulance at the head of the traffic jam. The wail of a fire truck's siren can remind you of the need for smoke detectors. The threats to your data are much more ethereal; you rarely see a smoldering heap of data destroyed by a virus. You must believe it though, because, as with seat belts and smoke detectors, the time to protect yourself is before the threat turns real.

Manipulation—Falsification

Manipulation is the changing of data in such a way as to make it untrue. Examples might be deleting orders, invoices, or receipts. You might also see changes in data such as inventory levels, prices, or customer credit limits. Whatever form it takes, this is an insidious problem because you don't often realize you have a problem until it has spread.

For the most part, you will contain this problem by limiting access to data on an ad hoc basis. For example, if your tables are stored on a Microsoft SQL Server, you would want to limit access to the ISQL/w program that lets users bypass your programs to get at the data.

Personal Gain

If prices are lowered or customer credit limits raised, people can sell more, affecting their commissions. If customer addresses can be changed, employees can have items sent to their houses and billed to your customers.

Covering Up Evidence

If inventory quantities can be changed, then items can be stolen and little notice taken of it until much later, most often too late to trace it back. If invoices can be deleted, then customers or friends can be shipped the product without having to pay for it.

Pranks

Pranksters can provide the biggest, and seemingly most innocent, headache of all. Customer names can be changed: "Smith, Jones, and Partners" might be changed to "Shark, Barracuda, and Bottom Feeders" as a lark with disastrous consequences. April

1st is a particularly vulnerable day. Let your users know that your computer system is no place for practical jokes.

Ignorance

Letting people in where they don't belong can lead to unintentionally devastating changes. When users find themselves in odd situations, they may be changing data in an attempt to get back out. Often they feel they shouldn't have been there, so they will be quiet about their foray out of a misplaced sense of guilt. Your security at both the program and raw data level should prevent inadvertent changes. The perfect example is users who think they are deleting files on their own workstation but have been inadvertently been placed in a network directory, deleting files there instead. This happens, but it is preventable.

Corruption

The actual loss of data is another threat you face. Tables and whole databases can be deleted, moved, or scrambled so their contents become unavailable. Here are a few sources of corruption.

Sabotage

Presenting itself in both specific and nonspecific forms, sabotage is both easy and difficult to handle. It is easy because simple policies will prevent all but the most determined saboteurs. It is hard because you must consider that someone you know and like, or perhaps don't know, might want to cause your data harm.

Pranks

Pranksters also present corruption problems. All programs access data in some form, and changing even the smallest detail can render all the data unreadable. For example, the popular Xbase format .DBF files have a header at the beginning of the file that contains formatting information. Changing even one byte in this header can make the file unreadable and very difficult to recover.

Viruses

Computer viruses are much in the news, and the threat is often overblown; witness the Michelangelo virus scare of a few years ago. The consequences of infection are so immense, however, that it is wise to protect yourself. This is fairly easy to do; we detail the procedure later, but briefly, you must limit access to outside data sources, disks, or online services, and force all data brought in through them past a good virus checker.

Theft

Difficult to detect, even when it has hurt your business, theft of data is a serious problem. Theft is accomplished with access to your sensitive data, either by copying the data to a removable source such as a floppy disk or by taking printed reports from your company.

Your Data May Be Worth More Than You Think

Some companies believe it would be more painful than devastating to lose data. Nothing could be further from the truth. Your business data—customer names, contacts, how much you sell to them and at what price—is a concentration of information that a competitor could use to run you out of business. Your data has all this information, and most often it can be distilled to fit on a few floppies or in a printed report that can be easily removed from your company in a briefcase.

Disgruntled and Departing Employees

Distilling the crucial data down to a couple of floppies or a handful of printed pages is not difficult and need not even be sophisticated. Who has access to your customer lists and sales reports? Even if you are careful with these, you must have seen shelf after shelf of books on computer databases at the local bookstore. These will guide a sufficiently intelligent person to the necessary commands to gather the data in just a short time—if you don't protect yourself.

Industrial Espionage

If your data is valuable and someone else could benefit from having it, then industrial espionage could happen to you. Protecting your data from this threat is not unlike the internal, employee problem, although it has a few twists.

Some Answers

After the preceding deluge of despair, you may be feeling down. The good news is that good security is not difficult to achieve. Here you'll see some different tools to address security concerns. It bears repeating, and we will repeat it, that security is only as good as your use of it. The most carefully crafted plan will fail miserably if people are not responsible for their roles and don't follow the plan. Make your plan workable and then ensure that it is followed.

The ABCs—Security Levels

The National Computer Security Center (NCSC), a branch of the United States National Security Agency (NSA), sets security levels for government computer purchases. These have become a de facto way of rating system security in commercial use, too. The ratings range from A ("I could tell you but then I'd have to kill you") to D ("open house"). A-level systems are custom built, and if you need one of these, you will have to obtain a list of authorized vendors and products. B and C are the most common level ratings. Each rating then has a number attached to it that specifies its user sensitivity: 2 is the normally sought level, for example, C2.

C2 requires a login procedure, specific resource control by the user, and audit tracking. B2 requires access control and does not allow users to set security levels on their own files. These things do not guarantee security and are primarily for government contract conformance.

What they do require that is a useful concept in this discussion is a written security plan and user manual. Documenting and distributing your plan is a good idea even if you do not need these NCSC certifications.

Using OS and NOS Security

Modern operating systems and network operating systems such as Novell's Netware, IBM's LAN Server, Microsoft's Windows NT, and all flavors of Unix provide some security in the form of user management, password checking, and auditing. It seems obvious, but this is the first place to start. Require all users to have their own account; force them to use a password.

Nobody Gets in Without a Password

Make certain that there are no accounts without passwords; look specifically for ones like **guest**. Remove any that are not specific to a particular user.

Take Special Care with *Supervisor* or *Admin*

These are special accounts that have full access to the network. They are like dynamite and should be carefully watched. One method of defusing this danger is to assign your administrative personnel as supervisor or admin equivalents, and then deactivate the supervisor/admin login. Most, if not all, systems will not allow you to delete this login, so what you can do is assign a random password to the account.

Since you need to type the password in twice to verify it, you can't simply assign a random string like "ripofu-9qwyr9." So what we recommend is that you take a magazine or book (this one will do) and pick a line at random and use it as the password, the whole line or as much as your system will allow.

> **CAUTION:** *Before you do this, make sure that your normal login has supervisor equivalence. You can best do this by logging in using your own login to change the supervisor password. If you can change the supervisor password, you have supervisor equivalence.*

Remember that the idea is to make the password unguessable, so favorite passages like "to be or not to be" or "the Lord is my shepherd" are not suitable. You do not need to remember the password, since the idea is that no one will be using the supervisor account.

In the rare event that you need to use the supervisor or admin login (some software requires that you use the actual account, not an equivalent one), you can change it to something usable and, when you have finished, use the same randomizing procedure to change it back.

Password Policies

Now that everyone has a password, what should it be? You should have a policy that specifies minimum length (your operating system should be able to enforce this) and a restriction on obvious passwords. What are obvious passwords? "Password" is one. Others include the user's name or nickname, family names such as spouse or children, and common key combinations like "asdf" or "aaaa." Chapter 9 goes into this topic in more detail.

Control Access

Use the operating system's access privileges to control security. Only allow users into files, directories, or other resources that they need to have access to. Set system flags for proper use. For example, Netware has delete inhibit (DI) and copy inhibit (CI) flags that can offer you a measure of protection for very little effort.

Database Server Security

Most database servers offer some security of their own. These range from very good to passable. You will want to review your options and make the best of them. One thing that database security can provide is a limited path to data. Databases are stored on your server as files, and if your server does not have database security, you may need to allow users access to those files. Access to this raw data is a weak security point. But servers that do have built-in security often set the server itself as the only one allowed to access the files. Manipulation of the data can then be done only through your secured server.

Lock Up Your Servers

In the previous discussion of supervisor passwords, we did not allow for what would happen if the supervisor account was lost; the only supervisor is unavailable, and you cannot access your server anymore. Most, if not all, operating systems have workarounds, which they do not make public, but one common point is physical access to the server. Since these workarounds are known, it is very important that you restrict access to the server. Lock it in a closet that only managers have access to.

By removing it from the common area, you also restrict another security problem: stealing the server. Anyone who can walk away with your data can also pursue cracking it in leisurely fashion.

Limit Access to Removable Media

Virtually all computer workstations have a floppy drive, and many network backup schemes rely on tape drives attached to workstations. These are vulnerable to data theft and corruption, through viruses.

Tape Drives

Many backup products rely on a tape drive attached to a workstation. These are often an excellent choice from a backup standpoint but present a vulnerability from a security vantage. Backup media of any sort should be stored in a fireproof safe, but these safes are not theft-proof; in fact, small ones come with a handy carrying handle. You should store your media in a secure location.

Floppy Drives

You should consider disabling the floppy drive on all but a few machines. Most modern workstations can be run without a floppy drive once the proper software has been installed. This protects you, to some extent, from theft of information. It also helps prevent unauthorized software installation.

VIRUS PROTECTION, TOO   You can screen anything that your users want to install for viruses. Use a virus checker on every disk that a user wishes to install, even if it is just a memo the user typed at home.

Limit Access to Computers

Security usually takes the form of logging in and then accessing your data through programs. The vulnerability is that users will often leave their computers without logging out. Consider a policy requiring users to log out when they are not using their computer or are going to leave it unattended for awhile.

Personnel

It is very important for security reasons to be aware of employment terminations, especially involuntary ones. As soon as employees are finished with their work, their user accounts should be deleted.

Make a Plan

In security, failing to plan is planning to fail; it won't happen by accident. Some people will be uncomfortable protecting their systems, but it must be done. Here are some rules for making a good security plan.

A Good Plan Is Workable

A plan that is difficult to do routinely will end up not being done routinely. An unworkable plan is worse than no plan; as with the emperor's new clothes, you may walk about serenely unaware until you are suddenly in the middle of an embarrassing situation. Try to make your plan work with the way people *really* work, not how they *should* work.

A Good Plan Is Routinely Reexamined

Don't be lulled into thinking that once you have a plan, you're done. You must routinely reexamine policies, threats, and workability. At least twice a year you should revisit the issue with company management.

The Danger of a Small Company Growing Up

Reexamining your policies is much more important if you are a growing company. Circumstances change rapidly as you go from a small family business to a larger enterprise. You change from a situation where security is from knowing and trusting users to not even knowing all the employees. If you are still operating on trust alone, you are leaving yourself open to a very unpleasant surprise.

By occasionally revisiting your plans, you can ask, "How have conditions changed since we last did this?" Have you added a lot of new employees, perhaps merged with another company? Have you added new networks, WAN links, or other capabilities that need security consideration?

A Good Plan Is Tested

As with the emperor, it is better to be embarrassed *en famile*. Get your best people to try to break the system. Offer rewards. Get users to give you feedback, and use it to polish your policies and practices.

A Good Plan Is Not Well Known

All plans have weaknesses; keep yours tight. Previously, we made the case for written policies; this is not a contradiction. What you need to do is publish your policies but keep the actual enforcement procedures private. For example, you might have a policy that prohibits the storing of company data on local workstation hard disks. This should be published. But if it were known that you enforced this by checking users' machines only every Thursday evening, this policy could be compromised easily.

A Final Word on Security

For the third, and last time for now, we want to emphasize the importance of actually enforcing policies. We close this chapter with a story of the potential consequences of not enforcing the rules.

Each of us has experienced the hassle of taking an airline flight: metal scanners, X rays, lines at the security checkpoints. Airport and airline employees are issued security passes, which they show at the security checkpoints. They can then pass without further inspection. At a California airport sometime in the '70s, an employee of a commuter airline was fired with just cause and his security pass was revoked. The next day he bought a ticket on this airline. Since the security detail recognized him, he was allowed to pass unchecked even though he no longer had a security pass. He boarded the airplane, and while it was in flight he produced a pistol and killed the pilot. The plane crashed, killing all aboard.

CHAPTER EIGHT

Computer Security

Throughout time, the need to secure and protect one's land, resources, and valuables from unwanted thieves, intruders, and other "undesirables" has remained a very real one. Whether it be walls, castles, gates, fences, or metal safes, keeping what's yours safe and secure has remained a continuing challenge. When it comes to computer systems, equipment, and data, this need for security is just as great, or perhaps even greater. This is due to the fact that we depend heavily on information, where a loss of computer services, or of a firm's data and records, could severely cripple, or even ruin, a business.

Because of the growth of the computer and information systems industry, and greater focus on networking and global communications, computer security is gaining in importance. Whether they are caused by a group of crafty students, a wily "hacker," or a disgruntled employee, breaches of computer security can be very costly and serious. A recent Ernst and Young survey showed the increasing importance of securing computers, networks, and data. For example, roughly half of the corporate respondents reported that they had lost important information over the past two years. Furthermore, a number of them had suffered losses exceeding $1 million. About 20 percent of the companies surveyed had an incidence of a network security breach, and at least 70 percent were hit by a virus. The overall feeling is that security risks are on the increase and that this is getting the attention of management.

The focus of this chapter is to examine many of the problems and considerations involved in computer security, and to provide insight into potential solutions.

What Is Computer Security?

The main objective of computer security is to protect computing resources from damage, alteration, theft, and loss. This includes computer equipment, storage media, software, computer printouts, and data.

Computer security encompasses a wide range of strategies and solutions, such as:

- **Access control**   Control of entry to a system

- **Discretionary access control**   Control of access to resources such as files and programs once admitted into a system

- **Viruses and computer "wildlife"**   Different kinds of viruses and other destructive programs, and how to prevent and control their effects

- **Encryption**   Encoding and decoding of information, so that only authorized persons will be able to access it

- **System planning and administration**   Planning, organization, and management of computing-related facilities, policies, and procedures to ensure the security of resources

- **Physical security**   Securing computer facilities and equipment

- **Biometrics** Use of unique characteristics to identify a user
- **Network and communications security** Communications security problems that arise through networks and telecommunications systems

This list is by no means exhaustive, but these are the major topics that should be included in any discussion of computer security.

Computer security is an important element of any computer system and facility, but it is often dismissed as something that can be taken care of later. A single security breach can, however, create serious damage or even ruin a business. The costs of recovery and lost productivity, not to mention strategic damage, can be substantial. In short, the role of computer security is an important one and should not be ignored, especially with the increased exposure due to network and telecommunications integration.

A Historical Perspective

The history of computer security can be traced back as far as recorded information. In fact, the need to secure information originated as early as 2000 B.C. The Egyptians were the first to use special hieroglyphics to code information, and as time passed, the civilizations of Babylon, Mesopotamia, and Greece all came up with ways to protect their written information. The coding of information, which is the basis of encryption, was used by Julius Caesar and throughout history during periods of war, including the Revolutionary and Civil Wars and the two world wars. One of the best-known coding machines was the German Enigma machine, which was used to create coded messages for the Germans during World War II. Eventually, through the efforts of Alan Turing and the Ultra project and others, the ability to decrypt messages generated by the Germans marked an important success for the Allies.

In the last ten years, the importance of computer security has been raised by a few well-publicized stories. There was the Internet worm in 1988, which spread to tens of thousands of computers, a result of the handiwork of Robert Morris. There was a cracker from Germany who broke into nearly 30 systems out of a self-professed goal of nearly 500, as profiled in the book *The Cuckoo's Egg* (Doubleday, 1989). Most recently, in February 1995, the arrest of the highly sought-after computer hacker Kevin Mitnick revealed criminal activities that included years of stealing codes, information, and other secret data. A more extensive list of security violations can be found in Peter G. Neumann's book, *Computer-Related Risks* (Addison-Wesley, 1995).

Clearly, the wide use of networked computing systems has sparked an awareness of the importance of computer security.

Access Control

One of the most important lines of defense against unwanted intruders is access control. Basically, the role of access control is to identify the person desiring access to a system and its data, and to verify that person's identity. This involves asking two basic questions:

- Who are you?
- Are you who you say you are?

The common way to control access to a system is to restrict entry to anyone without a valid username and password. For instance, if my username is HSU, that identifies me to the system. I then must enter a password that is associated with my account on the system. If the username and password are correct, then I am allowed access to the system. If it does not match, then I am denied entry. Some systems ask only for a password, while others ask for both a username (or login code) and a password.

More generally, access control can be described as a means of controlling access to a computer system or network. Without access control, anyone who wanted to could obtain entry to your computer system and do whatever he or she wanted to. Access control does not generally exist for most personal computers, but it is common on larger systems and networks.

There are three main ways of implementing access control. The first is to require the prospective user to produce some confidential information, such as the username and password previously mentioned. Another, more complicated method, is to require some kind of physical identification device such as an access card, key, or token. Finally, there are biometric systems, which uniquely identify someone based on a specific physical trait.

Since the latter two methods are more complicated and expensive, the most commonly used access control method is the password. Passwords are an easily implemented and effective means of allowing only authorized users into a system.

Passwords

A password is a simple yet effective form of access control. Without a valid password, it can be difficult for an intruder to break into a computer system. A password is simply a string of characters that only the system (and its administrator) and the user should know.

As long as a password remains secret, the account should remain secure from entry by unauthorized persons. However, since it is only a text string, once it is discovered (or stolen), the password offers no security—just as if the account on the system has no protection at all. Therefore, the most important considerations are to select passwords that are as secure as possible and to protect them from unauthorized users.

The need to protect passwords is a concern to both a system administrator and system users. An administrator must establish a viable system of password and/or username requirements for each account, and users must create "safe" passwords and protect them.

The number of types of logins can vary greatly from system to system. It can range from highly secure systems that require several levels of passwords (e.g., one for logging into a system, one for an individual account, and another for specific secure files), to those that require just a password to access an entire system. Most systems have a login sequence somewhere between these two extremes.

For instance, on a Digital VAX system, the user must enter a valid username, followed by a password. A similar method is implemented on Unix systems. The username and password must both match the information stored in the system's account/password file in order for someone to log in. Typically, while the username is echoed back to the user, the password does not display on the screen, so no one can just steal a peek at your screen to discover your password. The username or login identifier is usually some combination of your name, initials, or your account number, to form a unique identifier of your system account. The password is generally first issued to the user, then he or she is asked to change it to something that can be remembered and is private.

An example of an actual system and its login access control procedure is illustrated here. Suppose a user is required to enter a valid login name and password in order to gain access to the system. In other words, the system will prompt for the following information:

```
System XYZ
login: hsu
password: xxxxxxxx
```

Both login and password must correspond to each other and match the information contained in a valid password file. The login is typically a string that identifies the user, running from one to eight characters in length. The password, which is secret and not echoed to the screen, is stored, together with the login, in the /etc/password file on the system. The password is normally encrypted to prevent someone from illegally accessing the file and finding out what the passwords are.

The role of your user identification is also important in terms of what you can do on a system. Built into your account "description" or "profile" is a list of what you can and cannot do while on the system, called *discretionary access control,* which is covered later in this chapter. A particular user identification can also be tracked or audited to monitor whether you are doing something illegal on the system.

Getting back to passwords, it was mentioned that selecting effective passwords is half the battle. There are things that both the system administrator and the individual user can do to ensure that the most effective password is selected. Through warnings, messages, and broadcasts, the administrator can tell users what kinds of passwords are most effective. In addition, depending on the system's security system, an administrator can force changes in users' passwords, set minimum password lengths, and even prevent the use of passwords that might prove too easy to guess or the ongoing use of the same password.

But what is an "effective" password? Is it long or short, easy or difficult to understand, and what tips and techniques might be used to create the best possible password? The most effective password is one that the user can easily remember but would be difficult for a "cracker" to guess or break. Consider the fact that to try every combination of eight random characters would result in close to three trillion possible variations, which would literally take years to go through even with the help of a computer. Using an obvious, easily guessed password makes this task much simpler. It is also very important, regardless of the password created, to keep it away from the wrong persons.

Too many computer users pick passwords that can be easily figured out by people who work with them or know them. Inappropriate uses of passwords include such things as your first or last name, the name of your spouse, your kid's name, or the name of your dog. Using your initials, the name of your favorite book or television program, your phone number, or social security number would be equally dangerous.

The best passwords should follow the following guidelines:

- *Select long passwords.* The longer the password, the harder it will be for someone to guess or try all possible combinations. Most systems accept a password in the range of five to nine characters, with many allowing much longer ones. A long password enhances security.

- *The best passwords contain a combination of alphabetic and numeric characters.*

- *Using English words is discouraged.* Effective passwords include those that form an acronym for a phrase you know but that is not commonly known. For example, "Monday is Take Out Garbage Day" could produce the password "mitogd," which you can remember but would mean little to others. Or you could try "sounding out" something but spell it differently, such as "8hapedey," which could be cryptic looking but easy to remember (your birthday is in month 8, or August). Again, combining letters and numbers can improve the security of your password.

- *Don't use the same password for every system you access.* If security is breached on one of your systems, none of them are safe.

- *Never use names*, especially your own name, or that of your family members, town you live in, names for pets, and so on.

- *Don't pick a password you can't remember* because it is probably too complex or confusing. This will tend to make you write it down as a memory aid, which invites a security breach.

Developers of systems and system administrators recognize that even with the most conscientious users and numerous reminders, many still pick poor passwords and subject their accounts to breaches of security. In addition, there are system-oriented controls that can be implemented in some systems that can minimize changes based on illegal break-ins. These features, known as login/password controls, are effective in enhancing the security of user passwords. They include the following:

- **Password changes**   A user can change his or her password at any time. The constant changing of passwords helps prevent continued illegal system access by someone with a stolen password.

- **Required password changes**   A user is required to change his or her password on a regular basis, such as once a month. This prevents the extended use of the same password, which can result in security breaches if it is stolen or obtained illegally. On some systems, all passwords expire after a specified period of time (password aging), and all users logging in the next time must then change their password to something else. The user is given warnings before the mandatory change date, so that he or she knows the date is coming and can therefore think of a new password (quick password changes usually bring about poor choices). In addition, on some systems, there is a password history feature where previous passwords are recorded, and one is not allowed to reuse a password, but must enter a new one. This enhances security.

- **Minimum length**   The longer the password, the harder it is to guess. Also, the number of different tries it would take to guess a password using random characters increases significantly when the number of characters goes up. A system administrator can specify the minimum length of passwords required.

- **Multiple passwords**   Ordinarily, there is usually some form of login or username, which is associated with a private password. However, on systems requiring additional security, additional password controls could be implemented. These might include system passwords, which allow you access to specified terminals or systems but are an additional layer of access control on top of your usual login codes. There could also be additional passwords required for dial-up access or for accessing sensitive programs or files.

- **System-generated passwords**   There is also the option of having the computer generate passwords for users. The computer can generate secure passwords using many of the principles discussed in this chapter., The main disadvantage to this approach is that many users find these passwords hard to remember and will end up writing them down or recording them in other unsecure ways.

Aside from these methods, there are other ways to restrict access to a system that is secured by password. For example:

- **Login time limits**   A user is only allowed to log in during certain time periods, such as the working hours of an employee. Anyone trying to access the account "after hours" will be locked out.

■ **System messages** A system can provide warning messages when a person first gets to the login screen, strongly advising against unauthorized entry. In effect, your welcome message is saying "only authorized users are welcome." Some systems do not provide information such as the type of system being accessed, since that might provide information to hackers and others who are not welcome.

■ **Limits on logins** In an effort to prevent multiple tries at breaking into an account, a system will restrict the number of login attempts. For instance, if someone tries more then three times in a row unsuccessfully to log in, the connection will then be dropped. This prevents someone from trying different passwords and logins continuously.

■ **Last login** This merely reports the time/date of the last system login, and how many unsuccessful attempts since your last login. This can give you a clue if someone has accessed your account illegally or tried many times unsuccessfully to do so.

The second major consideration with passwords is protecting them from the wrong eyes. The world's best password is ineffective if you have it taped to the top of your computer screen or have it written down where anyone can read it. Some do's and don'ts with regard to passwords are as follows:

■ *In general, never give your password to anyone.* Aside from sending mail under your name, doing damage to your system files and other work, and other possible problems, you have absolutely no control over your account if someone else has your password. There have been cases where people have told others their passwords in e-mail messages, or even given out their passwords on the phone to someone masquerading as a system administrator conducting a "password survey."

■ *Never write your password down in a place where others can access it.* This includes taping it near your computer, on your desk, or on the side of your monitor. Whatever you do, don't write the words "system password" or something similar next to it, or any other identifying information such as the system dial-up number, for example.

■ *Never use the system-assigned password, such as "root", "demo", "test", and so on.*

■ *Change the password the first time you log into your account.* Don't stick with the default password that many systems give to all new users.

■ *Change your password frequently.* This will prevent problems even if someone obtains your password and attempts to use it. On some systems, all users are required to change their passwords on a regular basis.

Discretionary Access Control

Access control is effective in keeping unauthorized persons out of a system. Basically, it is like a security guard at the entrance to a building who allows persons in on the basis of their ID card or badge. However, once someone is "in," he or she should not be allowed to have free access to all of the programs, files, and information existing on the system. This would be like allowing someone into a corporation and then leaving all the doors unlocked, allowing anyone to roam freely throughout the building.

In much the same way, there needs to be some way to control who can do what on a computer system. Can someone run a particular program, read a certain file, modify information stored on the computer, or erase what someone else has done?

Discretionary access control, sometimes shortened to the acronym DAC, is built into many operating systems, and is an important part of any security scheme. This is basically a kind of access control where someone is given access to files and programs based on what kind of permissions are granted to that person or group. It is discretionary in that someone can specify the kind of access that he or she decides to give to other users of the system. This is different from a more restrictive form, *mandatory access control* (MAC), which provides much more rigid control on access to information in a system.

The idea behind discretionary access control is to regulate on a more specific level what you can do with your files and data. A common scheme implemented on many systems is to support three different kinds of access:

- **Read** Allows you to read a file.
- **Write** Allows you to create and make changes to a file.
- **Execute** This applies to programs. If you have execute rights, you can run the program.

Using just these three kinds of access, you can decide who can read your files, write to your files, and execute your programs. You might decide that only you can write (create and change) your files, but that everyone can read it. Or you can decide that no one can read or write your files.

Unix File System and DAC

Since Unix is such a widely used operating system, especially for use with networks, some examples from Unix would help to illustrate the concept of discretionary access control.

For instance, in most Unix system, there are rights given to three classes of users: the superuser (root), groups that contains a set of users, and users of a system. The superuser (root) account has wide-ranging powers on the system, with many rights and capabilities not available to other users. Security checks and other controls are not in force when it comes to the root superuser. This root account has nearly complete control over the operating system, so it is important to safeguard this account and password; otherwise, you are inviting disaster. The superuser account is considered by some a "security weakness" of Unix, since it can give someone virtually unlimited access to a system.

Groups are designed to group persons together so that rights, privileges, and access can be given to a specified set of users. For instance, you may want to limit access to a specific application development system to only those who are trained to use it. Or, certain sensitive files could be restricted to a select group of users who are authorized to read that information. A user on a Unix system can be assigned to one or more groups on the system.

Finally, there are users who have their own accounts on a Unix system. Even though all users have usernames and passwords, what a particular user can do on the system is controlled by the rights and privileges that user has on the Unix filesystem. More specifically, the Unix filesystem could be described as having the following parts, which are of greatest significance in terms of computer security.

If a user went into Unix and made a listing of the files in a certain directory using the ls command, a directory listing would appear. Aside from basic information such as the file type, file owner, size, time, and date, it also will show file permissions for your user account. For instance, a directory listing for a single file contains file permissions of the following form

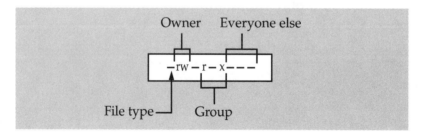

and would specify the following information (see also Table 8-1).

- File type
- Access for the file's owner
- Access for the users in the file's group
- All other users, with the obvious exception of the superuser

A directory listing would grant either one, two, or all three of the rights to the persons in the three categories mentioned. As an example,

-rw-r-x--- 1 user1   366 Jan 16 12:15 sample

Symbol	Description
File Type	
-	Plain file
d	Directory
c	Character device
b	Block device
1	Symbolic link (BSD Unix)
s	Socket (BSD Unix)
p	FIFO (System V Unix)
Permissions	
r	Read
w	Write
x	Execute
Permissions Groups	
	Supervision (all rights)
	Owner
	Group
	Everyone else

Table 8-1. *Unix Filesystem Permissions*

would mean that the file is a "plain file," which allows read and write access to the file's owner, read and execute rights to the group members, and no rights at all for all other users on the system, not including root, who is allowed all rights.

There are commands within Unix that allow a user to change file permissions using the chmod command (add, remove, replace permissions), provided that it is the owner of the file doing the changing. A Unix user can also use a four-digit octal number and chmod to change file permissions.

In Unix, there is also the need to specify permissions on directories within the filesystem. A directory can be assigned the permissions read (r), write (w), and execute (x), which define what can be done with that particular directory on the filesystem.

Encryption

We've discussed the problems of controlling who can gain access to a computer system or network and of maintaining control over who gets to read or do what while online. However, what if the information is of such a sensitive nature that it would be unwise to leave it in an easily accessible form? The answer? Encryption, or the coding of information.

This method has been used as far back as the earliest days of recorded history, when armies needed a secure means of sending messages back and forth, without revealing military secrets in case of interception by the enemy.

First, some definitions. While the concept of *encryption*, or the coding and decoding of information for security purposes, is simple, there are a number of related terms that need to be explained. The basic process involves the translation of original, readable information, called *cleartext* (or sometimes, *plaintext*) into a coded form known as *cipher*, or *codetext*. This coded information is sometimes known as a *cryptogram*. The exact reverse of the process, *decryption*, is simply the process of turning this coded information back into its original form.

The methods for coding (and subsequently decoding) this information can range from simple to complex. To accomplish this, some kind of encryption algorithm or method is required. It can be as simple as transposing (rearranging) letters or characters, or as complex as using a sophisticated equation combining both of these methods to create a complex code that can only be "unlocked" using a special key or set of keys.

While files bearing sensitive or crucial data are ideal candidates for encryption, password files in particular would be further protected using encryption.

There are two main kinds of encryption ciphers, or coding methods, which form the basis of most simple codes. These are *transposition* and *substitution*. Transposition is much like the "Jumble" game or the objective on one of those TV game shows where you must unscramble the letters to form a word. On the other hand, by rearranging the characters or symbols in a file, you can create a substitution cipher. In fact, aside from arranging individual characters, it is also possible to arrange bits, or even blocks or groups of characters, in order to create a coded message. In a transposition cipher, while the data itself does not change, it is simply arranged in a different format by being "scrambled." See Figure 8-1 for an example of a transposition cipher.

Another main form of an encryption cipher is *substitution*. Instead of merely rearranging the information, a substitution cipher changes each of the characters or bits to something else. There are many variations of substitution ciphers, one of which is named after Julius Caesar, who used a cipher that replaced each letter of the alphabet with the one three letters ahead. If the end of the alphabet is reached, it starts at the beginning again. A letter can be replaced with one a number of letters forward in the sequence. In Caesar's cipher, it was 3. You can use any substitute letter based on a certain ordered plan. See Figure 8-2 for an example of Julius Caesar's cipher. Chapter 9 looks in greater detail at encryption techniques for networks.

Biometrics and Specialized Technologies

Fans of "Star Trek" and other science fiction entertainment are likely to be familiar with biometrics. After all, where else can one hear about retina scans, voice identification, or handprint security?

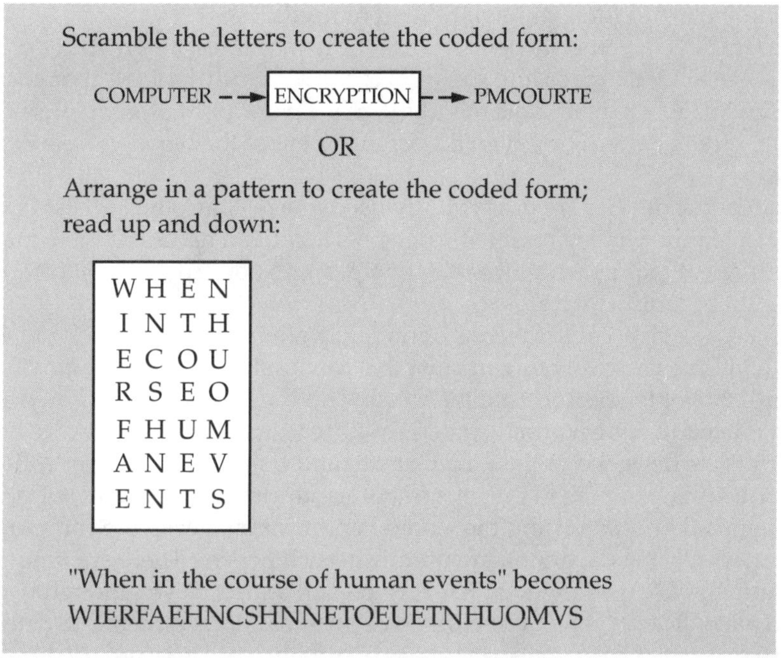

Scramble the letters to create the coded form:

COMPUTER – → ENCRYPTION – → PMCOURTE

OR

Arrange in a pattern to create the coded form;
read up and down:

```
W H E N
I N T H
E C O U
R S E O
F H U M
A N E V
E N T S
```

"When in the course of human events" becomes
WIERFAEHNCSHNNETOEUETNHUOMVS

Figure 8-1. *Transposition ciphers*

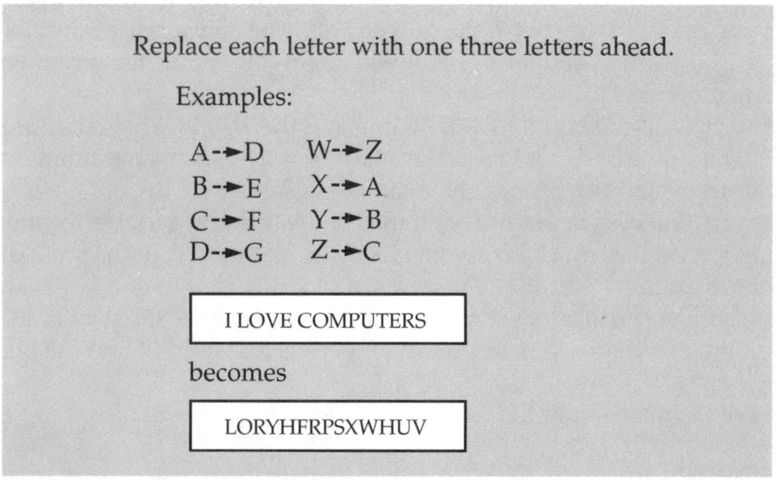

Replace each letter with one three letters ahead.

Examples:

A→D	W→Z
B→E	X→A
C→F	Y→B
D→G	Z→C

I LOVE COMPUTERS

becomes

LORYHFRPSXWHUV

Figure 8-2. *Julius Caesar's cipher*

However, biometrics, perhaps in their more common forms, are actually currently in use around the world for a variety of different needs.

On a general level, biometric devices are simply machines, designed for enforcing security of some kind, that measure some specific (frequently biological or physical) trait that is unique to a person. This might include a fingerprint, voice patterns, handwriting, typing patterns, or even the arrangement of the blood vessels in one's retina.

While biometric devices are not typically used unless controlling access is very critical, with a highly detailed check of a person's identity a necessity, there are a number of different biometric devices that any person knowledgeable in computer security should be familiar with.

Fingerprints are an accepted means of uniquely identifying an individual. Each person has a unique pattern of fingerprints that can be stored in a computer and then matched with that of the person seeking access. There are some sophisticated systems that can even tell if the fingerprint is indeed attached to a living person.

Handprints are designed to read the features and characteristics of an entire hand instead of just a finger. A person puts his or her handprint on the reader surface and a match is attempted between it and the stored handprint images in the computer.

Voice patterns, believe it or not, are unique to each person. There are unique acoustical and vocal patters inherent in every person's speech even though two people may "sound alike." The ability to recognize voice patterns allows someone to determine the identity of a person based on speaking a certain phrase. These are used frequently for financial applications, and only suffer from the possibility of errors if someone experiences a major change in voice (such as a cold or laryngitis).

The analysis of someone's writing or signature patterns includes not only the formation of letters and symbols but also such minute variations as how much pressure is applied when writing certain parts of a signature or word, or the timing of the pen against the paper and the breaks in the movements. The analysis is performed by a unique biometric pen and pad facility that will attempt to match the writer with the stored information.

All documents typed should look the same, but the way in which they are typed may not be. That is the basis for keystroke analysis systems, which examine such details as the speed and rhythm of your typing.

Retina scans, depicted in many a sci-fi movie, are actually a usable technology but have never gained as much acceptance as other methods. A retina scanner uses infrared light to examine the unique patterns of blood vessels in one's eye. This has received less acceptance than other methods primarily because there is some fear that a malfunctioning device could prove to be dangerous and might blind the person being scanned.

A listing of the main biometric techniques is found in Table 8-2.

Problem	Security Device/Method	Comments
Disaster		
Fire	Smoke detectors No smoking in computer center Fire extinguishers	Planning will help to avoid losses and damage
Floods	Water sensor Secure computer equipment Disaster planning	(Same as above)
Earthquake	Secure equipment in case of movement Keep equipment away from windows Disaster planning	(Same as above)
Electrical	Anit-static carpeting Surge protection devices UPS (uninterruptible power supply) Line filter on power supply Backup tapes and other media	(Same as above)
Unauthorized Entry/Damage		
	Locks and securing methods	Avoid damage and theft
	Secure disks	Removal of these disks will sound alarm
	Tokens	Authenticate one's identity before allowing access
	Access cards	Confirm identity of some desiring access

Table 8-2.   *Physical Security and Biometrics Problems*

Problem	Security Device/Method	Comments
Biometric Devices		
	Fingerprint identification	Well-accepted method
	Handprint	Less reliable than fingerprint authentication
	Voice patterns	Voice verification is accepted; voice change may affect reliability
	Signature/Writing	Less expensive than other methods; well accepted
	Keystroke analysis	Can be easily implemented into login sequence
	Retina scan	Accurate, but is least accepted method; fear of blinding

Table 8-2. *Physical Security and Biometrics Problems* (continued)

Physical Security

Another aspect of computer security is the physical security of computer facilities, communications links, and the actual computers and data media themselves. Keeping all this valuable hardware and storage media secure is another of the challenges of computer security.

What good is protecting your system using passwords and other means when someone can easily enter your facility and damage your computer system CPUs, disk drives, and other peripherals? Obtaining your data could involve stealing your tapes and disks or purposely destroying them right in your own facilities. There needs to be some kind of backup and contingency planning system to prevent loss in this kind of situation.

There are a number of different things that can help protect your physical computer resources and avoid the kinds of problems that can result in lost productivity, lost business, and frustration.

These steps are designed to prevent a wide range of problems. The most obvious is sabotage—damage from intruders, disgruntled employees, or anyone who has obtained illegal access to your system through telecommunications links. Sabotage, which can include stolen disks, erased files, or outright damage to computer equipment, can be prevented.

There are also ways to prevent intentional sabotage of your computing equipment and facilities. Allowing the right persons access and keeping undesirables out is one of the key aspects of ensuring the physical security of your facilities. Some of the different methods of preventing illegal access to your computer facilities include the use of locks and keys (the same as for any secure room); allowing access to computer terminals only with keys and passwords; requiring an access code to enter a room; using a key, token, or "smart card" to restrict access; and the use of biometrics devices.

Summary

Computer security is an especially important field for the 1990s. The increased importance of computer networks, the greater number of businesses relying on computer systems for their daily operations, and the sheer amount of information being handled on a daily basis through computer-based systems makes the security of computer systems, programs, and data a paramount concern for systems professionals. The impact of lost or damaged information on businesses and organizations could be staggering. However, through the use of various computer security methods and techniques, it is possible to secure your information (and systems) and allow access only to authorized users.

CHAPTER NINE

Network Security

A s computer networks continue to grow in size and integrate with other networks, the challenges of keeping data secure increase significantly. While networking and connectivity have made it easier to communicate and share information, they have also been a Pandora's box, exposing organizations to many more security attacks that can cripple or damage computing systems and data. Networks are commonly connected to the outside world through a variety of methods, such as bulletin boards, the Internet, and computer telephony integration.

This creates the potential for outsiders to gain access to your computing facilities even though they have no other relationship to your firm. Hackers, former employees, and others have the potential to link up with your computer facilities and work as though they were sitting in your computer center and they can do considerable damage. This chapter examines some technologies and techniques you can use to protect yourself from security attacks on your network.

Network Operating Systems

Briefly stated, network operating systems (NOSs) such as Novell's NetWare, IBM Corporation's LAN Server, and Microsoft Corporation's Windows NT Advanced Server provide network services to the LAN. Network operating systems have specialized features designed to meet network computing requirements, including such things as file, print, and device sharing, as well as server application processing in client/server systems. They also include administrative tools for data security; network management; problem determination; and administration of users, computers, and peripherals on the network.

On the server computer, there are three main components: an access system, a file management system, and a disk cache system. The first, access system, helps to control who uses what data and the access of multiple files. The next part, file management system, is designed to manage the reading and writing of data to and from hard disk drives on the network. Finally, there is the disk cache system, which manages the flow of information into hard disk caches. In addition, there are also functions that coordinate the security of shared resources as well as printing and communications needs. See Figure 9-1 for a diagram of a local area network, and Figure 9-2 for various LAN topologies.

Internetworking

Internetworking is another major development in local area networks. With so many LANs being set up in the various departments, branch offices, and locations of a firm, the need arises to link them together in some way. Internetworking is the answer, through the use of bridges and routers. This allows a LAN thousands of miles away to be reached as easily as one in the next office. See Figure 9-3 for an illustration of internetworking LANs into MANs and WANs.

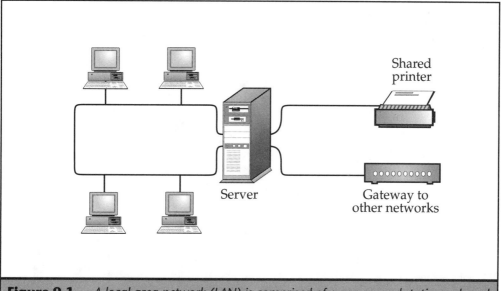

Figure 9-1. *A local area network (LAN) is comprised of a server, workstations, shared resources, and gateways to external networks*

Network Security

Network security is concerned with the security of your systems, programs, and data when they exist in a networked setup. If you have connected your machines to others in LANs or WANs or by modems, you have associated security risks.

Network security risks are greater than those for stand-alone systems. The same factors that make networks useful also contribute to an increased probability of security breaches. The effects of "sharing" on networks, from a security viewpoint, result in the potential of more users—friendly or not—accessing the system, of having network data intercepted, and for illegal access of data, programs, and resources from a remote location.

As a result, it has often been mentioned that networks add increased vulnerability to a computer system. The increased access, availability through phone lines and modems, the popularity of the Internet, and the increased volume of users from different locations all add to the complexity of network security. The fact that information has to travel from one place to another also increases the possibility of error and corruption.

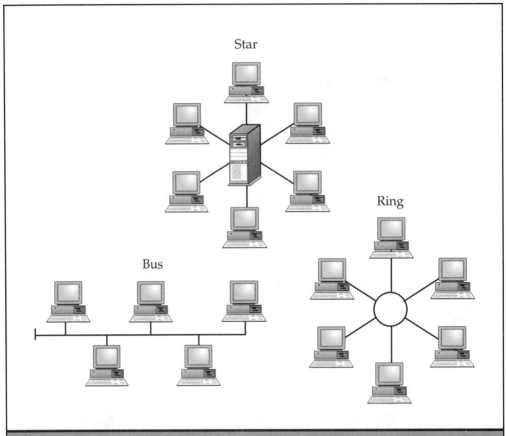

Figure 9-2. *A LAN can be set up in one of several different arrangements or topologies*

Strategies for Protection

How can a network be protected? The basic concepts can be broken down into several strategies:

■ **Create a secure network environment**   There are methods of monitoring users and what they can do on a system, access control, identification/ authentication, screening routers, use of firewalls, and so on.

■ **Encryption of data**   One problem with networks is that an intruder can tap into your system and steal data. This can be alleviated not only by using different media that resist tapping, but also by encrypting the information so that even if it is stolen it cannot be read.

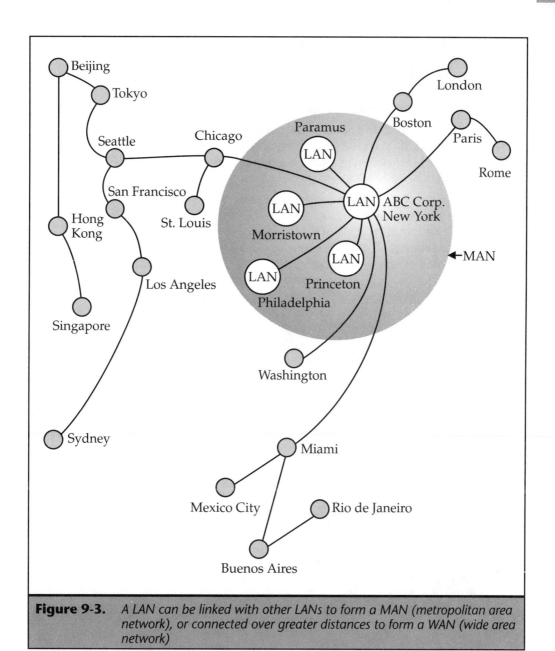

Figure 9-3. *A LAN can be linked with other LANs to form a MAN (metropolitan area network), or connected over greater distances to form a WAN (wide area network)*

■ **Modem security** A modem can be a means of illegal entry to your system if someone breaks your codes and passwords and gains access to your system. There are techniques that can be implemented to thwart illegal modem access.

■ **Disaster and contingency planning** What should be done if there is a disaster or a security problem that threatens a network? If there are solid contingency plans, backup measures, and other ways of dealing with disaster, it is far easier to recover from a security breach or a weather-related calamity. See Chapter 12 for an in-depth look at disaster recover planning.

■ **System planning and administration that considers security as an important element** While some of the other topics mentioned earlier could be considered inclusive within this topic, it is important to properly plan and administer your networks to prepare for any eventuality.

■ **Use a firewall to prevent communications threats** Security loopholes related to the Internet may allow intruders to do damage. Two of these include masquerading and denial of service. With *masquerading*, someone pretends to be someone else. This can be done through a wide range of strategies. These could be as simple as logging in using a stolen password or gaining entry to a computer facility through someone else's ID card, or as sophisticated as using a recording playback to gain access through a voice recognition system. *Denial of service* can be more serious, since it attempts to interrupt the operation of a computer system or facility, or slow service down so much that it seriously affects the operation of it. The well-known case of the Internet worm that traveled through many networks and systems is one type of denial of service, called *flooding* or *wedging,* that attempts to slow a system or network to an absolute crawl. There are other ways to bring about a denial of service, such as reformatting disk partitions, cutting off the supply of power, cutting network cables, or deleting important files.

Risks

Another way to examine the realm of network and communications security from a broad perspective is to look at it from the perspective of "risks." In other words, in what ways is a network more vulnerable and subject to breaches of security? They include the following:

■ **Communications equipment** Most network communications equipment can be a source of security weakness, whether one is talking about switching and signaling equipment, internetworking devices, file servers, or one of the many other parts of a LAN or larger network. Physical damage to this equipment can hurt or disable a network.

■ **Network media** The twisted pair or coaxial cables, wires, and other media used to connect networks are also vulnerable to damage, sabotage, and attack.

■ **Network connections** It is just as easy to access a system remotely as it is on site at the computing facility. Connections such as modems and dial-up connections are particularly vulnerable.

- **Network operating systems** Network operating systems help maintain security through the access control, authentication, and discretionary control features built into their systems. Have these feature been implemented into this network?

- **Virus attacks** The effect of a powerful virus or other computer "wildlife" can have a great effect on a network, because of the interdependence of system parts. If a server is hit with a virus, for example, it can affect an entire network. Viruses are covered more thoroughly in Chapter 11.

- **Physical security** Networks involve a lot of complex hardware, software, and specialized communications equipment in order to function and do their jobs. Problems with a network, even a small one, can cause significant problems, so guarding access to network computing facilities and equipment is of paramount concern.

System Planning and Administration

While there are many different techniques available for protecting a network, they can be less effective if there is no detailed security plan or clear policies on how to administer the network with security in mind. In short, there is an important need for effective system planning and administration if network security is to be maintained.

The complexity of networks requires a network security strategy that identifies components of a network that may be susceptible to security breaches. Some of these components are

- **Network servers** Is the server secure? Who is allowed access to the server and how much access? Is the server kept protected from disasters and other potential problems? A virus on the server can possibly bring down a network—is there any protection? Who has access as an administrator to the network?

- **Workstations (or clients)** What security is implemented on workstations, which ultimately access the server? Is there access control installed on the workstations?

- **Interconnection devices (repeaters, bridges, routers, gateways)** Properly implemented security will restrict access to different parts of a network, or to the entire network, only to those who are authorized to use it.

- **Network operating system (and related) software** There are security features built into network operating systems, and in various management and monitoring software, that can assist in the implementation of network security. Are they properly in place?

- **Application software running on a network** Does access to the program and data need to be protected or restricted?

- **Cabling and communications media** There is a need to protect the data running through communications media from interception, corruption, and other forms of sabotage. Damage to cables can also bring down a network.

- **Information being used and transmitted on a network** How safe is the information? What can be done?

- **Modems** What kinds of security weaknesses can be identified in terms of the modems and outside access currently being provided, if any?

- **People** What access do different staff members have on the network? This could include both physical and system access. What about former employees or consultants who work outside the office?

- **Documentation** What information is published, written down, or otherwise distributed about the network?

A complete facility/site security policy and plan needs to be written down and then carefully implemented into your computer network. The following questions should be used to evaluate one's current network setup and security procedures (if any), and what can be done to improve the current setup:

- What are possible threats to the network?

- How likely is a particular threat?

- What resources are particularly vulnerable?

- How critical is the resource to the functioning of the network?

- What measures can be used to improve the security of the particular resource?

- What backup, recovery, and other emergency procedures are defined and in place in the event of a security breach?

- How long has it been since network security has been reviewed?

Yet another approach is creating a *security analysis* of a network and determining which areas need particular attention in terms of the current or planned network structure. The following are some components of a security analysis to consider.

- **Physical security** Evaluate the security of your network hardware and software resources.

- **Access vulnerabilities** There are a number of points of entry to a network (called *ingress*). The workstations on a system, dial-up access points, connections, and even host computers are all access points to a network. Knowing where someone can break into your network is important, as important as knowing where someone can slip undetected through an unlocked door into your corporate headquarters.

- **Configuration problems**   A network server, for example, may come "out of the box" with passwords such as "demo" or "test," which are widely known to hackers or can be easily guessed. If these are connected to a critical account, they could have serious security ramifications, for example, allowing someone to obtain "superuser" status on a Unix-based network. Being sure that such loopholes do not exist is an important part of network security.

- **Insider hazards**   Probably no group of persons knows more about a network and has greater authorized access than those within the firm. Making it difficult for someone with proper access to break into and damage a system is an important security consideration.

There are many detailed issues to consider as you design your network security plan. The purpose of this section is to identify some of the major components which should be part of an overall security plan.

Access Control and Authentication

A network can be made more secure if it is known who is accessing the system and whether that person is indeed who he or she claims to be. Maintaining access control and authentication is an important part of LAN administration today.

Passwords and Accounts

It's very important on networked systems to determine who is using your network, when he or she is logged in, and to control what he or she can do while online. Fortunately, there are a number of features, many built into network operating systems, that can enhance the access control on your network.

A network, such as a LAN in a corporate or research setting, can be set up to allow access only to those with established accounts. While many users on stand-alone PCs, for example, are accustomed to booting up a computer and simply sitting down to use it, when a large network is involved, a network administrator can set it up so that there is no security, limited security, or a high level of security.

For instance, there can be general access accounts with no password, which allow anyone who knows how to log in to type in a name and have wide-ranging use of the system. A system may have accounts with limited rights for students and clerical staff and accounts with more rights for those who need them. There can also be a security setup where everyone must have a password-protected account, and no one is allows access without an account.

An Example: Novell NetWare 3.1x NOS

A popular network operating system such as Novell NetWare 3.1x, for example, offers the flexibility of designing a level of security appropriate for an organization's needs.

One aspect of the available security capabilities includes password security for accounts on the system.

For instance, using NetWare 3.1x, a system administrator can set up an account for a user with the following options:

- Password or no password required.
- Expiration date for account.
- Maximum number of workstations allowed access to using the same username.
- Forced periodic password changes.
- Requirement for unique passwords (must specify ten unique passwords before one can be reused).
- Intruder detection/lockout. Allows one to track the number of incorrect login attempts and can lock out a user who fails to log in properly a set number of times.

With Novell NetWare, a system administrator has a wide range of options even for implementing passwords. There are other features designed to enhance the security features of Novell NetWare. These include the creation of default account restrictions, so that an administrator may not need to assign security specifications to each user individually, which would be a very time-consuming and tedious job. In addition, there is the ability to create groups or workgroups, all of which share similar security rights and restrictions. There is also the feature of security equivalence, which allows one user to have the same or equivalent rights as another user. For instance, a person may not be the supervisor (system administrator) but can have rights equivalent to one. Finally, there is a supervisor utility, designated for those with supervisor (administrator) rights, called SECURITY, which identifies various possible security problems and vulnerabilities in system accounts.

Getting back to network security access control in general, many of the same principles described in Chapter 8 also apply to networks. In fact, powerful accounts such as SUPERVISOR on a Novell network or root on a Unix network can grant total access to someone with a stolen password. Therefore, all reasonable attempts should be made to keep your passwords effective and secure!

Some of the features that can be implemented on networks for access control, aside from single passwords, include

- **Multiple passwords** One password is required for entry to the network system, and another for a specific account, before access is allowed.
- **One-time passwords** A list of one-time passwords is generated by the system. The first time, the login must be X, the next time Y, then Z, and so on.
- **Time-based passwords** The correct password for access changes over time, based on the time and a secret user "key." As a result, the password changes

from minute to minute, making it harder to guess. The user is provided with a special device that displays the current password for that particular moment.

- **Smart cards** Access requires not only a password but also a physical "smart card" to verify access before allowing entry.

- **Challenge response system** This system uses a combination of a smart card and encryption to offer a secure access control/authentication system.

Passwords offer one measure of security in terms of network access control. However, they are certainly not foolproof, and on larger-scale networks where there is less control over security, these methods may be less effective. For instance, while protecting your network using passwords on a LAN may be reasonably successful, using the ftp or Telnet commands on the Internet may actually put your systems at risk! Some clever individuals are using what are known as "password sniffers" to monitor the data traffic being transmitted to a network, and will search for usernames and password strings that are sent to a system from a workstation to a server. They can then use this information to log in illegally.

Discretionary Access Control

Another important consideration in network security is the maintenance of effective discretionary access control. After all, there are a lot of programs, data, and resources on a network, and it would be generally unwise to have an "open door" policy for everyone, just because they have a valid password. Some important considerations with regard to discretionary access control on a network include the following:

- What programs and services can someone access?
- What files can someone access?
- Who can create, read, or delete a certain file?
- Who is the administrator or "superuser"?
- Who can create, delete, or manage users?
- What groups does someone belong to, and what are the associated rights?
- What rights does a user have when using a certain file or directory?

Many of these DAC decisions can be made by the system administrator or other network management personnel through the network operating system. The following is an example of what kinds of DAC security are offered through Novell NetWare 3.1x (which includes 3.11 and 3.12).

An Example: Novell NetWare 3.1x

Novell NetWare offers two areas of discretionary access control that help control what someone can do while on the system. These include both security-level assignments and directory/file level security. The combination of these, together with password/login security, makes for a very comprehensive and powerful network security system.

Security-level assignments provide different sets of rights and responsibilities depending on one's "position" or "role" within the network. Someone with an administrator (SUPERVISOR) role would have wide-ranging rights. On the other hand, an end user would have rather limited rights. These are general categories, and provide a number of broad network rights. The rights are as follows:

- **SUPERVISOR** Has all rights; can create equivalent supervisors; create all group managers; create and delete users; and have all rights on the system and on all volumes. This could be likened in some ways to a Unix "superuser," who has sweeping powers throughout the system.

- **Supervisor Equivalent** Holds supervisor rights, but is not the SUPERVISOR account. In general, this user is equivalent in rights and capabilities to the SUPERVISOR account.

- **Workgroup Manager** This is a type of user who has the rights to manage groups of users. He or she can create other user account managers, create and delete users, manage user accounts, and use the FCONSOLE utility on a limited basis.

- **User Account Manager** This type of account allows someone to function as an administrator over certain users and/or groups. A UAM can manage users, delete user accounts, and create other user account managers.

- **Print Queue Operator** A print queue operator holds specialized rights relating to the print queue. This user has functions that aid in operating or deleting the print queue.

- **Print Server Operator** A print server operator has rights to manage the print server. These include creating a notify list for printers, changing forms, changing queue priority, and downing the print server.

- **FCONSOLE Operator** This user has rights to manage the FCONSOLE utility. The FCONSOLE is primarily used to perform SUPERVISOR options.

- **End User** An end user, while not a specific class, allows someone to have whatever rights are granted to that person. These make up the bulk of users on a Novell network system.

The other two kinds of DAC control in Novell NetWare include directory and file rights. What a user can do with a specific directory or file can be controlled very specifically through the use of rights.

There are a total of nine rights that are supported in NetWare 3.1x. These basically apply to files and directories. Using these, a system administrator can carefully control what someone can do on the system.

S (Supervisor)   This grants all rights to a directory and its subdirectories.

R (Read)   This grants the right to read a file.

W (Write)   This grants the right to write or makes changes to a file.

C (Create)   This grants the right to write to and create new files or subdirectories.

E (Erase)   This grants the right to delete a file or subdirectories.

M (Modify)   This grants the right to modify filenames or attributes.

F (File Scan)   This grants the right to search a directory or subdirectory.

A (Access Control)   This grants the right to determine access rights, such as modifying disk space restrictions, changing directory rights, or changing trustee assignments.

There is additional sophistication in terms of the Novell NetWare directory tree structure and the determination of what rights can be inherited from locations higher up in the tree. This is sometimes known as the "flow of trustee assignments." The flow of inherited rights can be controlled by a special "filter" known as the IRM (Inherited Rights Mask), which specifies what rights can "filter down" and be inherited in subdirectories.

There are groups that can be created whose members have a common, shared set of rights. These groups can be created by the Supervisor, Supervisor Equivalent, and Workgroup Managers.

As is evident from this discussion, security is a crucial part of a LAN network, and network operating systems such as Novell NetWare 3.1x offer a wide range of features to allow for as much or as little security as is desired.

Authentication

Another important aspect of securing messages and other communications, aside from coding or encrypting the data, is the authentication of a message. While encryption has as its main goal the protection of the message from being read by the wrong persons, authentication has as its goal keeping the message from being altered or modified.

In general terms, the purpose of authentication is to ensure certain aspects of the message. These include the confirmation that the message has been received exactly as sent and that it came from the sender (and no one else), is not a repeated message, and went to the designated recipient. Some encryption methods such as DES support specific authentication tasks. In addition, the use of digital signature can help to ensure accurate authentication of messages.

Digital signatures are used to authenticate messages—in other words, to determine whether a message that has been received was actually written and created by a certain sender. For instance, if you receive a message from Joan asking you for some private information, you want to be sure it really came from her and not from someone else. A digital signature enables you to verify where and whom the message came from and to authenticate the message between the sender and the receiver. A digital signature could be likened to a written signature, except that it is electronic in form, cannot be forged, and cannot be changed without detection.

The ability to code information to make it secret and also to verify the sending and receiving of messages are important features. However, the effectiveness of any encryption method can bary greatly. A simple transposition or substitution cipher can be broken rather easily and could be considered weak. On the other hand, many of the cryptographic algorithms currently in commercial use involve complex mathematical computations and operations, and may require years, decades, or even centuries or millenniums to be broken. These could be considered cryptographically strong algorithms. Chapter 10 contains further exploration of authentication techniques.

Encryption

Encryption is used to protect data and information by coding it into a form that cannot be easily read or understood by unwanted intruders. The introductory chapter on computer security (Chapter 8) provided a general introduction to encryption and how it works, so that will not be repeated here. Instead, the focus will be on specific encryption methods that are commonly used on networks, and how they can prevent the interception and theft of valuable information from a network.

One of the most important issues in encryption and networks is the encryption of passwords and of messages that travel throughout the network. One of the problems of networked systems is that frequently passwords are sent through a network, whether for logging in or other related purposes. An unencrypted password can present a security hazard in that password sniffers and other forms of tapping/eavesdropping devices can be used to read the data being transmitted and can attempt to steal passwords being transmitted. In addition, a password file on a file server, for example, should not be kept in such a way that someone can steal it and then have access to various system accounts. Encrypting the password file is one defense against this problem. Some systems are designed to encrypt the password even when it is traveling through the network, so that no one can steal the password as it is being transmitted.

Encryption is also important when working with sensitive messages. An electronic mail message that contains highly sensitive information could be protected by a password and be restricted to reading by the recipient. But what happens if someone can intercept the message and then read this highly sensitive information? Encryption, or coding of the message, offers one solution to this problem. Chapter 10 takes a more in-depth look at this technology.

Modem Security

It is a familiar scene: a group of hackers sit huddled in a room, dialing phone numbers and guessing passwords in an attempt to break into a corporate or military computer system. What makes hacking easy to attempt (if not always succeed at) is the fact that there are modems providing access to many corporate computing facilities. By dialing a phone number, someone can establish a direct connection to a remote computer's modem and "talk" to the system as though he or she were right on site.

The accessibility of these systems through ordinary telephone numbers and even through global packet-switching networks has enabled anyone with a modem and phone line to have access to thousands of computers.

This is why modem security is an important consideration when allowing modem access to a facility. There are a number of techniques available to enhance the security of modems and make it as difficult as possible for illegal users to obtain entry to a computer system.

The main objective of effective modem security is to prevent unauthorized access to your network dial-up facilities, and restrict access to only authorized users. There are a number of methods that can help prevent access to a network through modem dial ups.

Security of Dial-up Modem Access

Before someone can obtain access to your system, he or she must first establish a connection with the network modem. Logically, the first line of defense is to keep the phone number away from unauthorized persons. Don't publish it, list it on your system, or give it out to anyone who calls technical support.

To add additional security to the system, a password can be added, effectively keeping out anyone without a valid "modem" password. This modem password is separate and distinct from system login passwords.

There are also modems known as "dial-back modems." These modems, upon receipt of a call, will not immediately establish a connection. Instead, they will ask for your login information. The modem will then drop the connection, and if the information is correct will call the authorized user back at a dial-up number stored on the system.

There are also modems that will encrypt the information being sent and received, so information cannot be intercepted or otherwise accessed in original form. This requires the purchase of special-purpose modems.

In addition, there are special "silent modems" that will not send the characteristic "connection established" signal until login has been completed. This will help prevent someone from searching through sequences of phone numbers for computer dial-ups.

Security of Dial-up System Access

Of course, a valid account and password should be required for access to your network. To ensure additional security, system messages identifying the systems should be kept to a minimum in order to give as little information as possible to an illegal user. Also, some systems now display strong warning messages threatening severe consequences for illegal access of a system.

Yet another method is to limit access to the time being spent on the network while attempting to connect. For instance, if someone has tried three times to log into the system and fails, the system could break the connection and require the person to dial up once again to attempt access.

Transmission Media Security

Another important vulnerability in terms of network security are the connections that tie a network together. Whether a medium-sized LAN or a large global WAN internetwork, the choice of communication links or medium can make an impact on how secure a network is. This is not difficult to understand, since any kind of link, whether a physical cable such as twisted pair or coaxial, or an unbounded media such as microwave, can have advantages and disadvantages in terms of security.

One important aspect is the transmission medium used. There are bounded (physical cable) and unbounded transmission mediums available, and they vary in their security strengths and weaknesses.

Earlier, you read a description of the major communications media in use for networks. These include twisted-pair telephone lines; coaxial cable; fiber optic; and unbounded media such as wireless networks, microwave technologies, and even satellite links.

All of these links vary in cost, advantages, and disadvantages, and the differences in terms of susceptibility to damage, sabotage, and eavesdropping. Some forms of media, such as twisted pair, are inexpensive and easy to work with but sensitive to interference. Coaxial is somewhat better in terms of interference, and fiber optic is even less susceptible to electro magnetic and other forms of interference. Of course, like any kind of physical cable, there are ways to cut or otherwise damage the physical cables, or to eavesdrop or tap into the data flowing through these media.

On the other hand, unbounded media, such as microwaves, radio waves, and infrared transmission, has problems of its own. Used more often for wide area networks and national/global operations due to high-cost considerations, these technologies, which don't use a physical wire, are not only more subject to weather and atmospheric problems, but also are quite sensitive to external interference, eavesdropping, and jamming of the waves. Unbounded media, while free from the limitations of physical cables, can create security problems if the information being transmitted is highly sensitive.

The security considerations of the media links between the components of a network are very critical, since the capturing of sensitive information can pose a problem, even if all other aspects of a network have been made very secure. See Figure 9-4 for an illustration of three main transmission cable types.

Firewalls and Other Network Protection Methods

There are other network security measures that can protect your networks and connected systems. These are designed to help prevent the spread of computer damage from network to network.

Firewalls

Networks, particularly larger internetworks (many smaller networks connected together), consist of a large interconnected system of hardware, software, resources,

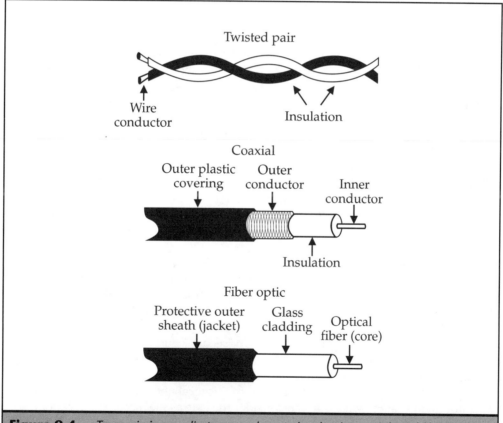

Figure 9-4. *Transmission media types such as twisted pair, coaxial, and fiber optic all have advantages and disadvantages with regard to security*

and data. A security breach on one network should not be allowed to spread from one network to another until the entire internetwork has been affected. This could cause grave harm to the operation of the computing facilities of an entire business.

A *firewall* is an effective means of preventing attackers from moving easily from network to network, spreading damage and destruction throughout. Like a physical firewall in a building, it is designed to restrict the flow of information from network to network.

A firewall for a network operates on the principle that not all segments on the system should necessarily be one huge "super-net." Rather, different networks are kept separate but can still communicate through routers or gateways. The implementation of a firewall would put limits on what data can "travel" through the firewall's "door" and enter the other network. Like a security guard at a corporate complex, it checks the ID of anyone coming into an adjacent network.

The need for a firewall is even more apparent when it comes to a large network such as the Internet, or a corporate network that connects many different computing centers or divisions. When there are hundreds of computers and networks being tied together, all accessible from dial-up links or other public means (or even from within the firm), then the potential for bringing about security breaches on a large scale is great.

From a security standpoint, using a firewall technology makes a lot of sense. An employee in the New York office does not really need access to the computing facilities in Los Angeles, unless there is a special reason for doing so. In that case, it can be granted. Similarly, an employee in the Accounting division may not regularly need access to the LAN used by the marketing department. Restricting access through firewall "gatekeepers" helps to ensure security on a broad scale.

A firewall uses a combination of software and hardware (including a router and computer) to make decisions about what kinds of requests can pass from an internal network from the outside (and vice versa). This includes such operations as electronic mail messages, file transfers, logins to a system, and the like. A firewall can block all access from the Internet or external network to this internal network, or it can be very selective, examining every message or communication that passes from one side to the other.

There are generally two parts to a firewall: a gate and a choke. The function of a gate is to move data between network and network. It works together with the choke, which functions as a filter, blocking data from going from one network to another. The choke and gate can be set up on one computer system, or alternatively a gate can be set up on a computer, and a choke on a router.

A firewall gate's main function is to act as a "security guard" for your network. It decides what information can be passed to and from the network. In effect, information coming from an external network must be destined for this gate computer, and any information being sent from this local network to the outside must pass through the gate as well. You can consider the gate as the "security checkpoint" for the local network.

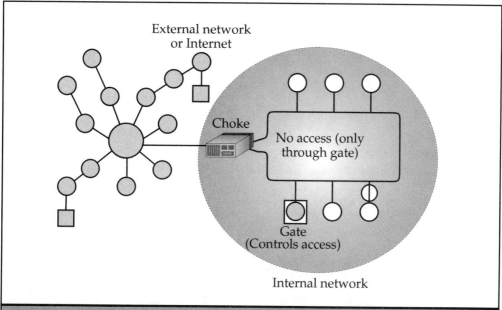

External network
or Internet

Choke

No access (only
through gate)

Gate
(Controls access)

Internal network

Figure 9-5. *A firewall restricts access to and from a network through the use of a choke and gate*

The choke, on the other hand, functions as a kind of security guard, checking "passports" and other documents for information being transmitted. It will pass information through if the source or destination is the gate computer, and block it if it is not. There can be more selective filtering, such as packets or messages of a certain type.

A firewall system can contain more than one choke and gate, if needed, in order to maximize security.

Firewalls are effective methods for controlling the access between two different networks that are interconnected. Much like the border between two adjacent countries, a firewall functions as an effective checkpoint for data moving to or from "foreign" but connected networks. See Figure 9-5 for a diagram of a typical firewall.

Summary

The realm of networking is expanding! Never before has there been such a demand for computers that offer the capabilities of connectivity. The entire range of networked systems from small LANs to huge WANs and the global Internet has presented enormous opportunity and capability to the corporate world. However, with all this promise and opportunity comes a great potential for serious computer security problems. In this chapter, the purpose was to provide a broad yet comprehensive overview of security problems and solutions in networked computer systems.

CHAPTER TEN

Authentication and Confidentiality on Networks

In this chapter, we'll explore cryptographic techniques used to provide authentication and confidentiality. Considering the large-scale integration of smaller LANs into larger LANs, LANs into WANs, and the rapid pace of interconnection to the Internet, it's more important than ever to positively identify people or companies you work with over your networks and to ensure that confidential information is not mistakenly revealed to unauthorized people.

First, we'll introduce the building blocks of the technology, and then we'll discuss the applications of these concepts in specific implementations used today. Among the topics for discussion are DES, IDEA, Kerberos, public key/private key, Diffie-Hellman, RSA, MD5, digital signatures, nonrepudiation, PGP, and Internet commerce. Sometimes the discussions of these technologies are mathematical in nature. However, knowledge of mathematics is not required to understand this chapter.

An Overview of the Technology and Its Applications

Since cryptography may be unfamiliar to many readers, we begin this chapter with an overview of the concepts and the terms used.

What Is Authentication?

Authentication refers to the process of verifying someone's identity. In real life, there are usually three ways to prove your identity: something that you *have*, *know*, or *are*.

For example, the keys on your key ring are something that you *have*, in order to enter your house or start your car. The password that you enter in order to log onto your computer is something that you *know*. When you are identified by your fingerprints or by your DNA, it is by something that you *are*. To authenticate the identity of a user over a LAN, your options are limited by the fact that all you have to work with is bit patterns that arrive over a wire.

Authentication by Possession

You can use a scheme that works on the basis of something the user *has*. One such product is SecurID by Security Dynamics, which operates using a portable hand-held authentication device that displays a different password every 60 seconds, matching a password that is simultaneously generated at the host computer. Although such systems work well, they are very rarely used because of the expense involved. In addition, this method obviously cannot authenticate an external third party contacting you from the Internet. In general, it is rare to identify LAN users by something that they have in their possession. In the future, smartcard technology may be used for authentication by possession.

Authentication by Intrinsic Characteristics

Human biology has given you several ways to uniquely identify yourself, such as fingerprints. However, authentication based on something that you *are* is not very practical for LANs. The technology required to implement biometric authentication is somewhat expensive and not generally available. For example, the military may be able to justify using a device that authenticates a person by scanning blood vessel patterns on the retina, but most businesses cannot afford the expense of this technology. In the future, video cameras mounted on users' PCs may be able to authenticate a person's identity.

Authentication by Knowledge

So, if you can't use something you possess and you can't use something you are, that leaves you with something you *know*, usually a password. However, using passwords over the LAN exposes you to what are called *replay attacks*. Any person monitoring the traffic over the LAN can record the passwords as they fly by using special password sniffer programs. In a world where passwords are the only means of authentication, once a password is stolen, your computer system and network may be totally vulnerable to intellectual property theft and destruction of data. Think about this the next time you log in to a system over the Internet using the same password you use on your own systems on your private network.

   This chapter will explore techniques that are used to positively verify the identity of the user without giving an electronic Peeping Tom the capability of seeing any information that would be useful to them.

What Is Confidentiality?

Confidentiality is the concept of keeping sensitive information from being disclosed to unauthorized people. In real life you might ask someone to step into a room and close the door in order to have a private chat. To send someone confidential information, you could write it down and then place the paper in a special tamper-evident envelope marked "personal and confidential." This would give you some degree of confidence that only the recipient would be aware of the contents of the envelope.

   The problem when sending data over a LAN or across the Internet is that the data you send is publicly exposed to many other computers connected to the network that forwards your message to the final destination. You've got to transform the information in some way that renders it meaningful only to the actual recipient. In other words, you have to *encrypt* the data.

What Is Encryption?

Encryption refers to the process of scrambling data so it appears to be random nonsense, while preserving it in a recoverable form. The recipient of an encrypted message can unscramble or decrypt the garbled message back into its original, comprehensible form. This concept is the basis for the science of cryptography—literally from the Greek words for "secret writing."

Keys, Plaintext, and Ciphertext

The method of scrambling the data—the *encryption algorithm*—is usually completely public. There are only a few encryption algorithms in use, with names like DES, IDEA, and RSA. These algorithms take the original information you want to protect, called the *plaintext* or *cleartext*, and scramble it using a numeric operator called a *key*. The resulting scrambled version is called the *ciphertext*. Even though others know the exact encryption algorithm you use, in order for them to unscramble your ciphertext, they must have the correct key to re-create your cleartext.

Secret Key Versus Public Key/Private Key

There are two basic classes of encryption algorithms: secret key and public key/private key. In *secret key encryption*, the same key is used to encrypt the data as is used to decrypt the data. Its called secret key encryption because you have to keep the key secret. Sometimes it's called *symmetric key encryption* because you use the same key both to encrypt and to decrypt. The secret key algorithms examined in this chapter are DES and IDEA.

The other major encryption technique is called *public key/private key*. Instead of using a single key, it uses a related pair of keys. Through some mathematical magic, whatever you encrypt with one of the keys can only be decrypted using the other. In general, you keep one of the keys to yourself—your "private key"—and you publish the other key in the pair—your "public key"—to the entire world. Later in this chapter we will examine the use of RSA, the most commonly used public key/private key algorithm.

The basic idea is that the confidentiality of encrypted data is protected because there are so many different possible key values that it is completely impractical to try them all to see which one works. To a cryptographer, "completely impractical" may mean, for example, that if you tried with the fastest computer in the world for as many centuries as there are atoms in the universe, you probably still wouldn't find the right key.

Basic Cryptography

Cryptographic techniques are used to provide both authentication and confidentiality. Therefore, the examination of these topics will begin with a review of some cryptographic fundamentals. Once past the basics, you will look at more advanced cryptographic techniques that allow us to do some pretty amazing things, such as proving you *know* a secret without divulging it and stamping a forgery-proof digital signature on a document.

Roman Cryptography

The need to send confidential messages is nothing new. Various cryptographic methods have been employed through the ages. One of the techniques developed by the ancient Romans to encode messages is called *alphabetic substitution*. A message could be encrypted with the key 5 by replacing every letter in the original message with the letter occurring five positions further down the alphabet (considering "a" to be after "z" when you got to the end). Thus every "a" in the original message would be replaced with an "f," every "b" would become a "g," and so on. The spaces between the words are simply discarded.

To make the substitution easy to perform, we can write the original alphabet on one line, and the replacement alphabet immediately below it, as shown in Figure 10-1

So let's use this table to encrypt a simple message. The original, or cleartext, message we'll use is "This is a secret." For each letter in the message, we find it in the alphabet on the first line and write down the letter immediately below it. This yields the ciphertext message "ymnxnxfxjhwjy." The decryption process is simply the reverse; for each letter in the ciphertext, find it in the alphabet on the second line and write down the letter immediately above it. The result is the cleartext message: "thisisasecret," which anybody can see means "This is a secret."

The Romans also invented encryption decoder rings that consisted of two disks with a pin stuck through the center of both disks. The alphabet was written around the rim of each disk, so that the user could rotate one disk against the other to the specified key position, and by finding the letter on one disk, the user could read off the shifted letter in the corresponding position on the other disk.

While this may seem like a fairly childish form of "secret writing" to us today, it's important to point out that it was successfully used for military intelligence signals in its day. Since that time, both the mathematical theory of cryptography and the tools available to automatically carry out the manipulations have evolved tremendously.

Source alphabet

a	b	c	d	e	f	g	h	i	j	k	l	m	n	o	p	q	r	s	t	u	v	w	x	y	z
f	g	h	i	j	k	l	m	n	o	p	q	r	s	t	u	v	w	x	y	z	a	b	c	d	e

Replacement alphabet

Figure 10-1. *Roman alphabetic substitution table for key 5*

Cryptography Is an Evolving Science

Even if we consider a cryptographic technique to be virtually unbreakable today, it is always possible that future developments in analysis and computing power could render existing strategies vulnerable. Cryptographers are keenly concerned that the methods they use will be as easy to crack tomorrow as Roman techniques are today.

One such unexpected method was recently publicized in the newspapers. A researcher familiar with standard techniques from genetic engineering was able to apply them to solve a computationally difficult mathematical problem. The "traveling salesman" problem asks what is the shortest route a traveling salesman can take to visit a large group of cities in the sales territory.

The computational difficulty in this problem comes from the fact that you have to calculate the length of all possible routes to assure yourself you have found the shortest one. When you have a very large number of cities, there are so many possible sequences of trips that the problem becomes virtually unsolvable. The researcher hit upon the idea of representing each leg of the journey by a particular genetic molecular building block. Using analytical techniques from molecular biology, he was able to arrive at results that numerically require an enormous number of processors working in parallel.

So how does this work? Simple. First, you chemically test for the presence of each city, and throw away the strings that don't have all the cities. Then you sort the molecular strings by size, and voilà, the smallest one represents the answer! (Now suppose for a moment that you could encode each possible password using a molecular sequence, and you had a way of testing if a particular password was the one you were looking for. . . .)

Secret Key (Symmetric Key) Encryption

Secret key encryption is what you normally think of when you hear the word encryption. It's called *secret key* because there is only one key and you obviously need to keep it secret. You feed the data and the key into the encryption routine, and out pops the scrambled ciphertext. You can let anyone see the scrambled ciphertext, and it remains an opaque, meaningless jumble. You can send the data across the Internet or you can save the data on a publicly accessible disk—all without compromising the security of the data. When you want the original data back, you feed the ciphertext and the key into the decryption routine, and out pops the original cleartext or plaintext. This concept is illustrated in Figure 10-2.

DES: The Data Encryption Standard

The most famous secret key or symmetric key encryption algorithm, DES was developed by IBM in the 1970s and was adopted by the U.S. government in November, 1976, after a search conducted for an official encryption standard. DES was

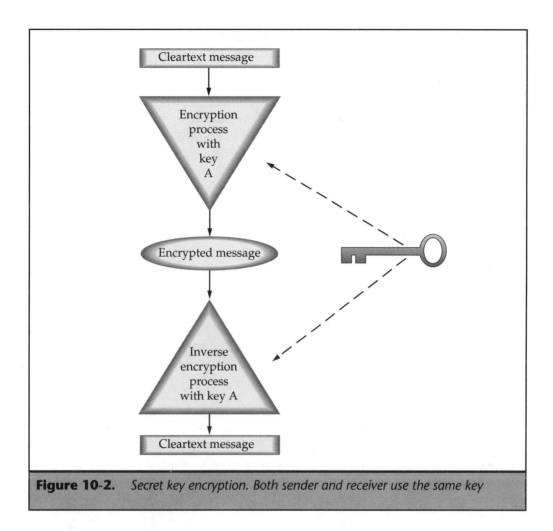

Figure 10-2. *Secret key encryption. Both sender and receiver use the same key*

subsequently blessed by the National Bureau of Standards and later the American National Standards Institute (ANSI).

DES uses a 56-bit key and encrypts data in 64-bit chunks. Why a 56-bit key? The true history is shrouded in government secrecy; cynics believe the 56-bit key was short enough for the technologically strong and well-funded National Security Agency (NSA) to crack it if necessary, but long enough to make DES impenetrable to almost anybody else.

DES works on 64-bit input data blocks that are put through a series of 16 rounds of scrambling. For each round, a 48-bit "per-round" key value is derived from the full 56-bit key. During each round, the 64 bits of data and the per-round key value are fed through a set of so-called "S" boxes and a *mangler* function that scrambles up the bits. In addition, before the rounds, after the rounds, and between each of the rounds, the

64 bits of data are permuted (the order of the bits is shuffled) in a particular way. During each step of the process, a unique round key is derived from the 56-bit master key.

At the end, the original 64 bits of input have been transformed into 64 bits of output that appear to be completely scrambled, but which can actually be transformed back into the input using the decryption algorithm (essentially encryption run in reverse) and, of course, the same key used to encrypt the data in the first place. Figure 10-3 shows the DES encryption algorithm.

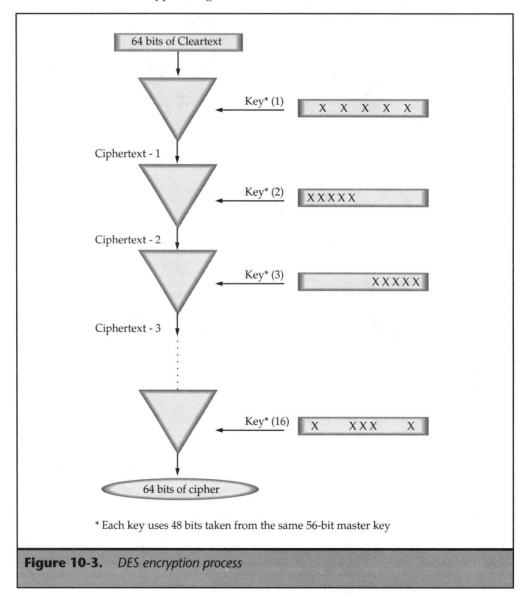

Figure 10-3. *DES encryption process*

Due to the permutations before, between, and after each round, DES is much slower to perform in software than in hardware. To perform a single permutation in software, you have to go through a loop 64 times, putting each of the 64 data bits in the right place one at a time. To perform a permutation in hardware, you just use a block of 64 input "pins" wired straight to 64 outputs, with the permutation defined by which input pin is wired to which output. The results can be read directly from the output pins.

This has had the effect of restricting would-be DES crackers to those with the resources to build special-purpose hardware. Most hackers today would have difficulty assembling the technology to build such a device.

Cracking DES

People who implement cryptographic systems ought to consider the *value* of the information being protected, and *how long* the data must be kept confidential. In 1977 it was estimated that it would have cost $20 million (in 1977 dollars!) to have built a special-purpose computer with custom-designed hardware that could "crack" a DES key in under 12 hours by simply trying every possible key by brute force until it found the one that worked. If it takes that level of effort to break, it would be considered "strong" encryption.

However, notebook computers today are more powerful than mainframes were in 1977. Because computers are so much more powerful now, the cost of producing a special-purpose DES-breaking computer has fallen to an estimated several hundreds of thousands of dollars today. Obviously, you do not want to protect interbank wire transfers of billions of dollars using such a technique.

On the other hand, if all you are doing is protecting someone's server access, once you've made it necessary to spend several hundreds of thousands of dollars to break, your encryption could well be described as "adequate." It's adequate because by then, you are at the point where it is much easier for an attacker to get your data by other means described in previous chapters, including

- Getting employed on the janitorial staff in the building containing the computer system
- Bribery
- Breaking in
- Dumpster diving
- Electronic eavesdropping
- Masquerading or impersonating trusted outsiders
- Researching the names of pets, family members, hobbies, and so on, looking for easy-to-guess passwords

Secure Today, Secure Tomorrow?

The other issue we mentioned is the retention period of confidential data. Suppose you are encrypting information today that needs to remain secret ten years from now. Over the past 20 years computers have doubled in processing power every two years or so. This trend is actually accelerating—the pace at which computers are getting faster is itself getting faster. As we saw with DES from 1977, this means that although it might not be possible today to break a code by trying all possible keys by brute force, it might well be possible in the future when computers will be *much* faster.

For every additional bit you add to the length of the key, you double the number of values that the key can assume. If computers are doubling in processing power every two years or less, to be conservative we should add one bit to the minimum key length for each year into the future that you wish the encrypted data to remain secure.

If DES No Longer Does the Job, What Should We Do Now?

Since it is now possible to build a DES-cracking special-purpose computer for a couple of hundred thousand dollars, DES is no longer considered to be adequately secure where "strong" encryption is required.

If a 56-bit key was considered to be adequate in 1976, then our conservative projection 20 years later suggests using a key length of 76 bits or more. If we need to be as secure today as DES was in 1976, why not just extend the key length of DES, or come up with a new algorithm with longer keys?

The problem here is that the roadside is littered with the skeletons of encryption schemes that were originally proposed as secure. Altering the DES algorithm is tricky, because if you try to extend the key length, the implementation of the algorithm must also change and you might subtly weaken the cryptographic strength of the algorithm. Researchers have shown that tiny changes in the DES design can seriously compromise the protection of the encrypted data against some sophisticated forms of mathematical attack. New encryption algorithms or changes to existing implementations may not show their vulnerabilities for several years. You would not want to discover this after you had already deployed a new encryption scheme on a mission-critical worldwide financial network.

Triple-DES

Because it's so difficult to be sure a new cryptographic algorithm actually is secure, and because the only cryptographic shortcoming of DES is its relatively short key length (not to mention the investment already made in hardware and software that reliably implements DES), one response to the key length problem has been to move to *triple-DES*. As the name suggests, three regular DES encryption steps are performed, but only *two* 56-bit DES keys are used in the most common version of triple-DES. Assuming the two keys are K1 and K2, the steps are

1. DES encrypt using K1.

2. Run the output of step 1 through a DES *de*cryption using K2.

3. Take the output of step 2 and *en*crypt using K1.

This process is called *EDE* because of the *Encrypt Decrypt Encrypt* steps. The middle step is a decryption so you can use a triple-DES implementation to perform regular DES encryption and decryption by setting K1=K2. Figure 10-4 illustrates how triple-DES works.

The downside to triple-DES is, of course, that it take three times more computing effort to perform than DES. On the other hand, the 112-bit key length of triple-DES is considered to be adequate well into the foreseeable future.

The "Meet-in-the-Middle" Attack

You might be curious about why we perform three DES encryption steps even though we use only two 56-bit DES keys. Why not just use *double-DES*—first DES encrypt using K1, and then DES encrypt *that* using K2?

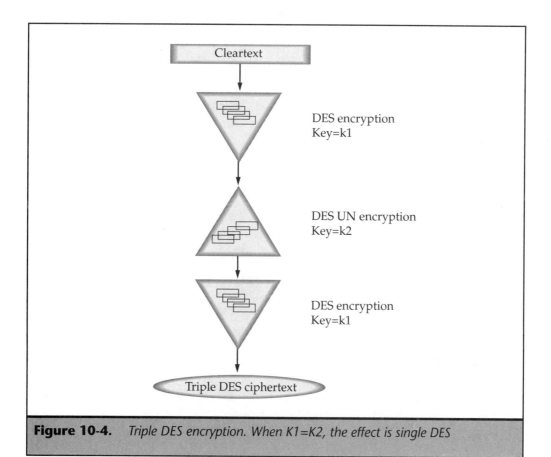

Figure 10-4. *Triple DES encryption. When K1=K2, the effect is single DES*

The answer lies in what is referred to as the "meet-in-the-middle" attack that can be mounted any time you use the output of one encryption as the input to a second encryption step. We start by assuming that you have several examples of cleartext and several of ciphertext to work with. From this you want to find out what pair of keys was used.

The primary concern about the security of DES revolves around the possibility of trying all possible 2^{56} different 56-bit DES keys until you find the correct one. This means that you can assume that you have a computer that can try all the 2^{56} possible keys and has enough storage capacity to store two tables that record each key tried and the corresponding encryption result.

The meet-in-the-middle attack on double-DES would proceed as follows. Select a plaintext/ciphertext pair. We are looking for the pair of keys K1 and K2 that were used in the two successive DES encryption steps. In the first table, for each of the 2^{56} possible candidates for K1, record the K1 candidate and encryption result. In the second table, for each of the 2^{56} possible candidates for K2, record this K2 candidate and the result of DES *de*crypting the final ciphertext using the candidate key.

If you then sort the first table by the result of the K1 encryption, and sort the second table by what you got by working backward by using K2 decryption from the final output, you can compare the output of the first encryption against the input of the second encryption. It turns out that there may be several K1/K2 pairs that will take that particular plaintext and double-DES encryption to the *middle* ciphertext value. To figure out which one of these K1/K2 pairs is correct, just try the pairs on an additional plaintext/ciphertext pair. The correct K1/K2 pair is the one that also works on other plaintext/ciphertext pairs. As it turns out, this is *much* faster than trying all 2^{112} possible K1/K2 pairs.

Now let's try to understand whether this type of attack is viable. Two tables may not sound like a lot of data at first, but these tables are actually very large. The tables would require 2^{56} rows, each containing a 56-bit value and a 64-bit value (15 bytes). Doing the multiplication, that's two tables of 2^{56} rows of 15 bytes. If a terabyte is 2^{40} bytes, this means there would be 2,000,000 terabytes of table! This does not even begin to consider the difficulty in sorting two 1,000,000 terabyte tables. Because this attack requires a comparison of all possible key; it would require an enormous amount of computing power and storage.

The meet-in-the-middle attack is considered to be a theoretical threat. The response of the cryptanalytic community to move into triple-DES indicates the level of commitment they have to keeping systems secure. Although it would appear that double-DES would be highly secure, triple-DES is much more secure.

A Word of Caution at This Point on Key Lengths

Just because your keys are long enough to preclude a brute force examination of all possible key values, don't think that you are necessarily secure. You might be "leaking" information about your keys that can give an attacker a shortcut.

For example, last year Netscape Communications was surprised when somebody disassembled their key generation program and discovered that they were generating their keys by recording random values from a limited set of variables reflecting the current state of the computer and then scrambling these variables. It was learned that trying all possible keys was not necessary; you only had to try the keys that could be constructed from a limited set of possible values fed into the key generator.

Of course, as soon as this loophole was discovered, it was quickly remedied by increasing the randomness of the key generator. This example points out the level of planning required when implementing cryptography because there is a never-ending stream of creative and clever people trying to find methods to undermine the security of computer systems.

IDEA (International Data Encryption Algorithm)

IDEA was developed by Xuejia Lai and James L. Massey at the Swiss Federal Institute of Technology. It was released in 1990 and enhanced in 1991. Like DES, IDEA is a conventional secret key encryption algorithm that uses one secret key to encrypt a 64-bit block of data. The same key is again used to decrypt the 64-bit ciphertext block to recover the original 64-bit cleartext block. Like triple-DES, IDEA was developed because DES was starting to show its age. IDEA operates with 128-bit (16-byte) keys, which cryptanalysts agree ought to be sufficient for many years.

Like DES, the IDEA algorithm operates in a series of rounds involving a sub-key generated for each round from the full encryption key, and like DES, a so-called "mangler" function is used to scramble the bits during each round. However, unlike DES, permutations are not used, which means the algorithm can be implemented easily in software as well as hardware.

The designers of IDEA appear to have been successful on all counts. The design has withstood the scrutiny of the cryptanalytic academic community; it has adequately long keys and it is fast to implement in both software and hardware.

The Benefit of IDEA Being an International Algorithm

One additional and very important benefit of IDEA was its development outside the United States. Developing and marketing encryption software in the United States has historically been problematic because U.S. law forbids the exportation of encryption technology without government approval. This approval is generally not granted broadly unless the key length is a toothless 48 bits or less. To put the situation in perspective, the exportation of encryption is covered under the same laws and classifications as the exportation of nuclear weapons.

Considering the global nature of the computer industry today, it has had the unfortunate negative effect of limiting the use of strong encryption in products sold in the United States. Furthermore, the government's policies have effectively limited the ability of U.S. software companies to compete in the worldwide market for encryption software. You can probably imagine the legal risks a software company assumes in shipping its products employing strong encryption to its customers in the United States, while at the same time attempting to ensure that the software will never be exported.

The government's policies regarding the export of cryptographic technology has been under heavy attack by much of the software industry as being outdated and ineffective. In fact, cryptographic algorithms and techniques are well known outside the United States; after all, IDEA was developed in Switzerland. There is no restriction on books that discuss cryptography in great detail. People of all nationalities, living in all corners of the earth, who want to learn all about advanced encryption can buy books on the subject and read. The algorithms used, and even code listings implementing those algorithms, are freely published. It's worth pointing out that such books are not restricted for export from the United States. To gain a better understanding of the U.S. government's role in cryptography, refer to Appendix B.

Applying Secret Key Techniques

In this section you will learn a variety of ways in which secret key techniques can be useful.

Encrypting a Whole Message

So far, we've discussed using DES, triple-DES, or IDEA to encrypt an 8-byte (64-bit) block of data. How do I encrypt an entire message?

The obvious approach is to break up the message into 64-bit blocks and encrypt each one using the agreed-upon key. This is a particularly dumb thing to do, because the same 64-bit input data block always maps to the same 64-bit ciphertext block. Even if an eavesdropper can't decrypt the ciphertext, people can certainly recognize when specific blocks are repeated. This gives away information about the content of the message. If the message reads either "approved *xxxx*" or "rejected *xxxx*," it won't take long for a snooper to figure out your code.

A better approach is to employ a method that ensures the same 64-bit block that appears several times in the plaintext gets encrypted to a different ciphertext block each time. This is done using a type of feedback loop where the results of encrypting the previous block are somehow folded into the calculation of the next ciphertext block. Cipher Block Chaining (CBC), Output Feedback Mode (OFB), and Cipher Feedback Mode (CFB) are some of the techniques that accomplish this. You also want to ensure that multiple copies of the sent message are encrypted differently each time. For further exploration on these topics, refer to the reading list at the end of this chapter.

How Often Can I Use the Same Key?

You could use the same key over and over to exchange messages with another party, but you will have to think about the following:

■ If someone else ever does happen to get their hands on your key, every message you have ever exchanged with the other side will now be readable.

■ The higher the volume you encrypt with a particular key, the more working material you are giving to eavesdroppers, increasing their odds of being successful.

Therefore, we generally establish either a session key that is used for only one message or one conversation with the other party, or we set up a mechanism to change keys on a regular basis to minimize the exposure.

Distribution of Secret Keys

If you know in advance who you are going to be communicating with, you can arrange to send them a pouch containing a bunch of keys on diskette or CD-ROM. No problem. This is in fact a perfectly standard and legitimate way to set up an encrypted channel between two fixed points.

However, suppose you have 1,000 people in an organization, and you need to be able to set up secure communications between any two of them. This turns out to be an unmanageable problem. You would need 499,500 separate keys—one for every possible pair of people. You also would have to make sure that each person always had the 999 keys necessary to communicate with the other people in the organization. Think of the administrative nightmare. Not only that, but this only allows for a single key for each pair of people—we haven't even thought about allowing for separate session keys! Figure 10-5 illustrates the number of keys needed for a group of seven people where each person needs to communicate secretly with any other member of

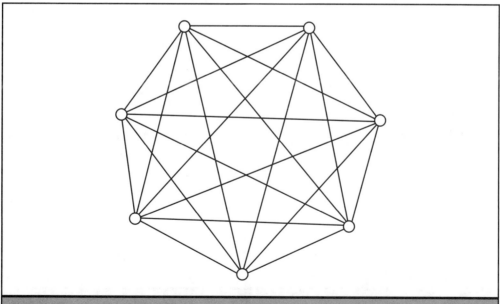

Figure 10-5. *Seven people sharing secret keys. Each person knows 6 keys, and there are 21 keys altogether*

the group. Each person must know 6 different keys, and there should be 21 keys available to the whole group.

Figure 10-6 is a table that indicates the number of keys required to support various size organizations implementing secret key cryptography.

Kerberos

Kerberos was invented at MIT to handle the problems of secret key management and distribution discussed above, where you have a large group of users belonging to a single group or institution. Kerberos is built around the concept of a secure, trusted key distribution center (KDC). Instead of having to know hundreds of secret keys, each user needs to know only *one* secret key—the key used to communicate with the KDC. The following scenario describes how Kerberos works.

Suppose Alice wants to communicate securely with Bob. Alice calls the KDC and says, "Hello KDC, Alice here. Please put me in touch with Bob."

The KDC selects a random session key *xxxxx* for the conversation between Alice and Bob, and makes a "ticket" that Alice will later give to Bob. This ticket says "Hi Bob, KDC here. The person giving you this ticket is Alice. Please use this session key *xxxxx* to talk to her." Interestingly enough, this ticket is encrypted with a secret key that only Bob and the KDC share. Let's call this ticket ENCRYPTED_TICKET_KDC_TO_BOB.

The message the KDC sends to Alice is encrypted with Alice's secret key that only Alice and the KDC share. It says, "Hello Alice, KDC here. Please use the session key *xxxxx* to talk to Bob. You'll need to introduce yourself by giving him this ticket from me—ENCRYPTED_TICKET_KDC_TO_BOB."

Alice decrypts the reply from the KDC, and recovers the session key *xxxxx* and the ticket to give to Bob. She can't make heads or tails of the ticket, since it's encrypted with the secret key that only Bob and the KDC know.

Alice then calls Bob and says, "Hi Bob, Alice here. The KDC gave me this ticket to give to you—ENCRYPTED_TICKET_KDC_TO_BOB."

Number of People	Each Person Must Know	Total Number of Keys
10	9	45
25	24	300
50	49	1,225
100	99	4,950
1,000	999	499,500
x	$x-1$	$\dfrac{x^2-x}{2}$

Figure 10-6.   *The management burden of secret key encryption*

Bob decrypts the ticket, knowing that only the KDC could have prepared it using the password he shares with it, and recovers Alice's name and the session key *xxxxx*.

From this point on, Alice and Bob can securely communicate with each other using the session key *xxxxx*. Note that Kerberos offers authentication in addition to confidentiality. Bob knows that Alice must be who she says she is, because only the real Alice would be able to decrypt the shared session key issued by the KDC. Similarly, Alice knows that Bob is the real Bob, because only he would be able to make sense of the ticket issued by the KDC. The flow of information between the KDC, Bob, and Alice is illustrated in Figure 10-7.

There are some additional wrinkles for added security, but this illustration gives the basic idea of how Kerberos works. By the way, the encryption method used in Kerberos is DES.

The centralized authority model of Kerberos means that we can easily add a new user, and conversely, if we need to remove a user, all we have to do is update the key distribution center, and instantly nobody will be able to set up any new connections to the now ex-user.

But what do we do if we want to establish random connections between any two people on the planet? For very large organizations, Kerberos can handle the volume by replicating KDCs and breaking up the organization into zones, but it was not intended to scale up to Internet size. Besides, there is no central authority on the worldwide Internet.

This brings us to the most amazing topic in cryptography—public key/private key cryptography embodied by Diffie-Hellman key exchange and the RSA algorithm.

Public Key/Private Key Cryptography

Up to now, you have seen how two parties who wish to communicate confidentially can either exchange keys through a physical distribution method or use a key distribution center. But instead, what if you were told that there was a way for two people, without any prior preparation, to establish a secret session key across a crowded room by holding up messages written on signs for all to see? Exactly such a method was discovered by Whitfield Diffie and Martin Hellman at Stanford University, and published in 1976.

The Diffie-Hellman Key-Exchange Algorithm

There's no real way to explain this without resorting to a bit of mathematics. Readers who are not interested in the math should skip ahead. Those who wish to explore this topic further should consult the books in the reading list at the end of this chapter.

First, pick a large prime number P, and a small number r that is a primitive root of P. (This just means that the numbers $r^1, r^2, r^3, \dots r^{P-1}$ are all different modulo P.) The numbers P and r are completely public. Somebody at the side could come up with P and r, and hold them up on a sign for everybody to see.

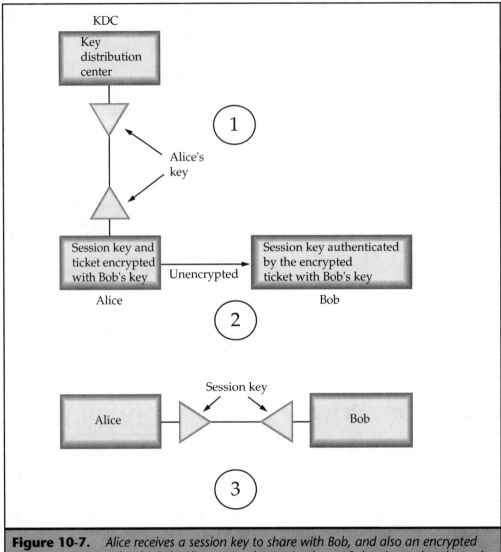

Figure 10-7. *Alice receives a session key to share with Bob, and also an encrypted ticket for Bob. Alice routes the session key to Bob, who authenticates it came from the KDC using his secret key*

Next, Alice picks a secret number A, and Bob picks a secret number B, both of which are in the range from 1 to P–1.

Alice keeps A secret, but she calculates the number $\alpha = r^A$ modulo P and writes it on a sign and holds it up.

Similarly, Bob keeps B secret, but he calculates $\beta = r^B$ modulo P, writes it on his sign, and holds it up for everybody to see.

Alice now computes β^A modulo P, and Bob computes α^B modulo P. These are both the same number, r^{AB} modulo P. This is their shared secret.

Diffie-Hellman works because it is mathematically very difficult to derive A if you only know P, r, and r^A, when P is a large enough number. The number P is usually chosen to be at least 500 bits long in order to make this computationally unfeasible.

What? A Key That's *500* Bits Long?!!

Yes. Welcome to public key cryptography. It works, but the keys are extremely long. This means public key cryptography calculations are somewhat time consuming. Therefore, you generally only use public key techniques to establish a regular DES, triple-DES, or IDEA secret key that you use from then on as a session key for the rest of your conversation.

Diffie-Hellman—Confidentiality Without Authentication

You know for sure that nobody can eavesdrop on the conversation you're having with the other person because you have an ironclad shared secret, but with Diffie-Hellman all by itself you can't be sure who it is that you're talking to! Consider this. If the room is so crowded Alice and Bob can't see each other and they can only see the sign being held up above a sea of heads, then all they know is that they have exchanged a shared secret with *someone*.

If there is a partition in the center of the room, there could be an impostor sending messages between Bob and Alice. By acting as a "man in the middle," this impostor will be able to freely communicate with both Alice and Bob, having exchanged one session key with Bob, and a different key with Alice. By relaying the information sent from Alice to Bob, the impostor has the opportunity to record everything that is said, and even can introduce false messages. This is referred to as the "man-in-the-middle" attack.

For this reason, Diffie-Hellman is usually used in conjunction with some sort of authentication scheme to make sure that the person you're exchanging the secret with really is the one you think you are talking to.

RSA—Public Key/Private Key

A further remarkable discovery in the domain of public key cryptography was made by Ron Rivest, Adi Shamir, and Len Adleman at MIT, and published in 1978, two years after Diffie-Hellman. When most people discuss public key/private key encryption, they usually are referring to the RSA algorithm. RSA encryption has the truly remarkable property that it operates using a *pair* of keys. Whatever you encrypt with one of the keys can only be decrypted using the other key.

The normal way that RSA is used is that each person generates a pair of RSA keys, keeps one of them secret (the private key), and then publishes the other key (the public key).

Mutual Authentication and Confidentiality Using RSA

Because of its remarkable properties, RSA can be used for either authentication or encryption, or both. Let's look closer.

Alice Sends Bob a Secret Little RSA Note

Let's have a little fun exploring the ins and outs of RSA with our friends Alice and Bob and a meddler named Newman.

Suppose Alice looks up Bob's public key and uses it to encrypt the message "Call me Darling, signed Alice." She can be sure that only Bob can understand this message, since once she has encrypted it, only Bob can decrypt it using his private key. When Bob gets the message, he decrypts it with his private key, and breaks into a smile. He encrypts the message "Alice, Darling! Love, Bob" using Alice's public key, and sends it back. Only Alice can decrypt the reply, again using her private key.

Spot any problem with the above scenario? Does Alice always smile when she gets Bob's reply? The answer is only "probably." *Anyone* could have sent the first message! It could have been Newman, playing a trick on Bob to get him to declare his love for Alice.

We didn't authenticate the sender as Alice. To fix this, Alice would first prepare her message "Call me Darling" by encrypting it with her private key, thus signing it. She would then send "Bob, the attached is from me, Alice ['Call me Darling' message encrypted with Alice's private key]", all encrypted with Bob's public key. Bob would decrypt the outer message using his private key, see the message saying the attachment was from Alice, and then decrypt the attachment using Alice's public key. Only Alice could have prepared the attachment, and only Bob could have understood the message. Bob replies enthusiastically. Is Alice guaranteed to smile when she gets Bob's reply?

Again, the answer is only "probably," because how do we know that the message "Call me Darling" that Alice encrypted with her private key was intended by Alice to go with that particular outer message addressed to Bob? It might have been sent earlier to Newman! Newman might be playing a trick on Bob by resending the attachment, making it seem as if it came directly from Alice.

To solve this last problem, all Alice needs to do is to put a timestamp and serial number on the outside envelope header part that is only encrypted with Bob's public key, and then repeat the text of the entire outside envelope header—timestamp, serial number, salutation, and all—at the beginning of the inner attachment encrypted with Alice's private key. Then Bob could fully authenticate that the envelope header matched the contents and came directly from Alice to him. He can then reply in full confidence, and using the same technique, to Alice. In this example, we have used RSA to handle both authentication and privacy.

Using RSA, if all we want to do is make a message private, we encrypt it using the public key of the recipient. Only the recipient can make sense of the message. If all we

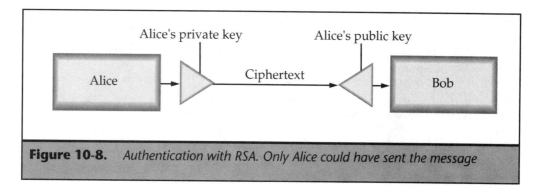

Figure 10-8.   *Authentication with RSA. Only Alice could have sent the message*

want to do is authenticate the identity of the sender, we encrypt the message using the private key of the sender. Anyone can decrypt the message using the public key of the sender, but only someone knowing the private key of the sender could have sent the message. Figures 10-8 and 10-9 illustrate these concepts. In both cases Alice sends a message to Bob. In Figure 10-8, Alice could be the only sender, using her private key, but anyone—even Newman!—could read it using her public key. In Figure 10-9, anyone could have sent the message using Bob's public key (again, even Newman could have sent it), but only Bob can read it using his private key.

The problems we had setting up a secure protocol for Alice and Bob to communicate without Newman's interference highlights the intricacies of designing a secure system, even using ironclad cryptographic algorithms.

Reducing the Effort Required to Send Messages with RSA

Since RSA keys typically start at 500 bits long and often are as big as 2,000 bits, and since working with RSA keys takes a *lot* of calculating, we may want to reduce the amount of data we encrypt using the RSA process.

Because of this, the way we would normally send a message would be to pick a random DES, triple-DES, or IDEA session key, and then use RSA techniques (perhaps

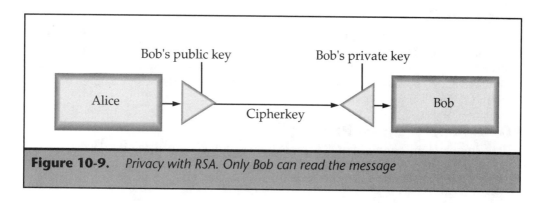

Figure 10-9.   *Privacy with RSA. Only Bob can read the message*

along the lines of how Alice ended up sending her last and most secure note to Bob) to send only a very short note containing the *session key* to the recipient, followed by the full text of the message encrypted under regular old DES, triple-DES, or IDEA and using the session key.

The recipient uses his or her own private key to open the RSA envelope and see who the alleged sender is. Using the sender's public key, the recipient opens and authenticates the inner attachment and recovers the session key. At this point the text of the message itself can be decrypted at high speed using the session key and regular secret key decryption.

Message Digest Functions

What if you only want to prove you sent a message that anybody could read?

To do this, you need to use what is called a *message digest* function. The most famous of these are MD5 written by Ron Rivest (the R in RSA), and the Secure Hash Algorithm (SHA) developed by the National Institute of Standards and Technology and based upon MD4 (also by Ron Rivest).

The idea is that you feed a message of any size into the function, and out pops a fixed length *digest*. MD5 produces a 128-bit digest, and SHA produces a 160-bit digest. The digest has the property that if you change even a single bit of the message that you put in, the digest will change in an unpredictable way. Each bit of the input object has an influence on each bit of the digest output. You can think of the digest as a kind of a digital fingerprint of the input message.

Digital Signatures

OK, so how can you sign a document to prove it came from you and has not been altered in any way?

To do this, you send the message in plain text between clearly defined *bookmarks*, and follow that by the digest of the text encrypted with your private key. If the receiver wants to authenticate that the message came from you and is intact, all he or she has to do is compute the message digest of the text between the bookmarks and compare that to the results obtained by using your public key to decrypt the original digest you sent with the message. If they match, the message is genuine.

Nonrepudiation

If you are in possession of a signed message from someone using public key/private key techniques that prove the origination of the sender, then you have achieved *nonrepudiation*—meaning that the sender cannot deny having sent the message. This is obviously very important, for example, if the message says "Please pay George one thousand dollars from my bank account."

PGP—Pretty Good Privacy

PGP, written by Phil Zimmermann, is more than pretty good privacy, it's darned excellent privacy!

PGP is an automated tool for the sending and receiving of both digitally signed and encrypted e-mail. The authentication process is handled using RSA public key/private key technology, with the user being free to select key lengths from 500 up to 2000 bits. The secret key or symmetric key encryption used for secret messages is IDEA, with its 128-bit keys, and the message digest algorithm used to accomplish digital signatures is MD5.

You may have received Internet e-mail messages that look like this:

```
-----BEGIN PGP SIGNED MESSAGE-----

This is the text of a message that is digitally signed.
You can prove that it came from me and is entirely intact.

-----BEGIN PGP SIGNATURE-----
Version: 2.6

lkjLKJKjKjL:kjkjKSFKs:LKJFKLDFJHDLKJDFKJDLKIuyjhgUHSFDDF
LKJDFKJDFLKJDFL:KJDFHJUEJHhjsdfijjjerilKdflkwejrashdrfljkerelkjare
KkdfjhkKHDFJHDHDjJJEIOREDLER:ELRE:RL:ERLE:lre;wleweHHdklds

-----END PGP SIGNATURE-----
```

If you had PGP, and you had the sender's public key in one of your PGP "key rings," you could automatically verify the authenticity and intact state of the message with the press of a key.

PGP and the Web of Trust

With Kerberos, or any other centralization key distributor, you have a central authority that you can trust to tell you whether another is bogus or genuine, and also set you up with a session key to talk to them. But what do you do on the Internet, where there is no centralized management?

PGP's solution is called the *web of trust*. The basic idea is that people keep *key rings* containing the public keys of other users. If you know Alice personally, then you can *sign* her public key, and thus assert that Alice's public key is genuine. If Bob receives the key that you have signed, and Bob trusts you, then he can also trust that Alice's key is genuine, even if he doesn't know Alice, since you signed Alice's key and Bob trusts you. Since Bob knows you, he will sign your public key, vouching for the fact that it really is your key. Thus there is an expanding web of trust where someone that knows Bob can trust Alice's key since Bob is vouching for you and you are vouching for Alice.

In this fashion you have people signing other people's keys, who have in turn signed yet other person's keys, and so on. Of course, there is also the concept of degree of trust. You are much more likely to trust a key that is directly signed by many people you know, rather than one signed by a person whose key is signed by someone one of your friends' cousin's wife's brother is vouching for.

People often make their PGP public keys available through other means, for example, by publishing them over the Internet on their companies' Web servers.

Thus PGP is the most widely used technique on the chaotic worldwide Internet to authenticate both the identity of the sender and the integrity of an e-mail message or to encrypt e-mail. Authentication is achieved using RSA to encrypt an MD5 message digest of the e-mail using the private key of the sender. Encrypted messages are sent by encrypting the e-mail message using the IDEA secret key algorithm, and then packaging the encrypted message with the IDEA key encrypted with the public key of the recipient.

Electronic Commerce on the Internet

The ability to conduct business on the Internet has been widely discussed in the news. The following paragraphs are intended to help the reader understand the technologies incorporated in setting up secure transactions over the Internet.

Many consider Netscape Communications, Inc. to be the leading technology provider for Internet commerce. Indeed, a great many of the news articles on Internet commerce have centered around Netscape's products. Therefore, the following discussion uses Netscape's implementation of cryptography as an example of how transactions may be conducted on the Internet.

Netscape accomplishes its encryption with a combination of RSA and secret key techniques. First, the public keys of a selected few certification authorities are built into the Netscape browser. If a business wishes to open itself up for secure access to Netscape users, it first must obtain an electronic certificate from one of these authorities. When it does this, it receives an RSA key pair, whose public key is digitally signed by the certification authority.

As an individual, when you use Netscape to connect to the company's Web server, it first responds by sending its certificate, which you can easily verify from the signature of the certification authority that is built into your Netscape browser. This authentication verifies that you are not communicating with a false business masquerading as somebody else on the Internet. After all, if you are about to give your credit card number to somebody over the Internet, you had better know who you are talking to.

Once you are satisfied that you really are talking to the company you want to do business with, you enter into a Diffie-Hellman–style key exchange to establish a secret session key to be used for the remainder of your conversation with the server. At this point you should be free to order your merchandise and give your credit card number knowing that the conversation you are having with the server at the other end is confidential. This protocol is called *Secure Sockets Layer* (SSL).

Using RSA to Improve the Security of Credit Card Transactions

One of the biggest problems surrounding the security of credit card transactions is that once your card number and expiration date have been obtained by a credit card thief, that person can order things over the telephone, charging these purchases to your credit card. Because the fraud level is so high in this type of transaction, the credit card companies actually charge businesses a significantly higher processing fee for "card not present" transactions than for transactions where the customer physically presents the card.

One method in use today implements a registration process where you register your encrypted credit card numbers with a transaction exchange broker. All communications with the broker can be authenticated and encrypted by both buyer and merchant.

After accessing the merchant's Web server, you can determine that you want to buy something. The merchant sends you an authenticated order ticket. You then respond with a positive response and a preferred method of payment containing an encrypted credit card authorization token for the broker and send it back to the merchant. The merchant can't figure out what you sent back because it's encrypted.

The merchant then packs this up, along with his own original order ticket message, which he also encrypts using the broker's public key, and sends the package of both messages to the broker. They decrypt everything, verify that both parties agree on the items and their price, and then contact the credit card company over leased phone lines to have the transaction authorized. Upon receiving the OK from the credit card company, the broker approves the sale to the merchant. Because all communications involving payment details are encrypted, there is no opportunity for eavesdroppers to commit fraud.

Notice that card details are never divulged to the merchant. This means the buyer no longer has to worry about the merchant or their employees selling credit card numbers out the back door. The credit card companies are happy because the opportunity for fraud has been drastically reduced—in fact, due to the much lower risk, the credit card companies actually charge lower transaction processing fees.

Summary

We hope this chapter helped you understand the fundamental concepts of network-based authentication and encryption. You should be able to understand common terms and concepts and the two basic algorithms used today: secret key and public key/private key. If you want to read more about these topics, please refer to the reading selection that follows.

Cryptography Reading List

1. *Applied Cryptography, Protocols, Algorithms, and Source Code in C (Second Edition)* by Bruce Schneier (John Wiley & Sons, 1995).

2. *Network Security: Data and Voice Communications* by Fred Simonds (McGraw-Hill, 1995).

3. *Network Security: Private Communication in a Public World* by Charlie Kaufman, Radia Perlman, and Mike Spencer (Prentice-Hall, 1995).

4. *Network and Internetwork Security: Principles and Practice* by William Stallings (Prentice-Hall, 1995).

5. *Security in Computing* by Charles P. Pfleeger (Prentice-Hall, 1988).

6. *PGP: Pretty Good Privacy* by Simson Garfinkel (O'Reilly & Associates, 1995).

7. *Firewalls and Internet Security: Repelling the Wily Hacker* by William R. Cheswick and Steven M. Bellovin (Addison-Wesley, 1994).

8. *Practical Unix Security* by Simson Garfinkel and Gene Spafford (O'Reilly & Associates, 1996).

CHAPTER ELEVEN

Computer Viruses and "Wildlife"

Back in the early days of computing, one of the original Mark II computers failed for no apparent reason. After some time spent checking and testing, technicians found the cause: a moth was stuck in the inner workings of the computer. This incident gave birth to the term "bug," which is used to this day to describe computer problems and glitches.

While bugs in computer programs and hardware may not be pleasant, there are other kinds of computer "bugs" that could be even more hazardous to the health of your computer and network. These are *viruses*—programs specifically designed to damage both your computer and the programs that run on them.

Even those who know little about computers have heard about these "nasty programs" with names like Friday the 13th, Michelangelo, Stoned, or Pakistani Brain. These are just a few of the many viruses in existence today, and there are literally thousands of different viral "strains." These numbers are growing every day, and recent studies, such as one conducted by Ernst and Young, point to the increasing threat of viruses and related "malware" programs.

The purpose of this chapter is to introduce you to the world of computer viruses: what they are, what they can do to your computer hardware and programs, the different kinds of viruses, and how you can keep your computer safe from them.

The need to understand and control the threat of viruses is especially important since a network, which can contain hundreds of computers, can be disrupted or even disabled by a computer virus. As a result, any discussion of network data integrity and security must give attention to viruses.

What Is a Computer Virus?

Computer viruses are programs that not only cause destruction to your computer but also can spread to, or infect, other systems with which they come into contact. *Virus*, which in Latin means poison, is an appropriate name since viruses act much like their biological counterparts, which infect cells and then spread their infection elsewhere. According to the dictionary, a virus is "a computer program usually hidden within another seemingly innocuous program that produces copies of itself and inserts them into other programs and that usually performs a malicious action . . ."

In a general sense, viruses are computer programs that run, like ordinary software, off the CPU, but have the additional ability to replicate, or make copies of themselves. A virus need not necessarily be destructive; some are more like innocent pranks, for example, merely displaying an amusing message. Destructive viruses and related destructive programs are called *malware.*

Unlike biological viruses, which attack living things and make them sick, computer viruses wreak havoc on your network or system. Some of the things a virus can do include reformatting your hard disk (wiping out all your data), erasing programs and files (which may be lost forever), adding garbage to files (effectively destroying them), or destroying your disk directories and FAT tables so that you can no longer use them to locate your files. Others print annoying messages such as "Jason

Lives," or "Disk Killer," or cause letters to fall off the screen, balls to bounce around your screen knocking away text, or an ambulance car to race across the bottom of your screen. As intriguing as these may seem, if you get hit with one, you won't think that it is very funny.

Computer viruses are similar to biological ones in another way as well. Aside from spreading to and infecting other systems, computer viruses also can mutate or evolve into variants to escape detection by various antivirus programs. For instance, the well-known Jerusalem virus, first discovered at Jerusalem's Hebrew University in 1987, has been modified to produce about a dozen "relatives," including Frere Jacques, Payday, and Fu Manchu.

Even though viruses are simply computer code (programs), they give the impression of being "alive" because they can do a lot more than simply crunch numbers or display something onscreen. They have within their binary bits the ability to do damage to computer hardware and software, to evade detection, and to spread their influence elsewhere. There are other kinds of destructive computer programs, such as *worms*, *Trojan horses*, and *logic bombs*, which are often viewed as being in the same category as viruses, although they are technically different.

Where Did Viruses Come From?

Viruses are the creation of computer hackers who wanted to prove that it was possible to write programs that could not only disrupt and damage computers, but also spread their destruction to other systems. In the 1940s, John von Neumann first noted that programs could be made to reproduce themselves and increase in size. There was little interest in his paper, "Theory and Organization of Complicated Automata," since computers were not yet in wide use, and the discussion was considered basically theoretical at the time. Some years later, in the 1950s, a group of scientists at Bell Laboratories began experimenting with a type of game in which one side's organisms (computer code) fought again the opponent's organisms. The side with the most organisms remaining was the winner of these "Core War" games.

Later on, in the 1960s, John Conway developed "living" software that could replicate itself. As the idea of "living" programs caught on over the years, the challenge of creating virus-type programs became widespread in the academic and research community, and students began coming up with all kinds of related programs, usually for harmless fun. This type of "biological computer" gaming later spread to other research centers at MIT and Xerox's PARC research center, and was largely kept a secret.

Throughout the 1970s, hackers made advances in these kinds of programs, giving them the power to do greater damage. However, actual virus attacks were still rare. At around the same time, computer crime was on the increase, including breaking into private accounts and making illegal bank transfers. By the 1980s, with the advent of the PC, viruses finally came onto the scene as a real threat.

One of the first documented viruses was written in 1983 by Fred Cohen, a University of Southern California student who wrote a program that, when installed on a hard disk, could replicate and expand itself and essentially make the computer "self-destruct." In 1985, one of the first malware programs was offered to the public, through electronic bulletin boards. Early malware programs included the Trojan horses NUKE-LA and EGABTR, as well as a number of other "traditional" viruses.

The year 1986 brought Ralf Burger's VIRDEM virus, and by 1987, dozens of viruses had emerged, with Pakistani Brain and Lehigh being among the most prevalent ones. The Pakistani Brain virus originated at the University of Delaware, while Lehigh, logically, came from Lehigh University. The following year, the Stoned virus arrived, followed in 1989 by the Dark Avenger virus. In just a few years, infections of computer systems had reached epidemic proportions, and currently there are hundreds, even thousands, of viruses throughout the world.

Public awareness of viruses increased with widespread publicity around Michelangelo, Friday the 13th (actually the Jerusalem), and others. The development of virus BBSs (bulletin boards), as well as virus-building toolkits, only increased worry over virus and malware attacks. The Internet takes these concerns to a much higher level.

The development of new virus technologies, such as those with stealth technologies or polymorphic capabilities to elude virus scanners, helped to bring virus technologies to a new level. The virus detection and protection industry has worked hard to keep up with the onslaught of viruses and to help protect the computing community, and it remains an ongoing battle.

How Widespread Are Viruses?

You may think that viruses are a limited phenomenon that only affects a few. This is not the case. Viruses are present throughout the world, and their numbers are increasing all the time. According to research conducted by Steve R. White, a researcher at the IBM Thomas J. Watson Research Center, currently there are 1,500 known viruses, and the number is increasing exponentially. It's estimated that by the year 2000, there will be 8,500,000 different computer virus strains in existence for IBM-PC and compatible machines. However, it is reassuring to know that only about 15 percent of all known virus strains actually exist in sufficient numbers to make them a threat.

Businesses are particularly concerned about the prevalence and effects of computer viruses. According to the National Computer Security Association (NCSA), the threat of viruses is growing. A recent survey of some 600,000 PCs and their users in the United States and Canada revealed that about 63 percent of the sites surveyed had experienced some kind of attack by viruses, and that 9 percent of these caused major problems. In addition, according to a recent Ernst and Young study, seven out of every ten companies surveyed experienced some kind of virus attack or problem over the past year. The incidence of virus and virus-related problems are cropping up especially in facilities that accommodate a large number of users.

The prevention, detection, and control of viruses and related destructive programs have been given a greater priority than ever before.

How Do Viruses Work?

There is, understandably, a great deal of fascination with viruses and how they work. Unlike ordinary software, which seems merely to follow instructions to perform some task or manipulate some system component, viruses are more interesting in that they take on the characteristics of a living phenomenon, which has a character and personality of its own. The fact that these programs are not written by teams of programmers in office complexes, but rather by hackers, only adds to their mystique.

It is therefore important to separate fact from fiction and describe in detail how virus programs work. It was mentioned previously that they are simply computer programs that work in a different way from normal, "clean" software. The destructive aspect makes the difference.

First, it is important to know that computer viruses are programs, and that they run on a computer just like your spreadsheet or database. In fact, viruses must be written for a certain processor (or processor family), and in general, for a certain type of operating system. As a result, if a virus is written for a PC or compatible running DOS on an Intel processor, it will not run on an Apple Macintosh. Most viruses are specific to a CPU and operating system, since they use functions and hardware routines that are unique to that configuration.

A virus could be said to exhibit several characteristics or features: infection, mutation, triggering, damage, and advanced features (stealth and polymorphism, for example). Each of these is a topic in itself.

Infection

An important component of any computer virus is how it infects a computer system. In fact, infection method is used to categorize the two main kinds of viruses: boot sector and file infector viruses.

Boot Sector Viruses

Boot sector viruses attack the boot sector of floppy disks and hard disks. The boot sector is where most of the instructions for powering-on or booting up the system are stored, and all disks, whether bootable or not, have one. The main method of infection occurs when a computer is booted through a boot disk, typically a floppy disk, whose boot sector is infected. See Figure 11-1 for a diagram illustrating how boot sector viruses work.

This boot sector is typically the first sector on a hard disk (or floppy disk), and is critical in that operations such as the loading of the operating system and the partitioning of a hard disk are initiated from this sector. In general, the boot sector gets

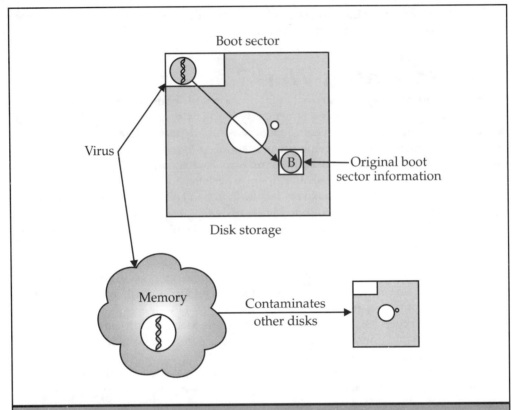

Boot sector

Virus

Original boot
sector information

Disk storage

Memory

Contaminates
other disks

Figure 11-1. *A boot sector virus overwrites and relocates the original boot sector. The virus also infects the memory, which can then spread the virus to other floppy disks*

control of a CPU before any other programs are run. Targeting the boot sector of a diskette is important since it allows the virus to immediately take control of a system.

The virus code replaces the original boot sector and puts its virus code in that location, which is typically about 512 bytes in size. Since this is a rather small amount of space, often the virus will locate other parts of the disk, mark them as "bad," and write additional virus code there. The original boot sector information, which is still vital to the functioning of the machine, is then placed in another area. What makes a boot sector virus work is that when DOS needs to access this original boot data, the virus redirects it to the new location where it is stored, without revealing that the new information has been moved.

In addition, part of the virus remains in memory, in order to ensure continued infection. If a new, noninfected diskette is placed into the machine's drives, the virus is written to the diskette. So, if many floppy disks pass through the system's drives through the normal course of use, there is the potential for infecting many diskettes, and when these are used in clean, uninfected computers, the process starts all over again.

One of the most prevalent boot sector viruses is the Pakistani Brain, which works by first moving the original boot information to another part of the disk, after which it copies itself into the boot sector and other vacant parts of the disk.

As a result, information concerning your hard disk's partition and file allocation tables are written over, causing you to lose access to your files. The next time the computer is booted up, the virus takes full control of the system, unleashing its destruction in the form of making incorrect accesses to the disk, modifying program requests, and making changes to memory.

Pakistani Brain and other boot sector viruses are remarkable not only in how they overtake a computer system, but also in how they protect themselves. The virus has a mechanism that will innocently display the original, correct boot sector data instead of its own virus code. If you try to remove or change the code, the virus will simply self-destruct, removing all traces of itself. Strangely enough, while Pakistani Brain has many features for escaping detection, it also frequently advertises its presence by using (C)BRAIN as its diskette volume label.

Boot sector viruses are also effective transmitters of infection. Any disk that is used in the drive of an infected computer is instantly contaminated, and when that disk is put into yet another system, the cycle continues.

Any attempt to remove this kind of virus from a disk is difficult, because the virus code may still exist in the system, hiding in inaccessible memory areas, even though the system checks out perfectly "clean."

Stoned is another widespread boot sector virus, which displays the message "Your PC is stoned—LEGALIZE MARIJUANA" in large letters, while at the same time destroying your directories and file allocation tables, making it impossible to access the files on your hard disk or floppy. Some of the boot sector viruses currently existing include the following:

BOUNCING BALL   A ball bounces around the screen, knocking off data. Also, the boot sector is overwritten by the virus. As a result, there are both visual effects and more serious system-wide effects from this kind of virus. The boot sector infection will affect the overall functioning of the system.

CHINESE FISH   This virus from Taiwan overwrites boot sectors and displays an identifying message.

DEVIL'S DANCE   This virus will infect all .COM files on a disk and overwrite the first sector of the hard disk when a warm boot is done. A message will also be displayed reading, "Have you ever danced under the weak light of the moon? Pray for your disk! The_Joker.... Ha Ha Ha Ha."

File Viruses

File viruses differ in that they attack the files on your disks. They attach themselves to executable files (usually .COM and .EXE) and wait until the program is run, at which point it starts working. The virus will attempt to infect other files, make itself memory resident, and proceed to do one of many other unpleasant things to your system. After the virus has finished its work, the regular program will execute, making it seem as though everything is fine.

How does a file virus work? The basic concept is that, unlike a boot sector virus, it does not move itself to a boot sector on a disk. Instead, it works by attaching, or appending, itself to executable files such as those with the extensions .EXE and .COM. There are three main kinds of file viruses: overwriting, pre- and post-pending, and companion file infectors. Each works in a different way (see Figure 11-2).

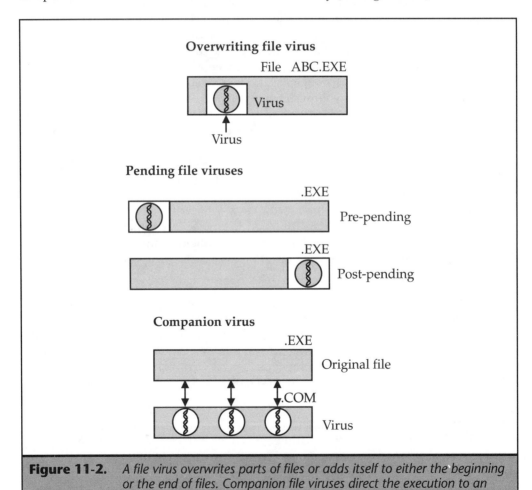

Figure 11-2. *A file virus overwrites parts of files or adds itself to either the beginning or the end of files. Companion file viruses direct the execution to an alternate "virus" file*

The *overwriting file infector* simply overwrites its code over a portion of the original program's code. This obviously can totally destroy the previous program. As an example, suppose you have a copy of a word processor that you wanted to infect. Once the code was written over, and especially if it is the beginning parts of the executable file, it would totally destroy the original program. Run the file, and the virus code will execute, but it is unlikely that the original program will ever work properly (or at all) again.

In general, while some overwriting file infectors will destroy the original program, some newer forms such as those using stealth technology, will attempt to hide its presence during execution by overwriting parts of the code that do not affect the overall running of the host program. As a result, after the virus code is run, then the program will execute, fooling the user into thinking that the virus is not really there. But it is.

One advantage to overwriting file viruses is that it does not change the length of the file, making the original file appear to be perfectly normal. However, any virus scanner or virus detection program can usually detect the presence of virus code that has been overwritten into a program.

A *pre-pending file virus* adds itself to the beginning of an executable file, while the *post-pending* type tacks the additional code onto the end of the file. It is generally easier to create (program) a post-pending file virus than a pre-pending one, but the final result is the same—the file now contains both the program code and the virus code.

The third type, *companion file virus*, creates, for an .EXE file, a corresponding .COM file that holds virus code. When someone runs the .EXE file, control is transferred to the hidden .COM file, which then will run the virus code. Upon completion, control will then return to the .EXE file, so that the user will not suspect anything is wrong. In effect, a companion file virus is much like a Trojan horse, which displays a harmless program while doing its destruction in the background.

There are two types of file infectors: *resident* and *non-resident file infectors*. A resident file infector stays in the memory of a machine, even after the execution of a virus file has been completed. This is usually accomplished through the use of a terminate and stay resident (TSR) function, or by putting itself in a place in memory that will not be used by other programs. This allows the virus to be continually active, able to infect files any time they are worked on (open, closed, or run).

A nonresident file infector (sometimes called a direct program infector) is less dangerous than its "resident" cousin. In effect, it only does its work of infection while the host file is being run. This gives it more limited opportunities for multiple infections. Non-resident file infectors can infect as much as an entire disk, or as little as a single directory, or file.

One widespread file virus, the Lehigh virus, works by attaching itself to COMMAND.COM (an important DOS file), in an area used as a run-time stack, and normally filled with zeroes. Once a computer is infected, the virus then sets out to attach copies of itself to the COMMAND.COM on any floppy disk in which it comes into contact. When you use this infected disk in a clean computer, it again infects that system, until four copies are infected in total. Then Lehigh begins to erase parts of your hard disk, rendering them unusable. The following are some of the file viruses that exist and what they can do to your system.

- **982** A program infector that erases CMOS RAM, making disks no longer accessible.

- **4096** This causes your computer to hang up.

- **Advent** The virus starts on Advent Sunday and adds one more candle each following Sunday. It displays "Merry Christmas" and plays "Oh Tannenbaum."

- **Amoeba** This virus writes over low-level tracks on a hard disk, with flashing messages to accompany it. A quote is placed in the overwritten sectors of the disk.

- **Autumn Leaves** This virus makes the letters on the screen fall down, accompanied by clicking noises.

- **Cancer** Cancer infects a program again and again, until it can no longer be loaded.

- **Datacrime la** This will announce its presence, then proceed to reformat the hard disk, and finally beeps continuously and endlessly.

There are many different varieties and mutations of these viruses that are out in the "wild."

Mutation

One goal of viruses is to escape detection from virus scanners and other antivirus software. How can this be accomplished? By emulating their biological counterparts and making variants (mutations) of themselves to confuse virus scanners and related software, and thereby escape detection.

A virus that creates copies of itself, yet whose "children" are mutated, different in key ways from the parent, is called a *polymorphic virus*. This technique is used to help create new strains of a virus that cannot be easily detected by virus scanners. There are even programs called *mutation engines* that can turn an ordinary virus into a polymorphic one. Figure 11-3 shows how mutation occurs in computer viruses.

Triggering

A virus does its "dirty work" as soon as it is set in motion. In order to get started, some kind of trigger must be designed and then set off. The most obvious kinds of triggers are those that are based on a certain date, such as Friday the 13th or March 6 (Michelangelo's birthday). Other triggers can be more subtle, such as after a program is run a certain number of times, or after a file virus has been copied from system to system a certain number of times.

The use of a trigger is also prevalent in bombs, which will be described later in this chapter.

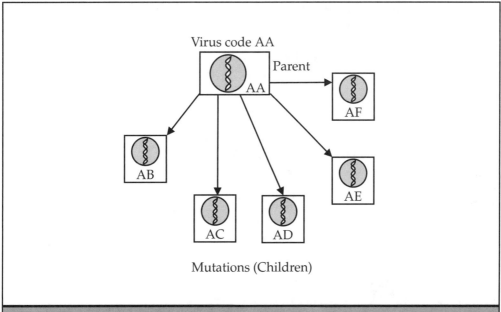

Figure 11-3. *A virus can create similar, yet different, "strains" of itself, which are then spread to other systems*

Damage

Alas, here is the part that worries most people. There are various forms of damage, from the innocuous to the deadly. This is because, among the thousands of viruses currently existing, there are many different kinds of damage that can be caused by viruses. These include the following.

Visual and Audio Effects

Messages are displayed to the screen, music is played, or graphical images are displayed to the screen. These can be cute, such as an ambulance car racing across your screen, or messages such as "Your PC is Stoned," or a smiling face, or the text on your screen falling down like leaves in autumn. There are some viruses that will play "Yankee Doodle," "Oh Tannenbaum," or a random selection from one of eight tunes. These may be amusing and harmless in themselves, but they could be masking behind-the-scenes destruction. However, some viruses actually do only these things. Others are a combination of some visual/audio effects and destruction.

Changes to Data

This may be more of a problem than you think. The virus can change some values in a file, which can cause problems that escape easy notice, although the effects can be damaging to the integrity of your data. There could be changes to figures in an accounting or spreadsheet file, which would be detrimental.

Deleting Files on a System

A virus can run rampant, deleting files and doing other related damage to your valuable information. A virus such as Jerusalem would delete any program you run on a Friday the 13th. Other viruses may erase sectors of a disk at random, or sectors of a file directory.

Destruction of the File System

Examples of damage in this category include overwriting normal, clean files with infected ones, effectively destroying previously stored information. Erasing or otherwise corrupting the FAT (file allocation table) can cause a loss of access to the files on a disk. Yet others will overwrite tracks on the hard disk, "hang" the system, completely reformat a hard disk (destroying the data), or prevent the booting up of your computer.

Don't Reformat!

Yet another ploy on the part of a virus writer is to get the user to panic and to do something drastic, such as reformat the system hard disk in an attempt to remove a virus. This is probably one of the worst things a person with an infected computer can do, and there are much more effective ways to both remove a virus and retrieve "lost" data.

Advanced Features

Computer viruses have evolved over time. The people who write viruses do so with the intent to escape detection for as long as possible. So, there are new strains of viruses designed to hide from virus scanners and antivirus software. Polymorphic and stealth viruses fall into this category.

A polymorphic virus, like its biological twin, can mutate into different strains, each new one slightly different from the ancestor. Each new strain differs in terms of the kind of coding scheme it uses to store and record the virus information. Since there are special strings of code that a virus scanner would look for to identify a particular virus, by changing the arrangement of how a virus is coded, it may be possible to escape detection by a virus scanner. This helps to protect the virus and keep it from being identified and, ultimately, removed from a disk.

A stealth virus is designed to keep its identity and location hidden from users and antivirus programs. A virus that announces its presence with visual and audio effects, such as "Your PC is Stoned," or "Type Happy Birthday Joshi," is easy to detect. These telltale messages make it clear that a virus exists and tells what kind of virus it is. One way to overcome this is to code any text into the program itself, so that a virus scanner cannot look into the file and immediately recognize the ASCII text stored there. Still other stealth techniques include the ability to hide the size of virus files, and also the existence of the files themselves, in order to escape detection.

Another stealth technique is to make a duplicate of clean, original information, and store it in a place that is accessible to the virus. When an antivirus program begins a search, the stealth virus will direct control to the original information while keeping its own identity and location a secret. As a result, the virus is free to continue on its path, doing whatever damage it had planned to do, while remaining undetected.

Other Computer Malware, or "Wildlife"

There are other kinds of viruses, or "living code," as they are sometimes called. You probably remember the case of Robert Morris, the Cornell University graduate student who wreaked havoc on hundreds of computer systems, all from a computer lab at Cornell. He sent a type of computer virus variant called a *worm* across the Internet, a network spanning over 60,000 computers. Traveling through the network, the worm made the computers run useless processes, in effect paralyzing their functions. Even though no data was destroyed, the effects of this mischief on thousands of computer systems ran into the millions of dollars and took enormous efforts to correct.

The term *virus* is often applied to any kind of "living code," but those in the field tend to separate viruses from other kinds of specialized destructive programs, often referred to as "malware," or "computer wildlife." So, it would be useful to go on a sort of "safari" and look at some of the other kinds of living software that can pose threats to your computer system or network. Figure 11-4 illustrates different types of computer malware.

Worms

A *worm* is a program that changes and destroys data like viruses but can also travel around and trigger damage from computer to computer through networks such as the Internet. A worm, after traveling to another computer system, can make many copies of itself, wasting enormous amounts of computer time, and can even bring an entire network of computers to a halt.

Creepers

Creepers are another term for worms, much like those set loose over the Internet. The name came from the message it displayed: "I'm the creeper, catch me if you can!"

Bombs

Bombs are similar to standard viruses in the damage they can do, but they differ in that they are set to go off at a certain date and/or time. Bombs have frequently been used by disgruntled employees to punish their boss or coworkers by destroying their computer data, and there have been cases where a ransom was demanded to avert an impending disaster.

Worm: Worms spread themselves to other computers through network links.

Bomb: Bombs are set to "detonate" on a trigger date or condition.

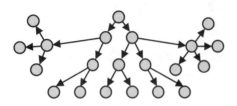

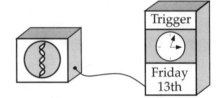

Trojan Horse: Trojan horses appear innocent, but the friendly visual or audio is designed to divert attention from the damage being done.

Trap Door: Trap doors allow someone to circumvent normal security procedures through a loophole left by an original system designer.

Game/Utility with nice graphics

Main security

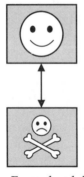

Erases hard disk
Destroys data
"Cleans out FAT"

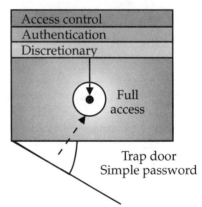

Trap door
Simple password

Figure 11-4. *The various types of computer malware*

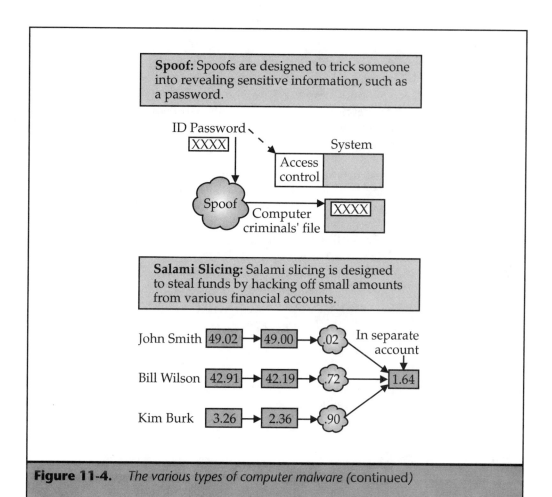

Figure 11-4. *The various types of computer malware* (continued)

Some viruses have a "bomb" element to them. The Joshi virus, for example, on January 5th prints the message "Type Happy Birthday Joshi" and will both lock up the system and seriously affect your hard disk unless "Happy Birthday Joshi" is typed. There has also been an increased awareness of the Jerusalem-B, which goes off every Friday the 13th and not only erases programs but also prints annoying black boxes to the screen.

What distinguishes a bomb from an ordinary virus is the "programmed trigger," which determines when the program is to spring into action. Once the program is triggered, the bomb can then do one of a multitude of different forms of damage to your system.

Trojan Horses

Trojan horses get their name from the wooden horse left outside the gates of Troy during the Trojan War. It appeared to be a peace offering, but instead was filled with scores of hostile Greek warriors. Computer Trojan horses work on much the same principle. A Trojan horse program usually appears quite harmless and innocent, and is disguised as a computer game, utility, or other routine program. When you run it, the Trojan horse goes to work keeping you engaged in the game or utility while it does damage in the background.

With a Trojan horse, destruction is often so well hidden that you have no idea serious damage is being done to your system. Examples of Trojan horses are programs that wreak havoc while you play "a nice game of chess," or a graphics enhancement program that erases programs while you admire a pretty graphics display. The following are some examples of Trojan horses.

12-Tricks

This Trojan horse, CORETEST.COM, is supposedly an innocent hard-disk speed diagnostic. In reality, it changes the FAT (file allocation tables) and then proceeds to reformat the hard disk.

AIDS

When this Trojan horse strikes, all directory entry names are encrypted, file extensions are changed, and free spaces are filled with blanks and line feed. This program tries to pass itself off as an "AIDS Information Diskette."

Trap Doors

Trap doors, sometimes known as back doors, are "easy entry points" to software, usually put in by system designers who use it to test or monitor the program without needing to go through all the security that has been implemented. For instance, a system designer might allow widespread access to a system using a single password, rather than needing to go through the many different layers of security that are implemented in the main program. What makes trap doors especially dangerous is that they are usually created for the use of the system designer and can offer full or wide-sweeping rights, giving a great deal of power to an illegal intruder who is granted access. Fortunately, most trap doors are taken out before a program is put into commercial use.

Spoofs

Spoofs are designed to trick someone into doing something on the system. For instance, a program might give a user the impression that he or she was accidentally logged out, and a login and password prompt would be displayed. An unsuspecting user would then type in his or her private login information, not to the system, but to someone who wants to record it and log in illegally.

Salami Slicing

No, this has nothing to do with delis and submarine sandwiches. It is a method by which tiny pieces of information are taken off computer accounts. A salami attack might take a few cents off someone's balance on a bank system, or change some numerical figures, and credit the difference to the intruder's account.

Bacteria

These are programs that rapidly replicate themselves and waste system resources in the process. They use up CPU time to create all these copies and disk space to store them. Eventually, much of the system's resources will be directed toward the reproduction of bacteria programs.

Rabbits

Rabbits are known to multiply rapidly, and so rabbit programs are those that make copies of themselves and spread throughout a system. Too many "baby rabbits" can clog up and effectively strangle a system.

Crabs

Crabs are programs that "eat away" at parts of the data or information displayed on a computer screen.

All of this sound interesting? Certainly, there is a lot of folklore and creativity associated with the whole realm of viruses and related malware programs. However, how can someone "catch" a virus? The next section will first describe the basics of how a system can become infected, and then some of the details of how a virus would invade parts of a computer system.

Catching a Virus

Catching a virus is easier than you may think. You can slip a floppy disk into the drive of an infected computer, and your disk can get "sick" instantly. Then, if you use your floppy in your own computer, you can easily infect your entire system (including your hard disk) as well.

Viruses are easily transmitted through "foreign" floppy disks. If someone gives you a disk with a program on it to try out, it could be infected. A computer service technician can pull out a diagnostic disk, which he had used on dozens of other computers previously, and use it on your system. That disk could very well have picked up viruses from one of those previous encounters. Public computer facilities, such as school computing labs and corporate facilities, can have viruses lurking in those PCs. While most shrink-wrapped commercial software is "clean," there have been cases where viruses have been found on those disks.

How do you protect yourself from the threat of computer viruses? One preventive measure is simply to keep unknown and questionable diskettes away from your computer. In addition, there are virus "scan" products that will check your floppy disks and hard disks for any evidence of viruses. So, if you have a questionable disk on your hands, you can simply scan it before using it.

You can also reduce your chances of infection by never loaning out program diskettes to anyone, and making it a rule to give out only copies, which you should promptly check for viruses or reformat upon return. Avoid letting other people use your system, since they may put infected diskettes into your drives, whether intentionally or by accident. Always boot from hard disks rather than floppies if you can. Finally, beware of programs that you download from BBS (bulletin board) systems and the Internet, since they could carry viruses.

Keeping Your Computer Well: An Overview

Antivirus software is designed to help prevent virus infections, scan for viruses on your system, remove viruses, and even give your system a preventive "vaccination" against virus attacks. While packages vary in their features, manner of operation, effectiveness, and suitability to your needs, these programs perform one or more of the following basic functions:

- ■ **Prevention** This feature is designed to keep viruses from infecting your system. Some of the techniques employed include preventing changes to executable (.COM and .EXE) files and sounding warnings if your file allocation tables or boot sectors are being changed, or if your hard disk is being readied for reformatting.

- ■ **Detection** This feature hunts for viruses on your disks and other parts of the system, and warns you if one is suspected to exist. By looking for the effects of a virus and also examining files and boot sectors, the telltale signs of a virus may be identified. The methods used include comparing the files to a preestablished algorithm or signature, or computing checksums (special numerical algorithms) for each file.

- ■ **Removal** This involves the removal of virus code from files and disks. One thing to keep in mind, however, is that it is frequently difficult to be sure if an entire virus infection has been removed, so frequently it is better to delete infected files and use a new, clean copy.

■ **Vaccination** Some antivirus software places special code into your executable (.COM and .EXE) files and then checks for changes in the signature or other irregularities when the program is run.

■ **Damage Control** Some antivirus programs try to minimize the damage caused by viruses. Preventive damage control includes giving you warnings about programs being placed into RAM, write-protecting your hard disk when new software is being run, and maintaining a copy of your file allocation table (FAT). The program may also save a copy of your CMOS memory (containing your SETUP information), in case it is wiped out by a virus.

Virus Scanning and Related Programs

There are several types of programs (or program techniques) for fighting the war on viruses. These are general categories of programs, and products marketed as "antivirus software" may contain one or more of these kinds of features. All of them are targeted toward the identification of viruses and/or the prevention of virus attacks.

One of the major tools in the fights against viruses and related programs is the virus scanner. Simply put, it allows for someone to go into a system and look for viruses, whether in the memory, hard disk, or on a floppy disk. In essence, it is like a detective spending time looking for key clues that will reveal the presence of a virus.

One of the main ways in which an antivirus scanner can find a virus is to look for *scan strings*, sometimes called *virus signatures*. These virus signatures are bytes of computer program code that uniquely identify a certain strain of a virus, and a virus scanner can search for this, or for other telltale segments of code.

This may seem like a rather straightforward process, but there are some issues that need to be addressed in relation to this operation. The important thing to note is that a virus scanner has a responsibility to its user (and purchaser) to be as accurate as possible.

Any reputable virus scanner should be able, to the best of its ability, to report any and all viruses that are located on that particular disk or system. In addition, it should avoid identifying false positives, such as looking for search strings that are common to many files, even those that do not in fact bear any kind of virus. This would identify the existence of a virus even if it is not there. Finally, because there are so many different strains of viruses, and new types and strains coming out all the time, it is important to be able to identify a wide range of viruses. It would not make sense to run one scan to look for boot sector viruses, another for file viruses, and yet another for those with stealth capabilities!

Getting back to virus scanners and search strings, a virus scanner is built to examine the code of a file (or boot sector), identify specific segments of code, and attempt to positively identify a virus. This string of information should be such that it is indicative of only one type of virus and is not found in ordinary files. The signature or string being searched for may not all reside in a particular location, or sequentially, nor does it have to be only one string of bytes. There are so many different variations that complicate the process.

A virus scanner determines what to look for by examining examples of virus code for, say, Stoned or Lehigh, and attempting to identify the unique strings that are clues to that virus's structure. Like biologists studying "living" viruses in a lab, computer virus researchers must study a virus code carefully to find ways to identify it "in the wild."

Of course, while virus researchers are out looking for ways to identify a virus, virus creators are also busy trying to outwit them. They find ways of rearranging code, down to the level of machine instructions, in an effort to accomplish the same damage, by changing the structure or sequence of the code to escape detection by scanners. A clever rearrangement will allow a virus scanner to pass over the code without identifying it as a virus. However, newer antivirus programs are clever enough to recognize these adjustments to the code and still flag a file as containing a virus.

A scanner program or antivirus program is also tested for its ability to actually find viruses and not come up with too many "false positives," or cases where a virus is not actually present but the scanner says there is one. This can cause undue frustration and panic on the part of someone who mistakenly thinks he or she has an infected disk. It would also waste a lot of time and cause aggravation to continually "find" viruses that are not really there.

A scanner program must also be up to date. Because new viruses are springing up all the time, and with mutation engines and polymorphic viruses constantly generating new strains, an outdated virus scanner will miss many new viruses, or label the finds as "unknown." It would be unfortunate if the virus is indeed known, but the virus software cannot identify or handle it properly. This could result in your computer becoming infected.

Integrity Checkers

Another class of antivirus program are *integrity checkers*. These are different from scanners in that they are designed to identify file and system changes based on the effect of viruses. Instead of looking to see whether virus code is present, they try to detect a virus based on what it does to a system.

Of course, a virus must be working and doing something for an integrity checker to work. This is one of the disadvantages of these programs, along with the fact that your system or network may already be infected by the time an integrity checker detects its presence. A dormant virus may escape the detection of an integrity checker.

A system integrity checker for viruses can compare the state of a file, for example, at one time to that at a later point in time. There are files on this integrity checker that hold information on the "original" condition of a file, whether file length and date/time or some more complex information such as a checksum. By comparing this stored information with a file's current state, it is possible to find out if the file has changed at all.

These kinds of programs can work either continuously or on a one-time basis. The continuous type will do this check each time a file is opened, for example. The one-time basis method will do this operation upon request by a user.

In general, integrity checkers can be very helpful in identifying changes in files. However, they can identify a more than desired number of "false positives," from a legitimate software upgrade, or from a change in a program's configuration. Because an integrity checker basically looks for changes in a file, it is less vulnerable to the effects of mutations and polymorphic viruses.

Behavior Blockers

The purpose of behavior blockers is to prevent damage by a virus. Instead of simply looking for or observing changes in files, it attempts to stop a virus dead in its tracks. If something funny or strange is about to happen, the behavior blocker will detect and warn the user. Some programs will attempt to confirm the activity before allowing it to proceed.

Sometimes a "suspected" activity is actually perfectly normal, so a "false alarm" is always possible. One file that calls another executable file could be the telltale sign of a companion virus, or it could be just an operation required by a certain software package. The user must then investigate the problem and decide what to do.

Another, more obvious virus-related problem might be the system-level request for a format of a hard disk. Of course, this is logical if someone just typed in a FORMAT command, but would be suspicious if it just came out of nowhere. A behavior blocker would identify and warn the user of any "impending doom" about to befall a system.

Virus Removal

Prevention of virus attacks is certainly important, but detecting already existing viruses by any of the methods described can stop them and prevent further damage. An effective regime of preventive measures and virus scanning would go a long way toward ensuring that your system is well. On the other hand, what happens if there is already a virus on your disk?

The obvious first thing to do is to remove the virus from the system—in other words, to disinfect it. There are a number of different ways to handle the removal of a virus, ranging from using DOS DEL or COPY to a commercial antivirus program.

Using DOS, one way to handle a virus, especially one attached to an executable file, is to delete it from the disk and then copy a clean version back to the disk. This is not 100 percent effective or foolproof, since the deletion merely removes the file from the FAT (file allocation table) and marks the previously used sectors as "available." The clean version that is then copied to the disk may not reside in the same sectors as the original infected file did, and the sectors that held the original infected file are not erased. However, since the old infected file will not be run in its infected form, it is generally a safe bet that the virus will not return.

In terms of boot sector viruses, the use of commands such as FDISK and SIGHS will help to restore the original boot information to the boot sector of your disk.

Disinfection programs, such as those featured as a part of many antivirus programs, must have information on how a particular virus works and then make changes to the disk (disinfect) as necessary. For a file virus, it needs to know how the virus operates, such as whether it appends virus code to the beginning or end of a file. The disinfection program then calculates where the virus code starts and ends, and where the program code should start and end. The virus code is removed from the file, the file is restored to its original form, and then the original sectors bearing the virus code are written over, to remove any possibility of it being used again. However, this process must be done very carefully, since if certain parts of the original file are inadvertently removed, the "cleaned" program may crash or simply not work properly again.

The stakes are higher with boot sector viruses, since a mistake in re-creating the boot sector and MBR (master boot record) can result not only in losing partitions, and even all the files on a hard disk, but the system may not boot at all! These problems can result if the displaced MBR information is taken from the wrong location or is led to the wrong place by the virus. The false MBR information would then be written back to the boot sector, effectively disabling the disk. Simultaneous infections by different viruses may further confuse an antivirus program that is looking to replace a boot sector with correct information but finds it in the wrong place. This could totally disable a hard disk.

Summary

Don't let any form of computer "wildlife" wreak havoc with your system! Now that you know what viruses are, what they can do, and how you can both prevent and manage virus problem, you have no excuse for letting your system become a haven for these dastardly computerized "bugs."

This chapter has offered a basic yet comprehensive introduction to the realm of viruses and living programs, all of which can be useful in understanding what viruses and related programs are, how they work, and how you can protect your systems from the onslaught of these computer-based, digital criminals.

CHAPTER TWELVE

Disaster Recovery Planning

Disaster recovery can be one of the most challenging operations you can encounter as a professional systems administrator. Following a disaster, you may not have your usual workplace to return to or any of the usual systems management tools you depend on to do your job. You might even have to do the work without your management team or people who work for you. How would you react if you were suddenly placed in a strange facility, without your normal working environment and team members, and then asked to perform difficult restore operations? Preparation is the key to succeeding when the odds are stacked against you.

Preparing for the Worst

As previously mentioned, there is no way to protect completely against every kind of threats to your data and systems, particularly large-scale environmental threats that can wipe out entire buildings. Therefore, it is prudent to think about what you would do in case such a disaster happens to you and you find yourself without any access to the network at your place of business. In the context of this book, disaster recovery planning is the process of determining what to do if catastrophe strikes your organization and you have to recover your network and its systems.

Unfortunately, disaster recovery planning is like exercising and dieting—much easier to think about than to do. With the amount of work most LAN administrators have, disaster recovery planning tends to get put off for some later time. One of the problems with disaster recovery planning for networks is trying to figure out where to start. This chapter provides an outline of the information you need in a disaster recovery plan and serves as a template for writing a plan. Armed with this knowledge, you can start budgeting time and resources for creating a comprehensive, usable disaster recovery plan.

Use Existing Resources

There may be resources available that you do not know about to help you plan for disasters. Large organizations sometimes have employees with job titles such as "disaster recovery planner" or "business continuity planner" assigned to the task of studying and planning to resume business functions following a catastrophe. Their jobs are not necessarily directed to restoring computer systems, but they certainly must know a lot about setting up real estate and services arrangements. If you have this type of resource within your organization, you can save a great deal of time by utilizing their skills and knowledge in your project.

Process, Not Product

Acquired skills require practice. It would be great to be able to pay a sum of money and become a jazz musician without practicing. It would also be fun to start downhill skiing on the steepest slopes without having to learn on shorter, gentler slopes. Like all things that need discipline and practice, recovering a network system after a disaster requires practice and analysis to be good at it and perform at a highly skilled level. Your current network probably took years to design and build; all of a sudden you will be asked to rebuild a network in a matter of days. This will take all the skill you have to succeed.

The mainframe environment has companies such as Comdisco and Sungard that provide hot-site services to resume processing of their customers' mainframe systems. Although these companies and services exist, they can't do their part without a great deal of work and preparation from their customers in structuring their systems and prioritizing the application systems that need rebuilding. Just because a hot-site provider has a room with a CPU does not mean they have the knowledge to make your systems work for you.

It's your data and your network. When you are called on to restore this stuff using new systems, spare parts, backup tapes, and any other pieces you need, the rest of your company will be counting on you to keep a cool head and make the best decisions possible. As much as you would like to buy a product that will do this for you, you can't. After all, nobody else knows your systems as well as you and your peers in your MIS organization. The pressure of trying to re-create a network from scratch when others, such as the president and CFO, are looking over your shoulder can be staggering; having a documented process to follow that you are familiar with can give you the vision you need to make it through the chaos.

Fortunately, you don't have to be a genius, but you do need to be well organized and disciplined. The problem with disasters is that they often surprise you, with little warning and no time to prepare. If you don't know what you are going to do in advance, you will probably wind up spinning your wheels trying to determine the best way to proceed. A prepared document can help avoid the additional pressure of explaining to others the reasons behind your decisions and defending yourself against second guessing and arguments.

Recovering from a disaster should be an exercise in teamwork, but the team will be extremely difficult to coordinate unless all team members can refer to a consistent set of policies and procedures. Whatever procedures you instigate for disaster recovery should be decisive and clearly communicated to all who need to know. A disaster recovery plan that changes often and is not communicated effectively is almost as bad as having no plan at all.

The Disaster Recovery Plan

The goal of the disaster recovery planning process is to produce a document called the *disaster recovery plan*. It provides the cohesion that enables your recovery group to function as a team by giving each member a specific list of responsibilities and procedures to follow. The remainder of this chapter is devoted to helping you with the preparation of your disaster recovery plan.

Data Availability

Disaster preparation begins with ensuring you have the data to restore. A disaster recovery plan doesn't necessarily include backup operations as part of its content, but a good, dependable backup operation should be a prerequisite to disaster recovery planning; otherwise, you are wasting your time thinking you can recover anything. So, while you are thinking about your plan, here are a few things you can do to prepare yourself if a disaster occurs:

- Run backup operations every day and verify that they completed.
- Rotate tapes off-site regularly to ensure recoverability from a site disaster.
- Become familiar with restoring data with your backup system.

Running backups without verification is not a good idea. As pointed out in Chapter 3, there are too many things that can go awry with backups. Obviously, the data that you will need to recover is supposedly on tapes or removable platters; if this data is missing or was never written to begin with, you will not recover it.

Regular off-site rotations of backup media can protect you from having all your data destroyed if you suffer a site disaster, such as a fire. By establishing a schedule for rotating tapes to an off-site facility, you ensure your ability to access data in an emergency.

Restore operations can hold unpleasant surprises; you are much better off knowing beforehand about any limitations in your backup system than finding out when you don't have the time for it.

Disaster Recovery Methodology

Once you have backup and data storage under control, you can start thinking about what you will need to do when a disaster hits you. There is a general methodology that you can use to formalize the process in your organization. While there are several variations of this form depending on which consultant you talk to, the basic concept is the same and is outlined below.

1. Risk analysis
2. Risk assessment
3. Application prioritization
4. Establishing recovery requirements
5. Document production
6. Plan testing and implementation
7. Plan distribution and maintenance

We'll now look at each one of these areas in more detail.

Risk Analysis

The first phase of disaster recovery planning, risk analysis, puts you in the position of an actuary for an insurance company. In this phase you are concerned with three simple questions: What is at risk?, What can go wrong?, and How likely is it to happen?

What Is at Risk?

The first of these questions, What is at risk?, needs to incorporate all of the components of your LAN that could be destroyed, resulting in lost connections, computers, or data. An architectural diagram of all the components in your network system should help build an inventory of items that may need to be replaced following a disaster. Keep in mind that software will need to be replaced, too, and that all relevant software products you use must be identified. This includes such things as file system utilities that you depend on to facilitate network operations.

A complete inventory list of a network illustrates clearly how complex your LAN is. Anybody who performs component inventories for networks understands the problems in tracking hardware and software used by end users. Fortunately, there are several products available to help you build an inventory of your systems from such companies as Seagate Software, McAfee, and others.

An omission in your inventory can easily result in failed restores after a disaster. The application system may not be ready for use if some of the parts are not available, so you want to continually be on the lookout for new items you may have missed. For example, an application for remote access will not work if the serial cables are not available to connect the modems.

One of the least pleasant things to consider, and one that is often overlooked, is the possibility that key people may become hurt by the disaster and that others may need to be called on to perform their duties. Cross-training on systems within your organization can help reduce the impact of one of your coworkers being unavailable. At the very least, the manuals for your organization's most important applications should be available at an off-site facility.

What Can Go Wrong?

The most fun in disaster recovery planning is answering the question, "What could possibly go wrong?" The answers to this question range from straightforward to almost unbelievable. Murphy's law has given us a litany of strange and unexpected disasters. For example, floods are fairly common, but few could have predicted the flooding of an underground tunnel system in the city of Chicago in 1992 that resulted from a pipe failure caused by a bridge repair construction project.

The most obvious types of disasters are natural disasters involving storms of all kinds or geological events such as earthquakes or volcanoes. There is potential for bad weather in every locale. In the past five years we have seen hurricanes destroy facilities along the gulf coast and Hawaii. Tornadoes and high winds destroy buildings every year in the central United States and Canada.

Flooding can happen almost anywhere when the existing drainage cannot handle the amount of rain or melting. Related to flooding is water damage; every year fires in buildings cause extensive water damage to computer systems when automatic sprinkler systems turn on to fight the blaze.

Fires themselves are some of the worst possible disasters. The heat and smoke and water surrounding fires is viciously damaging to computer systems. Storage media is easily ruined by the high temperatures and smoke. The cleanup of toxic residues after an office fire can take months, even years. The Environmental Protection Agency sometimes has to close buildings following fires due to the high concentration of toxins there. This means that you may not be able to get to your systems and data long after the fire has been put out. There are companies that specialize in setting up specialized clean room operations for fire victims where they will gain approval to send specialists wearing protective clothing into the burned building and retrieve data processing equipment and then attempt to recover the data from the disks.

You should plan for ways to access your network in case you are unable to get into your building for some reason, even though the building may still be standing and operational. Examples of events that can keep you from getting inside your building are chemical and industrial accidents and political demonstrations.

The fire does not even have to take place at your facility for the problem to be devastating. A fire destroyed the Ameritech central office in Hinsdale, Illinois, in May 1988, leaving some customers without phone service for months while the company repaired the damaged facility. Obviously, computer communications over phone lines that had been routed through this facility were seriously disrupted.

Unfortunately, terrorist attacks and other acts of willful damage by humans can destroy systems and facilities. This includes violent actions—for example, discharging weapons into computer equipment. Less exciting but just as damaging to your organization is loss of equipment by theft. There are also logical attacks to be aware of, where people destroy data intentionally by deleting or corrupting it. Viruses fall into this camp.

As discussed in previous chapters, human error is one of the most likely causes of missing or bad data. If such a mistake causes you to lose a system in your network, it has the same effect as any other kind of disaster and should be treated as such.

How Likely Is It to Happen?

If you had an infinite amount of resources and could protect yourself against all calamities, this question would not be interesting. But we don't have infinite resources, in fact, the resources are fairly scarce. Therefore we have to pick and choose the types of disasters we'll try to protect ourselves from. Obviously, you'll want to spend your precious resources on those disasters that have the highest probability of hurting your organization.

For example, we could try to protect our systems for the unlikely occurrence of a meteor falling on our building from outer space. This might not be as valuable as protecting our systems from flooding.

Answering the question: "How likely is it to happen?" also requires some budget consideration. It may help you to assume several different budget scenarios to understand what the cost trade-offs are for different levels of protection and preparation. In the end, you may feel exposed to certain threats that you cannot afford to protect yourself against, but at least you will know what they are so you can improve your plan in the future.

Risk Assessment

In a nutshell, risk assessment is the process of determining the cost to your organization of experiencing a disaster that impacts business operations. If a flood were to keep the business from running for five days, the company would lose five days of sales in addition to the physical damage to buildings and inventory. In this book we are primarily concerned with understanding the amount of financial loss that can be incurred by the interruption of network services.

For example, if your organization is marketing itself or does business on the Internet, what is the cost of having the web server unavailable? If the network that supports order entry is down, or if you have your inventory control system running on your network, what is the impact on the productivity of your organization?

The costs of a disaster can be broken down into the following categories:

- Real costs to replace computing equipment
- Production costs
- Opportunity costs
- Reputation costs

The real cost of equipment and software is easy to calculate and depends on having a good inventory of all the network components you will need.

Production costs can be determined by measuring the production output linked to your network. Your company has some good idea of the amount of work that is done each day and its relative value. Production loss due to network interruption can be calculated using this information.

Opportunity costs are lost revenues incurred by sales and marketing organizations when the network is unavailable. If the order entry system is lost and your organization can only process 25 percent of its normal daily sales volume, you have lost 75 percent of that sales volume.

Reputation costs are the most difficult to measure, but you may want to include them in your assessment nonetheless. They are incurred when customers lose faith in your organization and take their business elsewhere. Reputation costs go up when you have longer or more frequent delays in servicing your customers.

Application Prioritization

After the disaster strikes, and you start putting your systems back together, you'll want to know which applications to restore first. Don't waste time restoring the wrong systems and data when your business needs its bread and butter applications first.

This means you need to determine in advance what the bread and butter applications of the business are. If your organization is like most, you will have several "most important" applications, depending on whom you ask. The human resources department will say the payroll system is most important, sales management will tell you it's order entry, manufacturing will insist it's inventory control, and purchasing will tell you it's accounts payable. Unfortunately, not all of these systems can be the most important one, so it is essential that senior management help determine the order in which systems should be restored.

Hopefully, this information will be well understood by all department heads. Regardless, the disaster recovery plan should contain such a prioritized list of systems. This section of the plan should be signed by senior management to minimize disagreements.

Once you know what you are going to restore, you should take stock of everything you need to make those applications available. An application system on a network is comprised of server systems where the application stores its data, the workstation systems that process it, the printers or fax machines that are used for I/O, the network fabric that connects it all together, and the applications software. Client/server or distributed applications add an extra level of complexity by requiring various parts of the application to reside on separate machines.

You may be tempted to build a larger infrastructure than you need for your high-priority applications. For instance, if your network today has 50 workstations on it, you may immediately start working to rebuild all 50 workstations. However, if your top-priority applications only need five workstations, you should stop the workstation building at five and focus your efforts on making the application work. You will be much better off trying to get a small system running than a larger one, and you will save a lot of time in the process. In fact, when you are prioritizing the applications with senior management, you might also benefit from determining the minimum number of workstations you need to get the system online. You can always increase the size of the network after you are up and running.

One of the advantages of taking the application system approach is the amount of time required to restore an application compared to the amount of time required to restore a whole server. If the application only has 500MB of data and the server has 4GB, it's obvious that you could save a lot of time by just restoring the application.

However, this approach requires a little more detailed knowledge about your systems than you might currently have. First, you need to know where all the data is that the application uses and what system file dependencies there may be. If there are system files that contain information about the application, as is the case with Windows .ini files, you need to make sure that these files are also restored with the application. Second, you need to know how to operate your backup system to perform this type of selective restore. While this may not necessarily be difficult, you might not be familiar with this operation.

Consolidating Applications onto a Single Replacement Server

What you are likely to find as you move through this process is that the network you create following a disaster will be significantly different than the one that currently exists. For example, the two most important applications in your business may reside on different servers on different floors in your building. However, to decrease the time it takes to get a working network up and running, it may be fastest to put both of these applications on a single server.

NETWARE 3.X CONSOLIDATION   This looks innocent enough on the surface, but could be problematic in an actual implementation. For example, under NetWare 3.x, each server in the network has its own independent authorization database called the *bindery.* Every user on a NetWare 3.x system has a unique ID stored in the bindery of each server that they use. Files within the NetWare file system have user ID information stored with them in the file system. Access to files is granted when a match occurs between the user ID in the bindery and the ID associated with a file in the file system.

Unfortunately, NetWare 3.x does not allow binderies to be merged or combined. This means you can't consolidate the security and access privileges of two servers into one. As a result, some users may not have access to their files while others may find themselves with privileges they should not have.

This problem is outlined in Figure 12-1, which shows two servers, A and B, being consolidated onto a new, larger server A. The bindery from server A is used on the new server. Files from the old server A retain their original correct ownership, while files from server B bring the incorrect ownership information with them. When comparisons are made between server A's bindery and the file system rights for files from server B, there is a mismatch. Notice the file named John.two. When this file is transferred to the new server A, the associated ownership ID with the file grants rights to Carol, but not to John.

NETWARE 4.X CONSOLIDATION   The shortcomings with NetWare 3.x binderies was one of the underlying reasons why Novell developed NetWare Directory Services (NDS) for their 4.x products. In NetWare 4.x, there is a single common authentication system that is replicated across all servers in the network. Because all servers share the

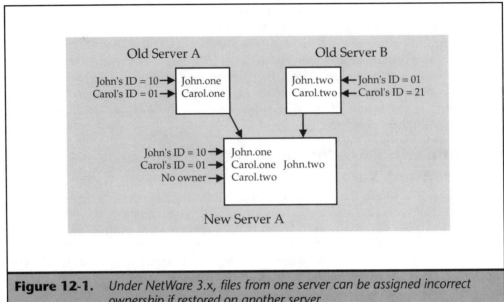

Figure 12-1. *Under NetWare 3.x, files from one server can be assigned incorrect ownership if restored on another server*

same user identification scheme, consolidating data onto a single server following a disaster is far less tricky.

One of the advantages of NDS is the fact that it can be replicated across servers in geographically separated locations. This makes it almost impossible for a site disaster to wipe out an organization's NDS. All that needs to be done to restore NDS in such an environment is to set up the replacement NetWare servers and let the NDS that exists replicate itself onto them. Figure 12-2 shows how NDS is replicated over a wide area network to a remote server, and how after a disaster it can be replicated back to replacement servers.

WINDOWS NT CONSOLIDATION   Windows NT has its own issues where server consolidation is concerned. Windows NT uses an internal identification and configuration system called the *registry.* It is similar to NetWare's bindery implementation because Windows NT servers have their own unique registry that is not shared or replicated across servers. Windows NT servers do, however, use the concept of access domains, which allows end users to more easily share resources within a local network.

Inside the registry are objects called *hives.* These contain configuration information that the NT system uses for low-level kernel functions like booting up and file access authorization. As Windows NT continues to evolve, there have been several significant changes to the Registry implementation, some of them not backward-compatible with previous versions of the Registry. Windows NT customers

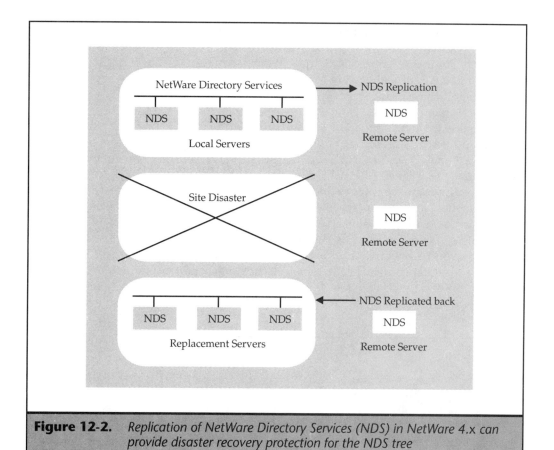

Figure 12-2. *Replication of NetWare Directory Services (NDS) in NetWare 4.x can provide disaster recovery protection for the NDS tree*

are advised to pay close attention to their operating system levels and try to keep them current and consistent across their organization.

Because Windows NT and Windows NT Server are relatively new products, there's not a great deal of expertise available to shed light on the issues of disaster recovery in a distributed network of NT systems. Still, what information is available is important, and the following sections should be useful to organizations that implement Windows NT.

One of the hives in NT is called the *hardware hive*. This contains information about all the systems devices, including disks, disk controllers, and video I/O. Incorrect information in the hardware hive will keep the system from booting. Therefore, you probably do not want to back up and restore the hardware hive in an NT system. The best way to re-create a hardware hive following a disaster is to reinstall Windows NT and let the installation process do the work for you.

As applications are installed in a Windows NT server, there is a good possibility that they will update the registry. This makes it somewhat difficult to take the registry from one NT system and restore it to another. It also makes it somewhat problematic to restore an application correctly on a different machine than the one it was initially installed on. For that reason, consolidating Windows NT servers following a disaster means that you will probably want to reinstall all the applications on the replacement server, rather than restoring their executable files (see Figure 12-3). Once the application is reinstalled, you can then restore the data files to the new system.

This makes the whole process a lot more difficult because instead of starting a complete restore to a new server, you will now have to select files to restore separately. In addition, you will want to make sure that you don't restore older executable files over the newly reinstalled executable files.

Another important concept to understand for disaster recovery of Windows NT networks is the *domain server* (see Figure 12-4). When NT servers are installed, you can choose to make them a domain server, a backup domain server, or a regular server. The domain server is used as an access authorization clearinghouse for the LAN. Whenever an end user wants to access a resource on the network, the server they are attempting to access verifies the attempt with the domain server. Should the domain server fail, the backup domain server will step in and resume authentication services for the network.

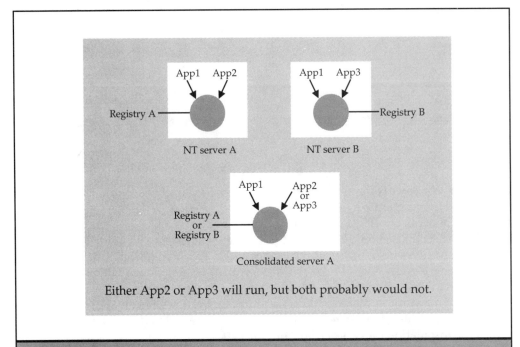

Figure 12-3. *Applications linked to the registry in Windows NT may not run on a different NT system following a redirected restore*

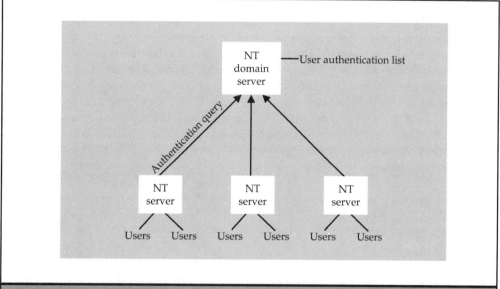

Figure 12-4.   *The domain server in a Windows NT network authorizes access to network resources*

Should both the domain server and the backup domain server fail, transparent access to information on the network would stop until a new domain server could be installed and brought on the network. Also, if you try to consolidate servers following a disaster, you want to make sure that the server you rebuild is either the domain server or the backup domain server.

So, it appears that recovering information from two different Windows NT machines onto one poses significant challenges. Considering the difficulty of the work involved following a disaster and the pressures you will be working under, it would be best if you restore your servers on a one-to-one basis, according to the priorities of the applications that reside on them. In addition, you would not have to reinstall all your applications if you can restore the registry information for the server that contains application-generated updates.

Establishing Recovery Requirements

The key to this phase of the disaster recovery planning process is to define an acceptable and achievable amount of time to get a functional network running again. As discussed in the previous section, the primary concern should be to get the most important applications running first. Management people in your organization will want to know when their applications will be running in order to plan the operations of the company.

It is very important to allow yourself an adequate amount of time and not to make unrealistic estimates about your abilities. You do not want to have a lot of people waiting around for you to finish your recovery operations; having such a distraction will probably hinder your work. The term for this time is called the *recovery time objective*, or *RTO*. The RTO you define should be tested to make sure it is realistic and attainable, not just by you but by others in your organization who may be called upon to do the work if you are not available.

Business management should work closely with the LAN administration staff to determine the RTO for your applications. Different applications will have different RTOs. Figure 12-5 shows six applications on three servers. The order to restore these applications would be

Server 2, Application 4
Server 1, Application 1; Server 3, Application 6
Server 1, Application 2
Server 3, Application 5

Make sure to give yourself time to get tapes from your off-site storage facility and to acquire the systems you will need. By the way, you should know well in advance how to issue purchase orders for equipment when your company is in complete disarray.

You may find it necessary to update the backup system to meet your RTO. A tape system that restores data at 2MB per second will get the job done much faster than one that performs at 500KB per second. Be careful not to assume you can do too many things at once; you may find yourself making unfortunate mistakes that slow you down if you do not pay close attention to the work at hand.

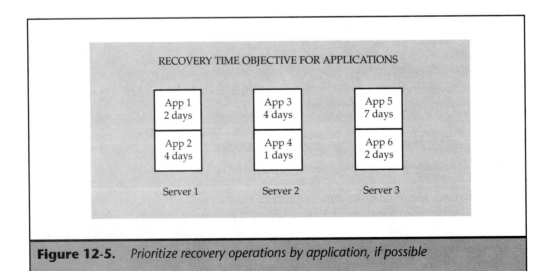

Figure 12-5.   *Prioritize recovery operations by application, if possible*

Producing the Actual Disaster Recovery Document

Creating a document that many people can follow and work together from is the crux of disaster recovery planning. Don't fool yourself; this will take significant effort on the part of several people, but it will help you learn things about your systems and it may just save your business some day.

Management Commitment

The resources required to write and maintain a disaster recovery plan are more than can be done in spare time and off-hours. An organization's management must support this initiative for it to succeed. One of the problems with disaster recovery planning for the networking environment is that networking technology changes so quickly that it is difficult to stay current. This includes new devices as well as new application systems that introduce their own level of complexity into the arena. As an example, consider recovering a large Unix relational database system. This type of work requires much more intricate knowledge of the database installation than a LAN administrator is likely to have; it usually requires a database administrator, who will also find it a challenge.

Given the fact that networking technology changes so rapidly, you should plan to update your disaster recovery plan periodically, like once a year. Although writing the initial plan will take a great deal of work, once you have it, updates are relatively easy.

Contents of the Disaster Recovery Plan

Try to define the following five areas of your network disaster recovery plan:

- Notification lists, phone numbers, maps, and addresses
- Priorities, responsibilities, relationships, and procedures
- Acquisition and purchasing information
- Network diagrams
- Systems, configurations, and tape backup

Make sure you know whom to notify first when a disaster occurs. As an example, if you have a fire, call the fire department first—not the CEO. There may be other people or organizations you identify that have special skills or knowledge that can help keep the damage to a minimum. If you don't have current phone numbers or addresses you could have a very hard time contacting the people who need to know.

Maps showing the locations of the temporary operations center and off-site facility could save you a lot of time. It may also be useful to show alternative access routes in case the primary routes are unavailable.

When you first start assembling your thoughts about how to respond to a disaster, focus on the priorities you have established. The clock is ticking; get started working on restoring the top-priority applications right away. People should be given clear direction and responsibilities. The relationship between tasks should be documented so you can identify any bottlenecks as they come up. Finally, detailed operations and tasks showing precise installation and recovery operations should be included and easy to read and follow. Phone numbers of support organizations you might need to call should also be included here.

As mentioned previously, know how to issue a purchase order and get equipment to your temporary operations center. This means providing your vendors with the address and any necessary shipping instructions. Do not assume that every vendor in the world will know about your plight and come to your rescue. You may want to have copies of invoices and receipts and the like to show proof of purchase. A list of serial numbers for hardware equipment could come in handy, too. Be advised that a great many of the products sold for the PC networking marketplace today are delivered through a large distribution system and the manufacturers and software developers of your products may have no idea that you are their customer. Don't expect to receive replacements for free, but you might be able to arrange a special purchase and shipping arrangements to replace your lost goods.

Network diagrams greatly simplify the task of constructing a network. A detailed diagram of the network you need for your first few applications can help you get up and running quickly. Making some labels for cabling and storing them off-site probably wouldn't take much time and could save a great deal of confusion later. The other advantage of a wiring diagram is that you can use contractors to install the wiring for you. Somebody who is experienced in setting up wiring and other network fabric devices, and does it for a living, may be able to do it better and faster than you can.

You may be hours or days ahead in the restore process if you can warehouse a few replacement systems that have the capacity to handle a variety of different tasks. Plan on installing a generic configuration that will at least allow you to run the high-priority applications without problems. If you don't know what kinds of configurations people have on their PCs, a LAN inventory product could help you gather that information. After your replacement network is running and you have a little time to breathe, you can restore your PCs to their previous configurations using the configuration information from the inventory reports.

Make sure you have a working tape backup system available to you; if possible, keep a spare system, including SCSI adapters, cables, and device driver software off-site. You may find that your local vendors do not have the products you need in stock, forcing you to wait for replacement parts to be shipped in before you can start restoring data. If you follow this advice, remember to upgrade this system when you upgrade your production backup systems; otherwise, you may find yourself with incompatible tape formats, databases, or other problems that will keep you from restoring data.

Plan Testing and Implementation

After the plan is written, test it. You and others need to have confidence that the plan will work. This requires you to become a skeptic of your own work so you can prove to yourself that it does. This is not necessarily easy to do psychologically, because you probably have invested a fair amount of personal time and energy in this process, but you will be much better off if you can be completely open-minded about the accuracy of the plan. So, test to find problems, not to verify that your plan will work. If there are mistakes in any of the information, take note of them and change the plan.

Testing the Plan in Parts

Don't just pull the plug on your network someday to see if you can recover it. There are much better ways to test a disaster recovery plan without causing major work interruptions in your organization. Some of the things you might not normally think to test could help you save a great deal of time later. For example, call the telephone numbers of your people on the phone lists in the plan to see if they are current; call your vendors to see if they have products in stock—they may have changed their inventory policy. Drive to the off-site facility yourself someday to know where it is and how to identify the building.

Of course, you also need to test the procedures you'll use for restoring data. Test the backup software to see if you can restore your high-priority applications the way you expect to. This should be done on a separate, isolated network to avoid problems with server licensing conflicts. For example, if you plan on merging two servers together by restoring one of them completely on the replacement server and then restoring just the user data files from the other one, you will have two servers with the same license of the server software on the network, which could result in licensing warning messages being broadcast throughout your network. Even if you use a new license of the network operating system for testing, there are still other conflicts such as duplicate server names and any other duplication problems that would cause problems with your production systems.

Once the data has been restored, test to see that users can access it. This requires a few workstations connected on the network to simulate real end users with accounts on the original servers. You may need to update your plan at this point to include administrative information on setting up user accounts. Test every restore operation in the plan individually and then test to see if it results in a working network system. You may even want to test the plan with others in your organization who are not as familiar with the products or procedures as you are.

Test the backup side of the plan every day by verifying that backups are completing correctly. Test this further by ensuring that several people in your organization can run backups correctly and verify their completion.

Plan Distribution and Maintenance

Finally, when you have a finished plan that has been tested, you need to distribute it to the people who need to have it. Try to control the release of this, so you don't have the confusion of multiple versions. Also, you should make sure you have extra copies of the plan to store at your off-site facility or some other place besides your work site. Keep a list of all the people and locations who have a copy of the plan. When you update the plan, replace them all and collect the previous versions.

Maintaining the plan is a straightforward process. Start with a review of the existing plan and go through it all, making changes to any piece of information that may have changed. At this time you should reevaluate your application systems and determine which ones are the most important to your organization. Changes to this part of your plan will cause ripple effects in the restore procedures. That should not be viewed as a big problem, however, because you will probably need to update the procedures section anyway due to other changes. If you've made changes to your backup system, make sure the information on how to use the new or updated backup system is included.

This process will take time, but it has some valuable benefits that you will receive even if you never have to use it. More people will know about your network than before. This will give your organization a much broader skill base to use to keep your network in good shape. It will also help grow a global perspective on the network within the MIS organization and can help identify current or future problem areas. One of the most difficult things about any distributed task, such as LAN management and administration, is communicating what is going on. Maintaining and testing a disaster recovery plan will help make that communication happen in your organization.

Running in a Temporary Facility

If your building is destroyed or you can't get access to it, you will need another location to set up a temporary business facility. This could be a vacant office space or a warehouse location that has the space available for you to move into on a temporary basis. While it may not be practical for you to reserve real estate for this, your organization should at least know how to lease space on a temporary basis and how to generate the paperwork to get you in the door and running.

Make sure you know what the power, communications, and space requirements are for your temporary network and communicate this to the people in your organization who will be responsible for establishing a temporary site for your business. Also, communicate any security concerns you may have about the temporary network. If your organization has confidential information on it that it needs to protect, the temporary facility should have the capability of installing physical security for the network.

Summary

A good disaster recovery plan begins with management's commitment to the process on an ongoing basis. Disaster recovery is a methodology and a process; it is not a product, although products and services can be purchased to assist you. Resources will be needed periodically in the future to ensure the plan continues to be valid.

Test your plan for accuracy and ease of use. When you test, try to be as objective as possible in determining where the weaknesses are and fix them. Keep in mind that the recovery of a network requires good backup tapes and equipment to run on, and you will need to understand how the equipment will get to you. The logistical problems with disaster recovery can be the most difficult part of the process. Thinking about them and preparing for them can save a great deal of time.

Know what is expected and the time frame you have to get the job done. Prioritize the restoration of your network by application systems. Restore the most important applications first and get them operational before moving on to other less important applications. Know how to generate the maximum impact from your efforts because you are far better off with a few systems running than a lot of systems *almost* running.

CHAPTER THIRTEEN

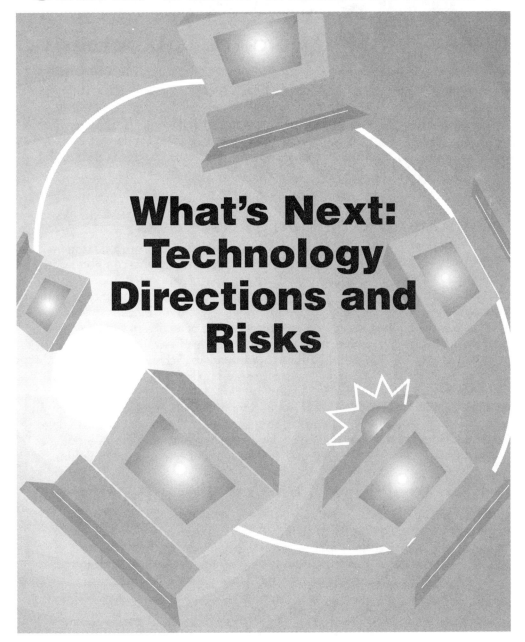

**What's Next:
Technology
Directions and
Risks**

In the risk analysis phase of disaster recovery planning, you try to think of all the ways there are to lose data. In the previous chapters, we looked at many of the existing threats to data that have resulted in data loss. In this chapter, we try to look into the future a little to predict areas where you may want to pay extra attention.

Future Considerations for Data Integrity and Security

As computers continue to evolve with the integration of networking, portability, and wireless communications technologies, the threats to data integrity and security continue to increase. This chapter examines some of the data integrity and security concerns associated with emerging technologies that are changing the way we use computers. The topics covered in this chapter include developments in LAN and WAN systems, portable computers, wireless communications, the Internet, and data warehousing.

The Continuing Evolution of Networks

One of the fundamental goals of computing technology is the desire to find more efficient ways to work. In the evolution of computing, the personal computer stands as a milestone, extending the efficiency and productivity benefits of computers to individuals. These benefits have been further enhanced by the ability to connect these personal computers in LANs, which extend these productivity benefits to workgroups.

Today, networks are used to reinforce the structure of an organization by establishing logical "proximity" where workers who are physically separated can efficiently work closely together through the network to exchange ideas and information. The successful deployment of workgroup software and the business requirement to quickly adapt to fast-changing markets practically ensures the continued evolution of networked personal computers. As a result, data integrity and security issues associated with these new technologies will also continue to evolve. Responsible information systems (IS) professionals implementing new technologies will want to identify the associated risks and establish adequate countermeasures.

Switching Devices and Virtual Networks

To accommodate requirements for increased data transmissions, organizations are implementing switching hubs and other network connection devices that have extremely high-speed backplane circuitry. The general idea of these switches is to provide isolated wire segments for individual computers on the network and to control data transfers between segments. By isolating systems on their own wire segment, the performance overhead of collisions on shared media is avoided, increasing the overall performance of the network. Figure 13-1 shows a simplified switch connection between two systems.

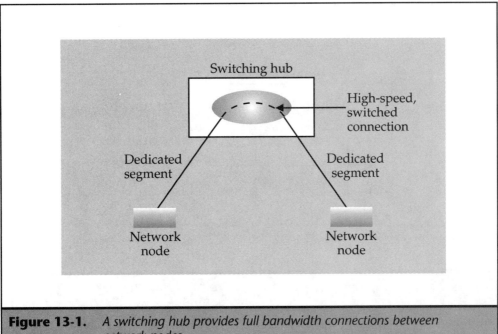

Figure 13-1. *A switching hub provides full bandwidth connections between network nodes*

This technology draws its inspiration from telephony technology, where a single telephone switch is capable of handling many private telephone conversations, as opposed to a common access party line, without noticeable degradation in service or sound quality.

In addition to the performance benefits switching hubs offer, they also enable customers to establish *virtual networks*. A virtual network is the logical separation of certain network segments into an isolated subgroup for the purposes of providing guaranteed performance or segregating users for security purposes. Figure 13-2 shows the segmentation of three segments into a virtual network. Virtual networks are established via software functionality in the hub and do not require changes to the hub's hardware.

Virtual networks can have a positive impact on data integrity by enabling higher performance backup and storage management over the network by dedicating extra bandwidth to these functions, as discussed briefly in Chapter 3. Some organizations have implemented separate backbone networks for their network backup. Virtual networks allow them to do the same thing, but with fewer cabling and equipment changes.

However, using virtual networks can create security risks also. If the virtual network is used to segregate access to various parts of the network, care must be taken to ensure that unauthorized users cannot get to segments where they are not authorized. At first this appears to be trivial; just configure the switch to not allow

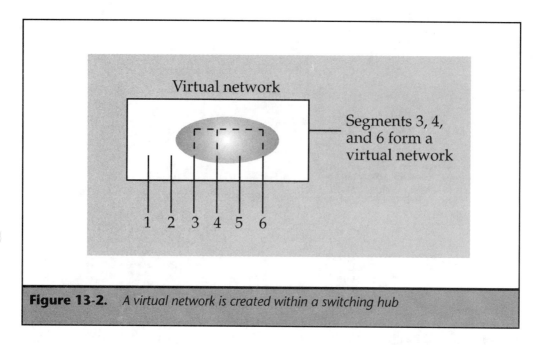

Figure 13-2. *A virtual network is created within a switching hub*

access to unauthorized users. However, you also need to make sure that unauthorized users cannot use a "Trojan horse" program to change the configuration of the switch, enabling them to get onto network segments where they do not belong. If the switch functionality can be changed by updating its MIB (management information base) from an SNMP (simple network management protocol) console application, you will want to also protect access to the network management console.

Just because hostile attackers can gain access to a network, it does not mean they will be able to infiltrate any of the machines where the interesting data is stored. Unfortunately, a Trojan horse infiltration could go unnoticed almost indefinitely, giving intruders a long time to break whatever security mechanisms are implemented on individual machines.

Another security exposure of virtual networks is the possibility of human errors making configuration changes to the hub, resulting in unauthorized access for some end users. It is not unheard of in this business for end users to discover they have access to files and systems they should not have access to. There is no reason to believe similar oversights will not occur with the administration of virtual networks.

Electronic Mail and Groupware

The most common enabler of person-to-person communications on networks is electronic mail or, more recently, groupware products. In the case of electronic mail, messages are transferred between electronic "post office" repositories. In the case of groupware, there are other mechanisms that copy data between locations. For example, Lotus Notes keeps databases of documents in each location that automatically replicate themselves to all other locations in the network on a regular basis.

The security threats to distributed electronic mail and groupware data are challenging. Systems that allow people to share information also make it easier for others to have unauthorized access to it. For starters, there is the obvious problem of trying to maintain physical security at sites where you do not have the control and monitoring capabilities needed to protect data from theft. It may also be more difficult to prevent break-ins where people enter a remote site and try to access data or systems through the network.

If the systems exist to transfer data, people will use them. Policies can be established to restrict the transmission of certain documents and files but cannot stop the system from functioning. These systems are designed to accelerate the sharing of ideas and information and therefore facilitate the transportation of messages and files within and between organizations. For that reason, organizations with sensitive information should make sure their employees stay vigilant about the information they share between locations if the other locations do not have adequate security safeguards in place.

The information a company needs to discuss and share within the organization is sometimes confidential, such as technology and product documents or marketing plans. Of course, this is exactly the sort of information that others might want to steal. So, if the organization is sharing this information across several locations, it also means that there are several more copies, which can turn into separate threads or conversations in those locations, all of them being sources of potential leaks.

In an attempt to communicate better with its customers, some organizations will even extend their e-mail systems beyond their boundaries by giving their customers or business partners an e-mail address of their own. There have been cases where broadcast email messages intended for internal use only and containing sensitive and embarrassing information have been sent to customers by mistake. Considering that many customers are in contact with an organization's competitors, this type of leak could be very damaging.

Physical security at remote or branch sites can be increased by using keyboard locks or higher levels of physical security. Lock-down mechanisms can be installed to dissuade potential thieves from stealing equipment. There are other security products that will prevent the system from booting up if the correct password information is not given, and some will even destroy the contents of the system disk if unauthorized access or theft is attempted.

Having several copies of information can also create version control problems where different people have different versions of a document or file that may contain different pieces of information, such as instructions, policies, or plans. As an example, consider an electronic mail message that is sent to several recipients who, in turn, start several "splinter" discussions about the original, but without the synchronization needed to keep all parties informed. The resulting final version of each of these splinter discussions can vary widely. Most people who have used electronic mail understand this phenomenon. Although it may seem like business as usual in many cases, it is an example of a data integrity problem.

The answers to such security and integrity concerns are not apparent. One potential solution to the version control issue discussed above is to use a groupware or conferencing product that organizes messages and documents in such a manner as to keep all relevant communications within a single logical viewing mechanism. Such products provide replication and synchronization services that maintain a consistent distributed repository of information.

Conferencing and groupware products such as Lotus Notes and Collabra Share that replicate information from one site to another provide the additional benefit of creating automatic backup copies of information in the various sites within the organization. If one site loses information that has been replicated to another site, it can be replicated back again. While such replication would probably not have the performance and capacity to completely back up a network, it could help save some important documents should a site disaster wipe out your systems. Figure 13-3 shows the replication of three separate databases across three servers.

However, as discussed previously, automated replication of data across the organization increases the security risk, and the best way to reduce that risk is to limit the sharing of data. So it appears that in distributed networks, data integrity and security mechanisms work against each other. You either share the information and

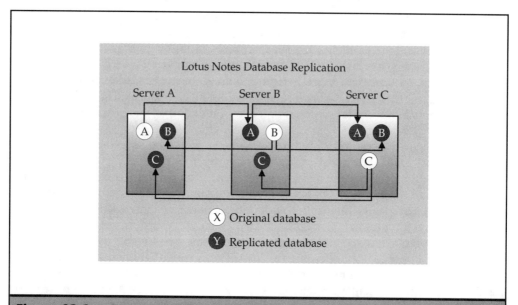

Figure 13-3.   *Data created on servers A, B, and C is replicated on the other systems*

have increased security risks, or you restrict the information and increase the data integrity risk of losing data. Figure 13-4 shows the inverse relationship between integrity and security: While security is optimized by allowing only one copy of the information, there is no means to recover the data after a disaster. Conversely, data integrity is increased by making redundant copies of the data; however, each of those copies is suspect to security attacks.

Distributed Databases

As organizations attempt to get the data closer to the workers who need it, they are starting to implement database systems that are distributed across various parts of their networks. Similar to conferencing and groupware products, these databases replicate themselves across networks (usually in part) to other machines in the network. The same sorts of data integrity and security concerns apply to distributed databases as those discussed above with a few additions. As discussed in Chapter 6, one of the primary data integrity problems with databases is backup.

The ability to back up and restore distributed databases is not well understood today and depends largely on the structure and organization of particular database products. Among the challenges to succeeding in this area is the problem of establishing a consistent, synchronized time between systems on the network.

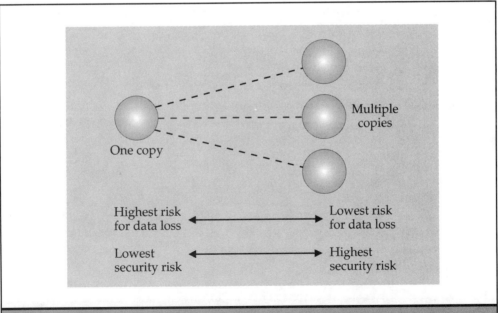

Figure 13-4. *Reducing the number of copies of data improves its security, but also decreases its recoverability*

Considering the speed and intricacy of database transactions, such a mechanism would need to be very accurate.

Figure 13-5 below shows two database servers that are supporting the same logical database. The internal clocks on the two systems are close, but not quite the same—for this example assume DB server 1 is half a minute slow and DB server 2 is half a minute fast. The backup process is designed to begin precisely at 12:01.

At t=12:00.30, DB server 2 locks its files and begins backing itself up. One minute later, DB server 1 does the same thing. In the meantime, updates have arrived that affect both DB servers. If the updates are made on server 1 and not on server 2, the database image written to tape will be out of synchronization and may not be usable if it is needed to be restored later.

Organizations attempting to implement distributed databases are warned to be careful and somewhat skeptical when evaluating this part of their implementation plan. If the database on one system is dependent on synchronized data from another database, the potential for large failures exists. There are few things as disturbing as finding out after building a large system that it cannot be reliably backed up and restored.

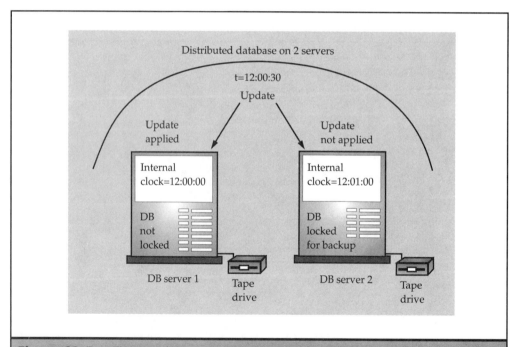

Figure 13-5.   *Time synchronization between database servers during backup results in an incorrect image of the database on backup tapes*

Laptop Risks

Laptop computers enable workers to take their work with them almost anywhere. While this has obvious benefits, it also has a serious downside: they are far more prone to damage and theft than other computer equipment.

Data Loss on Laptops

Airport X-ray systems seem harmless enough, but if you've ever had mysterious data loss or file corruptions on your laptop, you will question how harmless they really are. The security people at airports will tell you the X-ray equipment is safe, but the fact remains that the fundamental technology of X rays is to reflect higher-energy electromagnetic waves off an object. These waves have an associated momentum that imparts a force on the object. If the object happens to be a high-density magnetic storage device, data corruption can occur.

Figure 13-6 shows a magnetic disk surface before and after it is struck by X rays. The higher energy of X-ray particles that allows them to penetrate the outside surface of objects in order to view internal structures is reflected off the internal structure. When you consider the ever-increasing density of data on disk drives today, it is easy to see how particles on the disk could be pushed out of alignment, reducing the magnetic charge in a section of the disk, making it unreadable.

Therefore, laptop owners are advised to always try to use an alternative means to get their machines through security (this is not intended to suggest that illegal methods be used). Most airports today allow laptops to go through a power-up test at security checkpoints—a much safer method.

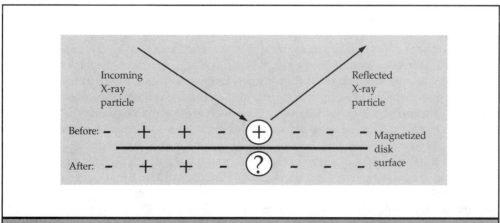

Figure 13-6. *X rays have momentum and can alter the readability of data on magnetic disk surfaces*

While laptops are made to travel, they are not made to take a beating. If your laptop is injured while traveling and it stops working, your data integrity is compromised 100 percent. For that reason, do not check laptops in baggage and always try to handle them yourself. I have seen one of my laptops tumble from the back of a courtesy vehicle as the driver was trying to adjust the load of baggage. It destroyed my laptop and severely hindered my activities. Most traveling cases for laptops are made for convenience more than protection. So don't expect your laptop case to protect the computer inside from physical impacts. For the best protection, you might want to consider using a hard-shell case reinforced with several inches of foam padding on the inside.

When a laptop fails, it can take much more time to get parts or find somebody who can repair it. Unlike desktop PCs, laptops are not standardized and use components that are specific to certain manufacturers and models. This can cause a serious integrity problem if you cannot access your data for a week or two while your system is being repaired.

Considering the exposure to damage and length of time it can take to repair a laptop and get its data back, you might think that backup systems for laptops would be widely used. In fact, backup of laptops is rarely done due to the slow speed of workstation backups and because owners often take them home. So, even though the threats to data on laptops are greater, backup of laptops tends to be woefully inadequate.

Laptops and Theft

One of the brute force methods used to steal data is to steal the machine the data is on. Laptops make it far easier for somebody to walk away with your data and your system. They also make it easier for you to forget your data someplace by leaving your laptop behind somewhere while you are in transit. The fact that laptops are used in the field by people who travel multiplies the possibilities of threats on data integrity and security.

You wouldn't allow a stranger to stand in your office and watch you type letters and memos. However, you often see people working on airplanes with their laptops where many people can read what they are working on. Is this a security threat? It depends on who the people are sitting around you, but the potential for releasing important information to the wrong people is much greater than in the office. Laptops left running and unattended are certainly inviting for competitors or others who have an interest in your business.

Although it seems like the stuff of suspense movies, leaving laptops in hotel rooms, especially during trade shows and conventions, can also be a threat to security. Hotel break-ins do occur and there are people who will do almost anything to find out something they think is important. You only have to look back to the Watergate scandal for an example. With the amount of money that can be made from well-timed business transactions and trade secrets, you should never take this risk too lightly.

One way to combat this sort of theft is to use a system that has password protection, similar to a keyboard lock on a PC. That way, even if somebody steals your system, they will not be able to get easy access to your files. At the file system level, one could use file encryption and password protection to discourage a thief from accessing sensitive files. At the machine level, you could use boot-up level security that restricts access to the machine prior to reading the boot record from the disk.

As small as laptops are, their parts are even smaller. Flash memory cards and hard disk cards for laptops are quite small and can easily be stolen. Even if the thief cannot use the information on the card, you may be left having to re-create all the lost data if you do not have a backup.

Many laptops are used to access remote LANs and systems and, therefore, contain lists of phone numbers and communication configuration information. This information could be very interesting to hackers and competitors who certainly wouldn't need your laptop to make use of it. Although your laptop would not be at risk, your remote systems would be. In addition, laptop users will often use keyboard configuration shortcuts to speed up the access to such remote systems. If somebody steals your laptop, or its disk, any hot-key login shortcuts make it much simpler to access your systems. For that reason, it is recommended that users not implement such sign-on hot keys on their laptop systems. If you access remote systems, bulletin boards, or external networks, make sure that you use virus protection software regularly to protect it from viruses in downloaded files.

Sometimes users store files containing their passwords on their systems. A hostile user who steals your laptop and recognizes this type of information can use it to attempt access to other systems in your company. It is common sense to not intentionally leave your laptop at a customer site overnight if you are planning to return the next day. Take it with you when you go as a matter of policy. Also, do not loan your laptop to others outside your organization. Laptops without internal diskette drives make it more difficult for somebody to steal information by copying files to diskette.

Version Control Issues

If you use more than one PC, and share data files among them, you have probably experienced version control problems. As you transfer data from the diskette copy to another machine, it is possible to make mistakes and keep the wrong file. Products such as Traveling Software's Lap Link are designed to help you synchronize files between a laptop and desktop system. IBM Corporation's DOS 7.0 and Microsoft Corporation's Windows 95 operating systems also provide some capabilities to manage versions between machines.

PDA Risks

Personal Digital Assistants, or PDAs, represent a new type of security and data integrity risk. Today, PDAs are typically deployed for specific applications, such as tracking shipments or sales force automation. They have not become broadly accepted as cross-application products. As such, they are more likely to use shortcuts and methods of communicating that have abbreviated login procedures for the sake of usability. They are a relatively new technology, and as has been true with PCs, might not get implemented with an eye to security.

For example, consider a nursing application where a field force of nurses visits patients in their homes. Let's assume they have an application for PDAs that can look up the patients' care history if needed. The nurses may not be skilled computer and telecommunications workers. Therefore, the system would be designed for the easiest use possible with a minimal, or no, login protection. Even if the information on the host machine were read-only, it is likely that the patients would not want others to have access to their medical history through a stolen PDA.

So, in building PDA applications, time should be taken to ensure adequate security measures are implemented. Too often in software development, the temptation is to first build a proof of concept that shows the basic functionality of the application and then to follow that with a series of refinements until the product is finally usable. In the rush to get a product in use, adequate security measures can be overlooked. You would not want to provide an easy-to-steal, easy-to-use doorway into your corporate data.

Of course, PDAs are even smaller than PCs. That means they are easier to misplace or to leave somewhere. Understanding that mistakes will happen from time to time, organizations that implement PDAs should assume they will become lost and provide the necessary security mechanisms. Not only that, but products or processes should also be identified to make backup copies of any important data that may reside on the PDA.

Mobile Computing

Mobile workers are constantly looking for ways to get the benefits of computing while out of the office. The ultimate device for such people is the wireless laptop computer, or PDA. Computer communications over cellular phone services are likely to become much more popular by the end of the decade as the cost of the technology and services decline.

The difficulty in dealing with electromagnetic interference is that it is very difficult for mobile workers to anticipate its sources. Another drawback with wireless communications for mobile computers is problems with the cellular service in an area. Most cellular phone users understand that there are some locations where transmission is problematic. In both cases, the use of a fallback system with a modem and regular phone line system could be a big advantage. Figure 13-7 shows a cluster of cells that cover a given geography and the areas between cells where coverage is too weak to be reliable.

Remote wireless applications with PDAs and laptops could likely use store and forward techniques to move data between the portable device and the host network.

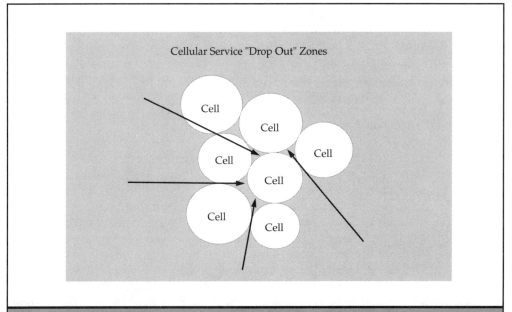

Figure 13-7. *The arrows indicate locations where cellular coverage is weak, resulting in lost connections*

The fact that your data is stored on an intermediate system for some time puts it at risk for both security and integrity. If an intermediate system can be "hacked" and the data stolen, you've got a serious security leak that could go unnoticed for an extended period of time. By the same token, if the failure of these intermediate systems keeps your applications from working, you've got an integrity problem.

If the intermediate system is private, it may help you implement security measures you are comfortable with. Unfortunately, it may be difficult to get assistance fixing the system should it fail if such a system is located where there is no or little MIS staff. On the other hand, if the intermediate system is provided by a service bureau, it should significantly decrease the downtime of the system, but its security would not be under your control—and potentially not reliable.

Wireless Networking

Sometimes it is very difficult, expensive, or even impossible to run cabling to install a network. In such a case, a wireless network solves the problem. The security and data integrity threats involved are related to the phenomenon of electromagnetic waves and radiation. The most obvious *security* threat is that the data transmissions can be intercepted by radio receivers and the data stolen. The most obvious *data integrity* threat is that electromagnetic interference could cause data to become corrupted in transmission.

Figure 13-8 shows a wireless transmitter on a computer next to a window. The radio waves from the transmitter are broadcast through the glass out into the surrounding environment where they can be eavesdropped on by sensitive antennaes.

There are logical and physical solutions to the security risk of somebody "listening" to your data transmissions. Unfortunately, the technology to "listen" to wireless transmissions exists and is extremely sophisticated and sensitive. In other words, if somebody wants to eavesdrop on your wireless transmissions, they can. The good news is that the same data encryption techniques used to prevent wiretapping on copper-wire networks work on wireless networks. Just because somebody can hear you doesn't mean they can understand what you are saying. There are also things that can be done to make electronic eavesdropping more difficult. The use of directional antennae and specialized reflective window coverings can significantly reduce the amount of network radio transmissions that escape from your building.

As for keeping the integrity of the transmission amid interference, the parity and checksum data built into transmission protocols greatly reduce the chance that interference will result in corrupt data transmissions. However, interference that is severe enough will stop the network from working altogether. Obviously, when the network doesn't allow you to access data, you've got a data integrity problem. For that reason, care should be taken before installing a wireless network to ensure the existing electromagnetic background "noise" is at an acceptable level. Things to watch out for are any broadcast or welding equipment and other heavy machinery that runs on electrical power feeds, including elevators.

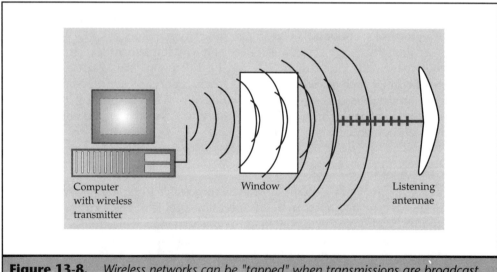

Computer
with wireless
transmitter

Window

Listening
antennae

Figure 13-8.   *Wireless networks can be "tapped" when transmissions are broadcast out of the building*

Public Networks and the Internet

The Internet has received a great deal of attention as the next great computing vehicle in the evolution of computers. It has also received a great deal of attention as the greatest risk to data security ever.

The problem with security on the Internet is the access others have to your internal networks and systems. The Internet works on the concept of open, free access to anyone who wants it. If you have a web server on the Internet, anyone with access to the Internet, anywhere in the world, can attempt to break into your system. The ways to do this are numerous and the means to prevent someone from trying do not exist. Common Internet programs and tools such as gopher, finger, Telnet, ftp, and e-mail have all been used creatively by hackers to access information they were not authorized to view.

Not only that, but a careful hacker can work virtually undetected. The freedom of access to the Internet today, combined with the lack of policing tools and personal privacy issues, makes it impossible to stop someone from trying to access your network through the Internet—repeatedly. There is a culture of "hacking" that discusses trade secrets and reads magazines devoted to exploring techniques for breaking into computing systems. Some are experts in cryptography and know far more about how it is implemented than most network administrators.

For this reason, a great deal of time and energy has been spent trying to understand the various ways Internet "firewalls" can be implemented to prevent unauthorized access to your network. The basic idea of a firewall is simple: place machines between your Internet web server and your internal network that prevent outsiders from establishing communications where your data is compromised. There is a great deal to consider when implementing a firewall for your organization, including the access to your network via various standard Internet access software packages such as gopher and ftp. You would be well served to study this topic in depth prior to establishing a web site.

Data Warehousing

Data warehousing is an extension of an older idea in computing called *decision support*. The basic idea of decision support systems is to give decision makers easy access to information about their organizations, competitors, markets, and other pertinent things so they can make better and faster decisions.

The challenge of decision support systems is supporting the ad hoc nature of the inquiries. This requires relational database technology and a fairly straightforward interface from which to seek out their queries. As it turns out, it also requires huge amounts of information from many sources outside the organization. From such considerations *data warehousing* was born.

The idea behind data warehousing is to collect enormous repositories of information from many different sources and to allow individuals to make database queries against the entire collection for the purpose of analyzing some aspect of the organization's business.

Data warehousing was first implemented commercially by direct marketing firms who had massive mailing lists and survey information at their disposal and also wished to increase the response rate of their mailings. These firms constantly look for the detailed threads of information that may help them characterize the type of customers who will buy a certain type of product. This kind of knowledge helps these companies target their efforts to a certain class of recipients, which reduces their cost while increasing their results.

For instance, a company may find that Canadian women between the ages of 30 and 40 who subscribe to *MAD* magazine and prefer drinking tea to coffee will respond at a very high rate to scratch-and-sniff cards in direct mail pieces. So, if the company sells products where the sense of smell could be exploited, they would use it for this target market.

In a similar fashion, other organizations are now starting to implement data warehousing to analyze their internal processes and markets. For instance, a company that sells hand lotion for men may discover that a decrease of 10 percent in new housing starts over a three-month period correlates with a 25 percent increase in inventory levels of their product. They may use this information in the future to control their manufacturing output to keep their inventory levels manageable.

So the question we pose here is this: what are the data integrity and security risks of data warehousing?

To begin with, data warehousing implies the existence of enormous databases compiled from many different information sources, internally and externally. The simple fact that there is so much data means that some of it will probably be bad. Also, there is no way to verify its accuracy and it may even be impossible to verify how recently the data was collected. This is an age where the exchange of information is big business and many organizations are involved with the buying and selling of databases. As these databases are exchanged, it is likely that mistakes will be made from time to time. This is an obvious data integrity risk.

Because the risk of having inaccurate records is high, data warehousing should not be used for collecting detailed information about any particular item. Detailed information should be extracted from their sources, where you can trace the origins of the data more accurately. Data warehouses are excellent for collecting statistics and performing trend analysis where the percentage of errors is low and the risk from record-level errors can be calculated and interpreted.

Another integrity risk comes from the fact that big databases are extremely difficult to back up and restore. Backing up a 5GB database is easy, and backing up a 50GB database is much more difficult, but backing up a 500GB database is almost impossible and the restore side is even worse. Yet this is the range of data warehouse databases. While the machinery to enable this is being rapidly developed using such techniques as symmetric multiprocessing, massively parallel processing, and clustering, the ability to protect it is running far behind. Administrators trying to find ways to back up data warehouses should consider purchasing 19mm VHS tape equipment used for scientific data recording. Although they are relatively quite expensive, they are probably the only devices with the performance and capacity for the job.

The big security risk in data warehousing comes from the environment of selling information to other organizations for a profit. Companies should think very carefully about the information they sell because once it is out of their control it could be sold illegally to competitors or stolen from a buyer who may not implement adequate security. Human errors also come into play; if there is the potential for a human to make an innocent mistake transferring information, it will probably happen. So, while it may look attractive to sell information very profitably, you must carefully consider the risk of doing so.

To protect your organization from purchasing innaccurate or outdated database information, the source of the information should be verified. If you can't determine the source, you may not want to trust it. Also you should try to understand precisely what the information represents or how it was gathered, especially where the potential exists for biased responses. For example, a database could be sold that contains survey information about people's attitudes about electronic banking. It might be useful to know that the survey was done on the Interent on the home page of a large bank. Considering the bank could have a marketing message associated with the survey and that the respondents all use computers on the Internet already, this would not suffice as an objective survey that samples evenly across various demographic groups.

Another thing to verify when collecting database information for data warehousing is the age of the data, or how current it is. You should always try to make sure that the information was collected as recently as possible unless, of course, you want to analyze information that varies over time. Information about sales performance, economic conditions, and public opinion changes frequently. Making decisions based on outdated information could miss new trends as they are emerging.

Similarly, one should be careful not to mix the wrong versions of data together. This means that if you receive some set of raw data from a supplier every six months, you will want to ensure that you receive the complete set. Otherwise, there might still be old data that hasn't been updated being used with the new data. Considering the number of sources and the amount of raw data in a data warehousing system, this could easily happen.

Security considerations in data warehousing are similar to those for most other networked systems, except for the scenarios discussed above when an organization is selling its own information to the outside world. One of the ways to reduce the likelihood of selling the wrong information is to automate the collection of it so people are less involved with it. Using automated scheduling tools and robotic media handlers, such as tape autoloaders, will reduce the opportunity for human error to occur.

It is probably a good idea to consult with your database administrator on a regular basis about the contents of the data your organization is selling to ensure that any changes made to your databases do not result in sensitive information being inadvertently leaked by mistake.

Beyond the Year 2000

As is common for most writings on computers, the contents of this book will be obsolete and need revising within a few years of its publication. Nonetheless, we hope it has been informative and educational to its readers.

As a final exercise, we'll try to predict the future a little further out in an attempt to start preparing for security and data integrity issues after the year 2000.

Today, leading experts in the field of cryptography and computer-related risks are not very hopeful about the ability to stop security breaches on networks. The Internet offers a wealth of wonderful potential, but also provides a perfect environment for hackers and thieves to make endless attempts to steal information with very little risk of being caught.

The concept of "guard dog" (with teeth) security programs, which may be able to counterattack hackers, will likely emerge as one of the best defenses against security attacks. Warnings to hackers that a "guard dog" exists at your site could suffice to keep most of them away. Such products would, of course, be controversial. The problems of "biting" an innocent web browser (even if they were hacking) would no doubt lead to complicated legal maneuverings. Still, throughout history, in games and in war, it has been shown that one of the best defensive strategies is to take a strong offensive position. Internet security may have to adopt a similar position to thwart its enormous security problems.

The nature of data integrity will not change after the turn of the century. The issue will still be trying to make redundant copies of data somehow so it can be recovered following some disaster. However, the amount of data to protect will cause real headaches. The level of data integrity protection you have depends on the capabilities of storage management systems to adequately protect data. If current trends continue, the cost of magnetic disk storage will be about five cents per megabyte, or about $50 per gigabyte of storage. At these prices, the amount of storage online in many organizations will be staggering. Backups will be extremely difficult.

Therefore, products for data archiving and migration as well as HSM will be needed just to keep the amount of online data small enough to be backed up. High-speed, long-distance I/O busses such as Fibre Channel and SSA will be implemented and support many of today's SCSI-type devices as LAN administrators continue to push for high-speed, centralized systems management.

Faster and higher-capacity devices and systems will be required by many organizations so they can complete their data protection operations overnight. Unfortunately, it does not appear that the speeds and capacities of removable storage devices are keeping pace with the capacities of network storage. The use of real-time backup to specialized storage servers will increase out of necessity as organizations find themselves with far too much data and not enough time to back it up using conventional methods.

The use of distributed databases will be more commonplace as organizations use them to build systems with faster response times and lower costs that best reflect the localized nature of their businesses. The sychronization technology to adequately back up such distributed database systems will be developed, but probably will be challenging to implement and maintain.

Hopefully, the future will see the emergence of enabling standards in storage management for data integrity and security that allow organizations to build reliable systems that they can manage adequately. Such standards always take a long time to develop and are accelerated by the interests and demands of the market. Readers are encouraged to talk to their vendors about standards implementations in data integrity and security in order to maintain an awareness of the importance of standards in these areas.

APPENDIX A

Excerpts from St. Bernard Software's White Paper on Open File Manager™

The following material contains edited excerpts from St. Bernard Software's white paper on their Open File Manager product.

Operating systems, including Novell NetWare, provide access control to server files. When an application opens a file it can choose the conditions under which other applications may be allowed access while the first application still has the file open. In many cases—including, for example, Microsoft Windows 3.11 Write—files are opened in deny write mode, allowing applications subsequently opening the file read access, but denying them the ability to write to the file. Other applications, for example Aldus PageMaker 5.0, open files in deny read mode, preventing other applications from reading or writing to the file.

It therefore follows that a Windows Write file could be backed up while Write had the file open, but a PageMaker file cannot be backed up while PageMaker has it open.

Data Integrity

Even if read access can be obtained, there are fundamental reasons why it is unsafe to back up an open file. The smallest unit of disk data that can be backed up is a single file, since neither the backup program nor the operating system has knowledge of the internal structure of a file that could belong to any one of an infinite number of possible applications.

The backup copy of a file needs to be an exact image of the original at a given point in time. Copying a file, however, is not an instantaneous process. The time taken will depend on the size of the file and the speed of the copy. This leads to a problem unless the backup program can ensure no other application modifies the file during the copy.

To copy a file, the backup program allocates an area of memory as a transfer buffer, and proceeds by alternately reading blocks of the source file into the buffer, and writing the buffer contents out to the backup device. Unless the file is very small, a number of read and write operations will be required to make a complete copy of the file.

Consider a file that is copied by ten read/write operations:

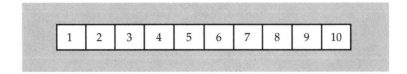

The backup program copies each block in turn. Halfway through the backup, while copying block 5, another application makes small changes to blocks 3 and 8, which together form part of a single transaction (e.g., a debit and a corresponding credit). It can be seen that the backup will capture the change to block 8 but not the change to block 3 since it has already been copied. Consequently, the backup copy contains a partial transaction that may well make the backup copy useless, since the application that owns it will probably consider the file corrupt.

The problem is particularly relevant in database applications where many users require simultaneous access to a given file, and a single transaction is likely to make a number of small changes in different places within the file.

Common Approaches Used by Backup Products for Copying Open Files

Existing backup products typically use one or more of the following methods in an attempt to minimize the open file problem.

Backup Program Opens the File in Deny Write Mode

Many backup programs attempt to open files in deny write mode themselves, thereby preventing any other application from obtaining write access while the file is backed up. This ensures a good copy of the file, but denies write access to other applications. Users are "locked out" of the file during the backup. This method only works if deny write access can be obtained. Often it cannot.

Skip the File and Optionally Retry It Later

If exclusive write access cannot be obtained, the backup software will skip the file and try to back it up later after waiting some time period or at the end of the backup. Again, this method only works if deny write access can eventually be obtained.

Open the File Without Exclusive Write Access (Deny None)

The problem with this approach is that another application or user can modify the file during backups, corrupting the backup copy. This approach allows the backup system to get a copy of the file, even though the copy may be worthless.

Use a Database Agent

Some database systems, such as Sybase and Oracle, provide API technology that allows backup products to safely back up their files while they are in use. This can successfully overcome problems with open files for that particular system's files. These backup products do not protect open files from other applications that may reside on the same system. This approach requires the backup vendor to develop a specific target agent that works with the database's API. Such agents take development resources from the backup software developer, and hence have an associated cost.

With the exception of database-specific target agents, none of the approaches outlined previously allows updates to be written to open files without compromising the integrity of the backup.

The St. Bernard Software Open File Manager™ Approach

Open File Manager is designed to work with a wide variety of industry-standard backup solutions. It complements other network backup software products by allowing them to safely back up open files on NetWare servers. Some significant points are described in the following sections.

Access to All Files for Backup

This feature enables backup of open files, even if they are already in use before backup starts and irrespective of the access mode or file locking status set by other applications. This includes the NetWare 3.*x* bindery and NetWare 4.*x* Directory Services.

Does Not Affect Access by Other Applications

Files opened by the backup system do not prevent or restrict access by other users or applications, including read/write access. Access rights are the same as if the backup program had no files open and normal access control is preserved for other applications.

Backup Data Does Not Change During Backup

Open File Manager ensures that the backup program receives a fixed copy of the file, which never changes during backup. The backup copy cannot be corrupted by another application.

Detection Mechanisms Prevent Partial Transactions in Backup

This feature ensures that another application is not part way through writing a transaction when backup begins. Operation is automatic and transparent to the backup program. Open File Manager detects, and works in conjunction with, the NetWare Transaction Tracking System (TTS) if it is being used.

Ability to Group Files into Logical Sets for Backup

Open File Manager allows configurable groups of files to be considered as a single unit for backup purposes. If any one file in the group is opened for backup, none of the files in the group will change until they have all been backed up. This feature allows database systems that are composed of groups of files to be backed up as a consistent set.

Open File Copy Feature

Open File Manager can also be used to make copies of open files for system management purposes other than backup. A system manager might, for example, wish to place a copy of a live database on another machine for training or experimental purposes.

This cannot be done if the database is in use, because "copy" commands generally require exclusive access to the source file to be sure it is not modified during the copy. Even if access is allowed, the problem of integrity over one or more files remains.

The problem could, of course, be solved by using Open File Manager with a backup program, where the backup system would perform a redirected restore of the database to the desired location.

In addition to this approach, Open File Manager provides a facility where the system manager logs in to the server containing the live database using a specific login ID that has been registered with Open File Manager. When this login ID performs a copy operation, Open File Manager will be invoked to allow the file to be copied elsewhere on the network without having to worry about integrity concerns. This technique also works for multiple file database systems, as described earlier, as long as all files in the database have been declared as a group to Open File Manager.

How Open File Manager Works

Open File Manager uses proprietary techniques that identify file access requests from the backup system by the specific login name reserved for backup. Other proprietary techniques provide unconditional file access to the backup program while allowing other applications to have normal access rights.

To ensure data integrity during backups, a pre-image cache, in the form of a standard disk file, is dynamically allocated. When a file is being backed up, updates are temporarily held while OFM writes the old data (that will be overwritten by the update) into the pre-image cache. After the cache is written to, the update is written to disk. As the backup progresses through the file, read requests for blocks that have been updated are satisfied from the pre-image cache. This way the file appears entirely static to the backup application, while it is in fact modified and seen normally by other applications.

As soon as the backup application closes the file, the pre-image data can be discarded. Since the amount of data that actually changes is generally small in relation to the file size, and because only one file is typically being backed up at a time, the amount of pre-image data is insignificant. System performance is only affected for access to the file currently being backed up, and in practice is unnoticeable.

The final technique is to ensure that a file is in a good state at the time access to it is allowed for backup. This is achieved by monitoring TTS (if used) in combination with file write activity.

If a file uses TTS either explicitly or implicitly, its current transactional status is determined; otherwise, the elapsed time since the last write operation is used to determine transaction breaks. In practice this is a very reliable method, since very few applications spread write activity for a single transaction because of the risk of power failure. A third mechanism is provided to allow an external application to "register" to provide transaction status. Open File Manager then automatically calls the registering application to obtain status when its files are about to be backed up. Using proprietary techniques, Open File Manager can hold file open requests from the backup application indefinitely without any detrimental effect, although typically the delay is only a fraction of a second, and goes entirely unnoticed.

Reliability

Open File Manager has been specifically designed to increase the reliability of backup products, without adding any additional risk to server data. Specifically, the product employs a number of techniques to ensure reliability and data integrity.

Disk Files Are Not Altered or Affected by Open File Manager

Open File Manager only affects data being read by the backup program. It does not cache disk writes; files are updated normally by applications. In the event that the server crashes, no more cache data will be lost than would have been the case if Open File Manager was not loaded. The ability to restore recent backup copies of all files is improved.

Will Not Cause "Disk Full" Problems

NetWare servers can become unstable if available disk space becomes low. Open File Manager includes a detection mechanism to automatically suspend operation and free pre-image data space if the available space falls below a minimum amount. This setting is configurable, and ensures Open File Manager will not cause disk space problems.

APPENDIX B

The Current Status of U.S. Government Activities in Cryptography

As discussed in Chapter 10, the U.S. government has had a major role in defining policies and technologies for authentication and encryption. This appendix is for those who are interested in knowing more about this. The following excerpt was edited and extracted from RSA Data Security, Inc.'s publication "Answers to Frequently Asked Questions About Today's Cryptography."

What Is NIST?

NIST is an acronym for the National Institute of Standards and Technology, a division of the U.S. Department of Commerce; it was formerly known as the National Bureau of Standards (NBS). Through its Computer Systems Laboratory it aims to promote open systems and interoperability that will spur development of computer-based economic activity. NIST issues standards and guidelines that it hopes will be adopted by all computer systems in the U.S., and also sponsors workshops and seminars. Official standards are produced as FIPS (Federal Information Processing Standards) publications.

In 1987, Congress passed the Computer Security Act, which authorized NIST to develop standards for ensuring the security of sensitive but unclassified information in government computer systems. It encouraged NIST to work with other government agencies and private industry in evaluating proposed computer security standards.

What Role Does NIST Play in Cryptography?

NIST issues standards for cryptographic routines; U.S. government agencies are required to use them, and the private sector often adopts them as well. In January 1977, NIST declared DES (Data Encryption Standard) the official U.S. encryption standard and published it as FIPS Publication 46; DES soon became a de facto standard throughout the U.S.

A few years ago, NIST was asked to choose a set of cryptographic standards for the U.S.; this has become known as the Capstone project. After a few years of rather secretive deliberations, and in cooperation with the NSA (National Security Agency), NIST issued proposals for various standards in cryptography, including digital signatures (DSS) and data encryption (the Clipper chip). These are pieces of the overall Capstone project.

NIST has been criticized for allowing the NSA too much power in setting cryptographic standards, since the interests of the NSA conflict with those of the Commerce Department and NIST. Yet the NSA has much more experience with cryptography, and has many more qualified cryptographers and cryptanalysts than does NIST; it would be unrealistic to expect NIST to forego such available assistance.

What Is the NSA?

The NSA is the National Security Agency, a highly secretive agency of the U.S. government that was created by Harry Truman in 1952; its very existence was kept secret for many years. The NSA has a mandate to listen to and decode all foreign communications of interest to the security of the United States. It also has used its power in various ways to slow the spread of publicly available cryptography in order to prevent national enemies from employing encryption methods too strong for the NSA to break.

As the premier cryptographic government agency, the NSA has huge financial and computer resources and employs a host of cryptographers. Developments in cryptography achieved at the NSA are not made public; this secrecy has led to many rumors about the NSA's ability to break popular cryptosystems like DES and also to rumors that the NSA has secretly placed weaknesses, called *trapdoors*, in government-endorsed cryptosystems, such as DES. These rumors have never been proved or disproved, and the criteria used by the NSA in selecting cryptography standards have never been made public.

Recent advances in the computer and telecommunications industries have placed NSA actions under unprecedented scrutiny, and the agency has become the target of heavy criticism for hindering U.S. industries that wish to use or sell strong cryptographic tools. The two main reasons for this increased criticism are the collapse of the Soviet Union and the development and spread of commercially available public-key cryptographic tools. Under pressure, the NSA may be forced to change its policies.

What Role Does the NSA Play in Commercial Cryptography?

The NSA's charter limits its activities to foreign intelligence. However, the NSA is concerned with the development of commercial cryptography because the availability of strong encryption tools through commercial channels could impede the NSA's mission of decoding international communications; in other words, the NSA is worried lest strong commercial cryptography fall into the wrong hands.

The NSA has stated that it has no objection to the use of secure cryptography by U.S. industry. It also has no objection to cryptographic tools used for authentication, as opposed to privacy. However, the NSA is widely viewed as following policies that have the practical effect of limiting and/or weakening the cryptographic tools used by law-abiding U.S. citizens and corporations.

The NSA exerts influence over commercial cryptography in several ways. First, it controls the export of cryptography from the U.S. The NSA generally does not approve export of products used for encryption unless the key size is strictly limited. It does, however, approve for export any products used for authentication only, no matter how large the key size, as long as the product cannot be converted to be used for encryption. The NSA has also blocked encryption methods from being published or patented, citing a national security threat. Additionally, the NSA serves an "advisory" role to NIST in the evaluation and selection of official U.S. government computer security standards; in this capacity, it has played a prominent, and controversial, role in the selection of DES and in the development of the group of standards known as the Capstone project, which includes DSS and the Clipper chip. The NSA can also exert market pressure on U.S. companies to produce (or refrain from producing) cryptographic goods, since the NSA itself is often a large customer of these companies.

Cryptography is in the public eye as never before and has become the subject of national public debate. The status of cryptography, and the NSA's role in it, will probably change over the next few years.

What Is Capstone?

Capstone is the U.S. government's long-term project to develop a set of standards for publicly available cryptography, as authorized by the Computer Security Act of 1987. The primary agencies responsible for Capstone are NIST and the NSA . The plan calls for the elements of Capstone to become official U.S. government standards, in which case both the government itself and all private companies doing business with the government would be required to use Capstone.

There are four major components of Capstone: a bulk data encryption algorithm, a digital signature algorithm, a key exchange protocol, and a hash function. The data encryption algorithm is called Skipjack, but is often referred to as Clipper, which is the encryption chip that includes Skipjack. The digital signature algorithm is DSS and the hash function is SHS. The key exchange protocol has not yet been announced.

All the parts of Capstone have 80-bit security: all the keys involved are 80 bits long and other aspects are also designed to withstand anything less than an "80-bit" attack, that is, an effort of 2^{80} operations. Eventually, the government plans to place the entire Capstone cryptographic system on a single chip.

What Is Clipper?

Clipper is an encryption chip developed and sponsored by the U.S. government as part of the Capstone project. Announced by the White House in April, 1993, Clipper was designed to balance the competing concerns of federal law-enforcement agencies with those of private citizens and industry. The law-enforcement agencies wish to have access to the communications of suspected criminals, for example by wire-tapping; these needs are threatened by secure cryptography.

Industry and individual citizens, however, want secure communications, and look to cryptography to provide them. Clipper technology attempts to balance these needs by using escrowed keys. The idea is that communications would be encrypted with a secure algorithm, but the keys would be kept by one or more third parties (the "escrow agencies"), and made available to law-enforcement agencies when authorized by a court-issued warrant. Thus, for example, personal communications would be impervious to recreational eavesdroppers, and commercial communications would be impervious to industrial espionage, and yet the FBI could listen in on suspected terrorists or gangsters.

Clipper has been proposed as a U.S. government standard; it would then be used by anyone doing business with the federal government, as well as for communications within the government. For anyone else, use of Clipper is strictly voluntary. AT&T has announced a secure telephone that uses the Clipper chip.

How Does the Clipper Chip Work?

The Clipper chip contains an encryption algorithm called Skipjack, whose details have not been made public. Each chip also contains a unique 80-bit unit key, which is escrowed in two parts at two escrow agencies; both parts must be known in order to recover the key. Also present is a serial number and an 80-bit "family key"; the latter is common to all Clipper chips. The chip is manufactured so that it cannot be reverse engineered; this means that the Skipjack algorithm and the keys cannot be read off the chip.

When two devices wish to communicate, they first agree on an 80-bit "session key." The method by which they choose this key is left up to the implementer's discretion; a public-key method such as RSA or Diffie-Hellman seems a likely choice. The message is encrypted with the key and sent; note that the key is not escrowed. In addition to the encrypted message, another piece of data, called the law-enforcement access field (LEAF), is created and sent. It includes the session key encrypted with the unit key, then concatenated with the serial number of the sender and an authentication string, and then, finally, all encrypted with the family key. The exact details of the law-enforcement field are classified.

The receiver decrypts the law-enforcement field, checks the authentication string, and decrypts the message with the key. Now suppose a law-enforcement agency wishes to tap the line. It uses the family key to decrypt the law-enforcement field; the agency now knows the serial number and has an encrypted version of the session key. It presents an authorization warrant to the two escrow agencies along with the serial number. The escrow agencies give the two parts of the unit key to the law-enforcement agency, which then decrypts to obtain the session key. Then the agency can use the session key to decrypt the actual message.

Who Are the Escrow Agencies?

It has not yet been decided which organizations will serve as the escrow agencies to keep the Clipper chip keys. No law-enforcement agency will be an escrow agency, and it is possible that at least one of the escrow agencies will be an organization outside the government.

It is essential that the escrow agencies keep the key databases extremely secure, since unauthorized access to both escrow databases could allow unauthorized eavesdropping on private communications. In fact, the escrow agencies are likely to be major targets for anyone trying to compromise the Clipper system; the Clipper chip factory is another likely target.

What Is Skipjack?

Skipjack is the encryption algorithm contained in the Clipper chip and was designed by the NSA. It uses an 80-bit key to encrypt 64-bit blocks of data which is the same key is used for the decryption. Skipjack can be used in the same modes as DES, and may be more secure than DES, since it uses 80-bit keys and scrambles the data for 32 steps, or "rounds"; by contrast, DES uses 56-bit keys and scrambles the data for only 16 rounds.

The details of Skipjack are classified. The decision not to make the details of the algorithm publicly available has been widely criticized. Many people are suspicious that Skipjack is not secure, either due to oversight by its designers, or by the deliberate introduction of a secret trapdoor. By contrast, there have been many attempts to find weaknesses in DES over the years, since its details are public. These numerous attempts (and the fact that they have failed) have made people confident in the security of DES. Since Skipjack is not public, the same scrutiny cannot be applied to it, and thus a corresponding level of confidence may not arise.

Aware of such criticism, the government invited a small group of independent cryptographers to examine the Skipjack algorithm. They issued a report that stated that, although their study was too limited to reach a definitive conclusion, they nevertheless believe that Skipjack is secure. Another consequence of Skipjack's classified status is that it cannot be implemented in software, but only in hardware by government-authorized chip manufacturers.

Why Is Clipper Controversial?

The Clipper chip proposal has aroused much controversy and has been the subject of much criticism. Unfortunately, two distinct issues have become confused in the large volume of public comment and discussion.

First, there is controversy about the whole idea of escrowed keys. Those in favor of escrowed keys see them as a way to provide secure communications for the public at large while allowing law-enforcement agencies to monitor the communications of suspected criminals. Those opposed to escrowed keys see them as an unnecessary and ineffective intrusion of the government into the private lives of citizens. They argue that escrowed keys infringe on their rights of privacy and free speech. It will take a lot of time and much public discussion for society to reach a consensus on what role, if any, escrowed keys should have.

The second area of controversy concerns various objections to the specific Clipper proposal, that is, objections to this particular implementation of escrowed keys, as opposed to the idea of escrowed keys in general. Common objections include that the Skipjack algorithm is not public and may not be secure; the key escrow agencies will be vulnerable to attack; there are not enough key escrow agencies; the keys on the Clipper chips are not generated in a sufficiently secure fashion; there will not be sufficient competition among implementers, resulting in expensive and slow chips; software implementations are not possible; and the key size is fixed and cannot be increased if necessary.

An alternative system has been proposed, called *fair public-key cryptography*, that also attempts to balance the privacy concerns of law-abiding citizens with the investigative concerns of law-enforcement agencies. It is similar in function and purpose to the Clipper chip proposal except that users can choose their own keys, which they register with the escrow agencies. Also, the system does not require secure hardware and can be implemented completely in software.

What Is the Current Status of Clipper?

Clipper is under review. Both the executive branch and Congress are considering it, and an advisory panel recently recommended a full year-long public discussion of cryptography policy. NIST has invited the public to send comments, as part of its own review.

What Is DSS?

DSS is the proposed Digital Signature Standard, which specifies a Digital Signature Algorithm (DSA) and is a part of the U.S. government's Capstone project. It was selected by NIST, in cooperation with the NSA, to be the digital authentication standard of the U.S. government. Whether the government should, in fact, adopt it as the official standard is still under debate. It is for authentication only.

Several articles in the press have discussed the industry dissatisfaction with DSS. It has, for the most part, been looked upon unfavorably by the computer industry, much of which has already standardized on RSA.

The most serious criticisms of DSS involve its security. DSS was originally proposed with a fixed 512-bit key size. After much criticism that this is not secure enough, NIST revised DSS to allow key sizes up to 1,024 bits. More critical, however, is the fact that DSS has not been around long enough to withstand repeated attempts to break it; although the discrete log problem on which DSS is based is old, the particular form of the problem used in DSS was first proposed for cryptographic use in 1989 and has not received much public study.

In general, any new cryptosystem could have serious flaws that are only discovered after years of scrutiny by cryptographers. In the absence of mathematical proofs of security, nothing builds confidence in a cryptosystem like sustained attempts to crack it. Although DSS may well turn out to be a strong cryptosystem, its relatively short history will leave doubts for years to come. In contrast, RSA has withstood over 15 years of vigorous examination for weaknesses.

Some researchers warned about the existence of "trapdoor" primes in DSS, which could enable a key to be easily broken. These trapdoor primes are relatively rare however, and are easily avoided if proper key generation procedures are followed.

There are also performance concerns. In the DSS system, signature generation is faster than signature verification; whereas in the RSA system, signature verification is faster than signature generation. NIST claims that it is an advantage of DSS that signing is faster, but many people in cryptography think that it is better for verification to be the faster operation.

Index

About the Authors...

Andrew R. MacBride happily lives and works in the San Francisco Bay Area. He worked at Sun Microsystems for several years on the design and implementation of networked object-oriented systems and user interfaces. Following this, he was a technical consultant for Component Integration Labs, Inc. Educated at the University of California, Berkeley, he has returned there to work on distributed database systems.

Joshua Susser is one of the principal designers of OpenDoc, and one of the implementors of OpenDoc on MacOS. He has worked at Apple Computer long enough to be able to talk about the "good old days," doing research on component systems in the Advanced Technology Group, and product development in developer tools and system software groups. Previously he worked at Xerox, building integrated applications and doing Smalltalk-80 system development. He currently resides in the San Francisco Bay Area.

Byte Guide to OpenDoc

Andrew MacBride &
Joshua Susser

Osborne **McGraw-Hill**

Berkeley New York St. Louis San Francisco
Auckland Bogotá Hamburg London Madrid
Mexico City Milan Montreal New Delhi Panama City
Paris São Paulo Singapore Sydney Tokyo Toronto

Osborne **McGraw-Hill**
2600 Tenth Street
Berkeley, California 94710
U.S.A.

For information on translations or book distributors outside the U.S.A., or to arrange bulk purchase discounts for sales promotions, premiums, or fundraisers, please contact Osborne **McGraw-Hill** at the above address.

Byte Guide to OpenDoc

1234567890 DOC 99876

ISBN 0-07-882118-5

Acquisitions Editor
Cindy Brown

Technical Reviewer
Jens Alfke

Project Editor
Vicki Van Ausdall

Copy Editor
Judy Ziajka

Proofreader
Jeff Barash

Computer Designer
Jani Beckwith

Illustrator
Lance Ravella

Series Design
Jani Beckwith

Quality Control Specialist
Joe Scuderi

Contents At A Glance

Contents

Foreword

It's been a real pleasure watching this book take shape. After years of work, there's a tremendous sense of enjoyment in seeing someone else explain the project you've labored on, and do it well.

As I was reading it, I began thinking about a time about a decade ago, a time when one of the authors, Joshua Susser, was working with me on a personal workstation system. The software was quite extensive, written almost entirely in Smalltalk-80.

We all loved working on the project, because we had such an extensive base of reusable software to start with. We could add functionality at a fearsome rate. At its peak, the system did a lot of the things that personal computers do today. It had a compound document system, an interface builder, a raft of productivity tools like outliners and spreadsheets and databases and mapping programs. It had drawing and painting programs, it had terminal emulators and networking. It had its own integrated file-system interface that provided hypertext linking between elements of its information base. It had just about everything you could ask for, and it ran on 4MB systems with small disk drives. It was cross-platform, and ran on Xerox workstations, Sun workstations, Macintosh, DOS machines, and a few other esoteric bits of hardware.

The entire thing was put together by a team that typically had about six programmers. Over the course of the six or so years that I worked on it, we released it to our customers at least 20 times. Our productivity numbers and bug rates were nothing short of fantastic.

It's easy to imagine that a piece of work like this would have taken over the world by now.

So why didn't it? Well, there were a number of reasons, but by far the most important one is this: it didn't work with anything else. As we worked on it, we told ourselves that this didn't matter, that if we just put enough features into the package it would catch on. After all, we were adding features at a rate that actually kept up nicely with most of the rest of the personal computer industry at the time. Eventually, people would "get it" and switch to start using our stuff.

That thinking was naive, of course. Even then, people had large investments in existing data formats and mainframe programs. Everybody needs to work with other people, and everybody needs to work with systems that are already in place. Often, people have no control over the decisions that drive the decisions that keep certain bits of software in general use.

If you think about your own software purchases, you'll probably see what I mean. When was the last time you really comparison shopped for software, instead of simply buying the latest upgrade? If you did do the comparison, how much did compatibility with everybody else affect your decision?

So it became clear, after a while, that mere technology wasn't the answer for our beloved workstation system. Leaving that glorious project was hard, but eventually the truth of the situation sunk in, and I was forced to go somewhere where I thought I could do more good. I resolved never to make that mistake again, if I could help it.

So now you have a book in your hands about OpenDoc. It's a great book, a clear explanation of how to go about a very hard task, making your software work with other people's software. It's a sort of primer for understanding the new world of components.

As you read the book, you're going to need to get used to the idea of being "polite" when you write software. Being polite means understanding what to do and what not to do when writing code. It means understanding that you can't just change the menus any time you want. It feels restrictive, at first, because you used to be able to do that sort of thing with impunity. It's a lot like learning, when you're two years old, that you can't just punch the other little kids when they don't share their toys with you.

This sort of thing has been going on for a long time. Every major advance in computing has been an exercise in enforcing a greater level of "politeness" so that programs could be created more quickly and reliably. High-level languages, operating systems, I/O redirection, subroutine libraries and toolboxes, and graphical interfaces are all examples of this process at work. As each became popular, a segment of the programming population complained that they were too restrictive, that quality software couldn't be done that way.

In every case, they've been proved wrong. Eventually, the advantages of working with other people's code outweigh the potential disadvantages that standardization imposes. Much as with human societies, the advantages of working together outweigh the delights of untrammeled individual freedom. There are exceptions, of course, where each of the technologies I just mentioned must be bypassed. By and large, though, it's better to use them than not.

What OpenDoc is doing is trying to lay down the basic rules of etiquette in a society of cooperating components. It's a conscious attempt to be fair, open, and non-proprietary, and yet still lay down enough rules to make cooperation work well. When you read this book, you'll be getting your first dose of that etiquette.

So as you read this book, remember the glorious project that was doomed by its isolation. A little cooperation, and a few rules of etiquette, and your favorite project can be spared the same fate. Working together is the key, and working together requires rules of conduct. OpenDoc provides those rules, and this book is your guide to the new etiquette.

Make Miss Manners proud.

—Kurt Piersol
OpenDoc Architect
Apple Computer, Inc.

Acknowledgments

Writing a book is a long process; I'd like to acknowledge some of the people who helped me along the way. Joshua Susser, my friend, wondered if I had any interest in writing a book with him. The answer was yes, and we're even still friends. Jens Alfke, our technical editor, kept us honest; Brad Shimmin got the project started and provided encouragement. The people at Osborne worked very hard on this project; special thanks to Vicki Van Ausdall, for efforts above and beyond the call of duty. The staff at Jumpin' Java kept me nourished during the writing of the book, while Todd Huge kept me entertained. Jed Harris, Neil Katin, Bart Calder, Robert Gahl, Lucy Sheldon, and Eve Margozzi got me involved with OpenDoc in the first place and served as mentors, coworkers, and friends.

Finally, a thank you to Scott, for his patience and support.

—Andrew MacBride

Thanks to

- Brad Shimmin for getting the book project going.

- The staff at Osborne for all their hard work and for putting up with us.

- The OpenDoc team at Apple, for being the best bunch of people I've ever worked with.

- The regulars on the OpenDoc-Interest mailing list, for showing what developers really needed to know about OpenDoc.

- Kurt Piersol for dreaming up OpenDoc and for not complaining too much about my driving on Highway 17.

- And of course Andrew for being such an awesome co-author.

—Joshua Susser

Introduction

As a software professional, life is complicated by a fast-moving industry and by the shifting demands and needs of your customers. Some days it seems quite enough to cope with the current crisis, much less think about the next one (or two, or five) that you might face. Unfortunately, it is a survival requirement to look ahead and plan for the changes, or else be overwhelmed by them.

Luckily, there are some technologies available to help solve the problems faced by users, software developers, and the IS professionals who support and manage them. This book is intended to help introduce the technology of OpenDoc to these audiences, and demonstrate some of the ways in which it can help people to do their jobs efficiently and productively.

End Users

These are the men and women whose requirements and needs drove the development of OpenDoc in the first place. In offices, homes, and schools, the push toward media-rich, collaborative computing has pushed current technology to its limit (and in some unfortunate cases, to its breaking point).

Developers

These are the people whose technology has been stretched, broken, and generally abused. The demands of the marketplace have led to ever-growing pressures on the current software tools and infrastructure, which have proven to be inadequate to the demands of media-rich, highly interactive applications. As a result, schedules slip, products are delayed, and finally the product ships: large, slow, and filled with bugs.

IS Professionals

As managers of software projects and also as the purchasers of software for corporate networks, IS professionals have to attempt to solve the problems of the first two groups. Trying to quench the thirst of the user base for new features, they attempt to upgrade to the latest version of critical software, only to discover that it is eight months late, uses twice the memory of the previous version, and is plagued by a number of intermittent, annoying flaws.

The hapless manager of such a project finds herself blamed for the lateness, even though the project was delayed twice because the marketing department had insisted on adding new features late in the product cycle due to competitive pressures.

The people responsible for the bottom line in either scenario will probably ask some difficult questions, such as

How did this happen? We always used to ship on time.

and

Can you tell me how to keep this from happening again?

Hopefully, this book will give you an answer to the second question.

Chapter 1: Overview of OpenDoc

This chapter explores the highest-level concepts related to OpenDoc, and it is aimed toward a broad audience. It starts with an overview of OpenDoc and of component software in general. It discusses some of the business reasons for moving toward a component software model, touching on the economic, productivity, and marketing benefits. It talks about some of the obstacles that may be faced in moving toward a component model but discusses the benefits, as well.

It then talks about the role of CI Labs, and a bit of the rationale for setting up a separate entity to guide the evolution of OpenDoc. It touches on some of the features of similar systems, such as Microsoft's OLE2 and Taligent's CommonPoint, including discussions of features, cross-platform availability, and "openness."

Next, the chapter moves on to talk about the founding members of CI Labs and what commitments each have made. It also discusses the role of sponsor companies.

Chapter 2: OpenDoc Concepts

This chapter builds on the high-level concepts of Chapter 1 and goes into more detail. It explains the human interface (HI) model and talks about some of the differences that the user might expect to see between the current application-centered model and the OpenDoc document-centered model, and it suggests ways to help minimize user confusion.

Part of the discussion will touch upon the way that OpenDoc documents are structured, and how that differs from the current models of application use. It compares the processing and memory requirements of a component-based document to the wholesale linking of large, monolithic applications. A discussion of content models defines how component boundaries are the separations between different content models (i.e., data plus the operations on that data). The chapter then talks about the shell/container model, and briefly mentions how existing applications can be retrofitted to play in the OpenDoc world.

The last part of the chapter touches briefly on the services provided by the various OpenDoc subsystems, leaving a more detailed treatment for Chapter 4.

Chapter 3: Development with OpenDoc

Chapter 3 provides an overview of the development environment and the development process, including the installation process for part editors. Installation of OpenDoc itself is discussed in Appendix B. Since there are in some cases multiple supported development environments, the discussion focuses on the common points, with pointers to sources of environment-specific information. It talks about differences and similarities with traditional application development.

The chapter focuses on issues that are specific to the OpenDoc environment, rather than being a general primer on software development. In particular, it talks about the impact of using SOM to build part editors and ways to minimize that impact. It also discusses the exception-handling and memory-management facilities in OpenDoc.

The discussion of developer resources talks about the registries maintained by CI Labs and points interested developers to the CI Labs WWW page. These registries include those for the OpenEvent (AppleEvent) suites, ISO 9070 names for user properties, and OpenDoc Extensions.

Chapter 4: Getting Started with OpenDoc

This chapter is aimed primarily at engineers and technical managers. The fourth chapter goes into more detail on the OpenDoc subsystems mentioned in Chapter 2, talking about each in brief, with a focus on the important concepts in each (e.g., drawing, frames, and facets in the Imaging subsystem; drafts in the Storage subsystem; and the dispatcher in the UI/Event subsystem). These concepts lead naturally into a discussion of creating a simple part, which is discussed more fully in Chapter 5.

Chapter 4 begins with a discussion of the persistent structure of an OpenDoc document and is followed by a discussion of the runtime structure. The chapter discusses the important protocols that the part must obey and touches on some of the important method calls that the part editor must make.

Users who have already installed the OpenDoc SDK can proceed to Chapter 5, "A Simple OpenDoc Part." Others should refer to Appendix B and the installation discussion contained there.

Chapter 5: A Simple OpenDoc Part

This chapter introduces the developer to the process of writing a sample part. It discusses SOM and C++ and how the two are used in the sample part editor. Next, it breaks the sample code up into pieces and discusses how the implementation relates to the abstract concepts presented earlier. It discusses initialization, opening a window, the layout subsystem, drawing, event handling, activation and user interaction, and storage. It then discusses how this simple code can be extended to add features.

At this point, readers can skip ahead to Chapter 7, "Adding Features," or can proceed to Chapter 6, "Cross-Platform Portability."

Chapter 6: Cross-Platform Portability

This chapter talks about general strategies for portability and compares and contrasts the simple part example (from Chapter 5) on the various OpenDoc platforms. It mentions the cross-platform tools that are available (and refers readers to sources of additional information). The chapter goes into more detail on how the sample code fits together, and strategies for increasing cross-platform portability.

Chapter 7: Adding Features

The focus of this chapter is adding features to the example part. At the completion of this chapter, the reader has a fairly complete OpenDoc part that supports the basic protocols and plays as a "good citizen" in the OpenDoc world. More importantly, it can serve as a model for new code that a developer might wish to write. It adds several important features, such as drag and drop, window display, multiple presentations, scripting, and undo/redo. It discusses linking and embedding but does not add these features to the sample part. It does, however, contain a memory-management discussion and sample code.

Chapter 8: Interoperability and Migration

This chapter talks about the process of migrating to OpenDoc, and that how that decision does not necessitate abandoning old systems; it demonstrates OpenDoc as a solution to some real-world problems.

It describes how legacy systems can be retrofitted to work with OpenDoc, either as parts, or as container applications. The chapter contains a scenario to make this discussion more clear.

Following this is a discussion of ComponentGlue for OLE interoperability, and interoperability with Taligent. Next comes a discussion of CORBA in general, and how OpenDoc will be able to take advantage of CORBA-networked services.

Finally, there is a discussion of standard parts and data formats, and how that helps OpenDoc work seamlessly across platforms.

Chapter 9: Underlying Technologies

This chapter is aimed at those who wish to know a bit more about the technology that makes OpenDoc work. It talks about the benefits of SOM (language neutrality, CORBA compliance), the advantages of scriptability, and the advantages of having a widely available cross-platform file format. It has four sections: a discussion of SOM, a discussion of Bento, a review of common scripting systems, and a description of how the ComponentGlue technology does its work.

Chapter 10: OpenDoc: Current Systems and Future Possibilities

The final chapter talks about some of the announced future directions for OpenDoc. It mentions how the OpenDoc framework is itself extensible, with replaceable subsystems and additional user-definable behaviors.

Chapter 10 talks about several projects that are using OpenDoc currently and some other speculation about how OpenDoc might fit into future software architectures.

It ends with an extensive list of additional resources available on the Internet and from the sponsors, members, and community-at-large.

Appendix A: Class Reference

This is a listing of classes, with a brief note about each. It refers to the official class reference for the most detailed information.

It contains a treatment of the ODPart class, which contains about 60 API calls plus a small number that are inherited or overridden. It has a sentence or two explaining each call, and provides a brief overview.

Appendix B: Installing OpenDoc

This appendix has an extensive discussion and hands-on tutorial on OpenDoc installation for MacOS and Windows. It also presents a PartMaker session on Windows. (A Macintosh PartMaker session was presented in Chapter 3.)

Appendix C: Example Source Code

This appendix contains selected methods from the example source code for the part that was developed in Chapters 5, 6, and 7. The chapter contains pointers to the location of the source code, available on the Internet.

Appendix D: Bibliography and Resources

This appendix presents the references that the authors have found helpful in writing this book as well as when developing software. It contains references to books, magazine articles, and web sites.

Appendix E: Platform Differences

This appendix discusses some of the differences among platform implementations. Most are due to the differing maturity levels of the platform implementations and are expected to disappear over time. Although the architecture is such that this is supposed to be minimal, there are still some pragmatic decisions that had to be made.

Putting it Together

Each chapter ends with a brief recap of the contents of the chapter, as well as some thoughts on how one might put the pieces together to form more coherent, focused ideas about how OpenDoc works.

Online Resources

There is a web site for this book at:

http://www.splash.net/books/opendoc/

It contains any updates and corrections as well as the source code for the example part presented in Chapters 5, 6, and 7.

CHAPTER 1

Overview of OpenDoc

A system that enables the development of component software and robust compound documents holds promise for solving some of the problems faced by users, corporate information science managers, and software developers. OpenDoc is such a system and has advantages over competing schemes in terms of its design, wide availability, and open systems foundation.

Software development is rapidly approaching a point where traditional models, practices, and methods begin to break down and become useless. In fact, some say software development is already at that point, given the now-customary delays that plague many large software projects. For the industry to continue as it has in the past would be foolish at best and disastrous at worst.

Information science (IS) managers responsible for the deployment of software across organizations are just as concerned about another type of software crisis. They face users' demands for software customized to their needs and upper management's desire to have the same software working across all hardware owned by the company. Both want software that allows all the employees of the organization to work together efficiently and well.

Many problems can be traced to a single cause: the ever-increasing number of features in each version of software. Each major revision of a product needs to contain new or improved features so customers can justify purchasing it. It must be able to differentiate itself from competitive products, as well as match their feature sets.

Naturally, this leads to increases in program size and complexity. This process ends with several programs doing many similar things with varying degrees of success. It can also end with products being too late to market to remain viable. Many manufacturers have attempted to address this issue by providing facilities for adding modules to their programs via plug-ins or extensions, but while this may be fine for an individual vendor, the modules are not universally useful, as Figure 1-1 illustrates.

The extension approach, though flawed, has proven that there is a market for component software. (Kai's Power Tools is one of many plug-in packages for Adobe Photoshop; XTensions, which add functions to QuarkXPress, are also very popular.) What is needed is a way to make such components widely available to a variety of programs, without components' requiring any knowledge of the uses to which they may be put. OpenDoc is a carefully planned, platform-neutral attempt

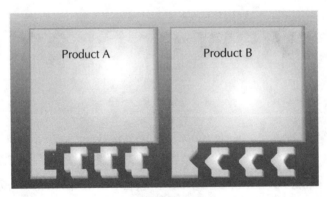

Some products can be *extended*, but . . .

most extensions are specific to a single product.

FIGURE 1-1. *Software extensions*

to solve this problem. It can make useful software components accessible by any other OpenDoc-, OLE-, or CommonPoint-aware application. Available across all major desktop and server operating systems, OpenDoc provides the structures and facilities to enable software developers to concentrate on their areas of expertise and yet add value to software for many different types of endeavors.

As software development has become more complex, many attempts have been made to simplify the development process. Each has been hailed as "revolutionary" and has promised to reduce the complexity of the software development effort (or at least to slow the rate of increase). Unstructured "spaghetti" code gave way to structured code, which gave way to the object-oriented techniques of today. Even as techniques have evolved to handle complexity, the demands of the marketplace for more features and peripheral support across more hardware platforms have offset these remedies. The economics of the industry, now dominated by a small number of large players (notably Microsoft), have made it difficult if not impossible for small developers to reach a broad consumer base. When the market is dominated by a few large, feature-rich programs, it suddenly becomes important to play by their rules, evade those same rules, or do both.

OpenDoc is an attempt to do both: it allows small companies to innovate within the framework set by larger competitors, such as Microsoft, yet not be dominated by their requirements. OpenDoc provides a well-designed system for creating compound documents (and component software in general), frees the software designer to concentrate on his or her particular added value, and perhaps most important, provides an economic model for the success of the small developer. OpenDoc enables the creation of software components across platforms, allowing custom solutions and easy collaboration.

This book introduces the concepts that underlie OpenDoc, demonstrates how to build both simple and more complicated OpenDoc components, and serves as a reference to other resources available to users of OpenDoc and developers of OpenDoc components.

What Is OpenDoc?

OpenDoc is an architecture and a collection of technologies that enables the creation of compound documents. It provides a practical method for creating software components rather than large, monolithic applications that attempt to do everything. Ever since the advent of object-oriented programming, reusability and standardization have been promised, but the approaches have always had problems. Now, however, the technology has evolved to the point where it is both practical and economically feasible to structure software this way. OpenDoc components work with any OpenDoc-enabled application, as shown in Figure 1-2.

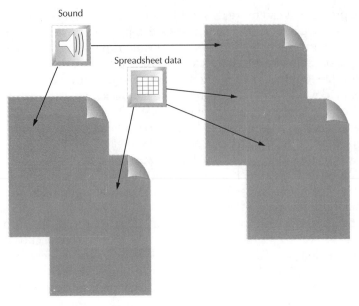

FIGURE 1-2.   *OpenDoc components*

Years of design and development work have made the OpenDoc architecture simple, yet complete. It is an integrated architecture rather than a collection of features added in an ad hoc fashion. It strikes a careful balance between mechanism and policy by providing most of the facilities that a developer or administrator may need plus a few carefully chosen policies to ensure that the facilities are used in the most logical fashion. There are many examples of well-structured OpenDoc components and development frameworks to make the creation of OpenDoc components easy.

The driving force behind OpenDoc is the advent of compound documents and multimedia, which have many properties that make component software approaches desirable. For this reason, the first release of OpenDoc technology focuses on making such documents easy to create, work with, and share.

Documents are the primary products of the OpenDoc technology, but there are differences between today's documents and the documents delivered by OpenDoc. Today, the term "document" refers to data, such as text or images, all in a single format and created or modified by a single program. This, in some sense, describes the most basic level of an OpenDoc document: a single content or data type with a single editor for that type. However, OpenDoc enables multiple content types to coexist peacefully in a container (the document), and operations on a particular content type to be handled by specialized applications called *component editors.*

Rather than try to contain all of the code for every conceivable type of content (an impossible task in any event), OpenDoc brings the required code into the computer memory when it is needed and then removes it when it is no longer needed. Figure 1-3 summarizes the differences between the old and new document styles.

Where Is OpenDoc Available?

OpenDoc is or will be available on all major personal computer and server operating systems. It is not locked into any particular platform and will be available from multiple sources.

There will be implementations available for the three major versions of Microsoft Windows: Windows 3.11, Windows NT, and Windows 95. This work is being done by IBM, with assistance from Novell.

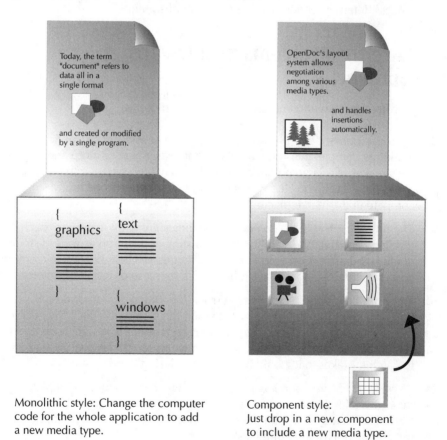

Today, the term "document" refers to data all in a single format

and created or modified by a single program.

OpenDoc's layout system allows negotiation among various media types.

and handles insertions automatically.

{ graphics

{ text }

} { windows }

Monolithic style: Change the computer code for the whole application to add a new media type.

Component style: Just drop in a new component to include a new media type.

FIGURE 1-3.   *A comparison of old and new document styles*

Apple Computer has implemented the OpenDoc architecture on MacOS and plans to make it a part of the standard system software in an update to System 7.5. It is currently available for download from the World Wide Web at URL **http://www.opendoc.apple.com.**

IBM is implementing OpenDoc for OS/2 under the Presentation Manager and integrating it with the Workplace Shell. IBM is also implementing OpenDoc under UNIX, with the first implementation on IBM's AIX using the X Window System.

Component Vision

The benefits of OpenDoc are not limited to compound documents or page layout. The mechanisms for collaboration, extensibility, and scripting embody solutions to several general problems in the software industry and thus extend to uses such as database access, Internet services, and high-end publishing.

What Are the Problems in Software Development?

Monolithic software development results in several problems:

- *The development effort is too big.* Completely revising an application of moderate complexity is now an effort that lasts a year or more and requires the services of a large number of people. Many companies can no longer afford the costs associated with such large, multiyear projects and still compete in the marketplace.

- *The revision effort is too complex.* Adding significant features at each revision can affect the stability of the existing application as well as strain quality assurance for the new software. Regression tests become ever more complex, threatening interoperability with the base of installed systems.

- *Programs are difficult to debug.* Errors in implementation or design become difficult to find and correct when the system in which they occur becomes too large for any one person to comprehend. A significant effort is required for multiperson development teams to remain coordinated and to catch mistakes that would be obvious to a single individual.

- *User demands are not being met.* Users want to be able to complete their jobs with the least amount of obstruction by the tools that they use. Complex interfaces or multiple tools that don't interoperate are barriers to the completion of a required task.

■ *Marketplace demands are not being met.*   The marketplace demands that companies be fast and flexible, with the ability to make changes quickly to support new hardware, access new network services, and meet competitive demands. Complex software development processes impede these efforts.

How Does Component Software Solve These Problems?

Component software solves many of the problems related to monolithic software development. Figure 1-4 summarizes these solutions.

Component software brings these solutions to the problems of monolithic software development:

■ *Small pieces*   The average component is small enough for a single developer or a small number of developers to create and maintain it.

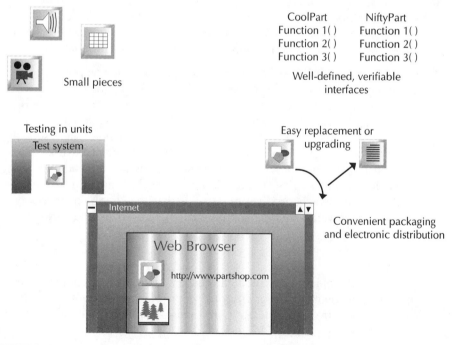

FIGURE 1-4.   *Solving problems with component software*

Problems can be solved in isolation before they occur in—and possibly destabilize—the project as a whole.

- *Well-defined, verifiable interfaces*   A software component has a set of well-defined interfaces through which it interacts with the outside world. Because of this, it is possible to verify that a component functions according to its specifications, enabling isolation of faults and helping to make the system as a whole more stable.

- *Testing in units*   Part of the work in writing component-based software is factoring the different functions that each component performs (i.e., identifying the discrete functions performed by that component). By separating the functions and placing each behind a well-defined application program interface (API), the developer lays the groundwork for easier (and thus less expensive) maintenance. It is much easier to replace a component when the interface that it presents is well defined and well understood. As with any set of tools, interchangeability and standardization lead to simpler maintenance.

- *Easy replacement and upgrading*   One of the benefits of the component software approach is the ability to implement incremental updates, enhancements, and bug fixes. Rather than releasing an entirely new version of an entire application, components can simply be added or replaced

- *Convenient packaging and electronic distribution*   The component approach is well suited to electronic distribution. While the core components of a large system can be sold through conventional channels, add-ons, updates, and plug-ins can be sold via less conventional means, such as the Internet, World Wide Web (WWW), or online services such as eWorld, America Online, CompuServe, and the Microsoft Network. Electronic distribution provides several benefits: lower overhead costs for packaging, manufacturing, and distribution (especially important for the smaller, lighter-weight products that can be developed using a component software framework); national and international coverage; and very low fixed costs.

TIP
Several major banks, credit card issuers, and software companies are working on methods for ensuring secure electronic payments, so the biggest current objection to e-payment—inability to actually make any money—is being addressed.

By creating a suite of components, a software manufacturer can create new products by rearranging the pieces that a customer owns and adding some new functionality. For example, a database manufacturer can sell components that provide a user interface and a new engine that provides additional database functions. Since customers are buying software that leverages their existing software, the useful life of the product is extended, and customers will be more likely to continue to buy from that company. Manufacturers outside the computer industry have used this technique for years to create brand loyalty. The product becomes a toolbox that stays useful and can meet the changing needs or desires of the client.

Because components are smaller and less complex than traditional applications, a company can get them to market more quickly, allowing the company increased flexibility and agility. There are precedents for this approach in the computer hardware business: Sun Microsystems initially was able to produce workstations quickly and cheaply by assembling off-the-shelf hardware and software components into its own unique system design. Dell Computer did a similar thing in the PC clone business, adding the innovation of mail-order sales. By incorporating standard parts, these companies were able to concentrate their R&D dollars in a few key areas that let each system as a whole excel.

Because OpenDoc is an open system that allows small components to be created and distributed easily, it will likely have strong third-party and shareware support. To this end, several resources are available on the Internet that foster the exchange of shareware components and product ideas. CI Labs, the nonprofit organization set up to promote OpenDoc, maintains a World Wide Web site that has links to OpenDoc resources. Its URL is **http://www.cilabs.org**.

OpenDoc Benefits and Capabilities

In today's heterogeneous computing environment, with Windows, Macintosh, OS/2, UNIX, PDA/organizer, and mainframe platforms coexisting, developers should be able to work on cross-platform solutions without having to duplicate their entire software development organization. Even given the prevalence of Windows-based computers on the desktop, the client/server demands of most environments make it beneficial to be able to move components across various computing platforms.

OpenDoc was designed from the very earliest stages to work across all major computing platforms, and the fact that its first release will span four different environments is a testament to this portability.

User Benefits

OpenDoc offers many user-centered design features, such as the consistency and uniformity of the interface, the scalablity of the interface, and the ability to use the "best-of-breed" in a particular problem domain. Almost any part of the system is replaceable in true plug-and-play style. OpenDoc provides uniform ways to embed and manipulate media types, making each a first-class citizen in the world of the document. The concepts of OpenDoc are extremely simple, so that novice users can accomplish their work quickly with a minimum of learning, and yet power users can extract every last bit of performance and sophistication from their documents.

People who use computers as a normal part of their jobs (an ever-increasing percentage of the work force) are demanding both more power and more flexibility from their computer systems. Computers have been a part of the office for long enough that the basic tasks of data entry, simple text processing, and calculation have given way to collaborative tasks, multimedia, and communication.

It is now commonplace to use multiple media in a single document or presentation. Because of this, the creator of a document must interact with multiple domain-specific applications, such as text editors, video capture software, and illustration programs, and attempt to integrate the content. To integrate the various pieces, the document creator has to try to find a single application that happens to have all of the functions that he or she requires to complete the project. Needless to say, finding such an application is extremely unlikely, and perhaps not even desirable. As the number of features increases, so does the steepness of the learning curve, until new users are unwilling or unable to learn the interface. OpenDoc provides a way to address these problems today and allow the software of tomorrow to take full advantage of the future hardware.

OpenDoc was designed with ease-of-use foremost in mind—enabling users to create complicated and rich documents more easily and quickly than would otherwise be possible. By viewing the document as a container for various media types, OpenDoc lends itself to the incorporation of the latest technology while maintaining the investment (in terms of time, money, and productivity) in current software.

In-place editing lets the document editor interact with content in the most natural manner: direct manipulation in the context of the surrounding media. This approach, for example, lets the user fine-tune the look of text as it relates to the image around which it is wrapped.

OpenDoc uses the concept of *drafts*—multiple versions of a document stored within the same file—to allow a natural work flow. Drafts are earlier versions of a document that can be reviewed during the course of the document's development. For the final version, the earlier drafts can be removed.

With drafts, the user can easily compare two different looks or scenarios, trace the evolution of a concept, or revert to an earlier version of a document. Drafts also allow a natural style of multiuser collaboration, without the fear of working at cross purposes and losing changes that have been made to a document. OpenDoc has an infrastructure in place that allows a third-party developer to design a mechanism to reconcile differences among drafts. Figure 1-5 illustrates the concept of drafts.

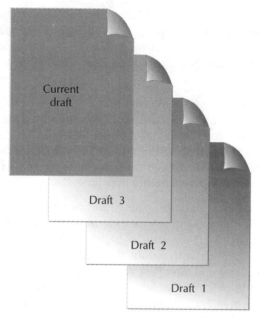

FIGURE 1-5. *Drafts in OpenDoc*

OpenDoc's cross-platform support enables users to mix and match the appropriate platforms for specific tasks without having to worry about the difficulties in migrating the document across hardware and operating system platforms.

Here is a summary of some of OpenDoc's key benefits for users:

■ *Customization of the work environment*   One of the consequences of software bloat—a multiplicity of features, leading to software that requires too much memory and is hard to learn—is redundancy. Many applications have overlapping feature sets. For example, most applications (for instance, mail, database, and spreadsheet applications) provide text editing. This means the user must learn how to use many slightly different text editors, and some will be less functional than desired. OpenDoc lets the user use one editor, which can be as powerful as he or she wants, uniformly across all text editing tasks on the system—an approach both simpler and more powerful. This approach also frees developers from having to implement a text editor and lets them focus on an area where they can add marketable value.

■ *Prepackaged components* OpenDoc's approach is to break domain-specific functions into separate components that can then be recombined to meet the specific needs of the document author. Users can be less concerned with the applications they use and can concentrate instead on the tasks they want to perform.

■ *Cross-platform portability* Because OpenDoc is available on all of today's major computing platforms and is inherently portable, users need be much less concerned with the hardware they use; they can use whatever is appropriate and available. This portability is important when sharing projects and data within departments, agencies, or companies: each user is free to use whatever systems are in place.

■ *Easy collaboration with others* More and more often, multiple members of a team must make contributions to a single project to ensure its success. For example, an advertising campaign may share visuals across the print and video markets and also require the work of specialists such as copy editors, producers, and directors. With current techniques, difficulties often occur related to multiple formats, sharing, versions, and change control. In addition, people in different professions work in different ways, and productivity can be increased by allowing people to customize their environments to match their work styles rather than the other way around.

Manager Benefits

Managers have several major needs: they require fast development of effectively custom software (every IS department is a vertical market of one), they must provide integration with existing and legacy systems, and they must be able to support end-users with widely varying requirements but still provide consistency across the organization. OpenDoc allows IS managers to create *stationery pads* that contain preconfigured controls, data, and links to network services such as databases. Figure 1-6 shows how OpenDoc can integrate a legacy system—in this case, a mainframe database—with new programs.

Here is a summary of some of OpenDoc's key benefits to mangers:

■ *Easy distribution of templates to users* Perhaps an IS manager's greatest challenge is providing support for large organizations of professionals who know little or nothing about the tools they must use. OpenDoc provides several tools to help provide consistent support across the organization. All solutions created with OpenDoc can be packaged as stationery: template documents that automatically create new documents with initial content as complex as needed. IS programmers can create custom solutions that can be accessed as easily as opening a document.

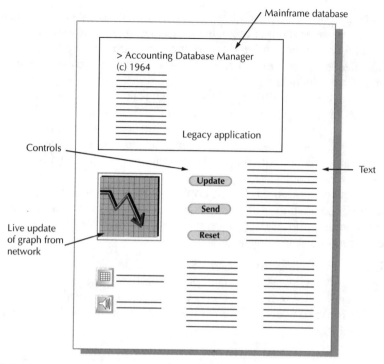

FIGURE 1-6. *Document templates and legacy systems*

■ *Integration with legacy applications* Using commercial off-the-shelf components integrated through OpenDoc's linking or scripting mechanisms, managers can quickly create custom applications as documents. Mix several database query components, some script buttons, a chart or two, and the manager instantly has a custom database front-end. Add to this a terminal emulator component and several more script buttons, and the manager has an easy-to-use interface to the old legacy mainframe, completely integrated with the latest tools.

■ *Control of document content types* A common problem in organizations is distributability of documents. A reader must have the necessary application to view the document created by the writer. This means either the writer is limited to simple applications the organization can afford to site-license or purchase for everyone, or a reader will sometimes (often?) receive documents he or she cannot view. OpenDoc provides support for *viewers*, component editors that can be used only to view a document, not to edit it. Most developers will provide freely distributed viewers, so content created with their editors can be viewed by everyone. For situations where a viewer is not enough, the kinds of components used in OpenDoc documents can be restricted to a particular group supported within the organization to ensure that all readers have the necessary editors to view and edit all documents.

One example of this sort of technology is the Acrobat Reader product from Adobe. It is given away freely and distributed widely—Adobe makes money on the software that creates portable document format (PDF) files. In a similar vein, developers of a format are strongly encouraged to create a reader for the format and distribute it for free (via the CI Labs WWW server, for example).

Another possibility is for the content of a document to be translated into a format compatible with the available viewers. In many cases, OpenDoc can do this without intervention on the part of the user—the user does not need to perform any special action.

■ *Cross-platform implementation*   Smart IS managers cannot simply replace their hardware investment to adopt the latest technology, and they have an interest in using whatever tools and hardware are available. Because OpenDoc is so widely available, it is a natural fit with an IS manager's requirements.

Developer Benefits

Developers have to support huge feature sets. Debugging large programs is difficult, and years now pass between major versions of products. Breaking software into components allows development of smaller, more manageable pieces that can be supported, upgraded, and released independently.

OpenDoc provides a rich set of underpinnings for developers, with extensive support for data storage, imaging, user interface, and document layout. A developer of an OpenDoc component need implement only a small number of functions in one API—approximately 60 or fewer, depending on the protocols in which the component participates. The procedure provides access to the policies and protocols that let OpenDoc components communicate and work together effectively.

Here is a summary of some of the key benefits of OpenDoc for developers:

■ *Portable storage format*   OpenDoc documents are stored in OpenDoc Standard Interchange Format (SIF), widely used across a variety of platforms. OpenDoc SIF is also known as Bento. Files are portable across platforms without requiring data transformation or translation. Bento provides support for multiple update streams to the same file, the ability to have drafts, and version control for storage files.

NOTE
The name Bento comes from the Japanese word for box.

At the same time, OpenDoc provides an extensible set of document storage formats and mechanisms. If Bento is not sufficient for a particular user's needs, the storage system can easily be replaced with a different one that supports other features (for example, a true object-oriented database). Documents stored in other formats may not be as portable as those using Bento, but the trade-off between functionality and portability is now a choice that can be made by the user, rather than a rigid policy.

This easy piecewise replaceability is a hallmark of OpenDoc. Every subsystem of OpenDoc is plug-replaceable to allow piecewise upgrading of OpenDoc itself, just as for OpenDoc-based products.

■ *Extensive document layout facilities*   The OpenDoc implementation has extensive facilities for document layout, freeing developers from having to re-invent a layout system. OpenDoc's layout system allows negotiation among various media types and handles insertions automatically. For example, OpenDoc automatically handles such cases as nonrectangular shapes, the embedding of graphics within text, and dynamic changes in shape or space requirements. Figure 1-7 illustrates automatic reformatting of a document upon the insertion of a new graphics component. A

FIGURE 1-7.   *Document layout in OpenDoc*

database interface can resize itself if more tables are added to the database or if objects are removed from the database.

- *Shared resource arbitration* OpenDoc provides shared resource arbitration not only for resources such as text insertion points and window frames, but also for hardware devices such as mouse pointers, serial ports, and graphics tablets. This feature solves problems that might occur when multiple components try to access the network simultaneously, and it also allows a more dynamic and interactive interface. One component might be watching for mouse clicks while another is monitoring the network and another is watching the keyboard for cursor movement commands. Systems such as OLE have no resource arbitration, so one piece of software must be in complete control at all times.

- *Event dispatching* OpenDoc provides a complete system for managing and dispatching events that occur during system use. These include user-generated events such as mouse clicks and keypresses as well as requests by other applications or components, via scripting, for example.

- *Easy solution building and testing* By breaking problems into smaller pieces, a developer can build and test partial solutions on the path to a complete implementation. It is easier to create a framework or outline of the whole application and plug in pieces as they become complete than to create the entire application at once

- *Use of SOM and IDL for language-neutral development* OpenDoc is based on IBM's System Object Model (SOM), which is endorsed by every major computer manufacturer, and provides methods for creating language-neutral distributed objects. SOM complies with the Common Object Request Broker Architecture (CORBA), which is endorsed by every major computer manufacturer and sponsored by the Object Management Group. The OMG is one of the largest standards organization in the world. CORBA is a set of standards for enabling widely different object systems to interoperate. It specifies a framework for letting these systems coexist on the same machine or on multiple machines over a network.

     SOM allows objects written in multiple languages to work together. One of the ways in which SOM accomplishes its goal is by using the Interface Definition Language (IDL), which specifies the way in which object boundaries are defined. The use of IDL permits a standardized way of interacting with objects and easy replacement of one object with another (perhaps from a different vendor) that supports the same interface. Defining *interfaces* (well-defined operations on data) in IDL allows legacy code to be encapsulated and reused. In addition, these interfaces allow objects to be dispatched across multiple machines on a network. Figure

1-8 shows objects written in multiple languages interoperating.

SOM and IDL allow developers to use whatever language that they want (or are required to use) to implement their components. There are CORBA- compliant systems using languages such as C and C++ as well as Smalltalk and Ada.

■ *Shorter time to market* For developers in rapidly changing and evolving markets such as the Internet and WWW, this architecture lets the software product evolve as swiftly as the surrounding technological environment. For example, a WWW browser based on OpenDoc technology or incorporating OpenDoc facilities can quickly be upgraded to handle new media types or layout styles. A plug-in module that understands MacroMind's Director format or Sun's Java language can be prototyped, debugged, and deployed much more quickly than an application that requires modification and retesting of the entire browser. From a business point of view, it makes sense to create many small, lightweight objects that can be mixed and matched to a particular market or market niche.

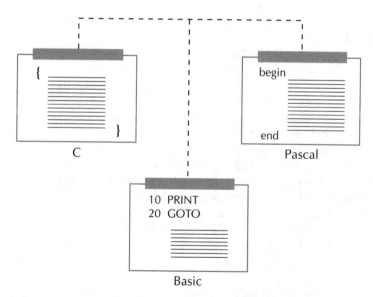

FIGURE 1-8. *SOM and IDL allow objects to interoperate*

Role of CI Labs

Component Integration Laboratories (CI Labs) is the organization set up to promote OpenDoc and ensure interoperability among the various platform implementations. It has several important roles to this end.

CI Labs was set up as a vendor-neutral organization to guide distributed component technologies to market and provide a forum in which entities—from large corporations to individuals—could share their ideas. CI Labs helps negotiate and integrate the various technologies provided to it and make these technologies available to its members. CI Labs also pursues standardization efforts to ensure that differing implementations continue to work together seamlessly.

CI Labs pursues an open process: companies are free to license the source code and provide new implementations of the technology, which can, in turn, be given to CI Labs for validation and adoption.

CI Labs is sponsored by Apple, Novell, and IBM. Additional members include such firms as Oracle, Adobe, Lotus, and Just Systems of Japan.

CI Labs also licenses technologies. It is responsible for several software component groups that make up the OpenDoc technologies: OpenDoc APIs, SOM, Open Scripting Architecture (OSA), and OpenDoc SIF (or Bento).

OpenDoc APIs are the platform-independent class libraries and facilities that enable compound documents. SOM is the CORBA-compliant mechanism that allows dynamic linking of objects and language-neutral implementation. OSA is the messaging specification that allows multiple scripting languages to interoperate to provide user scripting and program automation. OpenDoc SIF (or Bento) is the OpenDoc storage and interchange format. It allows efficient storage of the multiple data formats and streams used by compound documents and is part of the Recommended Practice for data exchange promoted by the Interactive Multimedia Association. The IMA is an industry group composed of the major hardware and software manufacturers of consumer and industrial electronics.

CI Labs also provides ComponentGlue, the gateway that allows OpenDoc to interoperate seamlessly with Microsoft's OLE interapplication communication technology.

CI Labs provides other important services to developers as well. It licenses source code and handles releases for all of the source code to OEMs. CI Labs also maintains registries of important components, types, and protocols, such as the following:

- Data type name registries
- Registries of OpenDoc extension suites
- Event registries for scripting

Apple, IBM, and Novell are sponsors of CI Labs, and each has made significant contributions and commitments to OpenDoc technology. As the original developer of the OpenDoc compound document architecture, Bento, and OSA, Apple is fully committed to making OpenDoc a part of the Macintosh user experience. IBM contributed a key technology in SOM and is the platform implementor for OS/2 and AIX. IBM is also responsible for porting OpenDoc to the Windows environments with the help of Novell. Novell in turn, has contributed its ComponentGlue technology to make interoperation with OLE simple, easy, and painless.

Competing and Complementary Systems

Systems similar to OpenDoc are also available in the marketplace. Microsoft's Object Linking and Embedding (OLE) and Taligent's CommonPoint are the best-known examples.

Using the ComponentGlue technology contained in OpenDoc, creators of OpenDoc components can guarantee the interoperability of their products with the large base of OLE-aware applications without the substantial investment in time and effort that OLE development requires. In addition, developers and users can leverage the substantial number of OLE custom controls (OCX) that currently exist.

OLE

OLE from Microsoft enables interapplication communication and limited types of embedding and linking. It allows one application to access data in another application and one application to issue a limited set of commands to another application. OLE is available only in binary form from Microsoft, which controls all aspects of the implementation.

OLE currently allows only one object to be fully active at any one time and requires all applications cooperating on a document to be fully loaded and resident. Thus, for example, a document containing text, a spreadsheet, and a slide presentation may require the simultaneous use of Microsoft Word, Microsoft Excel, and Microsoft

PowerPoint. This trio requires significant processing and memory resources. OLE also currently supports only rectangular embedding regions.

By contrast, OpenDoc supports OLE's entire feature set, while adding much richer scripting, automation, and storage alternatives. Because of OpenDoc's multivendor nature, all of the subsystems in OpenDoc are replaceable with whatever serves the customer's needs most efficiently from any one of a number of sources.

ComponentGlue technology turns OLE from a competing system into a complementary one; it is possible to get Windows 95 OLE certification via OpenDoc's OLE interoperability rather than having to write code to accommodate the notoriously baroque OLE interfaces.

CommonPoint

CommonPoint, from Taligent, is another similar and complementary system. The Taligent frameworks were designed from the outset to interoperate with OpenDoc.

The CommonPoint class library and application framework can be used to create OpenDoc parts, and CommonPoint applications can serve as containers for OpenDoc content.

Putting It Together

This chapter introduced the concepts of component software and compound documents and explained some of the ways in which OpenDoc can solve some common business problems. The next chapter explains how OpenDoc is structured and introduces some of its major pieces.

CHAPTER 2

OpenDoc Concepts

Chapter 1 introduced the basic concepts of OpenDoc: what it is, what its role is, and how it can be used. Now that you have an idea of what OpenDoc does, you probably want to know how it works and what software writen for it will look like. This chapter presents that information and provides the necessary technical foundation for understanding the rest of the chapters of the book.

This chapter discusses some of the basic concepts of OpenDoc: parts and frames, content models, the human interaction model, container applications, the document shell, and the various OpenDoc subsystems.

The section on parts and frames describes the most common and visible elements of a document. The content model section outlines the basic philosophy that should underlie the design of all part editors. The section on the human interaction model describes how OpenDoc both expands on and departs from more traditional application user interaction models. The section on container applications discusses how existing applications may be extended to embed OpenDoc parts. The document shell section describes the basic application model for OpenDoc documents. The final section describes the various subsystems of OpenDoc that developers use in writing part editors.

The material in this chapter is fundamental to understanding the technical aspects of OpenDoc. It should be read before continuing to the other technical chapters of this book.

Parts and Frames

The basic building blocks of OpenDoc documents are *parts* and *frames*. These are the objects with which users most often interact. Parts represent the data within a document, and frames represent the views of that data.

Parts and frames can most simply be thought of as an evolution of the typical window system found in any graphical user interface (GUI). Just as the invention of windowing systems enabled multiple documents to share a personal computer display without contention, frames allow multiple parts to share a single window (and document layout) without problems.

Each part contains a specific kind of data, such as text, graphics, or video. Frames describe the boundaries between those different kinds of data. One of the basic features of OpenDoc is *embedding*—the ability of one part to contain other parts. Container parts use frames to designate areas within their own layout space for use by their embedded parts. For each part in a document, there is a corresponding frame in which it is displayed. Figure 2-1 illustrates the concepts of parts and frames.

The analogy of parts and frames to documents is useful, but limited. The user can do much more with parts and frames than place a single view on one piece of data. What may have been one document in an old-style application can be factored into a number of cooperating parts. For example, a report can consist of text, graphics, spreadsheet, chart, and movie parts, and the parts can interact through linking, scripting, or extension interfaces.

Frames are also very flexible building blocks. Each part can have more than one frame. These multiple views can be used to display alternative presentations of the same data, such as wire-frame versus shaded graphics, or extra frames can be used to display tool palettes, continue contents that are split across multiple columns or pages, or provide expanded views in separate windows.

Content Models

Many of the basic concepts of OpenDoc came from the designers' experience with object-oriented programming (OOP). The most fundamental OOP concept is that

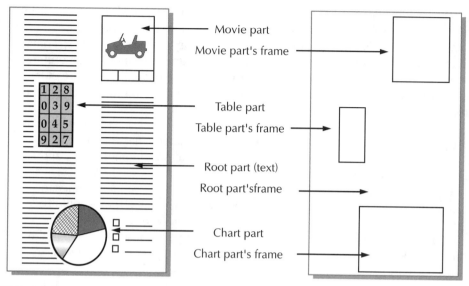

FIGURE 2-1. *Parts and frames*

of the object, which combines both data and functions into a single unit. OpenDoc itself is a system of objects—windows, frames, drafts, and parts—that a programmer manipulates in writing a part editor. Objects exist at more than one level of the OpenDoc system, however, and users also experience OpenDoc in a very object-oriented way.

Each part contains data and provides commands that operate on that data. The data in a part is factored into *content objects,* and the commands the user performs on those objects are called *content operations.* Together, the objects and operations of a part make up something called a *content model.*

Content Model Example

Here is an example of a content model: In a simple drawing editor, the user can interact with content objects that consist of *shapes, colors,* and *patterns.* Content operations can include *creating* and *deleting* shapes, *changing* their positions, colors, and sizes, and *reordering* them.

The important point about a content model is that it is a factoring that is meant to be meaningful to users but is not necessarily useful from the programmer's point of view. The implementation of a text editor may use highly optimized data structures to represent the text and style information and have intricate algorithms for manipulating that data. However, the user should be blissfully unaware of the run-arrays and piece-tables that make the part work and should see only the words and paragraphs, and that some of them are bold or italic.

The first task in designing a part editor is to consider the content model that its parts will present. What objects will the user manipulate? What actions will the user take upon them? These questions define the basic operation of a part, and all else should follow from there.

Of particular note is the relationship of a part editor's *semantic interface* to its content model. A well-architected part editor's semantic interface should be very close or identical to its content model. That is, the objects and operations supported in the semantic interface should be the same as those presented in the content model. This parallel design ensures that any action the user can perform directly can also be accomplished via scripting.

Human Interaction Model

OpenDoc uses a human interaction (HI) model that is a departure from preceding models. This different model is necessary to enable users to work with compound documents in a natural and effective way. However, although OpenDoc's model is different, it is not difficult to learn or use.

Compound document systems have been in use, at least experimentally, for almost two decades. Commercial implementations (such as Xerox's Star, NoteCards, and Analyst systems; and Go's PenPoint) have been sold for at least a decade (though with relatively limited popularity or availability). Thus, OpenDoc's designers had a good deal of applicable experience to draw upon. Most of the HI model for OpenDoc was designed at Apple Computer and was based on Apple's well-known user-centered design principles. A considerable amount of user testing went into creating and validating the HI model. As a result, the OpenDoc HI model is easy for both new and experienced users to learn and use.

A Portable Model

Like everything else in the OpenDoc architecture, the HI model was designed from the start to be portable across a range of operating systems. Different platforms have different base models, with differences ranging from minor to profound. Windows uses a two-button mouse, while MacOS uses a one-button mouse. In

Windows and MacOS, the frontmost window takes keyboard input, but in X Windows it is the window under the mouse cursor that does. Some systems have menu bars, and others do not. Tautologically speaking, there are as many differences as there are systems.

Thus, the OpenDoc HI model is as much a philosophy as a specification. In concrete terms, the OpenDoc HI model is an extension of the existing platform HI model, no matter what the platform. The user experience will be largely similar to the base platform HI, with a few differences that make OpenDoc work.

This approach has many advantages. It enables experienced users to easily make the transition to using OpenDoc. It also allows platform vendors to continue to differentiate their systems by providing unique value in their own HI. Finally, it allows OpenDoc to be ported to operating systems beyond its initial targets, potentially including operating systems not yet developed or established.

There are many detailed specifications that must be adhered to in writing OpenDoc software. However, the basic attributes of the HI model are few and simple. They are as follows:

- Document-centered focus

- In-place editing

- Selection of parts and contents

Document-Centered Focus

There are several fundamental differences between OpenDoc's HI model and previous HI models. The biggest difference is that in OpenDoc's model the focus of the user's attention is on documents and what is in them, not on applications and what they can do. This document-centric approach allows users to concentrate on a particular task without being distracted by searching for the right tool for the job.

This approach is particularly important in a compound-document system. The activation of an embedded part should be seamless and not distracting. The user does not want to worry about what software to use to edit the part; the user just wants to click the part and edit it.

Part Editors

In OpenDoc, the equivalent of an application is a *part editor*. Part editors are almost identical to traditional applications in their functions and responsibilities, but they operate in a different runtime environment. The biggest difference from the user's point of view is that, after installation, there is no direct interaction with the editor. Users do not launch editors as they would applications. Instead, editors are loaded automatically by OpenDoc as needed to edit parts.

Stationery

If users do not launch editors, how do they create new parts or documents? OpenDoc's answer to this question is *stationery*. Stationery pads are template documents that are used to generate both documents and embedded parts. Stationery documents are identical to regular documents with the difference that opening one "tears off" a new document (like tearing off a page from a physical pad of paper) and then opens that "page." Likewise, pasting or dragging stationery into a document embeds a copy of that stationery, rather than the stationery itself.

Since stationery is still a full-fledged document, the template can be as simple or as rich as desired. A stationery pad can generate an empty text document or a complex report consisting of a half-dozen parts, all with partially completed contents.

In-Place Editing

OpenDoc allows users to edit embedded parts wherever they occur in a document. This in-place editing is a fundamental feature of OpenDoc and a significant focus of the HI model. The goal of in-place editing is to allow the user to edit multiple kinds of contents without a jarring, disruptive transition.

For example, a relatively simple document may consist of a graphics part that embeds a table part, a chart part, and a text part. The user can edit the contents of any part simply by clicking it. In old-style applications, this operation would require running four separate applications, and the transition from editing text to editing the chart could involve many steps. In OpenDoc, the user just clicks the chart and begins editing.

In implementing in-place editing, several issues must be addressed: how parts are activated, how the user gains a sense of place, how the available command set is presented, and how a part editor integrates common and document-wide operations with its own commands. OpenDoc's HI model addresses all of these issues.

Part Activation

OpenDoc uses a style of activation referred to as *inside-out selection*. When a user clicks the mouse, the smallest frame containing the cursor is activated. (In outside-in selection, each click activates the next inactive part further down the hierarchy.) The advantage of this style is that it allows the user to easily activate parts and edit content. One click is needed to activate a part and select content within it, no matter how many levels deep the part is embedded. The disadvantage of this style is that it is sometimes difficult to select a part as a whole, rather than activate it. Approaches that facilitate easy selection of parts are discussed in "How Parts Are Selected" later in this chapter.

Figure 2-2 illustrates the difference between inside-out and outside-in selection.

Inside-out

Outside-in

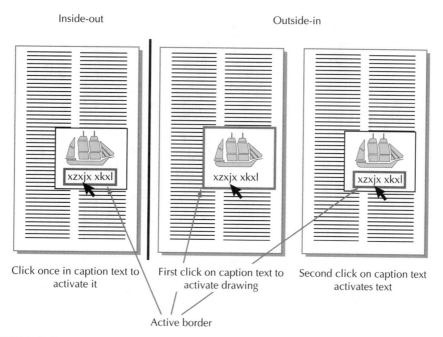

Click once in caption text to activate it

First click on caption text to activate drawing

Second click on caption text activates text

Active border

FIGURE 2-2.   *Inside-out versus outside-in selection to activate parts*

Sense of Place

Notice in Figure 2-3 that when the Memo window is active, it is displayed with a distinctive appearance, its selected contents are highlighted, and its commands appear in the menu bar. When the Memo window is inactive, its display is simpler, its selected contents are not highlighted, and the menu bar contains the commands for the window that is active—not those of the Memo window itself.

In a window-based GUI, users need to be guided to focus attention on the document that is being edited. Since many windows often are open at once, there must be visual cues that allow the user to predict where keystrokes will go and what items menu commands will affect. Window systems typically highlight the frontmost or *active window* with an appearance distinct from other windows to indicate which window operations will affect. Figure 2-3 shows active and inactive windows.

Notice in Figure 2-3 that the active Memo window is displayed with a distinctive appearance; its selected contents are highlighted and its commands appear in the menu bar.

In the same way, OpenDoc uses visual highlighting to indicate which part will be affected by user actions. When a user clicks a part, that part becomes the *active*

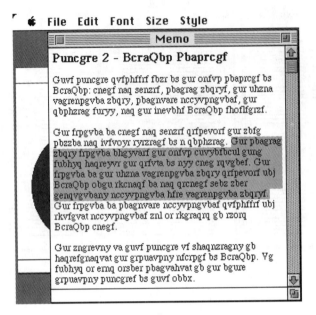

a. Memo window is active

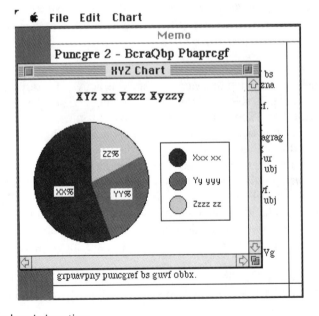

b. Memo window is inactive

FIGURE 2-3. *Active and inactive windows*

part. The activation of a part is indicated by the display of the *active border* around the frame of that part. Figure 2-4 show active and inactive frames.

Presentation of Part Commands

All but the simplest parts (such as buttons) are likely to need their own sets of menu commands. When a part becomes active, it should display its own menu commands. Since each part displays its own commands separately, there is no confusion about which part a command applies to.

As with menu commands, parts should display any tool palettes only when the part is active. This approach both helps avoid screen clutter and provides a strong connection between a palette and its part. Figure 2-5 shows how menus differ depending on the active part.

Integration of Common and Document Commands

Even though most part editors support a unique set of menu commands, some commands—such as Undo, Copy, Cut, and Paste—are common across most editors. In addition, some commands apply to the operation of the document as a whole and not to any specific part. In both these cases, the part editor should use the standard command in its menus rather than invent a new command.

Part editors can pretty much ignore document-wide commands. OpenDoc will create the menus for these commands and perform the command operations. So long as the editor doesn't disable the command, it will function automatically.

For common commands, OpenDoc creates the menu command, and the editor need only respond to it. This assures users of consistent behavior and makes editors easy to learn and use.

Selection of Parts and Contents

A significant piece of OpenDoc's HI model is the selection model. The structure of a compound document is richer than that of a simple document, and the ways in which users select content and parts must accommodate this extra complexity.

Selection Scope and Part Boundaries

An important constraint of the OpenDoc selection model is that a selection can exist only within the scope of a single part's content. A selection may include embedded parts in their entirety, but it may not start in one part and end in another. Otherwise, since only one part at a time has the active border and menus, the effect of a command would be impossible to predict. Figure 2-6 shows legal and illegal selections.

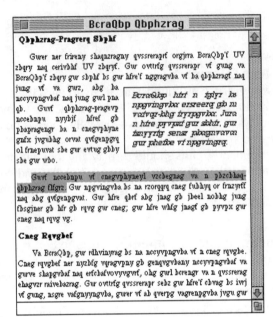

a. Root part is active

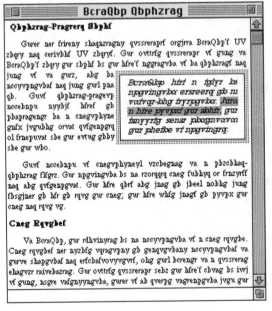

b. Embedded part is active

FIGURE 2-4. *Active and inactive frames*

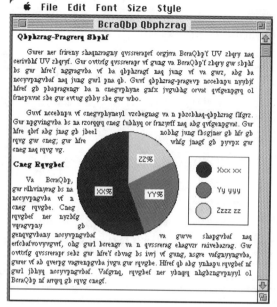

a. Root part's menus

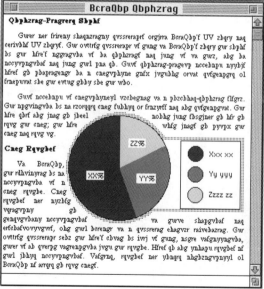

b. Embedded part's menus

FIGURE 2-5. *Different menus for different active parts*

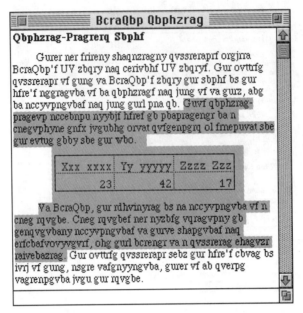

a. Legal selection

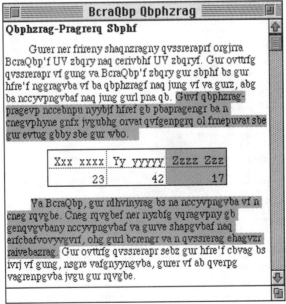

b. Illegal selection

FIGURE 2-6. *Legal and illegal selections*

How Parts Are Selected

Embedded parts behave similarly to other kinds of intrinsic content, including in the way they are selected and, for the most part, how the selection is displayed. However, some behaviors involved in selecting parts are not applicable to normal intrinsic content.

One difference is that clicking the active border of a frame selects that frame (and consequently activates the containing part). This feature provides a two-gesture method for selecting almost any frame in a document.

If the user wants to manipulate a frame more often than edit its content, the user can set the *bundled* flag on that frame (found in the Part Info dialog box). A bundled frame behaves as a single unit and does not allow the user to directly edit its contents. This behavior is similar to that typical of grouped objects in graphics editors: the user can manipulate only the group as a whole, not the individual objects within it. The result is that clicking a bundled frame selects it rather than activating its part.

Frames can also be selected by extending an existing selection. If a frame or other content is already selected, the selection can be extended to include other frames within the same containing part. In the MacOS, this operation is performed by holding down the SHIFT or COMMAND key and clicking the frame to be added.

The similarity of embedded parts to intrinsic content also includes selection appearance. Whenever possible, part editors should highlight selected parts using the same appearance as for other content, as shown in Figure 2-6a.

In some cases, using highlighting with a similar appearance may not be possible or desirable. For instance, the standard highlighting for selected text does not provide handles for manipulating an embedded frame. Figure 2-7 shows the use of different highlighting for part selection.

Container Applications

Applications that are not themselves part editors but which can embed OpenDoc parts are called *container applications*. These applications are more limited than part editors in their functionality, but they have a number of advantages over non-container applications. The biggest advantage is that, like part editors, their potential range of content is unlimited. Once an application can embed one kind of part, it can embed any kind of part.

Only a few modifications are needed to allow an application to embed parts. First, the application must be able to use OpenDoc storage to give the parts a place to store themselves in its documents. Second, it must pass events to OpenDoc to give parts a chance to respond to them. Third, it must tell parts to draw when they need to update. Except for a few details here and there, that's about all the work needed.

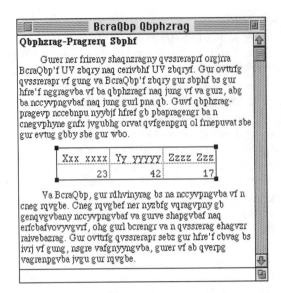

FIGURE 2-7. *Selection of parts using highlighting with a different appearance*

If you have an existing software base, you can use a variety of approaches to convert your applications to use OpenDoc. Although the procedure for converting an application to a part editor is fairly straightforward, it is a significant amount of work—about the same as producing a major revision of the program. In some cases, it may make more sense to extend your application to allow it to embed parts. In the short term, this will require much less work (about equivalent to the effort in adding QuickTime support to an application). As an experiment, for example, two engineers at a major Macintosh development company converted a popular, midrange word processor application in about a month.

A small number of current applications will make best use of OpenDoc by becoming container applications, but most current applications will work better as part editors. So for most software, converting to a container application should be considered an interim step toward full conversion to a part editor. Under OpenDoc, there are very few reasons to maintain software as an application and many for turning it into a part editor.

Document Shell

The simplest possible container application is one that has no intrinsic content of its own and embeds only a single part. This is in fact the standard way OpenDoc documents are launched. This simple application is referred to as the *document shell*. It is the basic interface between OpenDoc and the standard OS application runtime environment.

The application runtime environment varies greatly from platform to platform, so the discussion here of the document shell sticks to the basics that apply everywhere. For more detail, consult the documentation for OpenDoc on the relevant operating system.

To the OS, the document shell is just another application. It owns an address space for its memory use, puts up windows, and receives events and processing time. This design allows OpenDoc documents to exist side by side with old-style documents and applications. The two kinds of documents can even interact using standard OS facilities such as copying and pasting, dragging and dropping, and messaging.

To the user, OpenDoc documents also appear very similar to old-style documents. A single part can appear very much like a pre-OpenDoc application. This is one of the advantages of using the document shell approach: any part can act like an application, without any extra work. Instead of being embedded in another part, a part is just contained in the document shell. So for the effort of writing one part editor, you get something that can act like both a part and an application.

The standard document shell provides a base of functionality for all documents. It handles operations such as saving the document, closing windows, managing drafts, and creating the base Edit menu. Basically, all document-wide operations are implemented in the shell.

Like nearly everything else in OpenDoc, the shell is itself replaceable. It can be replaced by a shell with new or different features, such as support for collaboration management, document mailing, or authentication.

OpenDoc Subsystems

OpenDoc is factored into a number of subsystems. Each subsystem implements a portion of the OpenDoc functionality and may be replaced or upgraded independent of the others. Developers writing part editors have to deal with only a few of the subsystems directly. The other subsystems are usually used only by OpenDoc itself.

The subsystems of interest to part developers are Storage, Layout, Imaging, User Interface, and Messaging.

Storage Subsystem

OpenDoc gives the developer a platform-independent, structured storage model. Using the OpenDoc storage application program interface (API), the developer can completely avoid direct interaction with the underlying platform file system. The developer also gains many advantages in the features provided by OpenDoc storage.

The basic storage model gives each part a *storage unit* in which to store its persistent data. A storage unit is very much like a directory in a file system: it is a bundle of an arbitrary number of named data streams called *properties*. Each property can also hold multiple formats for its contents, each one a different *value*. Each value of a property represents the same data in a different data type. Figure 2-8 illustrates the storage model.

The Storage subsystem also provides a built-in version history of document contents. Users can create a new *draft* of a document as a snapshot of the document and then continue to work on it. All versions are stored in the same document, so the user cannot lose previous drafts. The contents of a draft are typically stored as deltas from the previous draft, so file size is efficiently kept to a minimum.

The storage APIs are used not only to save parts in documents but also for data transfer operations. This means that writing a part's contents to the clipboard, drag and drop, or a link uses the same calls as saving the part in its document. Not only does this result in fewer calls for the programmer to learn, but common code can be shared among data transfer operations.

Layout Subsystem

The Layout subsystem has a small number of classes, but they are rich in functionality. *Frame* and *facet* objects are used to describe the geometric arrangement of parts within a document. Frames allow parts to tell each other about their geometry and to negotiate shapes and sizes of embedded parts within the document's layout space. Facets allow parts to tell OpenDoc where frames are displayed in a window so OpenDoc can draw the frames properly and dispatch mouse events to them.

Imaging Subsystem

Classes in the Imaging subsystem are used to describe graphical objects used in screen display and printing. OpenDoc does not include a cross-platform graphics system; however, it does provide the abstractions necessary for parts to display themselves on any graphics system using platform-specific mechanisms.

OpenDoc provides *shape* and *transform* objects to describe the geometry of the location where parts are displayed. *Canvas* objects represent the underlying drawing environment provided by the platform's graphics system. All of these objects are platform-neutral abstractions for platform-specific structures.

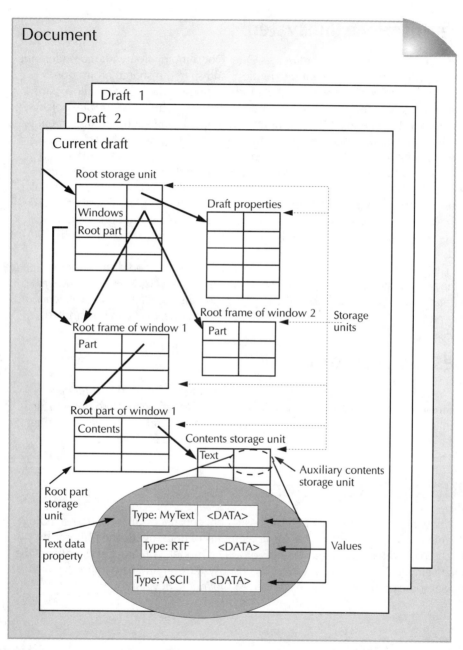

FIGURE 2-8. *Storage model*

User Interface Subsystem

The User Interface subsystem manages OpenDoc's interaction with the underlying platform window system, event distribution, and shared resource arbitration.

OpenDoc *window* objects hold platform window structures and allow parts to manipulate windows in a platform-neutral manner. The *WindowState* object contains a list of windows in a document and their arrangement on the screen.

The *Arbitrator* manages the ownership of resources that are shared among different parts. Each resource is represented by a *focus* object. Standard foci in OpenDoc include the selection focus, keyboard input focus, and menu focus. Since only one part can have the selection within its contents at a time, the Arbitrator helps parts decide which part gets the focus. Foci can represent abstract resources such as menu ownership or concrete resources such as a serial port. OpenDoc comes with a standard set of foci, but developers can add their own for other kinds of shared resources.

The *Dispatcher* takes input events provided by the OS and distributes them to the appropriate parts, based on layout information in facets or resource ownership as registered with the Arbitrator. Like the Arbitrator, the Dispatcher can be extended with new rules for distributing events, so new kinds of events can be handled.

Messaging Subsystem

The Messaging subsystem provides an interface for parts to send and receive semantic events. Each part can present a *semantic interface* to its contents. This interface allows users to control or extend the part's operation through scripting. It also allows parts to interact with each other in rich, content-specific ways.

Putting It Together

You now have an overview of all the basic concepts necessary for understanding OpenDoc. You've examined the basic elements of documents, the philosophy behind part editor design, the features of the HI model, container applications, the document shell, and some of OpenDoc's subsystems. In the next chapter you will look at some of the technologies related to OpenDoc development.

CHAPTER 3

Development with OpenDoc

Complete OpenDoc development environments are available on MacOS, Windows, OS/2, and AIX; in some cases, there are multiple supported development environments per platform. This chapter provides instructions on how to install an OpenDoc environment on your development platform (whatever it might be), discusses some OpenDoc-specific development issues, and introduces some of the resources available to developers and users of OpenDoc components.

The previous chapters presented the basic concepts of OpenDoc. Now the time has come to discuss how to install OpenDoc itself as well as the OpenDoc development environment. In addition, this chapter will cover OpenDoc-specific development issues and the present some of the resources available to help in the development and marketing of OpenDoc-based software.

This chapter addresses some of the issues that are specific to OpenDoc development, including the use of the System Object Model (SOM) to create components, memory and resource management, packaging, and installation. The chapter assumes that the reader is familiar with traditional application development and standard development tools such as compilers, linkers, and debuggers. The discussion here focuses on those areas where OpenDoc development differs from traditional application development.

Installing OpenDoc

Installing OpenDoc is fairly easy on any of the supported platforms: MacOS, Windows, OS/2, and AIX. You can use familiar installation programs to install the required software on your system. (In some cases, it will be installed for you when you install the operating system on your computer.) Appendix B details the installation procedure for Windows and MacOS systems. This information is subject to change, but is accurate as of the writing of this book.

Using PartMaker

This section walks you through a PartMaker session to familiarize you with some of the nuts and bolts of OpenDoc before delving into actual coding.

PartMaker, found in the Developer Starter Kit folder on the OpenDoc CD, allows you to get an overview of the development environment before addressing the OpenDoc application programmer interfaces (APIs) themselves. This example uses a Macintosh; however, PartMaker is available for Windows as well.

The Developer Starter Kit, shown in Figure 3-1, contains all of the items necessary to get started with OpenDoc development.

PartMaker creates source code for OpenDoc part editors from standard templates. Some supported parts are

- Draw Editor
- Picture Viewer
- SamplePart (C)
- SamplePart (C++)
- Sound Editor

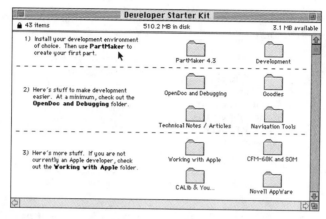

FIGURE 3-1. *Developer Starter Kit*

By using one of the supplied templates, you can create and build an OpenDoc part without having to write any code to the OpenDoc API. You can then use this code as a starting point for your own modifications. The OpenDoc programming interface is introduced in Chapter 4, and Chapters 5 and 7 lead you through the process of actually coding to the OpenDoc API.

As shown in Figure 3-2, open the PartMaker folder and activate the PartMaker application. After the application launches, you will be able to select a part

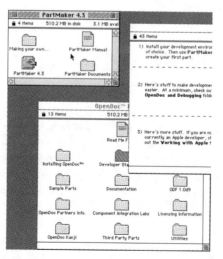

FIGURE 3-2. *PartMaker on the CD*

template from the PartMaker Documents folder. In this example, you'll use the C++ Sample Part, as shown here.

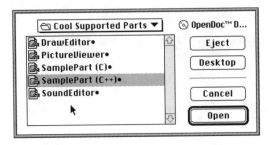

After you select the template, PartMaker displays a screen that provides information on PartMaker and a description of the part template.

The part you will create in this exercise is extremely simple, as it has no real content of its own, apart from a text string that it displays in its window. It does, however, implement the following OpenDoc features, discussed in detail in Chapter 5 and subsequent chapters:

- SOM interface with a C++ method implementation

- View types and presentations

- Adding display frames and facets

- Part drawing

- Part internalization and externalization

- Reference counting

- Storage

- Event handling

In the text entry fields in the PartMaker dialog box, enter a class name and company or organization name. These names will be used to create the C++ classes that implement your part's methods, so they should start with a letter and contain only letters and digits. In particular, they should not contain any white space (spaces, tabs, and so on). The default name will work fine, or you can exercise your imagination.

After entering the names in the text fields, as shown in Figure 3-3, press the Create Part button and select a name and location for the new part's folder or directory, as shown in Figure 3-4. The name you entered as the class name is a good choice.

PartMaker will create a folder on your hard drive in which it will place the source code, interface files, and project files for your part.

Open the folder, shown in Figure 3-5. You'll see several additional folders and two files, shown in Figure 3-6. You'll see a source code folder with the C++ files created by PartMaker. The _SOM_ folder contains the IDL interface to your part (SOM and IDL are discussed in greater detail later in this chapter). You'll also see a Macintosh Programmer's Workshop (MPW) makefile and a Metrowerks CodeWarrior 6 project file. (The Windows version generates equivalent project files for Microsoft and Borland compilers.) The Objects folder contains the object files generated by MPW-hosted compilers.

Double-click the project file to launch the compiler and the development environment.

As you see in Figure 3-7, PartMaker generated several C++ files for your part as well as the files for the SOM interface.

Press COMMAND-M (or select Make from the Project menu) and watch while your part is compiled, linked, and placed in your project folder.

The next section demonstrates how to install and run your newly created software component.

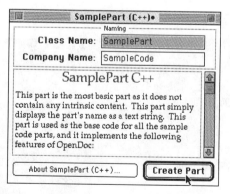

FIGURE 3-3. *Selecting a class name*

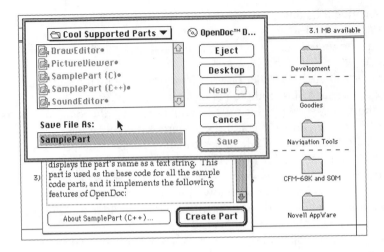

FIGURE 3-4. *Selecting a directory name*

Installing a Part

This section describes how to install a part on Macintosh and Windows systems. After you install the part, follow the instructions in Appendix B to test your new OpenDoc component.

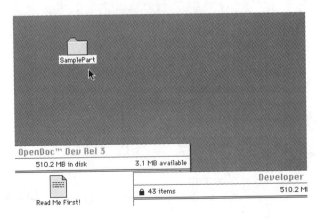

FIGURE 3-5. *The SamplePart folder*

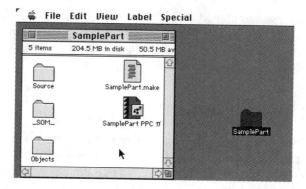

FIGURE 3-6. *Output of PartMaker*

Macintosh Installation

On a Macintosh system, installing an OpenDoc part is simple. You have two choices:

- Copy it into the Editors folder in your System Folder.
- Copy it into an Editors folder at the root of any mounted volume.

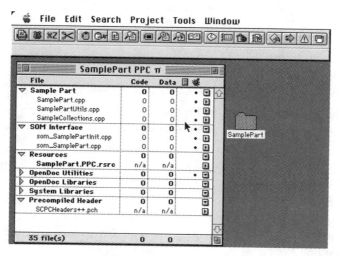

FIGURE 3-7. *Project file for SamplePart*

Before you can use SamplePart, you have to create a stationery file. To do so, drop the part editor onto the OpenDoc shell application in the OpenDoc Libraries folder in the Extensions folder. This will deposit a stationery file in the Stationery folder at the root of the startup volume.

Windows Installation

On a Windows system, let the system know about your part by running the program ODReg32.EXE, located on the OpenDoc for Windows CD. This program registers your part with the operating system and tells the OpenDoc shell where to find your part when you include it in a document.

Using SOM

The System Object Model (SOM) from IBM is the object infrastructure underneath OpenDoc. It provides language independence and efficient dynamic linking of objects, and can in the future be extended to operate transparently over a network. It complies with the CORBA specification from the Object Management Group.

SOM uses the Interface Definition Language (IDL) to provide this degree of flexibility. IDL, which is used to declare types and classes, is much like C++ in syntax and follows the same identifier and white space rules. It also has the same comment styles, character sets, and preprocessor capabilities. Experienced C or C++ programmers can become familiar with the IDL syntax in an hour or two.

OpenDoc is implemented as SOM classes in a shared dynamic link library, as are OpenDoc parts. This has several advantages:

- SOM objects are easily bound to and unbound from a running application. This functionality is a key part of OpenDoc, which allows new parts to be added to or removed from a document at the user's convenience.

- Modification and recompilation of a SOM library does not necessarily require the recompilation of all of its subclasses, nor of clients of that library.

- Parameter passing and communication are consistent across platforms and under different programming languages and compilers.

This section provides an overview of SOM and IDL, presents a simple example of an IDL interface, and discusses some of the ways in which SOM is used in OpenDoc development.

Overview of SOM

SOM consists of several pieces. These are the three most important, and are illustrated in Figure 3-8.

- *SOM runtime* The SOM runtime is implemented by the SOM kernel, which dispatches method calls to objects and passes arguments and return values. In a distributed system, the runtime also handles the required network operations when making calls to objects residing on a different machine.

- *SOM class libraries* These libraries provide extensions to the basic runtime environment. An example is a class library that provides facilities for high-level security or audit trails.

- *SOM compiler* The SOM compiler translates the abstract definitions of interfaces and methods into implementations in a specific target language. For example, the SOM compiler translates a declaration written in IDL into C++ code.

Here are a few important issues to keep in mind when developing or using SOM-based objects:

- Parameters in IDL have an attribute that helps enforce the usage rules intended by the designer of the class:

  - Input parameters are preceded by the keyword **in**.

  - Result parameters (similar to vars in Pascal or references in C++) are preceded by the keyword **out**.

  - Parameters used for both purposes follow the keyword **inout**.

- The implementation function for every SOM method has an initial Environment parameter, used to pass exceptions (errors) back to the caller of the method. When paired with some additional error-handling code, this allows more graceful failure conditions; for example, it provides the ability to disable certain functions when a network host is down, yet retain the use of the non-network-related functions. SOM does not yet directly support the throw/catch exception model found in C++, Modula-3, and some other languages.

- When SOM methods are implemented in C, each implementation function also has a somSelf parameter, similar to the **this** pointer in C++ or **self** in Smalltalk. This object specifier is the receiver of the message.

SOM kernel and runtime

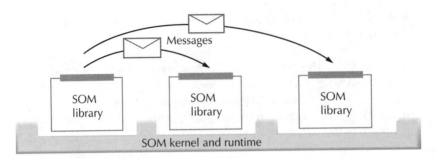

SOM class libraries

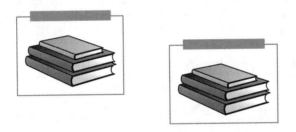

IDL compiler

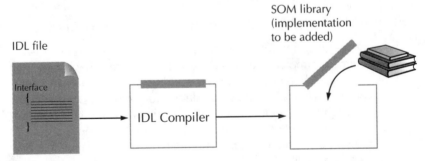

FIGURE 3-8. *Essential SOM components*

IDL Example

This example shows a simple IDL interface. It demonstrates how the declarations in the IDL file are translated by the IDL compiler into language-specific constructs in a language such as C++. The interface represents a currency object that can perform conversions based on exchange rates.

```
interface Currency {
    readonly attribute string name;
    float rate();
    float convert(in float amount);
};
```

The **name** attribute is a read-only attribute of the interface and returns the name of the actual currency that the object represents, such as yen, deutsch mark, franc, or pound. The **rate** method returns the rate used to calculate the conversion, expressed in terms of another currency such as dollars, yuan, rubles, or pesos. Finally, the **convert** method takes a floating-point decimal value and returns the appropriate value in the desired currency.

In C++, the translation would result in something like the following (these results are simplified and omit implementation details such as constructors):

```
class Currency_impl {
    char *Currency_name;
    float Currency_rate;
  public:
    char *name();
    float rate();
    float convert(float amount);
};
```

There are two private data members: Currency_name and Currency_rate. Their values are returned by the public methods **name** and **rate**. The **convert** method calculates the value of the currency conversion by using the preceding data. As you can see, there can be a very simple one-to-one correspondence between the abstract interface provided by the IDL file and its implementation in the target language. Other examples (in Chapters 5 and 7) provide more detail.

SOM and OpenDoc

OpenDoc development typically uses either of two development styles. In the first, the method implementations are included in the SOM method definition. In the second, the SOM method definitions *delegate* their implementation to C++ classes or other similar programming language constructs. (In this context, delegation means that one implementation provides its functions by calling functions in another class or module.)

In the first approach, the implementation of a SOM method can contain the entire implementation of that method. A part can thus be written as one or more SOM classes, with each SOM method containing the implementation for that method. Creating an OpenDoc component as a series of SOM classes allows you to include objects that are implemented in different programming languages (or implemented using legacy code—see Chapter 8) and that use different compilers. It also reduces the need to recompile many objects when changing only one, a feature that becomes especially important when dealing with large code bases and with multiple development teams.

In the second approach, you perform most development in a language such as C++ and create only one SOM class that contains the public interface for your OpenDoc component. Everything else, including all private methods and data fields and the implementation of your public methods, is implemented in a series of C++ classes. This approach, while not as flexible as the SOM approach, has advantages in that it reduces both code complexity and the memory footprint.

Upcoming compilers include a Direct-to-SOM feature that allows you to write code in line, without having to run a separate IDL compiler. This feature will allow greater flexibility and simplify the generated code; essentially, it combines the best aspects of both development approaches.

Exception Handling

As noted earlier, the inclusion of comprehensive exception handling makes OpenDoc a more error-tolerant system. Every piece of code using the OpenDoc foundation has access to enough information to handle unusual conditions, memory errors, and user errors. Although this feature is not unique to SOM nor to OpenDoc, the facilities provided by OpenDoc allow user code to recognize and handle unusual conditions and make error checking easier to implement.

The Environment parameter passed to every SOM method is used to return error and exception information. A method that needs to return an error makes a SOM call that stores the error data (which can be any arbitrary data structure) in the environment. The caller of a SOM method is responsible for checking the environment after every SOM method call to detect errors.

For example, after the following code fragment (which initializes part of the OpenDoc storage subsystem), code would appear that would ascertain whether or not the operation had failed. If it had failed, then the program could try an alternative, or fail gracefully.

```
Environment* ev;
ODSession* session = fSelf->GetStorageUnit(ev)->GetSession(ev);
```

OpenDoc includes an error-handling utility that makes this process almost automatic. This utility is discussed in Appendix C.

OpenDoc Memory Management

In the course of an OpenDoc session, many objects are created, moved, and destroyed. Because of this complex relationship, the runtime environment can have difficulty determining which objects are in active use, and which have been discarded. OpenDoc uses reference-counted objects to implement its memory-management scheme. This allows the OpenDoc runtime to keep track of whether an object is being used at a particular moment. When an object is no longer being used, the memory it consumes can be released and reused. Thus, every object that is a subclass of ODRefCntObject (which includes almost everything you'll encounter in OpenDoc) maintains a count of how many times it is being used. When the reference count drops to zero, then the object is not being used and can be safely deleted. Figure 3-9 gives a simple overview of reference counting.

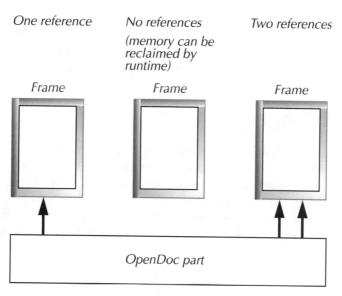

FIGURE 3-9. *A simple reference-counting example*

The memory-management protocol states that every time a new object is created, its reference count is set to 1. Any time another object needs to store a reference to that object, its reference count is increased by 1; similarly, when that object is no longer needed, its reference count is decreased by 1.

Chapter 7 provides a hands-on explanation of memory management.

Developer Resources

Many of the developer resources for OpenDoc are available on the World Wide Web (WWW). Two important sites are as follows:

- *Club OpenDoc* Sponsored by IBM, this site contains links to developer information, press releases, schedules, and marketing literature. This is where you would go to get the latest information on OpenDoc for Windows, OS/2, and AIX. This site has even been known to run a contest or two. It's available at

  http://torolab.ibm.com/clubopendoc/index.html

- *Apple's OpenDoc page* This site contains the latest OpenDoc release from Apple, along with developer information for MacOS. Surf over to it at

  http://opendoc.apple.com/mainpage.html

Another important resource is the OpenDoc newsgroup. Originally a mailing list at CI Labs, the traffic has grown to the point where it's best distributed as a newsgroup. You can find it on Usenet news as **comp.soft-sys.middleware.opendoc**.

Putting It Together

This chapter explained how to get started with OpenDoc development, including how to use PartMaker to create a simple part and how to install your new part on your system. It also discussed SOM and IDL and how they are used in OpenDoc. Finally, it touched on exception handling and memory management and provided pointers to OpenDoc information on the Internet. The next chapter goes into more depth on OpenDoc concepts that you need to understand before you actually implement a simple part.

CHAPTER 4

Getting Started with OpenDoc

This chapter provides more technical detail on how to write OpenDoc part editors. It is your first view of the specifics of the OpenDoc software and offers a glimpse of the OpenDoc application programming interface (API). This chapter presents some basic concepts used in OpenDoc programming, describes both persistent and runtime views of the OpenDoc application model, and lists some of the services provided by the OpenDoc libraries. It finishes with a brief description of the fundamentals for designing a part editor.

OpenDoc part editors are in many ways similar to modern window-based applications. Like applications, they present a graphical user interface, display content data, respond to user events, save and restore persistent data, and interoperate with other programs. Also, of course, each editor implements some kind of core functionality that provides its own particular value, such as text editing, database manipulation, or graphical rendering, just as applications do. OpenDoc steers clear of meddling with core functionality, but it does provide extensive support for those functions common to all editors. This support comprises the infrastructure for OpenDoc application code.

In a compound document system, application code shares system resources and facilities at a much finer granularity than do monolithic applications. A good portion of OpenDoc exists just to keep editors from getting in each other's way while they attempt to share the same window, event stream, and persistent storage. This is the part of OpenDoc that is often most challenging for developers to learn, as it is likely different from software environments with which most developers are familiar. The rest of OpenDoc consists of enabling technologies that make it easier to add features such as scripting and linking to part editors and also provides document features such as drafts. This part of OpenDoc is fairly typical and should provide no special challenges to developers.

The OpenDoc API is complex, and a complete discussion of it is beyond the scope of this book. What this book does present are the important pieces of the model; you will learn enough about the API to actually write a basic part editor. For more detailed information on OpenDoc programming, see the references in Appendix D, the annotated bibliography.

The rest of this chapter discusses the fundamentals of the OpenDoc application model, starting with the persistent structure of a document, continuing with the runtime software environment and the major OpenDoc service APIs, and ending with the development process for part editors.

Basic Concepts

This section discusses some of the basic concepts of OpenDoc: reference counting, ISO strings, name spaces, and types and tokens.

Reference Counting

OpenDoc uses a reference-counting strategy for memory management of objects that are shared among multiple clients. Reference-counted objects maintain a count of how many objects are using them. Clients notify an object when they acquire or release a reference to that object. When the reference count drops to zero, the object is no longer in use, and it can be deallocated.

A reference-counted object is created by a call to a Factory method, which returns the object with a reference count of 1. For example, calling ODShape::Copy returns a new shape with a reference count of 1. The object that called the Factory method now owns that reference to the object.

If a new client receives a reference to an existing reference-counted object, the client should call Acquire on the object to inform the object that it has another client. The Acquire method increments the reference count of the object.

When a client is done using a reference-counted object, it should call Release on the object. The Release method decrements the reference count. When the count reaches 0, the object knows it is no longer in use and may be deallocated. Some reference-counted objects are simple enough that they can deallocate themselves, while others must ask their factory objects to perform the deallocation for them. In either case, this detail is hidden from the client of the object.

If all clients have correctly called Acquire and Release on reference-counted objects they refer to, the object's reference count should indicate the number of clients at a given time. Figure 4-1 shows a graph of objects and the correct

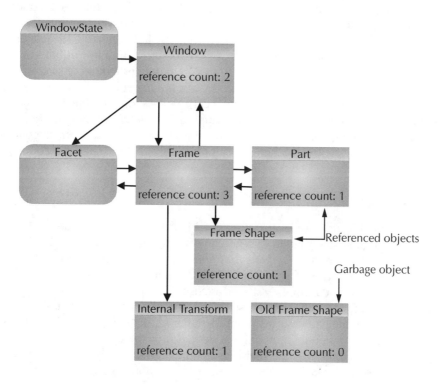

FIGURE 4-1.   *Reference-counted objects*

reference counts of the reference-counted objects. Note that the object with a reference count of 0 is garbage and may be deallocated.

The OpenDoc API has many calls for accessing a value of an object. For instance, ODWindow::GetPlatformWindow returns the toolbox window structure associated with an OpenDoc window object. These simple accessor calls are often called *getter methods* (and their corresponding calls to set the value are called *setter methods*). Getter method names almost always follow the form Get<*ValueName*>.

OpenDoc has a number of getters that not only return a reference-counted object, but also increment the reference count for the caller. By convention, all such calls begin with "Acquire" rather than "Get." ODFrame::AcquirePart, for instance, returns the part displayed by the frame with its reference count already incremented for the caller. Calls to getters that increment reference counts must be balanced with subsequent Release calls, just as regular calls to Acquire must be.

Reference counting of objects is a useful tool for memory management, but it is by no means a perfect solution. Care must always be taken to count references correctly. Otherwise, unused objects may never be deallocated—or even worse, objects will be deallocated when they still have clients. Using a reference-counting scheme has the advantage that it does not rely on a particular programming language and so allows OpenDoc to be used with any SOM-capable language.

For a developer programming in C++, OpenDoc provides a few utilities that make reference counting easier. The file TempObj.h defines a number of classes that help manage reference-counted objects. A TempObject holds a reference to a reference-counted object and automatically calls Release on the object when the TempObject is destructed. Not only is this approach more convenient for the developer than calling Release manually, but it is also safer to use with exceptions. The file ODUtils.h also defines a number of functions that help in reference counting.

ISO Strings

The International Standards Organization (ISO) has established a standard for "public text identifiers" formed from segmented strings. This standard is *ISO/IEC 9070:1991(E) Registration Procedures for Public Text Owner Identifiers*. Originally intended to provide a way of uniquely identifying published works such as catalogs, papers, and so forth, ISO strings are used by OpenDoc to uniquely identify type and property names. These segmented strings consist of a unique prefix followed by the particular name or identifier for the item. ISO 9070 defines a format for these strings and a protocol that defines how to become a naming authority. Naming authorities are registries of unique prefixes; the top-level naming authority designated by ISO is ANSI, the American National Standards Institute.

ANSI then registers additional naming authorities that can then manage their own unique collections of names.

OpenDoc uses ISO strings to create unique identifiers for type names, property names, and other entities. CI Labs has been established as an ISO 9070 naming authority, and will be able to register prefixes for OpenDoc developers. These developers may request a unique string prefix from CI Labs so developers can manage their own space of unique strings. Typically, this prefix consists of the CI Labs ISO 9070 prefix concatenated with the company name of the developer. For instance, the prefix for Apple Computer is

+//ISO 9070/ANSI::113722::US::CI LABS::Apple:

The following prefix is defined for OpenDoc as a whole:

+//ISO 9070/ANSI::113722::US::CI LABS::OpenDoc:

For more information, refer to the CI Labs web page at **http://www.cilabs.org/**.

Name Spaces

OpenDoc name spaces provide a general-purpose registry for objects and other values. Name spaces are used to map names to values, as in a hash table or dictionary. Each name space is identified by a unique ISO string name. Values within name spaces are also identified by ISO strings.

Name spaces can be used to share information among different part editors. For instance, a suite of editors that present a common set of tools for editing can place an ODExtension or some other SOM object in an agreed-upon name space. The various parts in a document that need to use the tools can obtain that object from the name space.

Name spaces are accessed through the NameSpaceManager. The NameSpaceManager is itself a name space that merely holds other name spaces. For more information on the NameSpaceManager, see Appendix A, which is the class reference.

Types and Tokens

ISO strings are also used at runtime to describe the types of objects used by OpenDoc. For instance, parts are displayed in frames according to the frame's *presentation*. For example, a clock part may have an analog presentation or a digital presentation. Rather than register the names of all these types individually with a central authority such as CI Labs, developers may use ISO strings to uniquely name the types. The data type ODType is defined as an ISO string and is used to specify these object types.

ISO strings are useful, but considerable overhead is involved in passing strings as parameters to functions (SOM requires that such parameters be copied) and comparing strings for equality. OpenDoc provides a simple registration mechanism that allows these types to be passed and compared as efficiently as integers. An ODTypeToken is a "magic cookie" that represents a particular ODType. Types may be converted to tokens by calling the session's Tokenize method. From then on, tokens may be used in place of types, with far less overhead involved in their use.

Persistent Structure

In an OpenDoc document, many parts may share the same persistent storage container. In terms of monolithic applications, this is equivalent to storing multiple documents in the same file. This sharing would certainly be impossible if the part editors did not cooperate to share the storage. Thus, OpenDoc provides a standard way of structuring a storage file and rules for sharing its storage space.

The OpenDoc class hierarchy includes the class ODPersistentObject. Classes derived from this class are capable of being stored persistently in document files. These persistent objects are ODFrame, ODLink, ODLinkSource, and ODPart. Persistent objects are reference counted, so their use must follow the restrictions described in the section "Reference Counting" earlier in this chapter.

Storage Units

The basic unit of persistent storage is called a *storage unit*. Each persistent object in a document (including parts) is given a storage unit in which to store its data. A storage unit consists of a number of named *properties*. Each property holds a number of *values*. Each value is the equivalent of a traditional file and presents a typical stream interface to its data. Figure 4-2 shows a typical storage unit with several properties and values.

A property represents a particular attribute of an object. The different values of a property each describe the same data, but in a different format, thus allowing parts (and other objects) to be stored in multiple representations. Storing several representations of a part's data is useful for document interchange. It allows a part to be stored in a high-fidelity, proprietary format and, possibly, lower-fidelity standard interchange formats at the same time.

For example, a text part may store in its contents property a value in its own format, one in Rich Text Format (RTF), and one in plain ASCII, all at the same time. If the document is given to a user who does not have the same editor that stored the part, then the user can use a different editor that can interpret one of the other

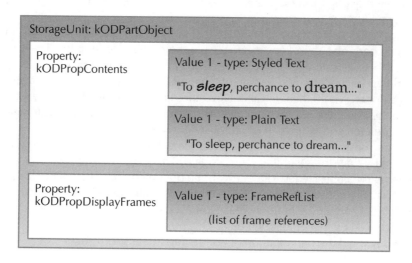

FIGURE 4-2.   *A storage unit*

formats of the part's data. The process of selecting an appropriate editor that can handle one of the stored formats of a part is called *binding* and is discussed more fully in the section "Editor Binding" later in this chapter.

NOTE
Each separate value should be a complete description of a part's contents and should be able to stand on its own. The data in a value should not be an incremental addition to the data in another. For example, if one value stores unstyled ASCII text, and a second value stores styled text, the second value should include both the text and the style information, not just the additional style information.

Persistent References

An important feature of OpenDoc storage is the ability to create references between stored objects. A part's persistent representation usually includes references to other objects. Because no one part editor is in control of the entire document's storage, it would be impossible to save a reference to storage units created by other parts without a special facility. OpenDoc provides that facility in the form of a *storage unit reference*.

In most cases, a stored part includes a list of the frames in which it is displayed. Containing parts also must keep references to their embedded frames. These references between storage units are generated and maintained by OpenDoc (for an example, see the "Storage" section of Chapter 5). When referenced storage units are repositioned within the file, OpenDoc automatically adjusts the references to maintain the connection. OpenDoc can also detect when a referenced storage unit has been deleted and returns an error if a stale reference is resolved.

Perhaps most importantly, when a part's storage unit is copied, storage units referenced by that storage unit are also copied. This feature is important for maintaining the cohesiveness of data within a document. Since a containing part does not usually understand the persistent formats of its embedded parts, copying embedded data would be impossible if OpenDoc did not locate and copy storage units referenced by that embedded data. This procedure allows compound data to be moved without the participation of editors for all parts moved.

Part Storage Organization

Each part is given its own storage unit when it is created. The part should create a *contents property* in which to store its contents. Parts may store their contents in several alternative formats as different values within the contents property. Parts should also store a list of any display frames in the *display frames property* of the storage unit. There are several other properties in a part's storage unit, but these are created, maintained, and used by OpenDoc itself, and the part usually does not care about them or their values. A list of the standard properties of part storage units can be found in the file StdProps.idl.

Very simple parts may store their contents entirely within one storage unit, but for more complex data, it is often useful to create additional storage units to help manage the complexity. This arrangement is recommended for all but the simplest parts. Figure 4-3 shows a part with an auxiliary contents storage unit.

Very complex parts may use OpenDoc structured storage to organize their contents. Storage units can be created for any number of objects within a part's contents. However, this rather advanced technique is not necessary for most part editors. Figure 4-4 illustrates the use of multiple storage units to store a part.

Whether a part stores its contents data in the main storage unit, an auxiliary storage unit, or many storage units, the contents property of the main storage unit is the only property that should contain contents data.

If all the data representing a part's contents is stored in one property, what is the purpose of the other properties in the storage unit? Contents data is only a piece of the information on a part you may wish to store persistently. You may also want to store descriptive data on the part itself or metadata that OpenDoc stores for its

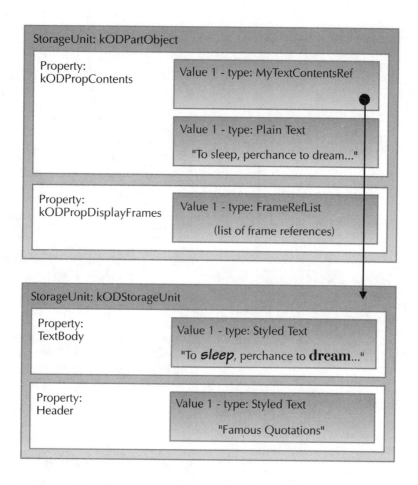

FIGURE 4-3.   *Auxiliary contents storage unit*

own use. This data includes the part's name if it has one, the modification date, and the user who last modified the part. Properties may also hold annotations to the part placed there by other parts. An example of such annotation is a dictionary of special words used in the part that is stored by a spelling checker. This data should be stored with the part, but it is not actually part of its contents.

Part annotation properties are named so they can be identified as annotations. Annotation property names (in ISO string format) should include the segment

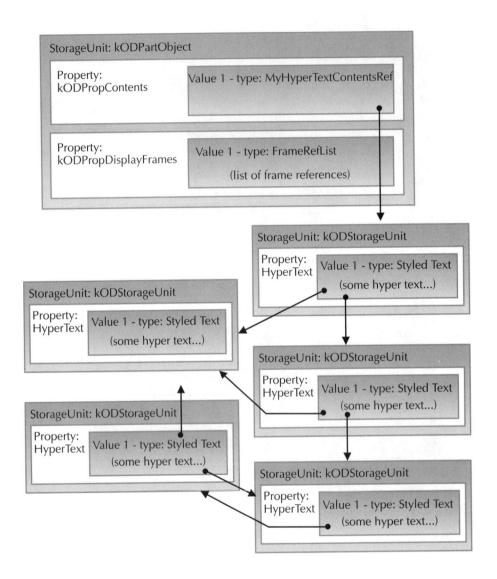

FIGURE 4-4. *Multiple contents storage units*

"Annotation:" before the actual property name. See the file StdProps.idl for examples.

The arrangement just described may sound complex, but generally it is fairly simple for editors to handle. The rule is that a part editor should store all content data in the contents property of the part's storage unit. A list of the frames in which the part is displayed should be stored in the display frames property. Unless the part is doing something unusual, the other properties may be safely ignored.

Editor Binding

OpenDoc uses a sophisticated rule for choosing which editor to use to edit a part. The process of choosing an editor is called *binding*. The binding process tries to find the best editor to use for a part, based on several criteria. First, OpenDoc attempts to present a part with no loss of fidelity. Second, OpenDoc respects a user's preference for editing a certain kind of data.

Every part is annotated with information on which editor was last used to edit it. Binding first attempts to use that editor to edit the part. If that editor is not available, one is chosen based on the kind of value in the part's contents property. If the contents property holds text in the RTF format, the user's preferred RTF editor is used to edit the part. If the user has not set such a preference, an arbitrary RTF editor is used. If the system does not have an RTF editor, OpenDoc looks for another value in the contents property, perhaps lower-fidelity, plain ASCII text. Again, OpenDoc tries to find the user's preferred editor first. If no editor can be found, the part can sometimes be translated into a format for which an editor does exist.

The point is that the contents property plays a special role in choosing which editor to use with a part. Thus, it is worth repeating: parts must always store their contents in the standard contents property.

Drafts

Storage units within a document are organized into *drafts*. Each draft represents a consistent, stored version of a document. A document may contain a virtually unlimited number of drafts.

In OpenDoc's standard document format (Bento), each draft is stored as a set of incremental changes from the previous draft. Only storage units that have been modified are actually stored in the new draft. All others are made available transparently from the previous draft. Storing versions in this manner is not only more efficient than keeping each version in a separate file, but one also avoids the risk of accidentally losing a version.

Draft Organization

A draft is just a bag of storage units, with no implicit organization. OpenDoc imposes a small amount of organization on a draft so the contents will be useful.

Each draft contains a special storage unit that can be located externally. This is the *root storage unit*. All storage units in a draft are transitively connected to the root storage unit by storage unit references. Any storage unit that becomes disconnected and can no longer be reached by following references is considered garbage and will eventually be removed from the draft.

The root storage unit contains several standard properties. The root part property holds a reference to the root part of the document. The window list property holds a list of the windows in the draft. There are other standard properties in the root storage unit, but they are typically not of interest to part developers.

The window list is the gateway to the rest of the draft. The root frame of every persistently stored window of a document is listed here. Each frame refers to information for reconstructing its window, and also to the root part of that window. A root part may have embedded frames, so from the root storage unit, it is a simple matter to walk the structure of a document and visit every part's storage unit.

Refer to Figure 2-8 in Chapter 2 for a rough view of the organization of a draft of a simple document.

Runtime Structure

The OpenDoc runtime environment is contained within an entity called a *session*. A session is merely the set of OpenDoc objects that can directly interact using SOM mechanisms. In the simple case, a session holds a single document and its contents, though it sometimes may hold more.

The runtime environment of an OpenDoc session is similar to that of an ordinary application. The basic model gives each session an address space in which all parts and other objects are allocated, though this can vary across different platform implementations. Variations on this model may include allocation of each part in its own address space, each part in its own process, and different parts distributed across different physical processors. For memory and process details for the runtime environment, check the documentation for the platform in question.

Whatever the basics of the runtime environment, the overall structure of the objects within a session is the same: a hierarchy of objects represents the persistent storage of documents, a session object holds all the objects of global interest to parts within that session, and a hierarchy of objects describes the visual layout of documents in that session.

Storage

Every part in a document has its own storage unit, allocated to it by its draft. At runtime, a part instance is given a reference to its storage unit object when the part is initialized. The storage unit is the part's connection to its draft and the rest of its document storage. Figure 4-5 shows the storage object hierarchy.

The runtime storage object hierarchy naturally parallels the persistent storage hierarchy. *Storage units* are contained by *drafts*, drafts are contained by *documents*, documents are contained by *containers*, and containers are managed by a *storage system*. From a given object, a part can obtain the container of that object; that is, given a storage unit, a part can call storageUnit->GetDraft(ev) to obtain the draft.

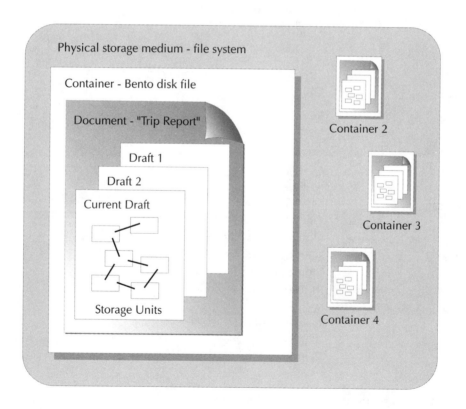

FIGURE 4-5. *Storage object hierarchy*

So from its own storage unit, a part can navigate the entire storage hierarchy. However, there is not much need for that sort of access. Most storage interactions occur with storage units and drafts.

In most programming tasks, editors interact with a draft rather than with the document itself. Certain drafts are more commonly used than others. The current draft is the draft the user is in the process of editing. It is the only draft in the document that may be modified. Other drafts are associated with drag-and-drop operations, the clipboard, and linking.

The Session Object

Each OpenDoc session has an object that represents the session itself. This is the session object. The session object is the place to find many objects and services that are used by parts. For detailed information on the session and its objects, refer to the class API descriptions in Appendix A.

Table 4-1 lists the session global objects.

Area	Objects
Core	Info NameSpaceManager
Data Transfer	Clipboard DragAndDrop LinkManager
Messaging	MessageInterface NameResolver ShellSemanticInterface
Storage	Binding StorageSystem Translation
User Interface	Arbitrator Dispatcher Undo WindowState

TABLE 4-1.   *Session Global Objects*

The following sections describe the session global objects in each area and the session services available. The getters and setters for session globals are shown in IDL. See Chapter 3 for an overview of IDL.

Core Area

These methods are part of the OpenDoc Core subsystem.

Info   The Info object assists in presenting the Part Info dialog box. Parts should use this object to display the dialog box when a user chooses the Part Info command.

```
ODInfo GetInfo();
void SetInfo(in ODInfo info);
```

NameSpaceManager   The NameSpaceManager object manages the various name spaces in a session. It is used by parts and other objects to create, delete, and access name spaces.

```
ODNameSpaceManager GetNameSpaceManager();
void SetNameSpaceManager(in ODNameSpaceManager nameSpaceManager);
```

Data-Transfer Area

The Clipboard, DragAndDrop, and LinkManager objects perform data transfer operations (copy, cut, and paste operations, drag-and-drop operations, and linking). Parts use the Clipboard and DragAndDrop objects to move and copy data. Parts do not directly use the LinkManager object, but rather interact with Link and LinkSource objects.

Clipboard   The Clipboard provides a temporary holding area for data.

```
ODClipboard GetClipboard();
void SetClipboard(in ODClipboard clipboard);
```

DragAndDrop   Users directly manipulate data via drag and drop.

```
ODDragAndDrop GetDragAndDrop();
void SetDragAndDrop(in ODDragAndDrop dragAndDrop);
```

LinkManager   The LinkManager maintains link integrity.

```
ODLinkManager GetLinkManager();
void SetLinkManager(in ODLinkManager linkManager);
```

Messaging Area

These methods deal with OpenDoc messaging.

MessageInterface   The MessageInterface object is used by parts to send semantic event messages. It provides a standard interface for the platform's messaging system.

```
ODMessageInterface GetMessageInterface();
void SetMessageInterface(in ODMessageInterface messageInterface);
```

NameResolver   The NameResolver object is used by OpenDoc to find content objects named by object specifiers in semantic events or scripts. Normally, parts do not use this object.

```
ODNameResolver GetNameResolver();
void SetNameResolver(in ODNameResolver nameResolver);
```

ShellSemanticInterface   The ShellSemanticInterface object holds the event handler functions for the session's shell. Parts do not use this object, though container applications register their handlers here.

```
ODSemanticInterface AcquireShellSemtInterface();
void SetShellSemtInterface(in ODSemanticInterface shellSemanticInterface);
```

Storage Area

These methods are part of the OpenDoc Storage subsystem.

Binding   The Binding object is used to find the right part editor to use to edit a part. It encapsulates the OpenDoc policy for editor selection based on the part's data type, editor availability, and user preference. Parts never need to use the binding object.

```
ODBinding GetBinding();
void SetBinding(in ODBinding binding);
```

StorageSystem   The StorageSystem object manages persistent storage for the entire session. It holds the containers of the documents for that session. Parts rarely have to use the StorageSystem object.

```
ODStorageSystem GetStorageSystem();
void SetStorageSystem(in ODStorageSystem storageSystem);
```

Translation   The Translation object assists in translating part data from one format to another. If a part receives transferred data that it cannot interpret, it can ask the Translation object for a format that it does support.

```
ODTranslation GetTranslation();
void SetTranslation(in ODTranslation translation);
```

User Interface Area
These methods are part of the OpenDoc UI subsystem.

Arbitrator   The Arbitrator is used by parts to negotiate for shared resources such as the menu bar, keyboard input, or selection. Each resource is represented by a focus, which is a tokenized ISO string naming the resource. If a part wants to use a shared resource, it must acquire the resource from the Arbitrator. Parts may also register new kinds of resources with the Arbitrator by installing FocusModules.

```
ODArbitrator GetArbitrator();
void SetArbitrator(in ODArbitrator arbitrator);
```

Dispatcher   The Dispatcher is the object that delivers events to the appropriate part. Parts don't often have to interact directly with the Dispatcher. Parts may make calls on the Dispatcher to register modules for special dispatching of events (by installing DispatchModules) or to redispatch events to other parts.

```
ODDispatcher GetDispatcher();
void SetDispatcher(in ODDispatcher dispatcher);
```

Undo   The Undo object manages the stack of undoable operations for the session. The OpenDoc HI specification requires the undo stack to be system wide, so that data is shared among all sessions on a desktop.

```
ODUndo GetUndo();
void SetUndo(in ODUndo undo);
```

WindowState   The WindowState object manages the list of a document's windows as well as some information related to the menu bar. Parts ask the WindowState object to create new window objects, control the layering of windows, and find OpenDoc Window objects for platform window structures. The WindowState object is also a factory for several User Interface-related objects.

```
ODWindowState GetWindowState();
void SetWindowState(in ODWindowState windowState);
```

Session Services

In addition to the getters and setters for the session globals, the Session object also has a handful of calls that provide certain services.

Tokenize   The Tokenize method converts a type string into a token and returns that token. If the same string has been tokenized before, the same token will be returned for subsequent calls.

```
ODTypeToken Tokenize(in ODType type);
```

GetType   The GetType returns the type string for a token. The function return value indicates whether a type was found for that token, and if so, the type is returned in the out parameter.

```
ODBoolean GetType(in ODTypeToken token,
                    out ODType type);
```

RemoveEntry   The RemoveEntry call removes a token table entry. Subsequent calls to GetType for tokens generated from this type will not succeed, and the next call to Tokenize for that type will return a different token.

```
void RemoveEntry(in ODType type);
```

GetUserName   The GetUserName call returns a string containing the name of the user of the document.

```
void GetUserName(out ODIText name);
```

UniqueUpdateID   The UniqueUpdateID call returns a unique ID used to identify a link change.

```
ODUpdateID UniqueUpdateID();
```

Layout Hierarchy

Each window of an OpenDoc document contains a separate hierarchy of objects that describe the layout of parts within that window. The organization of the layout hierarchy is somewhat complex, but this complexity allows greater flexibility in the creation of sophisticated document layouts. In fact, there are actually two distinct hierarchies of layout information in each window: a hierarchy of frame objects describes the embedding relationships among parts, and a hierarchy of facet objects describes where frames are displayed in a window or canvas.

The frame and facet hierarchies both are rooted in the window. The window owns a root frame and a root facet, and both are used to display the root part. Starting at one of these objects, either hierarchy can be traversed using appropriate iterators. The root frame of a window can be obtained with the call window->AcquireRootFrame(ev). The root facet can be obtained with the call window->GetRootFacet(ev).

The Facet Hierarchy

The facet hierarchy is a typical tree data structure, with children having upward links to parents. Figure 4-6 shows an example of a facet hierarchy for a simple window layout.

A facet knows which frame it displays, on which canvas it is displayed, the position on the canvas where it is displayed, and how the display should be

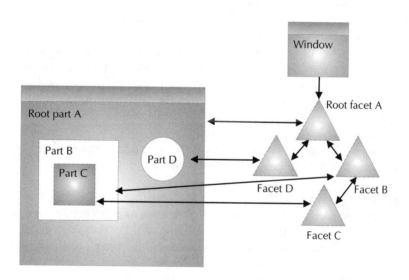

FIGURE 4-6. *Window and facet hierarchy*

clipped. A facet may have its own canvas, or it can use the canvas of its parent facet. In the simplest case, all facets in a window appear on the window canvas.

The facet hierarchy represents only the frames actually visible at any given time plus perhaps a few more which were recently visible but have not yet been purged. The number of frames in a document can be far greater than the number of facets visible. For this reason, iterating the facets in a window is not a reliable way to find all of a window's embedded frames.

The Frame Hierarchy

The organization of the frame hierarchy is somewhat more complex than that of the facet hierarchy. A frame does not have direct references to its embedded frames, but only to the part that it displays. The part maintains its list of embedded frames, and that list is available as an iterator through the ODPart call CreateEmbeddedFramesIterator.

The list of embedded frames is not kept in the containing frame for several reasons. Most importantly, the number of embedded frames can be quite large, perhaps tens of thousands for large documents. Keeping the embedded frame list in the containing frame would dictate a particular representation in memory, whereas the actual arrangement allows part editors the freedom to represent and manage the list as they choose. For example, for very large lists, the editor can keep in memory only the pieces of the list that are needed at any given time.

In addition, references to embedded frames must be stored persistently. But a part can store its contents in several data formats, and some of those formats may support embedding while others do not. A text editor that embeds may store its own format that supports embedding as well as a plain ASCII text format without embedding. Both of these representations are valid, but with one, embedded frame references in the containing frame would be invalid, as it does not use embedded frames. Clearly, the references to embedded frames can be meaningfully maintained only by the containing part itself.

An embedded frame does contain a direct reference to its containing frame, however, as the frame hierarchy in Figure 4-7 shows.

The Combined Hierarchy

As was mentioned earlier, a facet contains a reference to its frame. A frame may be displayed in several facets, and the frame maintains a list of these facets. Multiple facets can be used for a range of layout purposes, but the most common use is for creating split views. Figure 4-8 illustrates split views.

Putting everything together, the hierarchy looks like Figure 4-9.

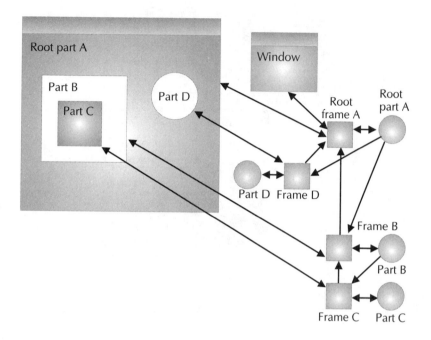

FIGURE 4-7. *Frame hierarchy*

Developing a Part Editor

You now have a good idea of what the environment looks like to a part editor. In this section, you will look at the process of actually writing a part editor. This section starts with an overview of the kinds of behavior an editor must support and then looks at the calls that must be implemented to provide that support. The calls discussed here are only a subset of the full Part API, but they are sufficient to illustrate the main points of the design.

Part Protocols

There are roughly 70 calls in the Part API. About half of these calls are optional or have default-inherited implementations. That leaves about 35 calls that must be implemented to write the simplest part possible.

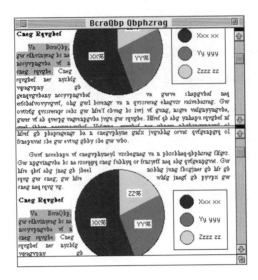

FIGURE 4-8. *Split views*

The calls in the Part API are organized into ten areas of functionality called *protocols*. The six protocols that all parts must implement are Initialization, Layout, Imaging, UI Events, Part Activation, and Part Persistence. The four optional protocols are Undo, DragAndDrop, Linking, and Embedding. A developer may choose not to implement an optional protocol if its functionality is not required. However, if any calls in an optional protocol are implemented, all of the calls must be implemented as a unit.

Required Protocols

This section discusses the required part protocols in order of the flow of part activity. First the part is created and initialized. It is put in a frame and then displayed in a facet. The part responds to user actions, possibly being activated as a result. Finally, the part is saved so it can be restored later.

Initialization   When a new part instance is created, it must be initialized to prepare it for operation. A new instance can be created for a new part or for an old part that was saved in a document. In either case, the initialization methods connect the part instance to its storage unit and prepare the instance to participate in the other protocols. OpenDoc requires the part's constructor never to return an

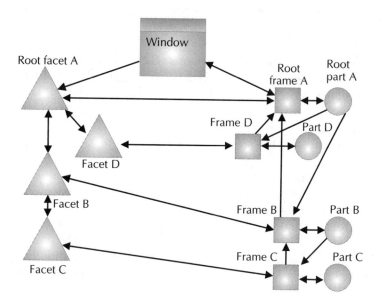

FIGURE 4-9. *Complete layout hierarchy*

exception, so any code that could fail must be placed in the initialization methods instead.

Layout   The Layout protocol consists of calls that manage a part's interaction with its display frames. Most of these calls are notifications regarding a change in a display frame's state, such as its frame shape or link status. In addition, some calls notify a part that a display frame has been added or removed and ask it to read and write the frame's PartInfo data.

Imaging   The Imaging protocol calls all operate on a part's facets. These calls include notifications of facet state change and the addition and removal of facets as well as the actual drawing of the part's contents on a particular facet.

UI Events   The calls in the UI Events protocol allow a part to respond to user actions.

Part Activation   Calls in the Part Activation protocol are used by the Arbitrator to manage a part's foci, including the selection focus, which controls which part is active.

Part Persistence   The Part Persistence protocol is really an extension of the basic Storage protocol of all persistent objects. These calls allow a part to read and write its persistent form.

Optional Protocols
The protocols described in this section are optional.

Undo   If a part editor uses the services of the Undo object, it must implement the Undo protocol. These calls are used by the Undo object to manage the data the part registers on the Undo stack. Any part that uses the Clipboard or drag-and-drop operations should implement this protocol.

DragAndDrop   For a part editor to receive data via drag-and-drop operations, it must implement the DragAndDrop protocol. These calls allow drag interaction and the dropping of data.

Linking   For a part editor to allow links to its content data, it must implement the Linking protocol. These calls are used to create and manage link objects.

Embedding   A part editor must implement the Embedding protocol if it is to contain other parts. These calls include notifications of embedded frame state changes and frame negotiation methods.

Important Calls

The previous section presented the basic organization of the Part API. This section briefly describes some important calls that are key in an editor's implementation. For a more complete description of an editor implementation, see Chapter 5. For a full description of the Part API, see Appendix A.

Initialization
A part object can be initialized in either of two ways. One method is used if the part is newly created and the other if the part existed previously and was stored persistently.

InitPart   The InitPart call is used to initialize a part instance when the part is first created. This call prepares the part instance to receive further calls.

```
void InitPart(in ODStorageUnit storageUnit,
              in ODPart partWrapper);
```

InitPartFromStorage   The InitPartFromStorage call is used to initialize a part instance when the part has been previously saved to persistent storage.

```
void InitPartFromStorage(in ODStorageUnit storageUnit,
                         in ODPart partWrapper);
```

ReleaseAll   The ReleaseAll call is the last call that will be made on a part instance before its destructor is called. The part should release all external resources, including references to reference-counted objects.

```
void ReleaseAll();
```

Layout
These methods are part of the OpenDoc Layout subsystem.

DisplayFrameAdded   The DisplayFrameAdded call notifies a part that it has been embedded in a new container, either a window or a containing part. The part should remember the new frame for future use, and prepare itself to be displayed in the new frame. Appendix A lists several related calls: DisplayFrameRemoved, DisplayFrameConnected, DisplayFrameClosed, and AttachSourceFrame.

```
void DisplayFrameAdded(in ODFrame frame);
```

Open   The Open call causes a part to display itself in a new window. This is used both when a document is opened to construct its window(s), and to open an embedded embedded part in a part window.

```
ODID Open(in ODFrame frame);
```

FrameShapeChanged   The FrameShapeChanged call notifies a part that the frame shape of one of its display frames has been changed. This can happen when the user resizes an embedded frame. The part should adjust the display of its contents for the new shape. Appendix A lists several similar notifications: ViewTypeChanged, PresentationChanged, SequenceChanged, LinkStatusChanged, and ContainingPartPropertiesUpdated.

```
void FrameShapeChanged(in ODFrame frame);
```

ReadPartInfo   The ReadPartInfo call is used by a display frame to request the part to read in the frame's PartInfo data from the frame's storage unit. This usually happens when a saved frame is internalized and connected to its part. Appendix A lists several related calls: WritePartInfo and ClonePartInfo.

```
ODInfoType ReadPartInfo(in ODFrame frame,
                        in ODStorageUnitView storageUnitView);
```

Imaging

These methods are part of the OpenDoc Imaging subsystem.

FacetAdded   The FacetAdded call notifies a part that one of its display frames is being displayed in a new facet. The part should prepare itself to display in the new facet. Appendix A lists a related call: RemoveFacet.

```
void FacetAdded(in ODFacet facet);
```

Draw   The Draw call tells a part to draw itself in one of its facets. There are many settings that can influence how a part draws its contents. For more information on part drawing, see Chapter 5.

```
void Draw(in ODFacet facet,
          in ODShape invalidShape);
```

UI Events

These two methods handle user-interface events.

HandleEvent   The HandleEvent call delivers a UI event to the part so it can respond to it. All mouse clicks and key presses, as well as other UI events, are delivered to the part via this call. Semantic events are delivered to the part via the part's semantic event handlers.

```
ODBoolean HandleEvent(inout ODEventData event,
                      in ODFrame frame,
                      in ODFacet facet,
                      inout ODEventInfo eventInfo);
```

AdjustMenus   When the user attempts to invoke a menu, the part which owns the menu focus will receive an AdjustMenus call. The part should then adjust the menu system to reflect the current state of the part.

```
void AdjustMenus(in ODFrame frame);
```

Part Persistence

These methods deal with persistent storage for an OpenDoc part editor.

Externalize   The Externalize call tells a part to save its state to its storage unit. This happens when the document is being saved.

```
void Externalize();
```

Undo

When the user performs an action that can be undone, the part records that information by creating an action data object and registering it with the global Undo object. The following calls all operate on the action data objects that a part has recorded.

UndoAction   The UndoAction call tells a part that it should undo an action. The part should revert its state to whatever it was before the action was performed.

```
void UndoAction(in ODActionData actionState);
```

RedoAction   The RedoAction call tells a part that it should redo an action. The part should perform the action again.

```
void RedoAction(in ODActionData actionState);
```

DisposeActionState   The DisposeActionState call tells a part to dispose of the action data object for a particular undoable action. This happens when the user performs an action that cannot be undone or when the document is closed. The part should commit the action (it will not be undone after this) and deallocate the action data.

```
void DisposeActionState(in ODActionData actionState,
                        in ODDoneState doneState);
```

Putting It Together

This chapter presented a great deal of technical detail about the OpenDoc programming enviroment. It discussed basic concepts such as reference counting and tokens, and described both the persistent and runtime structure of a document. Finally, it gave a brief overview of the design process involved in developing a part editor.

Chapter 5 will expand upon the information presented here and will describe the construction of a simple OpenDoc part editor.

CHAPTER 5

A Simple OpenDoc Part

This chapter introduces the OpenDoc Part application programmer interface (API) by explaining the structure of a simple OpenDoc part editor. After explaining how the different C++ and System Object Model (SOM) classes fit together and interact, it presents a detailed summary of each method and data structure.

Now that you've learned the basics of OpenDoc and the important subsystems of the OpenDoc Part API, it's time for a more detailed and complete presentation of an actual OpenDoc component.

The 1.0 release of OpenDoc has several examples and tools for creating sample parts. One of these is called SamplePart, and it demonstrates all of the functions and behaviors that are expected of a simple OpenDoc part. This chapter presents a very simple component, based on the SamplePart code from the OpenDoc 1.0 distribution. The SamplePart code implements the minimum set of methods for a useful part. In addition, the SamplePart code is supported by Apple and the other CI Labs partners and subsequent versions can be expected to incorporate any changes to the OpenDoc API.

The MacOS version of the part is based on the 1.0 version of OpenDoc, which shipped on November 10, 1995. The Windows version is based on the DR1 release of OpenDoc. The explanatory text in this chapter focuses mainly on the final version of the API as reflected in the MacOS implementation, and the code samples in Appendix C reflect the currently available implementations on both platforms. Since the Windows version of the OpenDoc API will eventually be brought into line with the MacOS version, we will note places in the Windows sample code that are likely to change.

The part that this chapter presents is called WebGauge. As its name implies, it displays some simple, useful statistics about a running World Wide Web (WWW) server. The main point of the exercise is to demonstrate how you can replace the WebGauge code with your own unique code for a particular business need. For example, the code can be adapted to display stock quotes in real time or monitor critical variables in a control system or network administration center.

WebGauge implements basic protocols that are required of all parts, such as storage management and initialization protocols. More advanced features, such as drag and drop and scripting, will be added later, in Chapter 7.

About WebGauge

WebGauge implements a small number of features. Some are concerned with WebGauge's content, which is a live summary of WWW server use (but could be any similar monitoring task). Most are concerned with WebGauge's ability to interact properly with other OpenDoc parts and with OpenDoc container applications.

Some of these functions are

- Initialization
- Basic event handling

- Activation

- Handling persistent storage

- Drawing summary information in the part window

- Handling layout and window presentation

- Allowing the part to take advantage of OpenDoc's dynamic binding capabilities

Some parts can handle having other parts embedded within them; these are referred to as *containing* parts. WebGauge, by contrast, is a *leaf* part and does not allow other parts to be embedded within it. (If you were to draw a tree structure of the parts of a document, a leaf part would be at the very end of the branches—thus the name.) The embedding protocols are described in Chapter 7.

Like SamplePart, WebGauge is structured with a wrapper class that encapsulates most of the complexities inherent in dealing with SOM and the Interface Definition Language (IDL). The purpose of a wrapper class is to allow certain housekeeping functions, such as dealing with SOM, to be segregated from the rest of the code. The specific functions of WebGauge are provided in a fairly portable C++ class called WebEngine, implemented on both MacOS and Windows. Chapter 6 provides a detailed look at the WebEngine class. Figure 5-1 provides a look at the structure of WebGauge.

SOM Interface to WebGauge

ODPart is the basic OpenDoc part class provided by the implementation of OpenDoc. All OpenDoc parts are subclasses of ODPart.

Many part developers have discovered that the easiest way to implement an OpenDoc part is to create a single SOM subclass that overrides all of the methods in ODPart and then delegates their implementation to a class or set of functions written in a language such as C or C++. WebGauge uses a C++ class that implements most (though not all) of the functions of ODPart.

The SOM wrapper class is extremely simple and calls the corresponding methods in the C++ implementation class. (For example, the SOM class method som_WebGauge::InitPart calls the similarly named WebGauge::InitPart method in the C++ class.) Adding features to WebGauge merely requires the addition of a method call to the C++ class and the method that implements the new feature,

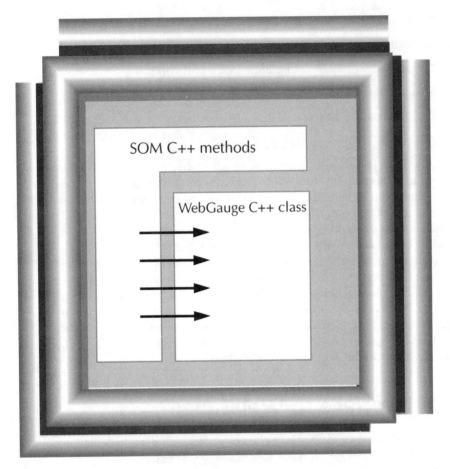

FIGURE 5-1.   *WebGauge structure*

without the need to rerun the SOM compiler to regenerate the interface. Figure 5-2 shows how an OpenDoc part is structured.

Some C++ compilers have a feature called Direct-to-SOM, which lets a developer implement SOM classes directly as though they were C++ classes. This

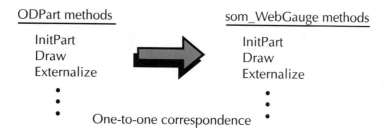

Implementation delegation

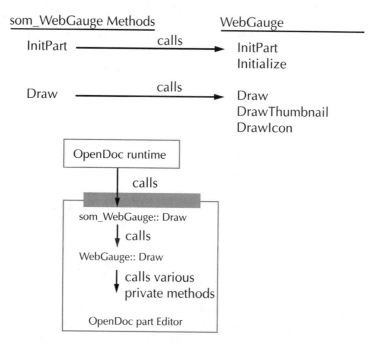

FIGURE 5-2.   *SOM and C++ in an OpenDoc part editor*

approach tends to make code much cleaner and obviates the need to run a separate SOM compiler.

The C++ Class

The rest of this chapter focuses on the C++ class that implements the bulk of WebGauge's functions. The code for this class is in Appendix C.

Appendix A provides a definition of the ODPart SOM class. As discussed in Chapter 4, ODPart is the fundamental SOM class that defines the interface between the OpenDoc runtime and an individual component. Look at that definition and you'll notice that there is an exact correspondence between the methods shown here and those in ODPart, with the addition of some private methods.

The following sections explain the operation of the methods in WebGauge. Each heading indicates the method name, and whether it is a method that overrides a method in ODPart, or is specific to WebGauge.

The following list shows the methods that correspond to ODPart methods.

InitPart	DisplayFrameAdded	Draw
InitPartFromStorage	DisplayFrameConnected	GeometryChanged
Release	DisplayFrameRemoved	HighlightChanged
ReleaseAll	DisplayFrameClosed	BeginRelinquishFocus
Purge	AttachSourceFrame	CommitRelinquishFocus
CloneInto	ViewTypeChanged	AbortRelinquishFocus
Externalize	FrameShapeChanged	FocusAcquired
ReadPartInfo	Open	FocusLost
WritePartInfo	FacetAdded	HandleEvent
ClonePartInfo	FacetRemoved	AdjustMenus

The following list shows the methods specific to WebGauge.

Constructor	CalcNewUsedShape	DrawFrameView
Destructor	UpdateFrame	DrawIconView
Initialize	GenerateThumbnail	DrawThumbnailView
InternalizeStateInfo	AcquireFramesWindow	RelinquishAllFoci
InternalizeContent	CreateWindow	PartActivated
ExternalizeStateInfo	CleanupWindow	ActivateFrame
ExternalizeContent	GetDefaultWindowProperties	WindowActivating
CleanseContentProperty	GetSavedWindowProperties	HandleMenuEvent
CheckAndAddProperties	CalcPartWindowSize	HandleMouseEvent
SetDirty	CalcPartWindowPosition	DoMouseEvent
CleanupDisplayFrame	GetActiveFacetForFrame	DoDialogBox

Global Variables

WebGauge has a few global variables, listed here. The function of each is explained as it comes up in the main body of the code.

```
extern     ODUShort              gGlobalsUsageCount;
extern     WebGaugeGlobals*      gGlobals;


struct WebGaugeGlobals {
    public:
    WebGaugeGlobals();
    ~WebGaugeGlobals() {}

    ODMenuBar*          fMenuBar;
    ODFocusSet*         fUIFocusSet;
    Handle              fThumbnail;

    ODTypeToken          fSelectionFocus;
    ODTypeToken          fMenuFocus;
    ODTypeToken          fModalFocus;
    ODTypeToken          fFrameView;
    ODTypeToken          fLargeIconView;
    ODTypeToken          fSmallIconView;
    ODTypeToken          fThumbnailView;
    ODTypeToken          fMainPresentation;

    ODScriptCode        fEditorsScript;
    ODLangCode          fEditorsLanguage;
};
```

Class Definition

The following is the C++ definition of the WebGauge class:

```
class WebGauge {
    public:
        WebGauge ();
        virtual ~WebGauge ();
```

```
// Initialization
void    InitPart (Environment    *ev,
            ODStorageUnit    *storageUnit,
            ODPart    *partWrapper);
void    InitPartFromStorage (Environment    *ev,
            ODStorageUnit    *storageUnit,
            ODPart    *partWrapper);


// Storage
void    Release (Environment    *ev);
void    ReleaseAll (Environment    *ev);
ODSize    Purge (Environment    *ev, ODSize    size);
void    Externalize (Environment    *ev);
void    CloneInto (Environment    *ev,
            ODDraftKey    key,
            ODStorageUnit    *destinationSU,
            ODFrame    *initiatingFrame);
void    WritePartInfo (Environment    *ev,
            ODInfoType    partInfo,
            ODStorageUnitView    *storageUnitView);
ODInfoType    ReadPartInfo (Environment    *ev,
                ODFrame    *frame,
                ODStorageUnitView    *storageUnitView);
void    ClonePartInfo (Environment    *ev,
            ODDraftKey    key,
            ODInfoType    partInfo,
            ODStorageUnitView    *storageUnitView,
            ODFrame    *scopeFrame);


// Layout
void    DisplayFrameAdded (Environment    *ev,
            ODFrame    *frame);
void    DisplayFrameRemoved (Environment    *ev,
            ODFrame    *frame);
void    DisplayFrameClosed (Environment    *ev,
            ODFrame    *frame);
void    DisplayFrameConnected (Environment    *ev,
            ODFrame    *frame);
void    AttachSourceFrame (Environment    *ev,
            ODFrame    *frame,
            ODFrame    *sourceFrame);
void    ViewTypeChanged (Environment    *ev,
```

```
                    ODFrame      *frame);
void      FrameShapeChanged (Environment      *ev,
                    ODFrame      *frame);
ODID      Open (Environment      *ev,
                    ODFrame      *frame);

// Imaging
void      Draw (Environment      *ev,
                    ODFacet      *facet,
                    ODShape      *invalidShape);
void      GeometryChanged (Environment      *ev,
                    ODFacet      *facet,
                    ODBoolean      clipShapeChanged,
                    ODBoolean      externalTransformChanged);
void      HighlightChanged (Environment      *ev,
                    ODFacet      *facet);
void      FacetAdded (Environment      *ev,
                    ODFacet      *facet);
void      FacetRemoved (Environment      *ev,
                    ODFacet      *facet);

// Activation
ODBoolean      BeginRelinquishFocus (Environment      *ev,
                        ODTypeToken      focus,
                        ODFrame      *ownerFrame,
                        ODFrame      *proposedFrame);
void      CommitRelinquishFocus (Environment      *ev,
                        ODTypeToken      focus,
                        ODFrame      *ownerFrame,
                        ODFrame      *proposedFrame);
void      AbortRelinquishFocus (Environment      *ev,
                        ODTypeToken      focus,
                        ODFrame      *ownerFrame,
                        ODFrame      *proposedFrame);
void      FocusAcquired (Environment      *ev,
                        ODTypeToken      focus,
                        ODFrame      *ownerFrame);
void      LostAcquired (Environment      *ev,
                        ODTypeToken      focus,
                        ODFrame      *ownerFrame);
```

```
        // Event Handling
ODBoolean    HandleEvent (Environment      *ev,
                ODEventData     *event,
                ODFrame     *frame,
                ODFacet     *facet,
                ODEventInfo     *eventInfo);
void    AdjustMenus (Environment     *ev,
                ODFrame     *frame);

protected:

        // Initialization
void    Initialize (Environment     *ev);

        // Storage
void    CheckAndAddProperties (Environment      *ev,
                ODStorageUnit     *storageUnit);
void    CleanseContentProperty (Environment      *ev,
                ODStorageUnit     *storageUnit);
void    InternalizeStateInfo (Environment      *ev,
                ODStorageUnit     *storageUnit);
void    InternalizeContent (Environment      *ev,
                ODStorageUnit     *storageUnit);
void    ExternalizeStateInfo (Environment      *ev,
                ODStorageUnit     *storageUnit,
                ODDraftKey     key,
                ODFrame     *scopeFrame);
void    ExternalizeContent (Environment      *ev,
                ODStorageUnit     *storageUnit);
void    SetDirty (Environment     *ev);

        // EventHandling
ODBoolean    HandleMenuEvent (Environment      *ev,
                ODEventData     *event,
                ODFrame     *frame);
ODBoolean    HandleMouseEvent (Environment      *ev,
                ODEventData     *event,
                ODFacet     *facet,
                ODEventInfo     *eventInfo);
ODBoolean    HandleWindowEvent (Environment      *ev,
                ODEventData     *event,
                ODFrame     *frame);
```

```
void     DoMouseEvent (Environment    *ev,
             ODFacet    *facet,
             Point    *point);
void     DoDialogBox (Environment    *ev,
             ODFrame    *frame,
             ODSShort   dialogID,
             ODUShort    errorNumber = 0);


// Imaging
void     DrawFrameView (Environment    *ev,
             ODFacet    *facet);
void     DrawIconView (Environment    *ev,
             ODFacet    *facet);
void     DrawThumbnailView (Environment    *ev,
             ODFacet    *facet);
void     GenerateThumbnail (Environment    *ev,
             ODFrame    *frame);


// Activation
void     PartActivated (Environment    *ev,
             ODFrame    *frame);
ODBoolean    ActivateFrame (Environment    *ev,
             ODFrame    *frame);
void     WindowActivating (Environment    *ev,
             ODFrame    *frame,
             ODBoolean    activating);


// Layout
ODWindow     *GetFrameWindow (Environment    *ev,
                 ODFrame    *frame):
ODWindow     *CreateWindow (Environment    *ev,
                 ODFrame    *frame,
                 ODType    frameType,
                 WindowProperties    *winProps);
WindowProperties    *GetDefaultWindowProperties
                    (Environment    *ev,
                     ODFrame    *frame);
WindowProperties    *GetSavedWindowProperties
                    (Environment    *ev,
                     ODFrame    *frame);
Rect    CalcPartWindowSize (Environment    *ev,
             ODFrame    *sourceFrame);
```

```
Rect     CalcPartWindowPosition (Environment      *ev,
             ODFrame     *frame,
             Rect     *partWindowBounds);
ODFacet     *GetActiveFacetForFrame (Environment     *ev,
             ODFrame     *frame);
ODShape     *CalcNewUsedShape (Environment     *ev,
             ODFrame     *frame);
void     UpdateFrame (Environment     *ev,
             ODFrame     *frame,
             ODTypeToken     view,
             ODShape     *usedShape);

private:

CFrameList     *fDisplayFrames;
ODBoolean     fDirty;
ODPart     *fSelf;
ODBoolean     fReadOnlyStorage;
};
```

The following sections explain each of the preceding methods and data members in detail.

Initialization

During the initialization phase, a part editor sets up its basic structure, reads its persistent data from storage, and prepares itself to start responding to user interaction. The following sections explain this process. When a user decides to begin working on a document, the OpenDoc shell creates a running part object corresponding to each piece of content visible in the document window. In the example here, this part object is an instance of the som_WebGauge class, which is in turn a subclass of ODPart.

After SOM loads the dynamic library for the class and allocates memory for the object, it calls the somInit method for that class. The somInit method is similar to a C++ constructor.

The OpenDoc runtime then calls one of two functions in WebGauge, depending on whether the instance is new or one that had been instantiated at some earlier point. If the part is a newly created one, the runtime calls InitPart. If the part is a previously created one, the runtime uses InitPartFromStorage. These methods contain other initialization code that WebGauge needs to set its internal state. These functions create a C++ object that corresponds to the WebGauge class shown in the preceding listing. The constructor for this class initializes its instance variables (zeroing them out or setting them to a Boolean false state).

Five methods are called to create a fully functioning WebGauge part:

- Constructor
- CheckAndAddProperties
- InitPart
- InitPartFromStorage
- Initialize

The following paragraphs discuss the implementation of each method in detail.

Constructor (WebGauge)

The WebGauge constructor method simply initializes the private data members of the class. The constructor is actually called from the SOM wrapper class' InitPart or InitPartFromStorage, since the SOM object cannot allocate memory in its own constructor (somInit method). The constructor then forwards the call to InitPart or InitPartFromStorage to the new C++ object.

CheckAndAddProperties (WebGauge)

The CheckAndAddProperties method makes sure that the appropriate properties have been initialized in the part's storage unit. It handles the content, default editor, and display frame properties.

InitPart (ODPart)

Every part must implement the InitPart method, which is called by the OpenDoc runtime when a part is newly created. It can safely allocate memory or set up data structures or perform any other action that might return an error.

As implemented in WebGauge, InitPart performs the following series of actions:

1. *Initializes the part-wrapper field*   OpenDoc needs to be able to change part editors at runtime to provide the default translation behavior. Because of this requirement, some methods require the part to pass in a reference to itself. The part-wrapper field contains this reference.

2. *Ensures that the storage unit can be written to*   OpenDoc writes state information in the storage unit when it instantiates the part, so the storage unit has to be accessible. (This is a new instance and thus cannot be created on a read-only medium.)

3. *Calls the common initialization code* Both InitPart and InitPartFromStorage use the common method Initialize to set up most state data.

4. *Sets the dirty flag* To let OpenDoc know that the part needs to be synchronized with its on-disk representation in case it needs to be externalized, WebGauge sets the isDirty flag to true.

If an exception occurs in any of the preceding steps, the CATCH_ALL macro makes sure it is passed back to SOM using the Environment pointer. Cleanup occurs in the destructor for the class.

InitPartFromStorage (ODPart)

The InitPartFromStorage method is similar to InitPart, except that it handles the case where a part is being re-created from its persistent storage. Since this can be the case for any part, every part must implement this method.

The InitPartFromStorage method follows the same steps as InitPart, except that it also reads state and content information from storage and handles the case where the storage unit for the part is read-only. (This situation might occur if the document is on a CD-ROM drive or some other read-only medium.)

In WebGauge, this method performs these steps:

1. *Initializes the part-wrapper field* OpenDoc needs to be able to change part editors at runtime to provide the default translation behavior. Because of this requirement, some methods require the part to pass a reference to itself. The part-wrapper field contains this reference.

2. *Checks whether the storage unit is read-only* If the storage unit is read-only, then the part should not attempt to write any information to it. It sets the fReadOnlyStorage flag, which is checked before writing in the Externalize method.

3. *Calls the common initialization code* Both InitPart and InitPartFromStorage use the common method Initialize to set up most state data.

4. *Reads the status information from the storage unit* The InternalizeStateInfo is called to update the status information in the running part. This information was saved the last time the part was stored on disk.

5. *Reads all of the content data from storage* This method reads WebGauge's persistent data from storage. This data includes the location of the WWW server log file and the refresh interval.

Initialize (WebGauge)

The Initialize method performs common initialization functions. It is called by both InitPart and InitPartFromStorage. In WebGauge, it performs the following actions:

1. *Stores a reference to the session object* The session object provides access to global objects and shared resources, such as the name-binding mechanism and the keyboard state. To obtain the session, it is necessary to pass the fSelf reference (which represents the WebGauge object) to the call to ODGetSession.

2. *Creates a frame collection* A utility function provides a way to store a list of frames, with automatic reference counting. This procedure is required since WebGauge can have multiple simultaneous representations and needs a way to keep track of multiple frames.

3. *Checks whether other instances are active* If the global variables have already been initialized by another instance of this part, then Initialize can increment the reference count and exit.

4. *Creates a menu bar* This global resource is shared among all instances of WebGauge currently running. It is copied from the global OpenDoc menu bar, and then items are added or removed as needed.

5. *Tokenizes various types and values* The types and values for several different objects are tokenized to provide a fast implementation of the selector methods. The event-handling and focus methods are called often, and tokenizing these data items results in increased performance.

6. *Creates sets of focus objects* Objects that must be acquired together (menu and mouse focus, for example) should be grouped as a single unit so the OpenDoc Arbitrator can allocate them together.

7. *Handles localization* If an alternate language package is installed, these calls set up the proper methods to handle localization. If more than one instance of a part is active, these calls share the same global objects. The end of the Initialize method merely updates the usage count and exits.

The part editor is now fully initialized and ready for activation and user interaction.

Opening a Window

Once the part editor is fully initialized, it is ready to be activated by the user or by other parts. There are two methods for opening a part into a window: Open and CreateWindow.

The OpenDoc runtime calls the Open method when the part is the root part of the document being opened, when the part is first created from stationery, and when an embedded part is opened as a separate window.

During a call to Open, WebGauge's CreateWindow method is called to create an actual window in the platform-specific graphics system. The information in the windowProperties parameter tells the method the specific window attributes needed by Open, such as its size, shape, color, and title string. CreateWindow then creates a platform-specific window, inserts it into the surrounding environment, and returns it in an ODWindow object.

The following chart shows the graphics systems commonly available on each OpenDoc platform.

Platform	Graphics System
Windows	GDI
MacOS	QuickDraw or QuickDraw GX
OS/2	Presentation Manager
AIX/Unix	X Window System

The following sections describe the operation of the Open and CreateWindow methods in detail.

Open   (ODPart)
The implementation of Open in WebGauge does the following:

1. *Sets up variables for window objects* This operation creates a place to store the window objects (such as the window wrapper itself and the window properties).

2. *Checks whether the document is new* If the document is new, then new window objects need to be created. If it is not new, then there should be stored references to the existing window objects.

3. *Checks whether the frame is an embedded frame* If the frame is an embedded frame (indicated by a kODNull frame parameter and the fact that it's not a root frame), then there should be existing frame objects. Otherwise, this method creates a new frame object in which to display the part's contents.

4. *Activates the window* Open calls some methods on the ODWindow wrapper. These set up the facets for drawing and then activate and select the window.

5. *Returns the window ID* WebGauge does some housekeeping and then returns a window ID to the OpenDoc runtime.

CreateWindow (WebGauge)

Open calls the CreateWindow utility method when WebGauge needs to create a platform window when the part is being opened into a frame.

This method does the following:

1. *Creates a platform window and an OpenDoc window object* WebGauge obtains a window from the underlying window system and associates it with an OpenDoc window wrapper object. It also performs some housekeeping to keep track of when windows and frames can be reused.

2. *Sets the disposal method* This flag determines whether this window is removed when the root part or frame is closed. If an error occurs, this method displays an error dialog box and returns an exception to the OpenDoc runtime.

Layout

As discussed in Chapters 1 and 2, parts determine their own size and shape based on their own requirements and the constraints of the other parts in their environment. For example, WebGauge might request a certain amount of screen area, but the containing part may be able to give WebGauge only 75 percent of the requested size. WebGauge has to accept this restriction and display its content accordingly.

WebGauge does not accept embedded parts, so the layout code is somewhat simpler that it would otherwise be. (The embedding protocol will be presented in Chapter 7.)

The Layout subsystem consists of six methods, discussed in the following paragraphs.

DisplayFrameAdded (ODPart)

DisplayFrameAdded is called when a new display frame is created for WebGauge. This method is called whenever the part is first instantiated (for example, when it is created from stationery).

The operations are as follows:

1. *Sets up the view and presentation type* As discussed in the section "Initialization," each part has preferred view and presentation types. If the frame doesn't already have these, then they are set to the preferred kinds for WebGauge.

2. *Stores part information and updates the frame list* A reference to a frame information object is stored in the part's part information field, and the frame is added to WebGauge's frame list.

DisplayFrameRemoved (ODPart)

DisplayFrameRemoved is called when a frame is permanently removed, or deleted, from a part. This occurs when a document is being closed, or when a document is invisible and its resources are being purged. Most of the functions involve removing references to the frame from frame lists, recursively removing embedded frames, and releasing other resources no longer needed by the part. WebGauge does not embed other parts, so this implementation is simple.

The actions are as follows:

1. *Relinquishes all foci owned by the frame* By querying the arbitrator, the method systematically removes the frame from any lists of foci owners. At the end, it should own no foci.

2. *Handles connections to source and attached frames* Calling CleanupDisplayFrame notifies the display frame that this frame is being removed.

3. *Frees the window storage consumed by the frame* This procedure deallocates the platform resources associated with the frame, including the platform window and ODWindow object.

4. *Performs housekeeping for the frame and the part* WebGauge zeros out the frame wrapper stored in the partInfo field and deletes it. WebGauge also removes the frame from the master list of all display frames for the part.

If any exceptions occur, the method displays an error dialog box and returns an exception to the OpenDoc runtime.

DisplayFrameConnected (ODPart)

OpenDoc calls the DisplayFrameConnected method when an existing display frame first becomes visible in its containing part. This method simply adds the frame to the list of display frames if it's not already there.

DisplayFrameClosed (ODPart)

The DisplayFrameClosed method is called if the part's frame is closed because the user closed the document. Apart from not deleting the source frame or part window, this method is similar to the DisplayFrameRemoved method explained earlier.

AttachSourceFrame (ODPart)

AttachSourceFrame is called when WebGauge's containing part is being opened up into a part window. In this case, the containing part looks through the list of parts embedded within it and calls AttachSourceFrame for each of them. This operation makes sure that each embedded part has a reference to its source frame.

FrameShapeChanged (ODPart)

If the shape of a WebGauge frame has been changed either by OpenDoc itself or through user action, then OpenDoc calls the FrameShapeChanged method to update the new shape. If the part has any dependent frames (which WebGauge does not, since it doesn't support embedding), then this method makes sure they have been updated by going through the frame list and calling each one's RequestFrameShape method.

Drawing to the Screen

Every part needs to implement a Draw method. The OpenDoc runtime calls this method when the display needs to be updated, as occurs, for example, when part of a frame is exposed after being hidden by another window. In addition, any part that updates live data (such as WebGauge) calls its own Draw method to refresh the display of that data. WebGauge summarizes WWW server traffic at a specific interval and thus calls its own Draw method to update the information presented to the user.

Parts display their contents in frames, so a part must have at least one frame per display window. The OpenDoc human interface model requires that an OpenDoc component be able to display itself in several different representations, such as an icon, small icon, thumbnail, or full view. These representations are determined by the GetViewType method.

In addition, a part can have different ways of presenting the same data. For example, WebGauge could display its logging data as text or as a graph. (This feature will be added in Chapter 7.) The types of presentation are determined by the GetPresentation method.

During rendering, the part must transform and clip its data to conform to the geometry of the screen area in which it draws its presentation—that is, it needs to render itself in an appropriate fashion for the type of output device. Whether a presentation is dynamic (for example, to a screen) or static (to a printer) is indicated by the isDynamic field of the canvas object on which the part does its rendering. Any additional information can be stored in the partInfo field of the appropriate frame or facet.

Once it has been notified that it needs to render itself to some output device, the part performs this series of actions:

1. Sets the platform-specific graphics environment. (For example, it may set up a grafPort in QuickDraw, an HDC in Windows, or a graphics context (GC) in the X Window System.)

2. Determines the view type and presentation type and uses this information to determine how to render the display.

3. Uses the platform-specific graphics calls to draw the display.

4. Performs any necessary cleanup.

The next sections explain each method used in drawing. The discussion is at a high enough level that it's appropriate across platforms, but drawing and graphics systems are extremely platform-specific—that is, they are implemented differently on different platforms. Chapter 6, "Cross-Platform Portability," provides more detailed information.

Draw (ODPart)

Draw is called both by the OpenDoc runtime and by the part itself if it needs to update its content asynchronously, as WebGauge does when its timer interval expires and it has new summary data to display. OpenDoc calls this method if it needs to update a previously obscured area of WebGauge's display.

Draw performs the following general operations on all platforms:

1. Gets a native graphics environment.

2. Determines the proper view and presentation types.

3. Uses native graphics calls to draw the content on the screen.

DrawFrameView (WebGauge)

The DrawFrameView method is called internally by WebGauge when the view type is equal to kODViewAsFrame. This is the *normal case,* where the part renders itself fully. WebGauge displays WWW server statistics and updates them at a specified interval.

This method obtains the platform-specific drawing items, sets the WebGauge font (Times), figures out what strings to draw, and then draws them on the screen.

DrawIconView (WebGauge)

DrawIconView does what its name implies: draws an icon on the screen to represent the content of the part. WebGauge displays a simple drawing. This method supports both large and small icon views of the content.

DrawThumbnailView (WebGauge)

DrawThumbnailView is slightly more complicated, as it is responsible for displaying a small ("thumbnail"-sized) representation of the part's contents. Since WebGauge's content is merely text, a thumbnail view wouldn't provide too much additional information. Thus, this method just displays a simple picture representative of the part's layout.

If the content of WebGauge were more complicated, then this method would be appropriate for displaying a scaled or transformed version of its content.

ViewTypeChanged (ODPart)

OpenDoc calls WebGauge's ViewTypeChanged method when the view type is changed, for example, from icon to frame. This method is also called when a display frame is added to the display list.

This method performs several operations to change the view type and notify all of the other interested parties:

1. *Determines the current view type* This is done by calling the GetViewType method on ODFrame.

2. *Loads appropriate icons or pictures* WebGauge has precomputed representations for icon views and thumbnail views; this method merely retrieves them.

3. *Updates the usedShape* Depending on the new view type, WebGauge changes usedShape for the frame to an appropriate value. It also invalidates the old frame.

4. *Updates any source or attached frames* WebGauge makes sure that the changes have propagated correctly.

GeometryChanged (ODPart)

GeometryChanged is a very simple method, called by OpenDoc when the geometry of the part is altered. In WebGauge, this method merely invalidates the clip shape of the facet, which causes the facet to be redrawn automatically. A more complicated part might need to perform additional processing here.

HighlightChanged (ODPart)

GeometryChanged and HighlightChanged are implemented in a somewhat similar fashion: the former invalidates the facet, causing it to be redrawn, and the latter does the same for the entire frame. In the case of WebGauge, HighlightChanged does nothing if the view type is set to frame, because no highlighting is performed on the WebGauge content.

FacetAdded (ODPart)

OpenDoc calls FacetAdded whenever a facet is added to WebGauge's display frames and also when a facet is opened as the root frame of a document. This method sets up the environment for the drawing methods to display the frame's contents and also handles edge cases where this is the first facet added to the part window.

FacetRemoved (ODPart)

True to its name, FacetRemoved is called when a facet is removed from the display frame. In some cases, if this is the last facet belonging to a frame, then this method also hides the frame's part window.

Event Handling

In addition to drawing itself to the screen, the part must be able to handle user-initiated actions that occur within its boundaries. These include any events controlled by a focus (such as keyboard input) that is owned by the part.

The OpenDoc shell and runtime handle the distribution of events to parts: the dispatcher object routes the event to the part and then inquires whether the part handles that particular kind of event. If the answer is no, then the shell, container application, or root part tries to handle the event.

The OpenDoc Dispatcher, part of the runtime system, locates a dispatch module for the event, which then calls a method belonging to WebGauge. WebGauge has methods that correspond to several different event types, such as mouse, keyboard, and menu events.

The following sections explain the different event types that a part might be asked to handle and discuss the methods that process these events.

Constants (WebGauge)

Parts such as WebGauge need to handle the following types of events, which are common across most systems with windows, keyboard, mouse, and so on:

```
kODEvtNull
kODEvtMouseDown
kODEvtMouseUp
kODEvtKeyDown
kODEvtKeyUp
kODEvtAutoKey
kODEvtUpdate
kODEvtActivate
```

```
kODEvtMenu
kODEvtWindow
kODEvtMouseEnter
kODEvtMouseWithin
kODEvtMouseLeave
kODEvtBGMouseDown
```

Parts that embed other parts need to handle some additional events, which are not relevant to the discussion of WebGauge.

A part has the freedom to interpret these events according to its needs and requirements: WebGauge ignores some of these events because they are not important to it.

HandleEvent (ODPart)

The HandleEvent method is very similar to event-switching methods in window-system platforms. This idiom is common across MacOS, Windows, and the X Window System.

The HandleEvent method processes an event and then branches to the appropriate method to handle the behavior caused by that event. If the part declines to handle the event, the method returns a Boolean value of kODFalse.

HandleMouseEvent (WebGauge)

The HandleMouseEvent method contains the platform-specific code to handle mouse events. If necessary, it activates and highlights the part by calling the ActivateFrame method.

Since WebGauge doesn't handle mouse events other than activation, the rest of the method merely notes where the pointer was when the pointer button was released (if the user has clicked the mouse button).

HandleMenuEvent (WebGauge)

The HandleMenuEvent method calls the appropriate platform-specific code to handle menu events (or keyboard shortcuts). It is similar to the other methods in that it consists of a switch statement that selects among the various choices.

AdjustMenus (ODPart)

The AdjustMenus method is called to change the menus displayed by the part. It can enable items, disable items, or add or remove them from the menus. It also makes sure that the text in the About... menu item is set correctly.

DoDialogBox (WebGauge)

The DoDialogBox method creates a dialog box. (In Windows systems, the HandleMenuEvent method handles this function.)

ViewAsWindow   (WebGauge)
ViewAsWindow is handled by the Open method, discussed in "Opening a Window" earlier in this chapter.

Activation and User Interaction

Activation enables a part to receive and process user events. It is accompanied by some visual indication that the part is active.

Some parts become active immediately upon initialization, if the part's persistent storage contains information telling the part to become active. Dragging and dropping data on a part (see Chapter 7) should also make a part become active.

The following paragraphs explain the methods that control the acquisition of focus, the highlighting of the active part, and the giving up of focus. A specific protocol must be followed to ensure that the part is activated properly.

BeginRelinquishFocus   (ODPart)
Sometimes a part may own a resource that is requested by another part: for example, the keyboard or mouse focus. The part is notified of this request when OpenDoc calls the BeginRelinquishFocus method. Note that this method doesn't actually relinquish the focus, but checks to see whether the request can be fulfilled. If WebGauge were displaying a modal dialog box, for example, it would not be able to relinquish exclusive control over the screen and mouse and would refuse a request to do so.

CommitRelinquishFocus   (ODPart)
CommitRelinquishFocus finishes the job begun with BeginRelinquishFocus (although the FocusLost method handles the actual work in WebGauge). In general, CommitRelinquishFocus should remove any highlighting performed by the part as well as disable menu items and other appropriate actions.

FocusLost   (ODPart)
The FocusLost method actually does the work of removing highlight indicators. In WebGauge's implementation, CommitRelinquishFocus calls this method; the OpenDoc runtime also calls it if the focus is lost due to other events.

AbortRelinquishFocus   (ODPart)
The AbortRelinquishFocus method is called by the OpenDoc runtime if the part that requested the focus no longer needs it, or if the process of transferring the focus cannot be completed and must be backed out. In some cases, parts may need to clean up after the BeginRelinquishFocus method, but WebGauge doesn't require any additional cleanup.

FocusAcquired (ODPart)

The FocusAcquired method is called when the Arbitrator decides to give a particular focus to a part. This method decides whether any additional foci need to become active (that is, are any additional members in the UI focus set) and requests them if they are. WebGauge calls the PartActivated method to perform the actual work.

PartActivated (WebGauge)

PartActivated is a simple method that does the work of activating the part. In the case of WebGauge, it merely sets the active border of the frame.

ActivateFrame (WebGauge)

ActivateFrame is called when a mouse-click event occurs within an inactive border. This method requests the keyboard-mouse-screen focus set by the Arbitrator and calls the PartActivated method.

WindowActivating (WebGauge)

WebGauge calls its WindowActivating method from HandleEvent when it receives an activate event from the OpenDoc runtime. This method makes sure that the selection focus and window state are consistent and then calls the ActivateFrame method.

Storage

OpenDoc has a document-centered architecture and avoids requiring the user to explicitly save work or load data. Thus, OpenDoc provides extensive support for persistent storage of data and has several fairly stringent requirements for parts. The following paragraphs explain the methods that make up the persistent storage interface and provide a usage scenario.

OpenDoc storage units (ODStorageUnit) provide portable, cross-platform storage by means of the OpenDoc Standard Interchange Format (SIF, also known as Bento). The interfaces and protocols that allow a part to manipulate that storage are fairly simple. Every piece of data that needs to exist across invocations of the part editor must be placed in a storage unit. In WebGauge, this data is the location of the WWW server's log file and the interval during which it samples the data.

Parts such as WebGauge need to respond to requests by the OpenDoc runtime to load and unload their contents from persistent storage. If a part's contents are not needed at the moment, the OpenDoc runtime may request that it unload them from memory to reduce runtime RAM requirements.

Before doing this, the part must ensure that its contents in memory and on disk are synchronized; otherwise, it must update the disk information before unloading the data.

Storage units can store many different representations of the same data, as well as many different types of content. For example, a part may contain a column of numbers and a simple drawing that can be exported in any of three data formats: GIF, PostScript, or an internal format. The part would be responsible for maintaining a portion of the storage unit for the numeric data and a portion for the graphical data; the graphics portion would contain all three representations of the drawing.

The storage unit can have an arbitrary number of properties (in the preceding example, the numeric property and the graphics property), and each property can have an arbitrary number of values (the numeric property has one value, and the graphics property has three).

For best results, parts should attempt to store several representations of their data if there is a possibility that their contents may be viewed with a different part editor. In the preceding example, the internal graphics format may be the most efficient for the part, but the creator may wish to keep the format private (it may be a trade secret, for instance). In this case, the part may provide a portable version (PostScript) and a simple version for quick or low-fidelity viewing (GIF).

Parts should store their contents in the order of greatest to least fidelity. In this example, the part would store the internal format first, then PostScript, and then GIF. In this way, if the part editor is unavailable, the recipient of the document will likely be able to view at least one of the formats with another editor.

Once the storage unit has been initialized according to the steps outlined in "Initialization" earlier in this chapter, the part needs to perform the following steps to externalize itself:

1. Call the Externalize method defined by the superclass of the part object. In the case of WebGauge, this method is in ODPersistentObject.

2. Obtain the fundamental (root) storage unit for the part.

3. Focus the storage unit on the editor status data and write the value in the storage unit.

4. Focus the storage unit on the highest-fidelity representation of the data and write this value in the storage unit.

5. For each of the remaining representations, focus the storage unit on the representation and write the value in the storage unit.

Initializing the part from persistent storage is essentially the same process in reverse, except that in the case of a new part, the storage unit will not contain any data. This process is described in "Initialization" earlier in this chapter.

The following methods implement WebGauge's persistent storage mechanism. Some are not implemented here, but are discussed further in Chapter 7.

Externalize   (ODPart)

Whenever it is necessary to write a part's contents to persistent storage, OpenDoc calls the Externalize method. This method stores all of the information required to re-create a part once it's loaded from disk.

Unlike most of the methods in WebGauge, the Externalize method has to call a method in the SOM wrapper for the part. All of the other functions are accomplished here, in Externalize.

This method performs the following actions:

1. *Checks flags and permissions* If the part is "dirty" (that is, if its contents have changed), and if the storage unit is not read-only, then the rest of the method executes.

2. *Gets the storage unit* The method retrieves a reference to the storage unit for the part using the GetStorageUnit function.

3. *Sets up storage unit properties and writes status information* Using internal methods, Externalize makes sure that the properties of the storage unit are set appropriately. It then writes its status information to storage.

4. *Writes content data* The ExternalizeContent information call writes the data in the storage unit.

5. *Performs cleanup* The method sets the isDirty flag to false.

CheckAndAddProperties   (WebGauge)

The CheckAndAddProperties method makes sure that the required properties are present in the storage unit and adds them if they aren't. It adds the contents and preferred properties if they aren't set up already and then performs a similar action for the display frame property. (The absence of appropriate properties doesn't necessarily imply damage to the storage unit—it may be newly created.)

CleanseContentProperty   (WebGauge)

If the part has any properties that it cannot write accurately, then it uses the CleanseContentProperty method to remove them from the contents property. After an editor switch, some properties may no longer be necessary or meaningful. Also, in some cases a part can write certain types of values only at certain times, though given its simple content model, WebGauge doesn't have to worry about this situation.

ExternalizeStateInfo (WebGauge)

The state information for the part (frames, display state, and so on) should be written in the storage unit using the ExternalizeStateInfo call. This method iterates through the part's list of display frames and writes each value in the storage unit so the part can be re-created in the same visible state as when it was externalized.

ExternalizeContent (WebGauge)

WebGauge stores its persistent information in the storage unit between invocations. This information consists of the last values for the summary information and the location of the WWW server's web log file.

CloneInto (ODPart)

The CloneInto method duplicates (clones) the part content in another storage unit. It adds properties, if necessary, writes the part's state information, and then writes the content of the part. For more discussion, see Chapter 7.

InternalizeContent (WebGauge)

The InternalizeContent method retrieves WebGauge's persistent information from the storage unit and reads it back into memory.

InternalizeStateInfo (WebGauge)

InternalizeStateInfo reads the part state information from the storage unit and uses it to re-create the visual state of the part. In some cases, this information may be incomplete or missing, so WebGauge needs to handle these cases.

ReadPartInfo (ODPart)

ReadPartInfo reads the part information from persistent storage and re-creates the partInfo fields in each display frame.

WritePartInfo (ODPart)

WritePartInfo writes the partInfo field for each display frame in the storage unit.

ClonePartInfo (ODPart)

The ClonePartInfo method duplicates (clones) the part information in another storage unit.

Release (ODPart)

Release reduces the reference count of an object every time someone who holds that object disposes it. When objects have a reference count of zero, they can be reclaimed by the system's memory allocator.

ReleaseAll   (ODPart)

ReleaseAll releases all references to all objects that the part holds. This method is called just before the part itself is deleted.

Purge   (ODPart)

Under low-memory conditions, OpenDoc may request that a part purge itself of unneeded resources. (This may not occur on certain platforms with more modern memory systems.) If requested, the part should free any resources that aren't needed and return the number of bytes freed to the OpenDoc runtime.

SetDirty   (WebGauge)

WebGauge calls the SetDirty method whenever the contents of the part differ from the state of the part in the storage unit. This method indicates that the two need to be synchronized if the part is externalized.

Putting It Together

This chapter presented a simple OpenDoc part on MacOS and on Windows. It discussed each method as well as other methods that perform similar or related functions. The next chapter elaborates on cross-platform portability issues and addresses more fully some of the questions raised by the discussions in this chapter.

CHAPTER 6

Cross-Platform Portability

This chapter discusses cross-platform portability issues in developing OpenDoc components and suggests a strategy that was used in the sample WebGauge part introduced in Chapter 5. Although the discussion focuses on MacOS and Windows implementations, the issues and strategies are applicable to development on OS/2 and Unix systems as well.

One of the key benefits of development with OpenDoc is that many cross-platform issues are addressed in the architecture itself. Often, the API provides abstractions that are implemented appropriately for each platform, freeing the software developer to concentrate on the implementation of his or her special added-value code. For example, a database expert is freer to develop interesting search algorithms if he or she doesn't have to re-implement event-handling code for each platform.

However, a few areas are not specifically covered by the OpenDoc architecture or 1.0 implementation. The graphics system is the most obvious example of an area in which some cross-platform knowledge is required to implement a part on multiple platforms. At some point in the future, some multiplatform graphics system may be added to OpenDoc, but people desiring to ship products soon must write code for platform-specific graphics APIs or use a cross-platform framework such as the OpenDoc Development Framework (ODF).

WebGauge uses a strategy to maximize portability and provide isolation to the platform-specific code: writing a C++ class that implements the added-value functions and plugs into the ODPart class.

Figure 6-1 shows the various portions of WebGauge. A large percentage of code comprises the implementation of the ODPart methods; this code is mostly portable among platforms. Another chunk of code, called WebEngine, implements the specific functions of WebGauge; this code handles the parsing of the WWW server logs and generates the summary statistics and is also largely portable. Finally, the code includes platform-specific routines to handle file input and output and graphics operations; these have distinct implementations, but are hidden in the WebEngine class. Thus, to add another platform to the list of platforms on which WebGauge runs, the developer merely needs to implement the specific WebEngine methods while leaving the bulk of the code alone. As Figure 6-1 shows, most of the code is portable.

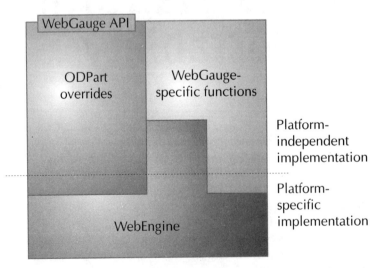

FIGURE 6-1. *Percentage of cross-platform versus platform-specific code*

The following sections examine the implementation of the WebEngine class in detail.

The ODPart Superstructure

The WebEngine class fits into the ODPart superstructure in the same way that ODPart fits into OpenDoc: it provides a well-defined API that is called to provide specific behavior. The full implementation is presented in Appendix C.

For example, look at the implementation of Initialize. Note how the behavior of WebGauge itself is defined by the WebEngine class that is instantiated during the Initialize method. We will look at all of the places where WebGauge calls WebEngine to implement its behavior.

Figure 6-2 shows the creation of a WebEngine object as a part of the WebGauge object instantiated by OpenDoc.

In general, the approach used here limits the number of places in the code where changes have to be made and allows an organization to add other platforms or fix bugs more easily. Once the platform-independent code is debugged and

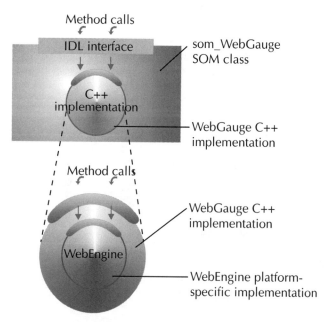

FIGURE 6-2.   *WebGauge and WebEngine*

solid, then bugs in the platform-specific code can be assigned to experts for the particular platform.

WebEngine Interface and Class Definition

The following code shows the C++ class definition of WebEngine.

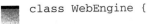

```
class WebEngine {

    public:
        WebEngine ();     //     constructor
        ~WebEngine ();    //     destructor

        // platform-specific routines
        void    Initialize ();
        void    drawStats (int, int);

        // platform-independent (ANSI portable)
        void    setWebLogFilename (char *);
        void    setErrorLogFilename (char *);
        int     getNumberOfHits ();
        int     getNumberOfErrors ();
        void    resetCounters ();

    private:
        // platform-independent (ANSI portable)
        int     countLines (char *);

        // private data members
        int     numHits;
        int     numErrors;
        char    *webLogFile;
        char    *errorLogFile;
};
```

We will first look at each of the platform-independent routines and data structures. Then we will turn our attention to the platform-specific code.

Setup and Cleanup

The constructor and destructor routines are called automatically when a C++ object is created or destroyed.

Constructor

The WebEngine constructor routine allocates and zeroes out some storage space for the filenames of the WWW server log and error files and sets the initial item counts to zero.

Destructor

The destructor routine frees any memory allocated within WebGauge that has not already been freed.

Platform-Independent Public Methods

Platform-independent public methods implement the simple processing functions that WebGauge provides. These public methods can all be called externally by outside code as well as internally by WebGauge itself.

As you can see, the code for these methods is extremely simple and highly portable, depending only on the ANSI-standard C/C++ headers <stdio.h>, <stdlib.h>, and <string.h>.

setWebLogFilename

The setWebLogFilename method uses a filename as an argument and makes the file represented by that filename the focus for operations that calculate the number of times the web server has been accessed. This number is also known as the number of hits or server hits.

Here is the code for setWebLogFilename:

```
void
WebEngine::setWebLogFilename (char *filename)
{
    // zap the memory
    memset (webLogFile, '0', strlen (filename) +1);
    strcpy (webLogFile, filename);


    return;
}
```

setErrorLogFilename

The setErrorLogFilename method uses a filename as an argument and makes the file represented by that filename the focus for operations that calculate the number of errors during the runtime of a web server.

Here is the code for setErrorLogFilename:

```
void
WebEngine::setErrorLogFilename (char *filename)
{
    // zap the memory
    memset (errorLogFile, '0', strlen (filename) +1);
    strcpy (errorLogFile, filename);


    return;
}
```

getNumberOfHits

The getNumberOfHits method returns the number of times that the web server has been accessed. To accomplish this, this method calls a private method, countLines.

Here is the code for getNumberOfHits:

```
int
WebEngine::getNumberOfHits (void)
{
    numHits = countLines (webLogFile);
    return numHits;
}
```

getNumberOfErrors

The getNumberOfErrors method returns the number of times that the web server generated an error. To accomplish this, this method calls a private method, countLines.

Here is the code for getNumberOfErrors:

```
int
WebEngine::getNumberOfErrors (void)
{
    numErrors = countLines (errorLogFile);
    return numErrors;
}
```

resetCounters

The resetCounters method resets the value of the access and error counters to zero.
Here is the code for resetCounters:

```
void
WebEngine::resetCounters (void)
{
    // reset hit and error counters
    numHits = 0;
    numErrors = 0;
    return;
}
```

Platform-Independent Private Methods

Platform-independent private methods are used internally by WebGauge and are
called by the implementations of the public methods.

countLines

The countLines method performs the simple function that WebGauge illustrates:
monitoring the activity of a WWW server. Web server logs are simple text files,
with a line added for each server event, whether it is a server access or an error.
Thus, a person can get a rough idea of web server activity simply by counting the
number of lines in the appropriate file.

Of course, more sophisticated processing of web server statistics (or of any
other data file) can be provided easily; this is the appropriate place to plug in the
implementation of your favorite analysis tool.

When a filename is passed to countLines, this method opens the file, starts
reading individual lines until it reaches the end of the file, and returns the number
of lines read.

Here is the code for countLines:

```
int
WebEngine::countLines (char *filename)
{
    // given a file, count the number of lines
    FILE *fp = fopen (filename, "r");
    if (fp == NULL)
    {
        perror ("open");
        exit (1);
    }
```

```
char *buf = new char [1024];
int         counter = 0;
while (fgets (buf, 512, fp) != NULL)
{
    counter++;
}
fclose (fp);
delete buf;
return counter;

}
```

Private Data Members

Private data members are operated on by the public and private methods of WebGauge. These are all simple scalar data types (numbers or characters). However, if you were to extend WebGauge to more sophisticated processing, you could store information on specific sites or specific types of errors in private data members, perhaps in arrays, B-trees, or dictionary-type data structures.

Here are the definitions of the data members webLogFile, errorLogFile, numHits, numErrors:

```
// private data members
int     numHits;
int     numErrors;
char    *webLogFile;
char    *errorLogFile;
```

Platform-Dependent Public Methods

This section describes the implementation of platform-specific routines on MacOS and Windows. As you'll see, this code is a small fraction of the whole. The code itself is available in Appendix C.

As discussed in Chapters 4 and 5, OpenDoc has many platform-independent functions, but graphics is one of the areas that must be implemented according to the platform. Luckily, it's possible to minimize the amount of code that directly depends on the underlying window system.

The following methods implement the initialization of the graphics routines and the actual drawing to the screen.

Initialize–Windows

The Initialize—Windows routine initializes the GDI and prepares a window and a graphics context in which to draw.

Initialize–Macintosh (QuickDraw)

QuickDraw initializes the QuickDraw routines for screen drawing and sets up a WindowPtr and Rect in which to draw.

DrawStats–Windows

DrawStats draws the web statistics to the window prepared in the Initialize call. Its arguments consist of two integers, which represent the number of server hits and the number of errors, respectively.

This method selects a pen and drawing color, moves to the proper location, and renders the data along with explanatory labels.

DrawStats–Macintosh (QuickDraw)

As with the Windows version, the arguments for DrawStats on the Macintosh consist of two integers that represent the web statistics of interest. This method selects a screen color, positions the drawing focus, and renders the data.

Integrating WebEngine with WebGauge

The calculation engine is finished. Now it's time to see how it is used by the WebGauge class to implement its functions.

Setup and Cleanup

The following WebGauge methods call the setup and cleanup methods in WebEngine.

WebGauge::InitPart

InitPart creates a WebEngine object and then calls several other methods. This method initializes the WebEngine object and then calls a public method to set up the files on which WebEngine operates.

WebGauge::InitPartFromStorage

InitPartFromStorage creates a WebEngine object from a previously created instance in persistent storage. This method is similar to InitPart.

InitPartFromStorage initializes the WebEngine object and then calls a public method to set up the files on which WebEngine operates, retrieving the appropriate value from persistent storage.

WebGauge::Purge

Purge, which is called in low-memory situations, removes some of the memory storage associated with the WebEngine object. It updates the values in persistent storage so the content of WebGauge is not lost.

Public Methods

The following WebGauge methods call public methods in WebEngine.

WebGauge::Draw

Draw calls one method in WebEngine. OpenDoc calls Draw whenever the contents of the screen need to be refreshed. Draw calls the drawStats method whenever an obscured portion of the WebGauge window is exposed or scrolled into view.

WebGauge::DrawFrameView

DrawFrameView also calls DrawStats. OpenDoc calls DrawFrameView whenever it renders into a frame (the normal case).

WebGauge::DrawIconView

DrawIconView calls the Pause method to tell WebEngine's built-in timer to stop updating its statistics because the screen is not being updated.

WebGauge::DrawThumbnailView

DrawThumbnailView calls getNumberOfHits and getNumberOfErrors method directly so it can render a thumbnail summary of the WebGauge data.

WebGauge::GeometryChanged

As with the Draw method, whenever the GeometryChanged method is called, WebGauge calls WebEngine::DrawStats.

WebGauge::Externalize

As with Purge, when Externalize is called, the WebGauge code must get persistent data (filenames and count data) from WebEngine and store it in the storage unit for the part.

Putting It Together

This chapter discussed a strategy for minimizing effort when creating a cross-platform part. This strategy involves creating a largely platform-independent class with separate implementations for platform-specific methods. Even if you're not developing a part for multiple platforms, this strategy provides the benefits of modular code and well-defined encapsulation of function. These features are important when you extend a part and add functions to it, as you will do in Chapter 7.

As we add features to our sample part in Chapter 7, we will continue the implementation strategy outlined here, and segregate platform-specific functions in independent classes and methods that can be re-implemented as your porting needs continue to grow.

CHAPTER 7

Adding Features

Chapter 5 discussed the implementation of WebGauge, a sample OpenDoc part editor. Chapter 6 talked about cross-platform portability and discussed some internal features of WebGauge on MacOS and Windows. This chapter will extend WebGauge by adding features such as drag and drop of data, undo, and changing the presentation of data, among others. We will talk about how to add these features in a platform-independent fashion. Finally, we will discuss some additional features that might be added to a more advanced part editor.

WebGauge, presented in Chapters 5 and 6, is a simple OpenDoc part editor that provides some of the most basic behaviors and functions. In this chapter, you will take that same simple part and add features to it that will make it more useful and versatile. Most of the features that you will add to WebGauge improve its user interface, both in terms of appearance and ease of use and convenience.

The first feature you will add is support for drag-and-drop operations to select web log and error log files. This feature is useful for any part that displays or uses file-based data.

NOTE:
Drag and drop or direct manipulation is a powerful user interface technique with which you are already familiar if you've used any of the popular computer operating systems. It lets users manipulate data files and objects by moving their representation on the screen with a pointing device. Good examples are dragging a file to a MacOS desktop printer icon or dragging a file to the Windows95 Recycle bin.

Next, you will add the capability to display WebGauge data in its own window, outside of the context of the containing document.

To make the data displayed by WebGauge more interesting, you will add a feature that allows the user to select either a text-based view or a simple graph. The graph shows the rate at which web accesses are being made or the frequency of errors.

The improved version of WebGauge is now scriptable and supports the OpenDoc SemanticInterface specification. Thus, you will add a scripting interface.

Finally, you will add the capability to undo actions such as changing settings or dragging and dropping files and to redo the same actions if desired.

This chapter also touches briefly on the linking and embedding protocols. In addition, during the course of adding the new features, you'll learn a bit about memory management and reference counting.

The presentation of material in this chapter is similar to that in Chapters 5 and 6. Each functional area is discussed, followed by the methods and functions most important to the main point of the chapter. The source code appears in Appendix C.

Adding Drag-and-Drop Functionality

The first behavior that we'd like to add to WebGauge is drag and drop. Drag and drop allows users to manipulate files and other items (such as printers) by moving the icons for these items around the screen.

Using Drag and Drop in WebGauge

WebGauge uses the simplest form of drag and drop: as an accelerator for a file-loading operation. The user can drop a logging file from a World Wide Web server onto WebGauge, and the part editor will incorporate the data and display a summary of server use. Figure 7-1 shows the sequence of events when a file is dropped onto WebGauge.

Although WebGauge accepts a drop action and incorporates that data, it does not act as a source of drag actions. In other words, WebGauge accepts data from another source but doesn't provide any data for other part editors. Given WebGauge's simple data model, it doesn't offer much that would be useful to other parts. For a part such as a video capture part, however, a drag source capability would be useful. Figure 7-2 illustrates a part editor that acts as a drag source.

WebGauge parses the file and determines whether it is in a format that it can understand. If not, WebGauge displays an error dialog box and keeps its current settings.

User Benefits

Because it has a very simple analog in the real world, direct manipulation (of which drag and drop is one of the best examples) is intuitive to both novice and experienced computer users.

Implementation

This section discusses the methods that need to be implemented to support drag and drop in WebGauge. Some of these methods override ODPart methods, and others are specific to the WebGauge implementation.

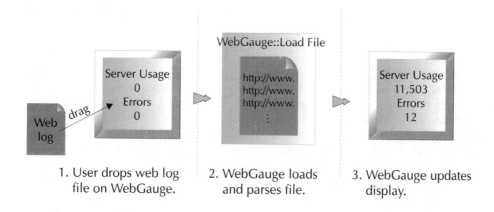

1. User drops web log file on WebGauge.

2. WebGauge loads and parses file.

3. WebGauge updates display.

FIGURE 7-1. *Performing a drag-and-drop operation with WebGauge*

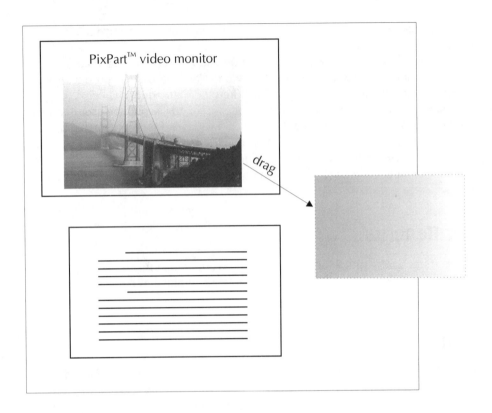

FIGURE 7-2. *Dragging from a video capture part editor*

IsDragSupported (WebGauge)

The IsDragSupported method is called during a drag operation when the part needs to know if the particular type of drag operation is supported. For example, a video editor can accept a drag operation that contains video data but would reject one that contains a spreadsheet. This method returns a Boolean (true or false) value. If a part does not support a particular data type, then the part does not highlight, indicating to the user that the drop operation is not supported.

WebGauge supports having files dragged onto it, if the files contain valid web log information or error log information. For each item dragged onto WebGauge, this routine examines the contents of the item's storage unit. If the contents property contains valid data, then the method returns true. Otherwise, it returns false.

CreateDragRegion (WebGauge)

The CreateDragRegion method is platform specific. It creates a graphics system-specific object to represent the shape of the area to be dragged. WebGauge does not support the dragging of its contents, so this method is not called. It does, however, serve as a placeholder should dragging behavior be added at some future time.

InitiateDrag (WebGauge)

If a part supports having its contents dragged, then InitiateDrag prepares the part's content and places *promises* (that is, placeholders for the data) in a temporary storage unit. Next, it calls the OpenDoc runtime to start the drag operation. Then it handles the result of the drag operation: did it succeed or fail?

WebGauge does not support the dragging of its contents, but this method is presented here to indicate where that behavior could be added in the future.

DragEnter (ODPart)

When an object being dragged enters a facet that belongs to this part, the OpenDoc runtime calls DragEnter to notify the part. This method calls the IsDragSupported method to see if the drag operation is acceptable. If it is, DragEnter highlights the facet by calling HighlightFacet. DragEnter returns a Boolean true value if the drag operation succeeds. Otherwise, it returns false.

DragWithin (ODPart)

If a part supports multiple drop targets (multiple areas within its confines that accept drag-and-drop operations, then it can use the DragWithin method to keep track of drag operation progress. This method is called when dragging is performed within a facet belonging to the part.

Since WebGauge doesn't support multiple drop zones, this method doesn't do anything, although it is presented for completeness.

DragLeave (ODPart)

The OpenDoc runtime calls the DragLeave method when a drag operation leaves a facet owned by the part. This method removes the highlighting (if any) on the facet.

Drop (ODPart)

When a dragged item is dropped onto the part, the OpenDoc runtime calls the Drop method to handle the result. Several steps need to be followed, in order, to ensure that the drop operation is performed correctly:

1. Remove drag highlighting. Since the drop operation is being processed, the highlight feedback needs to be removed.

2. Check the destination. If the drop destination is within the source part, then the drop operation fails (because nothing would happen). Similarly, if the destination does not support drag-and-drop operations (checked by calling IsDragSupported again), then the drop operation fails.

3. Handle the drop operation. The Drop method checks whether the drag is a copy or move operation and then creates a CDropAction object to handle data incorporation or processing. By using an action object, it is possible to undo the drop operation; see "Adding Undo and Redo Capabilities" later in this chapter for details.

The method returns true or false to indicate whether the drop operation succeeded or failed.

DropCompleted (ODPart)

The DropCompleted method is part of the infrastructure for asynchronous drag-and-drop operations, which the 1.0 implementation does not support. When implemented, this method will allow the source of a drag operation to be notified when the drop operation is completed.

CloneContents (WebGauge)

The CloneContents method handles the preparation of the part's contents for data interchange operations. It is called whenever the user chooses the Cut or Copy menu items or when a drag operation is initiated. It examines the source's storage unit and writes promises to the destination storage unit, which may be a clipboard-type holding area or the destination storage unit of a drop operation.

FulfillPromise (ODPart)

During a drag operation, sometimes a promise is returned instead of the actual data, especially if the amount of data is very large. This procedure tends to improve performance when the data is not needed immediately. The FulfillPromise method is called when the promise needs to be fulfilled: that is, when the part needs the actual data to do some processing or manipulation.

The implementation is simple: FulfillPromise retrieves the promise from the part's storage unit and then calls the Fulfill method for the promise object. This method then makes sure that the data is transferred from the source storage unit to the destination storage unit.

HighlightFacet (WebGauge)

The HighlightFacet method is platform specific (since it involves drawing bits to the screen). It is called when the highlight status of the facet needs to be changed. The facet highlight is generally a darker or thicker border drawn around the facet when something is dragged into it; this indicates that the part supports a particular operation. This method also removes the highlighting when it is no longer needed. As arguments, HighlightFacet takes an ODFacet and a Boolean value that indicates whether the facet is to be highlighted or unhighlighted.

Adding a Display Window

You've added drag-and-drop capabilities to WebGauge. Now you will start adding features that allow multiple presentations and views of the WebGauge data. The first of these (and the simplest to implement) is the capability to display part content in a separate window.

Using a Display Window in WebGauge

WebGauge can display itself in a separate window, as shown in Figure 7-3.

User Benefits

In some situations, it is more convenient to display part content in a separate window instead of as part of a larger document. For example, a long report may include graphs that indicate sales or accounts receivable. Viewing these graphs as small windows while hiding the rest of the document may be a good way to keep an eye on up-to-the-minute trends, while having the document context available when necessary.

Implementation

This section discusses the implementation of display-in-window capability in WebGauge. Adding this capability requires you to modify only one existing method in WebGauge.

Open   (ODPart)

This implementation expands upon the implementation of Open discussed in Chapter 5. Assuming an existing frame in a document, the Open method determines the proper bounding shape for the part's contents and creates a platform-specific window object based on those measurements and the default value for document windows. It then registers that window object with the OpenDoc runtime and notifies the frame that it must now display its content in that window.

This method returns the window ID of the new window.

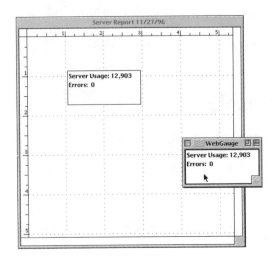

FIGURE 7-3. *WebGauge display in window*

Adding the Capability to Use Multiple Presentation Styles

You've given WebGauge the ability to display its intrinsic content in a separate window. Next, you'll add the code necessary to display WebGauge data in more than one presentation style. The original version of WebGauge allowed only a simple text display; you will now add the ability to display a graphical version of the data.

Using Multiple Presentation Styles in WebGauge

Figure 7-4 shows two views of WebGauge: one with a text display and the other with a graphical display.

User Benefits

Quite often, it is useful to view data in multiple formats. Sometimes the precision of exact figures is needed, and at other time the richness of graphical presentations is more helpful.

Implementation

This section discusses the methods that need to be implemented to support multiple presentation styles in WebGauge. Some of these methods override ODPart methods, and others are specific to the WebGauge implementation.

PresentationChanged   (ODPart)

The PresentationChanged method is called when the presentation style is changed. This method calls several implementation-specific methods to handle the swapping of one display type for another. In WebGauge's case, this method determines what information is needed to change from a text view to a graph view and back again. WebGauge caches the display information, so if the view is changed from a graph view to a text view and then back to a graph view, WebGauge can reuse the original display frame.

DisplayFrameAdded   (ODPart)

After the new display frame has been created (or reconstituted), then the DisplayFrameAdded method is called to notify the OpenDoc runtime that a new frame is to be associated with the part.

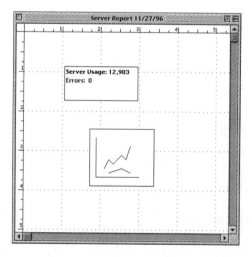

FIGURE 7-4. *Using multiple presentation styles*

Open **(ODPart)**

The Open method is modified to support the various presentation styles available to WebGauge in addition to the original text version.

CreateWindow **(WebGauge)**

The CreateWindow method does the actual work of creating new windows in response to requests from various OpenDoc routines.

Adding a Scripting Semantic Interface

WebGauge now has enough features that it's reasonable to think about adding a scripting interface. Making WebGauge scriptable enables its behavior to be controlled from other OpenDoc parts or from external applications that use the Open Scripting Architecture (OSA).

Using Scripting in WebGauge

Figure 7-5 shows a short script that tells WebGauge to reset its counters and change to graph mode.

User Benefits

Application integration through scripting is a simple yet powerful way to create custom solutions for MIS departments and the users they support.

Implementation

This section discusses the methods that need to be implemented to support scripting in WebGauge. Some of these methods override ODPart methods, and others are specific to the WebGauge implementation.

ConstructSemanticInterface **(WebGauge)**

The semantic interface for scripting is implemented as an OpenDoc extension. The ConstructSemanticInterface method initializes the interface object and installs the accessory functions necessary to connect it to the Open Scripting Architecture infrastructure.

FIGURE 7-5.   *Using scripting*

GetPropertyFromNULL   (WebGauge)

The first accessor function installed by ConstructSemanticInterface is GetPropertyFromNULL. This method returns a token that represents the contents property of the OpenDoc storage unit for the scripted part, which allows the Set and Get methods to access the actual data stored in the part.

HandleSetData   (WebGauge)

HandleSetData decodes the OSA event and uses the data transferred in the event to change the content of the part. One event that WebGauge understands is the command to change its web log filename. In this case, this method gets the new filename from the OSA event and then uses that filename as the basis for the statistics it displays.

HandleGetData   (WebGauge)

HandleGetData returns information requested from WebGauge. As with HandleSetData, one important piece of information is the filename for the web log. This routine returns that filename to the requestor.

Adding Undo and Redo Capabilities

Finally, you will add undo and redo features to WebGauge. Undo allows users to recover from errors that are noticed soon after they are made. For example, if the user deletes the wrong word when editing text, the user can use undo to restore the deleted word. Redo allows the user to change his or her mind yet again and redo the original action. OpenDoc supports multiple levels of undo and redo operations.

Using Undo and Redo in WebGauge

Figure 7-6 shows a sequence of events in WebGauge that can be undone or redone as the user wishes.

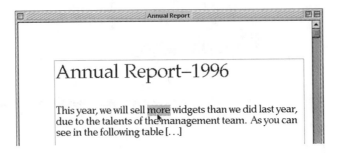

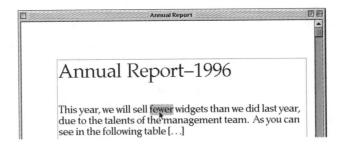

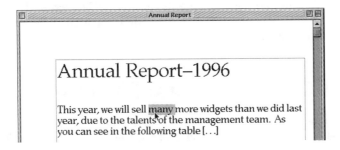

FIGURE 7-6. *Using undo and redo*

User Benefits

Undo and redo allow the user to make mistakes and then recover from them easily.

Implementation

This section discusses the methods that need to be implemented to support undo and redo in WebGauge. Some of these methods override ODPart methods, and others are specific to the WebGauge implementation.

UndoAction   (ODPart)
This UndoAction method calls the HandleUndo method for the action, causing it to be undone.

RedoAction   (ODPart)
The RedoAction method calls the HandleRedo method for the action, causing it to be redone.

DisposeActionState   (ODPart)
When OpenDoc no longer needs to keep track of an action, it calls the DisposeActionState method to dispose of the action object.

class CAction   (WebGauge)
The class CAction defines actions as objects with methods for undoing and redoing actions in general. Specific subclasses of this action class accomplish tasks such as cutting, copying, and pasting text.

Linking, Embedding, and Memory Management

Linking, embedding, and memory management are important topics, but extensive discussions of each are outside the scope of this book. However, this section briefly describes embedding and linking and gives examples of how these features can be added to a part with a richer content model than WebGauge's. This section also provides a short example of memory management in OpenDoc.

Using Embedding

A part that supports the embedding protocol can embed other parts within itself and is known as a container part. In general, a container part only handles embedded frames, and so the code needed to turn a leaf part into a container part is fairly straightforward. The embedded frames then interact with the parts they contain; most of the required frame behavior is already provided by OpenDoc. A container part has responsibilities in the following six areas:

■ *Content model and storage* A container part must have a content model that supports embedded frames and can store them properly in the part's storage unit. The content model should contain an element that represents embedded frames and be able to track and manipulate them. A drawing editor might represent an embedded frame as just another type of polygon (such as a square, circle, or curve) and be able to reuse positioning code that the drawing editor already contains. The part editor should maintain a list of these embedded objects and provide access to this list to other part editors via the CreateEmbeddedFramesIterator method. Finally, the container part should write persistent references to the embedded frames into its own storage unit, in its content property. When the part is re-created from storage, these references should be used to reconstruct the embedded frames.

■ *Layout management* This is the one of the most important areas for container parts because the containing part controls the sizes and locations of embedded frames. A container part should support frame negotiation and provide the embedded part's requested geometry, if possible. An embedded part may request an additional display frame, which could be used for alternate presentation styles or to show two views of the same data. In this case, the frames need to be synchronized with one another, using the AttachSourceFrame method. Finally, a container part is responsible for removing an embedded frame and all of its facets when the frame is no longer needed.

■ *Drawing* Embedded parts are displayed as icons, thumbnails, or complete frames. This display is controlled by the view type, which is set by the container part. (In general, embedded parts should be viewed as frames.) A container part must also support clipping, selection, and highlighting behavior for embedded frames. These should be consistent with the behaviors for the container part's native content. Last, the container part needs to handle interactions, such as overlapping or wrapping, between its native

content and the embedded frames. These policies are based on the
containing part's content and general style.

- *Event handling* A part that supports embedding needs to handle mouse
events in the embedded part's border. These events determine whether the
frame is selected or resized. If the embedded part is selected, then the
container part needs to handle the open, cut, and copy events for the
embedded frame. In general, these are the same events that a part needs to
handle for its own intrinsic or native content, so the code changes required
are minimal.

- *Data transfer* If the container part supports drag-and-drop and cut-and-
paste operations, then the routines that handle them must be modified
to handle the content elements that represent embedded frames. Any
operations that copy or move data should use the CloneInto method for
the embedded part.

- *Scripting* The elements in the content mode that represent embedded
frames must be accessible from the scripting interface; that is, they must
have content objects that can be identified and manipulated in the same
way as any other content object in the part.

For a more complete discussion of embedding and a checklist of additional
information, refer to the *OpenDoc Programmer's Guide*, listed in the annotated
bibliography in Appendix D.

Using Linking

The linking protocol allows a part to export updatable data or to import or embed
data from another part. Figure 7-7 shows an example in which parts share data
via linking.

A link is created when the user requests it during a paste or drag operation. The
part that contains the data source is called the source part, and the part at the other
end of the link is called the destination part. When the linking mechanism is used,
the data displayed at the link destination is updated automatically whenever the
data at the link source changes.

Linking in OpenDoc is implemented with a variation of the standard event
handling and storage code. The same techniques used in drag-and-drop operations
to manage the storage units are used in linking, along with additional methods to
synchronize the data transfer between the source and destination.

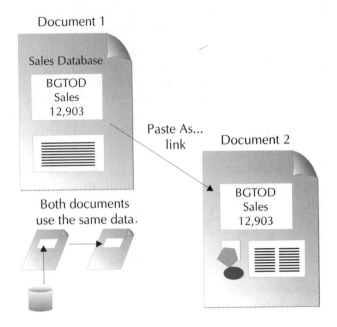

FIGURE 7-7. *Linking parts*

Memory-Management Example

For the most part, a part editor only needs to make sure that it frees or releases memory for objects it creates or obtains. (The OpenDoc runtime handles much of the memory management automatically.) The reference-counting protocol, discussed in Chapter 5, allows memory to be reclaimed when it is no longer being used.

Reference-counted objects store their reference count internally and return it as the result of the GetRefCount method. Reference counts are incremented whenever a part editor stores a reference to a reference-counted object. This is done by calling the object's Acquire method. Similarly, when that object is no longer needed by the part editor, the reference count is decremented by calling the Release method for that object. When the reference count reaches zero, the object becomes eligible for reclamation. The object's memory may not be freed immediately; the object may be kept for reuse until the part editor's Purge method is called. Every Acquire method call must be matched with a corresponding call to the Release method.

```
// acquire a clip shape for use in rendering
newClipShape = facet->AcquireClipShape(ev,renderCanvas);
// code using the acquired clip shape
// . . .
// decrement clip shape, clean up
newClipShape->Release(ev);
newClipShape = kODNULL;
```

Putting It Together

This chapter discussed some more advanced features of OpenDoc, such as drag and drop, multiple presentations, scripting, and undo and redo. It also touched on the linking and embedding protocols and presented an example of memory-management techniques. The next chapter tells you how to integrate OpenDoc into your existing software and computer systems.

CHAPTER 8

Interoperability and Migration

This chapter describes the process of moving to OpenDoc-based software. Migration to OpenDoc does not necessitate abandoning old systems; OpenDoc can be used as a solution to real-world problems that involve legacy systems and software. This chapter explains how legacy systems can be retrofitted to work with OpenDoc, either as parts or as container applications. This chapter also presents an extensive discussion of interoperability with OLE, Taligent, and other object technologies. Finally, this chapter discusses standard parts and data formats and how they help OpenDoc work seamlessly across platforms.

The preceding chapters presented a good introduction to OpenDoc: what it is, how it works, why it was developed, and who developed it. This chapter ties all of those threads together and discusses how OpenDoc is used in practice. Given the large base of installed, tested, valuable software already in use, techniques for making a transition to OpenDoc easier are a practical necessity. Some migrations are by necessity incomplete, and none are instant and painless. Nevertheless, OpenDoc can coexist with and enhance the functions of an organization's current software investment.

Of course, OpenDoc is not the only component software and compound document system available in the marketplace. Interoperability with OLE is one of OpenDoc's advantages and benefits. This chapter discusses this technology and uses a real-life example to explore how OpenDoc and OLE can be used together.

The first topic of this chapter is migration: moving from traditional applications to an OpenDoc-based component system. The chapter starts by discussing some major categories of business applications and then contrasts them with OpenDoc-enabled solutions to the same problems. The chapter also discusses some areas where OpenDoc provides solutions to problems that are difficult, if not impossible, to solve using traditional technologies. Finally, the chapter presents a detailed deployment scenario, showing how the solutions discussed at the beginning of the chapter can be applied in a real-world business.

The second main topic of this chapter is interoperability with current and future component software systems. First among these is OLE from Microsoft. Given the large installed base of OLE-capable systems, it is unrealistic to expect OLE to disappear. OLE will remain a strong competitor to open systems, and to OpenDoc in particular, for the foreseeable future. Recognizing this, OLE interoperability was designed into OpenDoc from the beginning. This chapter describes the ComponentGlue technology that enables OLE interoperability. ComponentGlue was developed by Novell and IBM and is promoted by CI Labs. The chapter discusses it from both technical and practical standpoints: how it works and how you use it.

There are yet other object and component systems also on the market. Taligent and NeXTStep/OpenStep are two of the best-publicized, and this chapter examines how they fit into an OpenDoc-centric environment.

OpenDoc is based on CORBA, so interoperability with that standard is not really an issue. There are, however, significant areas where it is valuable to know more about CORBA-based systems and their capabilities. This knowledge allows a designer or user of OpenDoc parts to leverage services that become available as OpenDoc and SOM (OpenDoc's CORBA implementation) evolve. Specifically, distribution and network services will become more important as network-based (that is, Internet-based) infrastructures continue to mature. A future release of OpenDoc will make explicit use of the network features enabled by distributed SOM. OpenDoc is well positioned to take advantage of these developments (perhaps more so than OLE is) because distribution was taken into account in the basic design. An open process is in place to make sure that the standards take into account the interests and concerns of a number of companies and organizations, rather than accept by fiat the dictates of a single company.

Migration from Other Systems

Once an MIS manager evaluates a technology and decides to adopt it in an organization, the manager is faced with the task of incorporating that technology without disrupting operations. Customers, both external and internal, cannot be deprived of services during the transition. The ideal approach is to make the transition to the new system in a piecewise fashion: replacing certain parts of the system while leaving others untouched, until the whole infrastructure has been upgraded.

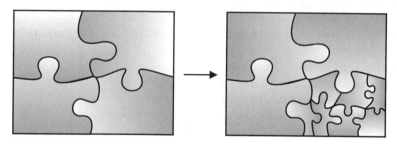

Subdivide and Conquer

The transition to object-oriented technology and component software should follow this approach. The three main steps in the transition are as follows:

- *Define interfaces.* Determine where a problem naturally breaks apart into functional units and formalize the interfaces between them. Make sure that pieces communicate only via the published interfaces. The Interface Definition Language (IDL) is a powerful tool in its own right, apart from its use with SOM. IDL can be used in the earliest stages of a transition, before any other modifications are made to the source code: IDL back-ends are or will be available for all of the popular implementation languages (C, C++, Ada, COBOL). Use IDL to declare interfaces, and then use the proper back-end to generate header files for the implementation.

- *Reimplement a particular interface.* The preceding step, if done properly, guarantees that the interactions of various systems pieces are governed solely by the interface definitions. Thus, any or all of those pieces can be replaced, so long as the replacement obeys the same interface rules.

■ *Repeat the preceding steps for all pieces.* Repeat the preceding steps, either for other pieces of the system or for previously encapsulated pieces to subdivide them further.

Keep these steps in mind as you review the next sections, which discuss some typical business applications and how they might look and behave in an OpenDoc context.

Overview of Current Business Applications

Current business applications generally fall into one of the following three broad (though somewhat arbitrary) categories: communication, presentation and report packages (including text processing programs), and database access and manipulation tools. The following sections discuss how the three categories of applications can work with and migrate to an OpenDoc-based environment.

Communication

Communication applications include e-mail, collaborative groupware, Internet software such as FTP, and World Wide Web browsers.

OpenDoc is most obviously useful in a communication context when communication tools such as e-mail, FTP, and video collaboration can be embedded in any other type of document. Other innovations arrive when OpenDoc documents can be manipulated using the communication tools. Imagine an e-mail composition window that is an OpenDoc document. Individual e-mail vendors have implemented such windows to handle multimedia composition; each scheme is specific to the e-mail program and handles a fixed set of data types. Figure 8-1 illustrates the differences between e-mail composed with and without OpenDoc.

Lotus Notes is another example of a communication product originally developed on a proprietary technology base that is now being made to work as components. Version 4 of Lotus Notes is now a component-based system; its first implementation is as OLE Custom Controls, but OpenDoc support is in the product roadmap from Lotus. Thanks to ComponentGlue, these Lotus Notes components will work in any OpenDoc document.

Presentations and Reports

Presentation and report applications include mainframe usage-reporting packages, personnel reports, and slide-creation packages.

The presentations and reports category is an area where OpenDoc can make a real difference in the way people do their work as well as in how work is presented. Current presentation packages, such as Microsoft's PowerPoint and Adobe Persuasion, are optimized for static presentations on overhead projectors. While both support computer-based presentations, the number of media types supported is small, and each has rather idiosyncratic controls. (In other words, they suffer from the same problems as most monolithic applications, as we discussed in Chapter 1.)

An OpenDoc-enabled presentation package would allow arbitrary data types and formats and could include live data feeds—something that can be accomplished now, but with some difficulty. Figure 8-2 contrasts a conventional presentation with one that uses OpenDoc components. Note how the content parts are embedded in a part that handles transition effects; none of them have to include any new code to handle the additional effects.

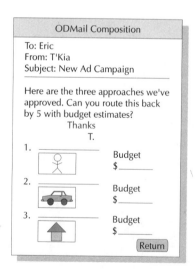

FIGURE 8-1. *E-mail composition with and without OpenDoc*

Databases

Database applications include database front-ends and back-ends, as well as the application-builder technology used to construct them.

With OpenDoc, many of the traditional application categories blur into one another—is a tool a presentation tool, a communication tool, or both? Database access is another area where OpenDoc can break down the traditional barriers between applications.

If a presentation is connected to a database to perform live updates, is that a fancy database front-end or a presentation tool with database access? If the user can e-mail that presentation to a colleague or collaborate over a network in real time, is the tool a database access tool or a communication tool?

Database access is an application category that becomes ubiquitous in an environment where OpenDoc parts are passed around freely. Even a simple terminal emulator part becomes valuable when it is connected to a corporate mainframe that contains a large database. Figure 8-3 shows some ways in which a database access part may be valuable to other application types.

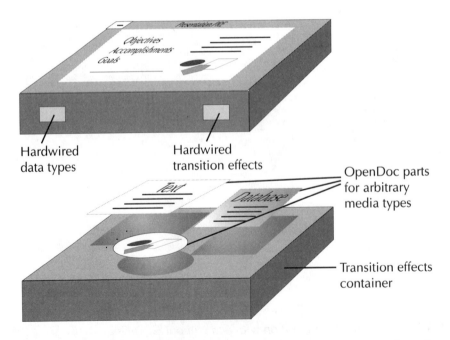

FIGURE 8-2.   *Conventional presentations versus presentations using OpenDoc*

New Categories of Applications

Breaking down barriers between applications and making data types usable in a myriad of contexts will lead to new areas of innovation. Because it is relatively simple to add scripting capabilities to OpenDoc parts, some interesting new ways of creating custom applications will no doubt be developed. Perhaps most important of all for innovation is being able to reuse pieces of old applications in new ways. For example, combining a simple database access part with scriptable button parts can lead to a new database interface, well-integrated with explanatory text, as shown in the survey application in Figure 8-4.

At this point in OpenDoc's development, it is difficult to imagine what clever software engineers will be able to invent. For additional discussion of some short-

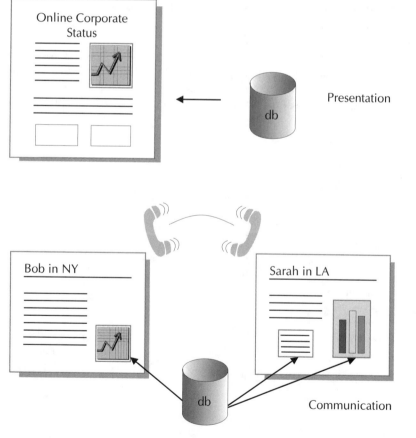

FIGURE 8-3. *Some uses of ubiquitous database access*

and medium-term possibilities, refer to Chapter 10 and the discussion of future uses of OpenDoc.

OpenDoc Deployment Scenario

This section presents a scenario in which a medium-sized MIS department decides to enhance its company's business applications so they work with OpenDoc as they upgrade their computer systems. This enhancement will give them the flexibility to upgrade additional pieces as resources permit and as new features are required.

Company Overview: Recreational SportShop, Inc.

This section explores some of the things that a fictional company (Recreational SportShop, Inc.) might do to move its operations from legacy systems toward an OpenDoc-based environment. It starts off with an overview of the hardware upgrades needed, and then focuses on the software.

RSS is a supplier of recreational equipment and supplies, based in Memphis, TN, near a famous worldwide shipping company. In business since the early 80s, RSS supplies complete packages of sporting goods, towels, and snack items to medium- and high-end gyms, resorts, and recreational facilities. RSS provides

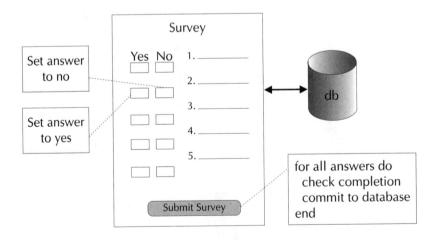

FIGURE 8-4. *Creating a new application from an old one*

customized starter packages as well as "subscriptions" for consumable items. Ordering and sales are done via an 800 number, and they have a well-regarded customer service and satisfaction program. This necessitates a fairly large call center and database system for order tracking, shipping, and customer feedback.

Overview of the Current System

The existing system consists of a mainframe and its storage system, connected to an array of terminals. The mainframe handles the bulk of the company's computing and data storage needs. It provides access to the customer database, the order database, and the customer-service database. It runs the ordering system as well as the order-tracking system and customer-service system. The mainframe holds the human-resources database and runs the human-resources applications such as payroll and benefits. Finally, it runs the corporate sales analysis and reporting tools. The Creative Services department, which creates brochures, marketing literature, and packaging, uses a locally networked group of Macintoshes.

While most of the equipment is still useful (although the alphanumeric terminals are approaching the end of their useful life), the MIS department wants a more decentralized system that can use commodity hardware and yet remains tightly integrated. It has decided on OpenDoc as the long-term strategy for typing together the various pieces of their business.

This is a fairly standard client/server redesign: substituting low-cost personal computers for terminals, turning the mainframe into a database and file server, and networking various isolated groups. Mainframes still have advantages when it comes to high-speed I/O (input/output) operations, and it's smart to retain them where it makes sense in a particular organization.

Figure 8-5 shows a diagram of the current computer system.

Transitional System

The transitional system shows the system with the addition of new hardware, but with mostly the same software. At this point, the only new pieces of software required are terminal emulator parts embedded in OpenDoc documents. Some employees in the call center are still using the same terminals while others have been upgraded to personal computers. A mixed environment allows training to take place on the new systems without seriously impacting the ability of the call center to get its work done. The mainframe is moving gradually away from providing computing power and applications to providing database services and files.

Figure 8-6 shows a diagram of the transitional system.

Long-term Goal

The long-term goal is accomplished mostly with new software rather than new hardware. Because the OpenDoc infrastructure is already in place, the additional software can be added as needed with no additional disruption of work required.

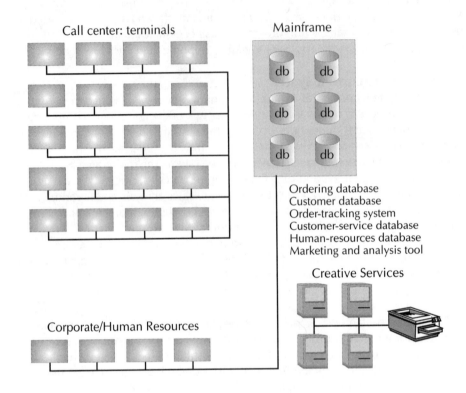

Call center: terminals

Mainframe

db db
db db
db db

Ordering database
Customer database
Order-tracking system
Customer-service database
Human-resources database
Marketing and analysis tool

Creative Services

Corporate/Human Resources

FIGURE 8-5. *Current computer system*

Figure 8-7 shows the diagram representing the MIS department's long-term goal for the computing services they provide.

The next sections will discuss the old tools and applications and show how they are integrated into the new system. In addition, it will talk about some of the new features that are enabled by using OpenDoc as the new foundation for the system.

Order Entry

The existing order-entry system is a text-based form on an alphanumeric terminal. The operator types in the catalog number, and a textual description of the item appears on the screen. Customer information (including order history and recurring orders) can be pulled up from another database, but it can be cumbersome, as it requires switching applications. The transitional system can keep the same interface, with the applications still running on the mainframe, but additional

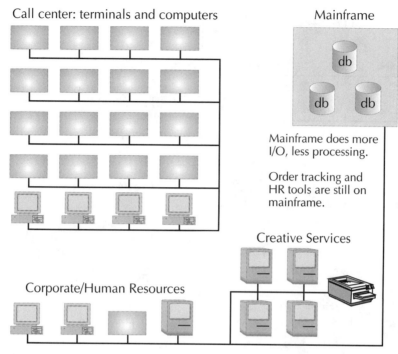

Call center: terminals and computers

Mainframe

Mainframe does more
I/O, less processing.

Order tracking and
HR tools are still on
mainframe.

Creative Services

Corporate/Human Resources

Marketing has local Macs and PCs,
and can access sales data on mainframe
and work collaboratively with
Creative Services.

Creative Services is now networked
with the rest of the company.

FIGURE 8-6. *Gradual transition to new systems*

information can appear on-screen, such as pictures of the items being ordered. By
embedding another terminal emulator part, the operator can view both databases
simultaneously.

Eventually, the application can be rewritten to run on the operator's computer
and pull information across the network from the mainframe. This reduces the load
on the mainframe and allows it to support more operators simultaneously. By using
OpenDoc, the company can decide to embed viewer parts for the online catalog
database—the operator can see the catalog items on the same screen on which he
or she is taking the order from the customer.

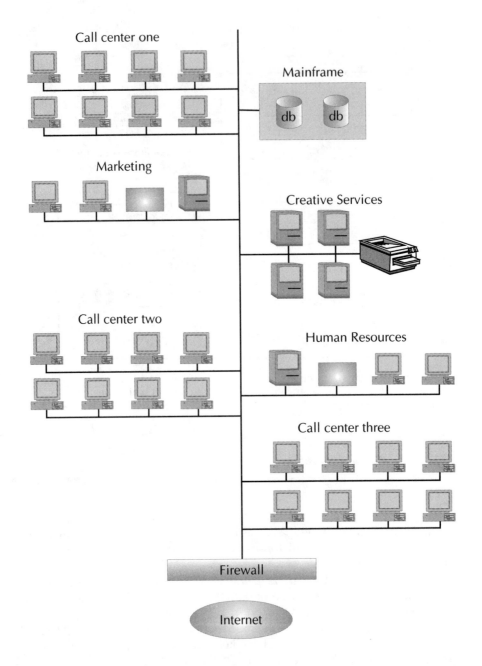

FIGURE 8-7. *Long-term goal of MIS department*

Old system

New system

FIGURE 8-8. *The old system versus the new system*

Order Tracking

The order-tracking system is closely integrated with the mainframe and is not scheduled for rewrite any time soon. It has minimal processing impact on the mainframe, and so this was not seen as a priority. A small terminal emulator part will suffice to integrate it with the new system interface.

Customer Service

The customer-service system needs multimedia capabilities—it needs to integrate pictures and movies with a display of the customer's order and order-tracking information. Previously, the customer-service representatives were limited to thumbing through a troubleshooting guide located at each work station. This had the disadvantage of being bulky, expensive to produce, and continually out of date. Although RSS supplies simple items such as balls and tennis raquets, it also supplies scuba equipment, sailboats, and computerized exercise equipment, so there is a need to have specific information for each model. Figure 8-9 shows a customer-service system with multimedia capabilities.

Human Resources

The human-resources system integrates the payroll and benefits information into one place, and gives the HR staff a single interface for all of the various databases.

Figure 8-10 shows a sample of the new HR system.

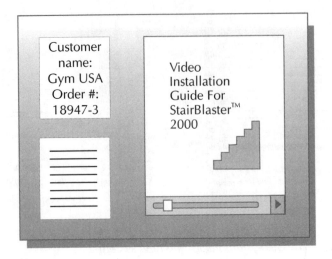

FIGURE 8-9. *Customer-service system with multimedia capabilities*

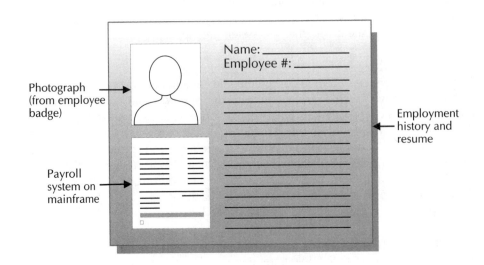

FIGURE 8-10. *Integration of multiple databases*

Marketing

The marketing and analysis staff can create more-detailed reports and keep a link to the corporate databases so that the data is continuously updated. Instead of having to create slides, reports, or memos, they can send e-mail to the staff and embed a live view of the data that the report attempts to interpret. Figure 8-11 shows one possible application of such a capability.

Reusing Part Suites

The MIS staff can create groups of related parts (a *part suite*) and provide customized versions for each department. A document consisting of a picture viewer, a database access part, some controls such as buttons or text-entry fields, and a text viewer would cover the majority of the applications examined above.

Interoperability with Other Systems

No system, no matter how successful, immediately sweeps all competitors into oblivion. OpenDoc will need to coexist with and interoperate with other systems for a long time to come. This chapter now turns to the other important component software and compound document systems currently available and discusses other important issues, such as network distribution and data format standards.

Interoperability with OLE

Given the likelihood that OLE and OpenDoc will coexist in the marketplace for a number of years, a knowledge of ComponentGlue technology is important. ComponentGlue acts as a gateway between OLE and OpenDoc. To an OLE-enabled application, an OpenDoc part in a ComponentGlue wrapper acts and appears just like an OLE component. Similarly, an OLE component can be embedded in an OpenDoc document within a ComponentGlue container, and it will behave just like any other part. This section discusses some technical details of how ComponentGlue works and some situations where mixed environments are important.

ComponentGlue Technical Overview

ComponentGlue works by providing a wrapper for the "foreign" component so that it and the environment interact as they normally would. The ComponentGlue wrapper translates each system's native method calls into the appropriate equivalents on the other side. Figure 8-12 shows an OpenDoc part in the OLE environment. Figure 8-13 shows an OLE component in the OpenDoc environment.

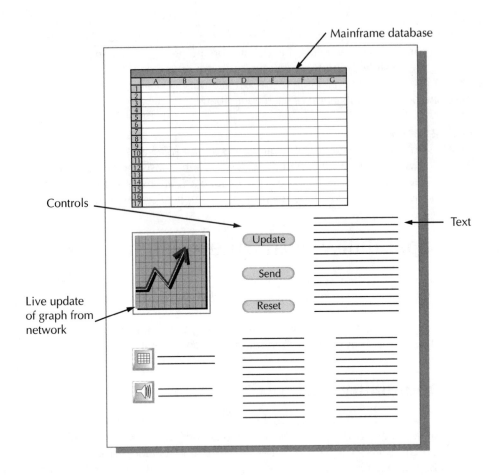

FIGURE 8-11. *Live reports*

Operating in a Mixed Environment

A mixed environment, such as the one shown in Figure 8-14, becomes important when legacy code is involved or when a component is available only for one system, not for others. For example, an organization might have paid to have an OLE Custom Control (OCX) written to control some aspect of its industrial control system. As OpenDoc is deployed in the organization, that control can still be used for its mission-critical purpose, while the environment in which it functions becomes more rich and varied.

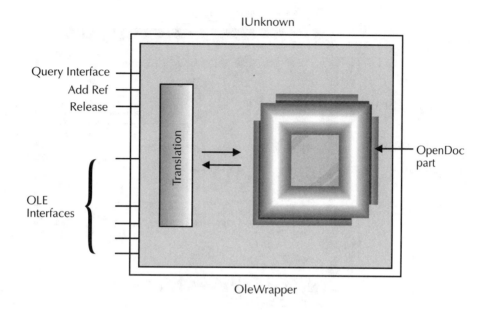

FIGURE 8-12.   *OpenDoc part in the OLE environment*

Interoperability with Taligent and OpenStep

Two of the other major players in the object technology market are Taligent and OpenStep.

Taligent frameworks were designed with OpenDoc interoperability in mind; Taligent itself is being rolled back into IBM, with Apple and Hewlett-Packard continuing to have rights to the technology. Certain aspects of the Taligent environment (especially the user metaphors) may become part of OpenDoc, though exact plans are currently unknown.

OpenStep (the open version of NeXTStep) has developed a following among financial institutions and among MIS shops in large corporations. For that reason alone, it needs to be taken into account when coming up with an object technology transition plan. In addition, OpenStep has a number of interesting technical features, along with backing from NeXT and Sun.

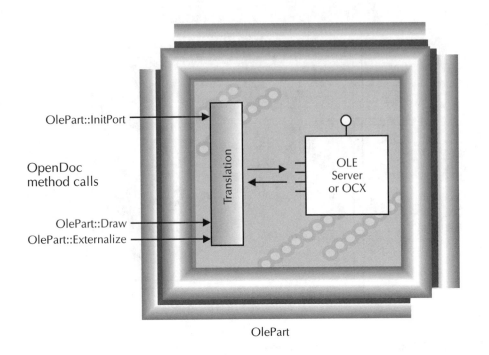

FIGURE 8-13. *OLE component in OpenDoc enviroment*

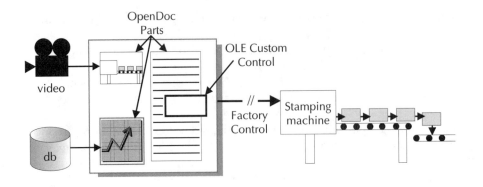

FIGURE 8-14. *OpenDoc and OLE components working together*

Taligent Technical Overview

Taligent's CommonPoint frameworks, numbering over 100, cover most areas required to write applications and create media-rich compound documents. There are frameworks to handle user interfaces, hide operating system differences, and provide collaboration services.

Taligent frameworks are implemented in C++, with versions planned for a variety of operating systems. As Figure 8-15 shows, CommonPoint provides an encapsulation layer above an operating system. Taligent calls this an application system.

Working with Taligent Frameworks

Taligent has the facilities in place to allow it to interoperate with OpenDoc. With Taligent's reabsorption by IBM, this link is likely to become even stronger. The following list provides some idea of how good the interoperation should be:

- *SOM and CORBA* Taligent plans to provide gateways to connect CommonPoint objects with other object systems via CORBA.

- *Component embedding and user interaction* Taligent documents will be able to embed OpenDoc parts, and vice versa. Because the user models for activation and manipulation are similar, interacting with a heterogeneous collection of components should be fairly seamless.

- *Storage* It should be possible to store a Taligent document in a Bento container, thus allowing OpenDoc and CommonPoint applications to share documents and exchange data.

- *Scripting* Taligent will support scripting that complies with Open Scripting Architecture (OSA). Thus, the same scripts that control a CommonPoint document will work with an OpenDoc document, provided that the semantic interfaces provide the same services.

- *Building OpenDoc parts with Taligent frameworks* It will be possible to build OpenDoc parts using the Taligent application frameworks.

Taligent is somewhat in limbo right now, as IBM takes control and decides how it fits into its object strategy. Taligent's technology may well end up as part of the next revision of OpenDoc, so you should keep its functions in mind.

OpenStep Technical Overview

OpenStep is the open, portable version of NeXT's award-winning NeXTStep. NeXTStep was largely designed and implemented by Guy Tribble, formerly of Apple and NeXT and now vice president of object technology at SunSoft. In 1993, Sun and NeXT announced a collaboration to make OpenStep available as part of

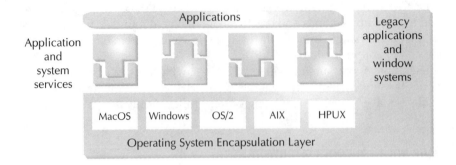

FIGURE 8-15. *CommonPoint frameworks*

Sun's DOE (now Neo) distributed object environment. Digital Equipment Corporation now also supports OpenStep on top of its ObjectBroker.

OpenStep provides all of the application-level resources that a developer needs, and since it has been around the longest, (NeXTStep 1.0 came out in the mid-eighties), it is the most stable and mature of the object platforms. On the other hand, it was invented before there were any other industry standards, so its interoperability with other systems is somewhat limited.

OpenStep's big claim to fame, and the reason it has become so popular with MIS departments, is its excellent application builder.

Working with OpenStep
Interoperability with OpenStep will require a gateway of some kind to translate its internal object format (Objective C) to a format palatable to the outside world. NeXT has plans to create such a gateway with both CORBA and OLE, though neither product has yet shipped.

Interoperability with CORBA

The Common Object Request Broker Architecture (CORBA) is an open standard promoted by the Object Management Group, a standards organization with more than five hundred member companies and organizations. Despite criticisms of "design by committee," the OMG has managed to come up with several good documents that specify in detail the architecture and requirements for a distributed object infrastructure. All of the CI Labs sponsors belong to the OMG, as do important industry leaders such as Hewlett-Packard and Sun Microsystems.

OpenDoc itself is poised to become part of the CORBA specification for Compound Document Services. The Object Management Group's technical committee voted to recommend this to the general membership, which is voting on the proposal.

SOM, one of the technologies on which OpenDoc is based (see Chapter 9), is an OMG-compliant Object Request Broker. As such, it will be able to take advantage of higher-level services defined by the OMG and implemented by IBM and third-party vendors.

The development of CORBA is a huge undertaking. The specification covers a wide variety of services, not all of which will be needed or implemented immediately.

Here are some of the major categories of CORBA services:

- Naming
- Events
- Life cycle
- Transactions
- Persistence
- Relationships
- Security
- System management

Because OpenDoc parts are IDL and SOM-based, they already have the infrastructure necessary to interact with CORBA object systems. As soon as networked versions of SOM become widely available, OpenDoc parts should be able to take advantage of distributed object services.

Standard Parts and Data Types

Although component software and cross-platform portability are central features of OpenDoc, there is another area in which cross-platform industry agreement is important: standard type and data formats. Although OpenDoc may provide tools to view GIF-format images and embed them in any arbitrary document, if another organization uses JPEG images exclusively, some form of translation is necessary. Although OpenDoc can handle this translation, it would also be nice to have a set of standard formats that every OpenDoc implementation understands. By providing a well-implemented default for each media type (such as bitmapped graphics, vector graphics, sound, and text), users and developers are encouraged to use those formats (if only from laziness!).

A proposal has been made to define a set of media types for OpenDoc. With a suggested list of standard formats, vendors can begin to ship a standard suite of part editors to make sure there is a universally recognized minimum level of document content.

Table 8-1 shows areas that would benefit from some of the suggested standard data formats. There are several areas in which the format has yet to be determined.

Content Area	Example Storage Format	Description
Plain text	ASCII	Unformatted text
Structured text	RTF	Rich formatted text
Structured graphics	CGM	Structured graphic
Images	GIF/JPEG	Bitmapped graphic
Audio	μ-law	Audio sample
Music	MIDI	Instrument control stream
Video	MPEG	Video sample
Page layout	TBD	Free-form container for parts with minimal page layout features
Page layout	TBD	Free-form container for parts with minimal page layout features
Table	TBD	Table of numbers
Matrix	TBD	Container part that displays rows and columns of embedded parts
Shrinkwrap	TBD	A container part allowing many parts to be embedded within, with only one displayed
Chart	TBD	Part displaying a chart
Form	TBD	Part providing the user with a customizable form layout

TABLE 8-1. *Proposed Standard Parts*

Putting It Together

This chapter tied together the themes explored in the previous seven chapters and used that information to describe the practical realities of working with an OpenDoc-based system. The next two chapters head off in very different directions: Chapter 9 delves into the technical details of how OpenDoc's underlying technologies work, and Chapter 10 wraps up the book with a discussion of future directions for OpenDoc and for OpenDoc-based software.

CHAPTER 9

Underlying Technologies

This chapter is aimed at those who wish to know a bit more about the technology that makes OpenDoc work. It discusses the implementation of the SOM object infrastructure and of Bento, a widely available cross-platform file format. It presents some of the issues surrounding scripting and the Open Scripting Architecture (OSA) and discusses how ComponentGlue OLE interoperability works.

The preceding chapters described OpenDoc technologies and explained some of the ways those technologies can be used. This chapter goes "under the hood" to look at the technologies that provide the basis for OpenDoc.

OpenDoc is built on top of four basic "pillar" technologies, each of which provides important support for the system:

- IBM's *System Object Model (SOM)* provides the object infrastructure beneath OpenDoc and is the means by which OpenDoc interoperates with other CORBA-compliant systems. OS/2 is based on SOM, so several million systems that use SOM are already in the field. This base provided a test bed and proving grounds for this technology.

- *Bento* is at the heart of the standard OpenDoc storage system implementation and provides the persistent structure for OpenDoc documents. Bento is freely available and is the basis for several non-OpenDoc storage formats. It has been adopted by the Interactive Multimedia Association as part of its multimedia data interchange specification.

- *Open Scripting Architecture (OSA)* has been in place since the introduction of AppleScript in 1990. Because it is an open architecture, other vendors have provided other OSA-compliant languages and scripting systems, all of which work with OpenDoc. Since dynamic languages are proving to be popular and useful in the Internet arena, OpenDoc's scripting and automation capabilities will be quite useful both now and in the future.

- Finally, *ComponentGlue* provides OpenDoc's gateway to the world of OLE and COM components and services. Because the object world is heterogeneous, this technology provides access to a large installed base of components and to new technologies that will arise. It allows these divergent worlds to coexist and take advantage of each other's capabilities.

The first section of this chapter recaps the SOM discussions in earlier chapters and then proceeds with a more detailed look at the runtime architecture and distributed SOM.

The next major section presents the basic concepts of Bento, along with a description of the Bento container format. Much of this discussion focuses on the Bento specification adopted by the Interactive Multimedia Association (IMA) as part of its Data Exchange Recommended Practice.

The section on OSA starts off with a general discussion of scripting and the OSA specification. Next, it looks at two OSA scripting systems: AppleScript and Frontier. Finally, it describes some other scripting systems (Tcl, Java and JavaScript, and Visual Basic) that are not currently OSA compliant, but which are important in the industry and which could, in theory, be adapted to work with OSA and therefore OpenDoc.

Ending the chapter is an examination of the implementation of ComponentGlue and how it allows OpenDoc and OLE components to work together.

SOM

Previous chapters mentioned SOM as the object system beneath OpenDoc without presenting many details of its operation. This section provides some of those details.

In the broadest sense, SOM provides a way to abstract object concepts away from a particular language and to apply these concepts in a language-independent fashion. Figure 9-1 shows a hypothetical object-oriented drawing package implemented in C++.

Using SOM, the drawing package could be rewritten and used in much the same way as in Figure 9-1, but with the advantage that it could be reused by any other application or component that is implemented in any language that has a binding for SOM. Figure 9-2 shows such a package.

The IDL compiler translates definitions written in IDL into an abstract syntax tree that embodies all of the information needed to define the structure of the interface. Next, language-specific emitter modules take that syntax tree and generate skeleton code in the target language, as shown in Figure 9-3. Adding this level of indirection (that is, the skeleton code) allows the SOM runtime to take method calls from the calling object and map them into the form required by the target object.

When a client requests an object service, the client invokes a method on the client stubs created by the IDL compiler. Thus, from a client's point of view, all calls are local. The code generated by the IDL compiler handles argument marshaling—translating method calls and the parameters for those methods into a

```
#include <drawing.h>

Pad    *myPad = newPad ();
Pad    *path = myPad ->getPath ();

path -> begin (10,10);
path -> drawto (100, 100);
path -> drawto (100,10);
path -> closepath ();
path -> stroke ();
path -> fill ("aquamarine");
```

FIGURE 9-1. *A language-specific drawing package*

```
ObjDrawPad    pad;
ObjDrawPath   path;
pad = ObjectDrawNameSpace -> find ("DrawPad");
path = pad -> getPath ();

path -> begin (10,10);
path -> drawto (100, 100);
path -> drawto (100,10);
path -> closepath ();
path -> stroke ();
path -> fill ("aquamarine");
```

FIGURE 9-2. *A language-independent drawing package*

universal format that can be sent to the server. This is necessary because SOM allows multiple languages to work together, and so arguments need to be flattened into a format that can then be "unflattened" in a multitude of ways, depending on the implementation language of the target server. Figure 9-4 shows how the marshaling process works.

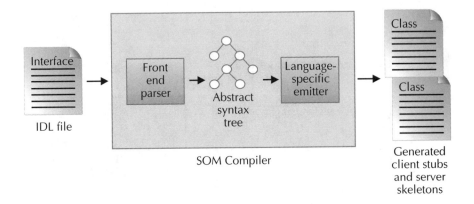

FIGURE 9-3. *SOM compiler, abstract syntax trees, and language emitters*

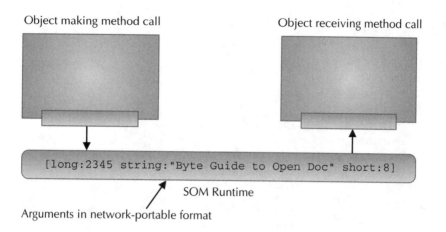

Object making method call   Object receiving method call

[long:2345 string:"Byte Guide to Open Doc" short:8]

SOM Runtime

Arguments in network-portable format

FIGURE 9-4. *Argument marshaling*

After a request is issued, the SOM runtime (also called the SOM kernel) needs to determine where to deliver the message. The runtime uses the object reference to determine the address of the destination object. The SOM runtime keeps track of all SOM classes registered with the system. In SOM as used in OpenDoc 1.0, this object is a dynamic library that is located, loaded, and mapped into the client's address space. Optimized versions of SOM can reduce the overhead of this operation to within the same order of magnitude as a C++ function call, so performance can be, by objective measures, quite good. In the best case, on a particular implementation optimized for the PowerPC processor, it can take *fewer* instructions than a C++ function call.

Once the target object is loaded and, if necessary, initialized, then the SOM runtime calls the unmarshaling code in the server skeleton of the target object. This code performs the necessary operations to translate the universal method and argument format into one appropriate for the target object's implementation.

Table 9-1 lists the CORBA 2.0 basic types. Table 9-2 lists the constructed and template types. All of the methods defined by IDL use the CORBA types. The constructed types (structs, unions, and enums) allow data types of arbitrary complexity. The constructed types allow the basic types to be used to create new types, as with a typedef.

Here is the CORBA 2.0 definition of Object:

```
interface Object {
    ImplementationDef get_implementation ();
    InterfaceDef get_interface ();
    boolean is_nil();
    Object duplicate ();
    void release ();
    boolean is_a (in string logical_type_id);
    boolean non_existent();
    boolean is_equivalent (in Object other_object);
    unsigned long hash(in unsigned long maximum);

    Status create_request (
        in Context ctx,
        in Identifier  operation,
        in NVList arg_list,
        inout NamedValue result,
        out Request request,
        in Flags req_flags
    );
};
```

All SOM objects implement this interface and can interoperate with other CORBA-compliant object systems.

Distributed SOM

Distributed SOM allows the objects whose services are being requested to reside in another process or on another machine across a network.

Short	Unsigned short
Long	Unsigned long
Float	Double
char	Unsigned char
Boolean	Octet
String	Any

TABLE 9-1. *CORBA 2.0 Basic Types*

Constructed Types	Template Types	Other Types
Struct	Sequence	Array
Union	String	
Enum		

TABLE 9-2. *Constructed Types*

The sequence of events involved in invoking a method is the same in both single-process SOM and in distributed SOM. In the latter case, however, the SOM runtime has a more elaborate location service and transport layer for locating and connecting to the remote object. The SOM Distribution Framework can use several over-the-wire protocols, including NetBIOS, IPX/SPX, and TCP/IP. CORBA 2.0 defines inter-ORB protocols, allowing heterogeneous object system deployment. The Internet Inter-ORB Protocol (IIOP) is a specification for connecting ORBs over the Internet using TCP/IP.

Other Frameworks

SOM also provides other frameworks for building SOM-based services and applications:

- *Replication Framework* The Replication Framework makes copies of an object available simultaneously to multiple clients and maintains consistency among all of the copies, propagating updates and providing fault-handling capabilities.

- *Persistence Framework* The Persistence Framework allows a user to save and restore SOM objects to any of a number of repositories, including file systems, relational databases, and object databases.

- *Emitter Framework* The Emitter Framework simplifies the process of creating additional SOM language bindings by providing a structured representation of an object interface definition.

- *Collection Classes Framework* The Collection Classes Framework provides widely used utility classes for data structures such as dictionaries, queues, sets, and a variety of lists. These are well tested and can be reused within applications or components.

- *Interface Repository Framework* The Interface Repository Framework generates a database of object definitions that can be queried dynamically at runtime to allow the client to perform dynamic method invocation.

Bento

Bento is used to implement OpenDoc's persistent storage system—the way documents are stored between editing sessions or accesses. Equally as important, Bento allows the storage of multiple data types in a structured form while occupying only one disk file or in-memory container. Bento containers are used for data exchange operations within OpenDoc (such as linking, clipboard operations, and drag-and-drop operations) and are also used in systems other than OpenDoc. In fact, Bento is available in over one hundred products. Bento has also been adopted by the IMA as the basis for its Data Exchange Recommended Practice. It is important to note that Bento is just one way to implement the OpenDoc storage system; other implementations, including the use of commercial databases, are possible.

Basic Concepts

Chapter 2 discussed the OpenDoc Storage subsystem and introduced the main concepts of Bento. This section delves deeper into how Bento works. Refer to Figure 2-8 in Chapter 2 to review the material that has already been presented.

Bento allows multiple streams of data to be stored and manipulated as a unit, without costing each stream its ability to be manipulated as a single stream. Bento's stream-oriented access means that most data-handling code originally written for file-system access can be rewritten to use Bento with minimal trouble.

A Bento file consists of a series of properties, each with a unique identifier within the Bento container. These Bento object IDs are integers from 0 to 2^{32}; 0 is not used, and values up to 2^{16} are reserved for use by Bento. Each of these properties has a name and one or more values. Each value has a type associated with it that describes the format of the data stored as the value.

For example, the property "My Favorite Song" might contain two representations of audio data: a low-quality, space-efficient version (such as 8-bit mu-law audio—common on the Internet) and a high-quality, large version (such as CD-quality audio). See Figure 9-5.

Bento containers contain a table of contents (TOC) that allows rapid, random access of data within the container.

Container Format

A Bento container is implemented as a series of byte codes. A parser reads the data from the physical storage medium (either disk or RAM) and then creates an in-memory representation of the container structure. (See Figure 9-6.)

Objects begin with the NewObject byte code, which contains tags for the object ID, property ID, and type ID. The parser proceeds, reading properties and

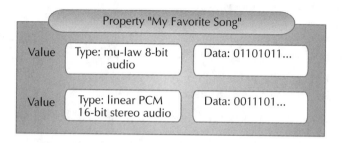

FIGURE 9-5. *Multiple representations of data*

values for the new object. Additional new objects are indicated by NewObject byte codes, until the end of the TOC is reached. At that point, the Bento container structure is in memory and ready to be manipulated by the higher-level routines of the OpenDoc Storage subsystem.

The Bento specification describes several standard properties that should be available in every implementation of Bento:

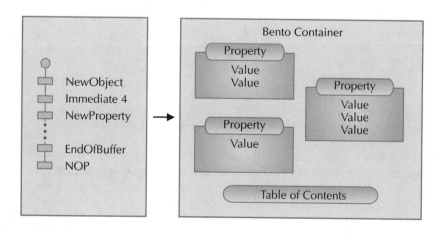

FIGURE 9-6. *Reading byte codes*

■ *TOC_Seed* The value of this property represents the next available user object ID for new objects.

■ *TOC_MinSeed* The value of this property represents the first user object ID in the container. In general, this value is 2^{16}.

■ *TOC_Object* The value of this property represents the table of contents itself. It consists of the TOC data in its entirety.

■ *TOC_Container* This property's value represents the container itself.

■ *TOC_Deleted* This property's value represents the amount of deleted space in the container. As objects are deleted from the container, the space that their values occupied is added to this count.

■ *TOC_Free* The value of this property is the amount of free space available in the container for reuse by new objects.

■ *Type_Name* The value of this property represents the globally unique name of a type.

■ *Property_Name* The value of this property represents the globally unique name of a property.

■ *Base_Type* The value of this property is used to construct structured types from the basic Bento types. Structured types consist of a list of base types. For example, a data structure representing a date might be constructed by combining simple types in the following manner:

```
struct MyDate {
    string    month;
    short     day;
    long      year;
};
```

■ *Object_Reference* The value of this property represents the object ID of another Bento object to which this object holds a reference.

The IMA's specification (noted in the bibliography in Appendix D) contains a thorough treatment of the Bento container format, including flowcharts and grammars. Refer to this and to the original Apple Bento specification (also noted in Appendix D) for a more extensive discussion of Bento.

OSA

Scripting is a powerful technique for building solutions to real-world problems; it enables existing applications and data to be tied together ad hoc. In the past, scripting was used only in well-defined closed systems and was not available ubiquitously across commonly deployed operating systems. Now, however, both problems have been addressed, and scripting languages continue to multiply.

   This section takes a look at scripting systems that conform to the Open Scripting Architecture and some others that are important for their technical merit, their installed base, or their patron. (Some fall into more than one of these categories.)

OSA-Compliant Scripting Languages

OSA provides a specification to govern the way scripting systems express an abstract interface in terms of the operations they support (semantic events) and the data they contain (content model). This abstraction enables different scripting languages to be plugged in to the same bus and have the same effect, even using widely different language constructs. Two of the OSA-compliant languages available are AppleScript and Frontier's UserTalk.

AppleScript
AppleScript was introduced by Apple Computer in 1990. It provides a simple, natural language-like syntax (English, Japanese, and French versions are available). The example in Figure 9-7 shows a simple script that empties the MacOS trash can.

Frontier's UserTalk
UserTalk is Frontier's scripting language. It currently is freely available on the Internet, thanks to its author, Dave Winer. It is a powerful language with a more traditional programming-language structure. Figure 9-8 functions identically to the preceding example: it empties the MacOS trash can.

   Interestingly, both of the example scripts shown in the figures were created by recording user actions. All that was necessary to do was to switch the script editor from AppleScript to UserTalk and perform the action again.

Other Scripting Languages

There are other scripting languages available in the industry. This section gives a brief overview of some of the popular ones. While these languages are not currenly

```
┌─────────────────────────────────────────────┐
│            etrash-applescript                │
│  ▽ Description:                               │
│  ┌─────────────────────────────────────────┐ │
│  │This script opens up the Trash, then      │ │
│  │empties it. It is an example of a simple   │ │
│  │AppleTalk script.                          │ │
│  └─────────────────────────────────────────┘ │
│  ┌───┐ ┌───┐ ┌───┐              ┌───┐        │
│  │ ● │ │ ■ │ │ ▶ │              │ ✓ │        │
│  └───┘ └───┘ └───┘              └───┘        │
│  Record  Stop  Run           Check Syntax    │
│  tell application "Finder"                    │
│        activate                               │
│        select trash                           │
│        open selection                         │
│        empty trash                            │
│  end tell                                     │
│  ┌────────────────┐                           │
│  │ AppleScript ▾  │                           │
│  └────────────────┘                           │
└─────────────────────────────────────────────┘
```

FIGURE 9-7.   *AppleScript*

available in OSA-compliant versions, there is no architectural reason that they couldn't be made to work within OSA at some point.

Tcl/Tk

Tcl (Tool Command Language) and Tk (the Tcl Toolkit) are extremely popular for creating simple scripts as well as complete applications. Tcl was developed at the University of California at Berkeley by Professor John Ousterhout and his research group. They were developing interactive tools for integrated circuit design and discovered that they were spending much of their time developing command languages to control those tools and tie them together. Finally, they hit upon the idea of creating Tcl, a reusable scripting and command language that could be

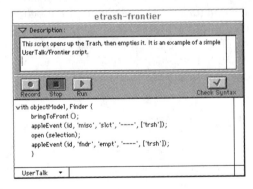

FIGURE 9-8.   *UserTalk*

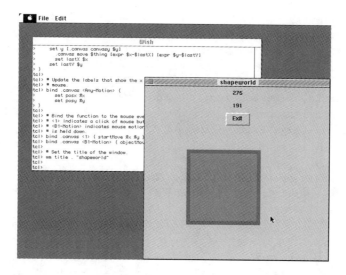

FIGURE 9-9. *A simple Tcl/Tk application*

embedded (as a C library) into any one of their tools. Tk came about as a way to create simple (or complex) graphical user interfaces by using Tcl commands rather than having to use the underlying window systems directly.

The Tcl/Tk developer community is large (in the tens of thousands) and the sources and implementations are freely available. Tcl/Tk was originally developed on Unix, but there are implmentations for most popular operating systems including Windows, OS/2, and MacOS.

Figure 9-9 shows a simple Tcl/Tk application.

Here is the script that creates this simple application.

```
#!/usr/local/bin/wish -f

# "shapeworld"
# This is a simple example of a wish (windowing shell) script;
# a geometric shape can be moved around the screen.

# These lines create two labels; they represent the x and y
# positions of the shape.
label .posx -textvariable posx
label .posy -textvariable posy
```

```
# Tell the geometry manager to add these two labels and place
# a 1 millimeter border around them.
pack .posx .posy -padx 1m -pady 1m

# Create a button, give it a label, and bind it to an
# exit procedure.  (Destroying the top-level widget
# exits the application.)
button .button -text "Exit" -command "destroy."
pack .button

# Create a canvas on which to place the shape; tell the
# geometry manager to start managing it.
canvas .canvas
pack .canvas

# Create a 4 centimeter square (green with grey fill)
set rect [.canvas create rectangle 0c 0c 4c 4c -width 2m \
    -outline aquamarine4 -fill gray60]

# Function to be executed when the mouse button goes down;
# stores the previous value of the x and y coordinates.
proc startMove {x y} {
    global lastX lastY
    set lastX [.canvas canvasx $x]
    set lastY [.canvas canvasy $y]
}


# Function to be executed when the mouse button is down
# and the mouse is moved; move the shape and store
# the new coordinates.
proc objectMove {thing x y} {
    global lastX lastY
    set x [.canvas canvasx $x]
    set y [.canvas canvasy $y]
    .canvas move $thing [expr $x-$lastX] [expr $y-$lastY]
    set lastX $x
    set lastY $y
}


# Update the labels that show the x and y position of the
# mouse.
bind .canvas <Any-Motion> {
```

```
        set posx %x
        set posy %y
}


# Bind the function to the mouse events:
# <1> indicates a click of mouse button 1,
# <B1-Motion> indicates mouse motion while button1
# is held down.
bind .canvas <1> { startMove %x %y }
bind .canvas <B1-Motion> { objectMove $rect %x %y }


# Set the title of the window.
wm title . "shapeworld"
```

For more information, check out the Tcl/Tk Usenet newsgroup **comp.lang.tcl**, or the World Wide Web home page at: **http://www.sunlabs.com/research/tcl/**.

The sources and binary distributions can be found on the SunLabs FTP server at **ftp://ftp.sunlabs.com/pub/tcl/**.

JavaScript

JavaScript is a language from Netscape that is built into the latest versions (2.0 and later) of the Netscape Navigator WWW browser. It is embedded into HTML documents and allows a page designer to embed scripts that react to mouse movement, mouse clicks, page navigation, and other system events. The syntax is similar to that of the Java language from Sun Microsystems, although there are significant differences in the runtime system. (Java has strict type checking and security features that JavaScript does not include.)

Netscape has a complete JavaScript handbook and tutorial on their World Wide Web site at **http://home.netscape.com**.

Figure 9-10 shows a simple JavaScript application, and here is a portion of the code that generated it.

```
<HTML>
<HEAD><TITLE>Interest Calculator</TITLE>

<SCRIPT LANGUAGE="JavaScript">
<!-- hide this script tag's contents from old browsers

function checkNumber(input, min, max, msg)
{
    msg = msg + " field has invalid data: " + input.value;

    var str = input.value;
```

```
for (var i = 0; i < str.length; i++) {
    var ch = str.substring(i, i + 1)
    if ((ch < "0" || "9" < ch) && ch != '.') {
        alert(msg);
        return false;
    }
}
var num = parseFloat(str)
if (num < min || max < num) {
    alert(msg + " not in range [" + min + ".." + max + "]");
    return false;
}
input.value = str;
return true;
}


function computeField(input)
{
    if (input.value != null && input.value.length != 0)
    input.value = "" + eval(input.value);
    computeForm(input.form);
}
```

JavaScript provides a bridge between Java applets and allows a page designer to embed simple behaviors directly in a web page. It remains to be seen whether or not it becomes an Internet standard, but it does appear to have momentum and strong backing.

Visual Basic
Visual Basic from Microsoft is an extremely popular scripting and programming language; Microsoft appears to be making significant progress in adapting it for

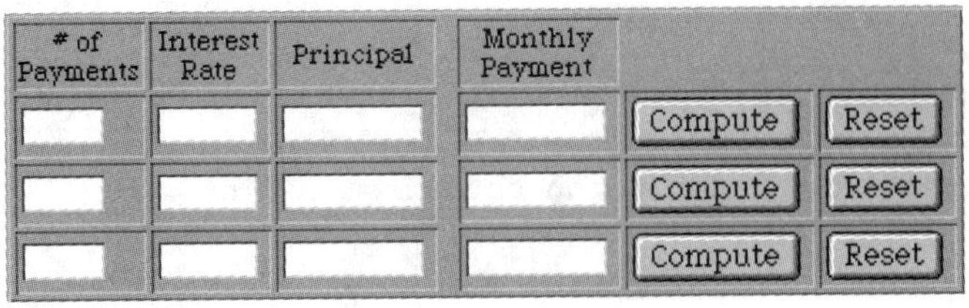

# of Payments	Interest Rate	Principal	Monthly Payment		
				Compute	Reset
				Compute	Reset
				Compute	Reset

FIGURE 9-10. *A simple JavaScript interest calculator*

web-based applications; it is already quite popular in MIS shops requiring custom applications.

An outgrowth of the Basic language that provided Microsoft's start in the 1970s, Visual Basic allows designers to create graphical user interfaces and do simple programming tasks. It has many features of more modern languages, although it is still recognizably Basic, and fairly comprehensible to anyone who has ever done programming in any Basic variant.

The following example (taken from the code samples section of the "Wild Web of Visual Basic" at **http://www.illuminet.net/~jsmith/home.html**) shows a small portion of the code required to create dialog boxes with Visual Basic.

```
Sub btnCD_Click (Index As Integer)
Dim BeginPage, EndPage, NumPage


    Select Case Index
        Case 0 'User chose Open
            CMDialog1.Filename = ""
            CMDialog1.Filter = "Text Files (*.TXT)|*.TXT|Batch Files
(*.BAT)|*.BAT|All Files (*.*)|*.*"
            CMDialog1.FilterIndex = 1
            CMDialog1.Action = 1
            Filename = CMDialog1.Filename
            OpenFile (Filename)
            txtCD.SetFocus
        Case 1 'User chose Save As
            CMDialog1.Filename = ""
            CMDialog1.Filter = "Text Files (*.TXT)|*.TXT|Batch Files
(*.BAT)|*.BAT|All Files (*.*)|*.*"
            CMDialog1.FilterIndex = 1
            CMDialog1.Action = 2
            Filename = CMDialog1.Filename
            CloseFile (Filename)
        Case 2 'User chose Color
            CMDialog1.CancelError = True
            On Error GoTo ErrHandler
            CMDialog1.Flags = &H1&
            CMDialog1.Action = 3
            frmCD.BackColor = CMDialog1.Color
```

For more information, check out the Usenet newsgroup **comp.lang.basic.visual**.

ComponentGlue

ComponentGlue provides a two-way gateway between OpenDoc components and OLE components. An OpenDoc container sees an OLE component as an OpenDoc part, and an OLE container sees OpenDoc parts as first-class OLE objects. In fact, Microsoft will provide its Windows 95 seal to applications that obtain OLE interoperability via OpenDoc and ComponentGlue. Let's take a look at how this technology works.

ComponentGlue provides a complete mapping between the functionality of OpenDoc and OLE. OpenDoc parts appear in the Windows Registry as OLE components, and an OpenDoc document can embed arbitrary OLE objects into itself, including OCXs (OLE Custom Controls). Figure B-5 and the illustration that precedes it in Appendix B show an OpenDoc document on Windows 95, along with a list of OLE embeddable parts. Within a document such as this, ComponentGlue allows cut and paste, drag and drop, and linking between OLE components and between OLE and OpenDoc components. CompoentGlue also maps OpenDoc semantic events to OLE automation and vice versa; scripting languages can control both types of components, regardless of heritage.

ComponentGlue provides two wrappers: on the OpenDoc side, there is OlePart. OlePart acts as an OLE container, and embeds OLE compoents. It provides the standard OLE interfaces such as IUnknown, IClassFactory, IOleItemContainer, and so forth.

OleWrapper encapsulates an OpenDoc part and allows it to act as an OLE server; this lets it be embedded into OLE documents as any other OLE object would be. It provides the key OLE server interfaces; among them are IUnknown, IDataObject, and IOleObject.

ComponentGlue is part of the Windows SDK; it will be available on the Macintosh in mid-1996 and then possibly on the OS/2 and AIX/Unix platforms by the end of the year.

Putting It Together

This chapter provided a higher level of technical detail regarding the operations of the technologies that underlie OpenDoc. For additional information, refer to the annotated bibliography in Appendix D.

Chapter 10 explores some future possibilities for OpenDoc and describes additional resources available to OpenDoc part developers and users.

CHAPTER 10

OpenDoc: Current Systems and Future Possibilities

This final chapter discusses some of the announced future directions for OpenDoc. It also discusses how the OpenDoc architecture, with its extensibility, provides the basis for replaceable subsystems and additional user-definable behaviors.

The OpenDoc architecture provides a platform on which third-party software vendors can build innovative solutions to problems; this chapter explores some of the products that are taking advantage of OpenDoc right now. The system is itself extensible, and, in a number of areas, new capabilities are being added to the base OpenDoc system; this chapter explores some of these as well. The chapter concludes with some speculation about future directions for OpenDoc in terms of applications and adoption.

The preceding nine chapters explained and illustrated the major points of the OpenDoc component software architecture, but the story is still incomplete. In a sense, describing OpenDoc is akin to describing a system of roads, freeways, traffic signals, and traffic laws, without discussing automobiles or trucks. OpenDoc provides foundations, facilities, and infrastructure; these are then used by software makers to deliver their technologies to users.

OpenDoc is just starting to become available to the general public; 1996 will mark the deployment of OpenDoc across all of the major operating systems. Despite having been available for only a short time, OpenDoc is already being used in a number of projects. These range from commercial ventures such as Oracle's PowerObjects product to educational projects such as SimCalc, being developed at the University of Massachusetts and the University of California at Berkeley.

In addition, service-oriented businesses are springing up, especially on the World Wide Web, that take advantage of OpenDoc. Kantara Development designed its PartMerchant site to facilitate commercial part development and distribution. Participants in the Java-OpenDoc Internet mailing list have come up with some interesting ideas to combine these two new technologies. Cyberdog, from Apple, enables applications to incorporate Internet-related features, making the network a ubiquitous resource.

Here's how the chapter is organized. It starts with a brief overview of some of the commercial products that plan to use OpenDoc: Adobe's Acrobat, Illustrator, and Photoshop; and Oracle's PowerObjects. Then it describes an educational project: SimCalc attempts to make the principles of calculus easier for students to understand. Next, it introduces Kantara Development's PartMerchant system for OpenDoc part distribution.

The chapter then moves to applications of the future. It describes a mailing list devoted to issues of integration between Sun Microsystems' Java language and OpenDoc. The future of computing is becoming inextricably interlinked with the Internet and so appears to depend on open, multiplatform, or platform-independent components. Applets, parts, OCXen, and scripts are driving the next stage of commercial and social developments in computing. Because of this, the chapter also discusses Cyberdog, which allows any OpenDoc-aware application to take advantage of the Internet.

OpenDoc has the technical merits and heritage to benefit from and facilitate the changes now taking place. Its technology can provide answers to many questions and solutions to many problems, if it is applied correctly.

We hope that this book has provided a good introduction to the technical aspects of OpenDoc as well as to the rationale behind its use and development. The next step for this technology depends on technically savvy managers and developers who see the advantages of OpenDoc and adopt it as a part of their long-term strategies.

Current Uses of OpenDoc

OpenDoc 1.0 for MacOS was released in November 1995 and on OS/2 in January of 1996. Windows and AIX versions are expected later in 1996. Already, more than a thousand developers have announced support for OpenDoc, and some are beginning to ship products based on OpenDoc. Table 10-1 is a partial list of these developers.

This section takes a look at two of the larger commercial vendors, along with educational and service-oriented projects currently underway.

Commercial Projects: Oracle PowerObjects and Adobe Illustrator, Photoshop, and Acrobat

Naturally, the OpenDoc sponsors and full members are some of the earliest companies to take advantage of OpenDoc; they believe it will be to their strategic

Genentech	Federal Express
America Online	Boeing Aircraft
Addison-Wesley	Viacom
Global Village	Jet Propulsion Laboratory
Ingram Micro	Knight-Ridder
Bank of America	TCI
Fireman's Fund Insurance	Claris
TRW	LucasFilm
Lockheed Martin	Virtus

TABLE 10-1. *OpenDoc Developers*

benefit to change their models of software development and distribution. In some cases, using OpenDoc is a way to ensure that their products and file formats become widely adopted and available on multiple platforms.

Oracle PowerObjects is a set of tools for building front ends to commercial relational databases. It will allow users to quickly and easily build custom database applications. PowerObjects will take advantage of OpenDoc technology to integrate it with more traditional compound document systems.

Adobe is planning to provide viewer and editor parts for the Adobe Illustrator, Photoshop, and Acrobat data formats.

Educational Project Example: SimCalc

Because OpenDoc is an open standard and will be widely available, it is a wise choice for educational markets. (This is especially true given Apple's strong position in the K to 12 educational market.) This section focuses on SimCalc, an ambitious project that makes extensive use of OpenDoc and whose proponents are very visible in the OpenDoc developer community.

Calculus, the "mathematics of change," is a means of describing mathematically many real-world problems. Being familiar with its concepts is an important part of living and working in a modern society, yet many students do not study it. For example, problems involving limits, rates, accumulations, and approximations appear in many real-world problems that involve

- Money
- Motion
- Planning
- Nutrition

Unfortunately, although the concepts involved can be taught in a hands-on, intuitive fashion, calculus is usually taught only after a whole series of prerequisites that tend to weed out all but engineering students and students with similar interests.

The SimCalc project attempts to make the concepts of calculus more accessible to mainstream students by combining new curriculum ideas with advanced computer simulations. The software being developed is intended for students from the third grade all the way through college. The project focuses especially on those students who would not otherwise have access to these important mathematical ideas.

Because of the broad audience and the need for specialization, the project uses a component architecture—OpenDoc—that allows plug-and-play animation and scriptability. These are just some of SimCalc's features:

- *Computer-based games* Students play such games as "UFO World," a space-theme game that simulates motions and trajectories.

- *Exploration* Students can manipulate objects in various "worlds" along with cartoon-like figures that "live" in the simulation.

- *Mixed computer and physical simulations* Students work with simulations, such as "Elevator World," that accurately reflect the real world and complete lab exercises to make the concepts more concrete.

Because SimCalc uses OpenDoc, the instructor has the freedom to create custom applications and exercises. In addition, e-mail capabilities can simplify data collection for lab exercises.

Service-Oriented Project Example: Kantara Development

The field of component software will offer new business opportunities. One company already making a place for itself in this wide-open field is Kantara Development, the focus of this section. Kantara is just one example of a business offering value-added services in addition to software.

Kantara Development has seen that there are some questions to be answered about OpenDoc and has tried to provide responses. Although OpenDoc has eliminated several limitations faced by traditional application developers, it has raised new questions:

- What happens when a user opens a document that contains parts for which he or she has no editors?

- Where might that user go to find a part viewer or editor?

- Where might that user find additional part editors or viewers?

- Which editors are available across all platforms?

- How do the economics of "partware" translate into a viable development market?

Kantara is providing both OpenDoc-based components (its HeronMail product) and, via PartMerchant, an infrastructure for buying and selling OpenDoc components.

The following sections present some of the services and products that Kantara provides.

PartMerchant

Kantara's PartMerchant (PM) is an Internet site dedicated to providing a secure, convenient way to purchase and download OpenDoc parts on demand. It will support all of the OpenDoc platforms: Windows, MacOS, OS/2, and AIX/Unix. The PartMerchant site is available 24 hours a day, 7 days a week, and purchases can be made rapidly. Because the web site is always available, users connected to the Internet can add any necessary functions to their applications quickly and without incurring the expense of traditional software distribution methods. In addition, developers can automatically obtain registrations from purchasers of their products. PartMerchant is available at **http://www.partmerchant.com**.

PM Finder

PM Finder is an OpenDoc extension that modifies OpenDoc's default behavior upon encountering a data type for which there is no editor or viewer. Instead of displaying a NullPart (a gray rectangle that indicates an unknown data type), PM Finder displays options for automatically retrieving the missing part from the PartMerchant web site.

If the user wishes, then PM Finder can connect to the PartMerchant web site and search for an appropriate editor or viewer. The user can select a free viewer for download or elect to purchase and then download the editor for the missing data type.

PM Fetch

PM Fetch is an OpenDoc component that provides a Buy button that can be incorporated into demo or trial versions of applications or components. For example, a viewer for the Portable Network Graphics format could have a Buy Editor button as part of the component's About... box. If the user wants to be able to manipulate rather than just view PNG graphics files, then he or she can be taken directly to the PartMerchant site where the editor is available for purchase. In addition, this capability can be used to offer new versions of products to current users.

Safety and Security

Currently, PartMerchant supports the CyberCash system for secure financial transactions over the Internet. Kantara plans to support other secure transaction methods in the future, including those from Digicash and First Virtual Holdings.

All of these secure payment systems make sure that sensitive financial data (such as credit card numbers) are protected. The PartMerchant site never receives the credit card number directly; instead, the transaction is encrypted and passes directly between the buyer and the bank, with PartMerchant receiving an authorization number when the transaction is approved.

odz: The OpenDoc Zine

PartMerchant provides a monthly forum called odz (pronounced "odds") to provide information to the OpenDoc development community. It contains interviews, articles on OpenDoc, and product reviews. The first issue is to be published early in 1996.

Support for Small Developers

PartMerchant provides a special category for products from small developers, who often want to sell small components at a low cost. Because PartMerchant provides all of the infrastructure required (including the processing of credit card orders), it allows developers to sells such products economically.

Other Services

In addition to the services currently available, Kantara plans several more services to help make the process of locating and purchasing OpenDoc parts easier:

- *Datatype services* The PartMerchant databases will be made available to developers who want to create parts that can query for the presence of other part editor or viewer types at runtime. For example, a presentation package might be able to query to learn what additional presentation effect modules are available. A package developer could upload additional modules and let the installed base upgrade itself incrementally.

   As a part of this plan, Kantara will be implementing a version control scheme for OpenDoc components. When enabled by the user, it would allow parts to check in with the PartMerchant web site and determine if they are the latest version available. If they are not, the user could choose to update the software.

- *Installation and updating* Kantara has stated that it will be working with other organizations to support standards for installing and updating components, allowing the version control system to automatically update components, if desired.

- *Licensing* Finally, Kantara will be working with corporations to bring licensing technologies to OpenDoc parts. Kantara plans a version of PM Finder that will be able to query internal corporate part repositories before venturing out to the Internet. It will also be able to keep track of licenses for part editors in use.

Kantara is only one example of a business that provides services to the OpenDoc developer and user community. In general, there are many opportunities for businesses, among them setting up infrastructure for purchasing and distributing OpenDoc parts, maintaining development suggestion lists, or writing about the needs and issues facing the OpenDoc community. OpenDoc and component software in general will open up new market niches in licensing, development, and marketing of software.

Future Uses of OpenDoc

This section explores some of the more cutting-edge and speculative applications of OpenDoc technology.

Java/OpenDoc List

Java and OpenDoc are complementary technologies, not competing ones. There is an Internet mailing list devoted to discussion involving the two technologies and how they can be combined to provide new and innovative solutions.

One of the most obvious interesting applications would be to provide an OpenDoc part that contained a Java interpreter. Java applets then become another data type (such as GIF, audio, or rich text) that can be embedded in any application. This should be available within the year, as people have already started work on it.

Once the CORBA bindings for Java have been finalized, then OpenDoc part editors will be able to be implemented in Java, allowing true portability across platforms. A developer, having already designed the IDL interface to her part editor, could write one implementation that could run portably on any platform that supported Java and OpenDoc.

To join the mailing list send mail to

java-opendoc-request@cuesys.com

Cyberdog and the Internet

Cyberdog, from Apple Computer, is the first in a new class of software enabled by OpenDoc: the cooperative part suite. A cooperative part suite is a set of parts that can be used together or separately to provide a scaleable set of functions for use in a variety of applications.

In Cyberdog's case, these functions are related to the Internet and to network operations, including parts that can handle all of the popular Internet protocols:

- File Transfer Protocol, FTP

- Hypertext Transfer Protocol, HTTP (the World Wide Web protocol)

- Network News Transfer Protocol , NNTP

- Post Office Protocol, POP

- Simple Mail Transfer Protocol, SMTP

- Gopher protocol

- Telnet

Figure 10-1 shows a Cyberdog connection dialog, with a list of some available Internet services.

A fairly stable alpha version of Cyberdog was released on the OpenDoc DR4 CD. (Because of the product's newness, note that some of the information presented here is preliminary and may change by the time Cyberdog is realized as a final product, expected sometime in 1996.)

Developers can create new objects and insert them into the Cyberdog framework at many levels: the user interface level, the protocol level, or the

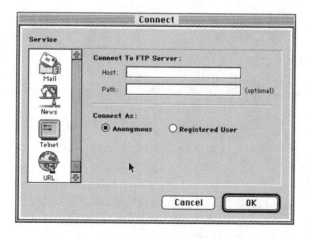

FIGURE 10-1. *Cyberdog connection dialog box*

network level. Developers can extend Cyberdog's core capabilities or add additional data types or access methods.

Cyberdog was designed to provide common facilities for some of the most common tasks associated with retrieving and organizing content from the Internet. Because of this, much of the code can be reused when adding a new service, and that service can itself be accessed from other components.

Cyberdog was also designed so that built-in services and newly added developer-created services are indistinguishable—both are first-class objects and can be used in any context. All components use the same public IDL interfaces and SOM classes as other OpenDoc parts, with some additions. This reusability means that developers can concentrate on pieces where they can add value—a theme throughout this book. A new display part, for example, can plug into Cyberdog to retrieve data; it need not duplicate any of the network functions already provided by the framework. Similarly, a developer of a new network protocol can use existing display or organizational components to display the retrieved data. For example, a display part can be reused to display electronic mail, files on a remote file server, or graphical representations of machines on a network. Normally, a new piece of display software would have to be written for each new protocol: Cyberdog allows reuse.

Cyberdog provides some organizational metaphors than can be used to provide some order to a user's Internet wanderings. Figure 10-2 shows a notebook part that provides a hierarchical way to store network addresses and items. Remember, this

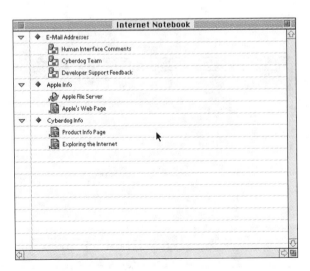

FIGURE 10-2. *Internet Notebook*

notebook can be embedded in any other OpenDoc document, providing instant access to network resources.

Cyberdog

The Cyberdog project has several key goals:

- To leverage OpenDoc's capabilities to integrate networked content with other types of data. Cyberdog is a way of embedding Internet data objects seamlessly into a document.

- To provide public, well-documented interfaces to its functions and allow developers to add new capabilities with a minimum of trouble.

- To encourage extensions to the base set of viewers and browsers, in part by making it easy to add new services without having to endure much of the drudgery of network programming. Developers can concentrate their effort where it will bring them the maximum return.

- To make it easy to add extensions to the system. Taking advantage of OpenDoc's dynamic extension capabilities and editor swapping, the developer can customize the document or application on the fly to match the requirements of the underlying data.

Protocol and Data Type Handling in Cyberdog

Cyberdog handles two categories of items: protocols and data types. Protocols consist of the standard Internet protocols (among them FTP, HTTP, and SMTP) and data types consist of GIF, JPEG, HTML, MIME, and so forth. These two abstractions are handled by different object classes, allowing any data type to be retrieved using any protocol.

Major Classes

Cyberdog objects inherit from three major abstract superclasses. Each defines the public interfaces that correspond to the tasks for that particular piece of the framework. Each is extensively subclassed to handle the many protocols and data types that Cyberdog understands. The three superclasses are

- *CyberStream*   CyberStream is an abstraction that represents the method for actually retrieving some data type over the network via a particular protocol such as FTP, gopher, or HTTP.

- *CyberItem*   A CyberItem is essentially an address of some data object on the network. When a CyberItem is combined with the CyberStream, the item can be retrieved and displayed to the user.

■ *CyberService* A CyberService represents the sum of the items necessary to implement a new network protocol or service. In Cyberdog, this represents a CyberStream and CyberItem pair.

Every protocol has a selection of the three Cyberdog superclasses associated with it. For example, a Cyberdog part that understands the World Wide Web would implement a WebItem, WebStream, and WebService object. Protocol classes are loaded and unloaded dynamically—a user never needs to know how the requested data was retrieved.

As with protocols, the appropriate data-handling machinery is swapped in as needed, using the standard OpenDoc machinery for selecting a part editor for a particular data type. In this case, the data comes from the network instead of from an OpenDoc storage unit on a local hard drive. If a data type is unknown, then Cyberdog can ask for input from the user; for example, a user might know that their new graphics editor part can handle a new format that comes in over the network and match it to that editor.

Cyberdog allows any OpenDoc document to be a starting point for Internet exploration; the Internet Pathfinder part, shown in Figure 10-3, is a top-level view on the networked world.

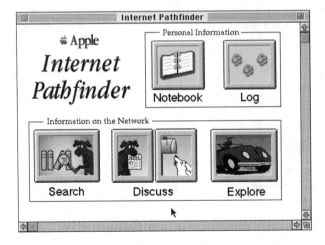

FIGURE 10-3. *Internet Pathfinder*

OpenDoc Everywhere

OpenDoc can be used in many different ways, and it remains to be seen what innovative developers and marketers will invent. This last section of the book will talk about some additional possibilities.

Object Management Group Compound Document Services

One of the most recent (and exciting) developments is the action of the Object Management Group's technical committee: it voted to recommend that OpenDoc be adopted as the CORBA standard for Compound Document Services. This would immediately make OpenDoc a major industry standard and give impetus to the hundreds of OMG members to actively support OpenDoc. As of this writing, the OMG membership is voting on the proposal; it is expected to pass.

OpenDoc as an HTML Replacement

Another possibility is to make OpenDoc technologies a part of a future version of HTML, the Hypertext Markup Language. The current version has a few shortcomings that OpenDoc might help address, as well as provide the following benefits:

- OpenDoc is designed to be portable across platforms and offers easy data exchange.

- It supports a complex and powerful embedding protocol.

- OpenDoc has a framework for infinitely extensible data types.

- HTML and OpenDoc can coexist, as shown by Cyberdog.

Corporate Information Services Based on OpenDoc

Chapter 8 gave an example of a corporate IS shop moving toward an OpenDoc-based system. Here are a few highlights and additional possibilities:

- Standard editors obtained from a server, automatically upgraded

- Key-server style checkout of user licenses for site-licensed editors

- Client parts that use legacy databases and systems

- Stationery and documents facilitating setup, training, and standard operations

- Drafts used to support document history, document tracking, and collaborative exchange

- Viewers and specialized editors allowing easy distribution of data while retaining strong security protection

- Combination of commercial off-the-shelf software with custom-made editors, scripts, and stationery allows for in-house creation of vertical solutions

Adopting OpenDoc is a way to improve productivity and capabilities through efficiency improvements and feature additions, while protecting an investment in legacy systems.

Putting It Together

This chapter described some innovative ways that current software vendors and developers are using OpenDoc. It also discussed some possible future uses for OpenDoc and component software.

Finally, a note about the "Putting It Together" sections at the end of each chapter. The name is no coincidence; the benefits from OpenDoc come from taking ideas and tools, both old and new, and putting them together in new ways. This book has explained the rationale, concepts, justifications, and technical details behind OpenDoc, from basic concepts and ideas, through a tutorial on building a part editor, and finally to applications of OpenDoc technology to real-world problems. The book has delved into a bit of technical detail and returned to speculate about the ways that OpenDoc might be used in the future.

OpenDoc is an exciting technology, and represents a first step towards the next generation of software. We hope that you will be able to put the pieces together in ways that will serve you well.

APPENDIX A

Class Reference

This appendix provides a class reference for OpenDoc, concentrating on the classes and subsystems discussed in this book.

Several tables help organize the classes because there are several different ways of looking at OpenDoc's structure:

- OpenDoc classes by subsystem
- OpenDoc classes that can be subclassed
- Abstract superclasses in OpenDoc

Following the tables is an alphabetical list of the OpenDoc classes: each entry contains the class name and its superclasses and subclasses, along with a list of the methods for that class. Each method is followed by a brief discussion of its function.

207

For a complete class reference including the arguments to each method, see the *OpenDoc Class Reference*, which is listed in Appendix D, "Bibliography and Resources."

One way to learn about OpenDoc is to examine each subsystem in isolation. Table A-1 shows the OpenDoc classes arranged by subsystem.

An implementor of an OpenDoc part can subclass a limited number of classes, shown in Table A-2. The remaining classes provide services and a client interface, but are not modified when a new part editor is written.

Finally, there are three abstract superclasses in OpenDoc: all other OpenDoc classes are subclasses of these three. These three classes are never instantiated directly; in other words, one might see instances of a class subclassed from ODRefCntObject, but would never see nor use an ODRefCntObject itself.

OpenDoc consists of 65 classes, which are listed in the following pages.

Methods followed by (MacOS) are specified to the Mac operating system. Those methods followed by (document shell) are called only by the document shell.

ODAddressDesc

Superclasses   ODDesc → ODObject

Subclasses   none

The ODAddressDesc class is a wrapper for an AEAddressDesc structure; this structure contains a target destination address descriptor.

InitODAddressDesc   Initializes the address descriptor.

ODAppleEvent

Superclasses   ODRecord → ODDescList→ ODDesc → ODObject

Subclasses   none

The ODAppleEvent class is a wrapper for an AppleEvent event structure.

InitODAppleEvent   Initializes the AppleEvent structure.

Binding	ODBinding	
Core	ODEmbeddedFramesIterator	ODSession
	ODExtension	ODPart
	ODInfo	ODPersistentObject
	ODNameSpace	ODRefCntObject
	ODNameSpaceManager	ODSettingsExtension
	ODObjectIterator	ODValueIterator
	ODObjectNameSpace	ODValueNameSpace
	ODObject	
Imaging	ODCanvas	ODTransform
	ODShape	
Layout	ODFacet	ODFrame
	ODFacetIterator	ODFrameFacetIterator
Messaging	ODAddressDesc	ODNameResolver
	ODAppleEvent	ODObjectSpec
	ODDesc	ODOSLToken
	ODDescList	ODRecord
	ODMessageInterface	ODSemanticInterface
Storage	ODClipboard	ODLinkSpec
	ODContainer	ODPlatformTypeListIterator
	ODDocument	ODPlatformTypeList
	ODDraft	ODStorageSystem
	ODDragAndDrop	ODStorageUnitCursor
	ODDragItemIterator	ODStorageUnitRefIterator
	ODLink	ODStorageUnitView
	ODLinkManager	ODTranslation
	ODLinkSource	ODTypeList
		ODTypeListIterator
User Interface	ODArbitrator	ODFocusSet
	ODDispatcher	ODFocusSetIterator
	ODDispatchModule	ODMenuBar
	ODFocusModule	ODUndo
	ODFocusOwnerIterator	ODWindow
		ODWindowIterator
		ODWindowState

TABLE A-1.   *OpenDoc Classes Arranged by Subsystem*

ODPart	ODEmbeddedFramesIterator	ODExtension
ODSemanticInterface	ODSettingsExtension	ODDispatchModule
ODFocusModule	ODTransform	

TABLE A-2. *OpenDoc Classes to Subclass*

ODPart	ODRefCntObject
ODPersistentObject	

TABLE A-3. *OpenDoc Abstract Superclasses*

ODArbitrator

Superclasses   ODObject

Subclasses   none

The ODArbitrator class manages the temporary ownership of shared resources (or foci) among parts.

Focus Module Registration

These methods involve registration of focus modules.

IsFocusRegistered   Indicates whether or not the specified focus is registered with the Arbitrator.

RegisterFocus   Registers a specified focus module for the focus.

UnregisterFocus   Breaks the connection between a given focus and the focus module that manages it.

GetFocusModule   Returns a focus module reference for a given focus.

Focus Ownership

These methods are used to determine focus module ownership.

IsFocusExclusive   Indicates whether or not the given focus is exclusive.

AcquireFocusOwner   Returns a reference to the frame that owns a particular exclusive focus.

CreateOwnerIterator   Creates an iterator that returns the frames that own a particular nonexclusive focus.

Focus Transfer

These methods involve focus transfer among parts.

RequestFocus   Requests that the focus ownership be assigned to the given frame.

RequestFocusSet   Requests ownership of each focus in the given focus set for the specified frame.

RelinquishFocus   Called to relinquish ownership of the given focus.

RelinquishFocusSet   Called to relinquish ownership of the given focus set.

TransferFocus   Called to transfer a focus from its current owner to another owner.

TransferFocusSet   Called to transfer a focus set from its current owner to another owner.

Focus Sets

This method deals with focus set creation.

CreateFocusSet   Creates and initializes a focus set.

ODBinding

Superclasses   ODObject

Subclasses   none
An instance of the ODBinding class represents the OpenDoc runtime binding system: this object matches parts in a document with the appropriate part editor.

ChooseEditorForPart   Specifies which editor will be used to edit a particular part in a document.

ODCanvas

Superclasses   ODObject

Subclasses   none
An ODCanvas object represents and wraps a drawing structure for a particular graphics system. This structure represents the environment in which images are created.

Canvas Properties

These methods involve the characteristics of a particular canvas.

AcquireBiasTransform   Returns a reference to the bias transform for the canvas.

SetBiasTransform   Associates a particular bias transform with the canvas.

GetFacet   Returns a reference to the facet for the canvas.

SetFacet   Assigns a particular facet to the canvas.

AcquireOwner   Returns a reference to the owner of the canvas. This method returns a reference to an OpenDoc part.

SetOwner   Makes a particular part the owner of the canvas.

IsDynamic   Indicates whether or not the canvas is dynamic.

IsOffscreen   Indicates whether or not the canvas is offscreen.

Drawing Structures

The following methods manipulate the drawing structures associated with the canvas.

GetPlatformCanvas   Returns a platform-specific drawing structure associated with the canvas.

SetPlatformCanvas   Specifies a platform-specific drawing structure for the canvas.

HasPlatformCanvas   Indicates whether the canvas contains (or can obtain) a drawing structure for the specified graphics system.

GetGXViewPort (MacOS)   Returns a QuickDraw GX drawing structure for the canvas. Requires QuickDraw GX.

GetQDPort (MacOS)   Returns a QuickDraw Classic drawing structure for the canvas.

Invalidating and Updating

These methods deal with invalidating and updating canvases and shapes.

AcquireUpdateShape   Returns the area of the canvas that will need to be updated. This method returns a reference to an object of type ODShape.

ResetUpdateShape   Resets the update shape for the canvas by setting it to be an empty shape.

Invalidate   Adds an area to the update shape for the canvas. This method is used to ensure that a particular area is redrawn if necessary.

Validate   Removes a particular area from the canvas' update shape.

Printing

Print jobs are controlled by the following methods.

GetPlatformPrintJob   For a particular graphics system, returns a print job for the canvas.

SetPlatformPrintJob   Associates a print job with the canvas. The graphics system must be specified.

HasPlatformPrintJob   For a particular graphics system, indicates whether or not the canvas has a print job associated with it.

ODClipboard

Superclasses   ODObject

Subclasses   none

The ODClipboard class represents an abstraction for transferring data among OpenDoc parts and between OpenDoc and other document systems.

Data Access

These methods deal with the data contained by the clipboard object.

Clear   Empties all data from the clipboard.

GetContentStorageUnit   This method returns a reference to the storage unit that contains the clipboard data.

Dialog Boxes

This method controls the Paste As... dialog box.

ShowPasteAsDialog (MacOS)   Displays the Paste As... dialog box and controls which options will be displayed there.

Drafts and Updates

These methods control the transfer of data to and from the clipboard object.

ExportClipboard (document shell)   Updates the contents of the system clipboard if the data it contains is different from the data contained by the clipboard object.

DraftClosing (document shell)   Called when the specified draft is going to be closed or its contents reverted to an earlier version.

DraftSaved (document shell)   Called to notify the clipboard object when a particular draft has been saved.

GetUpdateID Returns information about the current version of the clipboard object.

SetPlatformClipboard Updates the contents of the system clipboard if the data it contains is different from the data contained by the clipboard object. This method takes a type specifier, and transfers data of the specified type.

Undo and Redo

These methods notify the clipboard of the progress of undo and redo actions.

ActionDone Called at the completion of a Cut, Copy, or Paste action.

ActionUndone Called when a Cut, Copy, or Paste action is undone.

ActionRedone Called when a Cut, Copy, or Paste action is redone.

ODContainer

Superclasses ODRefCntObject → ODObject

Subclasses none

The ODContainer class represents a collection of OpenDoc documents, stored as a unit. It represents an abstract interface for manipulating the documents, regardless of the physical implementation (database, RAM, flat file) of the container.

Document and Storage System

These methods return references to specific objects associated with the container.

AcquireDocument (document shell) Given a document identifier, returns a particular document object.

GetStorageSystem   Returns a reference to the creator of this particular
container.

Names and Identifiers

These methods are concerned with names and identifiers for the container.

GetID   Returns an identifier for the container.

GetName   Returns the name of the container.

SetName (document shell)   Sets the name of the container.

ODDesc

Superclasses   ODObject

Subclasses   ODOSLToken, ODObjectSpec, ODAddressDesc, and ODDescList
The ODDesc class represents and wraps an AppleEvent descriptor structure.

InitODDesc   Initializes the descriptor.

GetDescType   Returns the descriptor type of the descriptor.

SetDescType   Sets the descriptor type of the descriptor.

GetRawData   Returns the raw data contained by the descriptor.

SetRawData   Overwrites any current data contained by the descriptor with new
raw data.

ODDescList

Superclasses   ODDesc → ODObject

Subclasses   ODRecord
   The ODDescList class represents and wraps an AEDescList structure, a list of other descriptor structures.

InitODDescList   Initializes the descriptor list.

ODDispatcher

Superclasses   ODObject

Subclasses   none
   The Dispacher object in OpenDoc is responsible for distributing events to part editors. The ODDispatcher class represents that object.

Events

These four methods deal with events and monitoring.

Dispatch (document shell)   Dispatches a specified event to the proper part.

Redispatch   Redispatches a specified event to the proper part.

AddMonitor   Adds a dispatch module monitor to the dispatch module dictionary.

RemoveMonitor   Removes a dispatch module monitor from the dispatch module dictionary.

Exiting

These methods control exit behavior for the document shell.

Exit (document shell)   Indicates to the dispatcher that the document shell should terminate. This method takes a Boolean (true or false) value.

ShouldExit (document shell)   Indicates whether or not the document shell should terminate.

Idle Time and Processor Time

These five methods allow parts to register requests for processor and idle time.

RegisterIdle (MacOS)   Adds the part and frame to the idle-time request list.

UnregisterIdle (MacOS)   Removes the part and frame from the idle-time request list.

GetSleepTime (MacOS, document shell)   Returns the amount of time that the document can sleep before it must wake up and continue processing idle-time requests from parts and frames.

SetIdleFrequency (MacOS)   Specifies the idle frequency for a particular part or frame.

Yield (MacOS)   Allows other parts to use available processor time.

Manipulating Dispatch Modules

These methods manipulate dispatch modules.

AddDispatchModule   For a given event type, adds the dispatch module to the dispatch module dictionary.

GetDispatchModule   For a given event type, returns a reference to the proper dispatch module.

RemoveDispatchModule   For a specified event type, removes the dispatch module from the dispatch module dictionary.

Pointer

These methods manipulate data structures associated with the mouse pointer.

GetMouseRegion (MacOS, document shell)   Returns a region associated with the current mouse position. This region is used to help dispatch mouse-motion events to the appropriate part editor.

SetMouseRegion (MacOS)   Sets the region to be used to dispatch mouse events.

InvalidateFacetUnderMouse (MacOS)   Invalidates the facet under the current position of the mouse pointer. The facet is set to kODNULL.

ODDispatchModule

Superclasses   ODObject

Subclasses   none
    An ODDispatch module distributes one or more types of events to OpenDoc part editors.

InitDispatchModule   Initializes the dispatch module.

Dispatch   Distributes a particular event to a part.

ODDocument

Superclasses   ODRefCntObject → ODObject

Subclasses   none
    The ODDocument class represents an OpenDoc document and its associated drafts.

Creating and Naming Drafts

These methods deal with creating and naming drafts.

CreateDraft (document shell)   Adds a new draft to the document. This becomes the most recent draft.

Exists   Indicates whether or not the document contains the specified draft.

SetName (document shell)   Sets the document's name.

Manipulating and Retrieving Drafts

The methods listed below involve the manipulation and retrieval of drafts.

CollapseDrafts (document shell)   Removes drafts from the document.

AcquireBaseDraft (document shell)   Returns a reference to the base draft of the document.

AcquireDraft (document shell)   Returns a reference to a particular draft of the document.

SaveToAPrevDraft (document shell)   Saves modifications of one or more drafts to a previous draft.

SetBaseDraftFromForeignDraft (document shell)   Changes the base draft of this document. This method takes a reference to a draft from another document.

GetContainer   Returns a reference to the document's creator.

GetID   Obtains the identifier for the document.

GetName   Returns the document's name.

ODDraft

Superclasses   ODRefCntObject → ODObject

Subclasses   none
   An ODDraft object represents a particular version of a document.

Cloning

These methods control the cloning of drafts.

BeginClone   Initiates a transaction to transfer data from one storage unit to another.

Clone   Transfers data between storage units.

WeakClone   Clones the object, maintaining weak persistent references.

EndClone   Commits the cloning transfer begun by BeginClone.

AbortClone   Aborts the cloning transaction.

Creation and Deletion

The ODDraft object acts as a factory for several different types of OpenDoc objects. These methods create and destroy these objects.

CreateFrame   Creates a new frame object.

AcquireFrame   Given a storage unit, returns a reference to the frame stored therein.

AcquireLink   Returns a reference to a particular link object associated with the storage unit.

CreateLinkSource   Produces a new link-source object.

AcquireLinkSource   Returns a reference to a particular link-source object associated with the storage unit.

CreateLinkSpec   Produces a new link-specification object for the specified part.

CreatePart   Creates a new part.

AcquirePart   Returns a reference to a particular part associated with the storage unit.

CreateStorageUnit   Creates a new storage unit.

AcquireStorageUnit   Given a storage unit identifier, returns a particular storage unit.

RemoveFrame   Removes a particular frame.

RemoveLink   Removes a particular link object.

RemoveLinkSource   Removes a particular link-source object.

RemovePart   Removes a particular part.

RemoveStorageUnit   Removes a particular storage unit.

Draft Attributes

This group of methods is used to view and manipulate certain attributes of the draft.

GetDocument (document shell)   Returns a reference to the draft's creator.

AcquireDraftProperties   This method returns a reference to the storage unit where the draft stores its properties and global data.

GetID (document shell)   Returns the draft's identifier.

IsValidID   Indicates whether or not a particular object identifier is valid.

GetPermissions   Obtains the current permissions for the specified draft.

GetPersistentObjectID   Obtains a persistent identifier for the draft.

AcquirePersistentObject   Using a persistent object identifier, returns a reference to the specified object.

Modifying Drafts

These methods are called to modify drafts.

Externalize (document shell)   Synchronizes the draft objects with the storage unit, writing out to persistent storage any updated information.

RemoveChanges (document shell)   Deletes all changes to the draft.

RemoveFromDocument (document shell)   Deletes the draft from the document.

ReleasePart   Releases a part associated with the draft.

SaveToAPrevious (document shell)   Copies draft contents to a previous draft in this document.

ChangedFromPrev (document shell)   Indicates whether or not this draft contains any changes relative to the previous draft.

SetChangedFromPrev   Indicates that this draft has changed from the previous one. This method takes a Boolean (true or false) value.

ODDragAndDrop

Superclasses   ODObject

Subclasses   none

The ODDragAndDrop class provides mechanisms for directly manipulating the contents of a document and moving items within parts, between parts, among OpenDoc documents, and between other applications and OpenDoc documents.

Clear   Empties the storage unit associated with the drag-and-drop operation.

StartDrag   Starts a drag-and-drop operation.

GetContentStorageUnit   Returns a reference to the storage unit associated with the drag-and-drop operation.

GetDragAttributes   Returns information about the drag-and-drop operation.

GetDragReference (MacOS)   On MacOS, returns the MacOS DragManager reference number corresponding to the drag-and-drop operation.

ShowPasteAsDialog (MacOS)   Displays the Paste As... dialog box and controls which options will be displayed there.

ODDragItemIterator

Superclasses   ODObject

Subclasses   none

An ODDragItemIterator allows clients to access each storage unit associated with a drag-and-drop operation.

First   Starts the iteration and returns the first item.

Next   Returns the next item in sequence.

IsNotComplete   Indicates whether not the iteration is incomplete.

ODEmbeddedFramesIterator

Superclasses   ODObject

Subclasses   none

An ODEmbeddedFramesIterator allows clients to access each frame directly embedded within a display frame of a part.

InitEmbeddedFramesIterator   Initializes the embedded-frames iterator.

First   Starts the iteration and returns the first item.

Next   Returns the next item in sequence.

IsNotComplete   Indicates whether not the iteration is incomplete.

CheckValid   Determines whether or not the iterator object is valid.

IsValid   Indicates whether or not the iterator is valid.

PartRemoved   Invalidates the iterator.

ODExtension

Superclasses   ODRefCntObject → ODObject

Subclasses   ODSemanticInterface and ODSettingsExtension
   The ODExtension class represents the extension of an OpenDoc object interface.

InitExtension   Initializes the extension.

GetBase   Returns a reference to the object that the extension is extending.

BaseRemoved   Invalidates the extension.

CheckValid   Generates an exception if the extension is invalid.

IsValid   Indicates whether or not the extension is valid.

ODFacet

Superclasses   ODObject

Subclasses   none
   The ODFacet class provides a way to keep track of transitory arrangements of parts and frames; it describes the position of screen elements for display and event dispatching.

Factory Methods

An ODFacet acts as factory for several other objects; the methods to create them are listed here.

CreateEmbeddedFacet   Creates an embedded facet for a specified frame.

CreateFacetIterator   Creates a facet iterator for any embedded facets.

CreateCanvas   Instantiates an ODCanvas.

CreateShape   Instantiates an ODShape.

CreateTransform   Instantiates an ODTransform.

Geometry

These methods manipulate facet geometry.

AcquireActiveShape   Returns a reference to the facet's active shape.

ChangeActiveShape   Sets a new active shape for the facet.

AcquireClipShape   Returns a reference to the facet's clip shape.

ChangeGeometry   Assigns the specified clip shape, external transform, or both, to the facet.

AcquireExternalTransform   Returns a reference to the facet's external transform.

GetCanvas   Returns a reference to the facet's canvas.

ChangeCanvas   Associates a particular canvas with the facet.

HasCanvas   Indicates whether or not the facet has its own canvas.

AcquireAggregateClipShape   Returns a reference to an ODShape object that represents the aggregate clip shape for the facet.

AcquireContentTransform   Returns a reference to an ODTransform object that represents the content transform of the facet.

AcquireFrameTransform   Returns a reference to an ODTransform object that represents the frame transform of the facet.

AcquireWindowAggregateClipShape   Returns a reference to an ODShape object that represents the window aggregate clip shape for the facet.

AcquireWindowContentTransform   Returns a reference to an ODTransform object that represents the window content transform of the facet.

AcquireWindowFrameTransform   Returns a reference to an ODTransform object that represents the window frame transform of the facet.

Imaging

These Imaging methods control the drawing behaviors of a facet.

IsSelected   Indicates whether or not the facet is selected.

SetSelected   Determines whether or not the facet is selected.

GetHighlight   Returns the highlight state for the facet.

ChangeHighlight   Modifies the highlight state for the facet.

Draw   Given a region of the facet, tells the facet's part to draw itself.

DrawActiveBorder   Sets the facet's active border.

DrawChildren   Refreshes all embedded child facets that need to be redrawn.

DrawChildrenAlways   Refreshes all embedded child facets.

DrawnIn   This method is called when the facet was drawn without an update event occurring.

Invalidate   Indicates that a specific area of the facet needs to be redrawn.

InvalidateActiveBorder   Indicates that the active border of the facet needs to be redrawn.

Validate   Indicates that a specific area of the facet no longer needs to be redrawn.

Update   Draws the facet along with any of its embedded children, as long as their clip shapes intersect the indicated region of the canvas.

Part Info

These methods manipulate the facet's part information field.

GetPartInfo   Returns the facet's part information.

SetPartInfo   Specifies the facet's part information.

Point Testing

These operations return information about points and positions relative to the facet.

ContainsPoint   Indicates whether or not the given point is within the facet.

ActiveBorderContainsPoint   Indicates whether or not the facet's frame is active and a point is within that active border.

Traversing the Facet Hierarchy

The following methods allow one to manipulate the facet hierarchy.

GetContainingFacet   Returns a reference to the facet's containing facet.

GetFrame   Returns a reference to the facet's frame.

GetWindow   Returns a reference to the window in which the facet is displayed.

RemoveFacet   Removes one of the facet's embedded facets.

MoveBefore   Changes the z-ordering of sibling facets; this method moves the facet in front of sibling facets.

MoveBehind   Changes the z-ordering of sibling facets; this method moves the facet behind sibling facets.

ODFacetIterator

Superclasses   ODObject

Subclasses   none
    An ODFacetIterator allows clients to access each facet embedded within a facet.

First   Starts the iteration and returns the first item.

Next   Returns the next item in sequence.

SkipChildren   Advances the iteration to the next sibling in the facet hierarchy; this is used if embedded children are to be skipped.

IsNotComplete   Indicates whether not the iteration is incomplete.

ODFocusModule

Superclasses   ODObject

Subclasses   none
    An ODFocusModule manages one or more types of ownership of a shared resource.

Initialization and Testing

These methods are used for initialization and testing of the focus module.

InitFocusModule   Initializes the focus module.

IsFocusExclusive   Indicates whether or not this is an exclusive focus.

Ownership and Transfer

These methods govern ownership and transfer of foci.

TransferFocusOwnership   Transfers focus ownership from one owner to another.

BeginRelinquishFocus   Indicates whether the current owner of the desired exclusive focus will give up ownership of it.

CommitRelinquishFocus   Finishes the focus transfer transaction by signalling the owner of the focus that it is about to lose ownership of it.

AbortRelinquishFocus   Cancels the focus transfer operation.

CreateOwnerIterator   Creates a focus-owner iterator that will return the owners of a particular nonexclusive focus.

AcquireFocusOwner   For a given exclusive focus, returns the frame that owns it.

SetFocusOwnership   Specifies that a given frame owns a particular focus.

UnsetFocusOwnership   Removes a frame as the owner of a focus.

ODFocusOwnerIterator

Superclasses   ODObject

Subclasses   none
    An ODFocusOwnerIterator allows clients to access each owner of a particular nonexclusive focus.

InitFocusOwnerIterator   Initializes the focus-owner iterator.

First   Starts the iteration and returns the first item.

Next   Returns the next item in sequence.

IsNotComplete   Indicates whether not the iteration is incomplete.

ODFocusSet

Superclasses   ODObject

Subclasses   none
    An ODFocusSet represents an arbitrary group of foci that are needed for a particular part's activation.

CreateIterator   Creates a focus-set iterator for the set.

Add   Adds a focus to the focus set.

Remove   Removes a particular focus from the focus set.

Contains   Indicates whether or not the specified focus is in the focus set.

ODFocusSetIterator

Superclasses   ODObject

Subclasses   none

An ODFocusSetIterator allows clients to access each focus in a focus set.

First   Starts the iteration and returns the first item.

Next   Returns the next item in sequence.

IsNotComplete   Indicates whether not the iteration is incomplete.

ODFrame

Superclasses   ODPersistentObject → ODRefCntObject → ODObject

Subclasses   none

The ODFrame class represents the screen area of an embedded part within the confines of its containing part.

Content Extent

These methods deal with changing and retrieving content extents.

GetContentExtent   Retrieves the frame's content extent.

ChangeContentExtent   Modifies the the frame's content extent.

Drag and Drop

The following four methods are involved with drag and drop.

IsDragging   Indicates whether or not the frame is currently being dragged.

SetDragging   Specifies that the frame is currently being dragged.

IsDroppable   Indicates whether or not the frame's part accepts drag-and-drop events in the frame.

SetDroppable   Specifies that the frame's part accepts drag-and-drop events in the frame.

Events

These methods deal with event propagation.

DoesPropagateEvents   Indicates whether or not the frame propagates unhandled events upwards to its containing part.

SetPropagateEvents   Specifies that the frame should propagate unhandled events upwards to its containing frame.

Facets

These methods act upon the frame's facets.

CreateFacetIterator   Creates a frame-facet iterator for the frame's facets.

FacetAdded   Adds a facet to the frame's facet list and notifies the frame's part that a facet has been added.

FacetRemoved Removes a facet from the frame's facet list and notifies the frame's part that a facet has been removed.

Frame Attributes

Frame attributes are modified by the following methods.

IsFrozen Indicates whether or not the frame is a bundled frame.

SetFrozen Designates this frame as a bundled frame.

IsInLimbo Indicates whether or not the frame is part of a part's content model.

SetInLimbo Removes this frame from the part's content model.

IsOverlaid Indicates whether or not the frame is an overlaid frame.

IsRoot If this method returns kODTrue, then the frame is the root frame.

Frame Closure and Removal

These two methods close and remove frames.

Close Allows the frame to be removed from memory but not from persistent storage.

Remove Allows the frame to be to removed from memory as well as from persistent storage.

Frame Hierarchy

These methods manipulate the frame hierarchy of which the frame is a member.

AcquireContainingFrame   Returns a reference to the frame's containing frame.

SetContainingFrame   Sets a frame as the containing frame of the frame.

AcquirePart   Returns a reference to a specified part within the frame.

ChangePart   Changes the part associated with the frame.

AcquireWindow   Returns a reference to the window in which the frame is displayed.

SetWindow   Designates the frame's window.

IsSubframe   Indicates whether or not the frame is a subframe.

SetSubframe   Sets the frame as a subframe of its containing frame.

Frame Geometry

The methods below deal with frame geomtery.

CreateShape   Creates a new ODShape.

AcquireFrameShape   Returns a reference to the frame's frame shape.

ChangeFrameShape   Changes the frame's frame shape.

AcquireUsedShape   Returns a reference to the frame's used shape.

ChangeUsedShape   Changes the used shape associated with this frame.

CreateTransform   Creates a new ODTransform.

AcquireInternalTransform   Returns a reference to the frame's internal transform.

ChangeInternalTransform   Modifies the frame's internal transform.

RequestFrameShape   Requests a new frame shape for the frame.

Groups

These methods deal with frame groups.

GetFrameGroup   Returns the frame's group identifier.

SetFrameGroup   Sets a group identifier for the frame.

GetSequenceNumber   Returns the frame's sequence number in its frame group.

ChangeSequenceNumber   Changes the frame's sequence number within its frame group.

Imaging

These methods control frame imaging.

GetViewType   Returns the view type for the frame.

SetViewType   Sets the frame's view type.

ChangeViewType   Modifies the frame's view type.

GetPresentation   Returns the presentation for the frame.

SetPresentation   Sets the frame's presentation type.

ChangePresentation   Modifies the frame's presentation type.

DrawActiveBorder   Draws the frame's active border.

Invalidate   Indicates that an area within the frame needs to be updated.

InvalidateActiveBorder   Indicates that the frame's active border needs to be updated.

Validate   Indicates that an area within the frame no longer needs to be updated.

Linking

These methods control linking behavior for the frame.

EditInLink   Indicates whether or not the destination of this link can be found. If so, then this routine returns kODTrue.

GetLinkStatus   Returns the frame's link status.

ChangeLinkStatus   Changes the frame's link status.

ContentUpdated   This method is called to notify the frame's containing part that the frame's content has changed.

Part Info

These methods deal with changing and retrieving part information.

GetPartInfo   Returns the frame's part info data.

SetPartInfo   Sets the frame's part info data.

ODFrameFacetIterator

Superclasses   ODObject

Subclasses   none
An ODFrameFacetIterator allows clients to access each facet in a frame.

First   Starts the iteration and returns the first item.

Next   Returns the next item in sequence.

IsNotComplete   Indicates whether not the iteration is incomplete.

ODInfo

Superclasses   ODObject

Subclasses   none
The ODInfo class represents a part's Get Info... dialog box, which contains information about the part's kind, properties, and so forth.

ShowPartFrameInfo   Puts the Part Info... dialog box on the screen.

ODLink

Superclasses   ODPersistentObject → ODRefCntObject → ODObject

Subclasses   none
ODLink objects represent the ends, or destinations, of an OpenDoc link.

Lock   Locks the link object to guarantee read-only access to the storage unit for the link.

Unlock   Removes a lock on the link object.

GetContentStorageUnit   Returns a reference to the link object's storage unit.

GetUpdateID   Obtains the version or generation number of the link's contents. This allows the link to track changes to the content.

GetChangeTime   Returns the last update time for the link source's content.

RegisterDependent   Adds a part to a list of parts to be notified when the link's contents change.

UnregisterDependent   Removes a part from a list of parts to be notified when the link's contents change.

ShowSourceContent   Requests that the source part make the source of the content visible.

ShowLinkDestinationInfo (MacOS)   Shows a Link Destination Info... dialog box for the destination of a link.

ODLinkManager

Superclasses   ODObject

Subclasses   none
    An ODLinkManager instance manages the process of creating and maintaining links between and within documents.

AnyLinkImported (document shell)   Indicates whether or not there have been any updates to link contents since the last time the document's content was saved.

UnsavedExportedLinks (document shell)   Indicates whether or not any outgoing links have been created since the last time the draft was saved.

DraftClosing (document shell)   Alerts the link manager that a particular draft is in the process of closing.

DraftOpened (document shell)   Alerts the link manager that a particular draft is being opened.

DraftSaved (document shell)   Alerts the link manager that a particular draft has been saved.

NewSectionID (MacOS, document shell)   Returns a new section identifier for the specified draft's document.

ReserveSectionID (MacOS, document shell)   Reserves a section identifier in the draft for the draft's document. This endures for the lifetime of the document.

ODLinkSource

Superclasses   ODPersistentObject → ODRefCntObject → ODObject

Subclasses   none

The ODLinkSource class represents the source of an OpenDoc link. Compare this to the ODLink class, which represents the destination. When a user creates a link between parts, the drafts create and maintain link-source objects.

Access Control

These four methods control access to the link-source object.

Lock   Gives the link source exclusive access to its content storage unit.

GetContentStorageUnit   Returns a reference to the link source's content storage unit.

Unlock   Surrenders the lock on the link source's content storage unit.

SetSourcePart   Designates a part as the source and maintainer of this link source.

Link-Source Dialog

This method controls the display of the Link Source Info... dialog box.

ShowLinkSourceInfo (MacOS)   Displays information about the link source in a dialog box.

Updating

These methods help maintain link integrity.

Clear   Removes the link source's content.

ContentUpdated   Notifies the link source that the link content has changed.

GetUpdateID   Gets the version number of the link source's content; this allows clients to tell if the content has changed.

GetChangeTime   Returns the last update time for the link source.

IsAutoUpdate   Indicates whether or not the link source is automatically updated.

SetAutoUpdate   If set, then the link source is updated automatically; otherwise, it must be updated manually.

ODLinkSpec

Superclasses   ODObject

Subclasses   none

The ODLinkSpec class allows a source part to signal that other parts can link to its content.

ReadLinkSpec   Reads data from a particular storage unit into a new link specification.

WriteLinkSpec   Writes link specification information into a particular storage unit.

ODMenuBar

Superclasses   ODRefCntObject → ODObject

Subclasses   none
The ODMenuBar class represents a menu bar, composed of menus from both the document shell and the active part.

Menu Bars

These operations deal with menu bars.

Copy   Copies the menu bar.

Display   Makes the menu bar the current displayed menu bar.

IsValid   Checks to see if the menu bar is equivalent to the menu bar from which it was copied.

Menu Items

The methods listed here operate on menu items.

GetItemString (MacOS)   Retrieves the text string for a given menu item.

SetItemString (MacOS)   Sets the text string for a given menu item.

EnableCommand (MacOS)   Enables or disables a given menu item.

CheckCommand (MacOS)   Displays or removes a checkmark next to a given menu item.

EnableAndCheckCommand (MacOS)   This method combines the operations of EnableCommand and CheckCommand—menu items are enabled or disabled, and checked or unchecked.

GetMenuAndItem (MacOS)   Given a command identifier, retrieves the corresponding menu/menu item designation.

GetCommand (MacOS)   Given a menu/menu item designation, retrieves the corresponding command identifier.

RegisterCommand (MacOS)   Pairs a command identifier with a menu/menu item designation.

UnregisterCommand (MacOS)   Breaks the association between a menu/menu item designation and a command identifier.

UnregisterAll (MacOS)   Removes all command identifiers associated with the menu bar.

Menu Queries

These commands return information about command identifiers.

IsCommandRegistered (MacOS)   Indicates whether or not the given command identifier is associated with the menu bar object.

IsCommandSynthetic (MacOS)   Indicates whether or not the given command identifier is synthetic.

Menus

These methods deal with menu manipulation.

AddMenuBefore   Given an existing menu on the menu bar, inserts a menu before it.

AddMenuLast   Adds a new menu to the end of the menu bar.

AddSubMenu (MacOS)   Adds a submenu to the menu bar.

DisableAll (MacOS)   This MacOS-specific method disables all menus in the menu bar, except for system menus.

EnableAll (MacOS)   This MacOS-specific method enables all menus in the menu bar, except for system menus.

GetMenu   Given a menu ID, this method returns a platform-specific menu structure.

RemoveMenu   Removes a given menu from the menu bar.

ODMessageInterface

Superclasses   ODObject

Subclasses   none
    An ODMessageInterface works with the ODSemanticInterface to provide interpart messaging. The ODMessageInterface provides methods to create and send semantic events.

CreateEvent   Creates an event.

CreatePartAddrDesc   Given a part, creates an address descriptor that represents its address.

CreatePartObjSpec   Given a part, creates an object specifier that refers to it.

ProcessSemanticEvent   Dispatches an event to the correct event handler.

Send   Sends an event to a particular part. This method may or may not wait for a reply.

ODNameResolver

Superclasses   ODObject

Subclasses   none

The ODNameResolver object helps resolve names and determine addresses for the targets of semantic events.

CallObjectAccessor   Calls the accessor function for the semantic interface of the calling part.

Resolve   Turns an object specifier into a token that identifies the target object.

CreateSwapToken   Creates a swap token: a token that allows a part to delegate object resolution to another part.

DisposeToken   Frees the memory associated with the token.

GetContextFromToken   Gets references to the part and the frame in whose context the specified token was created.

IsODToken   Indicates whether or not a particular token object is in OpenDoc token format.

GetUserToken   Given an OpenDoc token, returns a reference to the corresponding object descriptor.

ODNameSpace

Superclasses   ODObject

Subclasses   ODObjectNameSpace, ODValueNameSpace

An ODNameSpace provides a storage mechanism for key/value pairs and allows speedy retrieval of these entries.

Attributes

These methods manipulate the attributes of the name space itself.

GetName   Returns this name space's name.

GetParent   Returns a reference to this name space's parent name space.

GetType   Returns the name space's type.

SetType   Sets this name space's type.

Entries

These methods manipulate the entries in the name space.

Unregister   Removes a given entry from the name space.

Exists   Indicates whether or not a given key has a value associated with it.

Storage

Both these methods are concerned with name space storage.

ReadFromStorage   Reads the name space's content from a storage unit.

WriteToStorage   Writes the name space's content to a storage unit.

ODNameSpaceManager

Superclasses   ODObject

Subclasses   none
The ODNameSpaceManager class overseees the creation or deletion of OpenDoc name spaces.

CreateNameSpace   Creates a new name space.

DeleteNameSpace   Deletes a given name space.

HasNameSpace   Determines whether or not a given name space exists. If so, then this method returns a reference to it.

ODObject

Superclasses   none

Subclasses   All other OpenDoc classes
ODObject is the fundamental superclass on which all other OpenDoc classes are based. It contains certain methods dealing with object equality, extensions, and memory management that all subclasses must implement.

IsEqualTo   Indicates whether or not a given object is equal to this object.

AcquireExtension   Returns a reference to the specified OpenDoc extension.

HasExtension   Indicates whether or not the object supports a specified extension.

ReleaseExtension   Releases the given extension.

Purge   When called, releases any memory that can be released.

SubClassResponsibility   SubClassResponsibility is a method used in debugging: if a subclass failed to override a required ODObject method, then SubClassResponsibility throws an exception.

ODObjectIterator

Superclasses   ODObject

Subclasses   none
An ODObjectIterator allows clients to access each object in an object name space.

First   Starts the iteration and returns the first item from the name space.

Next   Returns the next item in sequence.

IsNotComplete   Indicates whether not the iteration is incomplete.

ODObjectNameSpace

Superclasses   ODNameSpace → ODObject

Subclasses   none
A subclass of ODNameSpace, an ODObjectNameSpace provides a way to store and retrieve object references.

CreateIterator   Creates an ODObjectIterator; allows client to access each object in this name space.

GetEntry   Returns an object reference if the given key matches an object in the name space.

Register   Adds a new key/object pair to the name space.

ODObjectSpec

Superclasses   ODDesc → ODObject

Subclassses   none
The ODObjectSpec class wraps a MacOS-specific object specifier structure.

InitODObjectSpec   Initializes the object specifier.

ODOSLToken

Superclasses   ODDesc → ODObject

Subclasses   none
The ODOSLToken class wraps an OpenDoc token structure.

InitODOSLToken   Initializes the token.

DuplicateODOSLToken   Creates a duplicate of this OpenDoc token, including all private data.

ODPart

Superclasses   ODPersistentObject → ODRefCntObject → ODObject

Subclasses   none

An ODPart object represents a part editor. This is the main class that developers subclass when writing a new part editor.

OpenDoc documents are made up of one or more parts, each with an associated part editor. A part is somewhat like a data file or traditional document: it provides the content, such as spreadsheet data. A part editor, on the other hand, is much like a traditional application in that it can display or modify the data in a part, save it to a persistent storage medium, and so forth. OpenDoc provides mechanisms for automatically matching a part with the correct part editor.

Developers must subclass ODPart when writing a new part editor. However, a developer need only implement certain methods: some are required by OpenDoc, and the others support the specific capabilities of the part editor.

Parts are created by drafts by calling the draft's CreatePart method. This method is called by the OpenDoc runtime or by another part.

Binding

These methods affect part-editor binding.

ChangeKind   Changes the part's preferred kind.

IsRealPart   Indicates whether or not this is an actual part (rather than a part wrapper).

GetRealPart   For a part wrapper, returns a reference to the part it encapsulates.

ReleaseRealPart   For a part wrapper, releases the part that it encapsulates.

Container Properties

These methods manipulate container properties.

AcquireContainingPartProperties   Writes the container properties associated with an embedded frame into a particular storage unit.

ContainingPartPropertiesUpdated   Notifies the part that the container properites of its containing part have changed.

Display Frame Manipulation

This group of methods manipulates display frames, including presentation styles and view types.

AttachSourceFrame   Associates a source frame with one of the part's display frames.

DisplayFrameAdded   Adds a new frame to the part's display frame list.

DisplayFrameClosed   Notifies the part of the closure of one of its display frames.

DisplayFrameConnected   Adds an exisiting frame to the part's display frame list.

DisplayFrameRemoved   Removes a specified frame from the part's display frame list.

PresentationChanged   Notifies the part that one of its display frame's presentations has changed.

ViewTypeChanged   Notifies the part that one of its display frame's view types has changed.

SequenceChanged   Notifies the part that its position in the display frame sequence has changed.

Open   Creates or activates a new window in which one of this part's frames is the root part.

Drag and Drop

These methods are associated with drag-and-drop operations.

DragEnter Begins tracking a drag operation.

DragWithin Tracks a drag operation within the part's border and provides graphical feedback for possible drop operations.

DragLeave Ends tracking a drag operation.

Drop Moves or copies the dragged content into the part.

DropCompleted Notifies the part that an asynchronous drag-and-drop operation is complete.

FulfillPromise Provides the content data represented by a promise.

Events

These methods handle various event-related actions.

AdjustMenus Prepares part menus for display.

HandleEvent Tries to handle a particular user event.

Frame Negotiation

These methods deal with frame negotiation.

FrameShapeChanged Notifies the part of a change in frame shape for one of its display frames.

RequestEmbeddedFrame   Creates a new embedded frame for the specified part.

RequestFrameShape   Negotiates a frame shape for an embedded part.

Imaging

These methods control part drawing and other imaging operations.

CanvasChanged   Transfers asynchronous imaging to a new canvas.

CanvasUpdated   Copies the contents of a particular canvas to that canvas' parent.

Draw   Draws the part's contents within the specified region of a facet.

GetPrintResolution   Returns the resolution requested for printing the contents of this part. This is expressed in dots per inch (e.g., 72 dpi, 300 dpi).

HighlightChanged   Updates the highlight state of a particular facet owned by the part.

Initialization and Storage

These methods handle initialization and storage of the part editor.

InitPart   Initializes the part.

InitPartFromStorage   Initializes the part from its persistent storage.

ReadPartInfo   Reads part info data for one of the part's display frames.

WritePartInfo   Writes part info data for one of the part's display frames.

ClonePartInfo   Clones part info data for one of the part's display frames.

ExternalizeKinds   Writes a list of the part kinds that the part supports.

Linking

These methods create and manipulate links.

CreateLink   Creates an ODLinkSource object for the part.

EmbeddedFrameUpdated   Updates all link-source objects concerned with changes to a particular embedded frame.

EditInLinkAttempted   Indicates whether or not an attempt was made to edit the content of the part from a link destination.

LinkStatusChanged   Notifies the part of a change to the link status of one of its display frames.

LinkUpdated   Updates the content at a link destination.

RevealLink   Shows the content at a link source.

Manipulating Embedded Frames

These methods manipulate frames embedded in the part.

AdjustBorderShape   Changes an embedded frame's active frame border.

CreateEmbeddedFramesIterator   Creates an iterator to give clients a way to iterate through this frame's embedded parts.

RemoveEmbeddedFrame   Removes a particular embedded frame from the part's canvas.

EmbeddedFrameSpec   Creates an object specifier for an embedded frame.

RevealFrame   Makes an embedded frame visible by scrolling the canvas until it comes into view.

UsedShapeChanged   Notifies the part that one of its embedded frame's used shape has changed.

Manipulating Facets

These methods manipulate facets.

FacetAdded   Notifies the part that one of its display frames has had a facet added to its facet list.

FacetRemoved   Notifies the part that one of its display frames has had a facet removed from its facet list.

GeometryChanged   Notifies the part of changes to clip shapes or external transforms of its facets.

Manipulating Foci

These methods manipulate foci.

AbortRelinquishFocus   Aborts a focus transfer operation.

BeginRelinquishFocus   Indicates whether or not the part will give up the requested focus, and if so, prepares the part to give up the requested focus.

CommitRelinquishFocus   Completes the focus transfer transaction.

FocusAcquired   Notifies the part that one of its display frames has acquired a requested focus.

FocusLost   Notifies the part that one of its display frames has lost a particular focus.

Undo

These five methods handle undo and redo actions.

RedoAction   Redoes a particular action.

UndoAction   Undoes a particular action.

DisposeActionState   Disposes of the undo action state.

ReadActionState   Reads undo action data from a particular storage unit.

WriteActionState   Writes undo action data to a particular storage unit.

ODPersistentObject

Superclasses   ODRefCntObject → ODObject

Subclasses   ODFrame, ODLink, ODLinkSource, and ODPart
An ODPersistentObject implements the protocols for saving and restoring objects to storage.

InitPersistentObject   Initializes the new persistent object.

InitPersistentObjectFromStorage   Initializes the persistent object from its stored content.

ReleaseAll   Removes all references to other reference-counted objects.

GetID   Returns the unique identifier for the persistent object.

GetStorageUnit   Returns a reference to the persistent object's storage unit.

Externalize   Stores to the storage unit all information needed to re-create the persistent object.

CloneInto   Clones this persistent object into a specified storage unit.

ODPlatformTypeList

Superclasses   ODObject

Subclasse   none
A ODPlatformTypeList is a list of OpenDoc platform types.

AddLast   Adds a platform type entry to the end of the list.

Remove   Removes a particular platform type entry from the end of the list.

Contains   Indicates whether or not the platform type list contains a particular entry.

Count   Returns the length of the platform type list.

CreatePlatformTypeListIterator   Creates an iterator for the list.

ODPlatformTypeListIterator

Superclasses   ODObject

Subclasses   none
An ODPlatformTypeListIterator allows clients to access each element in a platform type list.

First   Starts the iteration and returns the first item from the list.

Next   Returns the next item in the list.

IsNotComplete   Indicates whether not the iteration is incomplete.

ODRecord

Superclasses   ODDescList → ODDesc → ODObject

Subclasses   ODAppleEvent
    The ODRecord class is a wrapper for an AERecord structure; this structure contains a descriptor that can be used to construct events.

InitODRecord   Initializes the AERecord structure.

ODRefCntObject

Superclasses   ODObject

Subclasses   ODContainer, ODDocument, ODDraft, ODExtension, ODMenuBar, ODPersistentObject, ODShape, ODStorageUnit, ODTransform, and ODWindow
    ODRefCntObject is a base class that is subclassed by any class that wishes to implement reference counting. OpenDoc uses reference counting to help manage the memory for OpenDoc objects.

GetRefCount   Returns the object's reference count.

Acquire   Adds 1 to the object's reference count.

Release   Subtracts 1 from the object's reference count.

ODSemanticInterface

Superclasses   ODExtension → ODRefCntObject → ODObject

Subclasses   none

The ODSemanticInterface class is an OpenDoc extension that implements a semantic interface for parts. This allows parts to be manipulated by external entities via semantic events.

InitSemanticInterface   Initializes the semantic interface.

CallEventHandler   Calls the appropriate event handler for the event.

CallObjectAccessor   Returns an OpenDoc token that represents the target of the semantic event.

CallCountProc   Returns the number of elements of a particular type in a given container.

CallCompareProc   Compares two object descriptors.

CallGetMarkTokenProc   Returns a token than can be used to mark a large series of objects.

CallMarkProc   Using a mark token, marks a series of objects.

CallAdjustMarksProc   Removes marks from a particular series of previously marked objects.

CallDisposeTokenProc   Deletes part-specific data structures from a token.

CallGetErrDescProc   Returns a reference to a global error descriptor.

CallCoercionHandler   Casts a descriptor to a new type.

CallPredispatchProc   Calls the semantic interface's predispatch procedure. This procedure is in the part associated with the semantic interface.

UsingPredispatchProc   Indicates whether or not the predispatch procedure is being used.

GetOSLSupportFlags   Obtains flags that state which handlers the semantic interface supports.

SetOSLSupportFlags   Sets flags that state which handlers the semantic interface supports.

ODSession

Superclasses   ODObject

Subclasses   none
    The ODSession object initializes and shuts down the OpenDoc environment and provides methods to obtain global OpenDoc objects.

Initializing

This method starts an OpenDoc session.

InitSession   Initializes the session and creates instances of certain OpenDoc objects. This method is only called by the document shell.

Names and Identifiers

These methods return names and update identifiers.

GetUserName   Returns a string that corresponds to the name of the document's user (for example, "Nathaniel T. OpenDoc").

UniqueUpdateID   Obtains an update identifier (a 32-bit value) for the version of the clipboard or linked content.

Object Access

This group of methods each returns a reference to one of the global OpenDoc objects.

GetArbitrator   Returns a reference to the session's ODArbitrator instance.

GetBinding (document shell)   Returns a reference to the session's ODBinding instance.

GetClipboard   Returns a reference to the session's ODClipboard instance.

GetDispatcher   Returns a reference to the session's ODDispatcher instance.

GetDragAndDrop   Returns a reference to the session's ODDragAndDrop instance.

GetInfo   Returns a reference to the session's ODInfo instance.

GetLinkManager (document shell)   Returns a reference to the session's ODLinkManager instance.

GetMessageInterface   Returns a reference to the session's ODMessageInterface instance.

GetNameResolver   Returns a reference to the session's ODNameResolver instance.

GetNameSpaceManager   Returns a reference to the session's ODNameSpaceManager instance.

AcquireShellSemtInterface (document shell)   Returns a reference to the session's document shell semantic interface.

GetStorageSystem   Returns a reference to the session's ODStorageSystem instance.

GetTranslation   Returns a reference to the session's ODTranslation instance.

GetUndo   Returns a reference to the session's ODUndo instance.

GetWindowState   Returns a reference to the session's ODWindowState instance.

Setting Global Objects

These methods allow global objects to be replaced.

SetArbitrator   Specifies the session's arbitrator.

SetBinding   Specifies the session's binding object.

SetClipboard   Specifies the session's clipboard.

SetDispatcher   Specifies the session's dispatcher.

SetDragAndDrop   Specifies the session's drag-and-drop object.

SetInfo   Specifies the session's info object.

SetLinkManager   Specifies the session's link manager.

SetMessageInterface   Specifies the session's message interface.

SetNameResolver   Specifies the session's name resolver.

SetNameSpaceManager   Specifies the session's name-space manager.

SetShellSemtInterface (document shell)   Specifies the session's document shell semantic interface.

SetStorageSystem   Specifies the session's storage system.

SetTranslation   Specifies the session's translation object.

SetUndo   Specifies the session's undo object.

SetWindowState   Specifies the session's window-state object.

Tokens

These methods manipulate types and tokens.

Tokenize   Returns the tokenized version of a type name.

GetType   Given a type token, returns a type string, if possible.

RemoveEntry   Removes an entry from the table of type-to-token mappings.

■ ODSettingsExtension

Superclasses   ODExtension → ODRefCntObject → ODObject

Subclasses   none
    An ODSettingsExtension represents a dialog box that allows a user to manipulate part editor settings. If a part editor implments this extension, then the dialog box is available from the Part Info... dialog box.

InitSettingsExtension   Initializes the extension.

ShowSettings   Displays a dialog box that allows the use to modify part editor settings.

ODShape

Superclasses   ODRefCntObject → ODObject

Subclasses   none
ODShape objects represent geometric shapes; OpenDoc uses these shapes to manage part display.

Creating Shapes

These methods create and copy shape objects.

NewShape   Returns a new shape object.

Copy   Returns a copy of the given shape object.

Geometry Modes

These methods manipulate the shape's geometry mode.

GetGeometryMode   Returns the shape's current geometry mode.

SetGeometryMode   Specifies the shape's geometry mode.

Geometric Operations

All of the following calls modify the shape in some fashion.

Intersect   Performs an intersection operation between this shape and another.

Outset   Expands the boundaries of the shape in all directions, by the given amount.

Subtract   Subtracts a given shape from the shape.

Union   Performs a union operation between this shape and another.

Transform   Applies a given geometric transform to the shape.

InverseTransform   Applies the inverse of a given geometric transform to the shape.

Querying the Shape Object

These methods provide "20 Questions" (well, five) to use to obtain info about the shape's properties and attributes.

IsEmpty   Indicates whether or not the shape is an empty shape.

IsRectangular   Indicates whether or not the shape is a rectangle.

HasGeometry   Indicates whether or not the shape is a polygon.

IsSameAs   Indicates whether or not the shape is the same as a given shape.

ContainsPoint   Indicates whether or not a specified point is within the shape.

Shape Manipulation

These methods modify the shape object.

ReadShape   Reads shape information into the shape object.

WriteShape   Writes shape information from the shape object into a storage unit.

CopyFrom   Makes this shape equivalent to another shape.

Reset   Replaces the shape with an empty shape.

CopyPolygon   Returns a polygon that represents the shape.

SetPolygon   Replaces the internal representation with a shape corresponding to a given polygon.

GetBoundingBox   Determines the smallest rectangle that surrounds the shape.

SetRectangle   Replaces the internal representation with a shape corresponding to a given rectangle.

GetPlatformShape   Returns a platform-specific graphics structure that corresponds to the shape.

SetPlatformShape   Replaces the internal representation with a shape corresponding to a given platform-specific graphics structure.

GetQDRegion (MacOS)   Returns a read-only version of the shape as a QuickDraw region.

CopyQDRegion (MacOS)   Returns a version of the shape as a QuickDraw region.

SetQDRegion (MacOS)   Replaces the internal representation with a shape corresponding to a given QuickDraw region.

GetGXShape (MacOS)   Returns a QuickDraw GX structure that corresponds to the shape.

SetGXShape (MacOS)   Replaces the internal representation with a shape corresponding to a given QuickDrawGX structure.

ODStorageSystem

Superclasses   ODObject

Subclasses   none

The ODStorageSystem class represents the OpenDoc storage system and allows the user to create, manipulate, and destroy storage system objects.

CreateContainer (document shell)   Given a container type and ID, returns a new container reference.

AcquireContainer (document shell)   Given a container type and ID, returns a reference to an existing container.

CreatePlatformTypeList   Creates a new platform type list or copies one that already exists.

CreateTypeList   Creates a new type list or copies one that already exists.

GetSession   Returns a reference to the ODSession instance.

NeedSpace   Makes a request for memory from the storage unit.

ODStorageUnit

Superclasses   ODRefCntObject → ODObject

Subclasses   none

An ODStorageUnit class represents an OpenDoc persistent storage item.

Draft and Session Access

These methods give access to the storage unit's draft and session objects.

GetDraft   Returns a reference to the storage unit's draft.

GetSession   Returns a reference to the storage unit's session.

Global Operations and Access Control

The following methods control access to the storage unit and read or write its values all at once.

Lock   Provides exclusive access to the storage unit.

Unlock   Gives up exclusive access to the storage unit.

CloneInto   Duplicates each item in the storage unit; places each property/value pair into a destination storage unit.

Externalize   Writes out all property/value pairs to persistent storage; resolves all pending data transfers.

Internalize   Reads all property/value pairs from persistent storage into memory.

Manipulating Foci

These methods operate on storage-unit foci.

Exists   Indicates whether or not the storage unit contains a particular focus context.

ExistsWithCursor   Given a storage-unit cursor, indicates whether or not the storage unit contains the focus context represented by it.

Focus   Focuses the storage unit on a specified focus context.

FocusWithCursor   Given a storage-unit cursor, focuses the storage unit on it.

GetProperty   Returns the property name in the current focus.

Manipulating Persistent References

These methods manipulate persistent references.

GetIDFromStorageUnitRef   Returns a storage unit's storage-unit identifier.

GetStrongStorageUnitRef   Given a storage unit, creates a strong persistent reference to it.

GetWeakStorageUnitRef   Given a storage unit, creates a weak persistent reference to it.

IsStrongStorageUnitRef   Indicates whether or not a given reference is a strong reference.

IsWeakStorageUnitRef   Indicates whether or not a given reference is a weak reference.

IsValidStorageUnitRef   Indicates whether or not a given reference is valid.

SetStorageUnitRef   Given a storage unit, creates a new persistent reference to it.

RemoveStorageUnitRef   Invalidates a persistent reference.

Manipulating Promises

These methods manipulate promises (IOUs for data).

IsPromiseValue   Indicates whether or not the current value represents a promise.

GetPromiseValue   Gets a promise from the current value.

SetPromiseValue   Sets the current value to be a promise.

ClearAllPromises   Converts all promises in the storage unit to normal values.

ResolveAllPromises   Resolves all of the storage unit's promises.

Manipulating Storage Units

These methods manipulate the storage unit itself.

AddProperty   Adds a property to the current storage unit. This method takes an ODPropertyName for the new property's name and returns a storage unit reference.

AddValue   Adds a value of the indicated type to a property.

Remove   Deletes all property/value pairs from the current storage-unit context.

CountProperties   Counts the number of properties in this storage unit.

CountValues   Counts the number of values in this storage unit.

GetID   Returns the storage unit's storage-unit identifier.

GetName   Returns the storage unit's name.

SetName   Specifies a name for the storage unit.

GetSize   Returns the number of bytes used in the current storage-unit context.

Manipulating Values

These methods operate on values.

GetValue   Returns data read from the storage unit.

SetValue   Writes data to the storage unit.

DeleteValue   Removes data from the current value.

InsertValue   Adds data to the current value.

GetOffset   Returns the current value's offset.

SetOffset   Sets the current value's offset.

GetType   Returns the current value's type.

SetType   Sets the current value's type.

GetGenerationNumber   Returns the current value's generation number.

IncrementGenerationNumber   Increments the current value's generation number, then returns it.

Object Creation

These factory methods create new objects.

CreateCursor   Instantiates a new ODStorageUnitCursor object.

CreateCursorWithFocus   Instantiates a new ODStorageUnitCursor object, focused on the current value.

CreateStorageUnitRefIterator   Instantiates a new storage-unit reference iterator for the current value.

CreateView   Instantiates a new storage-unit view.

ODStorageUnitCursor

Superclasses   ODObject

Subclasses   none
   An ODStorageUnitCursor provides a shortcut for accessing frequently used data in a storage unit.

GetProperty   Returns the storage-unit cursor's property name.

SetProperty   Specifies the storage-unit cursor's property name.

GetValueIndex   Returns the storage-unit cursor's value index.

SetValueIndex   Specifies the storage-unit cursor's value index.

GetValueType   Returns the storage-unit cursor's value type.

SetValueType   Specifies the storage-unit cursor's value type.

ODStorageUnitRefIterator

Superclasses   ODObject

Subclasses   none
   An ODStorageUnitRefIterator allows clients to access each persistent reference in a storage unit value.

First   Starts the iteration and returns the first persistent reference, if any, in the storage unit.

Next   Returns the next item in the list.

IsNotComplete   Indicates whether or not the iteration is incomplete.

ODStorageUnitView

Superclasses   ODObject

Subclasses   none

An ODStorageUnitView provides most of the functions of an ODStorageUnit, except those involved with changing the focus. It allows a storage unit to be viewed and accessed by multiple threads because access is automatically serialized: the storage unit is locked during access.

Accessing Focus Contexts

These methods give access to the focus context.

GetCursor   Returns a reference to the ODStorageUnitCursor that represents the focus for the storage-unit view.

GetProperty   Returns the property name in the current focus.

Manipulating Persistent References

These methods manipulate persistent references in the storage-unit view's storage unit.

GetIDFromStorageUnitRef   Returns a storage unit's storage-unit identifier.

GetStrongStorageUnitRef   Given a storage unit, creates a strong persistent reference to it.

GetWeakStorageUnitRef   Given a storage unit, creates a weak persistent reference to it.

IsStrongStorageUnitRef   Indicates whether or not a given reference is a strong reference.

IsWeakStorageUnitRef   Indicates whether or not a given reference is a weak reference.

IsValidStorageUnitRef   Indicates whether or not a given reference is valid.

SetStorageUnitRef   Given a storage unit, creates a new persistent reference to it.

RemoveStorageUnitRef   Invalidates a persistent reference.

Manipulating Promises

These methods manipulate promises (IOUs for data) in the storage-unit view's storage unit.

IsPromiseValue   Indicates whether or not the current value represents a promise.

GetPromiseValue   Gets a promise from the current value.

SetPromiseValue   Sets the current value to be a promise.

Manipulating Storage Units

These methods manipulate the storage-unit view's storage unit.

GetStorageUnit   Returns a reference to the storage-unit view's creator.

AddProperty   Adds a property to the current storage-unit. This method takes an ODPropertyName for the new property's name and returns a storage-unit reference.

AddValue   Adds a value of the indicated type to a property.

Remove   Deletes all property/value pairs from the current storage-unit context.

GetID   Returns the storage unit's storage-unit identifier.

GetName   Returns the storage unit's name.

SetName   Specifies a name for the storage unit.

GetSize   Returns the number of bytes used in the current storage-unit context.

Manipulating Values

These methods operate on value in the storage-unit view's storage unit.

GetValue   Returns data read from the storage unit.

SetValue   Writes data to the storage unit.

DeleteValue   Removes data from the current value.

InsertValue   Adds data to the current value.

GetOffset   Returns the current value's offset.

SetOffset   Sets the current value's offset.

GetType   Returns the current value's type.

SetType   Sets the current value's type.

GetGenerationNumber   Returns the current value's generation number.

IncrementGenerationNumber   Increments the current value's generation number, then returns it.

Object Creation

The storage unit in this factory method is the creator of the storage-unit view.

CreateStorageUnitRefIterator   Instantiates a new storage-unit reference iterator for the current value.

Storage

These methods act upon the storage unit that created the storage-unit view.

CloneInto   Duplicates each item in the storage unit; places each property/value pair into a destination storage unit.

Externalize   Writes out all property/value pairs to persistent storage; resolves all pending data transfers.

Internalize   Reads all property/value pairs from persistent storage into memory.

ODTransform

Superclasses   ODRefCntObject → ODObject

Subclasses   none

An ODTransform represents a mapping of points from one coordinate space to another. This is used to scale, skew, or otherwise manipulate a geometric shape.

Applying Transforms

These methods control the application of the transform to shapes.

TransformShape   Applies the transform to the given shape.

InvertShape   Applies the inverse transform to the given shape.

TransformPoint   Applies the transform to the given point.

InvertPoint   Applies the inverse transform to the given point.

Changing Scaling Factors

These methods change the scaling factors for the transform.

GetScale   Obtains the horizontal and vertical scaling factors.

ScaleBy   Scales the transform by the given horizontal and vertical scaling factors.

ScaleDownBy   Scales the transform by the reciprocal of the given horizontal and vertical scaling factors.

Creation and Initialization

These methods create and initialize transform objects.

NewTransform   Returns a new transform. Initial value is the identity transform.

Copy   Returns a copy fo the current transform.

InitTransform   Initializes the transform. This is only required in derived classes of ODTransform, as the base implementation does not require it.

Matrix Manipulation

These methods manipulate a transform's matrix, if it contains one.

ReadFrom   Reads the matrix for this transform from a storage unit.

WriteTo   Writes the matrix for this transform into a storage unit.

GetMatrix   Copies the matrix for this transform into the specified data structure.

SetMatrix   Replaces the transform's matrix with another.

PostCompose   Postmultiplies the transform's matrix with another.

PreCompose   Premultiplies the transform's matrix with another.

CopyFrom   Copies the transform matrix from another transform.

Invert   Inverts the transform matrix.

Reset   Resets the matrix for this transform.

Querying the Transform

These methods return information about the transform object.

GetType   Returns the transform's type.

IsSameAs   Indicates whether or not this transform is identical to a specified transform.

HasMatrix   Indicates whether or not this transform describes its transformation using a matrix.

Translation Value Manipulation

These methods manipulate translation values.

GetOffset   Returns the transform's offset values.

SetOffset   Turns this transform into an offset.

GetPreScaleOffset   Returns the pre-scale offset.

MoveBy   Changes the translation matrix offsets by the specified amount.

IsQDOffset (MacOS)   Indicates whether or not this transform is a pure offset.

GetQDOffset (MacOS)   Returns a QuickDraw point that corresponds to the transform's offset value.

SetQDOffset (MacOS)   Turns this transform into an offset specified by QuickDraw point.

ODTranslation

Superclasses   ODObject

Subclasses   none
   The ODTranslation class provides translation services.

GetTranslationOf   Returns the types to which the given item can be translated.

CanTranslate   Indicates whether or not any translation is available.

Translate   Attempts to translate one data type into another.

TranslateView   For storage-unit views, attempts to translate one data type into another.

GetISOTypeFromPlatformType   Given a platform type, returns a corresponding ISO type.

GetPlatformTypeFromISOType   Given an ISO type, returns a corresponding platform type.

ODTypeList

Superclasses   ODObject

Subclasses   none
An ODTypeList is an ordered list of ODType structures.

AddLast   Adds an item to the end of the list.

Remove   Removes a given item from the list.

Contains   Indicates whether or not the list contains the given item.

Count   Calculates the number of elements in the list.

CreateTypeListIterator   Creates a type-list iterator to allow access to each element in the type list.

ODTypeListIterator

Superclasses   ODObject

Subclasses   none
An ODTypeListIterator allows clients to access each element of a type list.

First   Starts the iteration and returns the first element of the list.

Next   Returns the next item in the list.

IsNotComplete   Indicates whether not the iteration is incomplete.

ODUndo

Superclasses   ODObject

Subclasses   none

An ODUndo object maintains a list of recent commands and allows those commands to be undone.

AddActionToHistory   Adds an action and part reference to the undo stack.

AbortCurrentTransaction   Removes a transaction from the command stack.

ClearActionHistory   Clears the action history.

MarkActionHistory   Notes the top of the undo and redo stacks.

Undo (document shell)   Reverses the action at the top of the undo stack.

PeekUndoHistory   Retrieves information about the undo stack.

Redo (document shell)   Redoes the top action in the redo stack.

ClearRedoHistory   Clears the redo stack.

PeekRedoHistory   Retrieves information about the undo stack.

ODValueIterator

Superclasses   ODObject

Subclasses   none

An ODValueIterator allows clients to access each value in a value name space.

First   Begins the iteration and obtains the first entry in the name space.

Next   Returns the next item from the list.

IsNotComplete   Indicates whether not the iteration is incomplete.

ODValueNameSpace

Superclasses   ODNameSpace → ODObject

Subclasses   none
A subclass of ODNameSpace, an ODValueNameSpace provides a way to store and retrieve values.

CreateIterator   Creates an ODValueIterator; allows client to access each value in this name space.

GetEntry   Returns a value if the given key matches a value in the name space.

Register   Adds a new key/value pair to the name space.

ODWindow

Superclasses   ODRefCntObject → ODObject

Subclasses   none
An ODWindow wraps a platform-specific window data structure.

Manipulating Facets and Frames

These methods operate on facets and frames.

GetFacetUnderPoint   Given a point, returns a reference to the underlying facet.

GetRootFacet   Returns a reference to the window's root facet.

Open   Creates a new facet hierarchy in the window.

GetRootFrame   Returns a reference to the window's root frame.

AcquireSourceFrame   Returns a reference to the window's source frame.

SetSourceFrame   Sets the window's source frame.

AdjustWindowShape   Reshapes the root frame to match the window size.

Manipulating Windows

These methods manipulate platform-specific window structures.

Close (document shell)   Closes the window.

CloseAndRemove   Closes the window and removes the draft's root frame.

Hide   Hides the window.

Show   Shows the window.

Select (MacOS)   Brings this window to the top of the stacking order and selects it.

GetID   Returns the window's window identifier.

GetPlatformWindow   Returns a platform-specific window structure that represents this window.

Update (MacOS)   Updates the contents of this window immediately.

Querying Windows

These methods obtain information about the window state.

IsActive   Indicates whether or not this is an active window.

IsFloating   Indicates whether or not this is a floating window.

IsResizable   Indicates whether or not this is a resizable window.

IsRootWindow   Indicates whether or not this is a root window.

IsShown   Indicates whether or not this is a visible window.

ShouldDispose (MacOS)   Indicates whether or not the platform window structure should be deleted along with the ODWindow object.

ShouldSave   Indicates whether or not the window should be saved in its draft.

SetShouldSave   Specifies whether the window object should be saved in its draft.

ShouldShowLinks   Indicates whether or the window should highlight links.

SetShouldShowLinks   Specifies whether the window should highlight links.

ODWindowIterator

Superclasses   ODObject

Subclasses   none

An ODWindowIterator allows clients to access each window in a window-state object.

First Begins the iteration and returns a reference to the first window in the window-state object.

Last Begins the iteration and returns a reference to the last window in the window state.

Next Returns a reference to the next window in the sequence.

Previous Returns a reference to the previous window in the window sequence.

IsNotComplete Indicates whether not the iteration is incomplete.

ODWindowState

Superclasses ODObject

Subclasses none

The ODWindowState object maintains several different types of objects: a list of all open windows, a reference to the base menu bar, and a reference to the current menu bar. It contains methods to manipulate windows and menu bars and serves as a factory object for facets and canvases.

Factory Methods

These methods create new objects: windows, canvases, and facets.

RegisterWindow Given a platform-specific window, creates a new ODWindow and root frame.

RegisterWindowForFrame Given a platform-specific window and root frame, creates a new ODWindow.

CreateFacet   Creates a new ODFacet.

CreateCanvas   Creates a new ODCanvas.

Manipulating Menu Bars

These methods manipulate menu bars.

CreateMenuBar (document shell)   Creates and initializes a new ODMenuBar.

AcquireCurrentMenuBar (MacOS, document shell)   Returns a reference to the current menu bar.

AcquireBaseMenuBar (MacOS, document shell)   Returns a reference to the base menu bar.

CopyBaseMenuBar   Duplicates the base menu bar.

SetBaseMenuBar (document shell)   Makes a menu bar the base menu bar.

AdjustPartMenus   Prepares parts to display menus in the menu bar.

Manipulating Windows

These methods are used to manipulate windows.

ActivateFrontWindows (MacOS)   Activates the frontmost root window and the floating windows.

DeactivateFrontWindows (MacOS)   Deactivates the frontmost nonfloating window and the floating windows.

CloseWindows (document shell)   Closes all of a draft's windows.

OpenWindows (document shell)   Opens all of a draft's windows.

AcquireWindow   Given a window identifier, returns a reference to the corresponding window.

AcquireODWindow   Given a window structure, returns a reference to the corresponding ODWindow.

AcquireActiveWindow   Determines the frontmost nonfloating window and returns a reference to it.

AcquireFrontWindow (MacOS)   Determines the frontmost window and returns a reference to it.

AcquireFrontFloatingWindow (MacOS)   Determines the frontmost floating window and returns a reference to it.

AcquireFrontRootWindow (MacOS)   Determines the frontmost root window and returns a reference to it.

Externalize (document shell)   Writes window frames and window properties to persistent storage.

Internalize (document shell)   Reads window frame information and window properties into memory and opens those windows.

CreateWindowIterator   Creates a window iterator to give access to all windows in this window-state object.

SetDefaultWindowTitles (document shell)   Sets the titles for document windows.

Querying Windows

These methods return information about window attributes.

IsODWindow Indicates whether or not the window-state object has an ODWindow structure with the given platform-specific window.

GetWindowCount Returns the number of windows in the window-state object.

GetRootWindowCount Calculates the number of root windows for a particular draft.

GetTotalRootWindowCount Calculates the total number of root windows for all open drafts.

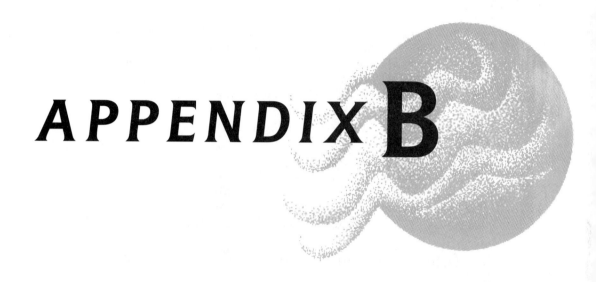

APPENDIX B

Installing OpenDoc

OpenDoc comes with an installation program tailored to the particular platform on which you are running OpenDoc. In the most general terms, it determines which components of OpenDoc you will need, based on your system configuration, then installs them on your hard drive. OpenDoc is packaged as dynamic shared libraries; these are added to your system and then the system is instructed on how to use these libraries to support OpenDoc documents.

One note about these installation instructions: these are the latest versions available as of the writing of this book. If you have problems, be sure to refer to the appropriate web site for the latest information:

- **http://opendoc.apple.com**
- **http://www.software.ibm.com/clubopendoc**

Windows

On Windows (3.1, 95, and NT), OpenDoc comes as a standalone package that contains the required applications and DLLs to support OpenDoc. These instructions are based on the Developer's Release 1 version of OpenDoc and the installer on the DR1 CD-ROM.

To install OpenDoc for Windows, you will need:

- Windows 3.11, Windows NT, or Windows 95
- A 486 or faster processor
- About 5MB of free space on the startup disk

The following description is based on an installation on Windows 95. The computer was a 90MHz Pentium system with 8MB of memory.

Step One: Running Setup and Choosing an Install Type

First, find the SETUP.EXE program on the DR1 CD-ROM. It should be on the root level. Run the program, and you will see a startup screen for the installer, shown in Figure B-1.

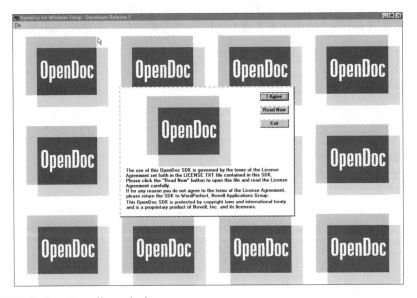

FIGURE B-1. *Installer splash screen*

At this point, you'll be able to choose either a standard installation or a custom installation.

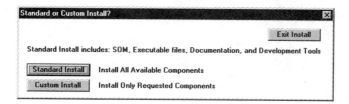

We're going to use the standard installation, but click the Custom button (which brings up the Custom Install dialog box, shown in Figure B-2) to examine the items that the installer will install. The installer installs OpenDoc executables (the OpenDoc shell and the registry-editing program), the complete set of OpenDoc documentation (including class references and additional tutorials), the C++ OpenDoc libraries and headers, and the System Object Model (SOM) runtime system.

Click on Cancel to return to the previous screen.

Select Standard Install and then select a drive on which you wish to install OpenDoc. The setup program will create two directories (ODWIN and SOM32) at the root of the selected drive.

FIGURE B-2. *Custom Install dialog box*

Step Two: Installation

At this point, the installer will put all of the proper items onto your hard drive. Under Windows 95, the installer will also install the proper types into the Windows Registry.

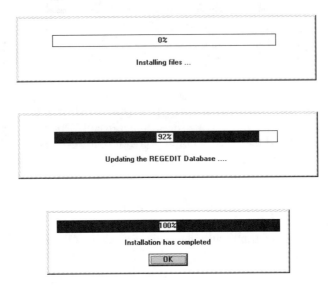

The installer creates four new program groups:

- Complete OpenDoc for Windows documentation
- OpenDoc recipes—tutorials for creating new parts
- SOM for Windows
- The main OpenDoc for Windows program group

Under Windows 95, the installer also places shortcuts to these program groups in your Start menu. The Documentation program group is shown in Figure B-3.

Step Three: Using OpenDoc

Navigate to the OpenDoc for Windows program group and read the README file you'll find there (shown in Figure B-4). It will give you any last-minute information that you'll need.

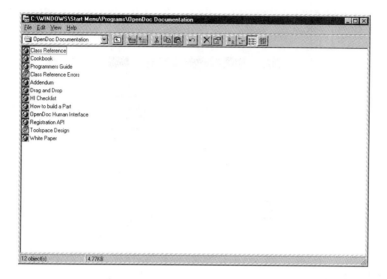

FIGURE B-3. *One of the program groups installed by the installer*

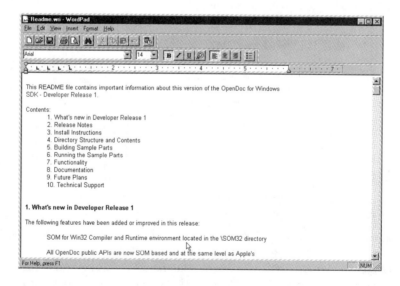

FIGURE B-4. *The contents of the README file*

Next, run the OpenDoc shell application. This will allow you to select the root part for your document.

Select the Draw part, and you will see the OpenDoc splash screen as the document is created. The resulting window can then embed any of the available OpenDoc part editors, including OLE components: ComponentGlue, built into OpenDoc for Windows, allows you to select any of the available OLE components. This illustration shows how you could embed a Netscape Navigator hypertext document into your new OpenDoc document.

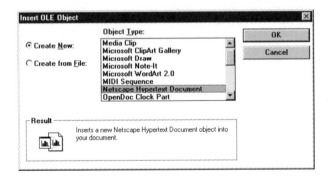

The blank document can be filled with any sort of content for which OpenDoc components are available. The following figure shows the document after the addition of a clock component and a movie-playing part. This particular movie, shown in Figure B-5, is an architectural rendering of a college campus. One interesting application of this would be to embed the renderings of a completed project into the blueprints for that project.

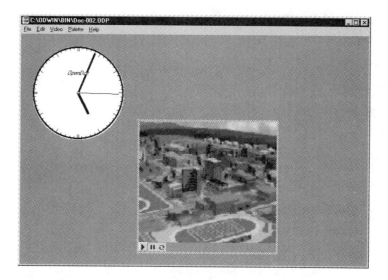

FIGURE B-5. *AVI video player in an OpenDoc document*

At this point, OpenDoc is fully installed on your system. The next section describes the installation procedures for MacOS.

MacOS

On MacOS, OpenDoc comes as a standalone package that can be installed on any version of the operating system later than 7.1.1 (7.1.2 for Power Macintosh). The package contains required system extensions and shared libraries to support OpenDoc. In later versions of the MacOS, OpenDoc will come pre-installed.

The Developer Release 4 CD contains the 1.0 version of OpenDoc for MacOS as well as documentation, sample code, and a number of parts from both Apple and third-party developers.

Step One: Running the Installer

Open the OpenDoc Developer Release 4 CD; you will see a README file and a series of folders:

■ Installing OpenDoc

■ Development

■ Documentation

■ OpenDoc Development Framework

■ OpenDoc International

■ Component Integration Labs

■ Licensing Information

■ OpenDoc Partners Info.

■ Demonstration Components

■ Cyberdog

■ Utilities

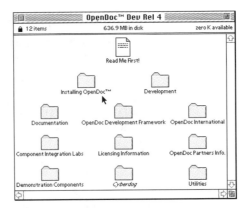

To install OpenDoc for MacOS, you will need:

■ System 7.1.1 (System 7.1.2 for Power Macintosh) or later

■ A Macintosh with a 68030 or better, any Power Macintosh, or compatible
system

■ About 5MB of free space on the startup disk

■ 8MB of RAM (suggested)

Open the Installing OpenDoc folder and double-click on the OpenDoc installer.

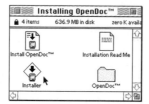

After presenting you with an OpenDoc splash screen, you'll see the first screen of the installer program. It will allow you to select the Easy Install, Custom Install, or Custom Remove options. As with the Windows version, the Custom Install option allows you to select the components you wish to install. Custom Remove will remove OpenDoc from your system and return it to its initial state. The default is Easy Install.

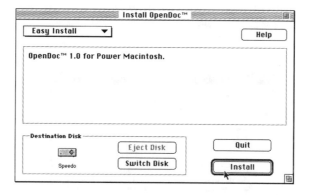

Using the Easy Install option, click the Install button and follow the directions given by the installer. While you will not have to restart your computer to use OpenDoc, the installer requires that no other applications be running during the installation process. It will give you the option to automatically quit your other applications.

During the installation, you will see the components that the installer is moving onto your hard drive; once the installation is complete, you will be given the option to do other installations, or quit.

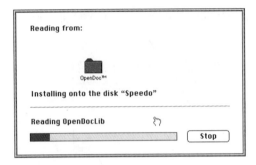

In the future, OpenDoc will come pre-installed on the system disk. OpenDoc is now ready to be used.

PartMaker for Windows

Chapter 3 gave details on how to use PartMaker to create OpenDoc parts; this appendix shows the process on Windows.

FIGURE B-6. *The PartMaker dialog box*

The PartMaker program can be found in the OpenDoc for Windows program group. At launch, it shows a dialog box (shown in Figure B-6) that allows you to select a class name and company name.

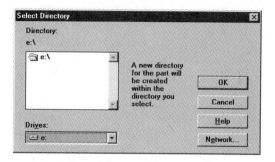

After clicking on the Create Part button, PartMaker will put up a dialog box requesting a destination for the new part editor source code. Select a destination and click on the OK button. PartMaker will then write the source code to the disk.

After the process completes, you will have template part editor source code that you can modify to create a new part editor.

Refer to Chapters 5 and 7 for part editor-writing information; Appendix C contains the source code for the example part presented there.

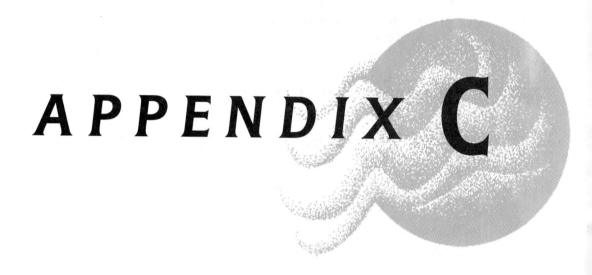

APPENDIX C

Example Source Code

This appendix contains a few selections from the example code for
WebGauge, presented in Chapters 5, 6, and 7. The complete code listing is
available online on the Internet, at

http://www.splash.net/books/opendoc/example/

The code is organized by method, alphabetically. In some cases, both
Macintosh and Windows implementations are shown.

NOTE
the Windows version of OpenDoc is still at the DR1 API level and,
for now, this part implementation does not use the same dual-class
structure as the MacOS version.

The code in this chapter was generated with PartMaker. Refer to Chapter 3 and to Appendix B for more discussion of PartMaker.

This appendix also documents two important routines in the Except.h exception-handling utility.

ConstructSemanticInterface

This routine allows the part to locate and initialize the semantic interface extension.

```
void WebGauge::ConstructSemanticInterface( Environment* ev )
{
    // The following lines must be used in strict order in order to initalize
    // The WebGaugeSI and SIHelper classes correctly.
    fSemanticInterface = new som_WebGaugeSI;
    THROW_IF_NULL(fSemanticInterface);

    SIHelper* semItfcHelper = new SIHelper;
    semItfcHelper->InitSIHelper(fSession, fSemanticInterface);

    // The Extension interface requires that a pointer to the real part, not the
    // part wrapper, be passed to InitExtension. Therefore, we get that
    // reference here.
    ODPart*   realPart = fSelf->GetRealPart(ev);
    fSemanticInterface->InitCPlusSemanticInterface(ev, realPart, semItfcHelper, fSession);
    fSelf->ReleaseRealPart(ev);

    SIHelper* helper = (SIHelper*) fSemanticInterface->GetSIHelper(ev);

    // We install one object accessor in order to get a token for the contents
    // property and two event handlers to handle get data and set data.

    ODObjectAccessorUPP theAccessorUPP;

    theAccessorUPP = NewODObjectAccessorProc(GetPropertyFromNULLStub);
    helper->InstallObjectAccessor(cProperty, typeNull, theAccessorUPP,
                                  (ODSLong) this);

    ODEventHandlerUPP theEventHandlerUPP;

    theEventHandlerUPP = NewODEventHandlerProc(HandleSetDataStub);
    helper->InstallEventHandler(kAECoreSuite, kAESetData, theEventHandlerUPP,
                                (ODSLong) this);

    theEventHandlerUPP = NewODEventHandlerProc(HandleGetDataStub);
    helper->InstallEventHandler(kAECoreSuite, kAEGetData, theEventHandlerUPP,
                                (ODSLong) this);
}
```

Drop

A drop operation completes a drag-and-drop transaction.

```
ODDropResult WebGauge::Drop( Environment*                ev,
                             ODDragItemIterator*       dropInfo,
                             ODFacet*                   facet,
                             ODPoint*                   where )
{
    SOM_Trace("WebGauge","Drop");

#ifndef qViewerBuild
    ODDropResult result = kODDropFail;

    // Remove the drag highlighting.
    this->HighlightFacet(ev, facet, kODFalse);

    ODULong dragAttributes = fSession->GetDragAndDrop(ev)->GetDragAttributes(ev);

    if ( dragAttributes & kODDropIsInSourcePart )
    {
        result = kODDropFail;
    }
    else if ( this->IsDragSupported(ev, dropInfo, facet) )
    {
        if ( !this->TryToEdit(ev, facet->GetFrame(ev)) )
            return kODDropFail;

        // Inspect the type of data being dragged to see if we can accept it.
        for ( ODStorageUnit* dropSU = dropInfo->First(ev) ; dropSU ;
            dropSU = dropInfo->Next(ev) )
        {
            if ( CWebGaugeContent::HasValidContent(ev, dropSU) )
            {
                result = (dragAttributes & kODDropIsMove) ? kODDropMove
                                                          : kODDropCopy;

                // Determine the nature of the drag (copy vs. move).
                if ( dragAttributes & kODDropIsPasteAs )
                {
                    ODBoolean pasteLink;
                    this->DoDropPasteAs(ev, facet, &pasteLink);

                    // We don't currently support linking, but we'll check
                    // this flag and set the result appropriately so that
                    // when support is added, we're handling it correctly.
                    if ( pasteLink )
                    {
                        // If we're pasting a link, we have to make sure it's
                        // a copy.  A move is not possible, because it would
                        // mean that we'd be removing the source of the link.
                        result = kODDropCopy;
```

```
                    }
                }
                else
                {
                    CWebGaugeContent* content = new CWebGaugeContent(this);
                    TempRefCounted contentTemp = content;
                    content->InitWebGaugeContent(ev, dropSU);

                    CDropAction* action = new CDropAction(this, content);
                    action->Perform(ev);
                }
            }
        }
    }

    return result;
#else
    return kODDropFail;
#endif
}
```

Draw

These code fragments show the Draw method.

Windows

This method draws a text string to the screen.

```
SOM_Scope void  SOMLINK
WGCo_WebGaugeDraw(WGCo_WebGauge *somSelf, Environment *ev,
        ODFacet* facet,
        ODShape* invalidShape)
{
    WGCo_WebGaugeData *somThis = WGCo_WebGaugeGetData(somSelf);

    HDC     hDC;
    CFocus    foc(facet, invalidShape, &hDC);

    ODFrame*    frame    = facet->GetFrame(ev);
    ODShape*    usedShape = frame->GetUsedShape(ev, kODNULL);
    RgnHandle    rgn    = usedShape->GetWinRegion(ev);

    usedShape->Release(ev);

    Rect        rct;
    RgnHandle    oldClip = kODNULL;
```

```
    RgnHandle     newClip = kODNULL;

    GetRgnBox(rgn, &rct);

    HBRUSH     fillBrush = CreateSolidBrush(GetBkColor(hDC));

    if (frame->IsRoot(ev))
    {
        oldClip = ::CreateRectRgn(0, 0, 0, 0);
        ::GetClipRgn(hDC, oldClip);
        Rect    r;
        ::GetClientRect(facet->GetWindow(ev)->GetPlatformWindow(ev), &r);
        newClip = ::CreateRectRgnIndirect(&r);
        ::SelectClipRgn(hDC, newClip);
        ::FillRect(hDC, &r, fillBrush);
    }
    else {
        ::FillRgn(hDC, rgn, fillBrush);
    }

    HPEN     framePen = ::CreatePen(PS_SOLID, 2, RGB(0, 0, 0));
    HGDIOBJ     oldPen = ::SelectObject(hDC, framePen);

    ::RoundRect(hDC, rct.left, rct.top, rct.right, rct.bottom, 40, 40);
    ::DeleteObject((HGDIOBJ)framePen);
    framePen = ::CreatePen(PS_SOLID, 5, RGB(0, 0, 0));
    oldPen = ::SelectObject(hDC, framePen);
    ::Ellipse(hDC, rct.left, rct.top, rct.right, rct.bottom);
    ::SelectObject(hDC, oldPen);
    ::DeleteObject((HGDIOBJ)framePen);

    SIZE     textSize;
    ::GetTextExtentPoint32(hDC, _fTextData, lstrlen(_fTextData), &textSize);
    int x = (rct.right - rct.left - textSize.cx) / 2;
    int y = (rct.bottom - rct.top - 12) / 2;
    ::TextOut(hDC, x, y, _fTextData, lstrlen(_fTextData));

    ::DeleteObject((HGDIOBJ)fillBrush);

    if (oldClip) {
        ::SelectClipRgn(hDC, oldClip);
        ::DeleteObject((HGDIOBJ)oldClip);
        ::DeleteObject((HGDIOBJ)newClip);
    }
}
```

MacOS

This is a version of the WebGauge Draw routine.

```
void WebGauge::Draw( Environment*        ev,
                     ODFacet*            facet,
```

```
                        ODShape*              invalidShape )
{
    SOM_Trace("WebGauge","Draw");

    ASSERT_NOT_NULL(facet);

    // Focus the port and origin for drawing in our facet.
    // Note that this instance of the CFocusDrawingEnv class
    // is being allocated on the stack. When the execution
    // leaves the scope of this method, the destructor (which
    // cleans up the drawing environment) is automatically
    // called.
    CFocus initiateDrawing(ev, facet, invalidShape);

    ODTypeToken view = facet->GetFrame(ev)->GetViewType(ev);

    if ( view == gGlobals->fLargeIconView || view == gGlobals->fSmallIconView )
        this->DrawIconView(ev, facet);
    else if ( view == gGlobals->fThumbnailView )
        this->DrawThumbnailView(ev, facet);
    else
        this->DrawFrameView(ev, facet);
}
```

Except.h

The Except.h utility provides auto-destruct base classes, easy ways to handle exceptions, and ways to recover from them. Here are two widely used utilities:

- CHECK_ENV   This routine automatically checks for exceptions that return from a method.

- CATCH_ALL   Upon exiting a function, this macro helps to clean up any exceptions.

Here is the MacOS version of CHECK_ENV.

```
void
CHECK_ENV( Environment *ev )
{
    if( ev->_major ) {
        const char *excpName = somExceptionId(ev);
        if( strcmp(excpName,ex_ODException) == 0 ) {
            ODException x = *(ODException*)somExceptionValue(ev);
            somExceptionFree(ev);
            ev->_major = NO_EXCEPTION;
            DoThrow(x.error, x.message);
        } else {
```

```
                WARN("Env has non-OpenDoc err: %s",excpName);
                somExceptionFree(ev);
                ev->_major = NO_EXCEPTION;
                DoThrow(kODErrSOMException,kODNULL);
            }
        }
    }
```

CHECK_ENV notifies the programmer if there is a non-OpenDoc error, perhaps from SOM or in the underlying operating system.

Here's the definition of the CATCH_ALL macro.

```
#define CATCH_ALL                                          \
                } catch(ODNativeException _exception)
```

Externalize

These routines write data to the part's storage unit.

Windows

This version takes the WebGauge content data and writes it to a storage unit for the part.

```
SOM_Scope void  SOMLINK
WGCo_WebGaugeExternalize(WGCo_WebGauge *somSelf, Environment *ev)
{
    WGCo_WebGaugeData *somThis = WGCo_WebGaugeGetData(somSelf);

    if (_fDirty != kODFalse)
    {
        WGCo_WebGauge_parent_ODPart_Externalize(somSelf,ev);

        ODStorageUnit* storageUnit = _fPartWrapper->GetStorageUnit(ev);
            // Get the reference to where we are writing to.

        storageUnit->Focus(ev, kODPropContents, kODPosSame, kWebGaugeKind, 0,
            kODPosSame);
            // First we focus on the property we want to write out.

        storageUnit->SetValue(ev, lstrlen(_fTextData), _fTextData);
            // Now we write out the property.

        _fDirty = kODFalse;
            // Flag our part as no longer being dirty.
    }
}
```

MacOS

The MacOS version is very similar to the Windows version in this case. Much of the total code base is portable.

```
void WebGauge::Externalize( Environment* ev )
{
    SOM_Trace("WebGauge","Externalize");

    TRY
        if ( fDirty && !fReadOnlyStorage )
        {
            // Get our storage unit.
            ODStorageUnit* storageUnit = fSelf->GetStorageUnit(ev);

            // Verify that the storage unit has the appropriate properties
            // and values to allow us to run. If not, add them.
            this->CheckAndAddProperties(ev, storageUnit);

            // Verify that there are no "bogus" values in the Content
            // property.
            this->CleanseContentProperty(ev, storageUnit);

            // Write out the part's state information.
            this->ExternalizeStateInfo(ev, storageUnit, kODNULLKey, kODNULL);

            // Write out the part's content.
            this->ExternalizeContent(ev, storageUnit, kODNULLKey, kODNULL);

            // Flag our part as no longer being dirty.
            fDirty = kODFalse;
        }

        // PRINTING: Externalize the page setup info. It might be dirty even
        // if fDirty is false, so don't put this in the if block above.
        if ( !fReadOnlyStorage && fPrinter )
        {
            TRY
                fPrinter->Externalize(ev);
            CATCH_ALL
                WARN("Err %d externalizing page setup", ErrorCode());
            ENDTRY
        }
    CATCH_ALL
        // Alert the user of the problem.
        this->DoDialogBox(ev, kODNULL, kErrorBoxID, kErrExternalizeFailed);
        // Change the exception value, so the DocShell doesn't display an
        // error dialog.
        SetErrorCode(kODErrAlreadyNotified);
        // Alert the caller.
        RERAISE;
    ENDTRY
}
```

InitPartFromStorage

These methods initialize parts that have already been created but then stored away.

Windows

This shows the InitPartFromStorage routine on Windows.

```
SOM_Scope void  SOMLINK
WGCo_WebGaugeInitPartFromStorage(WGCo_WebGauge *somSelf, Environment *ev,
        ODStorageUnit* storageUnit, ODPartWrapper* partWrapper)
{
    WGCo_WebGaugeData *somThis = WGCo_WebGaugeGetData(somSelf);
    if (somSelf->IsInitialized(ev))
        return;

    somSelf->InitPersistentObjectFromStorage(ev, storageUnit);

    _fPartWrapper = partWrapper;

    somSelf->MyCommonInitPart(ev);
    storageUnit->Focus(ev, kODPropContents, kODPosSame,
                    kWebGaugeKind, 0, kODPosSame);
    short    theSize = (short)storageUnit->GetSize(ev);
    storageUnit->GetValue(ev, theSize, _fTextData);
    _fTextData[theSize] = 0;
}
```

MacOS

This shows the InitPartFromStorage routine on a Macintosh.

```
void WebGauge::InitPartFromStorage( Environment*       ev,
                                    ODStorageUnit*    storageUnit,
                                    ODPart*            partWrapper )
{
    SOM_Trace("WebGauge","InitPartFromStorage");

    TRY
        // To allow editor swapping (translation) at runtime, OpenDoc requires
        // that we pass in a "reference" to ourselves when interacting with the
        // API (e.g., WindowState::RegisterWindow(), Dispatcher::RegisterIdle, etc).
        // The "partWrapper" passed to us here and in InitPart is the
        // "reference" OpenDoc is asking us to use.
        fSelf = partWrapper;
```

```
        // Are we being opened from a read-only draft? If so, we cannot
        // write anything back out to our storage unit.
        fReadOnlyStorage = ( ODGetDraft(ev, storageUnit)->
                                GetPermissions(ev) < kODDPSharedWrite );

        // Create the printer object.
        fPrinter = CPrinter::New(ev, storageUnit);

        // Call the common initialization code to get set up.
        this->Initialize(ev);

        // Read in the state the part was in when it was last Externalized.
        // This allows the part to present the same "environment" the user
        // had the part set up in the last time it was edited.
        this->InternalizeStateInfo(ev, storageUnit);

        // Read in the contents for your part editor.
        this->InternalizeContent(ev, storageUnit);

    CATCH_ALL
        // Clean up will occur in the destructor which will be called
        // shortly after we return the error.
        RERAISE;
    ENDTRY
}
```

InitPart

This routine initializes a new part.

MacOS

This initializes a new part on MacOS.

```
void WebGauge::InitPart( Environment*       ev,
                         ODStorageUnit*    storageUnit,
                         ODPart*            partWrapper )
{
    SOM_Trace("WebGauge","InitPart");

    TRY
        // To allow editor swapping (translation) at runtime, OpenDoc requires
        // that we pass in a "reference" to ourselves when interacting with the
        // API (e.g., WindowState::RegisterWindow(), Dispatcher::RegisterIdle, etc).
        // The "partWrapper" passed to us here and in InitPartFromStorage is the
        // "reference" OpenDoc is asking us to use.
```

```
        fSelf = partWrapper;

        // We are being created, either as part of generating stationery or
        // by some editor instantiating the part, so the destination storage
        // must be writeable.
        fReadOnlyStorage = kODFalse;

        // Create the printer object.
        fPrinter = CPrinter::New(ev, storageUnit);

        // Set up the default preferred kind.
        fPreferredKind = kWebGaugeKind;

        // Call the common initialization code to get set up.
        this->Initialize(ev);

        // Since we have just been created, our state/content info has
        // never been written out, so setting our "dirty" flag will
        // give us a chance to do that.
        this->SetDirty(ev);

    CATCH_ALL
        // Clean up will occur in the destructor which will be called
        // shortly after we return the error.
        RERAISE;
    ENDTRY
}
```

Windows

This demonstrates part initialization on Windows.

```
SOM_Scope void  SOMLINK
WGCo_WebGaugeInitPart(WGCo_WebGauge *somSelf, Environment *ev,
        ODStorageUnit* storageUnit, ODPartWrapper* partWrapper)
{
    WGCo_WebGaugeData *somThis = WGCo_WebGaugeGetData(somSelf);

    if (somSelf->IsInitialized(ev))
        return;

    somSelf->InitPersistentObject(ev, storageUnit);

    _fPartWrapper = partWrapper;

    somSelf->MyCommonInitPart(ev);

    storageUnit->AddProperty(ev, kODPropContents)->AddValue(ev, kWebGaugeKind);
        // For your edification, AddProperty & AddValue
        // implicitly focus.  Check the API for more info.
```

```
lstrcpy(_fTextData, "WebGaugePart content");

// Initialize your other fields here.

_fDirty = kODTrue;
}
```

Other Initialization Routines

These are the platform-specific initialization routines Initialize and MyCommonInitPart.

Windows

Serving the same purpose as the MacOS Initialize routine is the Windows routine MyCommonInitPart.

```
SOM_Scope void SOMLINK
WGCo_WebGaugeMyCommonInitPart(WGCo_WebGauge *somSelf, Environment* ev)
{
    WGCo_WebGaugeData *somThis = WGCo_WebGaugeGetData(somSelf);

    _fSession = _fPartWrapper->GetStorageUnit(ev)->GetSession(ev);
        // As your part grows, add your initialization that is common
        // between InitPart and InitPartFromStorage here.
        // Note that GetStorageUnit can be used, since just prior to
        // calling this method, InitPart called InitPersistentObject or
        // InitPartFromStorage called InitPersistentObjectFromStorage.

    _fFacets = new FacetList;

    _fSelectionFocus = _fSession->Tokenize(ev, kODSelectionFocus);
    _fMenuFocus      = _fSession->Tokenize(ev, kODMenuFocus);
    _fKeyFocus       = _fSession->Tokenize(ev, kODKeyFocus);
    _fModalFocus     = _fSession->Tokenize(ev, kODModalFocus);

    _fFocusSet = new ODFocusSet();
    _fFocusSet->InitFocusSet(ev);
    _fFocusSet->Add(ev, _fKeyFocus);
    _fFocusSet->Add(ev, _fMenuFocus);
    _fFocusSet->Add(ev, _fSelectionFocus);

    _fMenuBar = _fSession->GetWindowState(ev)->CopyBaseMenuBar(ev);

    _fMenu.menu = CreatePopupMenu();
    strcpy (_fMenu.strMenu, "WebGaugePart");
    if (!_fMenu.menu)
```

```
        OutputDebugStr("WebGauge::MyCommonMyInitPart -- couldn't create menu.");
            // Note that THROW won't work with SOM.  Therefore we are using
            // debug messages for these types of errors.

    _fMenuBar->AddMenuLast(ev, (ODMenuID)"WebGaugePart", &_fMenu,
            _fPartWrapper);

    }
```

MacOS

The MacOS initialization routine represents the common code factored from
InitPart and InitPartFromStorage.

```
void WebGauge::Initialize( Environment*    ev )
{
    SOM_Trace("WebGauge","Initialize");

    // Store the session in a member variable. This is merely for convenience.
    fSession = ODGetSession(ev, fSelf);

    // Create our content object (we should have one at all times).
    fContent = new CWebGaugeContent(this);
    fContent->InitWebGaugeContent(ev);

    // Create our settings object to track part settings.
    fSettings = new CSettings(this);
    fSettings->InitSettings(ev);

    // Create a list to keep track of the frames we are being
    // displayed in. Used for part maintenance (i.e., Purging memory).
    fDisplayFrames = new CList;

    // First check to see if the library's global variables have
    // been initialized (meaning another part instantiation is already
    // running).

    if ( gGlobalsUsageCount == 0 )
    {
        // Create our globals space. We store the globals in a struct so
        // that we can put them in temp mem. Otherwise, CFM loads the globals
        // with the data fragment of a CFM library in the application heap.
        gGlobals = new WebGaugeGlobals;

        // We will be using the following foci (shared resources) in this
        // part. For convenience, we tokenize the values here and store
        // them for equivalence tests in the activation methods.
        gGlobals->fSelectionFocus   = fSession->Tokenize(ev, kODSelectionFocus);
        gGlobals->fMenuFocus        = fSession->Tokenize(ev, kODMenuFocus);
        gGlobals->fModalFocus       = fSession->Tokenize(ev, kODModalFocus);
```

```
    // Also for convenience, we tokenize our part's main presentation
    // and the standard view types.
    gGlobals->fMainPresentation = fSession->Tokenize(ev, kMainPresentation);

    gGlobals->fFrameView      = fSession->Tokenize(ev, kODViewAsFrame);
    gGlobals->fLargeIconView  = fSession->Tokenize(ev, kODViewAsLargeIcon);
    gGlobals->fSmallIconView  = fSession->Tokenize(ev, kODViewAsSmallIcon);
    gGlobals->fThumbnailView  = fSession->Tokenize(ev, kODViewAsThumbnail);

    // This part supports TEXT data and files, so we must get the value types
    // OpenDoc associates with each. We do this through the Translation object.
    gGlobals->fTextDataValueType = fSession->GetTranslation(ev)->
                   GetISOTypeFromPlatformType(ev, 'TEXT',
                   kODPlatformDataType);

    // Value type for file information
    gGlobals->fAppleHFSFlavorValueType = fSession->GetTranslation(ev)->
                   GetISOTypeFromPlatformType(ev, 'hfs ',
                   kODPlatformDataType);

    // Lastly, we will package the menu and selection focus
    // so that we can request the "set" at activation time.
    gGlobals->fUIFocusSet = fSession->GetArbitrator(ev)->CreateFocusSet(ev);
    gGlobals->fUIFocusSet->Add(ev, gGlobals->fMenuFocus);
    gGlobals->fUIFocusSet->Add(ev, gGlobals->fSelectionFocus);

    // If we wanted to support keyboard input (such as supporting F1 - F4
    // for undo, cut, copy, paste -- which aren't supported automatically
    // by OpenDoc 1.0 -- or adding key input capability), we would need
    // to add a key focus for this, and we'd add it to our UI focus set.

    // Add our resource-based menus and register all the editor-specific
    // command numbers.
    this->BuildMenuBar(ev);

    // Determine what Script/Language the part is localized for.
    // This is important/necessary for creating OpenDoc's text objects.
    GetEditorScriptLanguage(ev, &gGlobals->fEditorsScript,
            &gGlobals->fEditorsLanguage);

    // Create an object to track promises on the clipboard and drag & drop.
    gGlobals->fClipboardPromises = new CPromiseSet;
    gGlobals->fDragPromises = new CPromiseSet;

    // The first client of the global variables is running.
    gGlobalsUsageCount = 1;
}
else
// If the globals have been initialized, we just bump the "usage" count so
// that we know how many part instances are using them.
{
    gGlobalsUsageCount++;
}
}
```

IsDragSupported

From the MacOS implementation, this routine returns a Boolean true if the part supports drag operations.

```
ODBoolean WebGauge::IsDragSupported( Environment*          ev,
                                     ODDragItemIterator*   dragInfo,
                                     ODFacet*              facet )
{
    SOM_Trace("WebGauge","DragEnter");

#ifndef qViewerBuild
    ODBoolean isSupported = kODFalse;

    if ( !fReadOnlyStorage &&
         (facet->GetFrame(ev)->GetLinkStatus(ev) != kODInLinkDestination) )
    {
        isSupported = kODTrue;
        ODULong count = 0;

        // Inspect the type of data being dragged to see if we can accept it.
        for ( ODStorageUnit* dragSU = dragInfo->First(ev) ; dragSU ;
              dragSU = dragInfo->Next(ev) )
        {
            // The recipe says that in order to accept a drag, we have to be
            // able to accept ALL of the contents of the drag.  Since we only
            // have one string, the most that we can handle is one item.
            if ( ++count > 1 )
            {
                isSupported = kODFalse;
                break;
            }

            // Determine if we support the drag content and if it would
            // need to be translated.
            ODBoolean itemHasValidData = CWebGaugeContent::HasValidContent(ev,
                    dragSU);

            // We have to be able to accept everything dropped on us, so see
            // if this item is acceptable, and if not, reject the entire drag.
            if ( !itemHasValidData )
            {
                isSupported = kODFalse;
                break;
            }
        }

    }

    return isSupported;
#else
    return kODFalse;
```

```
#endif
}
```

Open

This routine opens a new window for the part.

Windows

This routine (and the OpenDoc runtime system) opens up a window into which the Windows part can image.

```
SOM_Scope ODID  SOMLINK
WGCo_WebGaugeOpen(WGCo_WebGauge *somSelf, Environment *ev, ODFrame* frame)

// Creates and opens a presentation of the part in a frame
// in a new window.
//
// This method adds this part as the root part of the window.
// It bases the presentation in the new frame on the presentation
// in the old frame, or on a default presentation if there
// is no old frame.

{
    WGCo_WebGaugeData *somThis = WGCo_WebGaugeGetData(somSelf);

    ODWindow*    window = kODNULL;

    if (frame)
        window = _fSession->GetWindowState(ev)->GetWindow(ev, _fWindowID);

    if (window == kODNULL)
    {
        window = somSelf->MyMakeWindow(ev, frame);
        _fWindowID = window->GetID(ev);
        window->Open(ev);
        window->Show(ev);
    }

    window->Select(ev);

    return window->GetID(ev);
}
```

MacOS

This routine opens a new base (non-floating) window for the part editor.

```
ODID WebGauge::Open( Environment*     ev, ODFrame* frame )
{
    SOM_Trace("WebGauge","Open");

    ODID windowID;
    TempODWindow window(kODNULL);

    WindowProperties* windowProperties = kODNULL;
    ODVolatile(windowProperties);

    TRY
        // Because the frame parameter being passed to us can be one of
        // three things, we must determine what it is; either the root
        // frame of a existing document, the source frame for a part
        // window, or null if we are opening a new document.

        if ( frame == kODNULL )
        {
            // Calculate the bounding rectangle for a new window
            Rect windowRect = this->CalcPartWindowSize(ev, kODNULL);
            // Get the default setting for a document window.
            windowProperties = this->GetDefaultWindowProperties(ev, kODNULL,
                        &windowRect);
            // Create a Mac Window and register it with OpenDoc.
            window = this->CreateWindow(ev, kODNULL, kODFrameObject,
                        windowProperties);
        }
        else if ( frame->IsRoot(ev) )
        {
            // Get the previously saved settings for the document window.
            windowProperties = this->GetSavedWindowProperties(ev, frame);

            if ( windowProperties == kODNULL )
            {
                // Calculate the bounding rectangle for a new window
                Rect windowRect = this->CalcPartWindowSize(ev, frame);
                // Get the default setting for a document window.
                windowProperties = this->GetDefaultWindowProperties(ev,
                    kODNULL, &windowRect);
            }

            // Create a Mac Window and register it with OpenDoc.
            window = this->CreateWindow(ev, frame, kODFrameObject,
                        windowProperties);

            // We release the source frame here because we didn't call
            // EndGetWindowProperties and becuase we are done with it.
            ODReleaseObject(ev, windowProperties->sourceFrame);
        }
```

```
        else // frame is a source frame
        {
            window = this->AcquireFramesWindow(ev, frame);

            if ( window == kODNULL )
            {
                // Calculate the bounding rectangle for a new window
                Rect windowRect = this->CalcPartWindowSize(ev, frame);
                // Get the default setting for a document window.
                windowProperties = this->GetDefaultWindowProperties(ev, frame,
                        &windowRect);
                // Create a Mac Window and register it with OpenDoc.
                window = this->CreateWindow(ev, kODNULL, kODFrameObject,
                        windowProperties);

                // Tell the source frame that it is opened in a part window.
                CFrameInfo* frameInfo = CFrameInfo::GetFrameInfo(ev, frame);
                frameInfo->SetPartWindow(ev, window);

                this->ZoomPartWindow(ev, frame, window, kWindowOpening);
            }
        }

        // Create the window's root facet.
        window->Open(ev);
        // Make the window visible.
        window->Show(ev);
        // Activate and select the window.
        window->Select(ev);

        // Cleanup allocate memory.
        ODDeleteObject(windowProperties);

        // Get window id to return.
        windowID = (window ? window->GetID(ev) : kODNULLID);

    CATCH_ALL
        // If we threw early, the source frame's refcount may be too high.
        if ( windowProperties )
            ODSafeReleaseObject(windowProperties->sourceFrame);
        // Cleanup the created items.
        ODDeleteObject(windowProperties);
        windowID = kODNULLID;
        // Alert the caller.
        RERAISE;
    ENDTRY

    return windowID;
}
```

ViewTypeChanged

This routine is called after a request comes in to change the view type of the part
and its frame.

```
void WebGauge::ViewTypeChanged( Environment*    ev,
                                ODFrame*        frame )
{
    SOM_Trace("WebGauge","ViewTypeChanged");

    // Change this frame's used shape to match the new view setting.
    TempODShape newUsedShape = this->CalcNewUsedShape(ev, frame);

    frame->Invalidate(ev, kODNULL, kODNULL);
    frame->ChangeUsedShape(ev, newUsedShape, kODNULL);
    frame->Invalidate(ev, kODNULL, kODNULL);
}
```

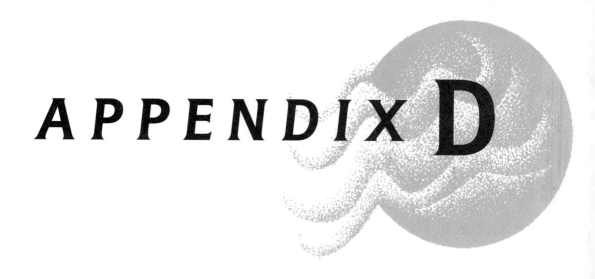

APPENDIX D

Bibliography and Resources

This appendix lists some of the books on the market that were helpful in writing Byte Guide to OpenDoc *or that provide additional useful information on OpenDoc and SOM/CORBA development. Many articles have been written about OpenDoc, and some of these are listed here, too. However, information changes frequently, so keep an eye on the Apple, IBM, and Component Integration Labs web sites for the latest updates.*

Books

Books are grouped into the following categories:

- General reference
- OpenDoc
- OLE
- SOM/DSOM
- CORBA
- Scripting and OSA

General Reference

The following books are useful as general references and are not necessarily specific to OpenDoc. All of them have come in handy in the authors' professional lives.

The Essential Distributed Objects Survival Guide
Orfali, Bob, Dan Harkey, and Jeri Edwards. *The Essential Distributed Objects Survival Guide.* New York: John Wiley, 1995.

This book contains extensive technical information and explanations of the various flavors of distributed object technology. It has excellent sections on OpenDoc, OLE, and CORBA. It is entertaining and serves as an excellent overview of current object technologies.

Interactive Multimedia Association Compatibility Project
IMA Architecture Technical Working Group. *Interactive Multimedia Association Compatibility Project: Architecture Technical Working Group—Recommended Practice for Data Exchange.* Annapolis, Md.: Interactive Multimedia Association, 1995.

This reference specifies Bento as the standard format for multimedia data exchange and contains an extremely good description of and specification for the Bento container format.

ISO/IEC 9070:1991(E) Registration Procedures for Public Text Owner Identifiers
ISO/IEC. *ISO/IEC 9070:1991(E) Registration Procedures for Public Text Owner Identifiers.* Geneva, Switzerland: ISO/IEC, 1991.

This standard defines the structure of ISO public text owner identifiers: in other words, names. OpenDoc type names are based on this standard.

The C Programming Language (Second Edition)
Kernighan, Brian W., and Dennis M. Ritchie. *The C Programming Language (Second Edition)*. Englewood Cliffs, N.J.: Prentice-Hall, 1988.

This classic reference defines the C programming language. The appendices alone are a must for any programmer.

Programming in C++
Dewhurst, Stephen C., and Kathy T. Stark. *Programming in C++*. Englewood Cliffs, N.J.: Prentice-Hall, 1989.

Another classic reference, this book is patterned after the Kernighan and Ritchie book. It is more approachable than *The C++ Annotated Reference Manual*.

The Annotated C++ Reference Manual
Stroustrup, Bjarne, and Margaret Ellis. *The Annotated C++ Reference Manual*. NewYork: Addison-Wesley, 1990.

This book is the standard reference and definition of the C++ language.

OpenDoc

This section lists the essential OpenDoc reference works.

OpenDoc Programmer's Guide for the Mac OS
Apple Computer, Inc. *OpenDoc Programmer's Guide for the Mac OS*. Reading, Mass.: Addison-Wesley, 1996.

This is the definitive source for programming OpenDoc on the MacOS. The book is also useful to developers using other platforms, as much of OpenDoc is platform independent. Of particular note is the fact that the human interface guidelines for part editors is included in this book.

OpenDoc Cookbook for the Mac OS
Apple Computer, Inc. *OpenDoc Cookbook for the Mac OS*. Reading, Mass.: Addison-Wesley, 1996.

This book expands upon the information presented in the *OpenDoc Programmer's Guide for the Mac OS*. It presents detailed recipes for solutions to common problems in developing OpenDoc part editors.

OpenDoc Class Reference for the Mac OS

Apple Computer, Inc. *OpenDoc Class Reference for the Mac OS*. Reading, Mass.: Addison-Wesley, 1996.

This is the complete documentation of the OpenDoc API. It is an absolute requirement for anyone involved in OpenDoc development. The entire class reference is included in electronic form on the OpenDoc SDK from Apple and also with the *OpenDoc Programmer's Guide for the Mac OS*.

OpenDoc Human Interface Specification for the Macintosh Implementation

Apple Computer, Inc. *OpenDoc Human Interface Specification for the Macintosh Implementation*. Cupertino, Calif.: Apple Computer, Inc., 1995.

The HI Spec defines the human interface for OpenDoc on the MacOS and is required reading for anyone implementing OpenDoc. However, it is not generally useful for part developers. However, developers integrating OpenDoc with existing systems may find the information useful. The HI spec is available on the OpenDoc SDK.

Bento Specification, Revision 1.0d5

Harris, Jed, and Ira Ruben. *Bento Specification, Revision 1.0d5*. Cupertino, Calif.: Apple Computer, Inc., 1993.

This specification is the primary Bento spec; although the version of Bento that OpenDoc uses has had additional features added to it, this is still the standard reference for the Bento implementations currently on the market.

OLE

The following book (along with *The Essential Distributed Objects Survival Guide*) was useful when writing about OLE.

OLE Wizardry

Murray, William H., and Chris H. Pappas. *OLE Wizardry*. Berkeley, Calif.: Osborne/McGraw-Hill, 1995.

This book is a helpful guide to some of the basic concepts and applications of OLE, though it avoids the extensive technical details of OLE itself.

SOM/DSOM

The books listed here are some of the better books on SOM and should be helpful to anyone wishing to make use of SOM in projects. Some are reference works and others contain tutorials.

Object-Oriented Programming Using SOM and DSOM

Lau, Christina. *Object-Oriented Programming Using SOM and DSOM.* New York: Van Nostrand Reinhold, 1994.

This is a good beginner's guide to programming with SOM. It is not an exhaustive reference, but it contains enough information for the reader to learn and use SOM for real applications. It answers many commonly asked questions and provides plenty of examples.

SOMobjects (SOM/DSOM 2.1) Reference [SC41-4632]

International Business Machines Co. *SOMobjects (SOM/DSOM 2.1) Reference [SC41-4632].* Armonk, N.Y.: IBM, 1995.

This is the standard reference guide for SOM and DSOM and is indispensable to anyone performing SOM development.

SOMobjects (SOM/DSOM 2.1) User Guide [SC41-4631]

International Business Machines Co. *SOMobjects (SOM/DSOM 2.1) User Guide [SC41-4631].* Armonk, N.Y.: IBM, 1995.

This is the standard user guide for SOM, and it contains good descriptions of the concepts behind SOM as well as helpful tips and information.

Objects for OS/2

Danforth, Scott, Paul Koenen, and Bruce Tate. *Objects for OS/2.* New York: Van Nostrand Reinhold, 1994.

The focus of this book is programming for OS/2 using object technology. It presents a lot of basic information on object-oriented programming and how OS/2 uses OOP techniques. It contains a good deal of discussion of SOM, though the book should not be considered a SOM reference.

CORBA

The following books by the Object Management Group (OMG) are the official standards and references for CORBA.

The Common Object Request Broker: Architecture and Specification

Object Management Group (OMG). *The Common Object Request Broker: Architecture and Specification.* Framingham, Mass.: OMG, 1995.

This volume describes the architectural features of CORBA and specifies how to build a compliant Object Request Broker. It covers IDL, the Interface Repository, inter-ORB communication (including IIOP), and CORBA 2.x ORB.

CORBAfacilities

Object Management Group (OMG). *CORBAfacilities.* Framingham, Mass.: OMG, 1995.

This volume describes the Common Facilities portion of the architecture. As of this writing, the OMG technical committee has voted to recommend the adoption of OpenDoc as the Compound Document Services portion of this architecture. (The proposal passed the technical committee and has been submitted for approval by the membership.)

CORBAservices

Object Management Group (OMG). *CORBAservices.* Framingham, Mass.: OMG, 1995.

This volume describes the Object Services portion of the architecture.

Scripting and OSA

Scripting and scripting languages are fascinating subjects in their own right and prove quite useful in the context of OpenDoc. Here are a few of the better books on the subject.

Inside Macintosh: Interapplication Communication

Apple Computer, Inc. *Inside Macintosh: Interapplication Communication.* Reading, Mass.: Addison-Wesley, 1993.

This book describes Apple Events and AppleScript, the technologies that later became the Open Scripting Architecture (OSA). Its focus is on the MacOS implementations of these technologies, but is also a good general reference for them.

Tcl and the Tk Toolkit

Ousterhout, John, K. *Tcl and the Tk Toolkit.* Reading, Mass.: Addison-Wesley, 1994.

This wonderfully lucid book talks about Tcl—Tool Command Language—and its window system toolkit, Tk. Written by Professor John Ousterhout of the University of California, Berkeley, and Sun Microsystems Laboratories, this book is the standard reference manual and language tutorial for Tcl and Tk. It is highly recommended.

Articles and White Papers

The articles listed here provide background and up-to-date technical information. Several magazines, including *BYTE* and *InfoWeek*, have also run articles providing general information on OpenDoc.

OpenDoc

These articles focus specifically on OpenDoc.

OpenDoc: Software Innovation and Opportunity

CI Labs. "OpenDoc: Software Innovation and Opportunity." Sunnyvale, Calif.: Component Integration Laboratories, 1995.

This white paper presents the business and technical reasons behind the development of OpenDoc and explains how OpenDoc can provide new, innovative ways of doing business.

The OpenDoc User Experience

Curbow, Dave, and Elizabeth Dykstra-Erickson. "The OpenDoc User Experience." *develop* 22 (June 1995): 83-93.

This article, written by members of the OpenDoc Human Interface team, gives a guided tour of the concepts and features of the OpenDoc user interface.

Getting Started with OpenDoc Storage

Lo, Vincent. "Getting Started with OpenDoc Storage." *develop* 24 (December 1995): 30-41.

Vincent Lo, the lead engineer for the OpenDoc Storage subsystem, presents a look at how the system works.

OpenDoc Technical White Paper
Novell. "OpenDoc Technical White Paper." Provo, Utah: Novell, 1995.

This white paper approaches OpenDoc from a Windows perspective and talks about how it fits into the PC marketplace.

A Close-Up of OpenDoc
Piersol, Kurt. "A Close-Up of OpenDoc." *BYTE* (March 1994): 183-187.

This early article, written by the chief architect of OpenDoc, provides a high-level view of OpenDoc and its design. It is a brief but interesting look at the system and is still useful as a starting place for understanding OpenDoc.

Building an OpenDoc Part Handler
Piersol, Kurt. "Building an OpenDoc Part Handler." *develop* 19 (September 1994): 6-16.

This article gives an example of what is involved in writing an OpenDoc part editor, and provides a simple working example.

Getting Started with OpenDoc Graphics
Piersol, Kurt. "Getting Started with OpenDoc Graphics." *develop* 21 (March 1995): 5-22.

This article explains some of the basic terminology and concepts of the OpenDoc graphics and imaging system and provides examples of some typical graphics operations.

Scripting

The following article is available in *HotWired* (**http://www.hotwired.com**), which is the online version of *Wired* magazine.

UserTalk Everywhere
Winer, Dave. "UserTalk Everywhere." San Francisco: HotWired Ventures, 1995.
http://www.hotwired.com/staff/userland/aretha/usertalkeverywhere_234.html

This column provides some good examples of how scripting languages can interact with and integrate various applications.

Web Sites

The following web sites also provide information on OpenDoc.

Apple Computer   http://www.opendoc.apple.com

Component Integration Labs   http://www.cilabs.org

IBM OpenDoc   http://www.software.ibm.com/clubopendoc/

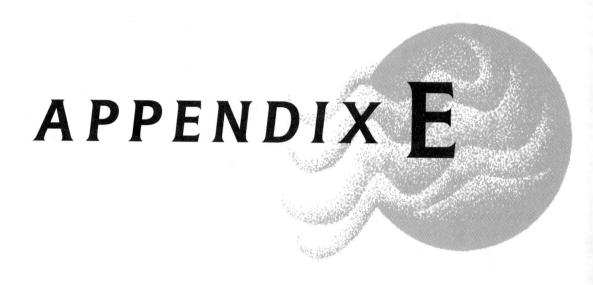

APPENDIX E

Platform Differences

S ince OpenDoc implementations have been coming out at different times (the Macintosh version in November 1995, the OS/2 version in January 1996, and the Windows version sometime later in 1996), there are still some platform implementation differences.

Here are a few important facts from the release notes:

■ The Windows DR1 version is still incomplete in several areas; these areas should be complete by the second developer's release, expected in mid-1996 or so. The Apple Event Manager is available for Windows, but the rest of OSA will follow in DR2, so scripting does not yet work in the Windows version. Although this version of OpenDoc runs on Windows 95, there is additional work necessary to completely integrate it with the Win95 shell. Finally, Direct-to-SOM compilers will remove the need to use SOM wrapper classes, making the implementation of the Windows part editor much clearer and simpler.

■ The OS/2 version of OpenDoc uses its own property notebook facilities to change OpenDoc part settings, rather than the dialog boxes used by other implementations. Much of this should be hidden by the implementation.

■ The 1.01 version of OpenDoc for the Macintosh will include some bug fixes and some minor UI changes: for example, the Editor Setup control panel will have a revised UI, and the OpenDoc splash screen will now only be shown once per day rather than every time OpenDoc is launched.

■ A beta version of Cyberdog is now available on the Cyberdog web site:

http://www.cyberdog.apple.com

Index

T